FUNDAMENTALS OF FINANCIAL MANAGEMENT

James C. Van Horne

Stanford University

Prentice-Hall, Inc., Englewood Cliffs, New Jersey 07632

5th Edition

FUNDAMENTALS OF FINANCIAL MANAGEMENT

Library of Congress Cataloging in Publication Data

VAN HORNE, JAMES C.
   Fundamentals of financial management.

   Includes bibliographies and index.
   1. Corporations—Finance.   I. Title.
HG4011.V36   1983   658.1′5   82-10123
ISBN 0-13-339465-4   AACR2

Fundamentals of Financial Management, 5th ed.
by James C. Van Horne

© 1983, 1980, 1977, 1974, 1971 by Prentice-Hall, Inc., Englewood Cliffs, N.J. 07632

Printed in the United States of America

10   9   8   7   6   5   4   3   2

Prentice-Hall International, Inc., *London*
Prentice-Hall of Australia Pty. Limited, *Sydney*
Prentice-Hall of Canada, Ltd., *Toronto*
Prentice-Hall of India Private Limited, *New Delhi*
Prentice-Hall of Japan, Inc., *Tokyo*
Prentice-Hall of Southeast Asia Pte. Ltd., *Singapore*
Whitehall Books Limited, Wellington, *New Zealand*

Preface

Just as financial managers seek a good return on their firms' investments, those who are about to study this introductory course in financial management will want a satisfactory return on the investment of their time. With a good yield as its objective, the book offers a basic understanding of

1. What business finance is
2. Allocation of funds within a business enterprise
3. Raising funds
4. Application of certain theoretical concepts to financial problems

Most of the concepts are expressed verbally, but elementary algebra is sometimes brought in for clearer understanding.

Structuring financial decisions continues to be the principal subject of the fifth edition. Unless financial managers focus on what is relevant, they will be hopelessly entwined in conflicting considerations, many of them trivial. In the pages that follow, they should find a lucid framework for approaching financial decisions. Theory will be explored not for its own sake, but for the help it can give in sorting out the important from the unimportant and in reaching better decisions.

A number of changes in this edition should enhance the learning experience and the reader's enthusiasm for financial management. Probably the most noticeable change is the comprehensive editing from start to finish. Explanations have been simplified, excess verbiage eliminated, and the writing style has been made more lively.

- The Economic Recovery Tax Act of 1981 is an essential part of the largely rewritten chapter 2.

- Inflation, as it affects financial market returns, receives increased attention.

- Amortizing a loan is a new section in chapter 4, which also has a new appendix on the use of a calculator in solving terminal and present values.

- The capital-asset pricing model is presented in a way that is easier to follow and apply.

- Cash and marketable security management incorporates new developments in financial markets, institutions, and practices.

- For judging credit policy decisions, chapter 10 suggests a method that is different from methods explained in previous editions.

- Accounts receivable management and inventory management are consolidated into one chapter.

- The treatment of short-term loans is reshaped in keeping with recent changes in financial markets and institutions.

- Capital budgeting (chapter 13) conforms to the Tax Act of 1981. A new section analyzes projects with different economic lives.

- Group-specific, or divisional, required returns are introduced in a restructured chapter 15. Among other improvements, there is a new appendix on adjusting the beta of a proxy company for leverage.

- The theory of dividend payout has been rewritten so that it is easier to follow, and newer arguments are incorporated. The effect of taxes and other imperfections is stressed. A new section reveals the things that managers consider when they decide on a dividend payout.

- Lease financing has been changed to reflect the Economic Recovery Tax Act of 1981.

- Improved examples in the valuation of convertible securities give the treatment more realism.

- Experience and research have made a better chapter 24, on mergers. A checklist illustrates the multitude of considerations in combining two companies. Tax-free transactions and empirical evidence on valuation vitalize the chapter.

- International financial management, chapter 25, is substantially revised, particularly the section on currency exposure management. The forward market, the effect of inflation and interest rates, and the interest-rate parity theorem are carefully examined.

- The smaller company and financial management is the subject of the entirely new chapter 26, which is devoted completely to this significant segment of our economy.

- The Bankruptcy Reform Act of 1978, having modified current procedures and practices, is the basis of the rewritten chapter 27, on failure and reorganization.

- Of the more than 200 problems at the end of the chapters, 35 percent are either new or revised. Less useful problems from the fourth edition have been eliminated.

- Other chapters have been carefully reviewed, updated, and improved. In many instances, the interest rates in the examples and problems are higher than in the earlier edition. Rather than use one interest rate throughout, I have used a wide range—6 percent to over 20 percent. Rates vary not only with the maturity and grade of debt instrument, but also with the recent volatility of interest rates overall. In this way the reader is able to apply the principles presented to a variety of interest rate scenarios.

I am grateful to a number of professors who have used the book and have offered helpful comments. In particular, I wish to thank Professors Eric L. Anderson, California State University, Los Angeles; Sheldon D. Balbirer, University of North Carolina, Greensboro; Edward J. Farragher, Eastern Michigan University; Peter G. Goulet, University of Northern Iowa; George A. Hachey, Jr., Merrimack College; Larry C. Nelson, Fisk University; and Raj A. Padmaraj, Bowling Green State University. Finally, I am grateful to Maurine Lewis, formerly of Prentice-Hall, who did a superb job editing the book.

JAMES C. VAN HORNE
Palo Alto, California

Contents

PRINCIPLES OF FINANCIAL RETURNS II

3

The role of financial markets for the business firm, 23

4

Compound interest and present value, 45

5

Foundations for valuation, 69

TOOLS OF FINANCIAL ANALYSIS AND PLANNING III

6

Financial analysis, 98

7

Funds analysis and financial planning, 136

WORKING CAPITAL MANAGEMENT IV

8

Current asset and liability structure decisions, 163

INVESTING IN CAPITAL ASSETS V

CAPITAL STRUCTURE AND DIVIDEND POLICIES VI

LONGER-TERM FINANCING—INSTRUMENTS AND MARKETS **VII**

19

Interface with suppliers of capital, 426

20

Term and lease financing, 445

21

Long-term debt, 470

INTRODUCTION

I

The role of financial management 1

At any moment in time, a business firm can be viewed as a pool of funds fed by a variety of sources: investors in the company's stock, creditors who lend it money, and past earnings retained in the business. Funds provided from these sources are committed to a number of uses: fixed assets used in production of a good or service, inventories used to facilitate production and sales, accounts receivable owed by customers, and cash and marketable securities used for transactions and liquidity purposes. At a given moment, the pool of funds of the firm is static; over time, it changes, and these changes are known as funds flows. In an ongoing business, funds flow continually throughout the enterprise. The term *financial management* connotes that these flows are directed according to some plan; it is with managing the flow of funds within the firm that this book deals.

In recent years, the role of the financial manager has expanded to involve the totality of the enterprise. Put another way, financial managers are now involved in general management, where before they primarily raised funds and managed the firm's cash position. The combination of increased competition among firms, persistent inflation, technological improvements that require considerable capital, increased national concern with environment, energy, and social issues, heightened government regulation of firms, and the growing importance of international operations have had an enormous influence in pushing the financial manager into a general management role. Moreover, these factors require considerable flexibility in order to cope with ever-present change. The "old way of doing things" simply is not good enough in a world where old ways quickly become obsolete. Competition requires continual adaption to changing conditions.

If you become a financial manager, your ability to adapt to change, efficiently plan the proper amount of funds to employ in the firm, oversee the allocation of these funds, and raise funds will affect the success of your firm and the overall economy as well. To the extent that funds are misallocated, the growth of the economy will be slowed. In an era of unfilled economic wants and scarcity, this may work to the detriment of society. Efficient allocation of resources in an economy is vital to optimal growth in that economy; it also is vital in assuring that individuals obtain the highest level of want satisfaction possible. Through effectively raising and allocating funds, the financial manager contributes to the fortunes of the firm and to the vitality and growth of the economy as a whole.

THE GOAL OF THE FIRM

Efficient management of the flow of funds within the firm implies the existence of some objective or goal, because judgment as to whether or not a financial decision is efficient must be made in the light of some standard. Although various objectives are possible, we assume in this book that the goal of the firm is to maximize the wealth of its present owners.

Ownership in a corporation is evidenced by shares of common stock. Each share indicates that its holder owns 1/nth of the company involved, where n is the total number of shares outstanding.[1] For our purposes, shareholder wealth is represented by the market price per share of the firm's stock. While the market price may not be a perfect measure of wealth for all stockholders, it is the best measure available. When a public market does not exist for the stock, an opportunity price must be used. By analyzing similar companies whose stock is traded publicly, one can approximate the market value of the company involved.

Profit maximization versus wealth maximization

Frequently, maximization of profits is regarded as the proper objective of the firm, but it is not as inclusive a goal as that of maximizing shareholder wealth. For one thing, total profits are not as important as earnings per share. Even maximization of earnings per share is not a fully appropriate objective, partly because it does not specify the timing or duration of expected returns. Is the investment project that will produce a $100,000 return 5 years from now more valuable than the project that will produce annual returns of $15,000 in each of the next five years? An answer to this question depends upon the time value of money to the firm and to investors at the margin. Few existing stockholders would think favorably of a project that promised its first return in 100 years, no matter how large this return. We must take into account the time pattern of returns in our analysis.

[1] For a discussion of the characteristics of common stock, see chapter 22.

Another shortcoming of the objective of maximizing earnings per share is that it does not consider the risk of the prospective earnings stream. Some investment projects are far more risky than others. As a result, the prospective stream of earnings per share would be more risky if these projects were undertaken. In addition, a company will be more or less risky depending upon the amount of debt in relation to equity in its capital structure. This financial risk also contributes to the overall risk to the investor. Two companies may have the same expected earnings per share, but if the earnings stream of one is subject to considerably more risk than the earnings stream of the other, the market price per share of its stock may be less.

Finally, this objective does not allow for the effect of dividend policy on the market price of the stock. If the objective were only to maximize earnings per share, the firm would never pay a dividend. At the very least, it could always improve earnings per share by retaining earnings and investing them in marketable securities. To the extent that the payment of dividends can affect the value of the stock, the maximization of earnings per share will not be a satisfactory objective by itself.

For the reasons given above, an objective of maximizing earnings per share may not be the same as maximizing market price per share. The market price of a firm's stock represents the focal judgment of all market participants as to the value of the particular firm. It takes into account present and prospective future earnings per share, the timing, duration, and risk of these earnings, the dividend policy of the firm, and other factors that bear upon the market price of the stock. The market price serves as a performance index or report card of the firm's progress; it indicates how well management is doing in behalf of its stockholders. Management is under continuous review. Stockholders who are dissatisfied with management's performance may sell their stock and invest in another company. This action, if taken by other dissatisfied stockholders, will put downward pressure on market price per share.

Social responsibility

Maximizing shareholder wealth does not imply that management should ignore social responsibility such as protecting the consumer, paying fair wages to employees, maintaining fair hiring practices and safe working conditions, supporting education, and becoming actively involved in environmental issues like clean air and water. Many people feel that a firm has no choice but to act in socially responsible ways; they argue that shareholder wealth and perhaps, the corporation's very existence depend upon its being socially responsible. Because the criteria for social responsibility are not clearly defined, however, it is difficult to formulate a consistent objective.

Social responsibility creates certain problems for the firm. It falls unevenly on different corporations, and it sometimes conflicts with the objective of wealth maximization. Certain social actions, from a long-range point of view, unmistakably are in the best interests of stockholders and should be undertaken. Other actions, less clear, may be detrimental both to profits and shareholder wealth in the long run. From the standpoint of society, this decline may produce a conflict. A socially desirable goal may be possible only through inefficient allocation of resources. As that inefficiency hampers growth of the economy, people will find their economic wants less satisfied. In an era of unfilled wants and scarcity, the allocation process is extremely important.

Many people feel that management should not be called upon to resolve the conflict posed above. Rather, society, with its broad general perspective, should make the decisions necessary in this area. Only society, acting through Congress and other representative governmental bodies, can judge the relative trade-off between the achievement of a social goal and the sacrifice in the efficiency of apportioning resources that may accompany realization of the goal. With these decisions made, corporations can engage in wealth maximization and thereby efficiently allocate resources, subject, of course, to certain governmental constraints. Under such a system, corporations can be viewed as producing both private and social goods, and the maxmization of shareholder wealth remains a viable corporate objective.

FUNCTION OF THE FINANCIAL MANAGER

As suggested earlier, the financial manager is concerned with (1) efficient allocation of funds within the enterprise and (2) raising funds on as favorable terms as possible. These functions are pursued with the objective of maximizing shareholder wealth. By and large, this book is organized according to the two functions mentioned above. Embodied in the first is consideration of the total amount of funds to employ in the enterprise.

The underpinnings

Before proceeding to examine the allocation and raising of funds, we take up certain background material and tools of analysis. In the next chapter, we examine the legal setting for financial management as it relates in particular to organizational form and taxes. The function of financial markets and interest rates is also pertinent background. These topics are discussed in chapter 3. In particular, our focus is on how business firms interact with financial markets. Certain concepts involving the time value of money and valuation are taken up in chapters 4 and 5, and an understanding here is essential to sound financial decisions. Indeed, the foundation for maximizing shareholder wealth is valuation. As a result, we take up the basics of the time value of money and valuation early on.

In order to raise funds efficiently and to allocate them, financial managers must plan carefully. For one thing, they must project future cash flows and then assess the likely effect of these flows on the financial condition of the firm. On the basis of these projections, they plan for adequate liquidity to pay bills and other obligations as they come due. These obligations may make it necessary to raise additional funds. In order to control performance, the financial manager needs to establish certain norms. These norms are then used to compare actual performance with planned performance. Because financial analysis, planning, and control underlie a good deal of the discussion in this book, we examine these topics in chapters 6 and 7.

Allocation of funds

The financial manager oversees the allocation of funds among alternative uses. This allocation must be made in accordance with the underlying objective of the firm: to maximize shareholder wealth. In part 4 we examine cash, marketable securities, accounts receivable, and inventories. We shall explore ways of efficiently managing these current assets in order to maximize profitability relative to the amount of funds tied up in the assets. Determining a proper level of liquidity is very much a part of this management. The optimal level of a current asset depends on the profitability and flexibility associated with that level in relation to the cost involved in maintaining it. In the past, the management of working capital dominated the role of the financial managers. Though this traditional function continues to be vital, their role has expanded to involve longer-term assets and liabilities.

In part 5, under capital investment, we consider the allocation of funds among fixed assets. Capital budgeting involves allocating capital to investment proposals whose benefits will be realized in the future. When a proposal embodies a current-asset component, the latter is treated as part of the capital-budgeting decision and not as a separate working-capital decision. Because the expected future benefits from an investment proposal are uncertain, risk necessarily is involved. Changes in the business-risk complexion of the firm can have a significant influence on its value in the marketplace. Because of this important effect, attention is devoted to the problem of measuring risk for a capital investment project. Capital is apportioned according to an acceptance criterion. The return required of the project must be in accord with the objective of maximizing shareholder wealth.

In part 8 we see mergers and acquisitions from the standpoint of the firm's allocation of funds. Many of the concepts applicable to capital budgeting are applicable here. Growth of a company can be internal, external, or both, domestic or international in flavor. Since the multinational firm has come into such prominence, it is particularly germane that we study growth through international operations. Nor do we overlook financial management of a smaller company and the things that make such management different from that in a large one. Finally, in this part, we take up failures and reorganizations, which involve a decision to liquidate a company or to rehabilitate it, often by changing its capital structure. This decision should be based on the same economic considerations that govern the allocation of capital.

In summary, the allocation of funds within the firm determines the total amount of assets of the firm, the composition of these assets, and the business-risk complexion of the firm. All of these factors greatly influence its value.

Raising funds

The second facet of financial management is the acquisition of funds. A wide variety of sources is available. Each has certain characteristics as to cost, maturity, availability, the encumbrance of assets, and other terms imposed by the supplier of capital. On the basis of these factors, the financial manager must determine the best mix of financing for the firm. Its implications upon shareholder wealth must be considered when this decision is made.

In part 6, we take up the appropriate capital structure of a firm. We look at the concept of leverage from a number of different angles in an effort to understand financial risk and how this risk is interrelated with operating risk. In addition, we analyze retained earnings as a source of funds. Because this source represents dividends foregone by stockholders, dividend policy very much impinges on financing policy and vice versa. In part 4 we examine the various sources of short-term financing; in part 7, the sources of long-term financing. Both parts reveal the features, concepts, and problems associated with alternative methods of financing.

Financial management, then, involves the allocation of funds within the firm and the acquisition of funds. The two are interrelated in that a decision to invest in a particular asset necessitates the financing of that asset, whereas the cost of financing affects the decision to invest. The focus of this book is upon the allocation and acquisition of funds; together, these activities determine the value of the firm to its shareholders. Mastering the concepts involved is the key to understanding the role of financial management.

QUESTIONS

1. The maximization-of-wealth objective suggests that management attempt to minimize dollar cost of production at a given level of output. Some costs of production are not paid for by the company (i.e., pollution). Is the objective of maximizing wealth functional from society's point of view? If the answer is no, which objective would you substitute in its place?

2. Contrast the objective of maximizing earnings and that of maximizing wealth.

3. Maximizing wealth implies maximizing the price of the stock of the firm. Scandals involving stock manipulations suggest that stock prices are not an infallible yardstick of performance. Discuss conditions created by management which maximize stock prices but which do not necessarily mean efficiency in financial decision making.

4. Is the goal of zero profits for some finite period (3 to 5 years, for example) ever consistent with the maximization-of-wealth objective? Explain.

5. Explain why judging the efficiency of any financial decision requires the existence of a goal.

6. What are the two major functions of the financial manager? How are they related?

7. Should the managers of a company own sizable amounts of stock in the company? What are the pros and the cons?

8. During the last two decades, a number of environmental, pollution, hiring, and other regulations have been imposed on businesses. In view of these changes, is maximization of shareholder wealth any longer a realistic objective?

9. As an investor, are not some managers paid too much? Do their rewards come at your expense?

10. How does the notion of risk and reward govern the behavior of financial managers?

SELECTED REFERENCES

BERANEK, WILLIAM, "Research Directions in Finance," *Quarterly Review of Economics and Business,* 21 (Spring 1981), 6–24.

BRANCH, BEN, "Corporate Objectives and Market Performance," *Financial Management,* 2 (Summer 1973), 24–29.

CISEL, DAVID H., and THOMAS M. CARROLL, "The Determinants of Executive Salaries: An Econometric Survey," *Review of Economics and Statistics,* 62 (February, 1980), 7–13.

COOLEY, PHILLIP L., "Managerial Pay and Financial Performances of Small Business," *Journal of Business,* (September 1979), 267–76.

DAVIS, KEITH, "Social Responsibility Is Inevitable," *California Management Review,* 19 (Fall 1976), 14–20.

DONALDSON, GORDON, "Financial Goals: Management vs. Stockholders," *Harvard Business Review,* 41(May–June 1963), 116–29.

FINDLAY, M. CHAPMAN III, and G. A. WHITMORE, "Beyond Shareholder Wealth Maximization," *Financial Management,* 3 (Winter 1974), 25–35.

FRUHAN, WILLIAM E., Jr., *Financial Strategy.* Homewood, Ill.: Irwin, 1979.

GERSTNER, LOUIS V., and HELEN M. ANDERSON, "The Chief Financial Officer as Activist," *Harvard Business Review,* 54 (September–October 1976), 100–106.

HILL, LAWRENCE W., "The Growth of the Corporate Finance Function," *Financial Executive,* 44 (July 1976), 33–43.

JENSEN, MICHAEL C., and WILLIAM H. MECKLING, "Theory of the Firm: Managerial Behavior, Agency Costs and Ownership Structure," *Journal of Financial Economics,* 3 (October 1976), 305–60.

SOLOMON, EZRA, *The Theory of Financial Management.* New York: Columbia University Press, 1963, chaps. 1 and 2.

WESTON, J. FRED, "Developments in Finance Theory," *Financial Management,* 10 (1981), 5–22.

The legal and tax environment 2

To understand the role of financial managers, we must be familiar with the legal setting in which they operate. When we look at one aspect of the setting, the basic form of business organization, we shall discover advantages and disadvantages of the various forms. Delving into another aspect, the tax environment, we shall not try to become experts, but we do hope to gain a basic understanding of the tax implications of various financial decisions to be considered in this book.

FORM OF ORGANIZATION

In the United States there are three basic forms of business organization: the sole proprietorship, the partnership, and the corporation. The sole proprietorship outnumbers the other two, but the corporation is largest in sales, assets, profits, and contribution to national income. As this section unfolds, we shall see several important advantages to the corporate form.

The sole proprietorship

The sole proprietorship is the oldest form of business organization. As the title suggests, a single person owns the business, holds title to all its assets, and is personally responsible for all of its liabilities. Because of its simplicity, a sole proprietorship can be established with few complications. Simplicity is its greatest virtue; its principal shortcoming is the proprietor's legal responsibility for all obligations the organization incurs. If the organization is sued, the proprietor as an individual is sued and has unlimited liability, which means that his or her personal property as well as the assets of the business may be seized to settle claims. Obviously, this liability places the individual in a risk-prone position.

Another problem with a sole proprietorship is the difficulty in raising capital. In general, this form of organization is not as attractive to creditors as are other forms of organizations. Moreover, the proprietorship has certain tax disadvantages. Fringe benefits, such as medical coverage and group insurance, are not regarded by the Internal Revenue Service as expenses of the firm and therefore are not deductible for tax purposes. A corporation often deducts these benefits. The proprietor must pay for them from income left over after paying taxes. In addition to these drawbacks, the proprietorship form makes the transfer of ownership more difficult than does the corporate form. In estate planning, no portion of the enterprise can be transferred to members of the family during the proprietor's lifetime. For these reasons, this form of organization does not afford the flexibility other forms do.

The partnership

A partnership is similar to a proprietorship in all aspects except that there is more than one owner. In a *general partnership* all partners have unlimited liability; they are jointly liable for the liabilities of the partnership. Because an individual partner can bind the partnership with obligations, general partners should be selected with care. In most cases there is a formal arrangement, or partnership agreement; this sets forth the powers of an individual partner, the distribution of profits, the amounts of capital to be invested by the partners, procedures for admitting new partners, and procedures for reconstituting the partnership in case of the death or withdrawal of a partner. Legally, the partnership is terminated if one of the partners dies or withdraws. In such cases, settlements invariably are "sticky," and reconstitution of the partnership is a difficult matter. For these reasons, many people view the partnership as an unattractive form of business organization.

The decision-making process of a partnership is often cumbersome. Unless the agreement specifies otherwise, important decisions must be made by majority vote. In most cases, group decisions are difficult, to say the least. On less weighty matters, individual partners may transact business for the firm but must be careful to keep the other partners informed. The powers of an individual partner will vary according to the formal or informal agreement among partners. Some partnerships specify a hierarchy of two or more layers of partners. This hierarchy determines the magnitude of decision an individual partner can make and the degree to which a partner can commit the firm.

In a number of states, *limited partnerships* are permitted. A limited partner contributes capital, and has liability confined to that amount of capital. There must, however, be at least one general partner in the partnership, whose liability is unlimited. Limited partners do not participate in the operation of the business; this is left to the general partners. The limited partners are strictly investors, and they share in the profits or losses of the partnership according to the terms of the partnership agreement. This type of arrangement is frequently used in financing real estate ventures.

The corporation

Because of the importance of the corporate form in the United States, the focus of this book is upon corporations. A corporation is an "impersonal" entity created by law; it can own assets and incur liabilities. In the famous *Dartmouth College* decision in 1819, Justice Marshall concluded that

a corporation is an artificial being, invisible, intangible, and existing only in contemplation of the law. Being a mere creature of law, it possesses only those properties which the charter of its creation confers upon it, either expressly or as incidental to its very existence.[1]

The principal feature of this form is that the corporation exists separately and apart from its owners. An owner's liability is limited to his investment. Limited liability represents an important advantage over the proprietorship and the general partnership. Capital can be raised in the corporation's name without exposing the owners to unlimited liability. Therefore, personal assets cannot be seized in the settlement of claims. Ownership itself is evidenced by shares of stock, with each stockholder owning that proportion of the enterprise represented by his shares in relation to the total number of shares outstanding. These shares are transferable, representing another important advantage of the corporate form. Moreover, the corporation can continue even though individual owners may die or wish to sell their stock.

A corporation is incorporated in a specific state. To establish a corporation, the owners must file an application with the secretary of state or some other state official. This application includes the location of the company, the purpose of the business, the names of the owners and directors, the names of the management, the number of shares of stock authorized, the paid-in capital, and the length of the corporation's life, which in most cases is perpetual. Upon approval by the appropriate state official, a *charter* is issued to establish the corporation as a legal entity and spell out the conditions under which it can exist.

Because of the advantages associated with limited liability, transferability of ownership, and the ability of the corporation to raise capital apart from its owners, the corporate form of business organization has grown enormously during the last century. With the large demands for capital that accompany an advanced economy, the proprietorship and partnership have proven unsatisfactory, and the corporation has emerged as the most important organizational form. A possible disadvantage of the corporation is the tax treatment, which we take up shortly. Even here, the disadvantage exists only under certain circumstances. Minor disadvantages include the length of time required to incorporate and the red tape involved, as well as the incorporation fee that must be paid to the state. Thus, a corporation is more difficult to establish than either a proprietorship or a partnership. For a moderate-sized organization, however, this is not a serious problem.

---

[1] *The Trustees of Dartmouth College v. Woodward*, 4 Wheaton 636 (1819).

CORPORATE INCOME TAXES

Few business decisions are not affected either directly or indirectly by taxes. Through their taxing power, federal, state, and local governments have a profound influence upon the behavior of business organizations and that of their owners. What might be an optimal business decision in the absence of taxes may prove to be a very inferior one with taxes. In this section we trace through some of the essentials of taxation. This basic understanding is used in later chapters when we consider specific financial decisions. We begin with the corporate income tax, then consider personal income taxes.

A corporation's taxable income is found by deducting from income all expenses, including depreciation and interest. There is a five-step graduated tax rate structure, the steps being

Corporate taxable income	Tax rate
$0 to $25,000	15%
$25,001 to $50,000	18%
$50,001 to $75,000	30%
$75,001 to $100,000	40%
Over $100,000	46%

If the annual taxable income of Arthur Brown Company were $110,000, its tax would be .15($25,000) + .18($25,000) + .30(25,000) + .40($25,000) + .46($10,000) = $30,350. For companies with significant profits, then, the marginal tax rate is 46 percent. This scaling of tax rates gives preferential treatment to small and moderate-sized corporations. With inflation, there is a considerable clamor to increase the graduation schedule so that more corporate income is subject to a lower tax. The most recent change in this direction occurred in the Economic Recovery Tax Act of 1981.

Corporations of any significant size are required to make quarterly tax payments on essentially a current basis. More specifically, they are required to pay 25 percent of their estimated taxes in any given year on April 15, June 15, September 15, and December 15 of that year. When actual income differs from that which has been estimated, adjustments are made. A company that is on a calendar-year basis of accounting, must make final settlement by April 15 of the subsequent year.

Depreciation

Because depreciation charges are deductible as an expense, they affect the amount of tax to be paid. The greater these charges, the lower the tax, all other things remaining constant. There are three methods for depreciating a capital asset: straight-line, declining-balance, and sum-of-the-years'-digits methods. The last two are forms of *accelerated* depreciation. Whatever method is used, it is necessary to start with the recovery period of the asset. Machinery, equipment, and real estate fall into defined classes, depending on their nature. These classes of property have periods, or depreciable lives of 3, 5, 10, and 15 years.

A general description of the classes follows. The reader should refer to the tax code for more detail.

3-year property includes automobiles, light trucks, machinery and equipment used in research and development, together with other assets with short economic lives (mid-point lives of 4 years or less).

5-year property includes all other machinery and equipment and certain structures.

10-year property encompasses public utility property having a midpoint economic life of 18–25 years, railroad tank cars, mobile homes, and certain real property.

15-year property takes in all depreciable real estate not assigned to the 10-year property class, as well as long-term public utility property.

The property category in which an asset falls determines its depreciable life for tax purposes.

To illustrate the various methods of depreciation, consider first straight-line depreciation. If an asset costing $15,000 falls in the five-year property class, annual depreciation charges using straight-line depreciation would be $15,000/5, or $3,000. The declining balance method of depreciation must specify some multiple. Let us assume initially that this multiple is two. With the double-declining-balance method, depreciation charges in any year are

$$2(BV/n) \tag{2-1}$$

where BV is the undepreciated book value of the asset at the start of the year, and n is the depreciable life of the asset. For a $15,000 asset, with a five-year life, depreciation charges in the first year would be

$$2(\$15,000/5) = \$6,000$$

Depreciation charges in the second year are based upon an undepreciated book value of $9,000; we arrive at the $9,000 by subtracting the first year's depreciation charges, $6,000, from the asset's original book value. Depreciation charges in the second year would therefore be

$$2(\$9,000/5) = \$3,600$$

In the third year they would be

$$2(\$5,400/5) = \$2,160$$

and so on.

Under the accelerated cost recovery system (ACRS) specified in the 1981 Tax Act, the declining balance method of depreciation is employed. For property placed in service through 1984, the multiple used is 1.50. For 1985, it is 1.75; and for 1986 and beyond, it is 2.00, or the double declining-balance method. Thus, the formula through 1984 is 1.5(1/n), where n is the number of years in the property class to which the asset is assigned. In the 5-year property class, the annual depreciation charge would be 1.5(1/5), or 30 percent of the depreciated book value balance at the beginning of the year. If the depreciable balance at the beginning of a year were $10,000, depreciation charges during the year would be $3,000; they would be $2,100 the next year, which is 30 percent of ($10,000 − $3,000), and so on. Under ACRS a half-year convention is followed the first year an asset is placed in service, however. That first year, one is able to deduct for tax purposes only one-half the amount indicated by the formula. In our example, this means a deduction of only 15 percent of the cost of the asset instead of 30 percent.

Finally, it is assumed under ACRS that users switch from the declining-balance method to either straight-line or sum-of-the-years' digits in the year that provides the quickest write off. With the sum-of-the-years' digits, we add up each year of the depreciable life of the asset to obtain the denominator. For a 5-year asset, the denominator is $1 + 2 + 3 + 4 + 5 = 15$. The numerator is the depreciable life for the first year, the depreciable life minus 1 for the second year, and so on. Thus, the first-year depreciation charge would be 5/15, followed by 4/15, 3/15, 2/15 and 1/15 for the remaining years. The ACRS under the 1981 Tax Act formally prescribes the percentage of the cost of a property that may be deducted each year. The following table shows the percentages for the first three property classes through 1984 and for 1985 when a multiplier of 1.75 will apply to the declining-balance method.

Recovery year	Through 1984 Property Class			1985 Property Class		
	3-year	5-year	10-year	3-year	5-year	10-year
1	25%	15%	8%	29%	18%	9%
2	38	22	14	47	33	19
3	37	21	12	24	25	16
4		21	10		16	14
5		21	10		8	12
6			10			10
7			9			8
8			9			6
9			9			4
10			9			2

Again, these percentages approximate (with rounding) the initial use of either the 150 percent or 175 percent declining-balance method, with a switch to either straight-line or sum-of-the-years'-digits method in the year that provides the quickest write off. For the 5-year property class through 1984, for example, first-year depreciation is 15 percent, which leaves 85 percent of the cost of the property to be recovered. Essentially straight-line depreciation is used thereafter, for 85 percent/4 = $21\frac{1}{4}$ percent. With rounding, 22 percent of the cost of the property is deductible in the second year, and 21 percent thereafter. For the 5-year property class for 1985, first-year depreciation is 1.75(1/5) = 35 percent divided by 2 and rounded, which comes to 18 percent. This leaves 82 percent of the cost of the property to be recovered. At this point, sum-of-the-years'-digits is used for the remaining years. The denominator is $1 + 2 + 3 + 4 = 10$, so for the second year of recovery, depreciation charges are 4/10, followed by 3/10, 2/10, and 1/10. For the second year, we have 40 percent × 82 percent = 32.8 percent, which is rounded to 33 percent. Similarly, the other percentages may be determined. Thus, the table above is used to determine depreciation charges for property placed in service through 1985.

Interest expense

Interest charges on debt issued by a corporation are treated as an expense and are deductible for tax purposes. This treatment contrasts with that for common- and preferred-stock dividends, which are not deductible for tax purposes. If a company is profitable and pays taxes, the use of debt in its financing mix results in a significant tax advantage relative to the use of preferred or common stock. If the marginal tax rate were 46 percent, the firm would need to earn approximately $1.85 before taxes for every $1 paid out in dividends [$1/(1 − tax rate)], versus only $1 for the payment of $1 of interest. Thus, we see the tax advantages associated with using debt.

Dividend income

A corporation may own stock in another company. If it receives a dividend on this stock, 85 percent of the dividend is tax exempt. The remaining 15 percent is taxed at the corporate income tax rate. A firm that receives $10,000 in dividend income pays taxes on only $1,500 of this income. At a tax rate of 46 percent, taxes would amount to $690 as opposed to $4,600 if the entire dividend income were treated as taxable income.

Carry-back and carry-forward

If a corporation sustains a net operating loss, this loss may be carried back three years and forward fifteen years to offset taxable income in those years. The loss must be applied first to the earliest preceding year. If a firm sustained an operating loss of $200,000 in 1983, it would first carry this loss back to 1980. If the company had net profits of $200,000 in that year and paid taxes of $72,750, it would recompute its taxes for 1980 to show zero profit for tax purposes. Consequently, the company would be eligible for a tax refund of $72,750. If the 1983 operating loss was greater than operating profits in 1980, the residual would be carried back to 1981 and taxes recomputed for that year. If part of the loss was not used in that year, it would be carried back to 1982. However, if the net operating loss was greater than net operating income in all three years, the residual would be carried forward in sequence to future profits in 1984 to 1998. Profits in each of these years would be reduced for tax purposes by the amount of the unused loss carry-forward. This feature of the tax law is designed to avoid penalizing the company with sharply fluctuating net operating income.

Capital gains and losses

When a capital asset is sold, a capital gain or loss is incurred. If the asset is held for less than one year, the gain or loss is defined as short-term; if held more than one year, it is long-term. Short-term capital losses are subtracted from short-term capital gains, and any net gain is added to the corporation's ordinary income, where it is subject to regular taxation. In contrast, long-term capital gains usually are subject to more favorable tax treatment. The effective tax rate on the excess of net long-term capital gains (long-term gains less long-term losses) over net short-term capital losses (short-term losses less short-term gains) is 28 percent.

A *capital gain* is defined as the sales price of an asset less its original cost. If a capital asset is sold for a price in excess of its depreciated book value but for less than its original cost, the excess is subject to the regular tax rate. A machine may be purchased for $15,000 and, at the end of the third year, sold for $10,000, at which time its depreciated book value is $6,000. The $4,000 difference between sales price and depreciated book value is taxed at the regular corporate tax rate. In other words, this difference is classified as ordinary income. It represents a recapture of depreciation and not a capital gain. In contrast, if the asset were sold for $18,000, $3,000 of the gain would be subject to the more favorable capital-gains tax rate, while $9,000 ($15,000−$6,000) would be treated as ordinary income for tax purposes. Thus, the sale of a capital asset is subject to the capital-gains tax only when the gain exceeds the total depreciation that has been taken.

If the depreciable property involved were a building or structural component, the recapture of depreciation treatment would be somewhat different. Here recapture of depreciation usually pertains to depreciation in excess of that which would have been taken under the straight-line method.

A capital loss cannot be deducted by the corporation for tax purposes; it can be used only to offset capital gains. If, after deducting all capital gains from all capital losses, a company has a net capital loss for the year, this net loss may be carried back for three years and forward for fifteen years to offset capital gains during that period.

Investment tax credit and R & D tax credit

The investment tax credit is available to corporations and individuals who invest in machinery and equipment. In general, it is not available for real estate investments. For the 3-year property class defined earlier, the tax credit is 6 percent, and it is available at the time the asset is placed into service. In 19x5 Zakor Tool Company purchased equipment costing $100,000, which fell in the 3-year property class. If the equipment were placed in service in 19x5, Zakor would be able to claim an investment tax credit of $6,000 in that year. This tax credit takes $6,000 off Zakor's 19x5 income taxes. Moreover, the credit does not alter the basis for depreciation; it remains at $100,000.

For assets in the 5-year property class and for public utility property in the 10-year class, 10 percent is applicable. In the example above, this would mean a tax credit of $10,000 instead of $6,000. The emphasis is on providing a greater incentive for investment in longer-term assets. The relative fast depreciation now allowed (with the Economic Recovery Tax Act of 1981) and the investment tax credit are designed to stimulate business investment in an inflationary environment.

A tax credit also is available for increased research and development activities. More specifically, incremental research and development wage costs involved in an experimental or laboratory sense are eligible for a 25 percent tax credit. By incremental, we mean expenditures above those incurred on average during the three prior years. If average R&D wage expenditures during the last three years were $150,000 and expenditures this year were $190,000, the increment in wages paid would be $40,000. With a 25 percent rate, the company would be eligible for a tax credit of $10,000 in the current year. The purpose of this tax credit is to stimulate technical innovation and productivity gains.

PERSONAL INCOME TAXES

The subject of personal taxes is extremely comprehensive, but here our main concern is with the personal taxes of individuals owning stock in corporations. Any income reported by a sole proprietorship or a partnership becomes income of the owners, and it is taxed at the personal tax rate. This rate is graduated according to the amount of taxable income, going from a marginal tax rate of 11 percent up to 50 percent for individuals having large taxable incomes. Individuals filing joint returns apply 11 percent to the $3,400 to $5,500 income bracket. That is, for taxable income below $3,400, there is no tax; for income in excess of $3,400, the tax rate is 11 percent up to $5,500 in total taxable income. Above $5,500, one falls into the $5,500 to $7,600 income bracket, where the tax rate is 12 percent on income within that bracket.[2] If two persons filing a joint return had taxable income of $7,000, they would pay the following taxes:

Tax on income between $3,400 and $5,500	$231
Tax on ($7,000 − $5,500) × 0.12	180
Total tax liability	$411

At the upper end, taxable income above $162,400 for individuals filing joint returns is subject to the top tax rate of 50 percent. In other words, after $162,400 in taxable income, the tax rate no longer is graduated but is flat. In order to negate "bracket creep," in which, owing to inflation rather than real income gains, individuals find themselves in higher and higher tax brackets, the Economic Recovery Tax Act of 1981 provided that income brackets be adjusted for inflation beginning in 1985. In this way, personal taxes will be largely based on real income rather than nominal income.

For the individual, the first $100 of dividend income is tax exempt; the rest is taxed at the ordinary income tax rate. If a joint return is filed, the exemption is

---

[2] The Economic Recovery Tax Act of 1981 instigated tax rate reductions to be phased in for three years. The tax rates discussed are for taxable income received after July 1, 1983, the last date of the phase-in.

$200. Interest income on debt instruments also is taxed at the ordinary income tax rate. A tax exemption on the first $450 ($900 in the case of a joint return) of such income can be taken after 1984.

Capital gains tax

As with the corporation, long-term capital gains for individuals are taxed more favorably than is ordinary income. Short-term capital gains, however, are treated as regular income and are taxed at the normal income tax rate. In order to establish a long-term capital gain, the asset must be held longer than one year. If the asset is a stock, the gain is simply the price for which the stock is sold, less the amount paid for it.

For individuals, the tax treatment of capital gains also is more favorable than that of ordinary income. Sixty percent of the gain is exempt from taxation. The remaining 40 percent is taxed at the individual's ordinary tax rate. Sandra Akers has sold some stock after holding it for two years, and her net capital gain is $1,100. If her marginal tax rate is 42 percent, she will pay a tax of $0.42(1 - 0.60)(\$1,100) = \$184.80$ on the gain. Because the maximum personal income tax rate is 50 percent, the maximum tax possible on capital gains is $0.50(1 - 0.60) = 20$ percent.

The difference in tax treatment between ordinary income and capital gains has significant implications for dividend and other financial decisions. We shall see in subsequent chapters that this tax differential is particularly important when it comes to certain valuation concepts.

Stock options

Executives of corporations often are given stock options as a performance incentive. An option is a contract that gives the holder the right to buy common stock in the company at some specified price and during some stated period of time. For example, Feldstein Focal Company may give its president, Mark Bender, a three-year option to purchase 10,000 shares of stock at $23 per share which is the current market price. The exercise price of this incentive stock option must be at least 100 percent of the fair market value of the stock on the day that it is granted. If the stock rises in price, Mr. Bender stands to gain; if it drops in price, he does not lose, because presumably he will not exercise his option. (His job may be in jeopardy, however!) At the end of three years, the stock is worth $51 per share. Mr. Bender exercises his option and buys 10,000 shares for $23 per share. If he then elects to sell some of his stock, the difference between the selling price and the exercise price ($51−$23) is treated as a capital gain and is subject to the favorable capital gains tax rate.

Subchapter S

Subchapter S of the Internal Revenue Code allows the owners of small corporations—those having 25 or fewer stockholders—to use the corporate organization form but to be taxed as though the firm were a proprietorship or a partnership. Thus, the owners are able to avail themselves of the legal advantages extended to corporations, but they are able to avoid any tax disadvantage that might result. They simply declare any corporate profits as personal income on a pro-rata basis and pay the appropriate tax on this income. This treatment eliminates the double taxation normally associated with dividend income—that is, the corporation paying dividends from after-tax income, and shareholders paying taxes on the dividend income they receive.

In addition, stockholders may deduct any operating losses on a pro-rata basis against their personal income. For start-up situations, this feature is particularly advantageous to investors with outside income, because they are able to get an immediate tax break on the early losses incurred by the new venture. Finally, any investment tax credit realized by the corporation may be passed on to the stockholders. Again, the advantage here is to investors with outside income.

SUMMARY

Of the three basic forms of business organization—the sole proprietorship, the partnership, and the corporation—the corporation has become most prominent because it offers a number of advantages. We observed these advantages together with aspects of the other two forms of business organization.

The tax environment has a profound influence upon business decisions. Certain basic features of the tax law apply to corporations, and these were explored. Depreciation, tax credits, interest expense, intercorporate dividends, the carry back-carry forward provision, and capital gains all affect the amount of taxes paid by the corporation.

Personal taxes affect debtholders and stockholders of a corporation through the interest, dividends, and capital gains they receive from their investment. Taxes affect employees and executives through their compensation and stock options. This chapter serves only as an introduction to the issue; relevant taxes and the implication of these taxes will be discussed throughout the book when we consider specific financial decisions.

QUESTIONS

1. What is the principal advantage of the corporate form of business organization? Discuss the importance of this advantage to the owner of a small family restaurant. Discuss the importance of this advantage to a wealthy entrepreneur who owns several businesses.

2. How does being a limited partner in a business enterprise differ from being a stockholder, assuming the same percentage of ownership?

3. What is the impact on earnings of the different methods of depreciation? Explain.

4. The method of depreciation does not alter the total amount of deductions from income during the life of an asset. What does it alter and why is that important?

5. If capital gains are taxed on a more favorable basis than ordinary income, why doesn't the business firm make sure that all of its profits are represented by capital gains?

6. If the owners of a new corporation number less than 25, does Subchapter S make sense for tax purposes?

7. Is there any theoretical justification for allowing the deduction of debt service charge from income for tax purposes, yet disallowing the deduction of dividends on preferred and common stock? Discuss.

8. Tax laws have become extremely complex. In addition, there is little theoretical or moral justification for a substantial number of tax incentives (loopholes). Why and how are these incentives created? In your opinion, is there any indication that these incentives will be eliminated?

9. What is the purpose of the carry-back and the carry-forward provisions in the tax laws?

10. If the investment tax credit were raised, what is the likely effect on business investment?

PROBLEMS

1. The Ross X-ray Company is going to purchase a new piece of equipment for $48,000. It has a depreciable life of three years and zero salvage value. Ross expects to earn $25,000 a year before depreciation and taxes from the use of the equipment in each of the three years. The company is interested in knowing the effects on profits of straight-line depreciation and sum-of-the-years'-digits depreciation.

   a) Determine the taxable income arising from the use of the equipment in each of the three years under both methods of depreciation.

   b) What is the total taxable income under both methods of depreciation?

   c) Which method of depreciation is preferable if the company is given a choice?

2. In 1980 the Kyle Company purchased, for $30,000, a special-purpose machine that was depreciable over five years and had an expected salvage value of zero. (The company used straight-line depreciation.) Three years later it sold the machine for $35,000.

   a) If the company had a marginal tax rate of 46 percent on income and 28 percent on capital gains, how much in taxes did it pay on the sale of the machine?

   b) If the machine were sold for $20,000, how much in taxes would have been paid?

3. Diefenbrock Cement Company is considering the purchase of the following assets:

	Cost	Property recovery category
Office equipment	$7,500	3 years
Trailer	12,000	5 years
High-tension winch	3,000	3 years
Mobile home office complex	47,000	10 years

   a) Determine the total investment tax credit that the company can claim if it purchases all of these assets.

b) What is depreciation in the first year on each of these assets if the company uses the double-declining-balance method?

4. Tripex Consolidated Industries owns $2 million in 9 percent bonds of Solow Electronics Company. It also owns 100,000 shares of preferred stock of Solow. In the year just past, Solow paid the stipulated interest on its bonds and dividends of $3 per share on its preferred stock. The marginal tax rate of Tripex is 46 percent. What taxes must Tripex pay on this interest and dividend income?

5. The Zeke White Construction Company was founded in 1978 and had the following taxable income through 1982:

1978	1979	1980	1981	1982
$0	$35,000	$68,000	−$120,000	$52,000

Compute the corporate income tax or tax refund in each year, assuming a tax rate of 17 percent on the first $25,000 of income; 20 percent on the next $25,000; 30 percent on the next $25,000; and 46 percent on all income over $100,000. (These rates were in effect for the period.)

6. Joe and Shirley Chin are executives in two separate companies. Together they have a taxable earned income of $178,000 this year. During the year, they sold their holdings of Xerox stock and realized a capital gain of $10,400 after holding the stock 9 years. If the Chins file a joint return, and the tax on $162,400 in taxable income is $62,589, what total taxes do they owe?

7. As a term project, evaluate the impact of continued inflation on the tax burden borne by a corporation vis-à-vis that borne by individuals.

PRINCIPLES OF FINANCIAL RETURNS

II

The role of financial markets for the business firm 3

In varying degrees, all business firms operate within the financial system. When a product or service is sold, the seller receives either cash or a financial asset in the form of an account receivable. In addition, the firm invests idle funds in marketable securities, and here it has direct contact with the financial markets. More importantly, most firms use financial markets to finance their investment in assets. In final analysis, the market prices of a company's securities are the test of whether it is a success or a failure. While business firms compete with each other in the product markets, they must continually interface with the financial markets. The financial system consists of a number of institutions and markets serving business firms, individuals, and governments. Because of the importance of this environment to the financial manager as well as to the individual as a consumer of financial services, this chapter is devoted to exploring the financial system.

THE PURPOSE OF FINANCIAL MARKETS

Financial assets exist in an economy because the savings of various individuals, corporations, and governments during a period of time differ from their investment in real assets. By real assets, we mean things such as houses, buildings, equipment, inventories, and durable goods. If savings equaled investment in real assets for all economic units in an economy over all periods of time, there would be no external financing, no financial assets, and no money and capital markets. Each economic unit would be self-sufficient; current expenditures and investment in real assets would be paid for out of current income. A financial asset is created only when the investment of an economic unit in real assets exceeds its savings, and it finances this excess by borrowing or issuing equity securities. Of course, another economic unit must be willing to lend. This interaction of borrowers with lenders determines interest rates. In the economy as a whole, savings-surplus economic units (those whose savings exceed their investment in real assets) provide funds to savings deficit units (those whose investment in real assets exceeds their savings). This exchange of funds is evidenced by pieces of paper representing a financial asset to the holder and a financial liability to the issuer.

Efficiency of financial markets

The purpose of financial markets in an economy is to allocate savings efficiently to ultimate users. If those economic units that saved were the same as those that engaged in capital formation, an economy could prosper without financial markets. In modern economies, however, the economic units most responsible for capital formation—nonfinancial corporations—use more than their total savings for investing in real assets. Households, on the other hand, have total savings in excess of total investment. The more diverse the patterns of desired savings and investment among economic units, the greater the need for efficient financial markets to channel savings to ultimate users. The ultimate investor in real assets and the ultimate saver should be brought together at the least possible cost and inconvenience.

Efficient financial markets are absolutely essential to assure adequate capital formation and economic growth in an economy. If there were no financial assets other than money, each economic unit could invest only to the extent that it saved. Without financial assets, then, an economic unit would be greatly constrained in its investment behavior. If the amounts required for investment in a real asset were large in relation to current savings, an economic unit simply would have to postpone investment until it had accumulated sufficient savings in the form of paper money. Because of the absence of financing, economic units that lacked sufficient savings would have to postpone or abandon many worthwhile investment opportunities.

In such a system, savings in the economy would not be channeled to the most promising investment opportunities, and capital would be less than optimally allocated. Economic units that lacked promising investment opportunities would have no alternative but to accumulate money. Likewise, economic units with very promising opportunities might not be able to accumulate sufficient savings rapidly enough to undertake the projects. Consequently, inferior investments might be undertaken by some economic units, while very promising opportunities would be postponed or abandoned by others. It is not difficult to see the value of being able to issue financial assets. Even with this ability, there are still degrees of efficiency with which savings are channeled to investment opportunities.

25
CHAPTER 3
The role
of financial
markets for
the business
firm

The more developed the financial markets of a country, the greater the efficiency. A number of institutions have evolved to improve this efficiency. One is the loan broker, whose purpose is to find savers and to bring them together with economic units needing funds. Because brokers are specialists, continually in the business of matching the need for funds with the supply, usually they are able to do it more efficiently and at a lower cost than are individual economic units themselves. Another institution that enhances the efficiency of the flow of savings is the secondary market, where existing securities can be bought or sold. With a viable secondary market, a purchaser of a financial instrument achieves marketability. If it needs to sell the security in the future, it will be able to do so. Thus, the existence of a strong secondary market enhances the primary market in which funds flow from ultimate savers to ultimate users. Investment bankers also enhance funds flows, and we study their role later in the chapter.

Financial intermediaries

Up to now, we have considered only the direct flow of savings from savers to users of funds. If there are financial intermediaries in an economy, the flow can be indirect. Financial intermediaries include institutions such as commercial banks, savings banks, savings and loan associations, life insurance companies, and pension and profit-sharing funds. These intermediaries come between ultimate borrowers and lenders by transforming direct claims into indirect ones. They purchase primary securities and, in turn, issue their own securities. The primary security that a savings and loan association purchases is a mortgage; the indirect claim issued is a savings account or a certificate of deposit. A life insurance company, on the other hand, purchases corporate bonds, among other things, and issues life insurance policies.

Financial intermediaries transform funds in a way that makes them more attractive. A variety of services and economies are provided. Economies of scale are possible and may be passed on to the borrower and lender in the form of lower cost of operations. A financial intermediary also is able to pool savings to purchase primary securities of varying sizes. Individual savers who would have difficulty investing in a $60,000 mortgage can put funds in a savings and loan association and indirectly invest in that mortgage. Diversification of risk is another service—something not always possible for the individual saver. Also, financial intermediaries are able to transform the maturity of a primary security into indirect securities of different maturities. As a result, the maturities may be more attractive to the ultimate lender than they would be if the loan were direct. Finally, the financial intermediary provides often needed expertise in investing in primary securities.

Thus, financial intermediaries tailor the denomination and type of indirect securities they issue to the desires of savers. Their purpose, of course, is to make a profit by purchasing primary securities yielding more than their expenses and the return they must pay on the indirect securities issued. In so doing, they channel funds from the ultimate lender to the ultimate borrower at a lower cost and/or with less inconvenience than would be possible if the ultimate lender directly purchased primary securities. Otherwise, they have no reason to exist.

FUNDS FLOWS THROUGH SECTORS OF THE ECONOMY

With the introduction of financial intermediaries, we have four main sectors in the economy: households, nonfinancial business firms, governments, and financial institutions. These four sectors form a matrix of claims against one another, as we see in Fig. 3-1, which shows a hypothetical balance sheet for each sector. Households are the ultimate owners of all business enterprises, whether they be nonfinancial corporations or private financial institutions. The distinct role of financial intermediaries is revealed in the nature of their assets, which are primarily financial; they hold a relatively small amount of real assets. On the right-hand side of their balance sheet, financial liabilities predominate. Financial institutions, then, are engaged in transforming direct claims into indirect ones that have a wider appeal.

Flow-of-funds matrix

We can study the flow of savings between sectors through the use of flow-of-funds data published by the Federal Reserve Bank. This system of social accounting provides an interlocking picture of funds flows in the economy.[1] Essentially, a source-and-use statement is prepared for each sector. The starting point is a balance sheet at the beginning of the period as well as one at the end. These balance sheets are similar to those in Fig. 3-1, but with financial assets categorized as *money* and as *other financial assets*—that is, paper claims—which are useful classifications. The flows are simply the changes in balance-sheet figures between the two moments in time. When source-and-use statements are combined, we obtain a matrix for the entire economy. Table 3-1 is a hypothetical matrix for a closed economy consisting of four sectors. Total uses of funds equals total sources for each sector; that is, the investment in real assets plus changes in financial assets must equal savings plus changes in financial liabilities.

We see also that business firms in aggregate invested in real assets to a greater extent than they saved. The difference was financed by issuing financial liabilities in excess of the increase in financial assets held. The existence of this large savings-deficit sector implies the existence of one or more savings-surplus sectors. When we analyze the matrix, we see that households were a savings-surplus sector and primarily responsible for financing the business firms sector on a net basis. In addition, financial institutions were a savings-surplus sector, although the excess of savings over investment for this sector was small. This sector acts almost entirely as an intermediary, increasing its holdings of financial assets by issuing financial liabilities. Finally, governments, the fourth category, were a savings deficit sector. Although governments make substantial expenditures for real assets, those expenditures, unfortunately, are not officially recorded. The budget deficit for governments is financed by an increase in financial liabilities in

---

[1] See James C. Van Horne, *Financial Market Rates and Flows* (Englewood Cliffs, N.J.: Prentice-Hall, 1978), chap. 2, for a further analysis of this system.

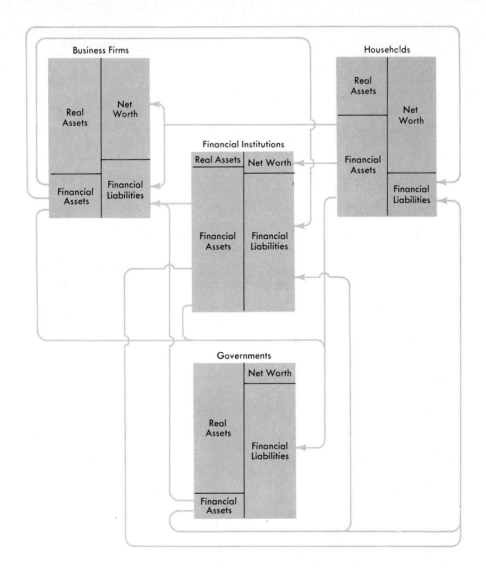

FIGURE 3-1
Relationship of
claims

TABLE 3-1 ╲ Matrix of flow of funds of entire economy, 19XX

	Households		Business firms		Financial institutions		Governments		All Sectors	
	U	S	U	S	U	S	U	S	U	S
Net worth (savings)		101		77		4		−3		179
Real assets (investment)	82		96		1				179	
Money	2		2			5	1		5	5
Other financial assets	37		18		60		17		132	
Financial liabilities		20		39		52		21		132
	121	121	116	116	61	61	18	18	316	316

excess of the increase in financial assets. Because the financial institutions sector contains commercial banks and the monetary authorities, it "provides" money to other sectors in the economy. The $5 source of money for this sector represents an increase in demand deposits and currency held by the public and governments as claims against commercial banks and the monetary authorities.

In the "All sectors" column, we see that total uses equal total sources. More important, total savings for all sectors in the economy equal the total increase in real assets. Likewise, the total change in financial assets equals the total change in financial liabilities. Thus, financial assets and financial liabilities cancel out in the economy as a whole. In other words, there is no such thing as saving through financial assets for the economy as a whole. The financial asset held by one economic unit is the financial liability of another. However, individual economic units can save through financial assets, and this is the process we wish to study. The fact that financial assets wash out when they are totaled for all economic units in the economy is a recognized identity. The important interaction is the one between issuers of financial claims and potential holders of those claims.

Funds flows for business firms

We know from our previous discussion that business firms are a savings deficit sector. When they invest more in real assets than they can pay for with their savings, they turn chiefly to households and financial institutions for funds. Households represent a direct flow; financial institutions, an indirect one. Of course, business firms finance each other through accounts receivable and other arrangements, but these funds flows wash out when we consider business firms in aggregate. The sources and uses of funds for the 1975–1980 period are shown in Table 3-2. We see that the principal use of funds by business firms is for plant and equipment. Of the total sources of funds, internal sources—comprised of retained earnings and depreciation allowances—account for about three-fifths, with external sources accounting for the remainder. Of the external sources, net new bond issues were the most important category, followed by mortgage debt and bank loans, both short-term and term, and by commercial paper.

FINANCIAL INSTITUTIONS

Among the number of institutions involved in the financial system, only a handful invest heavily in the securities of business firms. In what follows, we concentrate on those institutions involved in buying and selling corporate securities.

Deposit institutions

Commercial banks are by far the most important source of funds for business firms in the aggregate. Banks acquire demand and time deposits from individuals, companies, and governments and, in turn, make loans and investments. Among the loans made to business firms are seasonal and other short-term loans,

TABLE 3-2 \\ Sources and uses of corporate funds (in $ billions)

	1975	1976	1977	1978	1979	1980
Uses of funds:						
Plant and equipment	106.9	121.2	143.3	170.0	195.2	207.0
Land	10.0	11.1	11.9	13.0	14.5	16.0
Mineral rights	1.3	4.0	2.5	2.0	4.7	6.0
Direct foreign investment	6.0	3.9	5.0	3.8	4.0	3.5
Residential construction	2.0	3.0	4.8	4.2	4.3	2.0
Inventories adjusted for valuation	−10.4	10.8	19.2	19.7	17.1	14.5
Net trade and consumer credit	1.0	8.8	12.0	13.2	11.0	2.5
Demand deposits and currency	6.2	1.5	0.8	5.3	6.3	1.5
Time deposits	−3.0	−2.0	4.8	5.5	−2.0	3.0
U.S. governments	9.5	2.3	−5.8	−7.1	−2.1	4.0
Federal agencies	−0.8	0.0	−0.4	0.7	−0.5	1.0
Open market paper	2.2	4.1	7.6	7.5	8.0	1.0
State and local securities	−0.2	−1.1	0.0	0.2	0.0	−0.3
Repurchase agreements	−0.8	2.3	1.2	5.5	2.6	1.5
Foreign deposits	0.8	1.7	1.3	2.0	1.0	−0.5
Other assets	13.8	18.4	15.1	−1.2	−0.9	1.6
Total uses	144.5	190.0	223.3	244.3	263.2	264.3
Sources of funds:						
Internal cash generation	104.6	132.5	139.6	152.1	160.1	158.0
Mortgage debt	9.5	12.9	18.9	23.3	24.2	15.1
Bank term loans	−2.6	−2.1	2.2	11.7	19.6	12.0
Bank short-term loans	−8.4	5.9	19.1	19.9	24.3	16.9
Finance company loans	2.2	5.2	10.3	8.3	7.0	0.9
U.S. government loans	0.2	0.2	0.0	1.7	1.2	1.8
Net sales of open market paper	−2.7	2.7	2.3	3.9	9.9	12.4
Net new tax-exempt bond issues	2.6	2.5	3.5	3.2	3.6	3.1
Net new taxable bond issues	30.2	25.9	23.4	20.3	18.0	33.5
Net new stock issues	8.9	4.3	4.0	−0.1	−4.7	10.6
Total sources	144.5	190.0	223.3	244.3	263.2	264.3

Source of data: *Salomon Brothers 1981 Prospects for the Financial Markets.*

intermediate-term loans of up to five years, and mortgage loans. There are around 14,000 commercial banks in the nation, and their assets total over $1.3 trillion, a staggering sum indeed. Besides performing a banking function, commercial banks affect business firms through their trust departments, which invest in corporate bonds and stocks. They also make mortgage loans available to companies and manage pension funds.

Other deposit institutions include *savings and loan associations, mutual savings banks,* and *credit unions.* These institutions are primarily involved with individuals, acquiring their savings and making home loans as well as consumer loans.

Insurance companies

Insurance companies are in the business of collecting periodic premiums from those they insure in return for providing a payout should some event, usually adverse, occur. With the funds received in premium payments, insurance companies build reserves, which, together with a portion of their capital, are invested in financial assets. Insurance companies are of two types: (1) property and casualty and (2) life insurance.

Property and casualty companies insure against fires, thefts, car accidents, and similar unpleasantness. As these companies pay taxes at the full corporate income tax rate, they invest heavily in municipal bonds, which offer tax exempt interest income. To a lesser extent they invest also in corporate bonds and stocks.

Life insurance companies insure against the loss of life. Because the mortality of a large group of individuals is highly predictable, these companies are able to invest in long-term securities. Also, the income of these institutions is partially exempt from taxes, owing to the buildup of reserves over time. They seek therefore taxable investments with yields higher than those of tax-exempt municipal bonds. As a result, life insurance companies invest heavily in corporate bonds, which represent the largest single financial asset they hold. Next in importance comes mortgages, some of which are granted to business firms. Life insurance companies also invest in corporate stock, but their investment here accounts for less than 10 percent of the annual funds they have available for investment. In aggregate, life insurance companies are the second largest financial institution (after commercial banks), having total assets of around $400 billion.

Other financial intermediaries

Pension funds and other *retirement funds* are established to provide income to individuals when they retire. During the employees' working lives, they usually contribute to the fund, as does the employer. The fund invests these contributions and either pays out the cumulative amount periodically to the retired worker or arranges an annuity. Commercial banks, through their trust departments, and insurance companies have pension funds, as do the federal government, local governments, and certain other noninsurance organizations. Because of the long-term nature of their liabilities, pension funds are able to invest in longer-term securities. As a result, they invest heavily in corporate bonds and stocks. In fact, pension funds are the largest single institutional investor in corporate stocks. Although individuals hold the largest amount of corporate stock, accounting for about 60 percent of total holdings, in recent years they have not invested new funds in stock on a net basis. In many years, they have actually reduced their holdings. On the other hand, pension funds have accounted for about two-thirds of the net increase in corporate stock in recent years.

Mutual funds also invest heavily in corporate stocks. These funds accept monies contributed by a number of individuals and invest them in specific types of financial assets. The mutual fund is connected with a management company to which the fund pays a fee, frequently one-half percent per annum, for professional investment management. Each individual owns a specified percent of the mutual fund, which depends on that persons's original investment. Individuals can sell their shares at any time, as the mutual fund is required to redeem them. While most mutual funds invest in common stocks, "balanced funds" invest in both stocks and bonds. Various stock funds have different investment philosophies, ranging from income and safety to a highly aggressive pursuit of growth. In all cases, the individual obtains a diversified portfolio managed by professionals. Unfortunately, there is no evidence that such management results in consistently superior performance.

In the recent era of high interest rates, *money-market funds* have developed. These funds enable individuals to invest indirectly in money-market instruments in smaller denominations than is possible with the direct purchase of Treasury bills, commercial paper, bank certificates of deposit, or bankers' acceptances. A very important factor in financial markets, these funds have grown at the expense of deposit institutions.

Finance companies are private corporations established to make consumer installment loans, personal loans, and secured loans to business enterprises. These companies raise capital through stock issues as well as through borrowings, some of which is long-term but most of which comes from commercial banks. In turn, the finance company makes loans. As discussed in chapter 12, finance companies sometimes play an influential financing role for smaller, emerging companies.

Financial brokers

Certain financial institutions perform a necessary brokerage function. When brokers bring together parties who need funds with those who have savings, they are not performing a direct lending function, but rather are matching the demand and supply of funds.

Investment bankers are involved in the sale of corporate stocks and bonds. When a company decides to raise funds, an investment banker often will buy the issue and then turn around and sell it to investors. Because investment bankers are continually in the business of matching users of funds with suppliers, they can sell issues more efficiently than can the issuing companies. For this service the investment banker receives a fee in the form of the difference between the amount received from the sale of the securities to the public and the amount paid to the company. Much more will be said about the role of investment bankers in chapter 21, when we consider long-term financing.

Mortgage bankers are involved in acquiring and placing mortgages. These mortgages come either directly from individuals and businesses or, more typically, through builders and real estate agents. In turn, the mortgage banker locates institutional and other investors for the mortgages. Although mortgage bankers function as brokers and have no funds of their own committed, they typically

31
CHAPTER 3
**The role
of financial
markets for
the business
firm**

service mortgages for investors. This involves receiving payments and following through on loan delinquencies. For this service they receive fees.

Security exchanges and markets

Various security exchanges and markets facilitate the smooth functioning of the financial system. The purchase and sale of existing financial assets occur in the *secondary market*. Transactions in this market do not increase the total amount of financial assets outstanding, but the presence of viable secondary markets increases the liquidity of financial assets and therefore enhances the primary or direct market for securities. In this regard, *organized exchanges* such as the New York Stock Exchange, the American Stock Exchange, and the New York Bond Exchange provide a means by which buy and sell orders can be efficiently matched. In this matching, the forces of supply and demand determine price. In addition, the *over-the-counter market* serves as a secondary market for stocks and bonds not listed on an exchange. It is comprised of brokers and dealers who stand ready to buy and sell securities at quoted prices.

Increasing competition

Before closing this section, it is useful to note the trend toward greater and greater competition among financial institutions as well as overlaps in their activities. In an era of financial deregulation, many restrictions and barriers to entry have been removed. A number of institutions now are able to provide essentially banking services; these include brokerage houses, retail stores, mutual funds, and credit card companies. Inroads also have been made into investment banking. American Express Company, Prudential Insurance Company, and even Sears have acquired large investment banking houses. Economies of operation are often possible through offering the consumer of financial services a broad menu. The traditional boundaries between financial institutions no longer hold.

Without protected "turf," and with the high levels of interest rates—which have caused great declines in the value of fixed-interest rate loans and investments—many financial institutions have had trouble surviving. As a result, we have witnessed a number of mergers, failures, and changes in business focus. This consolidation phase will continue as financial institutions adjust, often painfully, to heightened competition.

ALLOCATION OF FUNDS THROUGH YIELDS

The allocation of savings in an economy occurs primarily on the basis of price, expressed in terms of expected yield. Economic units in need of funds must outbid others for their use. Although the allocation process is affected by capital rationing, government restrictions, and institutional constraints, yields are the primary mechanism whereby supply and demand are brought into balance for a particular financial instrument across financial markets. If risk is held constant, economic units willing to pay the highest yield are the ones entitled to the use of funds. If rationality prevails, the economic units bidding the highest prices will have the most promising investment opportunities. As a result, savings will tend to be allocated to the most efficient uses.

33

CHAPTER 3
**The role
of financial
markets for
the business
firm**

It is important to recognize that the equilibration process by which savings are allocated in an economy occurs not only on the basis of expected return but on the basis of risk as well. Different financial instruments have different degrees of risk. In order for them to compete for funds, these instruments must provide different expected returns, or yields. If all financial instruments had exactly the same risk characteristics, they would provide the same yield in market equilibrium. Because of differences in default risk, marketability, maturity, and taxability, however, different instruments pose different degrees of risk and provide different effective returns to the investor. (A fifth factor, callability, is considered in detail in chapter 21.)

Default risk

When we speak of default risk, we mean the danger that the borrower may not meet payments due on principal or interest. Investors demand a risk premium to invest in other than default-free securities. The greater the possibility that the borrower will default in his obligation, the greater the default risk and the premium demanded by the marketplace. Treasury securities usually are regarded as default-free, and other securities are judged in relation to them. The greater the default risk of a security issuer, then, the greater the expected return or yield of the security, all other things the same.[2]

For the typical investor, default risk is not judged directly but rather in terms of quality ratings assigned by Moody's Investor Service or Standard & Poor's. These investment agencies assign and publish letter grades for the use of investors. In their ratings, the agencies attempt to rank issues according to the probability of default. Analyzing an issue, an agency weighs a number of factors, including the cash-flow ability of the issuer to service debt, the amount and composition of existing debt, and the stability of cash flows. The highest-grade securities, judged to have negligible default risk, are rated triple A. The ratings used by the two agencies are shown in Table 3-3.

Marketability

Marketability of a security relates to the owner's ability to convert it into cash. There are two dimensions: the price realized and the amount of time required to sell the asset. The two are interrelated in that it is often possible to sell an asset in a short period of time if enough price concession is given. For financial instruments, marketability is judged in relation to the ability to sell a significant volume of securities in a short period of time without significant price concession. The more marketable the security, the greater the ability to execute a large trans-

---

[2] For an extended discussion of the influence of default risk on yields as well as a review of the various empirical studies, see Van Horne, *Financial Market Rates and Flows*, chap. 6.

TABLE 3-3 ╲ **Ratings by investment agencies**

	Moody's		Standard & Poor's
Aaa	Best quality	AAA	Highest grade
Aa	High quality	AA	High grade
A	Higher medium grade	A	Upper medium grade
Baa	Lower medium grade	BBB	Medium grade
Ba	Possess speculative elements	BB	Lower medium grade
B	Generally lack chracteristics of desirable investment	B	Speculative
Caa	Poor standing; may be in default	CCC-CC	Outright speculation
Ca	Speculative in a high degree; often in default	C	Reserved for income bonds
C	Lowest grade	DDD-D	In default, with rating indicating relative salvage value

action near the quoted price. In general, the lower the marketability of a security, the greater the yield necessary to attract investors. Thus, the yield differential between different securities of the same maturity is caused not only by differences in default risk but also by differences in marketability.

Maturity

The relationship between yield and maturity can be studied graphically by plotting yield and maturity for securities differing only in the length of time to maturity. In practice, this means holding constant the degree of default risk. An example of the yield-maturity relationship for default-free Treasury securities on two separate dates is shown in Fig. 3-2. Maturity is plotted on the horizontal axis and yield on the vertical; their relationship is described by a yield curve fitted to the observations.

Generally, when interest rates are expected to rise, the yield curve is upward-sloping, whereas it is humped and downward-sloping when they are expected to fall significantly. However, the yield differential between short- and long-term securities is greater for the steepest upward-sloping yield curve than the negative difference is for the steepest downward-sloping yield curve. In other words, there is a tendency toward positive-sloped yield curves. Most economists attribute this tendency to the presence of risk for those who invest in long-term securities vis-à-vis short-term securities. In general, the longer the maturity, the greater the risk of fluctuation in the market value of the security. Consequently, investors need to be offered a risk premium to induce them to invest in long-term securities. Only when interest rates are expected to fall significantly are they willing to invest in long-term securities yielding less than short- and intermediate-term securities.[3]

[3] For a much deeper discussion of this concept, see Van Horne, *Financial Market Rates and Flows*, chap. 4.

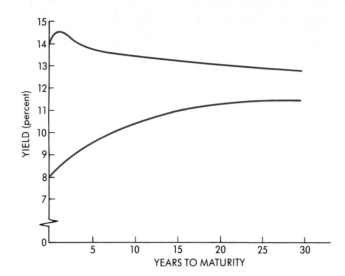

FIGURE 3-2
Example of Treasury yield curves

Taxability

Another factor affecting observed differences in market yields is the differential impact of taxes. The most important tax, and the only one we shall consider, is the income tax. The interest income on all but one category of securities is taxable to taxable investors. Interest income from state and local government securities is tax exempt; as a result, they sell in the market at lower yields to maturity than Treasury and corporate securities of the same maturity. A differential impact on yields arises also because interest income is taxed at the ordinary tax rate, while capital gains on securities held more than one year are taxed at the more favorable capital-gains tax rate. As a result, fixed income securities that sell at a discount from face value because of a low coupon rate in relation to prevailing yields are attractive to taxable investors. The reason is that part of the yield to maturity is a capital gain. If the face value of a bond is $1,000 and the current market price is $900, we know that the bond must rise in price to $1,000 at maturity. The $100 rise represents a capital gain, which is taxed at a more favorable rate than the interest income on the bond. Because of the desirability of discount bonds, their yield to maturity tends to be lower than the yield on comparable bonds with higher coupon rates. The greater the discount, the greater the capital-gains attraction and the lower its yield relative to what it would be if the coupon rate were such that the security sold at its face value.

Inflation

In addition to these factors, which affect the yield of one security relative to that of another, inflation expectations have a substantial influence on interest rates overall. It generally is agreed that the nominal rate of interest on a security embodies a premium for inflation. The higher the expected inflation, the higher the nominal yield on the security; and the lower the expected inflation, the lower the nominal yield. Many years ago Irving Fisher expressed the nominal rate of interest on a bond as the sum of the real rate of interest and the rate of price change expected to occur over the life of the instrument.[4] If the annual real rate of interest in the economy were 4 percent for prime risks, and inflation of 8 percent per annum were expected over the next ten years, this would imply a yield of 12 percent for ten-year, high-grade bonds. This states merely that lenders require a nominal rate of interest high enough to earn the real rate of interest.

It is important to differentiate between expected inflation and unexpected inflation. If inflation over the life of a security is exactly that which was anticipated when the terms of the loan were set, neither the borrower nor the lender gains (or loses) with respect to inflation. In other words, the terms of the loan reflect expected inflation, and the debt obligation is paid in keeping with the inflation that actually occurs. If part of the inflation which occurs is unanticipated, there is a redistributional effect from lender to borrower, or vice versa. With an unanticipated increase in inflation, the lender suffers by receiving a real rate of return lower than that anticipated at the time the terms of the loan were set.

To illustrate: the nominal rate of interest on a ten-year loan is 12 percent, of which 4 percent is the expected real rate and 8 percent is a premium for expected inflation. Over the ten years, inflation of 10 percent per annum actually occurs. As a result, the borrower's real interest cost is 2 percent instead of 4 percent. The lender loses, of course, because its real return is less than it anticipated at the time the loan contract was made. With an unanticipated decrease in inflation, the borrower loses in having to repay the loan in more "expensive" dollars than originally anticipated, whereas the lender gains.

Unanticipated increases in inflation result in a transfer of real wealth from net creditors to net debtors, whereas the opposite occurs with unanticipated decreases. A *net creditor* is defined as one whose financial assets exceed its financial liabilities; for the *net debtor*, the opposite holds. Whether a given company gains or loses with respect to inflation depends upon whether there is an unanticipated increase or decrease in inflation and whether the firm is a net debtor or a net creditor. In the aggregate, nonfinancial corporations have been consistent net debtors. Individually, companies can be net debtors or net creditors, and this can vary over time.

In the post-World War II period, a sizable portion of the inflation was unanticipated. Twenty years ago, no one would have thought present levels of inflation were possible. How much was unanticipated is difficult to say because we do not know what was expected, but it is not uncommon to see estimates that one-third of the inflation was unanticipated several years in advance. These estimates mean that nonfinancial corporations as net debtors, in the aggregate, have gained in the post-World War II period. Put another way, there has been a drop in the value of existing debt instruments, accruing to the benefit of the firm and its stockholders.

The important point here is that while nominal yields embody a premium for expected inflation, those expectations are not necessarily realized. In an uncertain world, unanticipated changes in inflation cause a relative redistribution of real return from lender to borrower, or vice versa.

---

[4] *Appreciation and Interest* (New York: MacMillan, 1896). Actually, Fisher expressed the nominal rate as $R + \alpha + R\alpha$, where R is the real rate, α is the expected rate of inflation, and $R\alpha$ is the product of the two. Like others, we ignore the product term, as it has not been found to be important.

Behavior of yields on corporate securities

Because of differences in default risk, marketability, maturity, and tax-ability, as well as because of changes in inflation expectations over time, the costs of funds to business firms vary. In Fig. 3-3 the yields on Aaa corporate bonds, Baa corporate bonds, and prime grade commercial paper are shown for the 1965–81

FIGURE 3-3 Yields for Aaa corporate bonds, Baa corporate bonds, and prime grade commercial paper, 1965–1981

period. Because of the difference in default risk, Baa bonds provide a higher yield than do Aaa bonds. Moreover, this differential tends to widen during recessionary periods as investors become more risk averse. This phenomenon is particularly evident in the 1974–1975 and the 1980–1981 periods. The difference in yield between Aaa bonds and prime commercial paper issued by corporations is due primarily to differences in maturity. As reflected in the figure, short-term interest rates, as typified by the commercial paper rate, fluctuate more than do long-term rates. This fluctuation is attributable to expectations of the future course of interest rates affecting short- and long-term rates in different ways. The maturity of a short-term instrument, by definition, is near. At maturity, the investor receives the face value of the instrument, assuming there is no default. Accordingly, short-term investors are less uncertain about fluctuations in the market value of their instruments than are holders of long-term securities.

The relevant expectations for commercial paper involve only the near future. The relevant expectations for bonds involve a much longer period. To illustrate the difference, suppose the economy were in a period of excessive inflation and that the monetary authorities had begun to tighten money. The accompanying reduction in the growth of the money supply would put upward pressure on short-term rates. By virtue of the monetary authorities' tightening of money, however, investors might believe that inflation would ultimately come under control and that interest rates would decline after a year or so. As a result, long-term bond yields might not rise and could actually decline somewhat in anticipation of short-term interest rates eventually moving down. Thus, the two rates might temporarily move in opposite directions. Over the long run, however, short and long rates tend to move in the same direction, as shown in the figure. The salient point in all of this discussion is that short-term rates reflect immediate supply and demand pressures in financial markets; long-term rates are much more influenced by long-run expectations.

Throughout the time span shown in the figure, the secular trend in interest rates was steadily upward. Each cyclical peak in interest rates exceeded the previous interest rate peak. This trend is primarily attributable to changing inflation and inflation expectations. In the mid-1960s, the rate of inflation was around 4 percent and reasonably stable; by the early 1980s, it averaged 10 percent and was quite volatile. This changing level and volatility of inflation, as well as the efforts of the monetary authorities to quell it, largely explains movements in the overall levels of interest rates in the 1965–1981 period reflected in the figure.

MONEY AND CAPITAL MARKETS

Different financial markets are classified according to the final maturity of the instrument involved. *Money* markets usually are regarded as including financial assets that are short-term, that are highly marketable, and that have a low degree of risk. These instruments are traded in highly impersonal markets, where funds move on the basis of price and risk alone. Thus, a short-term loan negotiated between a company and a bank is not considered a money-market instrument. *Capital* markets include instruments with longer terms to maturity and often less liquidity. The maturity boundary that divides the money and capital markets is rather arbitrary, ranging from one to five years, depending upon who is doing the classifying.

Highly sophisticated, the *money market* is comprised of commercial banks as well as a number of security dealers. It is a national market, but the focus of activity is New York City. Interest rates on money-market instruments are extremely sensitive to ever-changing supply and demand conditions. New information is quickly acted upon and transmitted to price. Funds transfers between buyers and sellers often are electronic, allowing prompt settlements on transactions.

The existence of an efficient money market serves the liquidity needs of the nation. Large amounts of securities can be exchanged quickly with little concession from the previous traded price. Given this liquidity, financial institutions as well as corporations and individuals are better able to manage and plan their overall portfolios of assets. Examples of money-market instruments include *Treasury bills, commercial paper, bankers' acceptances,* and *negotiable certificates of deposit.* These instruments are examined in some detail in chapter 9, when we consider the marketable-security position of the business firm. Our purpose here is to place these instruments in perspective with respect to financial markets overall.

The *capital markets,* comprised of a handful of distinctly different instruments, tend to be more varied than the money market. The market for *Treasury notes and bonds* is highly organized; dealers are strong, and the securities possess considerable marketability. The U.S. Treasury is the largest single borrower in the world and is engaged in continuous borrowing and refinancing. Because Treasury securities are free of default risk and are highly marketable, they command the lowest yields of all securities yielding taxable income. In contrast, the *mortgage market* is largely an aggregation of local markets, and only in recent years has it taken on some of the attributes of a national market. Interest rates, fees, and terms vary geographically to some extent. Although the liquidity of the mortgage has improved recently with certain government programs and the participation of financial institutions, it still is a far cry from a Treasury security when it comes to marketability. In addition, there are considerable legal requirements involved in the sale of a mortgage.

Another distinctly different capital market is the *municipal security market.* Because the interest income on a municipal bond is exempt from taxation, municipals are mainly of interest to individuals in high tax brackets and to corporations paying taxes at the full corporate tax rate. For this reason, the market for this security is segmented, and yields sometimes behave differently from those of other securities. Municipal securities have varying degrees of default risk, depending on the issuer.

Finally, the markets for *corporate bonds* and *corporate stock* are different from other capital markets. The income of corporate bonds is fully taxable, so their appeal is not to the same people who invest in municipal bonds. In general, corporate bonds are not nearly so marketable as Treasury bonds and somewhat less marketable than municipal bonds. Common stocks are evidence of ownership in a corporation, and their price behavior is substantially different from that of bonds. This behavior will be discussed in depth in chapter 5, when we consider the valuation of corporate bonds and stocks. It is clear from our brief examination of the capital markets, however, that its instruments are much more varied than those of the money market.

SUMMARY

Financial assets exist in an economy because an economic unit's investment in real assets frequently differs from its savings. An excess of investment over savings is financed by issuing a financial liability; a surplus of savings over investment in real assets is held in the form of financial assets. The purpose of financial markets is the efficient allocation of savings to ultimate users of funds.

A number of factors make financial markets efficient. Among the most important is the presence of financial intermediaries. A financial intermediary transforms the direct claim of an ultimate borrower into an indirect claim, which is sold to ultimate lenders. Intermediaries channel savings from ultimate savers to ultimate borrowers at a lower cost and with less inconvenience than is possible on a direct basis.

We can study the flow of savings from ultimate savers to ultimate borrowers through flow-of-funds data. We saw that for the economy as a whole, investment in real assets must equal savings. This is not true for individual economic units, which can have considerable divergence between savings and investment for a particular period. When practical, business firms usually support investment in real assets through internal financing, or savings. But since business is a savings-deficit sector, it makes extensive use of external financing—chiefly bond issues, stock issues, mortgage debt, and bank loans.

The greatest portion of funds received does not come directly from individuals but usually from commercial banks, life insurance companies, finance companies, pension funds, and mutual funds. In addition to these financial institutions, investment bankers and mortgage bankers are among the brokers who are valuable to a business firm. Finally, the secondary market is enhanced by the presence of strong security exchanges and an over-the-counter market.

The allocation of savings in an economy occurs primarily on the basis of expected return and risk. In turn, the overall risk of a security depends upon the likelihood of default, its marketability, its maturity, and certain tax considerations. In addition, expected inflation and unanticipated inflation have a major effect on all yields. Different financial instruments provide different yields over time because of variation in these factors. The differences in yields on Aaa corporate bonds, Baa corporate bonds, and prime commercial paper were studied in light of these factors.

Financial markets are classified into money or capital markets, depending upon their liquidity. Money markets include short-term, highly marketable financial assets with little risk. Capital markets are characterized by longer terms to maturity and much more variation among instruments with respect to marketability and default risk.

1. What is the purpose of financial markets? How can this purpose be accomplished efficiently?

2. Discuss the functions of financial intermediaries.

3. Business firms finance about two-thirds of their needs internally. As a result, many argue that professional management teams are isolated from investors; thus management teams run an enterprise for management, not for stockholders.

    a) What forces in the economy might break down management's isolation from investors?

    b) If management teams do in fact become isolated, what will be the impact on the efficiency of the economy?

4. The Braniff Airlines bankruptcy, the Equity Funding scandal, Penn Central's bankruptcy, the near collapse of Chrysler Corporation and International Harvester, and other incidents that have made headlines cause investors to revise their expectation of risk and return associated with financial instruments. What is the impact of such incidents on capital formation and on the economic development of our society?

5. What is the purpose of stock market exchanges such as the New York Stock Exchange?

6. What would be the effect of the following occurrences on the money and capital markets?

    a) The savings rate of individuals in the country declines.

    b) Individuals increase their savings at savings and loan associations and decrease their savings at banks.

    c) The government taxes capital gains at the ordinary income tax rate.

    d) Unanticipated inflation of substantial magnitude occurs, and price levels are rising rapidly.

    e) Savings institutions and lenders increase the transaction charge for savings and for making loans.

7. Suppose nonfinancial corporations had relatively great liquidity. Nonetheless, municipalities and the federal government developed a great demand for funds. What would be the effect on interest rates for corporate bonds? What would be the effect if corporations developed a large need for funds but first financed themselves by reducing their liquidity?

8. Can you name an innovation in financial instrument, institution, or practice? What is the characteristic of a financial innovation? Whom do they benefit?

9. Pick a financial intermediary with which you are familiar and explain its economic role. Does it make the financial markets more efficient?

10. What is the distinction between the money markets and the capital markets? Is the distinction real or artificial?

11. How do transaction costs affect the flow of funds and the efficiency of financial markets? Are transaction costs justified?

12. What are the major sources of external financing for business firms?

13. In addition to financial intermediaries, what other institutions and arrangements facilitate the flow of funds to and from business firms?

PROBLEMS

1. Loquat Foods Company is able to borrow at an interest rate of 14 percent for one year. For the year, market participants expect 10 percent inflation.

   a) What approximate real rate of return does the lender expect? What is the inflation premium embodied in the nominal interest rate?

   b) If inflation proves to be 7 percent for the year, does the lender suffer? Does the borrower suffer? Why?

   c) If inflation proves to be 13 percent, who gains and who loses?

2. Suppose that 91-day Treasury bills currently yield 9 percent to maturity and that 25-year Treasury bonds yield 10¼ percent. Lopez Pharmaceutical Company recently has issued long-term, 25-year bonds that yield 12 percent to maturity.

   a) If the yield on Treasury bills is taken to be the short-term, risk-free rate, what premium in yield is required for the default risk and lower marketability associated with the Lopez bonds?

   b) What premium in yield above the short-term risk-free rate is attributable to maturity?

3. For 19XX, suppose that the following changes in the balance sheets of business firms, households, and governments in the aggregate occur (in billions):

	Business firms	Households	Governments
Net worth (savings)	$220	$380	-$50
Real assets	275	280	
Money	5	10	2
Other financial assets	75	215	70
Financial liabilities	135	125	122

   a) Which sectors are savings-deficit sectors? Savings-surplus sectors? Why?

   b) From which sector do the savings-deficit sectors finance their deficits? How is it done?

4. In problem 3, suppose the economy is comprised of the three sectors described, along with a financial-institutions sector. For the year, the change in balance sheet for *all sectors* is as follows:

	Change
Net worth (savings)	$565
Real assets	565
Money	0 net ($17 use, $17 source)
Other financial assets	560
Financial liabilities	560

43

CHAPTER 3
The role
of financial
markets for
the business
firm

a)   Using a flow-of-funds matrix, derive the sources and uses of funds for the financial-institutions sector on the basis of the information presented in these two problems.

b)   What are the characteristics of the financial-institutions sector?

5. Companies X and Y have the following balance sheets at the latest year end (in thousands):

	Company X	Company Y
Cash	$1,000	$ 500
Receivables	7,000	2,000
Inventories	2,000	4,000
Net fixed assets	2,000	5,500
Total	12,000	12,000
Current liabilities	2,000	3,000
Long-term debt	1,000	5,000
Net worth	9,000	4,000
Total	12,000	12,000

a)   Are the companies net monetary creditors or debtors?

b)   If the rate of inflation should increase unexpectedly from 8 percent presently to 10 percent, who gains and who loses?

c)   If inflation unexpectedly drops from 8 percent to 6 percent, what happens?

6. From a recent Monday *Wall Street Journal,* collect yield information on yields for a long-term Treasury bond, a public utility bond (probably AA in quality), municipal bonds as described by the municipal bond index, Treasury bills, and commercial paper. (This information appears at the back of the paper under the Bond Market section, the Money Market Rates section, and the Treasury Issues section.) What reasons can you give for the differences in yield on these various instruments?

SELECTED REFERENCES

CARGILL, THOMAS F., *Money, The Financial System, and Monetary Policy.* Englewood Cliffs, N.J.: Prentice-Hall, 1979.

COOPER, S. KERRY, and DONALD R. FRASER, *The Financial Marketplace.* Reading, Mass.: Addison-Wesley, 1982.

DOUGALL, HERBERT E., and JACK E. GAUMNITZ, *Capital Markets and Institutions,* 4th ed. Englewood Cliffs, N.J.: Prentice-Hall, 1980.

HOMER, SIDNEY, and MARTIN L. LEIBOWITZ, *Inside the Yield Book.* Englewood Cliffs, N.J.: Prentice-Hall, 1972.

HORVITZ, PAUL M., *Monetary Policy and the Financial System,* 4th ed., Englewood Cliffs, N.J.: Prentice-Hall, 1979.

IBBOTSON, ROGER G., and REX A. SINQUEFIELD, *Stocks, Bonds, Bills, and Inflation.* Charlottesville, Va.: Financial Analysts Research Foundation, 1979.

JONES, FRANK J., *Macrofinance.* Cambridge, Mass.: Winthrop Publishers, 1978.

KAUFMAN, GEORGE G., *The U.S. Financial System: Money, Markets, and Institutions.* Englewood Cliffs, N.J.: Prentice-Hall, 1980.

KIDWELL, DAVID S., and RICHARD L. PETERSON, *Financial Institutions, Markets, and Money.* Hinsdale, Ill.: Dryden Press, 1981.

LIGHT, J. O., and WILLIAM L. WHITE, *The Financial System.* Homewood, Ill.: Irwin, 1979.

RITTER, LAWRENCE S., and WILLIAM L. SILBER, *Principles of Money, Banking, and Financial Markets,* 3d. ed. New York: Basic Books, 1980.

ROBINSON, ROLAND I., and DWAYNE WRIGHTSMAN, *Financial Markets: The Accumulation and Allocation of Wealth,* 2d. ed. New York: McGraw-Hill, 1980.

SMITH, PAUL F., *Money and Financial Intermediation.* Englewood Cliffs, N.J.: Prentice-Hall, 1978.

VAN HORNE, JAMES C., *Financial Market Rates and Flows.* Englewood Cliffs, N.J.: Prentice-Hall, 1978.

Compound interest and present value

4

Because finance is concerned with decisions involving monetary variables, and because the price of money is the interest rate, most financial decisions involve interest-rate considerations. This chapter deals with the mathematics of compound interest and present value. We have placed the material here because of the important role it plays in the development of the book. Although the discussion obviously is mathematical in orientation, we focus on only a handful of formulas, so that we may easily grasp the essentials. The examples frequently involve numbers that must be raised to the nth power, an operation that is difficult to work by hand, but most readers have access to a calculator, with which these examples can be easily verified.

COMPOUND INTEREST AND TERMINAL VALUES

The notion of compound interest is central to understanding the mathematics of finance. The term itself merely implies that interest paid on a loan or an investment is added to the principal. As a result, interest is earned on interest. This concept can be used to solve a class of problems illustrated in the following examples.

To begin with, consider a person who has $100 in a savings account. If the interest rate is 8 percent compounded annually, how much will the $100 be worth at the end of a year? Setting up the problem, we solve for the terminal value of the account at the end of the year (TV_1)

$$TV_1 = \$100(1 + .08) = \$108$$

For a deposit of 2 years, the $100 initial deposit will become $108 at the end of the first year at 8 percent interest. Going to the end of the second year, $108 becomes $116.64, as $8 in interest is earned on the initial $100 and $.64 is earned on the $8 in interest paid at the end of the first year. In other words, interest is earned on previously earned interest, hence the name compound interest. Therefore, the terminal value at the end of the second year is $100 times 1.08 squared, or times 1.1664. Thus

$$TV_2 = \$100(1.08)^2 = \$116.64$$

At the end of three years the depositor would have

$$TV_3 = \$100(1.08)^3 = \$125.97$$

Looked at in a different way, $100 grows to $108 at the end of the first year if the interest rate is 8 percent, and when we multiply this amount by 1.08 we obtain $116.64 at the end of the second year. Multiplying $116.64 by 1.08, we obtain $125.97 at the end of the third year.

Similarly, at the end of n years the terminal value of a deposit is

$$TV_n = X_0(1 + r)^n \tag{4-1}$$

where X_0 = amount of savings at the beginning
$\quad r$ = interest rate.

A calculator makes the equation very simple to use. Table 4-1, showing the termi-

TABLE 4-1 ╲ **Illustration of compound interest with $100
initial deposit and 8 percent interest**

Period	Beginning value	Interest earned during period (8 percent of beginning value)	Terminal value
1	$100.00	$ 8.00	$108.00
2	108.00	8.64	116.64
3	116.64	9.33	125.97
4	125.97	10.08	136.05
5	136.05	10.88	146.93
6	146.93	11.76	158.69
7	158.69	12.69	171.38
8	171.38	13.71	185.09
9	185.09	14.81	199.90
10	199.90	15.99	215.89

nal values for our example problem at the end of years 1 through 10, illustrates the concept of interest being earned on interest.

      Equation (4-1) is our fundamental formula for calculating terminal values. Obviously, the greater the interest rate r, and the greater the number of periods n, the greater the terminal value. In Figure 4-1 we graph the growth in terminal value for a $100 initial deposit with interest rates of 5, 10, and 15 percent. As can be seen, the greater the interest rate, the steeper the growth curve by which terminal value increases. Also, the greater the number of years during which compound interest can be earned, obviously the greater the terminal value.

      Although our concern has been with interest rates, the concept involved applies to compound growth of any sort. Suppose that the earnings of a firm are

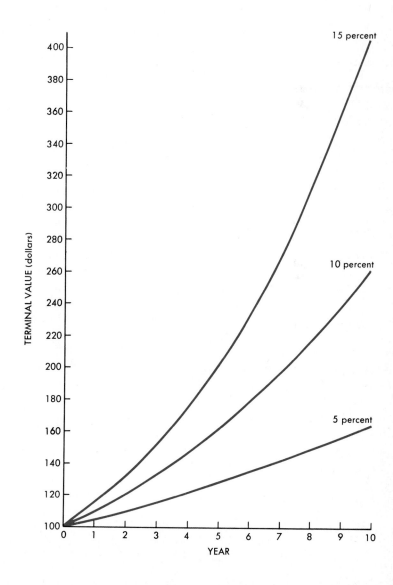

FIGURE 4-1
Compound values with $100 initial deposit and 5, 10, and 15 percent interest rates

$100,000, but we expect them to grow at a 10 percent compound rate. At the end of years 1 through 5 they will be as follows:

Year	Growth factor	Expected earnings
1	(1.10)	$110,000
2	$(1.10)^2$	121,000
3	$(1.10)^3$	133,100
4	$(1.10)^4$	146,410
5	$(1.10)^5$	161,051

Similarly, we can determine the level at the end of so many years for other problems involving compound growth. The principle is particularly important when we consider certain valuation models for common stock, as we shall do in the next chapter.

Tables of terminal values

Using Eq. (4-1), we can derive tables of terminal values (also known as future values). Table 4-2 is an example showing interest rates of 1 to 10 percent. In the 8% column, we note that the terminal value shown for $1 invested at this compound rate corresponds to our calculations for $100 in Table 4-1. Notice, too, that in rows tabulating two or more years, the proportional increase in terminal value becomes greater as the interest rate rises. This heightened growth is impressive when we look a century ahead. A dollar deposited today will be worth only $2.70 if the interest rate is 1 percent, but it will fatten to $13,780.59 if the interest rate is 10 percent. Behold (or let your heirs behold) the wonders of compound interest.

In 1790 John Jacob Astor bought approximately an acre of land on the east side of Manhattan Island for $58. Astor, who was considered a shrewd investor, made many such purchases. How much would his descendants have in 1990 if, instead of buying the land, Astor had invested the $58 at 6 percent compound interest? In Table 4-2 we see that $1 compounded at an interest rate of 6 percent is worth $339.30 in 100 years. Therefore, the value of $1 in 200 years is simply:

$$\$1 \times 339.30 \times 339.30 = \$115,124.49.$$

As the land was purchased for $58, we have a value of

$$\$58 \times 115,124.49 = \$6,677,220.42$$

in 1990 at a compound interest rate of 6 percent. This translates into a value of about $153 a square foot. Perhaps John Jacob would have been better off if he had forgone that particular purchase.

TABLE 4-2 ⟍ **Terminal value of $1 at the end of n years**

Year	1%	2%	3%	4%	5%	6%	7%	8%	9%	10%
1	1.0100	1.0200	1.0300	1.0400	1.0500	1.0600	1.0700	1.0800	1.0900	1.1000
2	1.0201	1.0404	1.0609	1.0816	1.1025	1.1236	1.1449	1.1664	1.1881	1.2100
3	1.0303	1.0612	1.0927	1.1249	1.1576	1.1910	1.2250	1.2597	1.2950	1.3310
4	1.0406	1.0824	1.1255	1.1699	1.2155	1.2625	1.3108	1.3605	1.4116	1.4641
5	1.0510	1.1041	1.1593	1.2167	1.2763	1.3382	1.4026	1.4693	1.5386	1.6105
6	1.0615	1.1262	1.1941	1.2653	1.3401	1.4185	1.5077	1.5869	1.6771	1.7716
7	1.0721	1.1487	1.2299	1.3159	1.4071	1.5036	1.6058	1.7138	1.8280	1.9487
8	1.0829	1.1717	1.2668	1.3686	1.4775	1.5938	1.7182	1.8509	1.9926	2.1436
9	1.0937	1.1951	1.3048	1.4233	1.5513	1.6895	1.8385	1.9990	2.1719	2.3579
10	1.1046	1.2190	1.3439	1.4802	1.6289	1.7908	1.9672	2.1589	2.3674	2.5937
11	1.1157	1.2434	1.3842	1.5395	1.7103	1.8983	2.1049	2.3316	2.5804	2.8531
12	1.1268	1.2682	1.4258	1.6010	1.7959	2.0122	2.2522	2.5182	2.8127	3.1384
13	1.1381	1.2936	1.4685	1.6651	1.8856	2.1329	2.4098	2.7196	3.0658	3.4523
14	1.1495	1.3195	1.5126	1.7317	1.9799	2.2609	2.5785	2.9372	3.3417	3.7975
15	1.1610	1.3459	1.5580	1.8009	2.0789	2.3966	2.7590	3.1772	3.6425	4.1772
20	1.2202	1.4859	1.8061	2.1911	2.6533	3.2071	3.8697	4.6610	5.6044	6.7275
25	1.2824	1.6406	2.0938	2.6658	3.3864	4.2919	5.4274	6.8485	8.6231	10.8347
50	1.6446	2.6916	4.3839	7.1067	11.4674	18.4201	29.4570	46.9016	74.3575	117.3907
100	2.7048	7.2446	19.2186	50.5049	131.5010	339.3014	867.7149	2,199.7569	5,529.0304	13,780.5890

Compound value with uniform payments or receipts

Consider now a situation in which an individual makes an initial deposit but adds to it a given amount at the end of each period. Continuing with our earlier example, suppose the initial deposit is $100 and the compound annual interest rate 8 percent, but the individual adds to it $50 per year. At the end of one year the terminal value would be

$$TV_1 = \$100(1.08) + \$50 = \$158$$

At the end of two years it would be

$$TV_2 = \$158(1.08) + \$50 = \$220.64$$

Although we could calculate the terminal value at the end of any period in this step-by-step manner, a more general formula is available for solution of the problem. It is

$$TV_n = \left(X_0 + \frac{X}{r}\right)(1 + r)^n - \frac{X}{r} \qquad (4\text{-}2)$$

49

where x is the increment which is added each period. For the example above, the terminal value at the end of two years would be

$$TV_2 = \left(\$100 + \frac{\$50}{.08}\right)(1.08)^2 - \frac{\$50}{.08}$$

$$= (\$100 + \$625)(1.1664) - \$625$$

$$= \$220.64$$

which, of course, is the same as calculated before. The terminal value at the end of five years would be

$$TV_5 = (\$100 + \$625)(1.08)^5 - \$625$$

$$= \$440.26$$

The formula in Eq. (4-2) is complicated, but it has widespread applicability. With the use of a calculator and with care to detail, one should have no difficulty. Remember that there is such a formula, but do not memorize it.

Annuities. An *annuity* can be defined as a series of uniform receipts occurring over a specified number of years, which result from an initial deposit. Figure 4-2 shows the cash-flow sequence for an annuity. An initial deposit is followed by a series of equal withdrawals over a given period of time. In our illustration we have assumed five years. Total withdrawals over the five years exceed the initial deposit because of the presence of compound interest.

Let us imagine that you inherit $10,000 and wish to have a steady income over the next ten years. A life insurance company sells annuities that will pay you, or your beneficiary if you should die, a fixed dollar amount annually for ten years. The insurance company calculates the amount of distribution on the basis of a 5 percent return. What is the annual amount it will pay? Referring to Eq. (4-2), the terminal value at the end of ten years would be zero, as everything would be paid out. We know also that X_0 is $10,000, r is .05, and n is 10. Therefore, we must solve for x, which we know will be negative, as it is a withdrawal. Setting the problem up in this manner, we have

$$0 = \left(\$10,000 - \frac{x}{.05}\right)(1.05)^{10} + \frac{x}{.05}$$

$$= (\$10,000 - 20x)(1.628894) + 20x$$

$$32.57788x - 20x = 16,288.94$$

$$12.57788x = 16,288.94$$

$$x = \$1,295.05$$

Thus, you are able to obtain $1,295.05 per year for ten years with an annuity.

Reversing our earlier problem, we also are able to determine the amount of initial deposit or balance that is necessary to afford a person a withdrawal of a

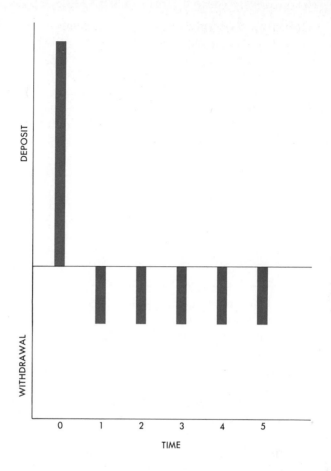

FIGURE 4-2
Cash flow of an annuity

certain amount over so many years. You may want to be able to withdraw $5,000 per year over the next ten years. If a savings institution pays 8 percent per annum, how much will you need to deposit for this to happen? In this case, x in Eq. (4-2) is $- \$5,000$. At the end of ten years there will be no terminal value, so $TV_n = 0$. With an interest rate of 8 percent, we have

$$0 = \left(X_0 - \frac{\$5,000}{.08} \right)(1.08)^{10} + \frac{\$5,000}{.08}$$

where we wish to solve for X_0. We have

$$0 = (X_0 - \$62,500)(2.1589) + \$62,500$$

$$2.1589X_0 = \$72,431$$

$$X_0 = \$33,550$$

Therefore, $33,550 must be deposited initially in order for the annuity to pay $5,000 at the end of each of the next ten years.

Compounding more than once a year

Up to now, we have assumed that interest was paid annually. It is easiest to work with this assumption. Now we consider the relationship between terminal value and interest rates for different periods of compounding. To begin, suppose that interest were paid semiannually. If one then deposited $100 in a savings account at 8 percent, the terminal value at the end of six months would be

$$TV_{1/2} = \$100\left(1 + \frac{.08}{2}\right) = \$104.00$$

In other words, at the end of one-half year one would receive 4 percent in interest, not 8 percent. At the end of a year the terminal value of the deposit would be

$$TV_1 = \$100\left(1 + \frac{.08}{2}\right)^2 = \$108.16$$

This amount compares with $108.00 if interest were paid only once a year. The $.16 difference is attributable to the fact that during the second six months, interest is earned on the $4.00 in interest paid at the end of the first six months. The more times during a year that interest is paid, the greater the terminal value at the end of a given year.

The general formula for solving for the terminal value at the end of year n where interest is paid m times a year is

$$TV_n = X_0\left(1 + \frac{r}{m}\right)^{mn} \tag{4-3}$$

To illustrate, suppose that in our previous example interest were paid quarterly and that we wished again to know the terminal value at the end of one year. It would be

$$TV_1 = \$100\left(1 + \frac{.08}{4}\right)^4 = \$108.24$$

which, of course, is higher than it would have been with semiannual or annual compounding.

The terminal value at the end of 3 years for the example above with quarterly interest payments is

$$TV_3 = \$100\left(1 + \frac{.08}{4}\right)^{12} = \$126.82$$

Compared to a terminal value with semiannual compounding of

$$TV_3 = \$100\left(1 + \frac{.08}{2}\right)^6 = \$126.53$$

and with annual compounding of

$$TV_3 = \$100\left(1 + \frac{.08}{1}\right)^3 = \$125.97$$

Thus, the more frequently each year interest is paid, the greater the terminal value. In Appendix A to this chapter we show how to determine terminal value when interest is compounded continuously. As m in Eq. (4-3) increases, terminal value increases at a decreasing rate until ultimately it approaches that achieved with continuous compounding. With continuous compounding, for example, the terminal value for our example problem is $127.12.

In summary, then, the terminal value of $100 at the end of three years with a 8 percent interest rate under various compounding intervals is as follows:[1]

Compounding	Terminal value
Annual	$125.97
Semiannual	126.53
Quarterly	126.82
Monthly	127.02
Continuous	127.12

We see that as the compounding interval shortens, terminal value increases but at a decreasing rate. The limit is continuous compounding. In order to attract deposits by paying a higher effective interest rate, many financial institutions have shortened their compounding period. In fact, certain institutions compound continuously.

To double your money!

Several rules of thumb apply to compound interest and doubling your money over a particular period of time. One is the rule of 72: divide 72 by the interest rate to find the number of years it will take you to double your money. If the interest rate on time deposits is 4 percent and you deposit $1 now, it will take roughly 18 years to double your money. If the interest rate is 6 percent, the number of years becomes 12; if 8 percent, 9 years. Referring to Table 4-2, we see that for annual compounding, $1 at a 6 percent rate is worth $2.01 in 12 years, and at an 8 percent rate it is worth $2.00 in 9 years. Therefore, the rule of 72 seems to give reasonable answers.

Indeed, for most interest rates one encounters, the rule of 72 gives a good approximation of the number of years required to double your money, but the answer is not exact. At 2 percent interest, the rule tells us our money will double in 36 years. In fact, our money will double in 35 years. At 24 percent interest, the rule tells us that we will double our money in 3 years. In fact, it will take a bit

[1] With monthly compounding, m in Eq. (4-3) is 12, and mn is 36.

longer—3.2 years with annual compounding. Also, when interest is paid more than once a year, it will take somewhat less time to double our money than with annual compounding. With quarterly compounding it will take 11.6 years to double our money if the interest rate is 6 percent as opposed to 11.9 years with annual compounding. (The rule of 72 tells us 12 years.)

Another rule of thumb is the 7-10 rule. This rule tells us that our money will double in 10 years at 7 percent interest and in 7 years at 10 percent interest. Turning to Table 4-2, we see that with annual compounding, $1 is worth $1.97 at the end of ten years at an interest rate of 7 percent, whereas it is worth $1.95 at the end of seven years at an interest rate of 10 percent. However, with quarterly compounding, $1 at the end of ten years at 7 percent interest is worth

$$TV_{10} = \$1\left(1 + \frac{.07}{4}\right)^{40} = \$2.002$$

and $1 at the end of seven years at 10 percent interest is worth

$$TV_{10} = \$1\left(1 + \frac{.10}{4}\right)^{28} = \$1.996$$

Therefore, the rule of 7-10 gives accurate results if the compounding interval is quarterly, but only approximate results if it is annual.

Both of these rules of thumb are useful to remember. They allow you to make certain compound-interest approximations in your head. Not only can you estimate the number of years it will require to double your money at a given interest rate, but also the interest rate required in order to double your money in a given number of years. For example, if you wish to know the interest rate necessary to double your money in eight years, the rule of 72 tells you it is 9 percent.

PRESENT VALUES

Having considered compound interest, we now are ready to take up present values. In any economy in which capital has value, a dollar today is worth more than a dollar to be received one year, two years, or three years from now. Therefore, we need a means for standardizing differences in timing of cash flows so that the time value of money is properly recognized. Calculating the present value of future cash flows allows us to isolate differences in the timing of these cash flows.

Perhaps you will be given an opportunity to receive, with complete certainty, $1,000 at the end of each of the next two years. If your opportunity cost of funds is 8 percent per annum, what is this proposal worth to you today? We might begin by asking, What amount today would grow to be $1,000 at the end of one year at 8 percent interest? In calculating the terminal value in the preceding section, we multiplied the initial deposit by $(1 + r)$, where r is the rate of interest, to obtain the terminal value. In this case, we are given the terminal value as well as the required interest rate and must solve for the appropriate beginning value. Consequently, we divide the terminal value by the required rate of interest, and this operation is known as *discounting*. For our example, the present value of $1,000 to be received at the end of one year is

$$PV = \frac{\$1,000}{(1.08)} = \$925.93$$

Similarly, the present value of $1,000 to be received at the end of two years is

$$PV = \frac{\$1,000}{(1.08)^2} = \$857.34$$

Thus, $1,000 received two years from now has a lower present value than $1,000 received one year from now. That is the whole idea of the time value of money. Overall then, the opportunity is worth $925.93 + $857.34 = $1,783.27 to us today.

In solving present-value problems, it is useful to express the interest factor separate from the amount to be received in the future. For example, our problem above involving $1,000 to be received at the end of two years can be expressed as

$$PV = \$1,000 \left[\frac{1}{(1.08)^2} \right] = \$857.34$$

In this way we are able to isolate the interest factor, and this isolation facilitates present-value calculations. In such calculations, the interest rate is known as the *discount rate*. The general formula for finding the present value of X_n to be received at the end of year n where k is the discount rate is

$$PV = X_n \left[\frac{1}{(1 + k)^n} \right] \tag{4-4}$$

Note that Eq. (4-4) for discounting is simply the reciprocal of the formula for finding the terminal value, Eq. (4-1), of x dollars so many years hence.

Figure 4-3 illustrates the present value of $100 received from one through ten years in the future with discount rates of 5, 10, and 15 percent. This graph shows that the present value of $100 decreases by a decreasing rate the further in the future it is to be received. The greater the interest rate, of course, the lower the present value but also the more pronounced the curve. At a 15 percent discount rate, $100 to be received ten years hence is worth only $24.72 today.

For an annuity involving a series of uniform receipts for a specified number of periods, the present value of the stream is

$$PV = \sum_{t=1}^{m} \frac{X}{(1 + k)^t} \tag{4-5}$$

where m is the number of periods over which receipts of X occur at the end of each period, and the capital Greek sigma denotes the sum of discounted receipts at the end of period 1 through period m. If $1,000 were expected at the end of each of the next two years and the discount rate were 8 percent, we would have

$$PV = \frac{\$1,000}{(1.08)} + \frac{\$1,000}{(1.08)^2} = \$925.93 + \$857.34 = \$1,783.27$$

Construction of present-value tables

Fortunately, one does not have to calculate present values by hand using Eq. (4-4). Present-value tables allow us easily to determine the present value of $1 received so many years from now at such and such a rate. To illustrate the construction of such a table, we make a few calculations using a discount rate of 10 percent. Suppose we wish to know the present value of $1 to be received one year from today. The formula is

$$PV = \frac{1}{(1 + 0.10)} = 0.90909$$

Similarly, if we wish to know the present value of $1 received two years from today, the formula is

$$PV = \frac{1}{(1 + 0.10)^2} = \frac{1}{1.21} = 0.82645$$

A present-value table relieves us of making these calculations every time we have a problem to solve; it is shown in Table A in the Appendix at the end of the book. We see in the table that for a 10 percent discount rate, the discount factors for one and two years in the future are 0.90909 and 0.82645, respectively—just as we calculated by hand.

If we had an uneven series of cash flows—$1 one year hence, $3 two years hence, and $2 three years from now—the present value of this series, using a 10 percent discount rate, would be:

PV of $1 to be received at the end of 1 year $1(0.90909) = $0.90909
PV of $3 to be received at the end of 2 years $3(0.82645) = 2.47935
PV of $2 to be received at the end of 3 years $2(0.75131) = 1.50262
$\qquad\qquad$ Present value of series $\qquad\qquad\qquad$ $4.89106

With a present-value table, we are able to calculate the present value for any series of future cash flows in the above manner.

The procedure can be simplified for a series if the cash flows in each future period are the same; that is, for an annuity. Suppose that in a series of future cash flows, $1 is to be received at the end of each of the next 3 years. The calculation of the present value of this stream, using the procedure above, is

$$\begin{aligned}
\text{PV of \$1 to be received in 1 year} &= \$0.90909 \\
\text{PV of \$1 to be received in 2 years} &= 0.82645 \\
\text{PV of \$1 to be received in 3 years} &= \underline{0.75131} \\
\text{Present value of series} &\quad \$2.48685
\end{aligned}$$

With an even series of future cash flows, it is unnecessary to go through these calculations. The discount factor, 2.48685, can be applied directly. Simply multiply $1 by 2.48685 to obtain $2.48685.

Present-value tables for even series of cash flows allow us to look up the appropriate compound discount factor (see Table A-8 at the end of the book). We note that the discount factor for an even series of cash flows for 3 years, using a 10 percent discount rate, is 2.4868, as we calculated. Thus, for an even series of cash flows, we simply multiply the appropriate discount factor times the cash flow.

Use of tables

Using the present-value tables A and B at the end of the book, we are able to calculate the present value of various future streams of cash flows. If we trace across any of the rows in Tables A and B, we see that the higher the discount rate the lower the discount factor. It is not a linear relationship, because the discount factor decreases less and less as the discount rate increases. Therefore, the present value of an amount of money to be received in the future decreases at a decreasing rate as the discount rate increases. The relationship is illustrated in Fig. 4-3. At a

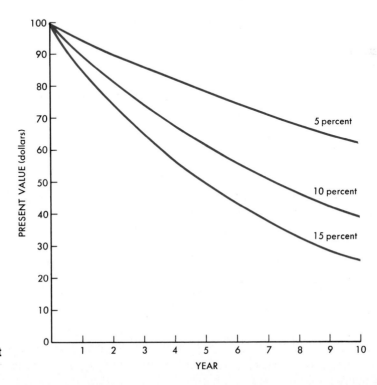

FIGURE 4-3
Present values with
$100 cash flow and
5, 10, and 15 percent
discount rates

zero rate of discount, the present value of $1 to be received in the future is $1. In other words, there is no time value of money. As the discount rate increases, however, the present value declines but at a decreasing rate. As the discount rate approaches infinity, the present value of the future $1 approaches zero.

As an additional illustration of the use of these tables, suppose that we wished to determine the present value of $500 to be received at the end of one year, $400 to be received at the end of 2 years, $300 to be received at the end of 3 years, and $200 to be received at the end of years 4 through 10, all at a discount rate of 12 percent. Here we have an uneven series for the first 3 years and an even series, or annuity, for years 4 through 10. Consequently, we use Table A for the first series and Table B for the second. For the first series, the present value is

$$
\begin{array}{lr}
PV \text{ of } \$500 \text{ at the end of 1 year} - \$500(.89286) & = \$446.43 \\
PV \text{ of } \$400 \text{ at the end of 2 years} - \$400(.79719) = & 313.88 \\
PV \text{ of } \$300 \text{ at the end of 3 years} - \$300(.71178) = & \underline{213.53} \\
& \$978.84
\end{array}
$$

For the second series, the annuity begins not at time 0, but at the beginning of the fourth year. Referring to Table B, we calculate the present value of an annuity of 10 years and subtract from it the present value of an annuity of 3 years to obtain the present value of an annuity from years 4 through 10.

$$
\begin{array}{lr}
PV \text{ of } \$200 \text{ for 10 years} - \$200(5.6502) = \$1,130.04 \\
PV \text{ of } \$200 \text{ for 3 years} - \$200(2.4018) \quad = & \underline{480.36} \\
& \$649.68
\end{array}
$$

Thus, the present value of the whole series is

$$
\begin{array}{lr}
PV \text{ of uneven series} & \$978.84 \\
PV \text{ of annuity} & \underline{649.68} \\
& \$1,628.53
\end{array}
$$

A wide variety of present-value problems could be illustrated. Be sure to do the problems at the end of this chapter.

In Appendix B to this chapter, we learn how to use an electronic calculator instead of present-value tables to determine present values and terminal values. There still are occasions when it is easier to use the tables, however, and that is the reason for our attention to them here.

Present value when interest is compounded more than once a year

When interest is compounded more than once a year, the formula for calculating present values must be revised along the same lines as for the calculation of terminal value. Instead of dividing the future cash flow by $(1 + k)^n$ as we do when annual compounding is involved, we determine the present value by

$$PV = \frac{x_n}{\left(1 + \dfrac{k}{m}\right)^{mn}} \qquad (4\text{-}6)$$

where, as before, x_n is the cash flow at the end of year n, m is the number of times a year interest is compounded, and k is the discount rate. The present value of $100 to be received at the end of year 3, the discount rate being 10 percent compounded quarterly, is

$$PV = \frac{\$100}{\left(1 + \dfrac{.10}{4}\right)^{(4)(3)}} = \$74.36$$

On the other hand, if the discount rate is compounded only annually, we have

$$PV = \frac{\$100}{(1.10)^3} = \$75.13$$

Thus, the fewer times a year the discount rate is compounded, the greater the present value. This relationship is just the opposite of that for terminal values. In Appendix A to this chapter, we show how to calculate present values when interest is compounded continuously. To illustrate the relationship between present value and the number of times a year the discount rate is compounded, consider again our example involving $100 to be received at the end of 3 years with a discount rate of 10 percent. The following present values result from various compounding intervals.[2]

Compounding	Present value
Annual	$75.13
Semiannual	74.62
Quarterly	74.36
Monthly	74.17
Continuous	74.08

We see that present value decreases but at a decreasing rate as the compounding interval shortens, the limit being continuous compounding.

While it is important to understand discounting where interest is compounded more than once a year, all of the present-value calculations in this book will involve annual compounding. However, the reader should be able to adjust any of the discount calculations undertaken for compounding more than once a year.

[2] For semiannual compounding, m is 2 in Eq. (4-6) and mn is 6. With monthly compounding, m is 12 and mn is 36.

Solving for the number of periods

In the preceding section we solved for the present value, given the interest rate, number of periods, and cash flows. In this section we wish to solve for the number of periods given the other three variables. To illustrate such a problem, suppose that for $10,000 you can acquire an asset that will generate cash inflows of $2,000 at the end of each year until it becomes obsolete, after which no more cash flows are generated and the asset has no salvage value. If the opportunity cost of funds is 18 percent, how long must the asset last to be a worthwhile investment? In this case, we have an annuity producing $2,000 a year. Setting up the problem, we have

$$\$10,000 = \frac{\$2,000}{(1.18)} + \frac{\$2,000}{(1.18)^2} + \cdots + \frac{\$2,000}{(1.18)^n}$$

We must determine that value of n where the cumulative sum on the righthand side of the equation equals $10,000. To do so, we first divide the amount of the investment, $10,000, by the annual cash flow, $2,000, and obtain 5.0. When we go to Table B at the back of the book, we find that for 18 percent the discount factor is 5.0081 for 14 years, whereas it is 4.9095 for 13 years. Therefore, the asset must last nearly 14 years if it is to be a worthwhile investment.

AMORTIZING A LOAN

Certain loans require the repayment of both interest and principal in a series of equal installments. Examples include mortgage loans, automobile loans, and some business loans. A bank may make you an $80,000 loan at 15 percent interest to be repaid in 10 equal annual installments. From the bank's standpoint, the cash flow stream represents an annuity with a cash outflow at time 0, followed by a series of even annual cash inflows. The amount of annual payment may be calculated by solving the following equation for x:

$$\$80,000 = \sum_{t=1}^{10} \frac{x}{(1.15)^t} \tag{4-6}$$

Looking under the 15 percent column in Table B at the back of the book, we see that the discount factor for an even stream of cash flows for 10 years is 5.0188. Therefore, we have

$$\$80,000 = 5.0188x$$

$$x = \$15,940$$

Thus, $15,940 is the annual payment necessary to pay off the loan in 10 years and return the lender 15 percent. In Table 4-3, the loan amortization schedule is shown. The interest payment is based on the amount owed at the beginning

TABLE 4-3 ❦ Loan amortization schedule (rounded to nearest dollar)

End of year	Payment	Interest	Principal repayment	Remaining principal amount owing
1	$15,940	$12,000	$ 3,940	$76,060
2	15,940	11,409	4,531	71,529
3	15,940	10,729	5,211	66,318
4	15,940	9,948	5,992	60,326
5	15,940	9,049	6,891	53,435
6	15,940	8,015	7,925	45,510
7	15,940	6,826	9,114	36,396
8	15,940	5,459	10,481	25,915
9	15,940	3,887	12,053	13,862
10	15,941	2,079	13,862	0

of the year. In the first year, it is 15 percent of $80,000, or $12,000. The principal payment in the first year is $15,940 minus $12,000, or $3,940. Therefore, the balance owing at the end of the year is $80,000 − $3,940 = $76,060, and this becomes the base on which the interest payment in the second year is calculated: $76,060 × 0.15 = $11,409. And so the process goes through successive iterations through year 10. Note that in the early years, the payment is comprised largely of interest, whereas at the end it is mainly principal. This relationship reflects the decline in interest as the principal amount is paid down. Similar to present-value tables, mortgage payment tables allow one to look up the amount of payment required.

SUMMARY

Mastering the concept of compound interest and growth is fundamental to understanding much of what goes on in financial management. In an economy where capital has value, interest rates are positive, and these rates must be embodied in any analysis involving future payments or receipts. In this chapter we considered the determination of terminal, or compound, values, as well as the determination of present values.

The terminal value at the end of year n for an initial deposit of X_0 that grows at a compound annual rate or r is

$$TV = X_0(1 + r)^n$$

This basic formula may be modified to take account of payment of interest more than once a year by

$$TV = X_0\left(1 + \frac{r}{m}\right)^{mn}$$

The greater the number of times a year interest is paid, the greater the terminal value.

We may also determine the terminal value when there are uniform payments or receipts over n years. Where receipts are involved, the situation is known as an *annuity*. Rules of thumb can be used to approximate the time required for one to double one's money, given a particular compound rate of interest.

The second major concept we considered was the determination of the present value of a future cash flow. It can be expressed as

$$PV = \frac{x_n}{(1 + k)^n}$$

where x_n is a cash flow at the end of year n, and k is the discount rate or interest rate required. As in the previous case, this formula may be modified for compounding more than once a year. We proceeded to show how present-value tables are constructed and used. Also, we considered how to solve for n, given the other three variables in the present-value equation. Finally, we showed how a loan may be amortized with equal installment payments and how to solve for the correct annual payment.

APPENDIX A ╲ Continuous Compounding

In practice, interest sometimes is compounded continuously. Certain valuation models in finance also employ continuous compounding. Therefore, it is useful to consider how it works. Recall from the chapter that the general formula for solving for the terminal value at the end of year n is

$$TV_n = X_0\left(1 + \frac{r}{m}\right)^{mn} \tag{4A-1}$$

where X_0 = the initial deposit
   r = the interest rate
   m = number of times a year interest is paid.

If interest were compounded daily on the basis of a 365-day year, the terminal value of an X_0 initial deposit at the end of n years would be

$$TV_n = X_0\left(1 + \frac{r}{365}\right)^{365n}$$

As m approaches infinity, the term $(1 + r/m)^{mn}$ approaches e^{rn}, where e is approximately 2.71828 and is defined as

$$e = \lim_{m \to \infty}\left(1 + \frac{1}{m}\right)^m \tag{4A-2}$$

where ∞ is the sign for infinity. To see that e approaches 2.71828 as m increases, simply increase m in the above expression from, say, 5 to 10 to 20 and solve for e. The terminal value at the end of n years of an initial deposit of X_0 where interest is compounded continuously at a rate of r is

$$TV_n = X_0 e^{rn} \tag{4A-3}$$

For our earlier example problem, the terminal value at the end of 3 years would be

$$TV_3 = \$100(2.71828)^{(.08)(3)} = \$127.12$$

This compares with a terminal value with annual compounding of

$$TV_3 = \$100(1.08)^3 = \$125.97$$

Continuous compounding results in the maximum possible terminal value at the end of n periods for a given rate of interest.

When interest is compounded continuously, the present value of a cash flow at the end of year n is

$$PV = \frac{X_n}{e^{rn}} \tag{4A-4}$$

The present value of $1,000 to be received at the end of ten years with a discount rate of 20 percent compounded continuously is

$$PV = \frac{\$1,000}{2.71828^{(.20)(10)}} = \$135.34$$

We see then that present-value calculations involving continuous compounding are merely the reciprocal of terminal-value calculations. While continuous compounding results in the maximum possible terminal value, it results in the minimum possible present value.

APPENDIX B ╲ Use of Electronic Calculators

With an electronic calculator, especially one equipped with a memory, we can easily and quickly compute the compound value and the present value of a series of cash flows.

Calculating terminal value

An investor deposits $3,000 in a bank account at the start of year 1, withdraws $1,000 at the start of year 2, and deposits $2,500 at the start of year 3. If the bank account earns interest at the rate of 5.875 percent compounded yearly, what is the compound value of the investment at the end of year 3?

With an electronic calculator, follow the accumulation process step by step.

Calculation step	Display shows
Enter the factor 1.05875	1.05875
Transfer it into the memory	1.05875 or 0.*
Enter the cash flow at start of year 1: + $3,000	3,000.
Multiply by the factor in the memory	3,176.25
Add the cash flow at start of year 2: − $1,000	2,176.25
Multiply by the factor in the memory	2,304.1046
Add the cash flow at start of year 3: + $2,500	4,804.1046
Multiply by the factor in the memory	5,086.3457

*Depending on type of calculator used.

In the above calculations, each multiplication by the factor 1.05875 carries the calculation forward by one year. The first multiplication finds and adds the interest earned during year 1. The negative cash flow, which occurs at the start of year 2, is then added, and the next multiplication finds and adds the interest earned during year 2. The positive cash flow at the start of year 3 is now added, and the last multiplication finds and adds the interest earned during year 3. Thus the compound value of the investment at the end of year 3 is $5,086.35.

Calculating a present value

We have seen that the easiest way of calculating the terminal value of a series of cash flows is to proceed step by step, moving forward one period at a time. Similarly, the easiest way of calculating the present value of a series of cash flows is to proceed step by step, moving *backward* one period at a time. This involves starting with the *last* cash flow of the series, *dividing* by the factor $(1 + k)$, adding the next-to-last cash flow, dividing by the factor again, and so on, ending with the cash flow (if any) at time 0.

An investment opportunity is expected to provide cash inflows of $6,000, $9,000 and $7,000, respectively at the end of each of the next 3 years. What is the present value of this series discounted at 10.5 percent per annum? The steps and results of this calculation are shown below.

Calculation step	Display shows
Enter the factor 1.105	1.105
Transfer it into the memory	1.105 or 0
Enter the cash flow at end of year 3: + $7,000	7,000.
Divide by the factor in the memory	6,334.8416
Add the cash flow at end of year 2: + $9,000	15,334.842
Divide by the factor in the memory	13,877.685
Add the cash flow at the end of year 1: + $6,000	19,877.685
Divide by the factor in the memory	17,988.855

In this table, each division by the factor 1.105 carries the calculation backward by one year. The third division carries it back to the start of the first year. As no cash flow at that time has been specified, this last division completes the calculation: the present value of the series is $17,988.85.

The use of an electronic calculator allows us to solve for problems without having to interpolate, as we must when we use present value tables. Therefore, the answers we obtain will often be more accurate.

QUESTIONS

1. What is compound interest? Why is it important?

2. What kinds of personal financial decisions have you made that involve compound interest?

3. In calculating the terminal value, we multiply by one plus the interest rate to the nth power, whereas to calculate the present value we divide by this amount. If the initial deposit and cash flow were $100, would the present value be the reciprocal of the terminal value?

4. What is an annuity? Is it worth more or less than a lump sum equal to the sum of the annuity payments?

5. What type of compounding would you prefer in your savings account? Why?

6. Contrast the calculation of terminal value with the calculation of present value. What is the difference?

7. What is the advantage of present-value tables over hand calculations?

8. If you were to receive a sum of money 5 years hence but wished to sell your contract for its present value, which type of compounding would you prefer? Why?

9. In order to solve for the number of periods in a present-value situation, what do you need to know?

10. The 7-10 rule of thumb suggests that an amount will double in seven years at a 10 percent compound annual rate or double in ten years at a 7 percent annual rate. Is this a useful rule and is it an accurate one?

11. Does present value decrease at a linear rate, at an increasing rate, or at a decreasing rate with the discount rate? Why?

12. Does present value decrease at a linear rate, at an increasing rate, or at a decreasing rate with the length of time in the future the payment is to be received? Why?

PROBLEMS

1. The following are exercises in terminal values:

   a) At the end of 3 years, how much is an initial deposit of $100 worth, assuming an annual interest rate of (1) 10 percent? (2) 100 percent? (3) 0 percent?

   b) At the end of 5 years, how much is an initial $500 deposit plus annual $100 payments worth, assuming an annual interest rate of (1) 10 percent? (2) 5 percent? (3) 0 percent?

   c) At the end of 3 years, how much is an initial $100 deposit worth, assuming a quarterly compounded interest rate of (1) 10 percent? (2) 100 percent?

   d) Why does your answer to part c differ from that to part a?

   e) At the end of 10 years, how much is a $100 initial deposit worth, assuming an interest rate of 10 percent compounded (1) annually? (2) semiannually? (3) quarterly? (4) continuously? (See the Appendix.)

2. The following are exercises in present values:

   a) $100 at the end of 3 years is worth how much today, assuming a discount rate of (1) 10 percent? (2) 100 percent? (3) 0 percent?

   b) What is the aggregate present value of $500 received at the end of each of the next 3 years, assuming a discount rate of (1) 4 percent? (2) 25 percent?

   c) $100 is received at the end of one year, $500 at the end of 2 years, and $1,000 at the end of 3 years. What is the aggregate present value of these receipts, assuming a discount rate of (1) 4 percent? (2) 25 percent?

   d) $1,000 is to be received at the end of one year, $500 at the end of 2 years, and $100 at the end of 3 years. What is the aggregate present value of these receipts assuming a discount rate of (1) 4 percent? (2) 25 percent?

   e) Compare your solutions in 2(c) with those in 2(d) and explain the reason for the differences.

3. Sally Ronk is considering two different savings plans. The first plan would have her deposit $500 every 6 months, and she would receive interest at a 7 percent annual rate, compounded semi-annually. Under the second plan she would deposit $1,000 every year with a rate of interest of $7\frac{1}{2}$ percent, compounded annually. The initial deposit with plan 1 would be made 6 months hence and with plan 2 one year hence.

   a) What is the terminal value of the first plan at the end of 10 years?

   b) What is the terminal value of the second plan at the end of 10 years?

   c) Which plan should Ronk use, assuming her only concern is with the value of her savings at the end of 10 years?

   d) Would your answer change if the rate of interest on the second plan were 7 percent?

4. Joe Hernandez has inherited $25,000 and wishes to purchase an annuity that will provide him with a steady income over the next twelve years. He has heard that the local savings and loan association is currently paying 6 percent on an annual basis. If he were to deposit his funds here, how much would he be able to withdraw annually (to the nearest dollar)?

5. You need to have $50,000 at the end of ten years. To accumulate this sum, you have decided to save a certain amount at the end of each of the next ten years and deposit it in the bank. The bank pays 8 percent interest compounded annually for long-term deposits. How much will you have to save each year (to the nearest dollar)?

6. Mr. Joel Dunway wishes to borrow $10,000 for 3 years. A group of individuals agrees to lend him this amount if he contracts to pay them $18,000 at the end of the three years. What is the implicit annual interest rate to the nearest percentage?

7. You have been offered a note with 4 years to maturity, which will pay $3,000 at the end of each of the four years. The price of the note to you is $10,200. What is the implicit interest rate you will receive to the nearest percentage?

8. Sales of the H. L. Cramer Company were $500,000, and they are expected to grow at a compound rate of 20 percent for the next 6 years. What will the sales be at the end of each of the next 6 years?

9. The H & L Bark Company is considering the purchase of a scraping machine that is expected to provide cash flows as follows:

Year	1	2	3	4	5	6	7	8	9	10
Cash flow	$1,200	$2,000	$2,400	$1,900	$1,600	$1,400	$1,400	$1,400	$1,400	$1,400

If the appropriate discount rate is 14 percent, what is the present value of this cash-flow stream?

10. Suppose you were to receive $1,000 at the end of 10 years. If your opportunity rate is 10 percent, what is the present value of this amount if interest is compounded annually? If compounded quarterly? if compounded continuously? (See the Appendix.)

11. In connection with the Bicentennial, the U.S. Treasury once contemplated offering a savings bond for $1,000, which would be worth $1 million in 100 years. Is such a large increase in value possible if the interest rate is only around 7 percent?

12. Patricia Van Auken is a prospective buyer of an apartment building on leased land. At the end of 20 years the land and the building revert to the lessor with no terminal value to the buyer. Annual rentals on the building are expected to be $126,000, while maintenance and other cash expenses are expected to average $60,000 per year. If Van Auken's opportunity cost of funds is 13 percent, what is the maximum price she should pay for the building?

13. Toby Markovich wishes to purchase an annuity contract that will pay him $7,000 a year for the rest of his life. Sierra Nevada Life Insurance Company figures that his life expectancy is 21 years, based on its actuary tables. The company imputes an interest rate of 6 percent in its annuity contracts.

a) How much will Markovich have to pay for the annuity?

b) How much would he have to pay if the interest rate were 8 percent?

14. The Happy Hang Glide Company is purchasing a building and has obtained a $190,000 mortgage loan for twenty years. The loan bears an interest rate of 17 percent and calls for equal annual installment payments at the end of each of the twenty years. What is the amount of the annual payment?

15. Barquez Mines, Inc., is considering investing in Peru. It makes a bid to the government to participate in the development of a mine, the profits of which will be realized at the end of 5 years. The mine is expected to produce $5 million in cash to Barquez at that time. Other than the bid at the outset, no other cash flows will occur, as the government will reimburse the company for all costs. If Barquez requires a return of 20 percent, what is the maximum bid it should make for the participation right if interest is compounded (*a*) annually? (*b*) semi-annually? (*c*) quarterly? (*d*) continuously?

SELECTED REFERENCES

CISSELL, ROBERT, HELEN CISSELL, and DAVID C. FLASPOHLER, *Mathematics of Finance,* 5th ed. Boston: Houghton, Mifflin, 1978.

DRAPER, JEAN E., and JANE S. KLINGMAN, *Mathematical Analysis,* 2nd ed. New York: Harper, 1972.

HAEUSSLER, ERNEST F., and RICHARD S. PAUL, *Introductory Mathematical Analysis for Students of Business and Economics,* 2nd ed. Reston, Va.: Reston Publishing Company, 1976.

HOWELL, JAMES E., and DANIEL TEICHROEW, *Mathematical Analysis for Business Decisions,* 2nd ed. Homewood, Ill.: Irwin, 1971.

KEMENY, JOHN G., ARTHUR SCHLEIFER, JR., J. LAURIE SNELL, and GERALD L. THOMPSON, *Finite Mathematics with Business Applications,* 2nd ed. Englewood Cliffs, N.J.: Prentice-Hall, 1972, chap. 7.

SHAO, STEPHEN P., *Mathematics for Management and Finance,* 3rd ed. Cincinnati: South-Western, 1974.

SNYDER, LLEWELLYN R., and WILLIAM F. JACKSON, *Essential Business Mathematics,* 7th ed. New York: McGraw-Hill, 1979.

VICHAS, ROBERT P., *Handbook of Financial Mathematics, Formulas, and Tables.* Englewood Cliffs, N.J.: Prentice-Hall, 1979.

Foundations for valuation 5

In the last chapter we investigated the wonders of compound interest as well as the time value of money. We now are able to apply these concepts to the valuation of different securities. By *valuation* we mean the process by which the market price of a security is determined. In particular, we are concerned with the valuation of bonds, preferred stocks, and common stocks, though the principles discussed apply to other financial instruments as well. These principles will underlie much of the later development of the book. Because the major decisions of a company are all related in their effect on valuation, we must understand how investors value the financial instruments of a company.

VALUATION IN GENERAL

A key factor in the valuation of any financial instrument is an implied positive relationship between risk and expected return. It has been shown that investors overall dislike risk. As a result, they must be offered additional expected return for taking greater risk. Assume for purposes of illustration that you are among investors who concentrate upon some common holding period—say one year. The return from holding a security is simply the change in market price, plus any cash payments received from the company, divided by the beginning price.

FIGURE 5-1
The security market line

You might buy a security for $100 that paid $7 in cash to you and was worth $106 one year hence. The return would be ($7 + $6)/$100 = 13 percent. Assume further that you are concerned with what we shall call *unavoidable risk*, the risk that cannot be avoided by diversification of the securities you hold. In other words, if you invest in a number of securities, some of the individual security risks cancel out. What is left over we call the unavoidable risk. Much more will be said about this later in the chapter; for now, our purpose is to illustrate a simple but fundamental concept.

If investors overall are averse to risk, there exists a relationship between the return they expect from holding a security and its unavoidable risk. This relationship, known as the *security market line*, is illustrated in Fig. 5-1. The expected one-year return is shown on the vertical axis, and unavoidable risk is on the horizontal. At zero risk, the security market line has an intercept on the vertical axis at a positive expected rate of return. As no risk is involved, this rate is known as the *risk-free rate*. As risk increases, the required rate of return increases in the manner depicted. Thus, there is a positive relationship between risk and expected return, which, as we shall see, governs the valuation of marketable securities.[1]

The slope of the security market line tells us the degree to which investors are risk-averse. The steeper the slope, the more averse they are to risk. If investors were not at all averse to risk, the security market line would be horizontal. In other words, they would require the same expected return on Treasury securities as they would on the securities of the most speculative of companies. As this equality of expected returns is not the case, we shall assume that the line has a positive slope.

Changes in security market line

We must be alert to the fact that the security market line depicts the tradeoff between expected return and unavoidable risk at a particular moment. This line can change over time with changes in interest rates and investor psychology. For one thing, the risk-free rate is expressed in nominal terms; that is, it is not adjusted

---

[1]The concepts underlying the security market line will be explored in more depth in the latter part of this chapter when we take up the valuation of common stocks.

for inflation. As we discussed in chapter 3, the nominal rate of interest can be thought of as comprised of the real rate of interest plus a premium for inflation. Suppose for purposes of illustration that the real rate of interest on short-term securities is 1 percent and the inflation premium 9 percent, making the nominal risk-free rate 10 percent. Now if there were an unanticipated burst in inflation of 3 percent, the inflation premium would go to 12 percent and the nominal rate to 13 percent. As a result, the security market line would shift upward. This shift might be depicted by the graph in the upper panel of Fig. 5-2. Note that the line shifts upward by a given amount throughout.

In the lower panel of the figure we show a hypothetical change in investor psychology from pessimism regarding the economy to optimism. Note here that the slope of the security market line decreases, as opposed to a shift throughout. The same expected return as before is required for a risk-free security. However, lower returns are required for all risky securities; the greater the unavoidable risk, the lower the return required relative to the pessimistic period. Thus, we must

FIGURE 5-2
Security market line with changes in interest rates and investor psychology

allow for the fact that the relationship between risk and expected return is not necessarily stable. The degree of risk aversion of the market can and does change over time. With these general valuation concepts in mind, we are able to explore in more detail the valuation of specific types of securities.

VALUATION OF FIXED-INCOME SECURITIES

A fixed-income security is one that pays a stated amount of money to the investor each period until it is retired by the issuing company. Before we can understand the valuation of such securities, certain terms must be discussed. For one thing, the instrument has a stated *face value*. This value is almost always $1,000 per bond and usually $50 or $100 per share of preferred stock. The bond also has a stated *maturity*, which is the time when the company must pay the holder the face value of the instrument. Preferred stock, on the other hand, has no stated maturity; like common stock, it is perpetual. Finally, *the coupon rate of interest* is stated, and it is paid each year. If the coupon rate is 12 percent on a $1,000 face value bond, the company pays the holder $120 each year until the bond matures. Remember that the terms of a fixed-income security are established at the time it is originally issued and cannot be changed.

Bond valuation

The terms of a bond call for the payment of a stated amount of interest over a given number of years, at the conclusion of which the face value of the instrument must be paid. The value of the instrument can be viewed as simply the present value of this cash-flow stream. The valuation equation for a bond that pays interest at the end of the year and has a face value of $1,000 is

$$P = \frac{C}{(1 + k)} + \frac{C}{(1 + k)^2} + \cdots + \frac{C}{(1 + k)^n} + \frac{\$1,000}{(1 + k)^n} \qquad (5\text{-}1)$$

where P is the present value of the payment stream, C is the annual interest payment as given by the coupon rate, n is the number of years to final maturity, and k is the required rate of return, given its risk. The latter also is known as the *yield to maturity*.

We may wish to determine the market price necessary for a bond with a 12 percent coupon and ten years to maturity to provide a return of 14 percent. This shift upward in market rates might occur if there were an unanticipated increase in inflation. The coupon rate corresponds to interest payments of $120 a year. Therefore,

$$P = \frac{\$120}{(1.14)} + \frac{\$120}{(1.14)^2} + \cdots + \frac{\$120}{(1.14)^{10}} + \frac{\$1,000}{(1.14)^{10}}$$

Referring to Table B at the back of the book, we find that the present-value discount factor for 10 years of annual payments at a 14 percent discount rate is 5.2161. From Table A, again at the back of the book, we find under the 14 percent column that the discount factor for a single payment 10 years in the future is .26974. Therefore, the value, P, of the bond is:

Period	Payment	Discount factor	Present value
1-10	$ 120	5.2161	$625.93
10	1,000	0.26974	269.74
		Value of bond	$895.67

Expressed differently, the value of the bond is simply the sum of the present value of the stream of future interest payments plus the present value of the final payment at maturity.

If, instead of 12 percent, the bond provided only a 10 percent return, the valuation equation would become

$$P = \frac{\$120}{(1.10)} + \frac{\$120}{(1.10)^2} + \cdots + \frac{\$120}{(1.10)^{10}} + \frac{\$1,000}{(1.10)^{10}}$$

Looking up the appropriate discount factors in Tables A and B at the back of the book, we find the following:

Period	Payment	Discount factor	Present value
1-10	$ 120	6.1446	$ 737.35
10	1,000	0.38554	385.54
		Value of bond	$1,122.89

In this case, the value of the bond is in excess of its $1,000 face value, whereas before it was less than its face value.

Behavior of bond values. On the basis of these examples, a number of observations can be made concerning the valuation of bonds.

1. When the required rate of return is more than the stated coupon rate, the value of the bond will be *less* than its face value. Such a bond is said to be selling at a *discount.*

2. When the required rate of return is less than the stated coupon rate, the value of the bond will be *greater* than its face value. Such a bond is said to be selling at a *premium.*

3. When the required rate of return equals the stated coupon rate, the value of the bond will equal to its face value.

4. If interest rates rise so that the required rate of return increases, the bond will decline in value. If interest rates fall, it will increase in value.

A further relationship, not apparent from the previous examples, needs to be illustrated separately.

5. For a given change in required return, the value of a bond will change by a greater amount, the longer its maturity.[2]

To illustrate, consider a five-year bond with annual interest payments of $120 a year and a required rate of return of 14 percent. Its valuation is

$$P = \frac{\$120}{(1.14)} + \frac{\$120}{(1.14)^2} + \cdots + \frac{\$120}{(1.14)^5} + \frac{\$1,000}{(1.14)^5} = \$931.34$$

which is determined in the same manner as illustrated before. Suppose now that interest rates fall so that the required rate of return is 10 percent. The value of the bond now is

$$P = \frac{\$120}{(1.10)} + \frac{\$120}{(1.10)^2} + \cdots + \frac{\$120}{(1.10)^5} + \frac{\$1,000}{(1.10)^5} = \$1,075.82$$

The increase in value for the bond is $1,075.82 − $931.34 = $144.48. Yet this illustration is exactly the same as our earlier one except for a maturity of 10 years instead of 5. In the former example the bond increased in value from $895.67 to $1,122.89. The absolute increase was $227.22. Thus, the change in value accompanying a decline in the required rate of return is greater for a 10-year bond than for a 5-year bond.

Similarly, one is able to take other maturities and demonstrate that, in general, the longer the maturity, the greater the price fluctuation associated with a given change in yield. One can think of the face value of $1,000 serving as an anchor. The closer it is to being realized, the less important are interest payments in determining the market price, and the less important is a change in required return on the market price of the security. In general, then, the longer the maturity of a bond, the greater the risk of price change to the investor when changes occur in the overall level of interest rates.

Paying interest more than once a year. If interest is paid more than once a year, Eq. (5-1) needs to be modified along the lines of our discussion in chapter 4. If interest is paid twice a year, or semiannually, we have

$$P = \frac{C/2}{[1 + (k/2)]} + \frac{C/2}{[1 + (k/2)]^2} + \frac{C/2}{[1 + (k/2)]^3} \tag{5-2}$$

$$+ \cdots + \frac{C/2}{[1 + (k/2)]^{2n}} + \frac{\$1,000}{[1 + (k/2)]^{2n}}$$

---

[2] For bonds selling at a discount with very long maturities, it is possible for prices to change by a lesser amount, the longer the maturity. This occurrence is unusual, so we shall not discuss it further. The interested reader may look into Michael H. Hopewell and George G. Kaufman, "Bond Price Volatility and Term to Maturity," *American Economic Review*, 63 (September 1973), 749–53.

For our first example above, we have

$$P = \frac{\$60}{(1.07)} + \frac{60}{(1.07)^2} + \frac{\$60}{(1.07)^3} + \cdots + \frac{\$60}{(1.07)^{20}} + \frac{\$1,000}{(1.07)^{20}}$$

We see that the discount rate is one-half of 14 percent, or 7 percent. Looking up the appropriate discount factors for 7 percent at the back of the book, we find the value of the bond to be

Period	Payment	Discount factor	Present value
1-20	$ 60	10.5940	$635.64
20	1,000	0.25842	258.42
			$894.06

where each period represents one-half year.

We see that the value of the bond with semiannual interest payments is slightly less than that with annual payments.[3] While the present value of the interest stream is greater, owing to earlier payment on average, the present value of the final $1,000 payment is less. The net result is a slight decrease in overall present value.

If interest on a bond is paid more than once a year, Eq. (5-2) can be modified in keeping with our discussion in the previous chapter; however, most bonds issued today have semiannual interest payments. Rather than having to solve for value by hand, we can turn to bond value tables. Given the maturity, coupon rate, and yield, we can look up the market price. Similarly, given any three of these four factors, we can look up the fourth.

Perpetual bonds and preferred stock

It is possible to have a bond that is a perpetuity. The British Consol, a bond issued in the early nineteenth century with no maturity date, carries the obligation of the British government to pay a fixed coupon perpetually. If an investment promises a fixed annual payment of C forever, its present value is

$$P = \frac{C}{k} \qquad (5\text{-}3)$$

Here k is the yield required on a perpetual investment. Suppose we could buy a security that paid $50 a year forever. If the appropriate yield, k, were 12 percent, the market value of the security would be

$$P = \frac{\$50}{.12} = \$416.67$$

[3] If the required rate of return were less than the coupon rate, semiannual payments would result in a slightly higher present value.

Preferred stock is a fixed-income security in the sense that it specifies a fixed dividend to be paid at regular intervals. The features of this financial instrument are discussed in chapter 23. While virtually all preferred-stock issues have a call feature and many are eventually retired, they have no maturity as such. Therefore, they can be treated as perpetuities when it comes to valuation. Thus, we have

$$P = \frac{D}{k} \qquad (5\text{-}4)$$

where P as before is the market price, D is the stated dividend per share, and k is the appropriate discount rate. If Hi-Lo Corporation had a 9 percent, $100 par value preferred-stock issue outstanding where the appropriate yield was 14 percent, its value per share would be

$$P = \frac{\$9}{.14} = \$64.29$$

Appropriate return for a fixed-income security

As illustrated in several instances above, the valuation of a fixed-income security simply involves capitalizing interest payments or preferred-stock dividends, using an appropriate discount rate. This rate can be thought to be comprised of the risk-free rate plus a premium for risk. Thus,

$$k = i + \theta \qquad (5\text{-}5)$$

where i = risk-free rate

θ = risk premium

If the security involved were a Treasury bill, there would be no risk of default, and we would expect θ to approximate zero.[4] Fixed-income securities of corporations obviously possess greater default risk than do Treasury bills. Therefore, there must exist a risk premium. The risk involved varies according to the company. Moreover, the financial instruments of an individual company possess more or less risk, depending upon their maturity, whether they are secured, and so forth. All of this is in keeping with our discussion in chapter 3 of the reasons that different interest rates prevail in the financial markets.

If we assume that investors overall are concerned with unavoidable risk, as described in the opening section of this chapter, the appropriate discount rate can be approximated by use of the security market line. Given the degree of risk, one traces up to the security market line in Fig. 5-1, then over to the vertical axis to obtain the appropriate required rate of return. Similar securities, such as 30-year bonds issued by electric utilities and rated Aa, will cluster at approximately the

---

[4] Even with Treasury bills, there are fluctuations in market price caused by changes in interest rates. Moreover, there is uncertainty about the return available upon reinvestment at maturity if one's holding period is longer than the maturity of the instrument. Nonetheless, Treasury bills are thought to represent a good proxy for the risk-free rate.

same degree of risk and, accordingly, require about the same rate of return. The risk associated with 5-year bonds of General Electric, however, will be considerably less than that associated with, say, the preferred stock of a new company in the electronics industry.

Our discussion of risk has been general, but it is possible to measure unavoidable risk and, as a result, approximate the required rate of return. As the work in this regard has been concerned primarily with the valuation of common stocks, we have deferred its illustration to the subsequent section. In closing, it is appropriate to stress that the same concepts that apply to the valuation of fixed-income securities apply also to the valuation of common stocks.

VALUATION OF COMMON STOCKS

The theory surrounding the valuation of common stocks has undergone profound change during the last two decades. It is a subject of considerable controversy, and no one method for valuation is universally accepted. Still, in recent years there has emerged growing acceptance of the idea that individual common stocks should be analyzed as a part of a total portfolio of common stocks the investor might hold. In other words, investors are not concerned with whether a particular stock goes up or down but with what happens to the overall value of their portfolios. We shall explore the valuation of common stocks in a portfolio context later in this section. First, however, we need to take up what is meant by the return to the common-stock investor.

Dividends and capital gains

If an investor's holding period were one year, most of us would agree that the return on investment in a common stock would be the sum of cash dividends received plus the selling price, all over the purchase price, minus one. More formally, the one-period return is

$$r = \frac{\text{Dividends} + \text{Ending price}}{\text{Beginning price}} - 1 \qquad (5\text{-}6)$$

On your next birthday, someone may give you a share of DSS Corporation worth $50 a share. The company is expected to pay a $2 dividend at the end of the year, and its market price after the payment of the dividend is expected to be $53\frac{1}{2}$ a share. Your expected return will be

$$k = \frac{\$2 + \$53.50}{\$50} - 1 = 11 \text{ percent}$$

Solving for the return. Another way to solve for the expected return is to set the problem up as follows

$$\$50 = \frac{\$2}{(1 + k)} + \frac{\$53.50}{(1 + k)}$$

In this formulation, we are interested in solving for the rate of return, k, which will equate the present value of the dividend and the terminal value at the end of year 1 with the beginning value. We want to determine the discount factor which, when multiplied by $2 plus $53.50, will equal the beginning value of $50. If we start with a discount rate of 11 percent, we find in Table A at the back of the book that the discount factor for one year is .90090. Therefore, the present value of the amounts to be received at the end of the year is .90090 × $55.50 = $50, or the exact value of the stock at the beginning of the year. Therefore, the expected return is 11 percent.

Now suppose that, instead of holding the security one year, you intend to hold it two years and sell it at the end of that time. Moreover, you expect the company to pay a $3 dividend at the end of year 2 and the market price of the stock to be $57 after this dividend is paid. Your expected return can be found by solving the following equation for k:

$$\$50 = \frac{\$2}{(1 + k)} + \frac{\$3}{(1 + k)^2} + \frac{57}{(1 + k)^2}$$

Here solving for k is more difficult. Suppose we start with two discount rates, 11 and 12 percent, because we have a "feel" from the numbers that the return will be somewhat higher than the 11 percent calculated before. Using this discount rates and Table A at the back of the book, we find:

Year	Discount rate	Discount factor	Cash flow	Present value
1	11%	.90090	$2	$ 1.8018
2	11	.81162	60	48.6972
			Total	$50.4990
1	12%	.89286	$2	$ 1.7857
2	12	.79719	60	47.8314
			Total	$49.6171

As the beginning value of $50 lies between these two total present-value figures, we know that the expected return falls between 11 and 12 percent. To approximate the actual rate, we interpolate as follows:

	Discount rate	Present value
	11%	$50.4990
	12	49.6171
Difference	1%	0.8819

$$\frac{0.4990}{0.8819} = 0.57 \qquad 11\% + 0.57\% = 11.57\%$$

Thus, the rate of return necessary to equate the present value of the expected dividends and terminal value with the beginning value is approximately 11.57 percent. With trial and error then, we can solve for the expected return on a particular investment. With practice, a person can come surprisingly close in selecting the discount rates from which to begin. Fortunately, computer programs and now even special calculators exist for solving for the rate of return, and these eliminate the need for the calculations illustrated above.

Multiple year holding period returns. For general purposes, the return formula for a two-year holding period can be expressed as

$$P_0 = \sum_{t=1}^{2} \frac{D_t}{(1 + k)^t} + \frac{P_2}{(1 + k)^2} \qquad (5\text{-}7)$$

where P_0 is the market price at time 0; D_t is the expected dividend at the end of period t; the capital Greek sigma denotes the sum of discounted dividends at the end of periods 1 and 2; and P_2 is the expected terminal value at the end of period 2.

If an investor's holding period were 10 years, the expected rate of return would be determined by solving the following equation for k:

$$P_0 = \sum_{t=1}^{10} \frac{D_t}{(1 + k)^t} + \frac{P_{10}}{(1 + k)^{10}} \qquad (5\text{-}8)$$

The investor might be a perpetual trust fund, and the trustee expects to hold the stock forever. In this case, the expected return would consist entirely of cash dividends and perhaps a liquidating dividend. Thus, the expected rate of return would be determined by solving the following equation for k:

$$P_0 = \sum_{t=1}^{\infty} \frac{D_t}{(1 + k)^t} \qquad (5\text{-}9)$$

where ∞ is the sign for infinity.

It is clear that the intended holding period of different investors will vary greatly. Some will hold a stock only a few days; others might expect to hold it forever. Investors with holding periods shorter than infinity expect to be able to sell the stock in the future at a price higher than they paid for it. This assumes, of course, that at that time there will be investors willing to buy it. In turn, these investors will base their judgments of what the stock is worth on expectations of future dividends and future terminal value beyond that point. That terminal value will depend upon the willingness of other investors at that time to buy the stock. The price they are willing to pay will depend upon their expectations of dividends and terminal value. And so the process goes through successive investors. Note that the total cash return to all successive investors in a stock is the sum of the dividends paid, including any liquidating dividend. Thus, cash dividends are all that stockholders as a whole receive from their investment; they are all the company pays out. Consequently, the foundation for the valuation of common stocks must be dividends.

The logical question to be raised at this time is, Why do the stocks of companies that pay no dividends have positive, often quite high values? The answer is that investors expect to sell the stock in the future at a price higher than they paid for it. Instead of a dividend income plus terminal value, they rely only upon the terminal value. In turn, terminal value will depend upon the expectations of the marketplace at the end of the horizon period. The ultimate expectation is that the firm eventually will pay dividends, either regular or liquidating ones, and that future investors will receive a cash return on their investment. In the interim investors are content with the expectation that they will be able to sell the stock at a subsequent time, because there will be a market for it. In the meantime, the company is reinvesting earnings and, everyone hopes, enhancing its future earning power and ultimate dividends.

Growth models

We saw that the return on investment is the rate of discount that equates the present value of the stream of expected future dividends with the current market price of the stock. If dividends of a company are expected to grow at a constant rate, g, in keeping, say, with a growth in earnings, Eq. (5-9) becomes

$$P_0 = \frac{D_0(1 + g)}{(1 + k)} + \frac{D_0(1 + g)^2}{(1 + k)^2} + \cdots + \frac{D_0(1 + g)^\infty}{(1 + k)^\infty} \tag{5-10}$$

where D_0 is the present dividend per share. Thus, the dividend expected in period n is equal to the most recent dividend times the compound growth factor, $(1 + g)^n$.

Assuming k is greater than g, Eq. (5-10) can be expressed as[5]

$$P_0 = \frac{D_1}{k - g} \tag{5-11}$$

Rearranging, the expected return becomes

[5] If we multiply both sides of Eq. (5-10) by $(1 + k)/(1 + g)$ and subtract Eq. (5-10) from the product, we obtain

$$\frac{P_0(1 + k)}{(1 + g)} - P_0 = D_0 - \frac{D_0(1 + g)^\infty}{(1 + k)^\infty}$$

Because k is greater than g, the second term on the right side will be zero. Consequently,

$$P_0\left[\frac{1 + k}{1 + g} - 1\right] = D_0$$

$$P_0\left[\frac{(1 + k) - (1 + g)}{1 + g}\right] = D_0$$

$$P_0[k - g] = D_0(1 + g)$$

$$P_0 = \frac{D_1}{k - g}$$

$$k = \frac{D_1}{P_0} + g \qquad (5\text{-}12)$$

The critical assumption in this valuation model is that dividends per share are expected to grow perpetually at a compound rate of g. For many companies, this assumption may be a fair approximation of reality. To illustrate the use of Eq. (5-12), suppose that A & G Company's dividend per share at $t = 1$ was expected to be \$3, that it was expected to grow at a 6 percent rate forever, and that the appropriate discount rate was 12 percent. The market price would be

$$P_0 = \frac{\$3}{.12 - .06} = \$50$$

When the pattern of expected growth is such that a perpetual growth model is not appropriate, modifications of Eq. (5-10) can be used. A number of valuation models are based upon the premise that the growth rate will taper off eventually. The transition might be from a present above-normal growth rate to one that is considered normal. If dividends per share were expected to grow at a 10 percent compound rate for 5 years and thereafter at a 6 percent rate, Eq. (5-10) would become

$$P_0 = \sum_{t=1}^{5} \frac{D_0(1.10)^t}{(1 + k)^t} + \sum_{t=6}^{\infty} \frac{D_5(1.06)^{t-5}}{(1 + k)^t} \qquad (5\text{-}13)$$

If the current dividend, D_0, were \$2 per share and the required rate of return, k, were 12 percent, we would solve for P_0 in the following manner:

End of Year	Dividend		Present value of dividend at 12 percent
1	$\$2(1.10) = \$2.20$	×	$.89286 = \$1.96$
2	$2(1.10)^2 = 2.42$	×	$.79719 = 1.93$
3	$2(1.10)^3 = 2.66$	×	$.71178 = 1.89$
4	$2(1.10)^4 = 2.93$	×	$.63552 = 1.86$
5	$2(1.10)^5 = 3.22$	×	$.56743 = 1.83$

Present value of dividends: first five years = \$9.47

Dividend at the end of year 6 = \$3.22 (1.06) = \$3.41

Market value at the end of year 5 = $\frac{D_6}{k - g} = \frac{\$3.41}{.12 - .06} = \$56.83$

Present value of \$56.83 at the end of year 5 = $\$56.83 \times .56743 = \$32.25$

$P_0 = \$9.47 + \$32.25 = \$41.72$

The transition from an above-normal to a normal rate of growth could be specified as more gradual than the rate above. We might expect dividends to grow at a 10 percent rate for 4 years, followed by an 8 percent rate for the next 4 years and a 6 percent growth rate thereafter. The more growth segments that are added, the more closely the growth in dividends will approach a curvilinear function. But even IBM cannot grow at an above-normal rate forever. Typically, companies tend to grow at a very high rate initially, after which their growth opportunities slow down to a rate that is normal for companies in general. If maturity is reached, the growth rate may stop altogether. For any growth model, Eq. (5-10) can be modified so that it portrays the expected stream of future dividends.

REQUIRED RATE OF RETURN ON A STOCK

We have seen that the expected return on a stock is the rate of discount that equates the present value of the stream of expected future dividends with the market price of the stock. Conversely, the market price of a stock might be thought to be the stream of expected future dividends discounted to their present value using the required rate of return. Frequently, the terms *required* and *expected* are used interchangeably. The two rates of return are the same in market equilibrium, but they are not the same when disequilibrium prevails. To appreciate the distinction and to understand the equilibrating process, we explore in detail the required rate of return for a stock.

Risk and return in a portfolio context

Picking up on our previous discussion of the security market line, we now want to consider how this line is derived and how the required rate of return is determined for a common stock. We do this in the context of Sharpe's capital-asset pricing model, which was developed in the 1960s. Like any model, this one is a simplification of reality. Nevertheless, it allows us to draw certain implications about the required rate of return for a stock, assuming the market for stocks overall is in equilibrium. As we shall see, the value of an individual security depends upon its risk in relation to the risk of other securities available for investment. Because a complete and mathematically rigorous presentation of the model is beyond the scope of an introductory book, we shall concentrate on the general aspects of the model and its important implications.[6] Certain corners have been cut in the interest of simplicity.

As with any model, there are assumptions to be made. First, we assume that capital markets are efficient in that investors are well informed, transaction costs are low, there are negligible restrictions on investment, and no investor is large enough to affect the market price of a stock. We assume also that investors are in general agreement about the likely performance of individual securities and that their expectations are based on a common holding period, say one year. There are two types of investment opportunities with which we will be concerned.[7] The first

---

[6] See William F. Sharpe, *Investments* 2d ed. (Englewood Cliffs, N.J.: Prentice-Hall, 1981), for a more complete discussion of the model.

[7] The immediate subsequent development draws upon William F. Sharpe, "Efficient Capital Markets with Risk," Research Paper (Stanford Graduate School of Business).

is a risk-free security whose return over the holding period is known with certainty. Frequently, the rate on Treasury bills is used as surrogate for the risk-free rate. The second is the market portfolio of common stocks. It is represented by all available stocks, weighted according to their market values outstanding. As the market portfolio is a somewhat unwieldy thing with which to work, most people use a surrogate such as Standard & Poor's 500-stock index, a broad gauged index reflecting performance of 500 New York Stock Exchange stocks.

Earlier we discussed the idea of *unavoidable risk*; it was defined as risk that cannot be avoided by efficient diversification. Because one cannot hold a more diversified portfolio than the market portfolio, it represents the limit to attainable diversification. Thus, the risk associated with the market portfolio is unavoidable, or "systematic." Put another way, the only risk remaining after efficient diversification is systematic in the sense that it affects all securities. In essence, this is the risk of market swings caused by things such as changes in the economy or the political situation. It affects all stocks, no matter how efficiently one is diversified.

The characteristic line

Now we are in a position to compare the expected return for an individual stock with the expected return for the market portfolio. In our comparison, it is useful to deal with returns in excess of the risk-free rate. The *excess return* is simply the expected return less the risk-free return. Figure 5-3 shows an example of a comparison of expected excess returns for a specific stock with those for the market portfolio. The colored line is known as the characteristic line; it depicts the expected relationship between excess returns for the stock and excess returns for the market portfolio. This expected relationship may be based upon past experience, in which case actual excess returns for the stock and for the market portfolio

**FIGURE 5-3
Relationship between
excess returns for stock
and excess returns for
market portfolio**

would be plotted on the graph, and a line would be drawn, best characterizing the historical relationship. Such a situation is illustrated by the scatter diagram shown in the figure. Each point represents the excess return of the stock and that of the S&P 500-stock index for a given month in the past, sixty in total. We see that when returns on the market portfolio are high, returns on the stock tend to be high as well. Instead of using historical return relationships, one might obtain future return estimates from security analysts who follow the stock. As this approach usually is restricted to investment organizations with a number of security analysts, we illustrate the relationship assuming the use of historical data.

In the figure, three measures are important. The first, known as the *alpha*, is simply the intercept of the characteristic line on the vertical axis. If the excess return for the market portfolio were expected to be zero, the alpha would be the expected excess return for the stock. In theory, the alpha for an individual stock should be zero.[8] Using past data to approximate the characteristic line, however, we might observe alphas that differ from zero if the market were in disequilibrium, if there were market imperfections, or if there were statistical problems in measurement. We assume for now, however, that the alpha for a particular stock is zero.

The second measure with which we are concerned, and the most important, is the *beta*. The beta is simply the slope of the characteristic line. If the slope is one, it means that excess returns for the stock vary proportionally with excess returns for the market portfolio. In other words, the stock has the same unavoidable risk as the market as a whole. If the market goes up and provides an excess return of 5 percent for a month, we would expect on average for the stock's excess return to be 5 percent as well. A slope steeper than one means that the stock's excess return varies more than proportionally with the excess return of the market portfolio. Put another way, it has more unavoidable risk than the market as a whole. This type of stock is often called an "aggressive" investment. A slope of less than one means that the stock has less unavoidable or systematic risk than the market as a whole. This type of stock is often called a "defensive" investment. Examples of the three types of relationships are shown in Fig. 5-4.

The greater the slope of the characteristic line for a stock, as depicted by its beta, the greater its systematic risk. This means that for both upward and downward movements in market excess returns, movements in excess returns for the individual stock are greater or less depending on its beta. Thus, the beta is a measure of a stock's systematic or unavoidable risk. This risk cannot be diversified away by investing in more stocks, as it depends upon such things as changes in the economy and in the political atmosphere, which affect all stocks. In summary, the beta of a stock represents its contribution to the risk of a highly diversified portfolio of stocks.

---

[8] If the alpha of a stock were above zero, market participants would recognize the opportunity for an expected return greater than that required for the systematic risk involved. They would buy the stock, and this buying pressure would raise the price of the stock and lower its expected return. As a result, the characteristic line would decline throughout. Such buying would continue until the stock provided the same expected return as other stocks with that systematic risk. At this point, the vertical intercept of the characteristic line would be zero. If the alpha of a stock is negative, market participants will sell it, and these sales will cause the market price to decline. With this decline, the stock's expected return will rise, as will the characteristic line until it passes through zero.

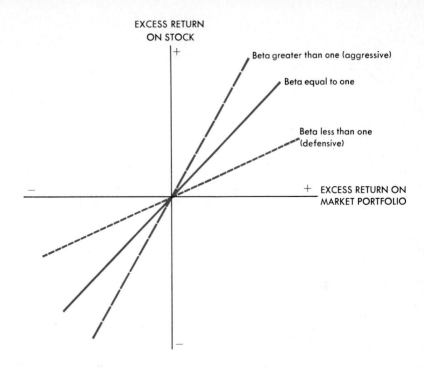

FIGURE 5-4
Examples of characteristic lines with different betas

Unsystematic risk

The last of the three measures with which we are concerned is the *unsystematic risk* of a stock. This risk is described by the dispersion of the estimates involved in predicting a stock's characteristic line. In Fig. 5-3 it is represented by the relative vertical distance of the dots from the solid line. If all of the points in the scatter diagram were plotted along the characteristic line, there would be no unsystematic risk. All risk would be market related. If the points are widely scattered around the characteristic line, this occurrence implies that a good deal of the total risk of the stock is company related. The greater the dispersion of the points in the figure, the greater the unsystematic risk of the stock. By diversification of stocks in one's portfolio, however, we can reduce unsystematic risk. It has been shown that unsystematic risk is reduced at a decreasing rate toward zero as more stocks are added to the portfolio. Thus, a substantial proportion of the unsystematic risk of a stock can be eliminated with a relatively moderate amount of diversification—say 10 or 15 stocks. For the well-diversified portfolio, unsystematic risk approaches zero. Conceptually, this can be illustrated as in Fig. 5-5. As the number of randomly selected securities held in the portfolio increases, the total risk of the portfolio is reduced in keeping with the reduction in unsystematic risk. However, this reduction is at a decreasing rate, as seen in the figure.

Thus, the total risk involved in holding a stock is comprised of two parts:

$$\text{Total risk} = \begin{array}{c} \text{Systematic risk} \\ \text{(Nondiversifiable)} \end{array} + \begin{array}{c} \text{Unsystematic risk} \\ \text{(Diversifiable)} \end{array} \qquad (5\text{-}14)$$

FIGURE 5-5
Total, unsystematic,
and systematic risk

The first part is due to the overall market risk—changes in the economy, tax reform by the Congress, a change in the world energy situation—risks that affect securities overall and, consequently, cannot be diversified away. In other words, even the investor who holds a well-diversified portfolio will be exposed to this type of risk. The second risk component, however, is unique to a particular company, being independent of economic, political, and other factors that affect securities in a systematic manner. A wildcat strike may affect only one company; a new competitor may produce essentially the same product; a technological breakthrough can make obsolete an existing product. For the typical stock, unsystematic risk accounts for somewhere around two-thirds of its total risk. By diversification, this kind of risk can be reduced or even eliminated if diversification is efficient. Therefore, not all of the risk involved in holding a stock is relevant; part of it can be diversified away.

Measuring the required rate of return

If we assume that financial markets are efficient and that investors as a whole are efficiently diversified, unsystematic risk is a minor matter. The major risk associated with a stock becomes its unavoidable or systematic risk. The greater the beta of a stock, the greater the risk of that stock, and the greater the return required. If we assume that unsystematic risk is diversified away, the required rate of return for stock j is

$$\overline{R}_j = i + (\overline{R}_m - i)\beta_j \tag{5-15}$$

where i is the risk-free rate, $\overline{R}_m$ is the expected return for the market portfolio, and β_j is the beta coefficient for stock j as defined earlier.

Put another way, the required rate of return for a stock is equal to the return required by the market for a riskless investment plus a risk premium. In turn, the risk premium is a function of: (1) the expected market return less the risk-free rate, which represents the risk premium required for the typical stock in the market; and (2) the beta coefficient. Suppose that the expected return on short-term Treasury securities is 10 percent, the expected return on the market portfolio is 15 percent, and the beta of Pro-Fli Corporation is 1.3. The beta indicates that Pro-Fli has more systematic risk than the typical stock. Given this information and using Eq. (5-15), we find that the required return on Pro-Fli's stock would be

$$\overline{R}_j = .10 + (.15 - .10)1.3 = 16.5 \text{ percent}$$

What this tells us is that on average the market expects Pro-Fli to show a 16.5 percent annual return. Because Pro-Fli has more systematic risk, this return is higher than that expected of the typical stock in the marketplace. For the typical stock, the expected return would be

$$\overline{R}_j = .10 + (.15 - .10)1.0 = 15.0 \text{ percent}$$

Suppose now that we are interested in a defensive stock whose beta coefficient is only 0.7. Its expected return is

$$\overline{R}_j = .10 + (.15 - .10)0.7 = 13.5 \text{ percent}$$

Obtaining information for the model. If the past is thought to be a good surrogate for the future, one can use past data on excess returns for the stock and for the market to calculate the beta. Several services provide betas on companies whose stocks are actively traded; these betas usually are based on weekly or monthly returns for the past three to five years. Services providing beta information include the Value Line Investment Survey; Merrill Lynch, Pierce, Fenner, and Smith; and Wells Fargo Bank. The obvious advantage is that one can obtain the historical beta for a stock without having to calculate it oneself. An example of betas for a sample of companies is shown in Table 5-1. The betas of most stocks range from .7 to 1.4, though some are lower and some are higher, as shown in the table. If one feels the past systematic risk of a stock is likely to prevail in the future, the historical beta can be used as a proxy for the expected beta coefficient.

In addition to the beta, the numbers used for the market return and for the risk-free rate must be the best possible estimates of the future. The past may or may not be a good proxy. If the past was represented by a period of relative economic stability but in the future considerable inflation is expected, averages of past market returns and past risk-free rates would be biased, low estimates of the future. In this case, it would be a mistake to use historical average returns in the calculation of the required return for a project. In another situation, realized market returns in the recent past might be very high and not expected to continue. As a result, the use of the historical past would result in too high an estimate of the future market return.

TABLE 5-1 \ **Betas for selected stocks (July, 1981)**

Stock	Beta
American Can Company	0.80
Campbell Red Lake (gold)	0.50
Control Data Corporation	1.60
Eastman Kodak	1.05
General Electric	0.95
Georgia-Pacific (forest products)	1.05
Hewlitt-Packard (electronics)	1.15
International Business Machines	0.95
Iowa-Illinois Gas & Electric	0.60
Northwest Airlines	1.30
Pillsbury Company	0.95
Ramada Inns	1.50
Reynolds Metals	1.25
Standard Oil of Indiana	1.10
U.S. Steel Corporation	1.00
Wrigley Company (chewing gum)	0.55

In situations of this sort, direct estimates of the risk-free rate and of the market return must be made. The risk-free rate is easy; one simply looks up the current rate of return on a short-term Treasury security. The market return is more difficult, but even here forecasts are available. These forecasts might be consensus estimates of security analysts, economists, and others who regularly predict such returns. Over the last 30 years or so, the annual return on the market portfolio, as represented by the Standard & Poor's Composite Index, has been around 11 percent. Having experienced the high inflation of recent years, most people would adjust the historical return upward to take account of expected inflation. Current estimates of the return on common stocks overall are in the 14 to 16 percent range.

Use of the risk premium. The excess return of the market portfolio (over the risk-free rate) is known as the market risk premium. It is represented by $(\overline{R}_m - i)$ in Equation (5-15). The expected excess return for the Standard & Poor's 500 market index has ranged from 4 to 6 percent. Instead of estimating the market portfolio return directly, one might simply add a risk premium to the prevailing risk-free rate. To illustrate, suppose the current rate of interest on Treasury bills is 10 percent. Moreover, suppose we feel that we are in a period of uncertainty, and there is considerable risk aversion in the market. Therefore, we estimate the risk premium to be in the upper part of the range; namely, 6 percent. Therefore, our estimated market return is $\overline{R}_m = .10 + .06 = 16$ percent. If, on the other hand, we feel that there is substantially less risk aversion in the market, we might use a risk premium of 4 percent, in which case the estimated market return is 14 percent.

The important thing is that the expected market return on common stocks and the risk-free rate employed in Equation (5-15) be current market estimates. With the volatile inflation of recent years, blind adherence to historical rates of return may result in faulty estimates of these data inputs to the capital-asset pricing model.

EQUILIBRIUM RETURNS AND STOCK PRICES

The capital-asset pricing model provides us a means by which to estimate the required rate of return on a security. This return then can be used as the discount rate in a dividend-capitalization model. You will recall that the market price per share of a stock can be expressed as the present value of the stream of expected future dividends.

$$P_0 = \sum_{t=1}^{\infty} \frac{D_t}{(1 + k)^t} \tag{5-16}$$

where D_t is the expected dividend in period t; k is the required rate of return for the stock, and Σ is the sum of the present value of future dividends going from period 1 to infinity.

Suppose that we wished to determine the value of the stock of Pro-Fli Corporation and that the perpetual dividend growth model was appropriate. This model is

$$P_0 = \frac{D_1}{k - g} \tag{5-17}$$

where g is the expected future growth rate in dividends per share. Suppose that Pro-Fli's expected dividend in period 1 is $2 per share, and that the expected annual growth rate in dividends per share is 10 percent. In previous computations we determined that the required rate of return for Pro-Fli was 16.5 percent. On the basis of these expectations, the value of the stock is

$$P_0 = \frac{\$2.00}{.165 - .100} = \$30.77$$

This represents the *equilibrium* price of the stock based on investor expectations about the company, about the market as a whole, and about the return available on a riskless asset.

These expectations can charge; and when they do, the value of the stock changes. Suppose that inflationary pressures in the economy abate, and we enter a period of relatively stable growth. As a result, interest rates decline, and investor risk aversion lessens. Moreover, suppose that Pro-Fli develops a new product line that has much less systematic risk than its existing product lines. However, the growth rate of the company also declines somewhat. The variables before and after these changes are

	Original	New
Risk-free rate	.10	.08
Market return	.15	.12
Pro-Fli Beta	1.30	1.10
Pro-Fli growth rate	.10	.09

The required rate of return for Pro-Fli's stock becomes

$$\overline{R}_j = .08 + (.12 - .08)1.10 = 12.4 \text{ percent}$$

Using this rate as k, the new value of the stock is

$$P_0 = \frac{\$2.00}{.124 - .09} = \$58.82$$

Thus, the combination of these events causes the value of the stock to go from $30.77 to $58.82, per share, almost doubling. Thus, the equilibrium price of a stock can change very quickly as expectations in the market place change.

Market-determined relationship

From these examples, we see that the greater the systematic or unavoidable risk of a stock, as denoted by its beta, the higher the return that is expected. Given the assumptions of the model, there exists a linear and positive relationship between the beta of a particular stock and its required rate of return. This relationship is known as the security market line, and it was illustrated for securities in general in Fig. 5-1. The work to date on devising return measures for combinations of fixed-income securities and common stocks leaves something to be desired. As a result, it is difficult in practice to derive satisfactory beta information for fixed-income securities and common stocks. In contrast, when the market portfolio is restricted to common stocks, beta information is well developed and readily available. For this reason, most of the work on the capital-asset pricing model has involved common stocks. The concept of the relationship between unavoidable risk and the required return is important, however, for both fixed-income securities and common stocks.

Returns in disequilibrium situations. We said earlier that in market equilibrium the required rate of return on a stock equals its expected return. What

FIGURE 5-6
Equilibrating process in cases of market disequilibrium

happens when this is not so? Suppose that in Fig. 5-6 the security market line is drawn on the basis of what investors as a whole know to be the appropriate relationship between the required rate of return and systematic or unavoidable risk. For some reason, two stocks—call them X and Y—are improperly priced. Stock X is underpriced relative to the security market line, while stock Y is overpriced.

As a result, stock X provides a higher expected return than the security market line for the systematic risk involved, while stock Y provides a lower expected return. Investors seeing the opportunity for superior returns by investing in stock X should rush to buy it. This action would drive the price up and the expected return down. How long would this continue? It would continue until the market price was driven up and the expected return down to the point at which the expected return was on the security market line. In the case of stock Y, investors holding this stock would sell it, recognizing that they could obtain a higher return for the same amount of systematic risk with other stocks. This selling pressure would drive Y's market price down and its expected return up until the expected return was on the security market line.

When the expected returns for these two stocks were both on the security market line, market equilibrium would again prevail. As a result, the expected returns for the two stocks would equal their required returns. Available evidence suggests that disequilibrium situations in stock prices do not long persist and that stock prices adjust rapidly to new information. With the vast amount of evidence indicating market efficiency, the security market concept becomes a useful means for determining the expected and required rate of return for a stock. This rate then can be used as the discount rate in the valuation procedures described earlier.

This brings to a close our examination of valuation. Given the expected cash payments together with the appropriate required rate of return for a financial instrument, we are able to determine its present value and, accordingly, attach a proper valuation to the investment.

SUMMARY

The valuation of any financial instrument involves a capitalization of its expected income stream by a discount rate appropriate for the risk involved. The important risk to the investor is that which cannot be avoided by diversification. This risk, known as *unavoidable risk*, is systematic in the sense that it affects all securities, although in different degrees. Unsystematic risk is company specific in that it does not depend upon general market movements. This risk is avoidable through proper diversification of one's portfolio. If we assume that investors as a whole are efficiently diversified in the securities they hold, the important risk to the investor is the security's systematic risk.

The degree of systematic risk a security possesses can be determined by drawing a *characteristic line*. This line depicts the relationship between expected returns in excess of the risk-free rate for the specific security involved and for the market portfolio. The slope of this line, known as *beta*, is a measure of systematic risk. The greater the beta, the greater the unavoidable risk of the security involved. The relationship between the required rate of return for a security and its beta is known as the *security market line*. It is linear and reflects a positive relationship between the return investors require and systematic risk. Thus, the required return is the risk-free rate plus some premium for systematic risk.

With the security-market-line concept, one is able to approximate the appropriate discount rate for both fixed-income securities and common stocks. Bonds and preferred stocks represent fixed-income securities in the sense that the cash payment, whether interest or preferred dividend, is established at issuance and is invariant. We illustrated the calculation of the present value of a bond under various assumptions as to the number of times a year interest is paid as well as the valuation of a perpetuity. In addition, the price behavior accompanying a change in interest rates was explored.

Expected future dividends are the foundation for the valuation of common stocks. The dividend-capitalization model embodies the notion of capital gains. We went on to consider various growth models in which dividends are expected to grow over time either at a constant rate or at different rates. In all cases, determination of value involves calculating the present value of the expected future stream of dividends. The key to valuation is determining the appropriate discount rate that properly takes account of risk. Several examples demonstrated how to calculate the required rate of return for a stock and how to obtain the necessary information. Once the discount rate is determined, it can be used in a dividend-capitalization model to determine the value of a stock.

QUESTIONS

1. Define the determination of the present value of an income stream approach to valuation.

2. Why do we treat bonds and preferred stock in the same way when it comes to valuation?

3. Why do bonds with long maturities fluctuate more in value than bonds with short maturities, given the same change in yield to maturity?

4. Why are dividends the basis for the valuation of common stock?

5. Suppose controlling stock of IBM Corporation were placed in a perpetual trust with an irrevocable clause that cash or liquidating dividends would never be paid. Earnings per share continued to grow. What would be the value of the company?

6. Why is the growth rate in earnings and dividends of a company likely to taper off in the future? Could not the growth rate increase as well? If it did, what would be the effect?

7. Explain the importance of the assumption of efficient capital markets when it comes to deriving the security market line.

8. Define the *characteristic line* and its *alpha* and *beta*.

9. Why is beta a measure of systematic risk? What is its meaning?

10. What is the required rate of return of a stock? How can it be measured?

11. Is the security market line constant over time?

12. What would be the effect of the following changes on the market price of a company's stock, all other things the same?

   a) Investors demand a higher required rate of return for stocks in general.

   b) The covariance between the company's rate of return and that for the market decreases.

   c) The standard deviation of the probability distribution of rates of return for the company's stock increases.

   d) Market expectations of the growth of future earnings of the company are revised downward.

13. Why should the required rate of return for preferred stock of a company be lower than that for its common stock?

14. In a world of complete certainty, would there be any difference between the debt and equity instruments of a company?

PROBLEMS

1. Gonzalez Electric Company has outstanding a 3-year, 10 percent bond issue with a face value of $1,000 per bond. Interest is payable annually. The bonds are privately held by Suresafe Fire Insurance Company. Suresafe wishes to sell the bonds and is negotiating with another party. It estimates that in current market conditions, the bonds should provide a return of 14 percent (yield to maturity). What price per bond should Suresafe be able to realize on their sale?

2. What would be the price per bond in problem 1 if interest payments were semiannual?

3. Superior Cement Company has an 8 percent preferred-stock issue outstanding, with each share having a $100 face value. Currently, the yield is 10 percent. What is the market price per share? If interest rates in general should rise so that the required return becomes 12 percent, what will happen to the market price per share?

4. The stock of the Health Corporation is currently selling for $20 a share and is expected to pay a $1 dividend at the end of the year. If you bought the stock now and sold it for $23 after receiving the dividend, what rate of return would you earn?

5. Delphi Products Corporation currently pays a dividend of $2 per share, and this dividend

is expected to grow at a 15 percent annual rate for 3 years, then at a 10 percent rate for the next 3 years, after which it is expected to grow at a 5 percent rate forever. What value would you place on the stock if an 18 percent rate of return were required?

6. Suppose that you were given the following data for past excess quarterly returns for Karochi Corporation and for the market portfolio:

Quarter	Excess returns Karochi	Excess returns market portfolio
1	.04	.05
2	.05	.10
3	−.04	−.06
4	−.05	−.10
5	.02	.02
6	.00	−.03
7	.02	.07
8	−.01	−.01
9	−.02	−.08
10	.04	.00
11	.07	.13
12	−.01	.04
13	.01	−.01
14	−.06	−.09
15	−.06	−.14
16	−.02	−.04
17	.07	.15
18	.02	.06
19	.04	.11
20	.03	.05
21	.01	.03
22	−.01	.01
23	−.01	−.03
24	.02	.04

On the basis of this information, graph the relationship between the two sets of excess returns and draw a characteristic line. What is the approximate alpha? The approximate beta? What can you say about the systematic risk of the stock, based upon past experience?

7. Assuming the capital-asset-pricing-model approach is appropriate, compute the required rate of return for each of the following stocks, given a risk-free rate of .07 and an expected return for the market portfolio of .13:

Stock	A	B	C	D	E
Beta	1.5	1.0	0.6	2.0	1.3

What implications can you draw?

8. North Great Timber Company will pay a dividend of $1.50 a share next year. After this, earnings and dividends are expected to grow at a 9 percent annual rate indefinitely. Investors presently require a rate of return of 13 percent. The company is considering several business strategies and wishes to determine the effect of these strategies on the market price per share of its stock.

   a) Continuing the present strategy will result in the expected growth rate and required rate of return shown above.

   b) Expanding timber holdings and sales will increase the expected dividend growth rate to 11 percent, but will increase the risk of the company. As a result, the rate of return required by investors will increase to 16 percent.

   c) Integrating into retail stores will increase the dividend growth rate to 10 percent and increase the required rate of return to 14 percent.

   From the standpoint of market price per share, which strategy is best?

9. On the basis of an analysis of past returns and of inflationary expectations, Marta Gomez feels that the expected return on stocks in general is 15 percent. The risk-free rate on short-term Treasury securities is now 10 percent. Ms. Gomez is particularly interested in the return prospects for Kessler Electronics Corporation. Based upon monthly data for the past 5 years, she has fitted a characteristic line to the responsiveness of excess returns of the stock to excess returns of Standard & Poor's 500-stock index and has found the slope of the line to be 1.67. If financial markets are believed to be efficient, what return can she expect from investing in Kessler Electronics Corporation?

10. Presently, the risk-free rate is 10 percent and the expected return on the market portfolio is 15 percent. The expected returns for four stocks are listed below, together with their expected betas.

	Stock	Expected return	Expected beta
1.	Stillman Zinc Corporation	17.0%	1.3
2.	Union Paint Company	14.5	0.8
3.	National Automobile Company	15.5	1.1
4.	Parker Electronics, Inc.	18.0	1.7

   a) On the basis of these expectations, which stocks are overvalued? Which are undervalued?

   b) If the risk-free rate were to rise to 12 percent and the expected return on the market portfolio to 16 percent, which stocks would be overvalued? Which would be undervalued? (Assume the betas stay the same.)

11. Zorro Zephyr Zest Company manufactures specialized windmills for a regional market in Wyoming. Demand for the product exceeds supply, but Zechariah Zorro, the president and principal stockholder, has been reluctant to grow other than with retained earnings. The market value of the stock is $20 per share, and at the end of the year the company is expected to pay a dividend of $1.40 per share. ZZZ currently earns 15 percent after taxes on equity capital, and this rate is expected to continue indefinitely into the future. It pays out 60 percent of its earnings in dividends and retains the other 40 percent. If all growth is based on the retention of earnings, what growth rate in earnings and dividends would you expect? What return on investment in the stock would you expect?

SELECTED REFERENCES

BAUMAN, W. SCOTT, "Investment Returns and Present Values," *Financial Analysts Journal,* 25 (November–December 1969), 107–18.

BLUME, MARSHALL E., "On the Assessment of Risk," *Journal of Finance,* 26 (March 1971), 1–10.

ELTON, EDWIN J., and MARTIN J. GRUBER, "Earnings Estimates and the Accuracy of Expectational Data," *Management Science,* 18 (April 1972), 409–24.

EVANS, JACK, and STEPHEN H. ARCHER, "Diversification and the Reduction of Dispersion: An Empirical Analysis," *Journal of Finance,* 23 (December 1968), 761–67.

FAMA, EUGENE F., "Components of Investment Performance," *Journal of Finance,* 27 (June 1972), 551–67.

———, *Foundations of Finance,* New York: Basic Books, 1976.

———, and MERTON H. MILLER, *The Theory of Finance.* New York: Holt, 1972.

IBBOTSON, ROGER G., and REX A. SINQUEFIELD, *Stocks, Bonds, Bills, and Inflation: Historical Returns.* Charlottesville, Va.: Financial Analysts Foundation, 1977.

LORIE, JAMES H., and MARY T. HAMILTON, *The Stock Market,* Homewood, Ill.: Irwin, 1973.

MAO, JAMES C. T., "The Valuation of Growth Stocks: The Investment Opportunities Approach," *Journal of Finance,* 21 (March 1966), 95–102.

MODIGLIANI, FRANCO, and GERALD A. POGUE, "An Introduction to Risk and Return," *Financial Analysts Journal,* 30 (March–April 1974), 68–80, and (May–June 1974), 69–86.

POGUE, GERALD A., and KISHORE LALL, "Corporate Finance: an Overview," *Sloan Management Review,* 15 (Spring 1974), 19–38.

ROGALSKI, RICHARD J. and SEHA M. TINIC, "Risk-Premium Curve vs. Capital Market Line: A Reexamination," *Financial Management,* 7 (Spring 1978), 73–84.

ROLL, RICHARD, "Performance Evaluation and Benchmark Errors," *Journal of Portfolio Management,* 6 (Summer 1980), 5–12.

ROSENBERG, BARR, "The Capital Asset Pricing Model and the Market Model," *Journal of Portfolio Management,* 7 (Winter 1981), 5–16.

ROSENBERG, BARR, and JAMES GUY, "Beta and Investment Fundamentals," *Financial Analysts Journal,* 32 (May–June 1976), 60–72.

SCHALLHEIM, JAMES, and ROBIN DeMAGISTRIS, "New Estimates of the Market Parameters," *Financial Management,* 9 (Autumn 1980), 60–68.

SHARPE, WILLIAM F., "Capital Asset Prices: A Theory of Market Equilibrium under Conditions of Risk," *Journal of Finance,* 19 (September 1964), 425–42.

———, "A Simplified Model for Portfolio Analysis," *Management Science,* 10 (January 1963), 277–93.

———, *Investments,* 2d. ed. Englewood Cliffs, N.J.: Prentice-Hall, 1981.

VAN HORNE, JAMES C., *Financial Market Rates and Flows.* Englewood Cliffs, N.J.: Prentice-Hall, 1978.

TOOLS
OF FINANCIAL
ANALYSIS
AND
PLANNING

III

Financial analysis

6

Financial analysis means different things to different people. Trade creditors are primarily interested in the liquidity of the firm being analyzed. Their claims are short-term, and the ability of the firm to pay these claims can best be judged by an analysis of its liquidity. The claims of bondholders, on the other hand, are long-term. Accordingly, they are interested in the cash-flow ability of the firm to service debt over a long period of time. The bondholder may evaluate this ability by analyzing the capital structure of the firm, the major sources and uses of funds, the firm's profitability over time, and projections of future profitability. Finally, an investor in a company's common stock is concerned principally with present and expected future earnings as well as with the stability of these earnings about a trend. As a result, the investor usually concentrates on analyzing the profitability of the firm.

The point of view of the analyst may be either external or internal. In the cases described earlier, it was external, involving suppliers of capital. From an internal standpoint, the firm needs to undertake financial analysis in order to plan and control effectively. To plan for the future, the financial manager must assess the firm's present financial position and evaluate opportunities in relation to their effect on this position. With respect to internal control, the financial manager is particularly concerned with return on investment in the various assets of the company and in the efficiency of asset management. Finally, in order to bargain effectively for outside funds, the financial manager needs to be attuned to all aspects of financial analysis that outside suppliers of capital use in evaluating the firm. We see, then, that the type of financial analysis varies according to the particular interests of the analyst.

FINANCIAL STATEMENTS

Financial analysis involves the use of financial statements. These statements attempt to do several things. First they portray the assets and liabilities of a business firm at a moment in time, usually at the end of a year or a quarter. This portrayal is known as the *balance sheet*. On the other hand, an *income statement* portrays the revenues, expenses, taxes, and profits of the firm for a particular period of time, again usually a year or a quarter. While the balance sheet represents a snapshot of the firm's financial position at a moment in time, the income statement depicts its profitability over time. From these statements certain derivative information can be obtained, such as a statement of retained earnings and a source-and-use-of-funds statement. (We consider the latter in the next chapter.)

Balance-sheet information

Table 6-1 shows the balance sheet of Aldine Manufacturing Company for the fiscal years ending March 31, 1983, and March 31,1982. The assets are listed in the upper panel according to their relative degree of liquidity. Cash and marketable securities are the most liquid of assets, and they appear first. On the other hand, fixed assets, long-term investment, and goodwill are the least liquid, and they appear last. Accounts receivable represent IOU's from customers, which should convert into cash within a given billing period, usually 30 to 60 days. Inventories, on the other hand, are used in the production of a product. The product first must be sold and a receivable generated before it can go the next step and be converted into cash. Goodwill is not a tangible asset. Rather, it represents the imputed value associated with a brand label, a product line, or the like. Its value, if realized at all, will come from future earnings of the firm.

The bottom panel of the table shows the liabilities and net worth of the company. These items are ordered according to the nearness with which they are likely to be paid. All current liabilities are payable within one year, whereas the long-term debt is payable beyond one year. Stockholders' equity will be paid only through regular dividends and, perhaps, a final liquidation dividend. Stockholders' equity, or *net worth* as it is called, consists of several subcategories. The first, common stock, represents stock purchased by investors and paid into the company in years gone by. As we discuss in chapter 22, a par value usually is assigned to the stock. In this case the par value is $1 per share, which means that on March 31, 1983, there were 420,828 shares of common stock outstanding. The paid-in capital section is the excess of monies paid for the stock above its par value. If the company were to sell an additional share of stock for $6, there would

TABLE 6-1 \ **Aldine Manufacturing Company balance sheet**

Assets (in thousands)	March 31, 1983	March, 31, 1982
Cash and marketable securities	$ 177,689	$ 175,042
Accounts receivable	678,279	740,705
Inventories, at lower cost (Fifo) or market	1,328,963	1,234,725
Prepaid expenses	20,756	17,197
Accumulated tax prepayments	35,203	29,165
Current assets	$2,240,890	$2,196,834
Fixed assets at cost	1,596,886	1,538,495
Less accumulated depreciation	856,829	791,205
Net fixed assets	$ 740,057	$ 747,290
Investment—Long-term	65,376	—
Goodwill	205,157	205,624
	$3,251,480	$3,149,748

Liabilities and net worth (in thousands)	March 31, 1983	March 31, 1982
Bank loans and notes payable	$ 448,508	$ 356,511
Accounts payable	148,427	136,793
Accrued taxes	36,203	127,455
Other accrued liabilities	190,938	164,285
Current liabilities	$ 824,076	$ 785,044
Long-term debt	630,783	626,460
Net worth		
Common stock, $1 par value	420,828	420,824
Paid-in capital	361,158	361,059
Retained earnings	1,014,635	956,361
Total net worth	$1,796,621	$1,738,244
	$3,251,480	$3,149,748

be a $1 increase in the common-stock section and a $5 increase in the paid-in capital section. Retained earnings represent a company's cumulative profits after dividends from the time of its inception. In this sense, it is a residual.

We see in the table that total assets equal total liabilities plus net worth. Indeed, that is an accounting identity. Also, it follows that assets minus liabilities equals net worth. For the most part, the liabilities of a firm are known with certainty. Most accounting questions concerning the balance sheet have to do with the numbers attached to the assets. We must remember that the figures are accounting numbers as opposed to estimates of the economic value of the assets. The value of fixed assets is based on their actual costs, not on what they would cost today (the replacement cost). Inventories are valued in the same manner. The receivable figure implies that all of these receivables will be collected. This may or may not be the case. Often it is necessary to go beyond the reported figures in order to analyze properly the financial condition of the firm. Depending on the analysis, the net-worth figure shown on the financial statement, which is a residual, may or may not be a reasonable approximation of the true net worth of the firm.

Income statement

The income statement in Table 6-2 shows Aldine's revenues and net profits for the two fiscal years. The cost of goods sold represents the cost of actually producing the product. Included here are purchases of raw materials and other items, labor costs associated with production, and other production-related expenses. Selling, general, and administrative expenses are shown separately from the costs of goods sold, so that we can analyze them directly. Depreciation was discussed in chapter 2, but remember that depreciation is based on historical costs, which in a period of inflation do not correspond to economic costs. Therefore, the profit figure may be distorted. The matter of inflation and financial analysis is explored in the Appendix to this chapter.

The last three rows of the income statement shown in Table 6-2 represent a simplified statement of retained earnings. Dividends are deducted from earnings after taxes to give the increase in retained earnings. The increase of $58,274 in fiscal year 1983 should agree with the balance-sheet figures shown in Table 6-1. On the two dates, retained earnings were $1,014,635 and $956,361, their difference being $58,274. Therefore, there is agreement. Note that retained earnings represent a residual. They do not imply funds available to the stockholders. Such availability depends on the firm's liquidity. With this background in mind, we are ready to examine financial analysis.

TABLE 6-2 \ **Aldine Manufacturing Company statement of earnings (in thousands)**

	Year Ended March 31, 1983	Year Ended March 31, 1982
Net sales	$3,992,758	$3,721,241
Cost of goods sold	2,680,298	2,499,965
Gross profit	$1,312,460	$1,221,276
Selling, general, and administrative expenses	801,395	726,959
Depreciation	111,509	113,989
Interest expense	85,274	69,764
Earnings before taxes	$ 314,282	$ 310,564
Income taxes (federal and state)	163,708	172,446
Earnings after taxes	$ 150,574	$ 138,118
Cash dividends	92,300	88,634
Increase in retained earnings	$ 58,274	$ 49,484

A POSSIBLE FRAMEWORK FOR ANALYSIS

A number of conceptual frameworks might be used in analyzing a firm. Many analysts have a favorite procedure for coming to some generalizations about the firm being analyzed. At the risk of treading on some rather sacred ground, we present a conceptual framework that lends itself to situations in which external financing is contemplated. The factors to be considered are shown in Fig. 6-1.

Taking them in order, our concern in the first case is with the trend and seasonal component of a firm's funds requirements. How much will be required in the future and what is the nature of these needs? Is there a seasonal component to the needs? Analytical tools used to answer these questions include source-and-use-of-funds statements and the cash budget, both of which are considered in chapter 7. The tools used to assess the financial condition and performance of the firm are financial ratios, a topic taken up in this chapter. With these ratios, the skilled analyst dissects the company being analyzed from a number of different angles, in the hope of obtaining valuable insight into its financial condition and profitability. The last factor in the first row of Fig. 6-1, *business risk*, relates to the risk inherent in the operations of the enterprise. Some companies are in highly volatile lines of endeavor, while others are in very stable lines. A machine tool company would fall in the volatile category, an electric utility in the stable. The analyst needs to estimate the degree of business risk of the firm being analyzed.

All three of these factors should be used in determining the financing needs of the firm. Moreover, they should be considered jointly. The greater the funds requirements, of course, the greater the total financing that will be necessary. The nature of the needs for funds influences the type of financing that should be used. If there is a seasonal component to the business, this component lends itself to short-term financing, and bank loans in particular. The basic business risk of the firm also strongly affects the type of financing that should be used. The greater the business risk, the less desirable debt financing usually becomes relative to

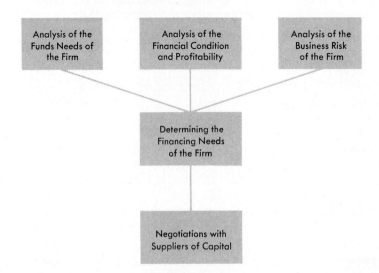

**FIGURE 6-1
Framework for
financial analysis**

common-stock financing. In other words, equity financing is safer in that there is no contractual obligation to pay interest and principal, as there is with debt. A firm with a high degree of business risk generally is ill advised to take on considerable financial risk as well. The financial condition and performance of the firm also influence the type of financing that should be used. The greater the liquidity, the stronger the overall financial condition; and the greater the profitability of the firm, the more risk can be incurred with respect to type of financing. That is, debt financing becomes more attractive with improvements in liquidity, financial condition, and profitability.

The last box in Fig. 6-1 indicates that it is not sufficient simply to determine the best financing plan from the standpoint of the firm and assume that it can be consummated. The plan needs to be sold to outside suppliers of capital. The firm may determine that it needs $1 million in short-term financing, but lenders may not go along with either the amount or the type of financing. In the end, the firm may have to compromise its plan to meet the realities of the marketplace. The interaction of the firm with these suppliers of capital determines the amount, terms, and price of financing. The fact that the firm must negotiate with outside suppliers of capital serves as a feedback mechanism to the other four factors in Fig. 6-1. Analysis cannot be undertaken in isolation from the fact that ultimately an appeal will have to be made to suppliers of capital. Similarly, suppliers of capital must keep an open mind to a company's approach to financing, even if it is different from their own.

Thus, there are a number of facets to financial analysis. Presumably, analysis will be in relation to some structural framework similar to that presented above. Otherwise, it is likely to be loose and will not really answer the questions for which it was intended. As we shall see, an integral part of financial analysis is the analysis of financial ratios; that will occupy our attention in the remainder of this chapter.

Use of financial ratios

To evaluate a firm's financial condition and performance, the financial analyst needs certain yardsticks. The yardstick frequently used is a ratio, or index, relating two pieces of financial data to each other. Analysis and interpretation of various ratios should give experienced, skilled analysts a better understanding of the financial condition and performance of the firm than they would obtain from analysis of the financial data alone.

Internal comparisons.   The analysis of financial ratios involves two types of comparison. First, the analyst can compare a present ratio with past and expected future ratios for the same company. The current ratio (the ratio of current assets to current liabilities) for the present year-end could be compared with the current ratio for the previous year-end. When financial ratios are arrayed on a spread sheet over a period of years, the analyst can study the composition of change and determine whether there has been an improvement or a deterioration in the firm's financial condition and performance over time. Financial ratios also

104
PART III
Tools of
financial
analysis and
planning

can be computed for projected, or *pro forma*, statements and compared with present and past ratios.

External comparisons and sources of industry ratios. The second method of comparison involves comparing the ratios of one firm with those of similar firms or with industry averages at the same point in time. Such a comparison gives insight into the relative financial condition and performance of the firm. Financial ratios for various industries are published by Robert Morris Associates, by Dun & Bradstreet, by Prentice-Hall (*Almanac of Business and Industrial Financial Ratios*), by the Federal Trade Commission and the Securities and Exchange Commission, and by various credit agencies and trade associations.[1] The analyst should avoid using "rules of thumb" indiscriminately for all industries. The criterion that all companies have at least a 2-to-1 current ratio is inappropriate. The analysis must be in relation to the type of business in which the firm is engaged and to the firm itself. Many sound companies have current ratios of less than 2 to 1. Only by comparing the financial ratios of one firm with those of similar firms can one make a realistic judgment.

To the extent possible, accounting data from different companies should be standardized. Apples cannot be compared with oranges. Even with standardized figures, the analyst should use caution in interpreting the comparisons.

Types of ratios

For our purposes, financial ratios can be divided into four types: liquidity, debt, profitability, and coverage ratios. No one ratio gives us sufficient information by which to judge the financial condition and performance of the firm. Only when we analyze a group of ratios are we able to make reasonable judgments. We must be sure to take into account any seasonal character of a business. Underlying trends may be assessed only through a comparison of raw figures and ratios at the same time of year. We would not compare a December 31 balance sheet with a May 31 balance sheet but would compare December 31 with December 31.

Although the number of financial ratios that might be computed increases geometrically with the amount of financial data, only the more important ratios are considered in this chapter. Actually, the ratios needed to assess the financial condition and performance of a company are relatively few. Computing unneeded ratios adds not only complexity to the problem but also confusion. To illustrate the ratios taken up in this chapter, we use the balance sheet and income statements of the Aldine Manufacturing Company shown in Tables 6-1 and 6-2.

[1] Robert Morris Associates, an association of bank credit and loan officers, publishes industry averages based upon financial statements supplied to banks by borrowers. Eleven ratios are computed annually for over 150 lines of business. In addition, each line of business is divided into 4 size categories. Dun & Bradstreet annually calculates 14 important ratios for over 100 lines of business. *Almanac of Business and Industrial Financial Ratios* (Englewood Cliffs, N.J.: Prentice-Hall, 1983) shows industry averages for some 22 financial ratios. Approximately 170 businesses and industries are listed, covering the complete spectrum. The data for this publication come from U.S. corporate tax filings with the Internal Revenue Service. *The Quarterly Financial Report for Manufacturing Corporations* is published jointly by the Federal Trade Commission and the Securities and Exchange Commission. This publication contains balance-sheet and income statement information by industry groupings and by asset size categories.

Current ratio

Liquidity ratios are used to judge a firm's ability to meet short-term obligations. From them, much insight can be obtained into the present cash solvency of the firm and its ability to remain solvent in the event of adversities. One of the most general and most frequently used of these ratios is the *current ratio*:

$$\frac{\text{Current assets}}{\text{Current liabilities}}$$

For Aldine, the ratio for the year 1983 year-end is

$$\frac{\$2,240,890}{\$824,076} = 2.72$$

Aldine is engaged in making household electrical appliances. Its current ratio is somewhat above the median ratio for the industry of 2.1. (The median for the industry is taken from Robert Morris Associates, *Statement Studies.*) Though comparisons with industry averages do not always reveal financial strength or weakness, they are meaningful in identifying companies that are out of line. Where a significant deviation occurs, the analyst will want to determine the reasons. Perhaps the industry is overly liquid, and the company being examined is basically sound despite a lower current ratio. In another situation, the company being analyzed may be too liquid, relative to the industry, with the result that it forgoes profitability. Whenever a "red flag" is raised, the analyst must search out the reasons behind it.

Supposedly, the higher the current ratio, the greater the ability of the firm to pay its bills; however, the ratio must be regarded as crude because it does not take into account the liquidity of the individual components of the current assets. A firm having current assets composed principally of cash and current receivables is generally regarded as more liquid than a firm whose current assets consist primarily of inventories.[2] Consequently, we must turn to "finer" tools of analysis if we are to evaluate critically the liquidity of the firm.

Acid-test ratio

A somewhat more accurate guide to liquidity is the *quick*, or *acid-test*, *ratio*:

$$\frac{\text{Current assets less Inventories}}{\text{Current liabilities}}$$

---

[2] We have defined *liquidity* as the ability to realize value in money, the most liquid of assets. Liquidity has two dimensions: (1) the time required to convert the asset into money and (2) the certainty of the realized price. To the extent that the price realized on receivables is as predictable as that realized on inventories, receivables would be a more liquid asset than inventories, owing to the shorter time required to convert the asset into money. If the price realized on receivables is more certain than that on inventories, receivables would be regarded as being even more liquid.

106

PART III
Tools of
financial
analysis and
planning

For Aldine, this ratio is

$$\frac{\$2,240,890 - \$1,328,963}{\$824,076} = 1.11$$

This ratio is the same as the current ratio except that it excludes inventories—presumably the least liquid portion of current assets—from the numerator. The ratio concentrates on cash, marketable securities, and receivables in relation to current obligations and thus provides a more penetrating measure of liquidity than does the current ratio. Aldine's acid-test ratio is slightly above the industry median of 1.1, indicating that it is in line with the industry.

Liquidity of receivables

When there are suspected imbalances or problems in various components of the current assets, the financial analyst will want to examine these components separately in assessing liquidity. Receivables, for example, may be far from current. To regard all receivables as liquid, when in fact a sizable portion may be past due, overstates the liquidity of the firm being analyzed. Receivables are liquid assets only insofar as they can be collected in a reasonable amount of time. For our analysis of receivables, we have two basic ratios, the first of which is the *average collection period ratio*:

Days credit sales outstanding

$$\frac{\text{Receivables} \times \text{Days in year}}{\text{Annual credit sales}}$$

For Aldine, this ratio is

$$\frac{\$678,279 \times 365}{\$3,992,758} = 62 \text{ days}$$

360

The average collection period tells us the average number of days receivables are outstanding.

The second ratio is the *receivable turnover ratio*:

$$\frac{\text{Annual credit sales}}{\text{Receivables}}$$

For Aldine, this ratio is

$$\frac{\$3,992,758}{\$678,279} = 5.89$$

These two ratios are inverses of each other. The number of days in the year, 365, divided by the average collection period, 62 days, gives the receivable turnover ratio, 5.89. The number of days in the year divided by the turnover ratio gives the average collection period. Thus, either of these two ratios can be employed.

When credit sales figures for a period are not available, we must resort to total sales figures. The receivable figure used in the calculation ordinarily represents year-end receivables. However, when sales are seasonal or have grown considerably over the year, using the year-end receivable balance may not be appropriate. With seasonality, an average of the monthly closing balances may be the most appropriate figure to use. With growth, the receivable balance at the end of the year will be deceptively high in relation to sales. In this case, an average of receivables at the beginning and at the end of the year might be appropriate if the growth in sales was steady throughout the year.

The median industry receivable turnover ratio is 8.1, which tells us that Aldine's receivables are considerably slower in turning over than is typical for the industry (62 days versus 45 days). This finding should cause the analyst concern. One thing to check is the billing terms given on sales. If the average collection period is 62 days and the terms given are 2/10, net 30,[3] a sizable proportion of the receivables are past due beyond the final due date of 30 days. On the other hand, if the terms are net 60, the typical receivable is being collected only two days after the final due date.

Although too high an average collection period is usually bad, a very low average collection period may not necessarily be good. It may be that credit policy is excessively restrictive. The receivables on the book may be of prime quality, yet sales may be curtailed unduly—and profits less than they might be—because of this policy. In this situation, credit standards for an acceptable account might be relaxed somewhat.

Another means by which we can obtain insight into the liquidity of receivables is through an *aging of accounts*. With this method, we categorize the receivables at a moment in time according to the proportions billed in previous months. We might have the following hypothetical aging of accounts receivable at December 31:

Proportion of receivables billed in

December	November	October	September	August and before	Total
67%	19%	7%	2%	5%	100%

If the billing terms are 2/10, net 30, this aging tells us that 67 percent of the receivables at December 31 are current, 19 percent are up to one month past due, 7 percent are one to two months past due, and so on. Depending upon the conclusions drawn from our analysis of the aging, we may want to examine more closely the credit and collection policies of the company. In the example above, we might be prompted to investigate the individual receivables that were billed in August and before, in order to determine if any should be charged off. The receivables shown on the books are only as good as the likelihood that they will be collected. An aging of accounts receivable gives us considerable more information than the

---

[3] The notation means that the supplier gives a 2 percent discount if the receivable invoice is paid within 10 days, and payment is due within 30 days if the discount is not taken.

TABLE 6-3 \\ Conversion matrix of credit sales to cash

Month	Credit sales	Jan.	Feb.	Mar.	Apr.	May	June
Oct.	$6,000	$ 600 (10%)[a]					
Nov.	4,000	900 (23%)	$ 300 (8%)	$ 125 (3%)			
Dec.	3,000	1,400 (47%)	700 (23%)	400 (13%)			
Jan.	5,000	700 (14%)	2,500 (50%)	1,200 (24%)	$ 600 (12%)		
Feb.	6,000		900 (15%)	3,200 (53%)	1,500 (25%)	$ 400 (7%)	
Mar.	7,000			1,200 (17%)	3,300 (47%)	1,900 (27%)	$ 600 (9%)
Apr.	8,000				1,110 (14%)	4,100 (51%)	1,900 (24%)
May	7,000					1,300 (19%)	3,300 (47%)
Jun.	5,000						700 (14%)
Total collections		$3,600	$4,400	$6,125	$6,500	$7,700	$6,500

[a]The percentages are in relation to credit sales shown in the second column.

calculation of the average collection period, because it pinpoints the trouble spots ·more specifically.

Both the average collection period and the aging of accounts receivable are affected by the pattern of sales. With rising sales, the average collection period and the aging will be more current than if sales are level, all other things the same. The reason is that a greater portion of sales is billed currently. On the other hand, when sales are declining over time, the average collection period and the aging will be less current than if sales are level. Here the reason is that a lower portion of sales is billed currently. Although the average collection period and the aging measures will not be significantly affected if there is only a modest and steady trend in sales, they will be affected if there is a rapid change in the pattern of sales or if there is a fluctuating pattern of sales behavior over time. For these situations, the average collection period and the aging schedule are not realistic portrayals of the liquidity of receivables. Adjustments in analysis should be made. For seasonal sales patterns, it is useful to compare the average collection period and aging at one point with the average collection period and aging at the same point in another year. We might compare the average collection period and an aging at the end of May with those at the end of May in another year.

The meaningful thing is to try to separate changes in the payment behavior of customers from changes in the pattern of sales. One way to do so is with a conversion matrix of receivables into cash.[4] Such a matrix is illustrated in Table 6-3. As we see, the matrix tells us the amount of credit sales in a given month and the months when the receivables so generated are collected. At the right of each

---

[4] Similar approaches have been proposed by W. G. Lewellen and R. W. Johnson, "Better Way to Monitor Accounts Receivable," Harvard Business Review, 50 (May–June 1972), 101–9; W. G. Lewellen and R. O. Edmister, "A General Model for Accounts Receivable Analysis and Control," Journal of Financial and Quantitative Analysis, 8 (March 1973), 195–206; and Bernell K. Stone, "The Payments-Pattern Approach to the Forecasting and Control of Accounts Receivable," Financial Management, 5 (Autumn 1976), 65–82. All three articles give a detailed analysis of the problem as it relates in particular to the average collection period and the aging of accounts receivable.

collection amount, the percentage that amount represents in relation to total credit sales is shown. At the bottom, total collections are shown for each month. The advantage of this type of calculation is that it permits the financial analyst to concentrate on the payment pattern of customers month-by-month as opposed to the combined payment and sales patterns. By tracing the collections in a month to the date of sales, we can determine if the firm's collection experience is improving or deteriorating. If sales change significantly over time, this isolation of payments behavior from sales behavior is critical. The principal limitation to the use of a conversion matrix is that such information is available only from the company and cannot be derived from financial statements. The same limitation applies to an aging of accounts receivable. In fact, the same information necessary to prepare an aging schedule can be used to derive a conversion matrix.

Duration of payables

From a creditor's point of view, it is desirable to obtain an *aging of accounts payable* or a *conversion matrix for payables*. These measures, combined with the less exact turnover of payables (annual credit purchases divided by payables), allows us to analyze payables in much the same manner as we analyze receivables. Also, we can compute the average age of a firm's accounts payable. The average age of payables is

$$\frac{\text{Accounts payable} \times 365}{\text{Purchase of raw materials}}$$

days purchases outstanding

where accounts payable is the average balance outstanding for the year, and the denominator is the credit purchase of raw material during the year. This information is valuable in evaluating the probability that a credit applicant will pay on time. If the average age of payables is 48 days, and the terms in the industry are net 30, we know that a portion of the applicant's payables are not being paid on time. A credit check of other suppliers will give insight into the severity of the problem.

Liquidity of inventories

We may compute the *inventory turnover ratio* as an indicator of the liquidity of inventory:

$$\frac{\text{Cost of goods sold}}{\text{Average inventory}}$$

For Aldine, the ratio is

$$\frac{\$2,680,298}{\$1,281,844} = 2.09$$

The figure for cost of goods sold used in the numerator is for the period being studied—usually one year; the average inventory figure used in the denominator

110
PART III
**Tools of
financial
analysis and
planning**

typically is an average of beginning and ending inventories for the period. As was true with receivables, however, it may be necessary to compute a more sophisticated average when there is a strong seasonal element. The inventory turnover ratio tells us the rapidity with which the inventory is turned over into receivables through sales. This ratio, like other ratios, must be judged in relation to past and expected future ratios of the firm in relation to ratios of similar firms, the industry average, or both.

Generally, the higher the inventory turnover, the more efficient the inventory management of a firm. Sometimes, a relatively high inventory turnover ratio may be the result of too low a level of inventory and frequent stockouts. It might also be the result of too many small orders for inventory replacement. Either of these situations may be more costly to the firm than carrying a larger investment in inventory and having a lower turnover ratio. Again, caution is necessary in interpreting the ratio. When the inventory turnover ratio is relatively low, it indicates slow-moving inventory or obsolescence of some of the stock. Obsolescence may necessitate substantial write-downs, which, in turn, would negate the treatment of inventory as a liquid asset. Because the turnover ratio is a somewhat crude measure, we would want to investigate any perceived inefficiency in inventory management. In this regard, it is helpful to compute the turnover of the major categories of inventory to see if there are imbalances, which may indicate excessive investment in specific components of the inventory. Once we have a hint of a problem, we must investigate it more specifically to determine its cause.

Aldine's inventory turnover ratio of 2.09 compares with a median turnover for the industry of 3.3. This unfavorable comparison suggests the company is less efficient in inventory management than is the industry and that Aldine holds excessive stock. A question also arises as to whether the inventory on the books is worth its stated value. If not, the liquidity of the firm is less than the current or quick ratio alone suggests. Once we have a hint of an inventory problem, we must investigate it along the lines of our previous discussion to determine its cause.

Summary of Aldine's liquidity

Although comparisons of Aldine's current and quick ratios with medians for the industry are favorable, a more detailed examination of receivables and inventory reveals some problems. The turnover ratios for both of these assets are significantly less than the median ratios for the industry. These findings suggest that the two assets are not entirely current, and this factor detracts from the favorable current and quick ratios. A sizable portion of receivables are slow, and there appear to be inefficiencies in inventory management. On the basis of our analysis, we conclude that these assets are not particularly liquid in the sense of turning over into cash in a reasonable period of time.

DEBT RATIOS

Extending our analysis to the long-term liquidity of the firm (i.e., its ability to meet long-term obligations), we may use several debt ratios. The *debt-to-net-worth* ratio is computed by simply dividing the total debt of the firm (including current liabilities) by its net worth.

$$\frac{\text{Total debt}}{\text{Net worth}}$$

For Aldine, the ratio is

$$\frac{\$1,454,859}{\$1,796,621} = 0.81$$

The median debt-to-worth ratio for the electrical appliance industry is 0.8, so Aldine is right in line with the industry. Presumably it would not experience difficulty with creditors because of an excessive debt ratio.

When intangible assets are significant, they frequently are deducted from net worth to obtain the tangible net worth of the firm. Depending upon the purpose for which the ratio is used, preferred stock sometimes is included as debt rather than as net worth. Preferred stock represents a prior claim from the standpoint of the investors in common stock; consequently, we might include preferred stock as debt when analyzing a firm. The ratio of debt to equity will vary according to the nature of the business and volatility of cash flows. An electric utility, with very stable cash flows, usually will have a higher debt ratio than will a machine tool company, whose cash flows are far less stable. A comparison of the debt ratio for a given company with those of similar firms gives us a general indication of the credit-worthiness and financial risk of the firm.

In addition to the ratio of total debt to equity, we may wish to compute the following ratio, which deals with only the long-term capitalization of the firm:

$$\frac{\text{Long-term debt}}{\text{Total capitalization}}$$

where total capitalization represents all long-term debt and net worth. For Aldine, the ratio is

$$\frac{\$630,783}{\$2,427,404} = .26$$

This measure tells us the relative importance of long-term debt in the capital structure. Again this ratio is in line with the median ratio of .24 for the industry. The debt ratios computed above have been based upon book-value figures; it is sometimes useful to calculate these ratios using market values. In summary, debt ratios tell us the relative proportions of capital contribution by creditors and by owners.

Cash flow to debt

A measure of the ability of a company to service its debt is the relationship of annual cash flow to the amount of debt outstanding. The cash flow of a company usually is defined as the cash generated from the operations of the company. In the case of a profitable company, it is comprised of net income and depreciation. The *cash flow-to-total liabilities* ratio is simply

112

PART III
Tools of
financial
analysis and
planning

$$\frac{\text{Cash flow}}{\text{Total Liabilities}} \quad \textit{After Tax}$$

For Aldine, the ratio is

$$\frac{\$262,083}{\$1,454,859} = 0.18$$

The cash flow is comprised of earnings after taxes of $150,574 and depreciation of $111,509, whereas total debt is composed of $824,076 in current liabilities and $630,783 in long-term debt. This ratio is useful in assessing the credit worthiness of a company seeking short- or intermediate-term debt, such as a bank loan. Another ratio is the cash flow-to-long-term debt ratio:

$$\frac{\text{Cash flow}}{\text{Long-term debt}}$$

Here we have the following for Aldine

$$\frac{\$262,083}{\$630,783} = 0.42$$

This ratio tends to be used in the evaluation of the bonds of a company. The two cash flow ratios described above have proven useful in predicting the deteriorating financial health of a company. Unfortunately, median ratios for the industry are not available for comparison.

PROFITABILITY RATIOS

Profitability ratios are of two types: those showing profitability in relation to sales, and those showing profitability in relation to investment. Together, these ratios indicate the firm's efficiency of operation.

Profitability in relation to sales

The first ratio we consider is the *gross profit margin*:

$$\frac{\text{Sales less cost of goods sold}}{\text{Sales}}$$

or simply gross profit divided by sales. For Aldine, the gross profit margin is

$$\frac{\$1,312,460}{\$3,992,758} = 32.9 \text{ percent}$$

This ratio tells us the profit of the firm relative to sales after we deduct the cost of producing the goods sold. It indicates the efficiency of operations as well as how products are priced. Aldine's gross profit margin is significantly above the median of 23.8 percent for the industry, indicating that it is relatively more efficient in producing appliances.

A more specific ratio of profitability is the *net profit margin:*

$$\frac{\text{Net profits after taxes}}{\text{Sales}}$$

For Aldine, this ratio is

$$\frac{\$150,574}{\$3,992,758} = 3.77 \text{ percent}$$

The net profit margin tells us the relative efficiency of the firm after taking into account all expenses and income taxes, but not extraordinary charges. Aldine's net profit margin is above the median margin (2.7 percent) for the industry, which indicates it is more profitable on a relative basis than are most other firms in the industry.

By considering both ratios jointly, we are able to gain considerable insight into the operations of the firm. If the gross profit margin essentially is unchanged over a period of several years, but the net profit margin has declined over the same period, we know that the cause is either higher expenses relative to sales or a higher tax rate. Therefore, we would analyze these factors more specifically to determine the cause of the problem. On the other hand, if the gross profit margin falls, we know that the cost of producing the goods relative to sales has increased. This occurrence, in turn, may be due to lower prices or to lower operating efficiency in relation to volume. If expenses are constant in relation to sales, we would know that the lower net profit margin is due entirely to the higher cost of producing the goods relative to sales.

Profitability in relation to investment

The second group of profitability ratios relates profits to investments. One of these measures is the *rate of return on common stock equity:*

$$\frac{\text{Net profits after taxes less preferred stock dividend}}{\text{Net worth less par value of preferred stock}}$$

For Aldine, the rate of return is

$$\frac{\$150,574}{\$1,796,621} = 8.38 \text{ percent}$$

This ratio tells us the earning power on shareholders' book investment and is frequently used in comparing two or more firms in an industry. Aldine's rate of return is somewhat below the median return (10.6 percent) for the industry. Thus, while Aldine has a higher profit margin on its sales than the industry has, it has

114

PART III
Tools of
financial
analysis and
planning

a lower return on its net worth. This phenomenon suggests that Aldine needs relatively greater assets to produce sales than do most other firms in the industry.

To investigate the problem more directly, we turn to the *return-on-assets ratio*:

$$\frac{\text{Net profits after taxes}}{\text{Total tangible assets}}$$

For Aldine, the ratio is

$$\frac{\$150,574}{\$3,046,323} = 4.94 \text{ percent}$$

where goodwill is deducted from total assets to obtain total tangible assets. This ratio compares with a median of 5.2 percent for the industry. Higher profitability per dollar of sales but a slightly lower return on assets tells us that Aldine must employ more assets to generate a dollar of sales than does the industry on the average.

Turnover and earning power

The relationship of sales to total assets is known as the *turnover ratio*:

$$\frac{\text{Sales}}{\text{Total tangible assets}}$$

Aldine's turnover for the 1983 fiscal year was

$$\frac{\$3,992,758}{\$3,046,323} = 1.31$$

The median turnover for the industry is 1.66, so it is clear that Aldine employs more assets per dollar of sales than does the industry on average. The turnover ratio tells us the relative efficiency with which a firm utilizes its resources to generate output. Aldine is less efficient than the industry in this regard. For our previous analysis of Aldine's liquidity, we may suspect excessive investments in receivables and inventories.

When we multiply the asset turnover of the firm by the net profit margin, we obtain the return-on-assets ratio, or *earning power* on total tangible assets:

$$\text{Earning power} = \frac{\text{Sales}}{\text{Total tangible assets}} \times \frac{\text{Net profits after taxes}}{\text{Sales}}$$

$$= \frac{\text{Net profits after taxes}}{\text{Total tangible assets}}$$

For Aldine, we have

$$\frac{\$3,992,758}{\$3,046,323} \times \frac{\$150,574}{\$3,992,758} = 4.94 \text{ percent}$$

**FIGURE 6-2
Determination of
earning power**

Neither the net profit margin nor the turnover ratio by itself provides an adequate measure of operating efficiency. The net profit margin ignores the utilization of assets, whereas the turnover ratio ignores profitability on sales. The return-on-assets ratio, or earning power, resolves these shortcomings. An improvement in the earning power of the firm will result if there is an increase in turnover on existing assets, an increase in the net profit margin, or both. The interrelation of these ratios is shown in Fig. 6-2. Two firms with different asset turnovers and net profit margins may have the same earning power. Firm *A*, with an asset turnover of 4 to 1 and a net profit margin of 3 percent, has the same earning power—12 percent—as Firm *B*, with an asset turnover of 1½ to 1 and a net profit margin of 8 percent.

With all of the profitability ratios, comparing one company to similar companies is extremely valuable. Only by comparison are we able to judge whether the profitability of a particular company is good or bad, and why. Absolute figures provide some insight, but it is relative performance that is most revealing.

COVERAGE RATIOS

Coverage ratios are designed to relate the financial charges of a firm to its ability to service them. Bond rating services such as Moody's Investors Service and Standard & Poor's make extensive use of these ratios. One of the most traditional of the coverage ratios is the *interest coverage ratio,* simply the ratio of earnings before interest and taxes for a particular reporting period to the amount of interest charges for the period. We must differentiate which interest charges should be used in the denominator. The *overall coverage method* stresses a company's meeting all fixed interest, regardless of the seniority of the claim. We have the following financial data for a hypothetical company:

Average earnings	$2,000,000
Interest on senior 10% bonds	−400,000
	$1,600,000
Interest on junior 12% bonds	160,000

116

PART III
Tools of
financial
analysis and
planning

The overall interest coverage would be $2,000,000/$560,000, or 3.57. This method implies that the credit-worthiness of the senior bonds is only as good as the firm's ability to cover all interest charges.

Of the various coverage ratios, the most objectionable is the *prior deductions method*. Using this method, we deduct interest on the senior bonds from average earnings and then divide the residual by the interest on the junior bonds. We find that the coverage on the junior bonds in our example is ten times ($1,600,000/$160,000). Thus, the junior bonds give the illusion of being more secure than the senior obligations. Clearly, this method is inappropriate.

The *cumulative deduction method* is, perhaps, the most widely used method of computing interest coverage. Under this method, coverage for the senior bonds would be five times. Coverage for the junior bonds is determined by adding the interest charges on both bonds and relating the total to average earnings. Thus, the coverage for the junior bonds would be $2,000,000/$560,000 = 3.57 times.

One of the principal shortcomings of an interest coverage ratio is that a firm's ability to service debt is related both to interest and principal payments. Moreover, these payments are not met out of earnings per se, but out of cash. Hence, a more appropriate coverage ratio relates the cash flow of the firm to the sum of interest and principal payments. The *cash-flow coverage ratio* may be expressed as

$$\frac{\text{Annual cash flow before interest and taxes}}{\text{Interest} + \text{Principal payments } [1/(1 - t)]}$$

where t is the income tax rate. As principal payments are made after taxes, it is necessary to adjust this figure by $1/(1 - t)$ so that it corresponds to interest payments, which are made before taxes.[5]

A broader type of analysis would evaluate the ability of the firm to cover all charges of a fixed nature in relation to its cash flow. In addition to interest and principal payments on debt obligations, we would include preferred-stock dividends, lease payments, and possibly even certain essential capital expenditures. As we will see in chapter 17, an analysis of this type is a far more realistic gauge than is a simple interest coverage ratio in determining whether a firm has the ability to meet its long-term obligations.

TREND OVER TIME

Up to now, our concern has been with presenting the various financial ratios, explaining their use in analysis, and comparing the ratios computed for our example company with industry averages. As we pointed out earlier, it also is valuable to compare the financial ratios for a given company over time. In this way, the analyst is able to detect any improvement or deterioration in its financial condition and performance.

[5] For an analysis of various approaches to coverage ratios when principal payments are involved, see M. Chapman Findlay III and Edward E. Williams, "Toward More Adequate Debt Service Coverage Ratios," *Financial Analysts Journal*, 31 (November–December 1975), 58–61.

To illustrate, Table 6-4 shows some of the financial ratios we have studied for Aldine Manufacturing Company over the 1974–83 period. As can be seen, the current and acid-test ratios tended to fluctuate through 1978 and then increase through 1982, falling off somewhat in 1983. Paralleling this behavior were movements in the average receivable collection period and the inventory turnover ratio. The former increased steadily from 1978 through 1982, after which it declined somewhat while the latter decreased steadily throughout. The trends here tell us that there has been a relative buildup in receivables and inventory. The turnover of both has slowed, which raises questions as to the quality of these assets. When a trend analysis of receivables and inventory is coupled with a comparison to median ratios for the industry, the only conclusion possible is that a problem exists. The analyst would want to investigate the credit policies of Aldine, the company's collection experience, and its bad-debt losses. Moreover, one should investigate inventory management, obsolescence of inventory, and any imbalances that might exist. Thus, despite the overall improvement in current and acid-test ratios in the Seventies, the apparent deterioration in receivables and inventory is a matter of concern and needs to be investigated in depth.

The debt-to-net-worth ratio has declined somewhat since 1976, indicating some improvement in overall condition from the standpoint of creditors, all other things the same. The gross profit margin and net profit margin have fluctuated over time. Since 1979, however, both ratios have shown steady improvement, which is encouraging. There is no particular disparity between the two series, which would indicate less efficiency in controlling expenses vis-à-vis the cost of producing appliances or vice versa. The return on assets has fluctuated over the 10-year period. Abstracting from these fluctuations, however, it is disturbing that the return on assets did not increase in the 1982–1983 period, a span during which the net profit margin showed steady improvement. With greater profitability in absolute terms, there must have been offsetting increases in total assets that caused the return on assets to remain relatively flat for the period. This reasoning is confirmed when we analyze the turnover ratio (Sales/Total assets). During the last 4 years it declined overall, indicating that more assets were needed to generate a dollar of

TABLE 6-4 ⟍ **Financial ratios of Aldine Manufacturing Company for fiscal years 1974–1983**

	1974	1975	1976	1977	1978	1979	1980	1981	1982	1983
Current ratio	2.21	2.09	2.11	2.06	1.98	2.19	2.41	2.37	2.79	2.72
Acid-test ratio	0.94	0.86	0.92	0.90	0.88	0.95	1.01	1.02	1.22	1.11
Average receivable collection period (days)	38	37	45	41	39	46	48	55	72	62
Inventory turnover	3.61	3.34	3.28	3.55	3.40	3.19	2.94	2.68	2.17	2.09
Total debt/Net worth	0.95	0.92	0.98	0.97	0.93	0.90	0.87	0.86	0.81	0.81
Gross profit margin	35.8%	32.6%	28.4%	29.7%	30.9%	27.4%	28.9%	30.6%	32.8%	32.9%
Net profit margin	4.63%	4.02%	2.68%	3.07%	3.36%	2.04%	2.67%	3.02%	3.71%	3.77%
Return on assets	8.45%	7.53%	4.82%	5.92%	6.47%	4.23%	4.97%	5.21%	4.69%	4.94%
Turnover ratio	1.82	1.87	1.85	1.93	1.93	2.07	1.83	1.72	1.26	1.31

118

PART III
Tools of
financial
analysis and
planning

sales. From our analysis of liquidity, we know that the primary cause was the large relative increase in receivables and inventory.

We see then that the analysis of the trend of financial ratios over time can give the analyst valuable insight into the changes that have occurred in a firm's financial condition and performance. When a trend analysis is combined with comparisons of similar companies and the industry average, the depth of analysis possible is magnified considerably.

COMMON SIZE AND INDEX ANALYSES

In addition to financial ratio analysis over time, often it is useful to express balance-sheet and income-statement items as percentages. The percentages can be related to totals, such as total assets or total sales, or to some base year. Called

TABLE 6-5 \ Riker Electronics Corporation balance sheet (in thousands)

	1980	1981	1982	1983
ASSETS:				
Cash	$ 2,507	$ 4,749	$ 11,310	$ 19,648
Accounts receivable	70,360	72,934	85,147	118,415
Inventory	77,380	86,100	91,378	118,563
Other current assets	6,316	5,637	6,082	5,891
Current assets	156,563	169,420	193,917	262,517
Fixed assets—net	79,187	91,868	94,652	115,461
Other long-term assets	4,695	5,017	5,899	5,491
Total assets	$240,445	$266,305	$294,468	$383,469
LIABILITIES AND NET WORTH:				
Accounts payable	35,661	31,857	37,460	62,725
Notes payable	20,501	25,623	14,680	17,298
Other current liabilities	11,054	7,330	8,132	15,741
Current liabilities	67,216	64,810	60,272	95,764
Long-term debt	888	979	1,276	1,917
Total liabilities	68,104	65,789	61,548	97,681
Preferred stock	0	0	0	2,088
Common stock	12,650	25,649	26,038	26,450
Paid-in capital	36,134	33,297	45,883	63,049
Retained earnings	123,557	141,570	160,999	194,201
Net worth	172,341	200,516	232,920	283,700
Total liabilities and net worth	$240,445	$266,305	$294,468	$383,469

TABLE 6-6 Riker Electronics Corporation income statement (in thousands)

	1980	1981	1982	1983
Sales	$323,780	$347,322	$375,088	$479,077
Cost of goods sold	148,127	161,478	184,507	223,690
Gross profit	175,653	185,844	190,581	255,387
Selling expenses	79,399	98,628	103,975	125,645
General and administrative expenses	43,573	45,667	45,275	61,719
Total expenses	122,972	144,295	149,250	187,364
Earnings before interest and taxes	52,681	41,549	41,331	68,023
Other income	1,757	4,204	2,963	3,017
Earnings before taxes	54,438	45,753	44,294	71,040
Taxes	28,853	22,650	20,413	32,579
Earnings after taxes	$ 25,585	$ 23,103	$ 23,881	$ 38,461

common size and *index* analyses, respectively, these evaluations of trends in financial statement percentages over time afford the analyst insight into the underlying movement of funds. Although source-and-use-of-funds statements yield a good portion of this insight, a deeper and broader understanding of a firm's funds flows is possible when the analysis is extended to include the above considerations. In order to illustrate these two types of analyses, we shall use the balance sheet and income statements of Riker Electronics Company for the 1980 through 1983 fiscal years. These statements are shown in Tables 6-5 and 6-6.

Statement items as percents of totals

In common-size analysis, we express the various components of a balance sheet as percentages of a company's total assets. In addition, this can be done for the income statement, but here items are related to sales. The gross and net profit margins, which we took up earlier, are examples of this type of expression, and it can be extended to all of the items on the income statement. The expression of individual financial statement items as percentage of totals usually offers insights not yielded by a review of the raw figures themselves.

To illustrate, common-size balance sheet and income statements are shown in Tables 6-7 and 6-8 for Riker Electronics Company for the fiscal years 1980 through 1983. In Table 6-7 we see that over the four-year span, the percent of current assets increased and that this was particularly true for cash. In addition, we see that accounts receivable showed a relative increase from 1982 to 1983. On the liability and net worth side of the balance sheet, the debt of the company declined on a relative basis from 1980 to 1983. However, with the large absolute increase in assets which occurred in 1983, the debt ratio increased from 1982 to 1983. This is particularly apparent in accounts payable, which increased substantially in both absolute and relative terms.

TABLE 6-7 \ Riker Electronics Corporation common-size balance sheet

	1980	1981	1982	1983
ASSETS:				
Cash	1.0	1.8	3.8	5.1
Accounts receivable	29.3	27.4	28.9	30.9
Inventory	32.2	32.3	31.0	30.9
Other current assets	2.6	2.1	2.1	1.5
Current assets	65.1	63.6	65.9	68.5
Fixed assets—net	32.9	34.5	32.1	30.1
Other long-term assets	2.0	1.9	2.0	1.4
Total assets	100.0	100.0	100.0	100.0
LIABILITIES AND NET WORTH:				
Accounts payable	14.8	12.0	12.7	16.4
Notes payable	8.5	9.6	5.0	4.5
Other current liabilities	4.6	2.8	2.8	4.1
Current liabilities	28.0	24.3	20.5	25.0
Long-term debt	0.4	0.4	0.4	0.5
Total liabilities	28.3	24.7	20.9	25.5
Preferred stock	0.0	0.0	0.0	0.5
Common stock	5.3	9.6	8.8	6.9
Paid-in capital	15.0	12.5	15.6	16.4
Retained earnings	51.4	53.2	54.7	50.6
Net worth	71.7	75.3	79.1	74.0
Total liabilities and net worth	100.0	100.0	100.0	100.0

TABLE 6-8 \ Riker Electronics Corporation common-size income statement

	1980	1981	1982	1983
Sales	100.0	100.0	100.0	100.0
Cost of goods sold	45.7	46.5	49.2	46.7
Gross profit	54.3	53.5	50.8	53.3
Selling expenses	24.5	28.4	27.7	26.2
General and administrative expenses	13.5	13.1	12.1	12.9
Total expenses	38.0	41.5	39.8	39.1
Earnings before interest and taxes	16.3	12.0	11.0	14.2
Other income	0.5	1.2	0.8	0.6
Earnings before taxes	16.8	13.2	11.8	14.8
Taxes	8.9	6.5	5.4	6.8
Earnings after taxes	7.9	6.7	6.4	8.0

The common-size income statement shown in Table 6-8 shows the gross profit margin fluctuating from year to year. When this is combined with selling, general, and administrative expenses, which also fluctuate over time, the end result is a relative profit picture which varies from year to year. While 1983 shows a sharp improvement over 1982 and 1981, it still is not as good as 1980 on a before-tax relative basis.

Statement items as indexes relative to a base year

The common-size balance sheet and income statement can be supplemented by the expression of items as trends from a base year. In the case of Riker Electronics Corporation, the base year is 1980, and all financial statement items are 100.0 for that year. Items for the three subsequent years are expressed as an index relative to that year. If a statement item were $22,500 compared with $15,000 in the base year, the index would be 150. Tables 6-9 and 6-10 show indexed balance-

TABLE 6-9 \ **Riker Electronics Corporation indexed balance sheet**

	1980	1981	1982	1983
ASSETS:				
Cash	100.0	189.4	451.1	783.7
Accounts receivable	100.0	103.7	121.0	168.3
Inventory	100.0	111.3	118.1	153.2
Other current assets	100.0	89.2	96.3	93.2
Current assets	100.0	108.2	123.9	167.7
Fixed assets—net	100.0	116.0	119.5	145.8
Other long-term assets	100.0	106.9	125.6	117.0
Total assets	100.0	110.8	122.5	159.5
LIABILITIES AND NET WORTH:				
Accounts payable	100.0	89.3	105.0	175.9
Notes payable	100.0	125.0	71.6	84.4
Other current liabilities	100.0	66.3	73.6	142.4
Current liabilities	100.0	96.4	89.7	142.5
Long-term debt	100.0	110.2	143.7	215.9
Total liabilities	100.0	96.6	90.4	143.4
Preferred stock	0.0	0.0	0.0	0.0
Common stock	100.0	202.8	205.8	209.1
Paid-in capital	100.0	92.1	127.0	174.5
Retained earnings	100.0	114.6	130.3	157.2
Net worth	100.0	116.3	135.2	165.8
Total liabilities and net worth	100.0	110.8	122.5	159.5

TABLE 6-10 \ **Riker Electronics Corporation indexed income statement**

	1980	1981	1982	1983
Sales	100.0	107.3	115.8	148.0
Cost of goods sold	100.0	109.0	124.6	151.0
Gross profit	100.0	105.8	108.5	145.4
Selling expenses	100.0	124.2	131.0	158.2
General and administrative expenses	100.0	104.8	103.9	141.6
Total expenses	100.0	117.3	121.4	152.4
Earnings before interest and taxes	100.0	78.9	78.5	129.1
Other income	100.0	239.3	168.6	171.7
Earnings before taxes	100.0	84.0	81.4	130.5
Taxes	100.0	78.5	70.7	112.9
Earnings after taxes	100.0	90.3	93.3	150.3

sheet and income statements. In Table 6-9 the buildup in cash from the base year is particularly apparent, and this agrees with our previous assessment. Note also the large increase in accounts receivable and inventories from 1982 to 1983. The latter was not apparent in the common-size analysis. To a lesser extent, there was a sizable increase in fixed assets. On the liability side of the balance sheet, we note the large increase in accounts payable as well as in other current liabilities that occurred from 1982 to 1983. This, coupled with retained earnings and the sale of common stock, financed the large increase in assets that occurred between these two points in time.

The indexed income statement in Table 6-10 gives much the same picture as the common-size income statement; namely, fluctuating behavior. The sharp improvement in 1983 profitability is more easily distinguished. Moreover, the indexed statement gives us information on the magnitude of absolute change in profits and expenses. With the common-size statement, we have no information about how total assets or total sales change over time.

In summary, the standardization of balance-sheet and income-statement items as percentages of totals and as indexes to a base year often gives us insights beyond those obtained from analyses of financial ratios. This supplemental information can be valuable in providing a better understanding of a company's underlying uses of funds and how those uses are financed over time.

SUMMARY

Financial analysis necessarily involves financial statements. In this regard, the important items on the balance sheet and the income statement were presented, and interrelationships were discussed. In financial analysis, one is concerned with the funds needs of the firm, its financial condition and performance, and its business risk. Upon analysis of these factors, one is able to determine the firm's financing needs and to negotiate with outside suppliers of capital. The framework proposed provides an interlocking means for structuring analysis.

Financial ratios are the tools used to analyze financial condition and performance. These ratios can be divided into four types: liquidity, debt, profitability, and coverage. No one ratio is sufficient in itself for realistic assessment of the financial condition and performance of a firm. With a group of ratios, however, reasonable judgments can be made. The number of ratios needed for this purpose is not particularly large—about a dozen.

Outside creditors and investors extensively employ the ratios taken up in this chapter. These ratios are also helpful for managerial control and for a better understanding of what outside suppliers of capital expect in financial condition and performance. The usefulness of the ratios depends upon the ingenuity and experience of the financial analyst who employs them. By themselves, financial ratios are fairly meaningless; they must be analyzed on a comparative basis. A comparison of ratios of the same firm over time uncovers leading clues in evaluating changes and trends in the firm's financial condition and profitability. The principles of trend analysis were illustrated.

Insight can be gained also by common-size and index analyses. In the former, we express the various balance-sheet items as a percentage of total assets and the income-statement items as a percentage of total sales. In the latter, balance-sheet and income-statement items are expressed as an index relative to an initial base year. In addition to historical comparisons for the same company, financial ratios may be judged in comparison with those of similar firms in the same line of business and, when appropriate, with an industry average. Much can be gleaned from a thorough analysis of financial ratios about the firm's financial condition and performance.

APPENDIX \ Inflation and Financial Analysis

In financial ratio analysis, inflationary forces may mask the results. Part of the financial performance of a company may result from management decisions, but part may be attributable to external factors over which management has little control. In particular, inflation may give rise to holding-period gains that are not attributable to management decisions. The problem with holding-period gains is that they vary with inflation, and this clouds the analysis of the overall results. To the extent the financial analyst wishes to differentiate performance based on conventional accounting data from economic profitability, he will need to adjust the accounting numbers.

The problem illustrated

Foster Tool Company, a wholesaler of tools, began business on December 31, 19X1, and had the following balance sheet at that time:

124

PART III
Tools of
financial
analysis and
planning

	Assets	Liabilities and net worth	
Cash	$ 40,000		
Inventory	100,000	Common stock	$240,000
Net fixed assets	100,000		
	$240,000		$240,000

The fixed assets have a depreciable life of 10 years, and inventory is reported on the first in-first out (FIFO) basis.[6] Sales occur entirely at the end of the first year of operation, and inflation for that year was 20 percent. For ease of understanding, we assume that inflation occurred at the beginning of 19X2 and that we live in a world of no taxes.

Operations for the first year are reported on an historical-cost basis and are as follows:

Income statement

Sales		$170,000
Cost of goods sold		
Beginning inventory	$100,000	
Purchases	120,000	
Ending inventory	(120,000)	100,000
Depreciation ($100,000/10)		10,000
Selling and administrative expenses		30,000
Net profit		$ 30,000

Note that the company's ending inventory is higher than its beginning inventory by the percentage increase in prices, namely 20 percent. The balance sheet of the company at December 31, 19X2, would be

	Assets	Liabilities and net worth	
Cash	$ 60,000		
Inventory	120,000	Common stock	$240,000
Net fixed assets	90,000	Retained earnings	30,000
	$270,000		$270,000

[6] This example draws on Lawrence Revsine, *Accounting in an Inflationary Environment* (Laventhol & Horwath, 1977).

If we compute two of the more widely used profitability ratios, we find them to be:

$$\text{Net profit margin } (\$30,000/\$170,000) = 17.65\%$$
$$\text{Return on assets } (\$30,000/\$240,000) = 12.50\%$$

In both cases the underlying economic profitability of the company is overstated. For one thing, with the FIFO method, inventories that are sold are assumed to have been purchased at the prices prevailing when the oldest items in the inventory were purchased. With inflation, these prices will be considerably below their replacement costs. In the case of Foster Tool Company, the inventories sold are valued at $100,000 for accounting purposes, whereas their replacement cost at the time they were sold was $120,000. The costing of inventories in this manner tends to understate economic costs and to overstate economic profits. A remedy is to use the last-in-first out (LIFO) method. With this method, the inventory most recently purchased is employed in the cost of goods sold. As a result, the value attached to the inventory approximates the replacement cost.

In addition to inventory valuation on a FIFO basis overstating economic profits, depreciation charges in our example are based on the original cost of the fixed assets, less accumulated depreciation. Again, with inflation, the original cost is less than the current replacement cost of these assets. If these assets increase in value by 20 percent, their replacement value is $120,000, and economic depreciation would be $12,000 instead of the $10,000 used for accounting depreciation purposes.

Restating the income statement of Foster Tool Company on a replacement-cost basis, we have for 19X2

Income Statement	
Sales	$170,000
Cost of goods sold (replacement cost)	120,000
Depreciation ($120,000/10)	12,000
Selling and administrative expenses	30,000
Net profit	$ 8,000

The profitability ratios are as follows when economic profits as opposed to profits on a historical-cost basis are used:

$$\text{Net profit margin } (\$8,000/\$170,000) = 4.70\%$$
$$\text{Return on assets } (\$8,000/\$240,000) = 3.33\%$$

We see, then, that the economic performance results are substantially lower than those originally supposed when accounting data were used.

In 19X3 no inflation occurs, and the income statement of the company is as follows on a historical-cost basis:

126

PART III
Tools of
financial
analysis and
planning

	Income statement	
Sales		$170,000
Cost of goods sold		
Beginning inventory	$120,000	
Purchases	120,000	
Ending inventory	(120,000)	120,000
Depreciation ($100,000/10)		10,000
Selling and administrative expenses		30,000
Net profit		$ 10,000

Therefore, the profits of the company drop substantially from the $30,000 reported the previous year, again using historical costs to compute the profit figure.

This "worsening" of the profit performance is primarily attributable to inflation, not to management. If we look at the income statement on a replacement-cost basis for 19X3, we find

	Income statement
Sales	$170,000
Cost of goods sold	120,000
Depreciation ($120,000/10)	12,000
Selling and administrative expenses	30,000
	$ 8,000

This profit figure is exactly the same as that for 19X2, again on a replacement-cost basis.

To compute the return-on-assets ratio on this basis we need to recast the 19X2 balance sheet to reflect replacement costs. This balance sheet becomes

Assets		Liabilities and net worth	
Cash	$ 60,000	Common stock	$240,000
Inventories	120,000	Retained earnings	8,000
Net fixed assets	108,000	Holding-period gain	40,000
	$288,000		$288,000

The gross fixed assets are adjusted upward for inflation by 20 percent to $120,000. When we subtract first-year economic depreciation of $12,000, we obtain net fixed assets of $108,000. The holding-period gain of $40,000 is comprised of the inventory profit of $20,000, which arises from the FIFO method, together with the increase in value of the fixed assets of $20,000. Both of these gains are attributable to inflation during 19X2. With $288,000 as the asset value, the profitability ratios for 19X3 using replacement-cost data are:

$$\text{Net profit margin } (\$8,000/\$170,000) = 4.70\%$$
$$\text{Return on assets } (\$8,000/\$288,000) = 2.78\%$$

While the net profit margin is the same as in 19X2, the return on assets is lower. This is because the denominator, beginning total assets, is larger than that for the previous year.

Implications

The example illustrates the problems involved when the analyst tries to compare the financial ratios of a company over time in the face of differing rates of inflation. We see that historical-cost accounting data are distorted from year to year as a result of inflation. Financial ratios, particularly those dealing with profitability, likewise are distorted. Some of the operating results are due to inflation, which is beyond managements' control. What may appear to be a significant change in profitability may, upon closer examination, be due to the vagaries of inflation. In most cases the financial analyst must not only recognize the underlying cause of the distortion but make appropriate modifications in assessing the financial performance of the company over time.

Not only a company's financial ratios but also intercompany comparisons may be distorted over time. When historical costs are used, the company with older fixed assets will often show a higher return on investment in an inflationary environment than will a company whose fixed assets were acquired more recently. Not only will the depreciation charges for the former company be less, which, in turn, will result in greater reported profits, but total assets will be lower. This combination of higher profits and lower investment will result in a higher return-on-investment ratio, all other things the same. This difference in return performance may be due entirely to assets being purchased at different times, not to the relative efficiency of management. The danger is that even though the company with older fixed assets is much less efficient in an economic sense, its return on investment, as based on conventional accounting data, may be as good as, if not better than, that of a more efficient producer. As a result, comparisons of return on investment ratios based on historical costs may lead to incorrect conclusions.

For both types of comparisons—intercompany and financial ratios of the same company over time—inflation can lead the financial analyst to derive faulty economic assessments. In periods of rapidly changing inflation, particular caution is necessary, and it is desirable to recompute financial ratios using replacement-cost accounting data. This can be done in the manner illustrated. The financial analyst then can differentiate between performance attributable to inflation and performance more directly under management's control. Only in this way can the analyst get a handle on economic return as opposed to accounting return. Oranges must be compared with oranges, and apples with apples, if the inferences derived are to be meaningful.

QUESTIONS

1. What is the purpose of financial statements? What are the major components of a financial statement?

2. Why is the analysis of trends in financial ratios important?

3. Zakor Manufacturing Company has a current ratio of 4 to 1 but is unable to pay its bills. Why?

4. Can a firm generate a 25 percent return on assets and still be technically insolvent? Explain.

5. The traditional definitions of *collection period* and *inventory turnover* are criticized because in both cases balance-sheet figures that are a result of the last month of sales are related to annual sales. Why do these definitions present problems? Suggest a solution.

6. Explain why a long-term creditor should be interested in liquidity ratios.

7. Which financial ratios would you be most likely to consult if you were the following? Why?

    a) A banker considering the financing of seasonal inventory

    b) A wealthy equity investor

    c) The manager of a pension fund considering the purchase of bonds

    d) The president of a consumer-products firm

8. Ratio analysis is valuable in assessing the financial position of a firm only when the ratios are compared with industry norms. In the current business environment, many corporations are conglomerates whose holdings cut across all industries. Suggest methods for analyzing conglomerates.

9. Why might it be possible for a company to make large operating profits, yet still be unable to meet debt payments when due? What financial ratios might be employed to detect such a condition?

10. Does increasing a firm's inventory turnover ratio increase its profitability? Why is this ratio computed using cost of goods sold (rather than sales, as is done by some compilers of financial statistics)?

11. Which financial ratios are likely to be affected if the firm's accounting statements are reported on a cost basis rather than on a market basis?

12. Which firm is more profitable? Firm A with a turnover of 10.0 and a net profit margin of 2 percent, or Firm B with a turnover of 2.0 and a net profit margin of 10 percent? Provide examples of both types of firms.

13. Why do short-term creditors, such as banks, emphasize balance-sheet analysis when considering loan requests? Should they also analyze projected income statements? Why?

14. How can index analysis be used to reinforce the insight gained from a trend analysis of financial ratios?

PROBLEMS

1. The data for various companies in the same industry and of about the same size are as follows:

Company	A	B	C	D	E	F
Sales (in millions)	$10	$20	$ 8	$ 5	$12	$17
Total assets (in millions)	8	10	6	2.5	4	8
Net income (in millions)	.7	2	.8	.5	1.5	1

Determine the asset turnover, net profit margin, and earning power for each of the companies.

2. Cordillera Carson Company has the following balance sheet and income statement for
   19X2 (in thousands):

Balance sheet	19X2
Cash	$ 400
Accounts receivable	1,300
Inventories ($1,800 for 19X1)	2,100
Current assets	3,800
Net fixed assets	3,320
Total assets	$7,120
Accounts payable	$ 320
Accruals	260
Short-term loans	1,100
Current liabilities	1,680
Long-term debt	2,000
Net worth	3,440
Total liabilities and net worth	$7,120

Income statement	
Net sales (all credit)	$12,680
Cost of goods sold*	8,930
Gross profit	3,750
Selling, general and admin. expenses	2,230
Interest expense	460
Profit before taxes	1,060
Taxes	490
Profit after taxes	$ 570

*Includes depreciation of $480

On the basis of this information, compute: (a) the current ratio; (b) the acid-test ratio;
(c) the average collection period; (d) the inventory turnover ratio; (e) the debt to net worth
ratio; (f) the long-term debt to total capitalization ratio; (g) the gross profit margin; (h) the
net profit margin; (i) the rate of return on common stock equity; and (j) the ratio of cash
flow to long-term debt.

3. Using the following information, complete the balance sheet below:

Long-term debt to net worth	.5 to 1
Total asset turnover	2.5 times
Average collection period*	18 days
Inventory turnover	9 times
Gross profit margin	10%
Acid-test ratio	1 to 1

*Assume a 360-day year, and all sales on credit.

130

PART III
Tools of
financial
analysis and
planning

Cash	$_____	Notes and payables	$100,000
Accounts receivable	_____	Long-term debt	_____
Inventory	_____	Common stock	$100,000
Plant and equipment	_____	Retained earnings	100,000
Total assets	$_____	Total liabilities and worth	$_____

4. Selected financial ratios for RMN Incorporated are as follows:

	1980	1981	1982
Current ratio	4.2	2.6	1.8
Quick ratio	2.1	1.0	0.6
Debt to total assets	23	33	47
Inventory turnover	8.7×	5.4×	3.5×
Average collection period	33	36	49
Fixed-assets turnover	11.6×	10.6×	12.3×
Total-assets turnover	3.2×	2.6×	1.9×
Profit margin on sales	3.8	2.5	1.4
Return on total assets	12.1	6.5	2.8
Return on net worth	15.7	9.7	5.4

a) Why did return on assets decline?

b) Was the increase in debt a result of greater current liabilities or of greater long-term debt? Explain.

5. The following information is available on the Vanier Corporation:

Balance sheet December 31, 19X6 (in thousands of dollars)			
Cash and marketable securities	$500	Accounts payable	$ 400
Accounts receivable	?	Bank loan	?
Inventories	?	Accruals	200
Current assets	?	Current liabilities	?
		Long-term debt	?
Net fixed assets	?	Common stock and retained earnings	3,750
Total assets	?	Total liabilities and net worth	?

Income statement for 19X6 (in thousands of dollars)

Credit sales	$8,000
Cost of goods sold	?
Gross profit	?
Selling and admin. expenses	?
Interest expense	400
Profit before taxes	?
Taxes (44 percent rate)	?
Profit after taxes	?

Other information

Current ratio	3 to 1
Depreciation	$500
Cash flow/long-term debt	0.40
Net profit margin	7%
Total liabilities/net worth	1 to 1
Average collection period	45 days
Inventory turnover ratio	3 to 1

Assuming sales and production are steady throughout the year and a 360-day year, complete the balance sheet and income statement for Vanier Corporation.

6. A company has total annual sales (all credit) of $400,000 and a gross profit margin of 20 percent. Its current assets are $80,000; current liabilities, $60,000; inventories, $30,000; and cash, $10,000.

   a) How much average inventory should be carried if management wants the inventory turnover to be 4?

   b) How rapidly (in how many days) must accounts receivable be collected if management wants to have an average of $50,000 invested in receivables? (Assume a 360-day year.)

7. Stella Stores, Inc., has sales of $6 million, an asset-turnover ratio of 6 for the year, and net profits of $120,000.

   a) What is the company's return on assets or earning power?

   b) The company is considering the installation of new point-of-sales cash registers throughout its stores. This equipment is expected to increase efficiency in inventory control, reduce clerical errors, and improve record keeping throughout the system. The new equipment will increase the investment in assets by 20 percent and is expected to increase the net profit margin from 2 to 3 percent. No change in sales is expected. What is the effect of the new equipment on the return-on-assets ratio or earning power?

132

**PART III
Tools of
financial
analysis and
planning**

8. The long-term-debt section of the balance sheet of the Diters Corporation appears as follows:

9¼% mortgage bonds of 2005	$2,500,000
12⅜% second mortgage bonds of 1998	1,500,000
10¼% debentures of 2001	1,000,000
14½% subordinated debentures of 2008	1,000,000
	$6,000,000

a) If the average earnings before interest and taxes of the Diters Corporation are $1.5 million, what is the overall interest coverage?

b) Using the cumulative deduction method, determine the coverage for each issue.

9. Tic Tac Homes has had the following balance-sheet statements the past four years (in thousands):

	19X1	19X2	19X3	19X4
Cash	$ 214	$ 93	$ 42	$ 38
Receivables	1,213	1,569	1,846	2,562
Inventories	2,102	2,893	3,678	4,261
Net fixed assets	2,219	2,346	2,388	2,692
Total assets	5,748	6,901	7,954	9,553

	19X1	19X2	19X3	19X4
Accounts payable	$1,131	$1,578	$1,848	$2,968
Notes payable	500	650	750	750
Accruals	656	861	1,289	1,743
Long-term debt	500	800	800	800
Common stock	200	200	200	200
Retained earnings	2,761	2,812	3,067	3,092
Total liabilities and net worth	5,748	6,901	7,954	9,553

Using index analysis, what are the major problems in the company's financial condition?

U.S. Republic Corporation balance sheet, December 31, 19X3

Assets		Liabilities and stockholders' equity	
Cash	$ 1,000,000	Notes payable—Bank	$ 4,000,000
Accounts receivable	5,000,000	Accounts payable	2,000,000
Inventory	7,000,000	Accrued wages and taxes	2,000,000
Fixed assets, net	15,000,000	Long-term debt	12,000,000
Excess over book value of assets acquired	2,000,000	Preferred stock	4,000,000
		Common stock	2,000,000
		Retained earnings	4,000,000
Total assets	$30,000,000	Total liabilities and net worth	$30,000,000

U.S. Republic Corporation statement of income and retained earnings, year ended December 31, 19X3

Net sales:		
Credit		$16,000,000
Cash		4,000,000
Total		$20,000,000
Cost and expenses:		
Cost of goods sold	$12,000,000	
Selling, general, and administrative expenses	2,000,000	
Depreciation	1,400,000	
Interest on long-term debt	600,000	16,000,000
Net income before taxes		$ 4,000,000
Taxes on income		2,000,000
Net income after taxes		$ 2,000,000
Less: Dividends on preferred stock		240,000
Net income available to common		$ 1,760,000
Add: Retained earnings at 1/1/X3		2,600,000
Subtotal		$ 4,360,000
Less: Dividends paid on common		−360,000
Retained earnings at 12/31/X3		$ 4,000,000

a) Fill in the 19X3 column in the data presented below.

134

PART III
Tools of
financial
analysis and
planning

U.S. Republic Corporation

Ratio	19X1	19X2	19X3	Industry norms
1. Current ratio	250%	200%		225%
2. Acid-test ratio	100%	90%		110%
3. Receivables turnover	5.0×	4.5×		6.0×
4. Inventory turnover	4.0×	3.0×		4.0×
5. Long-term debt/total capitalization	35%	40%		33%
6. Gross profit margin	39%	41%		40%
7. Net profit margin	17%	15%		15%
8. Rate of return on equity	15%	20%		20%
9. Return on tangible assets	15%	12%		10%
10. Tangible-asset turnover	.9×	.8×		1.0×
11. Overall interest coverage	11×	9×		10×
12. Cash Flow/long-term debt	0.46	0.39		0.40

b) Evaluate the position of the company from the above table. Cite specific ratio levels and trends as evidence.

c) Indicate which ratios would be of most interest to you and what your decision would be in each of the following situations:

(1) U.S. Republic wants to buy $500,000 worth of raw materials from you, with payment due in 90 days.

(2) U.S. Republic wants you, a large insurance company, to pay off its note at the bank and assume it on a 10-year maturity basis at a current rate of 14 percent.

(3) There are 100,000 shares outstanding, and the stock is selling for $80 a share. The company offers you 50,000 additional shares at this price.

11. Using historical costs, Patell Patterns, Inc., had the following income statement (in thousands of dollars) for the year, during which 15 percent inflation occurred:

Appendix problem

Sales		$5,000
Cost of goods sold		
Beginning inventory	$ 800	
Purchases	3,200	
Ending inventory	(920)	3,200
Depreciation		500
Selling and admin. expenses		800
Profit before taxes		620
Taxes (40 percent)		248
Profit after taxes		$ 372

At the beginning of the year, the fixed assets of the company amounted to $6 million on a historical cost basis, and they were depreciated on a straight-line basis with an average depreciable life of 12 years. The FIFO method is used for inventories.

a) Determine the income statement on a replacement cost basis.

b) What is the difference between the two methods?

SELECTED REFERENCES

Almanac of Business and Industrial Ratios, Englewood Cliffs, N.J.: Prentice-Hall, 1983.

ALTMAN, EDWARD I., "Financial Ratios, Discriminant Analysis and the Prediction of Corporate Bankruptcy," *Journal of Finance,* 23 (September 1968), 589–609.

———, ROBERT G. HALDEMAN, and P. NARAYNAN, "Zeta Analysis: A New Model to Identify Bankruptcy Risk of Corporations," *Journal of Banking and Finance,* 1 (June 1977).

ALTMAN, EDWARD I., and ARNOLD W. SAMETZ, eds., *Financial Crises.* New York: Wiley, 1977.

BACKER, MORTON, and MARTIN L. GOSMAN, "The Use of Financial Ratios in Credit Downgrade Decisions," *Financial Management,* 9 (Spring 1980), 53–56.

BEAVER, WILLIAM H., *Financial Reporting: An Accounting Revolution.* Englewood Cliffs, N.J.: Prentice-Hall, 1981.

CHEN, KUNG H., and THOMAS A. SHIMERDA, "An Empirical Analysis of Useful Financial Ratios," *Financial Management,* 10 (Spring 1981), 51–60.

DAMBOLENA, ISMAEL G., and SARKIS J. KHOURY, "Ratio Stability and Corporate Failure," *Journal of Finance,* 35 (September 1980), 1017–26.

EDMISTER, ROBERT O., "An Empirical Test of Financial Ratio Analysis for Small Business Failure Prediction," *Journal of Financial and Quantitative Analysis,* 7 (March 1972), 1477–93.

EMERY, GARY W. and KENNETH O. COGGER, "The Measurement of Liquidity," Working Paper, Washington University in St. Louis, 1980.

FINDLAY, M. CHAPMAN III, and EDWARD E. WILLIAMS, "Toward More Adequate Debt Service Coverage Ratios," *Financial Analysts Journal,* 31 (November–December 1975), 58–61.

FORD, JOHN KINGSTON, *A Framework for Financial Analysis.* Englewood Cliffs, N.J.: Prentice-Hall, 1981, chaps. 2 and 3.

FOSTER, GEORGE, *Financial Statement Analysis,* Englewood Cliffs, N.J.: Prentice-Hall, 1978.

HELFERT, ERICH A., *Techniques of Financial Analysis,* 5th ed. Homewood, Ill.: Irwin, 1981, chap. 2.

HORRIGAN, JAMES C., "A Short History of Financial Ratio Analysis," *Accounting Review,* 43 (April 1968), 284–94.

JAEDICKE, ROBERT K., and ROBERT T. SPROUSE, *Accounting Flows: Income, Funds, and Cash.* Englewood Cliffs, N.J.: Prentice-Hall, 1965, chap. 7.

JOHNSON, W. BRUCE, "The Cross-Sectional Stability of Financial Ratio Patterns," *Journal of Financial and Quantitative Analysis,* 14 (December 1979), 1035–48.

LEV, BARUCH, *Financial Statement Analysis: A New Approach,* Englewood Cliffs, N.J.: Prentice-Hall, 1974.

LEWELLEN, W. G., and R. O. EDMISTER, "A General Model for Accounts Receivable Analysis and Control," *Journal of Financial and Quantitative Analysis,* 8 (March 1973), 195–206.

LEWELLEN, W. G., and R. W. JOHNSON, "Better Way to Monitor Accounts Receivables," *Harvard Business Review,* 50 (May–June 1972), 101–109.

PINCHES, GEORGE E., J. CLAY SINGLETON, and ALI JAHANKHANI, "Fixed Coverage as a Determinant of Electric Utility Bond Ratings," *Financial Management,* 7 (Summer 1978), 45–55.

REVSINE, LAWRENCE, *Accounting in an Inflationary Environment.* Laventhol & Horwath, 1977.

RICHARDS, VERLYN D., and EUGENE J. LAUGHLIN, "A Cash Conversion Cycle Approach to Liquidity Analysis," *Financial Management,* 9 (Spring 1980), 32–38.

STONE, BERNELL K., "The Payments-Pattern Approach to the Forecasting of Accounts Receivable," *Financial Management,* 5 (Autumn 1976), 65–82.

Funds analysis and financial planning

7

The second portion of our examination of the tools of financial analysis and planning deals with the analysis of fund flows and financial forecasting. A funds-flow statement is a valuable aid to a financial manager or a creditor in evaluating the uses of funds by a firm and in determining how the firm finances those uses. In addition to studying past flows, the analyst can evaluate future flows by means of a funds statement based upon forecasts. Such a statement provides an efficient method for the financial manager to assess the firm's growth and its resulting financial needs, and to determine the best way to finance those needs. In particular, funds statements are very useful in planning intermediate- and long-term financing.

Closely related to a projected funds-flow statement are the cash budget and *pro forma* statements. The cash budget is indispensable to the financial manager in determining the short-term cash needs of the firm and, accordingly, in planning its short-term financing. When cash budgeting is extended to include a range of possible outcomes, the financial manager can evaluate the business risk and liquidity of the firm and plan a realistic margin of safety. This margin of safety might come from adjusting the firm's liquidity cushion, rearranging the maturity structure of its debt, arranging a line of credit with a bank, or a combination of the three. Cash budgets prepared for a range of possible outcomes are valuable also in appraising the ability of the firm to adjust to unexpected changes in cash flows.

The preparation of *pro forma* balance sheets and income statements enables the financial manager to analyze the effect of various policy decisions on the future financial condition and performance of the firm. We examine each of these tools in turn.

BUSINESS FIRM FLOW OF FUNDS

The flow of funds in a firm may be visualized as a continuous process. For every use of funds, there must be an offsetting source. In a broad sense, the assets of a firm represent the net uses of funds; its liabilities and net worth represent net sources. A funds-flow cycle for a typical manufacturing company is illustrated in Fig. 7-1. For the going concern, there is really no starting or stopping point. A finished product is a variety of inputs—namely, raw material, net fixed assets, and labor—ultimately paid for in cash. The product then is sold either for cash or on credit. A credit sale involves a receivable, which, when collected, becomes cash. If the selling price of the product exceeds all costs (including depreciation on assets) for a period of time, there is a profit for the period; if not, there is a loss. The reservoir of cash, the focal point in the figure, fluctuates over time with the production schedule, sales, collection of receivables, capital expenditures, and financing. On the other hand, reservoirs of raw materials, work in process, finished-goods inventory, accounts receivable, and trade payables fluctuate with sales, the production schedule, and policies with respect to managing receivables, inventories, and trade payables.

The funds statement is a method by which we study the net funds flow between two points in time. These points conform to beginning and ending financial statement dates for whatever period of examination is relevant—a quarter, a year, or five years. We must emphasize that the funds statement portrays net rather than gross changes between two comparable financial statements at different dates. For example, gross changes might be thought to include all changes that occur between the two statement dates, rather than the sum of these changes—the net change as defined. Although an analysis of the gross funds flow of a firm over time would be much more revealing than an analysis of net funds flow, we are usually constrained by the financial information available; namely, balance sheets and income statements that span particular periods of time. Funds may be defined in several different ways, depending upon the purpose of the analysis. Although they are often defined as cash, many analysts treat funds as working capital (current assets less current liabilities), a somewhat broader definition. Other definitions are possible although the two described are the most common by far. Depending upon the analyst's objective, the definition can be broadened or narrowed. Because a funds-flow analysis on a cash basis serves as a building block for analyses using broader definitions of funds, we begin by defining funds as cash.

SOURCE-AND-USE STATEMENTS

Basically, one prepares a funds statement on a cash basis by (1) classifying net balance-sheet changes that occur between two points in time: changes that increase cash and changes that decrease cash; (2) classifying, from the income

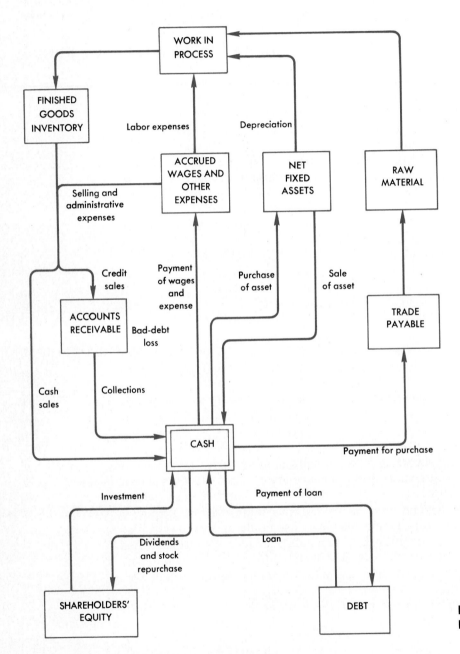

FIGURE 7-1
Funds flow within the firm

statement and the surplus statement, the factors that increase cash and the factors that decrease cash; and (3) consolidating this information in a source and use of funds statement form. In the first of these steps we simply place one balance sheet beside the other and compute the changes in the various accounts.

Sources of funds that increase cash are

1. A net decrease in any asset other than cash or fixed assets
2. A gross decrease in fixed assets
3. A net increase in any liability
4. Proceeds from the sale of preferred or common stock
5. Funds provided by operations

Funds provided by operations usually are not expressed directly on the income statement. To determine them, one must add back depreciation to net income after taxes. For Aldine Manufacturing Company, our example in the preceding chapter (Tables 6-1 and 6-2), we have (in thousands):

Net income after taxes	$150,574
Add noncash expenses: depreciation	111,509
Funds provided by operations	$262,083

Thus, the net income of Aldine understates funds provided by operations by $111,509. Depreciation is not a source of funds, for funds are generated only from operations.[1] If operating losses before depreciation are sustained, funds are not provided regardless of the magnitude of depreciation charges.

Uses of funds include

1. A net increase in any asset other than cash or fixed assets
2. A gross increase in fixed assets
3. A net decrease in any liability
4. A retirement or purchase of stock
5. Cash dividends

To avoid double counting, we compute gross additions to fixed assets in the following manner:

$$\frac{\text{Gross additions}}{\text{Fixed assets}} = NFA_1 + DPR_1 - NFA_0 \qquad (7\text{-}1)$$

where NFA_1 = net fixed assets at the ending financial statement date, NFA_0 = net fixed assets at the beginning statement date, and DPR_1 = depreciation during the

---

[1] For an extensive discussion of this concept, see Robert K. Jaedicke and Robert T. Sprouse, *Accounting Flows: Income, Funds, and Cash* (Englewood Cliffs, N.J.: Prentice-Hall, 1965), pp. 80–86.

TABLE 7-1 \ **Aldine Manufacturing Company sources and uses of funds March 31, 1982, to March 31, 1983 (in thousands)**

Sources		Uses	
Funds provided by operations:			
Net profit	$150,574	Dividends	$ 92,300
Depreciation	111,509	Additions to fixed assets	104,276
		Increase—inventories	94,238
Decrease—accounts receivable	62,426	Increase—prepaid expenses	3,559
Decrease—other assets	467	Increase—tax prepayments	6,038
Increase—bank loans	91,997	Increase—investments	65,376
Increase—accounts payable	11,634		
Increase—other accruals	26,653	Decrease—accrued taxes	91,252
Increase—long-term debt	4,323		
Increase—common stock and paid-in capital	103	Increase—cash position	2,647
	$459,686		$459,686

intervening period. As depreciation is part of the funds provided by operations, a source of funds, we must use gross changes in fixed assets as opposed to net changes in fixed assets.

Once all source and uses are computed, they may be arranged in statement form, so that we can analyze them better. Table 7-1 shows a source and use of funds statement for the Aldine Manufacturing Company for the fiscal year ended March 31, 1983. The balance sheet and income statement for this corporation, on which the funds statement is based, are shown in Tables 6-1 and 6-2 in chapter 6. When we subtract the total uses of funds in Table 7-1 from the total sources, the difference should equal the actual change in cash between the two statement dates. If it does not, then the analyst must search for the cause of the discrepancy. Frequently, discrepancies will be due to surplus adjustments; and the analyst should be alert to this possibility.

In Table 7-1 we see that the principal uses of funds for the 1983 fiscal year were additions to fixed assets, increases in inventories and in investments, and a sizable decrease in taxes payable. These uses were financed primarily by funds provided by operations in excess of dividends; a decrease in accounts receivable; and increases in bank loans, payables, and accruals. As sources exceeded slightly the uses of funds, the cash balance rose by $2,647. In a source and use of funds analysis it is useful to place cash dividends opposite net profits, and additions to fixed assets opposite depreciation. Doing this allows the analyst to evaluate easily both the amount of dividend payout and the net increase in fixed assets.

Funds as working capital

Financial analysts frequently prepare also a source and use of working capital statement. This statement is very similar to the source and use of funds statement, but the residual is net-working capital instead of cash. A statement of

TABLE 7-2 \ **Aldine Manufacturing Company sources and uses of working capital March 31, 1982, to March 31, 1983 (in thousands)**

Sources		Uses	
Funds provided by operations:			
Net profit	$150,574	Dividends	$ 92,300
Depreciation	111,509	Additions to fixed assets	104,276
Decrease—other assets	467	Increase—investments	65,376
Increase—long-term debt	4,323	Increase—working capital	5,024
Increase—common stock and paid-in capital	103		
	$266,976		$266,976

the source and use of working capital for Aldine Manufacturing Company for the year ended March 31, 1983, is shown in Table 7-2. We see that the only difference between this statement and a funds statement on a cash basis is the omission of changes in the various components of current assets and current liabilities. This statement is analyzed much the same as the source and use funds statement is. Bankers frequently use a source and use of working capital statement, for they often require a borrower to maintain some sort of minimum working capital. Other lenders and management use it for internal control.

FASB position

At the time of this writing, the Financial Accounting Standards Board is considering possible changes in the reporting of sources and uses of funds in year-end financial statements. Presently, companies may report funds flows either on a cash basis or on a working capital basis. Most use working capital. The board may require reports to be on a cash basis. Funds provided by operations would be expanded to show as separate items all receipts from customers, other income, payments to suppliers, expenses, interest, and taxes. Sources and uses of funds would be reported according to the enterprise's three main activities: operations, investment in assets, and financing. Such a change would represent a considerable departure from the format shown in Table 7-1. These and other changes in the FASB discussion memorandum may affect the reporting of funds flows in the future.

Implications of technique

The analysis of cash and working-capital funds statements gives us a rich insight into the financial operations of a firm—an insight that will be especially valuable to you as a financial manager analyzing past and future expansion plans of the firm and their impact on liquidity. You can detect imbalances in the uses of funds and undertake appropriate actions. An analysis spanning the past several years might reveal a growth in inventories out of proportion with the growth of other assets and with sales. Upon analysis, you might find that the problem was

142

PART III
Tools of
financial
analysis and
planning

due to inefficiencies in inventory management. Thus, a funds statement alerts you to problems that you can analyze in detail and take proper actions to correct. When a company has a number of divisions, individual funds statements may prove useful. These statements enable top management to appraise the performance of divisions in relation to the funds committed to them.

Another use of funds statements is in the evaluation of the firm's financing. An analysis of the major sources of funds in the past reveals what portion of the firm's growth was financed internally and what portion externally. In evaluating the firm's financing, you will wish to evaluate the ratio of dividends to earnings relative to the firm's total need for funds. Funds statements are useful also in judging whether the firm has expanded at too fast a rate and whether financing is strained. You can determine if trade credit has increased out of proportion to increases in current assets and to sales. If trade credit has increased at a significantly faster rate, you would wish to evaluate the consequences of increased slowness in trade payments on the credit standing of the firm and its ability to finance in the future. It is also revealing to analyze the mix of short- and long-term financing in relation to the funds needs of the firm. If these needs are primarily for fixed assets and permanent increases in working capital, you might be disturbed if a significant portion of total financing came from short-term sources.

An analysis of a funds statement for the future will be extremely valuable to you as a financial manager planning the intermediate- and long-term financing of your firm. It reveals the firm's total prospective need for funds, the expected timing of these needs, and their nature; that is, whether the increased investment is primarily for inventories, fixed assets, and so forth. Given this information, along with the expected changes in trade payables and the various accruals, you can arrange your firm's financing more effectively. In addition, you can determine the expected closing cash position of the firm simply by adjusting the beginning cash balance for the change in cash reflected on the projected source and use statement. In essence, the projected change in cash is a residual. Alternatively, you can forecast future cash positions of the firm through a cash budget, where direct estimates of future cash flows are made.

CASH-FLOW FORECASTING

A cash budget is arrived at through a projection of future cash receipts and cash disbursements of the firm over various intervals of time. It reveals the timing and amount of expected cash inflows and outflows over the period studied. With this information, the financial manager is better able to determine the future cash needs of the firm, plan for the financing of these needs, and exercise control over the cash and liquidity of the firm.

Cash budgets may be made for almost any period of time. For near-term forecasts, monthly periods probably are most frequently used because they take into account seasonal variations in cash flows. When cash flows are extremely volatile but predictable, budgets at more frequent intervals may be necessary for determining peak cash requirements. By the same token, when cash flows are relatively stable, budgeting at quarterly or even longer intervals may be justified. Generally, the farther in the future the period for which one is trying to predict cash flows, the more uncertain the forecast. The expense of preparing monthly cash budgets usually is warranted only for predictions concerning the near future. As we shall see, the cash budget is only as useful as the accuracy of the forecasts that are relied on in its preparation.

The forecast of sales

The key to the accuracy of most cash budgets is the forecast of sales. This forecast can be based upon an internal analysis, an external one, or both. With an internal approach, sales representatives are asked to project sales for the forthcoming period. The product sales managers screen these estimates and consolidate them into sales estimates for product lines. The estimates for the various product lines are then combined into an overall sales estimate for the firm. The basic problem with an internal approach is that it can be too myopic. Often, significant trends in the economy and in the industry are overlooked.

For this reason, many companies use an external analysis as well. With an external approach, economic analysts make forecasts of the economy and of industry sales for several years to come. They may use regression analysis to estimate the association between industry sales and the economy in general. After these basic predictions of business conditions and industry sales, the next step is to estimate market share by individual products, prices that are likely to prevail, and the expected reception of new products. Usually, these estimates are made in conjunction with marketing managers, even though the ultimate responsibility should lie with the economic forecasting department. From this information, an external forecast of sales can be prepared.

When the internal forecast of sales differs from the external one, as it is likely to do, a compromise must be reached. Past experience will show which of the two forecasts is more accurate. In general, the external forecast should serve as a foundation for the final sales forecast, often modified by the internal forecast. For example, the firm might expect several large orders from customers, and these orders might not show up in the external forecast. A final sales forecast based on both internal and external analyses is usually more accurate than is either an internal or an external forecast by itself. The final sales forecast should be based upon prospective demand, not modified initially by internal constraints such as physical capacity. The decision to remove these constraints will depend upon the forecast. The value of accurate sales forecasts cannot be overestimated, for most of the other forecasts, in some measure, are based upon expected sales.

Collections and other cash receipts

The sales forecast out of the way, the next job is to determine the cash receipts from these sales. For cash sales, cash is received at the time of the sale; for credit sales, the receipts do not come until later. How much later will depend upon the billing terms given, the type of customer, and the credit and collection policies of the firm. Continental Sheetmetal Company offers terms of net 30, meaning that payment is due within 30 days after the invoice date. Assume also that in the company's experience, 90 percent of receivables are collected, on the average, one month from the date of the sale, and 10 percent are collected 2 months from the date of the sale, with no bad-debt losses. Moreover, on the average, 10 percent of total sales are cash sales.

TABLE 7-3 \\ Schedule of sales receipts (in thousands)

	Nov.	Dec.	Jan.	Feb.	Mar.	Apr.	May	June
Total sales	$300.0	$350.0	$250.0	$200.0	$250.0	$300.0	$350.0	$380.0
Credit sales	270.0	315.0	225.0	180.0	225.0	270.0	315.0	342.0
Collections— one month		243.0	283.5	202.5	162.0	202.5	243.0	283.5
Collections— two months			27.0	31.5	22.5	18.0	22.5	27.0
Total collections			$310.5	$234.0	$184.5	$220.5	$265.5	$310.5
Cash sales			25.0	20.0	25.0	30.0	35.0	38.0
Total sales receipts			$355.5	$254.0	$209.5	$250.5	$300.5	$348.5

If the sales forecasts are those shown in the first line of Table 7-3, we can compute a schedule of the expected sales receipts based upon the above assumptions. This schedule appears in Table 7-3. For January, we see that total sales are estimated to be $250,000, of which $25,000 are cash sales. Of the $225,000 in credit sales, 90 percent, or $202,500, is expected to be collected in February; and 10 percent, or $22,500, is expected to be collected in March. Similarly, sales in other months are estimated according to the same percentages. The firm should be ready to change its assumptions with respect to collections when there is an underlying shift in the payment habits of its customers. If there is a slowdown in the economy, certain customers are likely to become slower in their trade payments. The firm must take account of this change if its cash budget is to be realistic.

From this example, it is easy to see the effect of a variation in sales upon the magnitude and timing of cash receipts, all other things held constant. For most firms, there is a degree of correlation between sales and collection experience. In times of recession and sales decline, the average collection period is likely to lengthen; bad-debt losses are likely to increase. Thus, the collection experience of a firm may reinforce a decline in sales, magnifying the downward impact upon total sales receipts.

Cash receipts may arise from the sale of assets, as well as from sales of the product. If Continental intends to sell $40,000 in fixed assets in February, total cash receipts that month would be $294,000. For the most part, the sale of assets is planned in advance and easily predicted for purposes of cash budgeting.

Cash disbursements

Next comes a forecast of cash disbursements. Given the sales forecast, management may choose either to gear production closely to sales or to produce at a relatively constant rate over time. When production is geared to sales, inventory carrying costs generally are lower, but total production costs are higher than they are when work continues steadily. If sales fluctuate, finished-goods inventories build up during certain periods and require storage. Because storage is uneven throughout the year, inventory carrying costs are generally higher than they would be if production were geared to sales. On the other hand, steady production typically is more efficient. Which alternative is best will depend upon the cost of carrying inventory when production is geared to sales compared to the savings available if production is steady. The final production schedule embodies decisions with respect to inventory management, a topic taken up in chapter 11.

Production outlays. Once a production schedule has been established, estimates can be made of the needs in materials, labor, and additional fixed assets. As with receivables, there is a lag between the time a purchase is made and the time of actual cash payment. If suppliers give average billing terms of net 30, and the firm's policy is to pay its bills at the end of this period, there is approximately a one-month lag between a purchase and the payment. If the production program of Continental Sheetmetal calls for the manufacture of goods in the month preceding forecasted sales, we might have a schedule of expenses like that in Table 7-4. As we see, there is a one-month lag between the time of purchase and the payment for the purchase.

TABLE 7-4 \ **Schedule of expenses (in thousands)** Payments

	Dec.	Jan.	Feb.	Mar.	Apr.	May	June
Purchases	$100	$ 80	$100	$120	$140	$150	$150
Cash payment for purchases		100	80	100	120	140	150
Wages paid	70	80	80	90	90	95	100
Other expenses		50	50	50	50	50	50
Total cash expenses		$230	$210	$240	$260	$285	$300

Wages are assumed to increase with the amount of production. Generally, wages are more stable over time than are purchases. When production dips slightly, workers are usually not laid off. When production picks up, labor becomes more efficient with relatively little increase in total wages. Only after a certain point overtime work is required or new workers have to be hired to meet the increased production schedule. Included in other expenses are: general, administrative, and selling expenses; property taxes; interest expenses; power, light, and heat expenses; maintenance expenses; and indirect labor and material expenses. These expenses tend to be reasonably predictable over the short run.

Other disbursements. In addition to cash expenses, we must take into account capital expenditures, dividends, federal income taxes, and any other cash outflows. Because capital expenditures are planned in advance, they usually are predictable for the short-term cash budget. As the forecast becomes more distant, however, prediction of these expenditures becomes less certain. Dividend payments for most companies are stable and are paid on specific dates. Estimation of federal income taxes must be based upon projected profits for the period under review. Other cash outlays might consist of the repurchase of stock or payment of long-term debt. These outlays are combined with total cash expenses to obtain the schedule of total cash disbursements shown in Table 7-5.

TABLE 7-5 \ **Schedule of cash disbursements (in thousands)**

	Jan.	Feb.	Mar.	Apr.	May	June
Total cash expenses	$230	$210	$240	$260	$285	$300
Capital expenditures		150	50			
Dividend payments			20			20
Income taxes	30			30		
Total cash disbursements	$260	$360	$310	$290	$285	$320

Net cash flow and cash balance

Once we are satisfied that we have taken into account all foreseeable cash inflows and outflows, we combine the cash receipts and cash disbursements schedules to obtain the net cash inflow or outflow for each month. The net cash flow may then be added to beginning cash in January, which is assumed to be $100,000, and the projected cash position computed month by month for the period under review. This final schedule is shown in Table 7-6.

The cash budget shown indicates that the firm is expected to have a cash deficit in April and May. Its deficit is caused by a decline in collections through March, capital expenditures totaling $200,000 in February and March, and a cash dividend of $20,000 in March. With the increase in collections in May and June, the cash balance without financing rises to $13,500 in June. The cash budget indicates that peak cash requirements occur in April. If the firm has a policy of maintaining a minimum cash balance of $75,000 and of borrowing from its bank to maintain this minimum, it will need to borrow an additional $66,000 in March. Additional borrowings will peak at $105,500 in April, after which they will decline to $61,500 in June, if all goes according to prediction.

Alternative means of meeting the cash deficit are available. The firm may be able to delay its capital expenditures or its payments for purchases. Indeed, one of the principal purposes of a cash budget is to determine the timing and magnitude of prospective financing needs so that the most appropriate method of financing can be arranged. A decision to obtain long-term financing should be

TABLE 7-6 \ **Net cash flow and cash balance (in thousands)**

	Jan.	Feb.	Mar.	Apr.	May	June
Total cash receipts	$335.5	$294.0*	$ 209.5	$250.5	$300.5	$348.5
Total cash disbursements	260.0	360.0	310.0	290.0	285.0	320.0
Net cash flow	$ 75.5	$(66.0)	$(100.5)	$(39.5)	$ 15.5	$ 28.5
Beginning cash without financing		100.0	175.5	109.5	9.0	(30.5)	(15.0)
Ending cash without financing	175.5	109.5	9.0	(30.5)	(15.0)	13.5

*Includes receipts of $254,000 and cash sale of assets of $40,000

based upon long-range funds requirements and upon considerations apart from a cash forecast. In addition to helping the financial manager plan for short-term financing, the cash budget is valuable in managing the firm's cash position. On the basis of a cash budget, the manager can plan to invest excess funds in marketable securities. The result is an efficient transfer of funds from cash to marketable securities and back.

RANGE OF CASH-FLOW ESTIMATES

Often, there is a tendency to place considerable faith in the cash budget simply because it is expressed in figures. We stress again that a cash budget represents merely an *estimate* of future cash flows. Depending upon the care devoted to preparing the budget and the volatility of cash flows resulting from the nature of the business, actual cash flows will deviate more or less widely from those that were expected. In the face of uncertainty, we must provide information about the range of possible outcomes. Analyzing cash flows under only one set of assumptions, as is the case with conventional cash budgeting, results in a faulty perspective of the future.

Deviations from expected cash flows

To take into account deviations from expected cash flows, it is desirable to work out additional cash budgets. We might want to base one cash forecast upon the assumption of a maximum probable decline in business, and another upon the assumption of the maximum probable increase in business. By bringing possible events into the open for discussion, management is better able to plan for contingencies. Not only will such discussion sharpen its perspective on the probability of occurrence of a particular event, but it will give management a better understanding of the magnitude of its impact on the firm's cash flows.[2] Given the preparation of a cash budget based upon expected cash flows, it is often a simple matter to trace through a change in one or a series of figures in order to take into account a large number of possibilities. Examples of a change in assumptions include a decline in sales or an increase in the average collection period. For each set of assumptions and resulting cash budget, a probability of occurrence should be attached.

The final product might be a series of distributions of end-of-the-month cash without financing. Figure 7-2 shows relative frequency distributions for the months of January through June. Bar graphs are used. The most likely values of ending cash are depicted by the highest bar; these conform with the values shown in Table 7-6. We note that while several of the distributions are reasonably symmetrical, others are skewed. In particular, the distributions for March and April are skewed to the left. As a result, the need for cash during these months might be considerably greater than that depicted in Table 7-6. It is clear that the type of information portrayed in Fig. 7-2 better enables management to plan for con-

[2] See Gordon Donaldson, "Strategy For Financial Emergencies," *Harvard Business Review*, 47 (November–December 1969), 69.

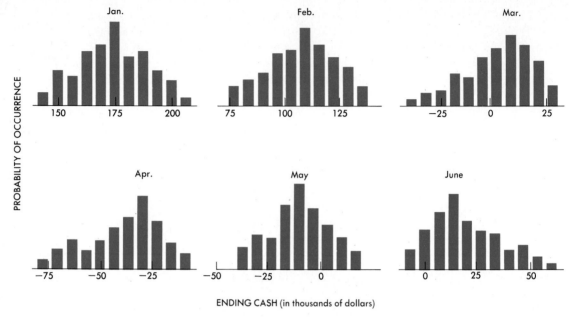

PROBABILITY OF OCCURRENCE

ENDING CASH (in thousands of dollars)

FIGURE 7-2 Distributions of ending cash

tingencies than does information giving only single-point estimates of monthly cash flows.[3]

Use of probabilistic information

The expected cash position plus the distribution of possible outcomes gives us a considerable amount of information. We can see the additional funds required or the funds released under various possible outcomes. This information enables us to determine more accurately the minimum cash balance, maturity structure of debt, and borrowing power necessary to give the firm a margin of safety.

We also can analyze the ability of the firm to adjust to deviations from the expected outcomes. If sales should fall off, how flexible are our expenses? What can be cut? By how much? How quickly? How much effort should be devoted to the collection of receivables? If there is an unexpected increase in business, what additional purchases will be required, and when? Can labor be expanded? Can the present plant handle the additional demand? How much in funds will be needed to finance the buildup? Answers to these questions provide valuable insight into the efficiency and flexibility of the firm under a variety of conditions.[4]

[3] For an additional discussion of probabilistic cash-flow information, see James L. Pappas and George P. Huber, "Probabilistic Short-Term Financial Planning," *Financial Management*, 2 (Autumn 1973), 36–44.

[4] Donaldson, "Strategy for Financial Emergencies," pp. 71–79, develops a framework for evaluating the resources available to meet adverse financial contingencies. These resources include surplus cash, unused lines of credit, negotiated bank loans, long-term debt, new equity, the reduction of planned outflows, and the liquidation of certain assets. Once these resources have been determined, together with the time necessary to put them to use, a strategy of response can be formulated. This strategy lays out the sequence in which resources will be brought into play to deal with an unanticipated event.

From the standpoint of internal planning, it is far better to allow for a range of possible outcomes than to rely solely upon the expected outcome. This allowance is particularly necessary for firms whose business is relatively unstable in character. If the firm bases its plans upon expected cash flows only, it is likely to be caught flat-footed if there is a significant deviation from the expected outcome, and it will have difficulty making an adjustment. An unforeseen deficit in cash may be difficult to finance on short notice. Therefore, it is absolutely essential for the firm to be honest with itself and attempt to minimize the costs associated with deviations from expected outcomes. It may do this by taking the steps necessary to assure accuracy and by preparing additional cash budgets to take into account the range of possible outcomes. When significant deviations from expected outcomes occur, the cash budget should be revised in keeping with new information.

FORECASTING FINANCIAL STATEMENTS

In addition to projecting the cash flow of a firm over time, it often is useful to prepare a projected, or *pro forma,* balance sheet and income statement for selected future dates. A cash budget gives us information only as to the prospective future cash positions of the firm, whereas *pro forma* statements embody forecasts of all assets and liabilities as well as of income-statement items. Much of the information that goes into the preparation of the cash budget can be used to derive a *pro forma* statement. In practice, the *pro forma* income statement usually precedes the cash budget. In this way the financial manager is able to use the tax estimates derived therefrom in the cash budget.

Pro forma income statement

The *pro forma* income statement is a projection of income for a period of time in the future. As was true with our cash budget, the sales forecast is the key to scheduling production and estimating production costs. The analyst may wish to evaluate each component of the cost of goods sold. A detailed analysis of purchases, production wages, and overhead costs is likely to produce the most accurate forecasts. Often, however, costs of goods sold are estimated on the basis of past ratios of costs of goods sold to sales.

Selling and administrative expenses are estimated next. Because both of these expenses usually are budgeted in advance, estimates of them are fairly accurate. Typically, these expenses are not overly sensitive to changes in sales in the very short run, particularly to reductions in sales. Next, we estimate other income and expenses as well as interest expenses to obtain net income before taxes. Income taxes are then computed—based upon the applicable tax rate—and deducted, to arrive at estimated net income after taxes. All of these estimates are then combined into an income statement.

To illustrate for Continental Sheetmetal Company, suppose that projected sales for January through June in Table 7-3 are $1,730,000, as reflected in our cash budget in Table 7-3. In the cash budget, the cost of goods sold is not depicted directly. However, we know that purchases fall into this category. For financial statement purposes, the purchases associated with January through June sales are those for December through May, because production occurs in the month pre-

150

PART III
Tools of
financial
analysis and
planning

ceding forecasted sales. Purchases are shown in Table 7-4, and they total $690,000 for December through May. Wages also are a cost of goods sold, and here, too, the relevant period for financial statement purposes is December through May. For this period, wages totaling $505,000 are expected to be paid. (See Table 7-4.) We stated earlier that depreciation of $110,000 was expected for the January–June period. Other expenses (selling and administrative) are expected to be $50,000 a month and are also shown in Table 7-4. For the 6-months' period they total $300,000. Finally, let us assume a federal plus state income tax rate of 48 percent. Given this information, we can derive a *pro forma* income statement for the January–June period (in thousands):

Sales		$1,730
Cost of goods sold:		
Purchases	$690	
Wages	505	
Depreciation	110	$1,305
Gross profit		425
Selling and administrative expenses		300
Profit before taxes		125
Taxes		60
Profit after taxes		$ 65

The *pro forma* income statement need not be based on a cash budget. Instead, one can make direct estimates of all of the items. By first estimating a sales level, one can multiply historical ratios of cost of goods sold and various expense items by the level in order to derive the statement. Where historical ratios no longer are appropriate, new estimates should be employed.

Pro forma balance sheet

To illustrate the preparation of a *pro forma* balance sheet, suppose that we wish to prepare one for Continental Sheetmetal for June 30 and that the company has the following balance sheet the previous December 31:

Assets (in thousands)		Liabilities (in thousands)	
Cash	$ 100	Bank borrowings	$ 50
Receivables	342	Accounts payable	200
Inventory	350	Accrued wages and expenses	250
		Accrued income taxes	70
Current assets	$ 792	Current liabilities	$ 570
Net fixed assets	800	Net worth	1,022
Total assets	$1,592	Total liabilities and net worth	$1,592

Receivables at June 30 can be estimated by adding to the receivable balance at December 31 the total projected credit sales from January through June, less total projected credit collections for the period. On the basis of the information in the cash budget, receivables at June 30 would be $342,000 + $31,500, or $373,500.

    Forecasting assets.   If a cash budget is not available, the receivable balance may be estimated on the basis of a turnover ratio. This ratio, which depicts the relationship between credit sales and receivables, should be based upon past experience. To obtain the estimated level of receivables, projected sales simply are divided by the turnover ratio. If the sales forecast and turnover ratio are realistic, the method will produce a reasonable approximation of the receivable balance. The estimated investment in inventories at June 30 may be based upon the production schedule, which, in turn, is based upon the sales forecast. This schedule should show expected purchases, the expected use of inventory in production, and the expected level of finished goods. On the basis of this information, together with the beginning inventory level, a *pro forma* estimate of inventory can be made. Rather than use the production schedule, estimates of future inventory can be based upon a turnover ratio of cost of goods sold to inventory. This ratio is applied in the same manner as that for receivables. Suppose that on the basis of a turnover ratio, we estimate inventory to be $420,000 on June 30, a figure that represents a moderate increase over the inventory level of December 31, in keeping with the buildup in sales.

    Future net fixed assets are estimated by adding planned expenditures to existing net fixed assets and subtracting from this sum depreciation for the period, plus any sale of fixed assets at book value. From the cash budget, we note that capital expenditures are estimated at $200,000 over the period and that $40,000 in fixed assets will be sold at what we assume to be their depreciated book values. If depreciation for the period is expected to be $110,000, the expected net addition to fixed assets would be $50,000, ($200,000 − $40,000 − $110,000), and projected net fixed assets at June 30 would be $850,000. Because capital expenditures are planned in advance, fixed assets generally are fairly easy to forecast.

    Forecasting liabilities and net worth.   Turning now to the liabilities, accounts payable are estimated by adding total projected purchases for January through June, less total projected cash payments for purchases for the period, to the December 31 balance. Our estimate of accounts payable, therefore, is $200,000 + $50,000, or $250,000. The calculation of accrued wages and expenses is based upon the production schedule and the historical relationship between these accruals and production. We assume the estimate of accrued wages and expenses to be $240,000. Accrued income taxes are estimated by adding to the current balance taxes on forecasted income for the 6-months' period, less the actual payment of taxes. If income taxes for the period are forecast at $60,000, as shown in the *pro forma* income statement, and the firm is scheduled to make $60,000 in actual payments, estimated accrued income taxes at June 30 would be $70,000.

    Net worth at June 30 would be the net worth at December 31 plus profits after taxes for the period, less the amount of cash dividends paid. If profits after taxes are estimated at $65,000 in the *pro-forma* income statement, net worth at June 30 would be $1,022,000 plus $65,000 minus dividends of $40,000, or

152

PART III
Tools of
financial
analysis and
planning

$1,047,000. Two items remain: cash and bank loans. We see from the cash budget that estimated cash at June 30 would be $13,500 without additional financing. If the firm has the policy of maintaining a minimum cash balance of $75,000 and borrowing from its bank to maintain this balance, cash at June 30 would be $75,000, and bank borrowings would increase by $61,500 to $111,500. In general, cash and notes payable serve as balancing factors in the preparation of *pro forma* balance sheets, whereby assets and liabilities plus net worth are brought into balance.

Once we have estimated all the components of the *pro forma* balance sheet, they are combined into a balance sheet format. The *pro forma* balance sheet at June 30 is:

Assets (in thousands)		Liabilities (in thousands)	
Cash	$ 75.0	Bank borrowings	$ 111.5
Receivables	373.5	Accounts payable	250.0
Inventories	420.0	Accrued wages and expenses	240.0
		Accrued income taxes	70.0
Current assets	$ 868.5	Current liabilities	$ 671.5
Net fixed assets	850.0	Net worth	1,047.0
Total assets	$1,718.5	Total liabilities and net worth	$1,718.5

As before, the cash-budget method is but one way to prepare a *pro forma* statement; one can also make direct estimates of all of the items on the balance sheet by projecting financial ratios into the future and then making estimates on the basis of these ratios. Receivables, inventories, accounts payable, and accrued wages and expenses frequently are based upon historical relationships to sales and production when a cash budget is not available. For example, if the average collection period is 45 days, turnover would be eight times a year. If receivables were $500,000 but the firm were predicting a $2 million increase in sales for the coming year, it would take approximately $2 million/8 = $250,000 in additional receivables to support the added sales. Thus the level of receivables one year hence might be forecast at $750,000.

Pro forma statements allow us to study the composition of expected future balance sheets and income statements. Financial ratios may be computed for analysis of the statements; these ratios and the raw figures may be compared with those for present and past balance sheets. Using this information, the financial manager can analyze the direction of change in the financial condition and performance of the firm over the past, the present, and the future. If the firm is accustomed to making accurate estimates, the preparation of a cash budget, *pro forma* statements, or both literally forces it to plan ahead and to coordinate policy in the various areas of operation. Continual revision of these forecasts keeps the firm alert to changing conditions in its environment and in its internal operations.

Again, it is useful to prepare more than one set of *pro forma* statements in order to take into account the range of possible outcomes.

SUMMARY

Continuing our examination of the analytical tools of the financial manager, we looked at source and use of funds statements, the cash budget, and *pro forma* statements. The source and use of funds statement gives the financial analyst considerable insight into the uses of funds and how these uses are financed over a specific period of time. Funds-flow analysis is valuable in analyzing the commitment of funds to assets and in planning the firm's intermediate- and long-term financing. The flow of funds studied, however, represents net rather than gross transactions between two points in time.

A cash budget is a forecast of a firm's future cash receipts and cash disbursements. This forecast is particularly useful to the financial manager in determining the probable cash balances of the firm over the near future and in planning for the financing of prospective cash needs. In addition to analyzing expected cash flows, the financial manager should take into account possible deviations from the expected outcome. An analysis of the range of possible outcomes enables management to better assess the efficiency and flexibility of the firm and to determine the appropriate margin of safety.

Finally, we considered the preparation of *pro forma* income statements and balance sheets. These statements offer financial managers insight into the prospective future financial condition and performance of their firms, giving them yet another tool for financial planning and control.

QUESTIONS

1. Contrast the source and use of funds statements with a cash budget as planning tools.

2. In constructing a cash budget, which variable is most important in order to arrive at accurate projections? Explain.

3. Discuss the benefits that can be derived by the firm from cash budgeting.

4. Explain why a decrease in cash constitutes a source of funds while an increase in cash is a use of funds in the source and use statement.

5. Explain why selling inventory to credit customers is considered as a source of funds when in fact no funds were generated.

6. Why do most audited financial reports to the stockholders include a source and use of funds statement in addition to the balance sheet and income statement?

7. Is depreciation a source of funds? Under what conditions might the "source" dry up?

8. Why do bankers closely analyze the source and use of funds statement in considering credit applications?

154

PART III
Tools of
financial
analysis and
planning

9. Which of the following are sources of funds and which are uses of funds?

   a) Sale of land

   b) Quarterly dividend payment

   c) Lease payment

   d) Decrease in raw-materials inventory

   e) Increase in depreciation charges

   f) Sale of government bonds

10. What are the major points of difference between a cash budget and the source and use of funds statement?

11. On what items should the financial manager concentrate to improve the accuracy of the cash budget? Explain your reasoning.

12. Is the cash budget a better measure of liquidity than traditional measures such as the current ratio and quick ratio?

13. Why is the sales forecast so important in preparing the cash budget?

14. What is the principal purpose of *pro forma* statements? Being a projection of the future, how do they differ from the cash budget?

PROBLEMS

1. Galow Fish Canning Company reports the following changes from the previous year end. Categorize these items as either a source of funds or a use of funds.

Item		Item	
Cash	− $100	Accounts payable	$300
Accounts receivable	700	Accruals	− 100
Inventory	− 300	Long-term debt	− 200
Gross fixed assets	900	Net profit	600
Depreciation	1,000	Dividends	400

2. Serap-Jones Inc. had the following financial statements for 1982 and 1983. Prepare a source and use of funds statement and evaluate your findings.

	1982	1983
ASSETS		
Cash	$ 53,000	$ 31,000
Marketable securities	87,000	0
Accounts receivable	346,000	528,000
Inventories	432,000	683,000
Current assets	918,000	1,242,000
Net fixed assets	1,113,000	1,398,000
Total	$2,031,000	$2,640,000
LIABILITIES AND EQUITY		
Accounts payable	$ 413,000	$ 627,000
Accruals	226,000	314,000
Bank borrowings	100,000	235,000
Current liabilities	739,000	1,176,000
Common stock	100,000	100,000
Retained earnings	1,192,000	1,364,000
	$2,031,000	$2,640,000

Note: Depreciation was $189,000 for 1983, and no dividends were paid.

3.

Kohn Corporation comparative balance sheets at Dec. 31 (in millions)

Assets	19X1	19X2	Liabilities and net worth	19X1	19X2
Cash	$ 5	$ 3	Notes payable	$ 20	$ 0
Accounts receivable	15	22	Accounts payable	5	8
Inventories	12	15	Accrued wages	2	2
Fixed assets, net	50	55	Accrued taxes	3	5
Other assets	8	5	Long-term debt	0	15
			Common stock	20	26
			Retained earnings	40	44
Total assets	$ 90	$100	Total liabilities and net worth	$ 90	$100

156

PART III
Tools of
financial
analysis and
planning

Kohn Corporation statement of income and retained earnings, year ended December 31, 19X2 (in millions)

Net sales		$50
Expenses		
Cost of goods sold	$25	
Selling, general, and administrative expenses	5	
Depreciation	5	
Interest	1	36
Net income before taxes		$14
Less: Taxes		7
Net income		$ 7
Add: Retained earnings at 12/31/X1		40
Subtotal		$47
Less: Dividends		3
Retained earnings at 12/31/X2		$44

a) Prepare a source and use of funds statement on a cash basis for 19X2 for the Kohn Corporation.

b) Prepare a source and use of working capital statement for 19X2 for the Kohn Corporation.

4. Financial statements for the Sennet Corporation follow.

Sennet Corporation balance sheet at December 31 (in millions)

	19X1	19X2		19X1	19X2
Cash	$ 4	$ 5	Accounts payable	$ 8	$10
Accounts receivable	7	10	Notes payable	5	5
Inventory	12	15	Accrued wages	2	3
Total current assets	$23	$30	Accrued taxes	3	2
Net plant	40	40	Total current liabilities	$18	$20
			Long-term debt	20	20
			Common stock	10	10
			Retained earnings	15	20
Total	$63	$70	Total	$63	$70

Sennet Corporation income statement 19X2 (in millions)

Sales		$100
Cost of goods sold	$50	
Selling, general, and administrative expenses	15	
Depreciation	3	
Interest	2	70
Net income before taxes		$ 30
Taxes		15
Net income		$ 15

a) Prepare a source and use of funds statement for Sennet.

b) Prepare a source and use of working capital statement.

5. At December 31, the balance sheet of Rodriguez Malting Company was the following (in thousands):

Cash	$ 50	Accounts payable	$ 360
Accounts receivable	530	Bank loan	400
Inventories	545	Accruals	212
Current assets	$1,125	Current liabilities	$ 972
Net fixed assets	1,836	Long-term debt	450
		Common stock	100
		Retained earnings	1,439
Total assets	$2,961	Total liabilities and net worth	$2,961

The company has received a large order and anticipates the need to go to its bank in order to increase its borrowings. As a result, it needs to forecast its cash requirements for January, February, and March.

Typically, the company collects 20 percent of its sales in the month of sale, 70 percent the subsequent month, and 10 percent in the second month after the sale. All sales are credit sales.

Purchases of raw materials to produce malt are made in the month prior to the sale and amount to 60 percent of sales in the subsequent month. Payments for these purchases occur in the month after the purchase. Labor costs, including overtime, are expected to be $150,000 in January, $200,000 in February, and $160,000 in March. Selling, adminis-

158

PART III

Tools of
financial
analysis and
planning

trative, tax, and other cash expenses are expected to be $100,000 per month for January through March. Actual sales in November and December and projected sales for January through April are as follows (in thousands):

November	$500	February	$1,000
December	600	March	650
January	600	April	750

On the basis of this information,

a) Prepare a cash budget for the months of January, February, and March.

b) Determine the amount of additional bank borrowings necessary to maintain a cash balance of $50,000 at all times.

c) Prepare a *pro forma* balance sheet for March 31. (It should be noted that the company maintains a safety stock of inventory.)

6. Prepare a cash budget for the Ace Manufacturing Company, indicating receipts and disbursements for May, June, and July. The firm wishes to maintain, at all times, a minimum cash balance of $20,000. Determine whether or not borrowing will be necessary during the period and if it is, when and for how much. As of April 30, the firm had a balance of $20,000 in cash.

Actual sales		Forecasted sales	
January	$50,000	May	$ 70,000
February	50,000	June	80,000
March	60,000	July	100,000
April	60,000	August	100,000

Accounts receivable: 50 percent of total sales are for cash. The remaining 50 percent will be collected equally during the following two months (the firm incurs a negligible bad-debt loss).

Cost of goods manufactured: 70 percent of sales. 90 percent of this cost is paid during the first month after incurrence; the remaining 10 percent is paid the following month.

Selling and administrative expenses: $10,000 per month plus 10 percent of sales. All of these expenses are paid during the month of incurrence.

Interest payments: A semiannual interest payment on $150,000 of bonds outstanding (12 percent coupon) is paid during July. An annual $50,000 sinking-fund payment is also made at that time.

Dividends: A $10,000 dividend payment will be declared and made in July.

Capital expenditures: $40,000 will be invested in plant and equipment in June.

Taxes: Income tax payments of $1,000 will be made in July.

7. Downeast Nautical Company expects sales of $2.4 million next year and the same amount the following year. Sales are spread evenly throughout the year. On the basis of the following information, prepare a *pro forma* balance sheet and income statement for year end:

Cash: Minimum of 4 percent of annual sales.

Accounts receivable: 60-day average collection period based on annual sales.

Inventories: Turnover of eight times a year.

Net fixed assets: $500,000 now. Capital expenditures equal to depreciation.

Accounts payable: one month's purchases.

Accruals: 3 percent of sales.

Bank borrowings: $50,000 now. Can borrow up to $250,000.

Long-term debt: $300,000 now, payable $75,000 at year end.

Common stock: $100,000. No additions planned.

Retained earnings: $500,000 now.

Net profit margin: 8 percent of sales.

Dividends: None.

Cost of goods sold: 60 percent of sales.

Purchases: 50 percent of cost of goods sold.

Income taxes: 50 percent of before-tax profits.

8. Given the information that follows, prepare a cash budget for the Central City Department Store for the first 6 months of 19X2.

a) All prices and costs remain constant.

b) Sales are 75 percent for credit and 25 percent for cash.

c) With respect to credit sales, 60 percent are collected in the month after the sale, 30 percent in the second month, and 10 percent in the third. Bad-debt losses are insignificant.

d) Sales, actual and estimated, are

October 19X1	$300,000	March 19X2	$200,000
November 19X1	350,000	April 19X2	300,000
December 19X1	400,000	May 19X2	250,000
January 19X2	150,000	June 19X2	200,000
February 19X2	200.000	July 19X2	300,000

e) Payments for purchases of merchandise are 80 percent of the following month's anticipated sales.

160

PART III
Tools of
financial
analysis and
planning

f) Wages and salaries are

January	$30,000	March	$50,000	May	$40,000
February	40,000	April	50,000	June	35,000

g) Rent is $2,000 a month.

h) Interest of $7,500 is due on the last day of each calendar quarter.

i) A tax prepayment of $50,000 for 19X2 income is due in April.

j) A capital investment of $30,000 is planned in June, to be paid for then.

k) The company has a cash balance of $100,000 at December 31, 19X1, which is the minimum desired level for cash. Funds can be borrowed in multiples of $5,000. (Ignore interest on such borrowings.)

9. Use the cash budget worked out in problem 8 and the following additional information to prepare a *pro forma* income statement for the first half of 19X2 for the Central City Department Store. (Note that the store maintains a safety stock of inventory.)

a) Inventory at 12/31/X1 was $200,000.

b) Depreciation is taken on a straight-line basis on $250,000 of assets with an average remaining life of 10 years and no salvage value.

c) The tax rate is 50 percent.

10. Given the following information and that contained in problems 8 and 9, construct a *pro forma* balance sheet as of June 30, 19X2, for the Central City Department Store. (Assume that accounts payable stay the same as at December 31, 19X1.)

Central City Department Store balance sheet at December 31, 19X1

Assets		Liabilities and equity	
Cash	$100,000	Accounts payable	$130,000
Accounts receivable	427,500	Bonds	500,000
Inventory	200,000		
		Common stock and	
Fixed assets, net	250,000	retained earnings	347,500
	$977,500		$977,500

SELECTED REFERENCES

CHAMBERS, JOHN C., SATINDER K. MULLICK, and DONALD D. SMITH, "How to Choose the Right Forecasting Technique," *Harvard Business Review,* 49 (July–August 1971), 45–74.

DONALDSON, GORDON, "Strategy for Financial Emergencies," *Harvard Business Review,* 47 (November–December 1969), 67–79.

HELFERT, ERICH A., *Techniques of Financial Analysis,* 5th ed. Homewood, Ill.: Irwin, 1981, chaps. 1 and 3.

HUNT, PEARSON, "Funds Position: Keystone in Financial Planning." *Harvard Business Review,* 53 (May–June), 106–15.

JAEDICKE, ROBERT K., and ROBERT T. SPROUSE, *Accounting Flows: Income, Funds, and Cash.* Englewood Cliffs, N.J.: Prentice-Hall 1965, chaps. 5 and 6.

JUDELSON, DAVID N., "Financial Controls that Work," *Financial Executive,* 45 (January, 1977), 22–27.

PAN, JUDY, DONALD R. NICHOLS, and O. MAURICE JOY, "Sales Forecasting Practices of Large U.S. Industrial Firms," *Financial Management,* 6 (Fall 1977), 72–77.

PAPPAS, JAMES L., and GEORGE P. HUBER, "Probabilistic Short-Term Financial Planning," *Financial Management,* 2 (Autumn 1973), 36–44.

PARKER, GEORGE G. C., and EDILBERTO L. SEGURA, "How to Get a Better Forecast," *Harvard Business Review,* 49 (March–April 1971), 99–109.

SMITH, KEITH V., *Guide to Working Capital Management.* New York: McGraw-Hill, 1979, chap. 2.

WORKING CAPITAL MANAGEMENT

IV

Current asset and liability structure decisions 8

Current assets, by accounting definition, are assets normally converted into cash within one year. Working capital management usually is considered to involve the administration of these assets—namely, cash and marketable securities, receivables, and inventories—and the administration of current liabilities. Administration of *fixed assets* (assets normally not converted into cash within the year), on the other hand, is usually considered to fall within the realm of capital budgeting, which we take up in part V. By and large, investment in current assets is more divisible than investment in fixed assets, a fact that has implications for flexibility in financing. Differences in divisibility as well as in durability of economic life are the essential features that distinguish current from fixed assets.

Determining the appropriate levels of current assets and current liabilities, which determine the level of working capital, involves fundamental decisions on the firm's liquidity and the maturity composition of its debt. In turn, these decisions are influenced by a tradeoff between profitability and risk. In a broad sense, the appropriate decision variable to examine on the asset side of the balance sheet is the maturity composition, or liquidity, of the firm's assets—that is, the turnover of these assets into cash. Decisions that affect the asset liquidity of the firm include

163

the management of cash and marketable securities, credit policy and procedures, inventory management and control, and the administration of fixed assets. For purposes of illustration, we hold constant the last three factors; the efficiency in managing them is taken up elsewhere in the book.[1] We assume also that the cash and marketable securities held by the firm (hereafter called liquid assets) yield a return lower than the return on investment in other assets.

Profitability and risk

For current assets, then, the lower the proportion of liquid assets to total assets, the greater the firm's return on total investment. Profitability with respect to the level of current liabilities relates to differences in costs between various methods of financing and to the use of financing during periods when it is not needed. To the extent that the explicit costs of short-term financing are less than those of intermediate- and long-term financing, the greater the proportion of short-term debt to total debt, the higher the profitability of the firm.

Although short-term rates sometimes exceed long-term rates, generally they are less. Even when they are higher, the situation is likely to be only temporary. Over an extended period of time we would expect to pay more in interest cost with long-term debt than we would with short-term borrowings which are continually rolled over at maturity. Moreover, the use of short-term debt as opposed to longer-term debt is likely to result in higher profits because debt will be paid off during periods when it is not needed.

The profitability assumptions above suggest a low proportion of current assets to total assets and a high proportion of current liabilities to total liabilities. This strategy, of course, will result in a low level of working capital or, conceivably, even negative working capital. Offsetting the profitability of this strategy is the risk to the firm. For our purposes, risk is the probability of technical insolvency. In a legal sense, insolvency occurs whenever the assets of a firm are less than its liabilities—negative net worth. Technical insolvency, on the other hand, occurs whenever a firm is unable to meet its cash obligations.[2]

In this chapter we study the extent to which possible adverse deviations from expected net cash flows (cash inflows less cash outflows) are protected by the liquid assets of the firm. The risk involved with various levels of current assets and current liabilities must be evaluated in relation to the profitability associated with those levels. The discussion that follows concerns the financing of current assets and the level of those assets that should be maintained.

THE MATURITY STRUCTURE OF FINANCING

The way in which the assets of a company are financed involves a tradeoff between risk and profitability. For purposes of analysis, we assume that the company has an established policy of payment for purchases, labor, taxes, and other

[1] See chapter 10 and part V.
[2] James E. Walter, "Determination of Technical Solvency," *Journal of Business*, 30 (January 1957), 30–43.

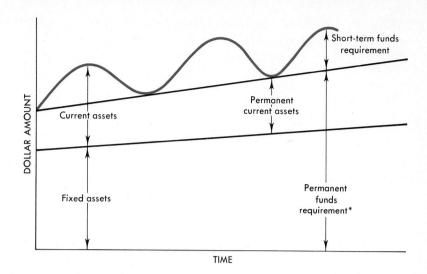

**FIGURE 8-1
Funds requirement; hedging
financing policy**

expenses. Thus, the amounts of accounts payable and accruals included in current liabilities are not active decision variables.[3] These liabilities finance a portion of the current assets of the firm and tend to fluctuate with the production schedule and, in the case of taxes, with profits. As the underlying investment in current assets grows, accounts payable and accruals also tend to grow, in part financing the buildup in assets. Our concern is with how assets not supported by accounts payable and accruals are financed.

Hedging approach

If the firm adopts a hedging approach to financing, each asset would be offset with a financing instrument of the same approximate maturity. Short-term or seasonal variations in current assets would be financed with short-term debt; the permanent component of current assets would be financed with long-term debt or equity. The situation is illustrated in Fig. 8-1. If total funds requirements behave in the manner shown, only the short-term fluctuations shown at the top of the figure would be financed with short-term debt. To finance short-term requirements with long-term debt would necessitate the payment of interest for the use of funds during times when they were not needed. This occurrence can be illustrated by drawing a straight line across the seasonal humps in Fig. 8-1 to represent the total amount of long-term debt and equity. It is apparent that financing would be employed in periods of seasonal lull when it was not needed. With a hedging approach to financing, the borrowing and payment schedule for short-term financing would be arranged to correspond to the expected swings in current assets, less payables and accruals. Fixed assets and the permanent component of

---

[3] Delaying the payment of accounts payable can be a decision variable for financing purposes. However, there are limits to the extent to which a firm can "stretch" its payables. For simplicity, we assume in the above analysis that the firm has a definite policy for paying bills, such as taking advantage of all cash discounts and paying all other bills at the end of the credit period. See chapter 11 for a discussion of trade credit as a means of financing.

current assets would be financed with long-term debt, equity, and the permanent component of current liabilities.

A hedging approach to financing suggests that apart from current install-ments on long-term debt, a firm would show no current borrowings at the seasonal troughs in Fig. 8-1. Short-term borrowings would be paid off with surplus cash. As the firm moved into a period of seasonal funds needs, it would borrow on a short-term basis, again paying the borrowings off as surplus cash was generated. In this way, financing would be employed only when it was needed. Permanent funds requirements would be financed with long-term debt and equity. In a growth situation, permanent financing would be increased in keeping with increases in permanent funds requirements.

Short- versus long-term financing

Although an exact synchronization of the schedule of expected future net cash flows and the payment schedule of debt is appropriate under conditions of certainty, it usually is not appropriate under uncertainty. Net cash flows will deviate from expected flows in keeping with the business risk of the firm. As a result, the schedule of maturities of the debt contracts is very significant in a risk-profitability tradeoff. The question is: what margin of safety should be built into the maturity schedule in order to allow for adverse fluctuations in cash flows? This depends on the tradeoff between risk and profitability.

The relative risks involved. In general, the shorter the maturity schedule of a firm's debt obligations, the greater the risk that it will be unable to meet principal and interest payments. On the other hand, the longer the maturity sched-ule, the less risky the financing of the firm, all other things the same.

A company may borrow on a short-term basis in order to build a new plant. The cash flows from the plant are not sufficient in the short run to pay off the loan. As a result, the company bears the risk that the lender may not renew the loan at maturity. This risk could be reduced by financing the plant on a long-term basis, the expected cash flows being sufficient to retire the debt in an orderly manner. Thus, committing funds to a long-term asset and borrowing short carries the risk that the firm may not be able to renew its borrowings. If the company should fall on hard times, creditors might regard renewal as too risky and demand immediate payment. In turn, this would cause the firm either to retrench or to go into bank-ruptcy.

In addition to this sort of risk, there also is the uncertainty associated with interest costs. When the firm finances with long-term debt, it knows precisely its interest costs over the time period it needs the funds. If it finances with short-term debt, it is uncertain of interest costs upon refinancing. In a sense, then, the uncer-tainty of interest costs represents risk to the borrower. We know that short-term interest rates fluctuate far more than long-term interest rates. During the past decade, the interest rate on short-term commercial paper issued by corporations ranged from approximately 5 percent to 20 percent. A firm forced to refinance its short-term debt in a period of rising interest rates may pay an overall interest cost on short-term debt that is higher than it would have been on long-term debt. Therefore, the absence of knowledge of future short-term interest costs may repre-sent risk to a company.

FIGURE 8-2
Typical yield curve
for high-grade
corporate bonds

The tradeoff with costs. Differences in risk between short- and long-term financing must be balanced against differences in interest costs. The longer the maturity schedule of a firm's debt, the more costly the financing is likely to be. For one thing, the explicit cost of long-term financing usually is more than that of short-term financing. Figure 8-2 illustrates the typical relationship which prevailed from 1970 to the present between interest rates and maturity for high-grade corporate bonds. The line is known as a *yield curve*, and it tells us the yield associated with a given maturity. As shown, the yield curve is upward sloping, which suggests that long-term borrowings are more costly than short-term borrowings. In addition to the higher expected interests costs of long-term borrowings, the firm may pay interest on debt over periods of time when the funds are not needed. Put another way, short-term financing gives the firm flexibility. If there is a probability that the firm's need for funds will decrease, the use of short-term debt permits debt to be paid off in keeping with the diminished need for funds. Thus, there is an expected cost inducement to finance funds requirements on a short-term basis.

Consequently, we have a tradeoff between risk and profitability. We have seen that in general short-term debt has greater risk than long-term debt, but also less cost. The margin of safety provided by the firm can be thought of as the lag between the firm's expected net cash flow and the contractual payments on its debt. This margin of safety will depend upon the risk preferences of management. In turn, its decision on the maturity composition of the firm's debt will determine the portion of current assets financed by current liabilities and the portion financed on a long-term basis.

To allow for a margin of safety, management might decide upon the proportions of short-term and long-term financing shown in Fig. 8-3. Here, we see, the firm finances a portion of its expected seasonal funds requirement, less payables and accruals, on a long-term basis. If the expected net cash flows do occur, it will pay interest on debt during seasonal troughs when the funds are not needed. In contrast, if an aggressive financing policy were adopted, the situation might look

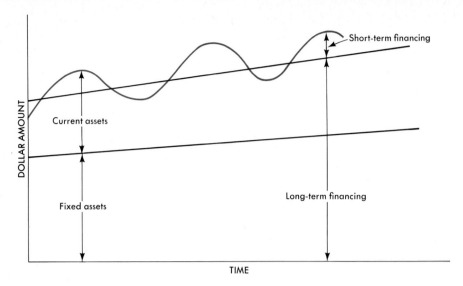

FIGURE 8-3 Funds requirement—conservative financing policy

like that shown in Fig. 8-4. Here we see that there is a "negative" margin of safety. The firm has financed part of its permanent current assets with short-term debt. As a result, it must refinance this debt at maturity, and this involves an element of risk. The greater the portion of the permanent funds requirements financed with short-term debt, the more aggressive the financing is said to be. Therefore, the margin of safety associated with financing policy can be either positive, negative, or zero. Zero would be the case with a hedging policy, illustrated in Fig. 8-1.

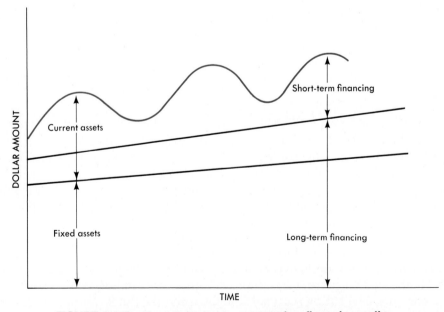

FIGURE 8-4 Funds requirement—aggressive financing policy

169

CHAPTER 8
Current asset
and liability
structure
decisions

As we shall see in the subsequent section, however, the firm also can create a margin of safety by increasing the proportion of liquid assets. Thus, the firm can reduce the risk of cash insolvency either by increasing the maturity schedule of its debt or by decreasing the relative "maturity" of its assets. At the end of the chapter we explore the interdependence of these two facets.

THE AMOUNT OF CURRENT ASSETS

In determining the appropriate level of current assets, management must again consider the tradeoff between profitability and risk. To illustrate this tradeoff, we hold constant the amount of the firm's fixed assets and vary the amount of current assets. Moreover, we assume that the management of receivables and inventories is efficient and consistent throughout the range of output under consideration. In other words, at every level of output, the investment in receivables and inventories is predetermined.[4] As a result, we are concerned only with the cash and marketable securities portion of the current assets of the firm.[5]

Risk-profitability tradeoff

Under these assumptions there exists a risk-return tradeoff with respect to the relative proportion of current assets held by the firm. In general, the greater the ratio of current assets to total assets, the less risky the company's working capital policy. This makes sense in that the firm will have sufficient cash and cash equivalents to pay its bills the greater the cushion. On the other hand, the lower the ratio, the more aggressive—and risky—the company's working capital policy. At any sales level, the greater the firm's proportion of current assets, the lower its relative profitability. What happens is that the firm has money tied up in idle or near idle current assets. As a result, its profitability is not as high as it would be if the funds were invested in assets providing a higher return.

To illustrate these concepts, suppose that with its existing fixed assets a firm can produce up to 100,000 units of output a year. Production is continuous throughout the period under consideration, in which there is a particular level of output. For each level of output, the firm can have a number of different levels of current assets. We assume initially three current-asset alternatives. The relationship between output and current-asset level for these alternatives is illustrated in Fig. 8-5. We see from the figure that the greater the output, the greater the need for investment in current assets. However, the relationship is not linear; current assets increase at a decreasing rate with output. This relationship is based upon the notion that it takes a greater proportional investment in current assets when only a few units of output are produced than it does later on when the firm can use its current assets more efficiently. Fixed assets are assumed not to vary with output.

---

[4] The efficiency of management of receivables and inventory is examined in chapter 10. The quality of these assets, as determined by the efficiency of their management, has a significant bearing upon the liquidity of the firm.

[5] The allocation of funds between cash and marketable securities, near cash, is taken up in chapter 9.

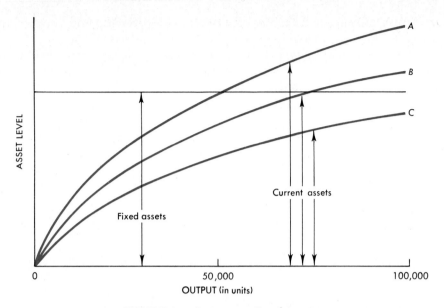

FIGURE 8-5 Current to fixed assets

Of the three alternatives, alternative *A* is the most conservative level of current assets, for the ratio of current assets to fixed assets is greatest at every level of output. The greater the proportion of current to fixed assets, the greater the liquidity of the firm and the lower the risk of technical insolvency, all other things held constant. Alternative *C* is the most aggressive policy, because the ratio of current assets to fixed assets is lowest at all levels of output. The probability of technical insolvency is greatest under alternative *C* if net cash flows are less than expected.

Suppose that for the forthcoming year a firm expects sales of $2 million on 80,000 units of output and expects to realize a profit margin before interest and taxes of 10 percent, or $200,000 in total profits. We assume that this figure will not vary with the levels of current assets considered. Fixed assets are $500,000 for the period under review, and management is considering current asset positions of $400,000, $500,000, or $600,000. Given this information, we are able to make the profitability calculations shown in Table 8-1. As evidenced in this table, the greater the proportion of current assets to fixed assets, the lower the rate of return. Alternative *A*, the most conservative plan, gives the firm the greatest liquidity cushion to meet unexpected needs for funds. It also provides the lowest rate of return of the three alternatives. Alternative *C*, on the other hand, provides the highest rate of return but has the lowest liquidity and, correspondingly, the greatest risk.

Some qualifications

This is a very simple example of the tradeoff between risk and profitability. Our assumptions were such that changes in the level of current assets were comprised entirely of changes in liquid assets—cash and marketable securities. We

TABLE 8-1 \ **Profitability under alternative current-asset positions**

	A	B	C
Sales	$2,000,000	$2,000,000	$2,000,000
Earnings before interest and taxes	200,000	200,000	200,000
Current assets	600,000	500,000	400,000
Fixed assets	500,000	500,000	500,000
Total assets	1,100,000	1,000,000	900,000
Asset turnover (sales/total assets)	1.82:1	2:1	2.22:1
Rate of return (earnings/total assets)	18.2%	20%	22.2%

should recognize that the generalizations possible become far more complicated when it comes to changes in accounts receivable and inventory. Although receivables do not provide the buffer against running out of cash that cash and marketable securities do, they provide more of a buffer than do inventories or fixed assets. By the same token, the profit foregone by holding receivables generally is less than that for holding cash or marketable securities, but greater than that for holding inventories and fixed assets. Though we may have some idea of the relative ordering of receivables and inventories with respect to risk and profits foregone, the differences are extremely difficult to quantify. In subsequent chapters we deal with the optimal level of each of these assets, taking into consideration both profitability and risk. For now, we continue to restrict our definition of liquid assets to cash and marketable securities.

COMBINING LIABILITY-STRUCTURE AND CURRENT-ASSET DECISIONS

In the preceding sections we examined two broad facets of working capital management: how to finance current assets and what proportion of liquid assets to maintain. The two facets are interdependent. All other things held constant, a firm with a high proportion of liquid assets is better able to finance its current assets on a short-term basis than is a firm with a low proportion of liquid assets. On the other hand, a firm that finances its current assets entirely with equity will have less need for liquidity than it would if it financed these assets entirely with short-term borrowings. Because of their interdependence, these two facets of working-capital management must be considered jointly.

Uncertainty and the margin of safety

If the firm knows its future cash flows with certainty, it will be able to arrange its maturity schedule of debt to correspond exactly with its schedule of future net cash flows. As a result, profits will be maximized, for there will be no need to hold low-yielding liquid assets nor to have more long-term financing than is absolutely necessary. When cash flows are subject to uncertainty, however, the situation is changed. As discussed in chapter 7, cash forecasts can be prepared for a range of possible outcomes, with a probability attached to each. This information enables management to assess the possibility of technical insolvency and to plan accordingly for a margin of safety. The greater the dispersion of the probability distribution of possible net cash flows, the greater the margin of safety that management will wish to provide.

We assume initially that the firm cannot borrow on short notice to meet unexpected cash drains. As a result, it can provide a margin of safety only by (1) increasing the proportion of liquid assets, and (2) lengthening the maturity schedule of financing. Both of these actions affect profitability. In the first choice, funds are committed to low-yielding assets; in the second, the firm may pay interest on borrowings over periods of time when the funds are not needed. In addition, long-term debt has a higher expected interest cost than does short-term debt.

Risk and profitability

A decision on the appropriate margin of safety will be governed by considerations of risk and profitability and by the utility preferences of management with respect to bearing risk. To the extent that the cost of running out of cash is measurable, the optimal margin of safety can be determined by comparing the expected costs of running out of cash with the profits foregone when a particular solution is used to avoid that possibility. The expected cost of a cash stockout is the cost associated with a particular stockout times its probability of occurrence. Suppose that associated with a particular solution there is a 10 percent probability for a cash stockout of $50,000, and a 5 percent probability that the stockout will be $100,000. If the costs of these stockouts are $10,000 and $25,000, respectively, the expected costs will be 0.10($10,000) = $1,000 and 0.05($25,000) = $1,250, respectively. The total expected cost of cash stockout for that solution is $2,250.

The optimal solution could be determined by comparing the reduction in the expected cost of cash stockout accompanying a particular solution with the opportunity cost of implementing that solution. The optimal solution is at the point where the marginal opportunity cost equals the marginal decrease in the expected cost of cash stockout. The difficulty with this approach, however, is in estimating the cost of a cash stockout. Costs such as deterioration in a firm's credit standing and the inability to pay certain obligations are intangible and defy precise quantification.

Because of this difficulty, it may be easier for management to consider subjectively the costs associated with various cash stockouts and then simply specify a tolerable level of risk. Suppose we find that there is a 5 percent probability that the cash balance of the firm will be −$300,000 or less during the next several periods. If management is willing to tolerate a 5 percent probability of running out of cash, the firm should increase its liquid assets by $300,000. If it does so, there will be only a 5 percent probability that possible deviations from expected cash flows will result in the firm's running out of cash. The firm may be able to achieve the same results by lengthening its maturity schedule of financing. By refinancing existing debt that matures within 2 years into intermediate-term debt maturing in 5 to 7 years, the firm may be able to reduce the probability of technical insolvency to 5 percent. Likewise, various combinations of liquidity increase and debt lengthening may achieve this result.

173

CHAPTER 8
Current asset
and liability
structure
decisions

Each solution (increasing liquidity, lengthening the maturity structure, or a combination of the two), will cost the firm something in profit-making ability. For a given risk tolerance, management may determine which solution is least costly and then implement that solution. On the other hand, management might determine the least costly solution for various levels of risk. Then management could formulate risk tolerances on the basis of the cost involved in providing a margin of safety. Presumably these tolerances would be in keeping with an objective of maximizing shareholder wealth. The approach, however, has been to provide an information framework specifying risk and profitability that management can use to make informal and rational decisions.

If the firm can borrow in times of emergency, the above analysis needs to be modified. The greater the ability of the firm to borrow, the less it needs to provide for a margin of safety by the means discussed previously. Certain companies can arrange for lines of credit or revolving credits that enable them to borrow on short notice.[6] When a company has access to such credit, it must compare the cost of these arrangements (compensating balances, interest costs, and use of debt capacity) with the cost of other solutions. There are, of course, limits on how much a firm may borrow on short notice. Consequently, it must provide for some margin of safety on the basis of the considerations discussed above.

SUMMARY

Working capital management involves deciding upon the amount and composition of current assets and how to finance these assets. These decisions involve tradeoffs between risk and profitability. The greater the relative proportion of liquid assets, the less the risk of running out of cash, all other things being equal. Profitability, unfortunately, also will be less. The longer the composite maturity schedule of securities used to finance the firm, the less the risk of cash insolvency, all other things being equal. Again, the profits of the firm are likely to be less. Resolution of the tradeoff between risk and profitability with respect to these decisions depends upon the risk preferences of management.

In this chapter we have been concerned with working capital management in a broad sense. We assumed the efficient management of the various components of current assets. The efficiency of credit and collection procedures and inventory control have a significant bearing upon the liquidity of the firm. Moreover, we did not differentiate between cash and marketable securities "near cash" or consider the optimal split between these two assets. In the three subsequent chapters we analyze specifically the management of cash and marketable securities, the management of receivables, and the management of inventories. Still later in this part, we consider methods of short- and intermediate-term financing.

QUESTIONS

1. Evaluate the following statement: "Returns on current assets are insignificant; therefore, a business firm should minimize its investment in these assets."

[6] For a discussion of these methods, see chap. 12.

2. The amount of current assets that a firm maintains will be determined by the tradeoff between risk and profitability.

   a) Is there a unique combination of risk and profitability for each level of current assets?

   b) Discuss the factors that affect the risk associated with holding current assets.

3. Utilities hold 10 percent of total assets in current assets; retail trade industries hold 60 percent of total assets in current assets. Explain how industry characteristics account for this difference.

4. Some firms finance their permanent working capital with short-term liabilities (commercial paper and short-term notes). Explain the impact of this decision on the profitability and risk parameters of these firms.

5. Suppose a firm finances its seasonal (temporary) current assets with long-term funds. What is the impact of this decision on the profitability and risk parameters of this firm?

6. Risk associated with the amount of current assets is assumed to decrease with increased levels of current assets. Is this assumption correct for all levels of current assets? Explain.

7. Can you compare the net working capital position with the cash budget to measure the ability of a firm to meet maturing obligations?

8. At times, long-term interest rates are lower than short-term rates, yet the discussion in the chapter suggests that long-term financing is more expensive. If long-term rates are lower, should not the firm finance itself entirely with long-term debt?

9. How does shortening the maturity composition of outstanding debt increase the firm's risk? Why does increasing the liquidity of the firm's assets reduce that risk?

10. Why do firms invest in any current assets at all if the returns on those assets are less than the returns from fixed assets?

11. What are the costs of maintaining too large a net working capital position? Too small a net working capital position?

12. What are the main disadvantages of the use of the net working capital position as an indication of a firm's financial solvency?

PROBLEMS

1. The Anderson Corporation has a sales level of $280,000 with a 10 percent profit margin before interest and taxes. To generate this sales volume, the firm maintains a fixed-asset investment of $100,000. Currently, the firm maintains $50,000 in current assets.

   a) Determine the asset turnover for the firm and compute the rate of return on assets before taxes.

   b) Compute the rate of return on assets at different levels of current assets starting with $10,000 and increasing in $15,000 increments to $100,000.

   c) What implicit assumption is being made about sales in part b? Appraise the significance of this assumption along with the policy to choose the level of current assets that will maximize the return on investments as computed in part b.

2. Pressler Cardboard Company estimates the following quarterly net cash flows for the company as a whole over the next 2 years (in millions of dollars):

175

CHAPTER 8
Current asset
and liability
structure
decisions

	19X1				19X2			
	1	2	3	4	1	2	3	4
	1.2	2.1	(2.7)	(1.9)	1.7	1.6	(3.6)	(1.0)

The company started in 19X1 with $1.5 million in liquid assets.

a) What is the cumulative liquid asset balance at quarter-end, in the absence of financing?

b) How much temporary and how much permanent financing should Pressler take on if it wishes to maintain an expected liquid asset balance of at least $1.5 million throughout the 2-year time span?

3. The Malkiel Corporation has made the 3-year projection of its asset investment given in the following table. It has found that payables and accruals tend to equal one-third of current assets. It currently has $50 million in equity and the remainder of its capitalization in long-term debt. The earnings retained amount to $1 million/quarter.

a) Graph the time path of total and fixed assets.

Date	Fixed assets	Current assets
3/31/X1 (now)	$50 (*in millions*)	$21 (*in millions*)
6/30/X1	51	30
9/30/X1	52	25
12/31/X1	53	21
3/31/X2	54	22
6/30/X2	55	31
9/30/X2	56	26
12/31/X2	57	22
3/31/X3	58	23
6/30/X3	59	32
9/30/X3	60	27
12/31/X3	61	23

b) Devise a financing plan, assuming your objective is to use a hedging approach.

c) If short-term rates average 10 percent and long-term rates average 12 percent, how much would the firm save if its entire current assets were financed by short-term debt?

4. Barnstap Aviation Company, founded 3 years ago, sells fuel and certain parts to private plane users at El Teton Airport, a small municipal airport in the Central Valley of California. The company has been successful in filling an economic need and has experienced good profitability. Up to the present time, it has been unable to obtain term financing. As a result, it has had to finance itself by "stretching" its accounts payable and recently by borrowing from a local finance company. At the end of June, Barnstap had the following debt and net worth:

Accounts payable	$60,000
Short-term debt	40,000
Net worth	60,000
	$160,000

Willie Brown, president of Barnstap, estimates that the effective cost of stretching payables is 30 percent per annum, comprised of cash discounts foregone and, in certain cases, payment of higher prices than would otherwise prevail. Only $30,000 of the total payables is stretched; that is, the company has $30,000 in normal payables at the end of June, which are not subject to the 30 percent cost. The rate of interest on the finance company loan is 24 percent. It appears that both sources of financing will be available in the future at the same effective rates of interest.

The company has a seasonal element to its business, with peak requirements in June. In June just passed, it required $100,000 in payables and debt. By the end of December its requirements will decline by 30 percent. Mr. Brown estimates that the company's requirements for payables and debt will be the following next June under three possible states of the economy:

State	Boom	Normal	Recession
Requirements	$160,000	$120,000	$90,000

For December of next year, funds requirements will decline by 30 percent from the requirements shown above for the three possible states of the economy.

Recently the company has been exploring the use of a term loan. Monument Southern Life Insurance Company has offered a 5-year term loan at 18 percent interest. The amount is $80,000, and the insurance company will not lend more nor less.

Mr. Brown wishes to evaluate the interest costs of the term loan in relation to the present method of financing at four times: June 30 and December 31 of this year, and June 30 and December 31 of next year. For ease of calculation, we assume that the amounts are outstanding 6 months, as increases and decreases in total financing requirements are steady. Moreover, 30 percent of the total payables and debt requirements are normal payables, for which there is no effective interest cost. The company would then borrow up to $40,000 from the finance company at 24 percent, with anything over that amount obtained from stretching accounts payable at an effective rate of 30 percent.

Which financing alternative has the lower six-month interest costs for each of the four dates and under each of the three possible states of the economy? Why?

SELECTED REFERENCES

BUDIN, MORRIS, and ROBERT J. VAN HANDEL, "A Rule-of-Thumb Theory of Cash Holdings by Firm," *Journal of Financial and Quantitative Analysis,* 10 (March 1975), 85–108.

EMERY, GARY W., and KENNETH O. COGGER, "The Measurement of Liquidity," Working Paper, Washington University in St. Louis, 1980.

LAMBRIX, R. J., and S. S. SINGHVI, "Managing the Working Capital Cycle," *Financial Executive,* 47 (June 1979), 32–41.

MEHTA, DILEEP R., *Working Capital Management.* Englewood Cliffs, N.J.: Prentice-Hall, 1974.

MORRIS, JAMES R., "On Corporate Debt Maturity Strategies," *Journal of Finance,* 31 (March 1976), 29–37.

PETTY, J. WILLIAM, and DAVID F. SCOTT, "The Analysis of Corporate Liquidity," *Journal of Economics and Business,* 32 (Spring/Summer 1980), 206–18.

SILVERS, J. B., "Liquidity, Risk and Duration Patterns of Corporate Financing," *Financial Management,* 5 (Autumn 1976), 54–64.

SMITH, KEITH V., *Guide to Working Capital Management.* New York: McGraw-Hill, 1979.

VAN HORNE, JAMES C., "A Risk-Return Analysis of a Firm's Working-Capital Position," *Engineering Economist,* 14 (Winter 1969), 71–89.

WALKER, ERNEST W., "Towards a Theory of Working Capital," *Engineering Economist,* 9 (January–February 1964), 21–35.

WALTER, JAMES E., "Determination of Technical Solvency," *Journal of Business,* 30 (January 1957), 30–43.

177

CHAPTER 8
Current asset
and liability
structure
decisions

Cash and marketable securities 9

We have been occupied with the overall level of liquid and current assets of the firm. By examining the tradeoff between profitability and risk, we were able to determine in a general way the proper amount of liquid assets the firm should carry. *(Liquid assets* were defined as cash and marketable securities.) Once the overall level of liquid assets is determined, other questions arise. How much will be carried in cash? How much will be carried in marketable securities? We are going to find out how to answer these questions. We shall also find out how to improve the efficiency of cash management and how to invest excess funds in marketable securities.

THE FUNCTION OF CASH MANAGEMENT

There are three motives for holding cash: the transactions motive, the precautionary motive, and the speculative motive.[1] The transactions motive is the need for cash to meet payments arising in the ordinary course of business— for things such as purchases, labor, taxes, and dividends. The precautionary motive for holding cash has to do with maintaining a cushion or buffer to meet un-

[1]John Maynard Keynes, *The General Theory of Employment, Interest, and Money* (New York: Harcourt Brace Jovanovich, 1936), pp. 170–74.

expected contingencies. The more predictable the cash flows of the business, the fewer precautionary balances needed. Ready borrowing power to meet emergency cash drains also reduces the need for this type of balance. It is important to point out that not all of the firm's transactions and precautionary balances need to be held in cash; indeed, a portion may be held in marketable securities—near-money assets.

The speculative motive relates to holding cash in order to take advantage of expected changes in security prices. When we expect interest rates to rise and security prices to fall, this motive would suggest that the firm should hold cash until the rise in interest rates ceases. When interest rates are expected to fall, cash may be invested in securities; the firm will benefit by any subsequent fall in interest rates and rise in security prices. For the most part, companies do not hold cash for the purpose of taking advantage of expected changes in interest rates. Consequently, we concentrate only upon the transactions and precautionary motives of the firm, with these balances held both in cash and in marketable securities.

Cash management involves managing the monies of the firm in order to attain maximum cash availability and maximum interest income on any idle funds. At one end, the function starts when a customer writes a check to pay the firm on its accounts receivable. The function ends when a supplier, employee, or the government realizes collected funds from the firm on an account payable or accrual. All activities between these two points fall within the realm of cash management. The firm's efforts to make customers pay their bills at a certain time fall within accounts receivable management. On the other hand, the firm's decision about when to pay its bills involves accounts payable and accrual management.

The treasurer's office of a company usually manages cash. A cash budget, instrumental in the process (see chap. 7), tells us how much cash we are likely to have, when, and for how long. Thus, it serves as a foundation for cash planning and control. In addition to the cash budget, the firm needs systematic information on cash as well as some kind of control system. Usually the information is computer based as opposed to manually based. In either case, it is necessary to obtain frequent reports—preferably daily or even more frequently—on cash balances in each bank account, on the cash disbursed, on the average daily balances, and on the marketable-security position of the firm as well as a detailed report on changes in this position. Also, it is useful to have information on major anticipated cash receipts and cash disbursements. All of this information is essential if a firm is to manage its cash in an efficient manner.

ACCELERATING COLLECTIONS

The various collection and disbursement methods by which a firm can improve its cash-management efficiency constitute two sides of the same coin. They exercise a joint impact on the overall efficiency of cash management. The general idea is to collect accounts receivable as soon as possible, but pay accounts payable as late as is consistent with maintaining the firm's credit standing with suppliers. Today, most companies of reasonable size use sophisticated techniques to speed collections and tightly control disbursements.[2] Let us see how they do it.

We consider first the acceleration of collections, which simply means reducing the delay between the time customers pay bills and the time the checks are collected and become usable funds for the firm. A number of methods that speed up this collection process and maximize available cash are designed to do one or all of the following: (1) speed the mailing time of payments from customers to the firm, (2) reduce the time during which payments received by the firm remain uncollected funds, and (3) speed the movement of funds to the disbursement banks.

The second item, representing float, has two aspects. The first is the time it takes a company to process checks internally. This interval extends from the moment a check is received to the moment it is deposited with a bank for credit to the company's account. The second aspect of float involves the time consumed in clearing the check through the banking system. A check becomes collected funds when it is presented to the drawee bank and actually paid by that bank. In order to streamline the availability of credit, the Federal Reserve System has established a schedule specifying availability for all checks deposited with it for collection. This schedule is based upon the average time required for a check deposited with a particular Federal Reserve bank to be collected in a particular geographical area of the country. The maximum period for which credit is deferred is two days. This means that even if a check is not actually collected through the Federal Reserve System within two days, it becomes collected funds because the Federal Reserve carries the float. Float is important to the financial manager because usually a company cannot make withdrawals on a deposit until the checks in that deposit are collected. As the name of the game is usable funds, the financial manager wants to reduce float as much as possible. Within the banking system, float has steadily declined on a relative basis as more sophisticated check-clearing methods are used by commercial banks and the Federal Reserve System. In what follows, we examine various ways to speed up the collection process in order to have more usable funds.

Concentration banking

Concentration banking is a means of accelerating the flow of funds of a firm by establishing strategic collection centers. Instead of a single collection center located at the company headquarters, multiple collection centers are established. The purpose is to shorten the period between the time customers mail in their payments and the time when the company has the use of the funds. Customers in a particular geographic area are instructed to remit their payments to a collection center in that area. Location of the collection centers usually is based upon the geographic areas served and the volume of billings in an area. When payments are received, they are deposited in the collection center's local bank. Surplus funds are then wire transferred from these local bank accounts to a concentration bank

[2] For a survey documenting this generalization, see Lawrence J. Gitman, Edward A. Moses, and I. Thomas White, "An Assessment of Corporate Cash Management Practices," *Financial Management*, 8 (Spring 1979), 32–41.

or banks. A bank of concentration is one with which the company has a major account—usually a disbursement account. A company headquartered in New York City might have but one concentration bank, a New York bank.

The advantage of a system of decentralized billings and collections over a centralized system is twofold.

1. The time required for mailing is reduced. Because the collection center bills customers in its area, these customers usually receive their bills earlier than if bills were mailed from the head office. In turn, when customers pay their bills, the mailing time to the nearest collection center is shorter than the time required for the typical remittance to go to the head office.

2. The time required to collect checks is reduced, because remittances deposited in the collection center's local bank usually are drawn on banks in that general area.

With the recent high levels of interest rates, it is not difficult to see the opportunity cost of tying up funds. Profits from the investment of the released funds must be compared with any additional costs of a decentralized system over a centralized one. Also consider any differences between the two systems in total compensating balances. The greater the number of collection centers, the more local bank accounts that must be maintained.

Lock-box system

Another means of accelerating the flow of funds is a lock-box arrangement. With concentration banking, a collection center receives remittances, processes them, and deposits them in a bank. The purpose of a lock-box arrangement is to eliminate the time between the receipt of remittances by the company and their deposit in the bank. A lock-box arrangement usually is on a regional basis, with the company choosing regional banks according to its billing patterns. Before determining the regions to be used, a feasibility study is made of the availability of checks that would be deposited under alternative plans. If a company divided the country into five sections on the basis of a feasibility study, it might pick New York City for the Northeast, Atlanta for the Southeast, Chicago for the Midwest, Dallas for the Southwest, and San Francisco for the West Coast.

The company rents a local post-office box and authorizes its bank in each of these cities to pick up remittances in the box. Customers are billed with instructions to mail their remittance to the lock-box. The bank picks up the mail several times a day and deposits the checks in the company's account. The checks are recorded and cleared for collection. The company receives a deposit slip and a list of payments, together with any material in the envelope. This procedure frees the company from handling and depositing the checks.

The main advantage of a lock-box system is that checks are deposited at banks sooner and become collected balances sooner than if they were processed by the company prior to deposit. In other words, the lag between the time checks are received by the company and the time they actually are deposited at the bank is eliminated. The principal disadvantage of a lock-box arrangement is the cost. The bank provides a number of services in addition to the usual clearing of checks and requires compensation for them, usually preferring increased deposits. Because the cost is almost directly proportional to the number of checks deposited, lock-box arrangements usually are not profitable if the average remittance is small.

The appropriate rule for deciding whether or not to use a lock-box system—or, for that matter, concentration banking—is simply to compare the added cost of the more efficient system with the marginal income that can be generated from the released funds. If costs are less than income, the system is profitable; if not, the system is not a profitable undertaking. The degree of profitability depends primarily upon the geographical dispersion of customers, the size of the typical remittance, and the earnings rate on the released funds.

Other procedures

Frequently, firms give special attention to handling large remittances so that they may be deposited in a bank as quickly as possible. This special handling may involve personal pickup of these checks or the use of airmail or special delivery. When a small number of remittances account for a large proportion of total deposits, it may be worthwhile to initiate controls to accelerate the deposit and collection of large checks. Instead of processing all checks for collection through the Federal Reserve System, some commercial banks offer special services that present high-dollar-volume checks directly to the drawee bank. The benefit is a speedup in collection of these checks, and it is passed on to the bank customer in having usable funds more quickly.

Some companies maintain too many bank accounts, thereby creating unnecessary pockets of idle funds. A company that has an account in every city where it has either a sales office or a production facility might be able to reduce cash balances considerably if it were to eliminate some of these accounts. The banking activities of a sales office can often be handled from a larger account with little loss in service or availability of funds. Even though small accounts may create a degree of goodwill with bankers, they make little sense in the overall cash management of the firm. By closing such unnecessary accounts, a firm may be able to release funds that it then can put to profitable use.

CONTROL OF DISBURSEMENTS

Effective control of disbursements can also result in a faster turnover of cash. Whereas the underlying objective of collections is maximum acceleration, the objective in disbursements is to slow them down as much as possible. The combination of fast collections and slow disbursements will result in maximum availability of funds.

Maximizing the float

One way of maximizing cash availability is "playing the float." For disbursements, float is the difference between the total dollar amount of checks drawn on a bank account and the amount shown on the bank's books. It is possible, of course, for a company to have a negative balance on its books and a positive bank balance, because checks outstanding have not been collected from the account on which they are drawn. If the size of float can be estimated accurately, bank balances can be reduced and the funds invested to earn a positive return.

A company with multiple banks should be able to shift funds quickly to banks from which disbursements are made, to prevent excessive balances from building up temporarily in a particular bank. The idea is to have adequate cash at the various banks, but not to let excessive balances build up. This requires daily information on collected balances. Excess funds then are transferred to the disbursement banks, either to pay bills or to invest in marketable securities. Many companies have developed sophisticated computer systems to provide the necessary information and to transfer excess funds automatically. Instead of developing one's own system, a firm can hire outside computer services to provide the described functions.

One procedure for tightly controlling disbursements is to centralize payables into a single account, presumably at the company's headquarters. In this way, disbursements can be made at the precise time they are desired. Needless to say, operating procedures for disbursements should be well established. If cash discounts are taken on accounts payable, procedures should aim toward eliminating or minimizing the loss of discounts due to clerical inefficiencies. The timing of payments is important. For maximum use of cash, payments should be made on the due dates, not before.

A company can delay disbursements through the use of drafts. Unlike an ordinary check, the draft is not payable on demand. When it is presented to the issuer's bank for collection, the bank must present it to the issuer for acceptance. The funds then are deposited by the issuing firm to cover payment of the draft. The advantage of the draft arrangement is that it delays the time the firm actually has to have funds on deposit to cover the draft. Consequently, it allows the firm to maintain smaller deposits at its banks. A possible disadvantage of a draft system is that certain suppliers may prefer checks. Also, banks do not like to process drafts because they require special attention, usually manual. As a result, banks typically impose a much higher service charge to process them than they do to process ordinary checks.

When a company has multiple bank accounts located throughout the country, the opportunities for "playing the float" expand. Taking advantage of inefficiencies in the check-clearing processes of the Federal Reserve System and of certain commercial banks, as well as inefficiencies in the postal system, a firm may maximize the time the checks it writes remain outstanding. Various models have been proposed to maximize disbursement float through the selection of geographically optimal disbursing banks.[3] The idea is to locate disbursing banks and to draw checks on them in a way that will maximize the time a check will remain outstanding. A check payable to a supplier in Arizona might be drawn on a bank in Portland, Maine. The solution depends on the location of, and the amount of billings from, suppliers, on procedural delays in the bank system associated with various supplier location-disbursing bank location combinations, and on the cost of banking services, whether it be compensating balances or fees.

[3] See Lawrence J. Gitman, D. Keith Forrester, and John R. Forrester, Jr., "Maximizing Cash Disbursement Float," *Financial Management*, 5 (Summer 1976), 15–24, for such an approach.

By maximizing disbursement float, the firm can reduce the amount of cash it holds and employ these funds in more profitable ways. One firm's gain, however, is another's loss. Maximizing disbursement float means that suppliers will not have collectible funds as early as would otherwise be the case. To the extent they look with disfavor on such payment habits, supplier relations may be hurt. If so, this factor must be taken into account in planning disbursements.

Payroll disbursements

Many companies maintain a separate account for payroll disbursements. In order to minimize the balance in this account, one must predict when the payroll checks issued will be presented for payment. If payday falls on a Friday, not all of the checks will be cashed on that day. Consequently, the firm need not have funds on deposit to cover its entire payroll.[4] Even on Monday, some checks will not be presented because of delays in their deposit. Based upon its experience, the firm should be able to construct a distribution of when, on the average, checks are presented for collection. An example is shown in Fig. 9-1. With this information, the firm can approximate the funds it needs to have on deposit to cover payroll checks. Similar to the payroll account, a separate account for dividends is one that many firms establish. Here, too, the idea is to predict when such checks will be presented for payment, so that the firm can minimize the cash balance in the account.

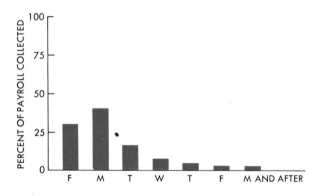

**FIGURE 9-1
Percentage of payroll
checks collected**

Electronic funds transfer and banking

In recent years substantial changes have been made in the way bills are paid. This progress has come about because of changes in financial institution regulation and because of advances in computer information systems as well as in electronic communications. Regulatory changes have focused on permitting greater competition among financial institutions. Commercial banks have been authorized to offer a variety of savings accounts and time deposits not only to individuals but to businesses and to state and local governments. On the other

[4] See James McN. Stancill, *The Management of Working Capital* (Scranton, Pa.: Intext, 1971), pp. 19–22.

hand, nonbank deposit institutions have been allowed to issue accounts which have most of the attributes of checking accounts. For both types of institutions, the purpose of savings deposits has been extended to allow their partial use as a payments mechanism. Preauthorized transfers between checking and savings accounts have permitted customers to make more efficient use of their checking accounts and to draw interest on idle funds.

The second aspect of the changing environment is the increased sophistication in computer applications to cash management and in electronic funds transfers. As individuals, we all are aware of plastic cards with magnetic coding which can be used to obtain cash, to transfer funds from one account to another, to pay bills, to borrow, and to do other things. These transactions can occur at a financial institution, at an unmanned electronic payments machine which is open 24 hours a day, and at certain retail stores. At stores, one is able to pay for a purchase with such a card, as funds are transferred electronically from the customer to the store. The advantage to retailers is obvious; they are assured that the payments for the purchase are good, and they are immediate. Retailers also can reduce the possibility of bad checks by using guarantee systems that a number of banks offer. With such a system, a customer's check is scanned electronically and verified by computer that it is good. Because the bank guarantees the checks it verifies, the retailer is not exposed to bad-check losses. Electronic banking also is used to deposit payrolls automatically in employee accounts, to make dividend and other payments, and to transfer funds nationally and internationally. The net result is faster and more efficient financial services.

Because electronic banking is capital intensive, the cost per transaction is reduced as volume increases. Indeed, this has occurred in recent years; and much of the saving is passed along to users of financial services. The customer benefits from the intense competition among financial institutions and large retailers which provide financial services. For the firm, electronic banking means less time in the collection of receivables, more efficient control of cash, and perhaps a reduction in servicing costs.

Thus, the use of electronic banking techniques can result in greater economization of money balances. In turn, the movement toward these techniques depends in part on the level of interest rates in financial markets. The greater the interest rate, of course, the greater the opportunity cost of holding cash and the more attractive electronic banking techniques become, all other things the same. The use of a new cash-management technique, however, typically involves significant start-up costs. As a result, once a new method is in place, there is a tendency to keep it even if interest rates should decline somewhat thereafter.

Earlier, we said that optimizing cash availability involves accelerating collections as much as possible and delaying payments as long as is realistically possible. Because delaying payments may damage the firm's credit standing, the resulting cost to the firm must be taken into account. In the future, we can expect to see further improvements in electronic money-payment transactions. As we move toward a "checkless society," the time during which funds remain uncollected will become shorter. In a checkless society, where transfers are made entirely through computers, payments would be immediate. There would be no uncollected funds, for one party's account would be debited the instant another's was credited. While the firm's deposits would be collected faster, so too would the checks it wrote. Whether it gained or lost would depend upon the typical float on checks deposited relative to the float for checks written.

CASH BALANCES TO MAINTAIN

Most business firms establish a target level of cash balances to maintain. They do not want to carry excess cash, for interest can be earned on the investment of these funds in marketable securities. The greater the interest rate on investments, of course, the greater the opportunity cost to maintaining idle balances. The optimal level of cash should be the larger of (1) the transactions balances required when cash management is efficient, and (2) the compensating-balance requirements of commercial banks with which the firm has deposit accounts.

Transactions balances are determined in keeping with considerations taken up earlier in the chapter. Also, we suggested that the higher the interest rate, the greater the opportunity cost of holding cash and the greater the corresponding desire to reduce the firm's holding, all other things the same. A number of cash-management models have been developed for determining an optimal split between cash and marketable securities. These models embody the demand for cash, the interest rate on marketable securities, and the cost of transfers between marketable securities and cash. The appendix to this chapter presents two of the more widely used models.

Compensating balances and fees

Establishing a minimum level of cash balances depends in part upon the compensating-balance requirements of banks. These requirements are set on the basis of the profitability of the accounts. A bank begins by calculating the average collected balances shown on its books over a period of time. This balance often is higher than the cash balance shown on the company's books. From the average collected balance, the bank subtracts the percentage of deposits it is required to maintain at the Federal Reserve—around 16 percent. The residual constitutes the earnings base on which income is generated. Total income is determined by multiplying the base times the earnings rate of the bank. This rate fluctuates in keeping with money-market conditions.

Once the income from an account is determined, the cost of the account must be computed. Most banks have a schedule of costs on a per item basis for such transactions as transfers and processing checks. The account is analyzed for a typical month, during which all transactions are multiplied by the per item cost and totaled. If the total cost is less than the total income from the account, the account is profitable; if more, it is unprofitable. The minimum average level of cash balances required is the point at which the account is just profitable. Because banks differ in the earnings rate they use as well as in their costs and method of account analysis, the determination of compensating balances varies. The firm, therefore, may be wise to shop around and find the bank that requires the lowest compensating balances for a given level of activity. If a firm has a lending arrangement with a bank, the firm may well be required to maintain balances in excess of those required to compensate the bank for the activity in its account. Because we consider compensation for a lending arrangement in chapter 11, no discussion of this form of compensation will be undertaken at this time.

In recent years, there has been a marked trend toward paying cash for services rendered by a bank instead of maintaining compensating balances. The advantage to the firm is that it may be able to earn more on funds used for compensating balances than the fee for the services. The higher the interest rate in the money markets, the greater the opportunity cost of compensating balances and the greater the advantage of service charges. It is an easy matter to determine if the firm would be better off with service charges as opposed to maintaining compensating balances. One simply compares the charges with the earnings on the funds released. Where a service offered can better be paid for by a fee, the firm should be alert to take advantage of the situation and to reduce its compensating balances.

Another development is the zero balance account, from which funds are automatically transferred into securities when there are excesses and reversed when there are deficits. Sometimes a deficit is filled by a prearranged overdraft (borrowing) arrangement with the bank. With a zero balance account, as the name implies, funds are not tied up unnecessarily. Activity in the account usually is supported by fees. With the sweeping changes in regulations which have occurred in recent years, individuals are able to avail themselves of accounts that not only serve transactions purposes but pay interest. These include NOW accounts—savings accounts with automatic transfers to checking accounts—and money market mutual funds with check writing privileges. With so many changes, it seems likely that corporations eventually will be able to earn interest on transaction accounts.

INVESTMENT IN MARKETABLE SECURITIES

In general, excess cash above some target level needed for transactions or compensating balances is invested in marketable securities. In this section we explore the types of marketable securities available to a company as near-money investments, allowing for varying yields and for fluctuations in market price. The yield available on a security depends on its maturity, its default risk, its marketability, and perhaps its tax situation if it is selling at a price less than its face value. All of these influences were explored in chapter 3, when we reviewed the role of interest rates in financial markets. Now we investigate various money-market instruments which, by definition, are highly marketable, subject to little default risk, and usually mature in less than a year. After we have discussed the various instruments available for investment, we will conclude with some observations on the overall management of the marketable-security portfolio.

Treasury securities

U.S. Treasury obligations constitute the largest segment of the money markets. The principal securities issued are bills, tax-anticipation bills, notes, and bonds. Treasury bills are auctioned weekly by the Treasury with maturities of 91 days and 182 days. In addition, nine-month and one-year bills are sold every month. All sales by the Treasury are by auction. Smaller investors can enter a "noncompetitive" bid, which is filled at the average price of successful competitive bids. Treasury bills carry no coupon but are sold on a discount basis. Denominations range from $10,000 to $1 million. These securities are extremely popular with companies as short-term investments, in part because of the large amount outstanding. The market is very active, and the transaction costs involved in the sale of Treasury bills in the secondary market are small.

The original maturity on Treasury notes is one to ten years, whereas the original maturity on Treasury bonds is over ten years. With the passage of time, of course, a number of these securities have maturities of less than one year and serve the needs of short-term investors. Notes and bonds are coupon issues, and there is an active market for them. Overall, Treasury securities are the safest and most marketable investments. Therefore, they provide the lowest yield for a given maturity of the various instruments we consider.

Agency securities

Obligations of various agencies of the federal government are guaranteed by the agency issuing the security but not by the U.S. government as such. Principal agencies issuing securities are the Federal Housing Administration and the Government National Mortgage Association (Ginnie Mae). In addition, there are a number of government-sponsored, quasi-private agencies. Their securities are not guaranteed by the federal government, nor is there any stated "moral" obligation, but there is an implied backing. It would be hard to imagine the federal government allowing them to fail. Major government-sponsored agencies include the Banks for Cooperatives, Federal Intermediate Credit Banks, Federal Land Banks, Federal Home Loan Banks, and Federal National Mortgage Association (Fannie Mae). The first three agencies are part of the Farm Credit Bank System, which issues consolidated system-wide discount short-term notes and bonds in behalf of these agencies. Over time, consolidated borrowings will replace borrowings by the individual agencies.

Agency securities have a fairly high degree of marketability; they are sold in the secondary market through the same security dealers as are Treasury securities. With the sharp increase in agency financing in recent years, marketability has been enhanced considerably. Although interest income on these securities is subject to federal income taxes, issues of the Farm Credit Agencies are not subject to state and local income taxes. Maturities range from several days up to approximately fifteen years. About half of the securities outstanding mature in less than a year.

Bankers' acceptances

Bankers' acceptances are drafts that are accepted by banks, and they are used in financing foreign and domestic trade. The credit-worthiness of bankers' acceptances is judged relative to the bank accepting the draft, not relative to the drawer. Acceptances generally have maturities of less than six months and are of very high quality. They are traded in an over-the-counter market dominated by five principal dealers. The rates on bankers' acceptances tend to be slightly higher than rates on Treasury bills of like maturity; and both are sold on a discount basis.

Commercial paper

Commercial paper consists of short-term unsecured promissory notes issued by finance companies and certain industrial concerns. Commercial paper can be sold either directly or through dealers. A number of large sales finance companies have found it profitable, because of the volume, to sell their paper directly to investors, thus bypassing dealers. Among companies selling paper on this basis are the C.I.T. Financial Corporation, Ford Motor Credit Company, General Motors Acceptance Corporation (GMAC), and Sears Roebuck Acceptance Corporation.

Paper sold through dealers is issued by industrial companies and smaller finance companies. The dealer organization for commercial paper is dominated by three firms. Overall, the total volume of paper sold through dealers is considerably less than the total volume sold directly. Dealers very carefully screen the creditworthiness of potential issuers. In a sense, dealers stand behind the paper they place with investors.

Rates on commercial paper are somewhat higher than rates on Treasury bills of the same maturity and about the same as the rates available on bankers' acceptances. Paper sold directly generally commands a lower yield than paper sold through dealers. Usually, commercial paper is sold on a discount basis, and maturities generally range from 30 to 270 days. Most paper is held to maturity, for there is essentially no secondary market. Direct sellers of commercial paper will repurchase the paper on request. Arrangements may also be made through dealers for repurchase of paper sold through them. Commercial paper is sold only in fairly large denominations, usually at least $25,000.

Repurchase agreements

In an effort to tap important sources of financing, government security dealers offer repurchase agreements to corporations. The repurchase agreement, or "repo" is the sale of short-term securities by the dealer to the investor whereby the dealer agrees to repurchase the securities at a specified future time. The investor receives a given yield while holding the security. The length of the holding period itself is tailored to the needs of the investor. Thus, repurchase agreements give the investor a great deal of flexibility with respect to maturity. Rates on repurchase agreements are related to the rates on Treasury bills, federal funds, and loans to government security dealers by commercial banks. There is little marketability to the instrument, but the usual maturity is only a few days. Because the instrument involved is a U.S. Treasury security, there is no default risk.

Negotiable certificates of deposit

A short-term investment that originated in 1961, the certificate (CD) is evidence of the deposit of funds at a commercial bank for a specified period of time and at a specified rate of interest. The most common denomination is $100,000, so its appeal is mostly to large investors. Money-market banks quote rates on CDs; these rates are changed periodically in keeping with changes in other money-market rates. The maximum rate that banks are allowed to pay, however, is regulated by the Federal Reserve System under Regulation Q. Yields on CDs are greater than those on Treasury bills and repos and about the same as those on bankers' acceptances and commercial paper. Original maturities of CDs generally range from 30 to 360 days. A fair secondary market has developed for the CDs of the large money-market banks. Default risk is that of the bank failing, a possibility that is remote in most cases. Banks also issue nonnegotiable certificates smaller than $100,000.

Eurodollars

Although most Eurodollars are deposited in Europe, the term applies to any dollar deposit in foreign banks or in foreign branches of U.S. banks. There exists a substantial, very active market for the deposit and lending of Eurodollars. This market is a wholesale one in that the amounts involved are at least $100,000 in size. Moreover, the market is free of government regulation, as it is truly international in scope. The rates quoted on deposits vary according to the maturity of the deposit, while the rates on loans depend on maturity and default risk. For a given maturity, the lending rate always exceeds the deposit rate. The bank makes its money on the spread.

As a marketable security, the Eurodollar time deposit is like a negotiable certificate of deposit. Most deposits have a maturity of less than a year, and they can be sold in the market prior to maturity. For a given maturity of 3 or 6 months, the rate on the Eurodollar deposit exceeds that on a negotiable certificate of deposit. During the last several years the spread has been around ½ percent. Call money deposits are available, allowing investors to get their money back on demand, and there are one-day (overnight) deposits. For the large corporation with ready contact with international money centers, the Eurodollar deposit can be an important investment.

Preferred stock

Some companies carry preferred stocks in their marketable security portfolios. As we shall see in chapter 22, the market price of this instrument fluctuates more than that of the short-term instruments discussed above. This fluctuation occurs because the maturity of a preferred stock is perpetual, and changes in interest rates have a pronounced impact on its market price. Default risk is greater because a preferred-stock dividend can be omitted by a company when its financial condition deteriorates. For these reasons, we usually do not think of preferred stock as being a marketable security for a corporation.

The corporate investor does gain a considerable tax advantage, in that 85 percent of preferred-stock dividends are exempt from taxation. Some financial managers are willing to bear the added risk in order to secure this after-tax yield, much higher than can be achieved with short-term marketable securities. Moreover, many companies actively trade in and out of preferred stocks, so that the holding period for any given stock is short. By selling a stock that has just paid its dividend, then investing in one that is about to pay a dividend, it is possible to receive a large number of preferred-stock dividends during a year for a particular level of investment.[5] The transactions costs that must be borne by the investor in such a strategy could be more than offset by the tax advantage. In final analysis, however, the substantially greater risk to the corporate investor and its liquidity needs must be balanced against the increased after-tax yield.

Portfolio management

The decision to invest excess cash in marketable securities involves not only the amount to invest but also the type of security in which to invest. To some extent, the two decisions are interdependent. Both should be based upon an evaluation of expected net cash flows and the certainty of these cash flows. If future cash-flow patterns are known with reasonable certainty and the yield curve is upward sloping in the sense of longer-term securities yielding more than shorter-term ones, a company may wish to arrange its portfolio so that securities will mature approximately when the funds will be needed. Such a cash-flow pattern gives the firm a great deal of flexibility in maximizing the average return on the entire portfolio, for it is unlikely that significant amounts of securities will have to be sold unexpectedly.

Suppose that the liquidity position of a firm were expected to fluctuate in the manner shown by the dotted line in Fig. 9-2. Although the figure shows only four months, we assume that the dotted line is not expected to decline below $900,000 over the next 12 months. Based on these projections, an appropriate investment strategy might be that shown by the horizontal bars in the figure. The bottom portion is represented by a 360-day investment in a certificate of deposit, followed by a Federal Home Loan Bank bond with about ten months to final maturity. Next the firm has invested in 91-day Treasury bills, and these are expected to be renewed, or rolled over, at maturity. The other investments shown in the figure are designed to match the fluctuating pattern of cash flows shown. Finally, the remaining areas under the dotted line are assumed to be filled as much as possible with repurchase agreements. With repos, maturities of only one or a few days can be tailored to the availability of funds for investment. Overall, then, the firm is able to match the maturities of its investments in marketable securities with its expected cash-flow patterns. In this way it is able to maximize its return on investment insofar as maturity decisions alone will allow.

Again, we have assumed an upward sloping yield curve. If the yield curve is downward sloping, the maturity matching strategy outlined above may not be appropriate. The company may wish to invest in securities having maturities shorter than the intended holding period, then to reinvest at maturity. In this way, it can avail itself of the higher initial yield on shorter-term securities, but it does not know what the securities will yield upon reinvestment at maturity. Another key factor is the degree of certainty one has in the cash-flow projections. With a

---

[5] For an analysis of this strategy in relation to the risk involved, see Michael D. Joehnk, Oswald D. Bowlin, and J. William Petty, "Preferred Dividend Rolls: A Viable Strategy for Corporate Money Managers?" *Financial Management*, 9 (Summer 1980), 78–87.

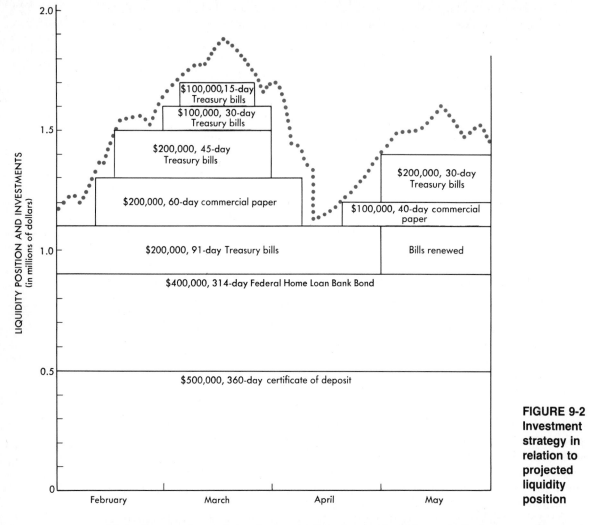

FIGURE 9-2
Investment
strategy in
relation to
projected
liquidity
position

high degree of certainty, the maturity of a marketable security becomes its most important characteristic.[6] If future cash flows are fairly uncertain, the most important characteristics of a security become its marketability and risk with respect to fluctuations in market value. Treasury bills and short-term repos are perhaps best suited for the emergency liquidity needs of the firm. Higher yields can be achieved by investing in longer-term, less-marketable securities with greater default risk. Although the firm should always be concerned with marketability, some possibility of loss of principal is tolerable provided the expected return is high enough. In addition to risk and marketability, transaction costs are a factor with uncertain cash flows. If securities must be sold unexpectedly, transaction costs will be incurred, reducing the net return. Thus, the firm faces the familiar tradeoff between risk and profitability.

[6] This statement assumes that all of the securities considered are of reasonably high quality from the standpoint of default risk. Otherwise they would not fall within the usual definition of a marketable security.

The larger the security portfolio, the more chance there is for specialization and economies of operation. A large enough security portfolio may justify a staff solely responsible for managing it. Such a staff can undertake research, plan diversification, keep abreast of market conditions, and continually analyze and improve the firm's position. When investment is a specialized function in a firm, the number of different securities considered for investment is likely to be diverse. Moreover, continual effort can be devoted to achieving the highest yield possible in keeping with cash needs of the firm. Trading techniques in such a firm tend to be very sophisticated. For companies with smaller security positions, there may be no economic justification for a staff. Indeed, a single individual may handle investments on a part-time basis. For this type of company, the diversity of securities in the portfolio will probably be limited.

SUMMARY

In the management of cash, we should attempt to accelerate collections and slow up disbursements so that a maximum of cash is available. Collections can be accelerated by means of concentration banking, a lock-box system, and certain other procedures. Disbursements should be handled to give maximum transfer flexibility and the optimum timing of payments. This applies to payments for purchases as well as to payroll disbursements. The development of electronic funds transfers and electronic banking has greatly improved the efficiency of cash management by reducing float.

The appropriate level of cash to maintain will be the higher of (1) that required for transactions purposes and (2) the compensating-balance requirements of commercial banks with which the firm has accounts. Usually the latter dominates; the requirement itself depends on the activity in the firm's accounts. The level of transactions balances desirable depends in part upon the opportunity cost of holding cash as typified by the interest rate on marketable securities. In the Appendix, we see models that allow us to take this as well as other factors into account in determining an optimal level of cash.

Among the numerous marketable securities in which the firm can invest are Treasury securities, government agency securities, bankers' acceptances, commercial paper, repurchase agreements, certificates of deposit, Eurodollar deposits and preferred stock. In the management of the marketable-security portfolio, one tries to match to some degree the maturities of investments with the likely future need for funds.

APPENDIX \ CASH-MANAGEMENT MODELS

Given the overall liquidity of the firm (its transactions and precautionary balances), we must determine an optimal split between cash and marketable securities. In turn, this split tells us the average levels of cash and marketable securities to maintain. The optimal level of cash depends on the firm's needs for cash, the predictability of these needs, the interest rate on marketable securities, and the cost of effecting a transfer between marketable securities and cash. A number of formal models have been developed to provide solutions to the cash-management problem. This appendix presents two of the more widely used models. The first approaches the problem under the assumption of a high degree of certainty as to the future cash needs of the firm. The second assumes just the opposite—that the future cash needs of the firm are highly uncertain. Let us examine these models.

Inventory model

Under conditions of certainty, the economic-order-quantity formula used in inventory management may be used to determine the optimal average amount of transactions balances to maintain. This model provides a useful conceptual foundation for the cash-management problem.[7] In the model, the carrying cost of holding cash—namely, the interest foregone on marketable securities—is balanced against the fixed cost of transferring marketable securities to cash, or vice versa. The model is illustrated by the sawtoothed lines in Fig. 9-3.

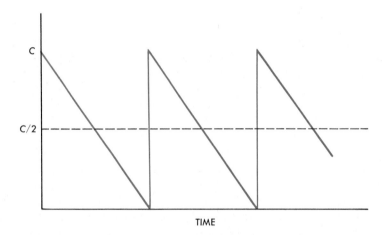

**FIGURE 9-3
Inventory model
applied to
cash management**

In the figure, we assume that the firm has a steady demand for cash over some period of time, say one month. The firm obtains cash during this period by selling marketable securities. Suppose it starts out with C dollars in cash and, when this amount is expended, replenishes it by selling C dollars of marketable securities. Thus, the transfer of funds from securities to cash occurs whenever cash touches zero. If a cushion is desired or if lead times are necessary to effect a transaction, the threshold for initiating a transfer can be higher. The principle is the same regardless of whether or not a cushion is used.

The objective is to specify the value of C that minimizes total costs—that is, the sum of the fixed costs associated with transfers and the opportunity cost of earnings foregone by holding cash balances. These costs can be expressed as

$$b\left(\frac{T}{C}\right) + i\left(\frac{C}{2}\right) \tag{9A-1}$$

[7] The model was first applied to the problem of cash management by William J. Baumol, "The Transactions Demand for Cash: An Inventory Theoretic Approach," *Quarterly Journal of Economics*, 46 (November 1952), 545–56. It has been further refined and developed by a number of others.

where b is the fixed cost of a transaction that is assumed to be independent of the amount transfered, T is the total demand for cash over the period of time involved, and i is the interest rate on marketable securities for the period involved (assumed to be constant). T/C represents the number of transactions during the period, and when it is multiplied by the fixed cost per transaction, we obtain the total fixed cost for the period. $C/2$ represents the average cash balance, and when it is multiplied by the interest rate, we obtain the earnings foregone by virtue of holding cash. The larger the C, the larger the average cash balance, $C/2$, and the smaller the average investment in securities and earnings from these securities. Thus, there is a higher opportunity cost of interest income foregone. However, the larger the C, the fewer the transfers, T/C, that occur, and the lower the transfer costs. The object is to balance these two costs so that total costs are minimized.

The optimal level of C is found to be

$$C^* = \sqrt{\frac{2bT}{i}} \qquad (9A\text{-}2)$$

Thus, cash will be demanded in relation to the square root of the dollar volume of cash payments. This phenomenon implies that as the level of cash payments increases, the amount of transactions cash the firm needs to hold increases by a lesser percentage. In other words, economies of scale are possible. The implication is that the firm should try to consolidate individual bank accounts into as few as possible in order to realize economies of scale in cash management. We see from Eq. (9A-2) that C^* varies directly with order cost, b, and inversely with the interest rate on marketable securities, i. However, the relationship is dampened by the square-root sign in both cases.

To illustrate the use of the economic-order-quantity (EOQ) formula, consider a firm with estimated cash payments of \$6 million for a one-month period, the payments expected to be steady over the period. The fixed cost per transaction is \$100 and the interest rate on marketable securities is 6 percent per annum, or 0.5 percent for the one-month period. Therefore,

$$C = \sqrt{\frac{2bT}{i}} = \sqrt{\frac{2(100)(6,000,000)}{.005}} = \$489,898$$

Thus, the optimal transaction size is \$489,898 and the average cash balance will be \$489,898/2 = \$244,949. This means that the firm should make \$6,000,000/\$489,898 = 12 plus transactions of marketable securities to cash during the month.

It is useful now to consider in more detail the two costs involved. The interest rate is fairly straightforward; it simply represents the rate of interest on securities that would be sold to replenish cash. The fixed cost associated with a transaction is more difficult to measure because it consists of both explicit and implied costs. Included are the fixed component of transaction costs, the time it takes the treasurer or other official to place an order with an investment trader, the time consumed in recording the transaction, the secretarial time needed to type the transaction and the purchase order, the time needed to record the transaction on the books, and the time needed to record the safekeeping notification. With a number of transactions, the procedures for placing an order can be streamlined to reduce the average fixed cost per transaction. Nevertheless, these costs do exist and too often are either overlooked or underestimated.

One limitation to the use of the model is that cash payments are seldom completely predictable. For modest degrees of uncertainty, one need only add a cushion so that a transfer from marketable securities to cash is triggered at some level of cash above zero. In general, the EOQ model gives the financial manager a benchmark for judging the optimal cash balance. It does not have to be used as a precise rule to govern behavior. The model merely suggests what would be the optimal balance under a set of assumptions. The actual balance may be more if the assumptions do not entirely hold.

Stochastic model

In those cases in which the uncertainty of cash payments is large, the EOQ model may not be applicable and other models should be used to determine optimal behavior. If cash balances fluctuate randomly, one can apply control theory to the problem. Assume that the demand for cash is stochastic and un- known in advance. We then can set control limits such that when cash reaches an upper limit, a transfer of cash to marketable securities is consummated; and when it hits a lower limit, a transfer from marketable securities to cash is triggered. As long as the cash balance stays between these limits, no transactions take place.

How the limits are set depends in part upon the fixed costs associated with a securities transaction and the opportunity cost of holding cash. As before, we assume these costs are known and that the fixed cost of selling a marketable security is the same as that for buying it. In essence, we want to satisfy the demand for cash at the lowest possible total cost. Although there are a number of applica- tions of control theory to the problem, we take up a relatively simple one. The Miller-Orr model specifies two control limits—h dollars as an upper bound and zero dollars as a lower bound.[8] The model is illustrated in Fig. 9-4. When the cash balance touches the upper bound, $h - z$ dollars of marketable securities are bought and the new balance becomes z dollars. When the cash balance touches zero, z dollars of marketable securities are sold and the new balance again becomes z. As long as the cash balance fluctuates somewhere between the upper and lower control limits, no action is taken. The situation is illustrated in the figure. The minimum bound can be set at some amount higher than zero, and h and z will move up in the figure. We will use zero as the lower bound for purposes of illustration, recognizing that a firm can set the lower bound at some positive amount. This obviously would be necessary if there were delays in transfer.

The solution for the optimal values of h and z depends not only upon the fixed and opportunity costs but also upon the degree of likely fluctuation in cash balances. The optimal value of z, the return-to-point for security transactions, is

$$z = \sqrt[3]{\frac{3b\sigma^2}{4i}} \qquad (9A\text{-}3)$$

[8] See Merton H. Miller and Daniel Orr, "A Model of the Demand for Money by Firms," *Quarterly Journal of Economics*, 80 (August 1966), 413–35.

FIGURE 9-4
Control-limits model

where b = fixed cost associated with a security transaction
σ^2 = variance of daily net cash flows (a measure of the dispersion of these flows)
i = interest rate per day on marketable securities.

The optimal value of h is simply 3z. With these control limits set, the model minimizes the total costs (fixed and opportunity) of cash management. Again, the critical assumption is that cash flows are random. The average cash balance cannot be determined exactly in advance, but it is approximately $(z + h)/3$. As experience unfolds, however, it can be easily calculated.

We have presented two models for determining an optimal level of cash balances under the self-imposed constraint. The EOQ model assumes that the demand for cash is predictable; the control-limit model assumes it is random. For most firms, the first model is more applicable than the second, owing to near-term cash flows being relatively predictable. When there is only moderate uncertainty, the EOQ model can be modified to incorporate a cushion. The second model serves primarily as a benchmark for determining cash balances under a rather extreme assumption as to their predictability. The average cash balance generally will be much higher when this model is used as opposed to the EOQ one. Thus, when cash balances of a firm are higher than those dictated by a control-limit model and the demand for cash is relatively predictable, we know cash is too high.

QUESTIONS

1. Explain the concept of concentration banking.

2. Explain how the lock-box system can improve the efficiency of cash management.

3. Money-market instruments are used an an investment vehicle for idle cash. Discuss the primary criterion for asset selection in investing temporary idle cash.

4. The assumed objective of a business firm is to maximize the wealth of stockholders, which

implies that priorities should be assigned to assets on the basis of profitability. Reconcile this statement with the fact that corporations keep 5 to 10 percent of assets in idle cash.

5. Discuss the impact of lock-box banking on corporate cash balances.

6. Explain the application of the economic-order-quantity model to managing cash balances. (See Appendix.)

7. Discuss the primary criterion for assigning priorities to assets that will serve as investment vehicles for a firm's temporary excess liquidity.

8. If the general level of interest rates is expected to fall, what maturity of securities should the firm invest in? If interest rates are expected to rise?

9. How can diversification reduce the risk of investment in marketable securities? What are the limits of such risk reduction?

10. Assuming that the return on real assets of a company exceeds the return on marketable securities, why should a company hold any marketable securities?

11. Under what conditions would it be possible for a company to hold no cash or marketable securities? Are these conditions realistic?

PROBLEMS

1. Speedway Owl Company franchises Gas and Go stations in North Carolina and Virginia. All payments by franchisees for gasoline and oil products are by check, which average $420,000 a day. Presently, the overall time between the mailing of the check by the franchisee to Speedway Owl and the time the company has collected or available funds at its bank is 6 days.

   a) How much money is tied up in this interval of time?

   b) To reduce this delay, the company is considering pickups daily from the stations. In all, 3 cars would be needed and 3 additional people hired. This daily pickup would cost $93,000 on an annual basis, and it would reduce the overall delay by 2 days. Currently, the opportunity cost of funds is 9 percent, that being the interest rate on marketable securities. Should the company inaugurate the pickup plan?

   c) Rather than mail checks to its bank, the company could deliver them by messenger service. This procedure would reduce the overall delay by one day and cost $10,300 annually. Should the company undertake this plan?

2. The Zindler Company currently has a centralized billing system. Payments are made by all customers to the central billing location. It requires, on the average, 4 days for customers' mailed payments to reach the central location. An additional one and one-half days are required to process payments before the deposit can be made. The firm has a daily average collection of $500,000.

   The company has recently investigated the possibility of initiating a lock-box system. It has estimated that with such a system, customers' mailed payments would reach the receipt location two and one-half days sooner. Further, the processing time could be reduced by an additional day, because each lock-box bank would pick up mailed deposits twice daily.

   a) Determine the reduction in cash balances that can be achieved through the use of a lock-box system.

b) Determine the opportunity cost of the present system, assuming a 5 percent return on short-term instruments.

c) If the annual cost of the lock-box system were $75,000, should such a system be initiated?

3. The List Company, which can earn 7 percent on money-market instruments, currently has a lock-box arrangement with a New Orleans bank for its southern customers. The bank handles $3 million a day in return for a compensating balance of $2 million.

a) The List Company has discovered that it could divide the southern region into a southwestern region (with $1 million a day in collections, which could be handled by a Dallas bank for a $1 million compensating balance) and a southeastern region (with $2 million a day in collections, which could be handled by an Atlanta bank for a $2 million compensating balance). In each case, collections would be one-half day quicker than with the New Orleans arrangement. What would be the annual savings (or cost) of dividing the southern region?

b) In an effort to retain the business, the New Orleans bank has offered to handle the collections strictly on a fee basis (no compensating balance). What would be the maximum fee the New Orleans bank could charge and still retain List's business?

4. The Frazini Food Company has a weekly payroll of $150,000 paid on Friday. On average, its employees cash their checks in the following manner:

Day check cleared on company's account	Percent of checks cashed
Friday	20
Monday	40
Tuesday	25
Wednesday	10
Thursday	5

As treasurer of the company, how would you arrange your payroll account? Are any problems involved?

5. Assuming an upward-sloping yield curve for marketable securities, devise a profit-maximizing maturity schedule for investment in marketable securities by Joey Brown Stereo Company, based on the following considerations. The company wishes to maintain cash balances of $100,000 at all times. There are no transaction costs for investing in, or selling, marketable securities. In the absence of any investment in marketable securities, cash balances are expected to be

Jan.	$300,000	May	$700,000	Sept.	$200,000
Feb.	500,000	June	800,000	Oct.	200,000
Mar.	600,000	July	400,000	Nov.	100,000
Apr.	500,000	Aug.	300,000	Dec.	100,000

Your schedule should indicate the amounts to be invested and the months over which the investments will be held. The maturity of the investment should correspond to the intended holding period.

Why might not such a schedule be in the best interest of the company?

Appendix problems

6. The Schriver Company expects to have $1 million in cash outlays for next year. The firm believes that it will face an opportunity interest rate of 5 percent and will incur a cost of $100 each time it transfers from marketable securities to cash. Cash outlays are expected to be steady over the year. Using the inventory model

   a) Determine the optimal transfer size for the Schriver Company.

   b) What is the total cost for the use of cash needed for transactions demand?

   c) What will be the cash cycle for the firm (velocity)?

   d) What will be the average cash balance for the firm?

7. Assume that the Schriver Company (Problem 6) began the year with $1 million in cash.

   a) How much would initially be invested in securities?

   b) How much would be invested in securities after 231 days?

8. The Verloom Berloop Tulip Bulb Company has experienced a stochastic demand for its product, with the result that cash balances fluctuate randomly. The standard deviation of daily net cash flows, σ, is $1,000. The company wishes to make the transfer of funds from cash to marketable securities and vice versa as automatic as possible. It has heard that this can be done by imposing upper- and lower-bound control limits. The current interest rate on marketable securities is 6 percent. The fixed cost associated with each transfer is $100, and transfers are instantaneous.

   a) What are the optimal upper- and lower-bound control limits? (Assume a 360-day year.) Hint: On a calculator, treat the $1,000 as 1 and solve for the cube root by trial and error. Move the decimal point of the final answer two places to the right.

   b) What happens at these control limits?

SELECTED REFERENCES

BATLIN, C. A., and SUSAN HINKO, "Lockbox Management and Value Maximization," *Financial Management,* 10 (Winter 1981), 39–44.

BAUMOL, WILLIAM J., "The Transactions Demand for Cash: An Inventory Theoretic Approach," *Quarterly Journal of Economics,* 46 (November 1952), 545–56.

EMERY, GARY, "Some Empirical Evidence on the Properties of Daily Cash Flow," *Financial Management,* 10 (Spring 1981), 21–28.

FROST, PETER A., "Banking Services, Minimum Cash Balances and the Firm's Demand for Money," *Journal of Finance,* 25 (December 1970), 1029–39.

GALE, BRADLEY T., and BEN BRANCH, "Cash Flow Analysis: More Important than Ever," *Harvard Business Review,* 59 (July–August 1981), 131–36.

GITMAN, LAWRENCE J., EDWARD A. MOSES, and I. THOMAS WHITE, "An Assessment of Corporate Cash Management Practices," *Financial Management,* 8 (Spring 1979), 32–41.

GITMAN, LAWRENCE J., D. KEITH FORRESTER, and JOHN R. FORRESTER, JR., "Maximizing Cash Disbursement Float," *Financial Management,* 5 (Summer 1976), 15–24.

HARTLEY, W. C. F., and YALE L. MELTZER, *Cash Management.* Englewood Cliffs, N.J.: Prentice-Hall, 1979.

JOEHNK, MICHAEL D., OSWALD D. BOWLIN, and J. WILLIAM PETTY, "Preferred Dividend Rolls: A Viable Strategy for Corporate Money Managers?," *Financial Management,* 9 (Summer 1980), 78–87.

MAIER, STEVEN F., DAVID W. ROBINSON, and JAMES H. VANDER WEIDE, "A Short-Term Disbursement Forecasting Model," *Financial Management,* 10 (Spring 1981), 9–20.

MEHTA, DILEEP R., *Working Capital Management.* Englewood Cliffs, N.J.: Prentice-Hall, 1974, chaps. 6–8.

MILLER, MERTON H., and DANIEL ORR, "The Demand for Money by Firms: Extension of Analytic Results," *Journal of Finance,* 23 (December 1968), 735–59.

———, "A Model of the Demand for Money by Firms," *Quarterly Journal of Economics,* 80 (August 1966), 413–35.

MULLINS, DAVID W. JR., and RICHARD B. HOMONOFF, "Applications of Inventory Cash Management Models," in Stewart C. Myers, ed., *Modern Developments in Financial Management.* New York: Praeger, 1976.

NAUSS, ROBERT M., and ROBERT E. MARKLAND, "Solving Lock Box Location Problems," *Financial Management,* 8 (Spring 1979), 21–31.

SMITH, KEITH V., *Guide to Working Capital Management.* New York: McGraw-Hill, 1979, chaps. 3 and 4.

STANCILL, JAMES McN., *The Management of Working Capital.* Scranton, Pa.: Intext, 1971, chaps. 2 and 3.

STONE, BERNELL K., and NED C. HILL, "Cash Transfer Scheduling for Efficient Cash Concentration," *Financial Management,* 9 (Autumn, 1980), 35–43.

———, "The Design of a Cash Concentration System," *Journal of Financial and Quantitative Analysis,* 16 (September 1981), 301–22.

STONE, BERNELL K. and ROBERT A. WOOD, "Daily Cash Forecasting: A Simple Method for Implementing the Distribution Approach," *Financial Management,* 6 (Fall 1977), 40–50.

VAN HORNE, JAMES C., *Financial Market Rates and Flows.* Englewood Cliffs, N.J.: Prentice-Hall, 1978.

WRIGHT, F. K., "Minimizing the Costs of Liquidity," *Australian Journal of Management,* 3 (October 1978), 203–24.

Accounts receivable and inventories

10

In chapter 8, we saw that the investment of funds in accounts receivable involves a tradeoff between profitability and risk. The optimum investment is determined by comparing benefits to be derived from a particular level of investment with the costs of maintaining that level. This chapter will reveal the key variables involved in managing receivables efficiently, and it will show how they can be varied to obtain the optimal investment. We consider first the credit and collection policies of the firm as a whole and then discuss credit and collection procedures for the individual account. The last part of the chapter investigates techniques for efficiently managing inventories. It relates these methods to the financial manager's concern with controlling investment.

CREDIT AND COLLECTION POLICIES

Economic conditions and the firm's credit policies are the chief influences on the level of a firm's accounts receivables. Economic conditions, of course, are largely beyond the control of the financial manager. As with other current assets, however, the manager can vary the level of receivables in keeping with the tradeoff between profitability and risk. Lowering quality standards may stimulate demand which, in turn, should lead to higher profits. But there is a cost to carrying the additional receivables, as well as a greater risk of bad-debt losses, It is this tradeoff we wish to examine.

The policy variables we consider include the quality of the trade accounts accepted, the length of the credit period, the cash discount, and the collection program of the firm. Together, these elements largely determine the average collection period and the proportion of bad-debt losses. We analyze each element in turn, holding constant certain of the others, as well as all exogenous variables that affect the average collection period and the percentage of bad-debt losses. In addition, we assume that the evaluation of risk is sufficiently standardized that degrees of risk for different accounts can be compared objectively.

Credit standards

Credit policy can have a significant influence upon sales. If competitors extend credit liberally and we do not, our policy may have a dampening effect upon the marketing effort. Credit is one of many factors that influence the demand for a firm's product. Consequently, the degree to which credit can promote demand depends upon what other factors are being employed. In theory, the firm should lower its quality standard for accounts accepted as long as the profitability of sales generated exceeds the added costs of the receivables. What are the costs of relaxing credit standards? Some arise from an enlarged credit department, the clerical work involved in checking additional accounts, and servicing the added volume of receivables. We assume that these costs are deducted from the profitability of additional sales to give a net profitability figure for computational purposes. Another cost comes from the increased probability of bad-debt losses. We postpone consideration of this cost to a subsequent section; we assume for now that there are no bad-debt losses.

Finally, there is the opportunity cost of the additional receivables, resulting from (1) increased sales, and (2) a slower average collection period. If new customers are attracted by the relaxed credit standards, collecting from these customers is likely to be slower than collecting from existing customers. In addition, a more liberal extension of credit may cause certain existing customers to be less conscientious about paying their bills on time.

An example of the tradeoff. To assess the profitability of a more liberal extension of credit, we must know the profitability of additional sales, the added demand for products arising from the relaxed credit standards, the increased slowness of the average collection period, and the required return on investment. Suppose a firm's product sells for $10 a unit, of which $7 represents variable costs before taxes, including credit department costs. The firm is operating at less than full capacity, and an increase in sales can be accommodated without any increase in fixed costs. Therefore, the contribution margin of an additional unit of sales is the selling price less variables costs involved in producing the unit, or $10 − $7 = $3.

Presently, annual credit sales are running at a level of $2.4 million, and there is no underlying trend in such sales. The firm may liberalize credit, which will result in an average collection experience of new customers of two months. Existing customers are not expected to alter their payment habits. The relaxation in credit standards is expected to produce a 25 percent increase in sales, to $3 million annually. The $600,000 increase represents 60,000 additional units if we assume that the price per unit stays the same. Finally, assume that the firm's opportunity cost of carrying the additional receivables is 20 percent before taxes.

This information reduces our evaluation to a tradeoff between the added profitability on the additional sales and the opportunity cost of the increased investment in receivables. The increased investment arises solely from new, slower-paying customers; we have assumed existing customers continue to pay in one month. With the additional sales of $600,000 and receivable turnover of six times a year (12 months divided by the average collection period of 2 months), the additional receivables are $600,000/6 = $100,000. For these additional receivables, the firm invests the variable costs tied up in them. For our example, $0.70 of every $1.00 in sales represents variable costs. Therefore, the added investment in receivables is 0.70 × $100,000 = $70,000. With these inputs, we are able to make the calculations shown in Table 10-1. Inasmuch as the profitability on additional sales, $180,000, far exceeds the required return on the additional investment in receivables, $14,000, the firm would be well advised to relax its credit standards. An optimal credit policy would involve extending trade credit more liberally until the marginal profitability on additional sales equals the required return on the additional investment in receivables necessary to generate those sales. However, as we take on poorer credit risks, we also increase the risk of the firm, as depicted by the variance of the expected cash-flow stream. This increase in risk is largely reflected in additional bad-debt losses, a subject we deal with shortly.

TABLE 10-1 ╲ **Profitability versus required return—credit standard change**

Profitability of additional sales	=	$3 × 60,000 units = $180,000
Additional receivables	=	(Additional sales/Receivable turnover) $600,000/6 = $100,000
Investment in additional receivables	=	(Variable costs/Sales price) (Additional receivables) (0.70)($100,000) = $70,000
Required return on additional investment	=	0.20 × $70,000 = $14,000

Credit terms

Credit period.   Credit terms involve both the length of credit period and the discount given. The terms "2/10, net 30" mean that a 2 percent discount is given if the bill is paid before the tenth day after the date of invoice; payment is due by the thirtieth day. The credit period, then, is 30 days. Although the customs of the industry frequently dictate the terms given, the credit period is another means by which a firm may be able to affect product demand, hoping to increase demand by extending the credit period. As before, the tradeoff is between the profitability of additional sales and the required return on the additional investment in receivables.

Let us say that the firm in our example increases its credit period from thirty to sixty days. The average collection period for existing customers goes from one month to two months. The more liberal credit period results in increased sales of $360,000, and these new customers also pay, on average, in two months. The total additional receivables are comprised of two parts. The first part represents the receivables associated with the increased sales. In our example, there are $360,000 in additional sales. With a receivable turnover of six times a year, the additional receivables associated with the new sales are $360,000/6 = $60,000. For these additional receivables, the investment by the firm is the variable costs tied up in them. For our example, we have ($7/$10)($60,000) = $42,000.

The second part of the total additional receivables represents the slowing in collections associated with original sales. The old receivables are collected in a slower manner resulting in a higher receivable level. With $2.4 million in original sales, the level of receivables with a turnover of 12 times a year is $2,400,000/12 = $200,000. The new level with a turnover of six times a year is $2,400,000/6 = $400,000. Thus, there are $200,000 in additional receivables associated with the original sales. For this addition, the relevant investment using marginal analysis is the full $200,000. In other words, the use of variable costs pertains only to new sales. The incremental $200,000 in receivables on original sales would have been collected earlier had it not been for the change in credit standards. Therefore, the firm must increase its investment in receivables by $200,000.

Based on these inputs, our calculations are shown in Table 10-2. The appropriate comparison is the profitability of additional sales with the opportunity cost of the additional investment in receivables. Inasmuch as the profitability on additional sales, $108,000, exceeds the required return on the investment in additional receivables, $48,400, the change in credit period from thirty to sixty days is worthwhile. The profitability of the additional sales more than offsets the added investment in receivables, the bulk of which comes from existing customers slowing their payments.

TABLE 10-2 ⟍ **Profitability versus required return—credit period change**

Profitability of additional sales	=	$3 × 36,000 units = $108,000
Additional receivables associated with new sales	=	(New sales/Receivable turnover) $360,000/6 = $60,000
Additional investment in receivables associated with new sales	=	(Variable costs/Sales price)(Additional receivables) (0.70)($60,000) = $42,000
Present level of receivables	=	(Annual sales/Receivable turnover) $2.4 million/12 = $200,000
New level of receivables associated with original sales	=	$2.4 million/6 = $400,000
Additional investment in receivables associated with original sales	=	$400,000 − $200,000 = $200,000
Total additional investment in receivables	=	$42,000 + $200,000 = $242,000
Carrying cost of additional investment	=	0.20 × $242,000 = $48,400

Discount given. Varying the discount involves an attempt to speed up the payment of receivables. Here we must determine whether a speedup in collections would more than offset the cost of an increase in the discount. If it would, the present discount policy should be changed. Suppose the firm has annual credit sales of $3 million and an average collection period of two months, and that the sales terms are net 45 days, with no discount given. Consequently, the average receivable balance is $500,000. By instigating terms of 2/10, net 45, the average collection period is reduced to one month, and 50 percent of the customers (in dollar volume) take advantage of the 2 percent discount. The opportunity cost of the discount to the firm is .02 × 0.5 × $3 million, or $30,000 annually. The turn-over of receivables has improved to 12 times a year, so that average receivables are reduced from $500,000 to $250,000.

Thus, the firm realizes $250,000 from accelerated collections. The value of the funds released is their opportunity cost. If we assume a 20 percent rate of return, the opportunity saving is $50,000. In this case the opportunity saving arising from a speedup in collections is greater than the cost of the discount. The firm should adopt a 2 percent discount. If the speedup in collections had not resulted in sufficient opportunity savings to offset the cost of discount, the dis-count policy would not be changed. It is possible, of course, that discounts other than 2 percent may result in an even greater difference between the opportunity saving and the cost of the discount.

Default risk

In the above examples we assumed no bad-debt losses. Our concern in this section is not only with the slowness of collection but also with the portion of the receivables defaulting. Different credit standard policies will involve both of these factors. Suppose that we are considering the present credit standard policy (sales of $2,400,000) together with two new ones and that these policies are expected to produce the following results:

	Present policy	Policy A	Policy B
Demand (sales)	$2,400,000	$3,000,000	$3,180,000
Default losses on incremental sales (percentage)	2	10	25
Average collection period on incremental sales	1 month	2 months	6 months

We assume that after six months an account is turned over to a collection agency and that, on average, 2 percent of the original sales of $2.4 million is never received by the firm, 10 percent is never received on the $600,000 in additional sales under policy A, and 25 percent on the $180,000 in additional sales under policy B is never received. Similarly, the one-month average collection period

TABLE 10-3 ✎ **Profitability versus required return—bad-debt losses and collection period changes**

		Policy A	Policy B
1.	Additional sales	$600,000	$180,000
2.	Profitability of additional sales (30%)	180,000	54,000
3.	Additional bad-debt losses (Additional sales × bad-debt percentage)	60,000	45,000
4.	Additional receivables (Additional sales/Receivable turnover)	100,000	90,000
5.	Investment in additional receivables (0.7 × additional receivables)	70,000	63,000
6.	Required return on additional investment (20 percent)	14,000	12,600
7.	Bad-debt losses plus additional required return	74,000	57,600
8.	Incremental profitability (2) − (7)	106,000	(3,600)

pertains to the original sales, two months to the $600,000 in additional sales under policy A, and six months to the $180,000 in additional sales under policy B.

The incremental profitability calculations associated with these two new credit standard policies are shown in Table 10-3. We would want to adopt policy A but would not want to go as far as policy B in relaxing our credit standards. The marginal benefit is positive in moving from the present policy to policy A but negative in going from policy A to policy B. It is possible, of course, that a relaxation of credit standards that fell on one side or the other of policy A would provide an even greater marginal benefit; the optimal policy is the one that provides the greatest marginal benefit.

Collection policy and procedures

The firm determines its overall collection policy by the combination of collection procedures it undertakes. These procedures include things such as letters, phone calls, personal calls, and legal action. One of the principal policy variables is the amount expended on collection procedures. Within a range, the greater the relative amount expended, the lower the proportion of bad-debt losses and the shorter the average collection period, all other things the same.

The relationships are not linear. Initial collection expenditures are likely to cause little reduction in bad-debt losses. Additional expenditures begin to have a significant effect up to a point; then they tend to have little effect in further reducing these losses. The hypothesized relationship between expenditures and bad-debt losses is shown in Fig. 10-1. The relationship between the average collection period and the level of collection expenditure is likely to be similar to that shown in the figure.

If sales are independent of the collection effort, the appropriate level of collection expenditure again involves a tradeoff—this time between the level of expenditure on the one hand and the reduction in the cost of bad-debt losses and

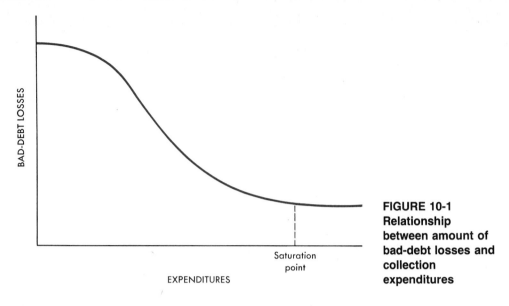

FIGURE 10-1 Relationship between amount of bad-debt losses and collection expenditures

BAD-DEBT LOSSES

Saturation point

EXPENDITURES

reduction in investment in receivables on the other. Calculations are the same as for the discount given and for default losses illustrated earlier. The reader easily can verify the tradeoff.

Because a receivable is only as good as the likelihood that it will be paid, a firm cannot afford to wait too long before initiating collection procedures. On the other hand, if it initiates procedures too soon, it may anger reasonably good customers who, for some reason, fail to make payments by the due date. Procedures, whatever they are, should be firmly established. Initially, a letter is usually sent, followed perhaps by additional letters that become ever more serious in tone. Next may come a telephone call from the credit manager and then, perhaps, one from the company's attorney. Some companies have collection personnel who make personal calls on the account.

If all else fails, the account may be turned over to a collection agency. The agency's fees are quite substantial—frequently one-half the amount of the receivable—but such a procedure may be the only feasible alternative, particularly for a small account. Direct legal action is costly, sometimes serves no real purpose, and may only force the account into bankruptcy. When payment cannot be collected, compromise settlements may provide a higher percentage of collection.

Credit and collection policies—summary

We see that the credit and collection policies of a firm involve several decisions: (1) the quality of account accepted, (2) the credit period, (3) the cash discount given, and (4) the level of collection expenditures. In each case, the decision should involve a comparison of possible gains from a change in policy and the cost of the change. Optimal credit and collection policies would be those that resulted in the marginal gains equaling the marginal costs.

To maximize profits arising from credit and collection policies, the firm should vary these policies jointly until it achieves an optimal solution. That solution will determine the best combination of credit standards, credit period, cash discount policy, special terms, and level of collection expenditures. For most policy variables, profits increase at a decreasing rate up to a point and then decrease as the policy is varied from no effort to an extreme effort. Figure 10-2 depicts this relationship with the quality of accounts rejected. When there are no credit standards, when all applicants are accepted, sales are maximized, but they are offset by large bad-debt losses as well as by the opportunity cost of carrying a very large receivable position. The latter is due to a long average collection period. As credit standards are initiated and applicants rejected, revenue from sales declines, but so do the average collection period and bad-debt losses. Because the latter two decline initially at a faster rate than do sales, profits increase. As credit standards are tightened increasingly, sales revenue declines at an increasing rate. At the same time, the average collection period and bad-debt losses decrease at a decreasing rate. Fewer and fewer bad credit risks are eliminated. Because of the combination of these influences, total profits of the firm increase at a diminishing rate with stricter credit standards up to a point, after which they decline. The optimal policy with respect to credit standards is represented by point x in the figure. In turn, this policy determines the level of accounts receivable held by the firm.

The analysis in the last several sections has purposely been rather general, to provide insight into the chief concepts of credit and collection policies. Obviously, a policy decision should be based upon a far more specific evaluation than that contained in the examples above. Estimating the increased demand and increased slowness of collections that might accompany a relaxation of credit standards is difficult. Nevertheless, management must make estimates of these relationships if it is to appraise realistically its existing policies.

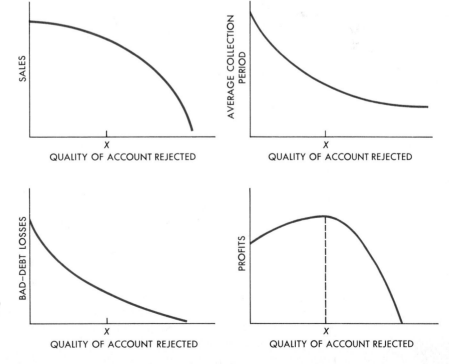

**FIGURE 10-2
Relationship of sales,
average collection
period, bad-debt losses,
and profits to the
quality of account
rejected**

ANALYZING THE CREDIT APPLICANT

Having established the terms of sale to be offered, the firm must evaluate individual credit applicants and consider the possibilities of a bad debt or slow payment. The credit evaluation procedure involves three related steps: obtaining information on the applicant, analyzing this information to determine the applicant's credit-worthiness, and making the credit decision. The credit decision, in turn, establishes whether credit should be extended and what its maximum amount should be.

Sources of information

A number of sources supply credit information; but for some accounts, especially small ones, the cost of collecting it may outweigh the potential profitability of the account. The firm extending credit may have to be satisfied with a limited amount of information on which to base a decision. In addition to cost, the firm must consider the time it takes to investigate a credit applicant. A shipment to a prospective customer cannot be delayed unnecessarily pending an elaborate credit investigation. Thus, the amount of information collected needs to be considered in relation to the time and expense required. Depending upon these considerations, the credit analyst may use one or more of the following sources of information.

Financial statement. At the time of the prospective sale, the seller may request a financial statement, one of the most desirable sources of information for credit analysis. Frequently, there is a correlation between a company's refusal to provide a statement and its weak financial position. Audited statements are preferable; and interim statements are helpful, particularly for companies having seasonal patterns of sales.

Credit ratings and reports. In addition to financial statements, credit ratings are available from various mercantile agencies. Dun & Bradstreet is perhaps the best known and most comprehensive of these agencies. It provides credit ratings to subscribers for a vast number of business firms throughout the nation. A key to its individual ratings is shown in Figure 10-3. As we see in the figure, D&B ratings give the credit analyst an indication of the estimated size of net worth and a credit appraisal for companies of a particular size, ranging from "high" to "limited." D&B also indicates when the information available is insufficient to provide a rating for a given business. In addition to its rating service, D&B provides credit reports containing a brief history of a company and its principal officers, the nature of the business, certain financial information, and a trade check of suppliers—the length of their experience with the company and whether payments are discount, prompt, or past due. The quality of the D&B reports varies with the information available externally and the willingness of the company being checked to cooperate with the D&B reporter.

TRW Inc., in conjunction with the National Association of Credit Management, has developed a data base on some seven million businesses. Typically, the

New Key to Ratings

ESTIMATED FINANCIAL STRENGTH			COMPOSITE CREDIT APPRAISAL			
			HIGH	GOOD	FAIR	LIMITED
5A	Over	$50,000,000	1	2	3	4
4A	$10,000,000 to	50,000,000	1	2	3	4
3A	1,000,000 to	10,000,000	1	2	3	4
2A	750,000 to	1,000,000	1	2	3	4
1A	500,000 to	750,000	1	2	3	4
BA	300,000 to	500,000	1	2	3	4
BB	200,000 to	300,000	1	2	3	4
CB	125,000 to	200,000	1	2	3	4
CC	75,000 to	125,000	1	2	3	4
DC	50,000 to	75,000	1	2	3	4
DD	35,000 to	50,000	1	2	3	4
EE	20,000 to	35,000	1	2	3	4
FF	10,000 to	20,000	1	2	3	4
GG	5,000 to	10,000	1	2	3	4
HH	Up to	5,000	1	2	3	4

CLASSIFICATION FOR BOTH
ESTIMATED FINANCIAL STRENGTH AND CREDIT APPRAISAL

FINANCIAL STRENGTH BRACKET	EXPLANATION
1 $125,000 and Over	When only the numeral (1 or 2) appears, it is an indication that the estimated financial strength, while not definitely classified, is presumed to be within the range of the ($) figures in the corresponding bracket and that a condition is believed to exist which warrants credit in keeping with that assumption.
2 20,000 to 125,000	

NOT CLASSIFIED OR ABSENCE OF RATING

The absence of a rating, expressed by two hyphens (--), is not to be construed as unfavorable but signifies circumstances difficult to classify within condensed rating symbols. It suggests the advisability of obtaining a report for additional information.

FIGURE 10-3
Dun & Bradstreet key to ratings

information is not as extensive as that of Dun & Bradstreet, but it is of considerable use in credit analysis. TRW information is computer-based, so teletype credit reports can be obtained through an automated retrieval system in a matter of minutes.

Bank checking. Another source of information for the firm is a credit check through a bank. Many banks have large credit departments that undertake credit checks as a service for their customers. By calling or writing a bank in which the credit applicant has an account, a firm's bank is able to obtain information on the average cash balance carried, loan accommodations, experience, and sometimes financial information. Because banks generally are more willing to share information with other banks than with a direct inquirer, it usually is best for the firm to initiate the credit check through its own bank rather than to inquire directly.

Trade checking. Credit information frequently is exchanged among companies selling to the same customer. Through various credit organizations, credit people in a particular area become a closely knit group. A company can ask other suppliers about their experiences with an account.

The company's own experience. A study of the promptness of past payments, including any seasonal patterns, is very useful. Frequently, the credit department will make written assessments of the quality of the management of a company to whom credit may be extended. These assessments are very important, for they pertain to the first of the famous "three C's" of credit: *character, collateral,* and *capacity*. The person who made the sale to a prospective customer frequently can offer useful impressions of management and operations. Caution is necessary in interpreting this information, because a salesperson has a natural bias toward granting credit and making the sale.

Credit analysis

Having collected credit information, the firm must make a credit analysis of the applicant. In practice, the collection of information and its analysis are closely related. If, on the basis of initial credit information, a large account appears to be relatively risky, the credit analyst will want to obtain further information. Presumably, the expected value of the additional information will exceed the cost of acquiring it. Given the financial statements of an applicant, the credit analyst should undertake a ratio analysis, as described in chapter 6. The analyst will be particularly interested in the applicant's liquidity and ability to pay bills on time.

In addition to analyzing financial statements, the credit analyst will consider the financial strength of the firm, the character of the company and its management, and various other matters. Then the analyst attempts to determine the ability of the applicant to service trade credit, the probability of an applicant's not paying on time and of a bad-debt loss. On the basis of this information together with information about the profit margin of the product or service being sold, a decision is reached as to whether or not to extend credit.

The amount of information collected should be determined in relation to the expected profit from an order and the cost of investigation. More sophisticated analysis should be undertaken only when there is a chance that a credit decision based upon the previous stage of investigation will be changed. If an analysis of a Dun & Bradstreet report resulted in an extremely unfavorable picture of the applicant, an investigation of the applicant's bank and its trade suppliers might have little prospect of changing the reject decision. Therefore, the added cost associated with this stage of investigation would not be worthwhile. With incremental stages of investigation each having a cost, they can be justified only if the information obtained has value in changing a prior decision.[1] Rather than perform all stages of investigation regardless of the profitability of the order, the firm should undertake investigation in stages and go to a new stage only when the expected net benefits of the additional information exceed the cost of acquiring it.

Although quantitative approaches have been developed to measure ability to service trade credit, the final decision for most companies extending trade credit rests upon the credit analyst's judgment in evaluating available information. Numerical evaluations are successful in consumer credit, where various characteristics of an individual are quantitatively rated and a credit decision is made on the basis of the total score. The plastic credit cards many of us hold are often given out on the basis of a credit scoring system in which things such as age, occupation,

---

[1] For such an analysis, see Dileep Mehta, "The Formulation of Credit Policy Models," *Management Science,* 15 (October 1968), 30–50.

duration of employment, home ownership, years of residence, telephone, and annual income are taken into account. Numerical ratings systems also are being used by companies extending trade credit.[2] With the overall growth of trade credit, a number of companies are finding it worthwhile to use numerical credit-scoring systems to screen out clear accept and reject applicants. Credit analysts, then, can devote their energies to evaluating marginal applicants.

Credit decision

Once the credit analyst has marshaled the necessary evidence and has analyzed it, a decision must be reached as to the disposition of the account. In an initial sale, the first decision to be made is whether or not to ship the goods and extend credit. If repeat sales are likely, the company will probably want to establish procedures so that it does not have to evaluate the extension of credit each time an order is received. One means for streamlining the procedure is to establish a *line of credit* for an account. A line of credit is a maximum limit on the amount the firm will permit to be owing at any one time. In essence, it represents the maximum risk exposure that the firm will allow itself to undergo for an account. The establishment of a credit line streamlines the procedure for shipping goods, but the line must be reevaluated periodically in order to keep abreast of developments in the account. What was a satisfactory risk exposure today may be more or less than satisfactory a year from today. Despite comprehensive credit procedures, there will always be special cases that must be dealt with individually. Here, too, a firm can streamline the operation by defining responsibilities clearly.

INVENTORY MANAGEMENT AND CONTROL

Inventories form a link between production and sale of a product. A manufacturing company must maintain a certain amount of inventory during production, the inventory known as goods in process. Although other types of inventory—namely, in-transit, raw-materials, and finished-goods inventories—are not necessary in the strictest sense, they allow the firm to be flexible. Inventory in transit—that is, inventory between various stages of production or storage—permits efficient production scheduling and utilization of resources. Without this type of inventory, each stage of production would have to wait for the preceding stage to complete a unit. Resultant delays and idle time give the firm an incentive to maintain in-transit inventory.

Raw-materials inventory gives the firm flexibility in its purchasing. Without it, the firm must exist on a hand-to-mouth basis, buying raw materials strictly in keeping with its production schedule. Finished-goods inventory allows the firm

[2] See William P. Poggess, "Screen-Test Your Credit Risks," in Keith V. Smith, ed., *Working Capital Management* (New York: West Publishing, 1974), pp. 109–20; and Robert O. Edmister and Gary G. Schlarbaum, "Credit Policy in Lending Institutions," *Journal of Financial and Quantitative Analysis,* 9 (June 1974), 335–56. For a discussion of the updating of the underlying sample used in a credit scoring system, see Michael S. Long, "Credit Screening System Selection," *Journal of Financial and Quantitative Analysis,* 11 (June 1976), 313–28.

flexibility in its production scheduling and in its marketing. Production does not need to be geared directly to sales. Large inventories allow efficient servicing of customer demands. If a certain product is temporarily out of stock, present as well as future sales to the customer may be lost. Thus, there is an incentive to maintain stocks of all three types of inventory.

The advantages of increased inventories, then, are several. The firm can effect economies of production and purchasing and can fill orders more quickly. In short, the firm is more flexible. The obvious disadvantages are the total cost of holding the inventory, including storage and handling costs, and the required return on capital tied up in the investment in inventory. Like accounts receivable, inventories should be increased as long as the resulting savings exceed the total cost of holding the added inventory. The balance finally reached depends upon the estimates of actual savings, the cost of carrying additional inventory, and the efficiency of inventory control. Obviously, this balance requires coordination of the production, marketing, and finance areas of the firm in keeping with an overall objective.

Economic order quantity

The economic order quantity (EOQ) is an important concept in the purchase of raw materials and in the storage of finished-goods and in-transit inventories. In our analysis, we wish to determine the optimal order quantity for a particular item of inventory, given its forecasted usage, ordering cost, and carrying cost. Ordering can mean either the purchase of the item or its production. Assume for the moment that the usage of a particular item of inventory is known with certainty. This usage is stationary or steady throughout the period of time being analyzed. In other words, if usage is 2,600 items for a 6-months' period, 100 items are used each week. Moreover, usage is assumed to be independent of the level of inventory.

We assume that ordering costs, O, are constant regardless of the size of the order. In the purchase of raw materials or other items, these costs represent the clerical costs involved in placing an order as well as certain costs of receiving and checking the goods once they arrive. For finished-goods inventories, ordering costs involve scheduling a production run. When start-up costs are large—as they are in a machined piece of metal, for example—ordering costs can be quite significant. For in-transit inventories, ordering costs are likely to involve nothing more than record keeping. The total ordering cost for a period is simply the number of orders for that period, times the cost per order.

Carrying costs per period, C, represent the cost of inventory storage, handling, and insurance, together with the required rate of return on the investment in inventory. These costs are assumed to be constant per unit of inventory, per unit of time. Thus, the total carrying cost for a period is the average number of units of inventory for the period, times the carrying cost per unit. In addition, we assume for now that inventory orders are filled without delay. Because out-of-stock items can be replaced immediately, there is no need to maintain a buffer or safety stock. Although the assumptions made up to now may seem overly restrictive, they are necessary for an initial understanding of the conceptual framework that follows. Subsequently, we shall relax some of them.

If the usage of an inventory item is perfectly steady over a period of time and

FIGURE 10-4
Order-quantity example

there is no safety stock, average inventory (in units) can be expressed as

$$\text{Average inventory} = \frac{Q}{2} \tag{10-1}$$

where Q is the quantity (in units) ordered and is assumed to be constant for the period. The above problem is illustrated in Fig. 10-4. Although the quantity demanded is a step function, we assume for analytical purposes that it can be approximated by a straight line. We see that zero inventory always indicates that further inventory must be ordered.

The carrying cost of inventory is the carrying cost per unit times the average number of units of inventory, or $CQ/2$. The total number of orders for a period of time is simply the total usage (in units) of an item of inventory for that period, S, divided by Q. Consequently, total ordering costs are represented by the ordering cost per order, times the number of orders, or SO/Q. Total inventory costs, then, are the carrying costs plus ordering costs, or

$$\frac{CQ}{2} + \frac{SO}{Q} \tag{10-2}$$

We see from Eq. (10-2) that the higher the order quantity, Q, the higher the carrying costs but the lower the total ordering costs. The lower the order quantity, the lower the carrying costs but the higher the total ordering costs. We are concerned with the tradeoff between the economies of increased order size and the added cost of carrying additional inventory.

Optimal order quantity.   From Eq. (10-2) we can obtain the optimal order quantity, Q^*:

$$Q^* = \sqrt{\frac{2SO}{C}} \tag{10-3}$$

215

This equation is known as the economic-lot-size formula. To illustrate its use, suppose that usage of an inventory item is 2,000 units during a 100-day period, ordering costs are $100 an order, and carrying costs are $10 per unit per 100 days. The most economic order quantity, then, is

$$Q^* = \sqrt{\frac{2(2,000)(100)}{10}} = 200 \text{ units}$$

With an order quantity of 200 units, the firm would order (2,000/200), or ten times, during the period under consideration or, in other words, every ten days. We see from Eq. (10-3) that Q^* varies directly with total usage, S, and order cost, O, and inversely with the carrying cost, C. However, the relationship is dampened by the square-root sign in both cases. As usage increases, then, the optimal order size and the average level of inventory increase by a lesser percentage. In other words, economies of scale are possible.

In our example, we have assumed that inventory can be ordered and received without delay. Usually, there is a time lapse between placement of a purchase order and receipt of the inventory, or in the time it takes to manufacture an item after an order is placed. This lead time must be considered. If it is constant and known with certainty, the optimal order quantity is not affected. In the above example, the firm would still order 200 units at a time and place ten orders during the specified time period, or every ten days. If the lead time for delivery were three days, the firm simply would place its order seven days after delivery of the previous order.

The EOQ function is shown in Fig. 10-5. In the figure, we plot ordering costs, carrying costs, and total costs—the sum of the first two costs. We see that whereas carrying costs vary directly with the size of the order, ordering costs vary inversely with size of the order. The total cost line declines at first as the fixed

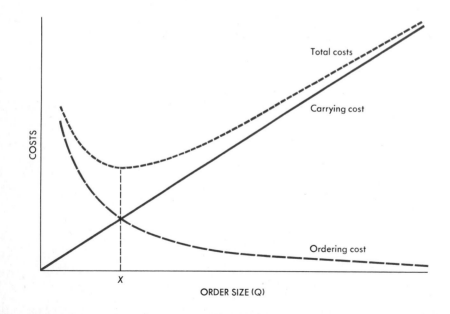

FIGURE 10-5
Economic-order-quantity
relationship

costs of ordering are spread over more units. The total cost line begins to rise when the decrease in average ordering cost is more than offset by the additional carrying costs. Point X, then, represents the economic order quantity, which minimizes the total cost of inventory. The EOQ formula taken up in this section is a very useful tool for inventory control. In purchasing raw materials or other items of inventory, it tells us the amount to order and the best timing of our orders. For finished-goods inventory, it enables us to exercise better control over the timing and size of production runs. In general, the EOQ model gives us a rule for deciding when to replenish inventories and the amount to replenish.

SAFETY STOCKS AND OTHER CONSIDERATIONS

In practice, the demand or usage of inventory generally is not known with certainty; usually it fluctuates during a given period of time. Typically, the demand for finished-goods inventory is subject to the greatest uncertainty. In general, the usage of raw-materials inventory and in-transit inventory, both of which depend upon the production scheduling, is more predicatble. In addition to demand, the lead time required to receive delivery of inventory once an order is placed usually is subject to some variation. Owing to these fluctuations, it is not feasible usually to allow expected inventory to fall to zero before a new order is anticipated, as the firm could do when usage and lead time were known with certainty. A safety stock is necessary.

Order point and safety stock

Before discussing safety stocks, it is necessary to consider at what point inventory will be ordered. Suppose that demand for inventory is known with certainty, but that it takes 5 days before an order is received. In our previous illustration of the economic-order-quantity formula, we found that the EOQ for our example firm was 200 units, resulting in an order being placed every 10 days. If usage is steady, the firm now would need to order 5 days before it ran out of stock, or at 100 units of stock on hand. Thus, the order point is 100 units. When the new order is received 5 days later, the firm will just have exhausted its existing stock. This example of an order point is illustrated in Fig. 10-6.

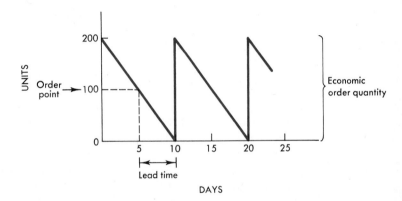

FIGURE 10-6
Order point when lead time is certain

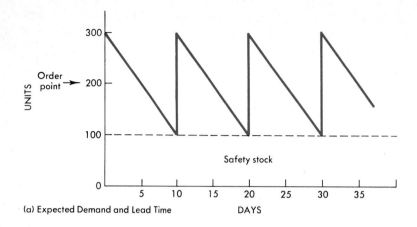

(a) Expected Demand and Lead Time

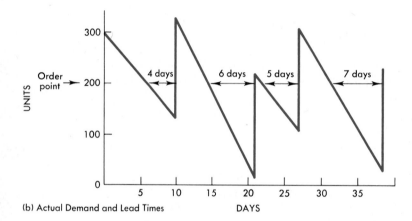

(b) Actual Demand and Lead Times

FIGURE 10-7
Safety stock when demand and lead time are uncertain

When we allow for uncertainty in demand for inventory as well as in lead time, a safety stock becomes advisable. The concept here is illustrated in Figure 10-7. In the upper panel of the figure we show what would happen if the firm had a safety stock of 100 units and if expected demand of 200 units every 10 days and lead time of 5 days were to occur. Note that with a safety stock of 100 units, the order point must be set at 200 units of inventory on hand as opposed to the previous 100 units. In other words, the order point determines the amount of safety stock held.

The bottom panel of the figure shows the actual experience for our hypothetical firm. In the first segment of demand, we see that actual usage is somewhat less than expected. (The slope of the line is less than the expected demand line in the upper panel.) At the order point of 200 units of inventory held, an order is placed for 200 units of additional inventory. Instead of taking the expected 5 days for the inventory to be replenished, we see that it takes only 4 days. The second segment of usage is much greater than expected and, as a result, inventory is rapidly used up. At 200 units of remaining inventory, a 200-unit order again is placed, but here it takes 6 days for the inventory to be received. As a result of both of these factors, heavy inroads are made into the safety stock.

In the third segment of demand, usage is about the same as expected; that is, the slopes of expected and actual usage lines are about the same. Because inventory was so low at the end of the previous segment of usage, an order is placed almost immediately. The lead time turns out to be 5 days. In the last segment of demand, usage is slightly greater than expected. The lead time necessary to receive the order is seven days, much longer than expected. The combination of these two factors again causes the firm to go into its safety stock. The example illustrates the importance of safety stock in absorbing random fluctuations in usage and in lead times. Without such stock, the firm would have run out of inventory on two occasions.

The amount of safety stock

The proper amount of safety stock to maintain depends upon several things. The greater the uncertainty associated with forecasted demand for inventory, the greater the safety stock the firm will wish to carry, all other things the same. Put another way, the risk of running out of stock is greater, the larger the unforeseen fluctuations in usage. Similarly, the greater the uncertainty of lead time to replenish stock, the greater the risk of running out of stock, and the more safety stock the firm will wish to maintain, all other things being equal. Another factor influencing the safety-stock decision is the cost of running out of inventory. The cost of being out of raw-materials and in-transit inventories is a delay in production. How much does it cost when production closes down temporarily? Where fixed costs are large, this cost will be quite high, as can be imagined in the case of an aluminum extrusion plant. The cost of running out of finished goods is customer dissatisfaction. Not only will the immediate sale be lost, but future sales will be endangered if customers take their business elsewhere. Although this opportunity cost is difficult to measure, it must be recognized by management and incorporated into the safety-stock decision. The greater the costs of running out of stock, of course, the greater the safety stock management will wish to maintain, all other things the same.

The final factor to consider is the cost of carrying additional inventory. If it were not for this cost, a firm could maintain whatever safety stock was necessary to avoid all possibility of running out of inventory. The greater the cost of carrying inventory, the more costly it is to maintain a safety stock, all other things being equal. Determination of the proper amount of safety stock involves balancing the probability and cost of a stockout against the cost of carrying enough safety stock to avoid this possibility. Ultimately, the question reduces to the probability of inventory stockout that management is willing to tolerate. In a typical situation, this probability is reduced at a decreasing rate as more safety stock is added. A firm may be able to reduce the probability of inventory stockout by 20 percent if it adds 100 units of safety stock, but only by an additional 10 percent if it adds another 100 units. There comes a point when it becomes very expensive to reduce further the probability of stockout. Management will not wish to add safety stock beyond the point at which incremental carrying costs exceed the incremental benefits to be derived from avoiding a stockout.

Relation to financial management

Although inventory management usually is not the direct operating responsibility of the financial manager, the investment of funds in inventory is a very important aspect of financial management. Consequently, the financial manager must be familiar with ways to control inventories effectively so that capital may be allocated efficiently. The greater the opportunity cost of funds invested in inventory, the lower the optimal level of average inventory and the lower the optimal order quantity, all other things held constant. This statement can be verified by increasing the carrying costs, C, in Eq. (10-3). The EOQ model also can be used by the financial manager in planning for inventory financing.

When demand or usage of inventory is uncertain, the financial manager may try to effect policies that will reduce the average lead time required to receive inventory once an order is placed. The lower the average lead time, the lower the safety stock needed and the lower the total investment in inventory, all other things held constant. The greater the opportunity cost of funds invested in inventory, the greater the incentive to reduce this lead time. The purchasing department may try to find new vendors that promise quicker delivery, or it may pressure existing vendors to deliver faster. The production department may be able to deliver finished goods faster by producing a smaller run. In either case, there is a tradeoff between the added cost involved in reducing the lead time and the opportunity cost of funds tied up in inventory. This discussion serves to point out the value of inventory management to the financial manager.

SUMMARY

Credit and collection policies encompass the quality of accounts accepted, the credit period extended, the cash discount given, and the level of collection expenditures. In each case, the credit decision involves a tradeoff between the additional profitability and the cost resulting from a change in any of these elements. By liberalizing the quality requirements for accounts, the firm might hope to make more on the additional sales than it spends to carry the additional receivables plus the additional bad-debt losses. To maximize profits arising from credit and collection policies, the firm should vary these policies jointly until an optimal solution is obtained. The firm's credit and collection policies, together with its credit and collection procedures, determine the magnitude and quality of its receivable position.

In evaluating a credit applicant, the credit analyst obtains financial and other information about the applicant, analyzes this information, and reaches a credit decision. If the account is new, the firm must decide whether or not to accept the order. With repeat orders, the firm must usually decide upon the maximum credit to extend. This maximum, known as a line of credit, is based upon the credit worthiness of the applicant.

The optimal level of inventories should be judged in relation to the flexibility inventories afford. If we hold constant the efficiency of inventory management, the lower the level of inventories, the less the flexibility of the firm. The higher the amount of inventories, the greater the flexibility of the firm. In evaluating the level of inventories, management must balance the benefits of economies of production, purchasing, and increased product demand against the cost of carrying the additional inventory. Of particular concern to the financial manager is the cost of funds invested in inventory.

In this chapter we examined several tools of inventory control. One is the economic order quantity (EOQ), whereby we determine the optimal size of order to place on the basis of the demand or usage of the inventory, the ordering costs, and the carrying costs. Under conditions of uncertainty, the firm must usually provide for a safety stock, owing to fluctuations in demand for inventory and in lead times. By varying the point at which orders are placed, one varies the safety stock that is held.

QUESTIONS

1. Is it always good policy to reduce the firm's bad-debt losses by "getting rid of the deadbeats"?

2. What are the probable effects on sales and profits of each of the following credit policies?

   a) A high percentage of bad-debt loss, but normal receivable turnover and rejection rate.

   b) A high percentage of past-due accounts and a low credit rejection rate.

   c) A low percentage of past-due accounts, but high receivable rejection and turnover rates.

   d) A low percentage of past-due accounts and a low rejection rate, but a high turnover rate.

3. Is an increase in the collection period necessarily bad? Explain.

4. Explain the difference between a bad-debt expense, the provision for bad debt, and a writeoff against the provision for bad debt.

5. What are the principal factors which can be varied in setting credit policy?

6. If credit standards for the quality of account accepted are changed, what things are affected?

7. Why is a saturation point reached in spending money on collections?

8. What is the purpose of establishing a line of credit for an account? What are the benefits of this arrangement?

9. The analysis of inventory policy is analogous to the analysis of credit policy. Propose a measure to analyze inventory policy which is analogous to aging of accounts receivable.

10. What are the principal implications to the financial manager of ordering costs, storage costs, and cost of capital as they relate to inventory?

11. Explain how efficient inventory management affects the liquidity and profitability of the firm.

12. The EOQ model does not provide any information about the safety stock that should be carried by a firm. Develop a conceptual model that will aid management in determining the correct amount of safety stock.

13. How can the firm reduce its investment in inventories? What costs might the firm incur from a policy of very low inventory investment?

14. Explain how a large seasonal demand complicates inventory management and production scheduling.

15. Do inventories represent an investment in the same sense as fixed assets?

16. Should the required rate of return for investment in inventories of raw materials be the same as that for finished goods?

PROBLEMS

1. To increase sales from their present annual $24 million, Jefferson Knu Monroe Company, a wholesaler, may try more liberal credit standards. Currently, the firm has an average collection period of thirty days. It believes that with increasingly liberal credit standards, the following will result:

Credit policy	A	B	C	D
Increase in sales from previous level (in millions)	$2.8	$1.8	$1.2	$0.6
Avg. collection period for incremental sales (days)	45	60	90	144

The prices of its products average $20 per unit, and variable costs average $18 per unit. No bad-debt losses are expected. If the company has a pre-tax opportunity cost of funds of 30 percent, which credit policy should be pursued? (Assume a 360-day year.)

2. Upon reflection, Jefferson Knu Monroe Company has estimated that the following pattern of bad-debt losses will prevail if it initiates more liberal credit terms:

Credit policy	A	B	C	D
Bad debt losses on incremental sales	3%	6%	10%	15%

Given the other assumptions in problem 1, which credit policy should be pursued?

3. Recalculate problem 2, assuming the following pattern of bad-debt losses:

Credit policy	A	B	C	D
Bad-debt losses on incremental sales	1.5%	3.0%	5.0%	7.5%

Which policy now would be best?

4. Durham-Feltz Corporation presently gives terms of net 30 days. It has $60 million in sales and its average collection period is 45 days. To stimulate demand, the company may give terms of net 60 days. If it does instigate these terms, sales are expected to increase by 15 percent. After the change, the average collection period is expected to be 75 days, with no difference in payment habits between old and new customers. Variable costs are $0.80 for every $1.00 of sales, and the company's required rate of return on investment in receivables is 20 percent. Should the company extend its credit period? (Assume a 360-day year.)

5. The Chickee Corporation has a 12 percent opportunity cost of funds and currently sells on terms of n/10, EOM. (This means that goods shipped before the end of the month must be paid for by the tenth of the following month.) The firm has sales of $10 million a year, which are 80 percent on credit and spread evenly over the year. The average collection period is currently 60 days. If Chickee offered terms of 2/10, net 30, 60 percent of its customers would take the discount, and the average collection period would be reduced to 40 days. Should Chickee change its terms from net/10, EOM to 2/10, net 30?

6. The Pottsville Manufacturing Corporation is considering extending trade credit to the San Jose Company. Examination of the records of San Jose has produced the following financial statements.

San Jose Company balance sheet (in millions)

	19X1	19X2	19X3
Assets:			
Current assets:			
Cash	$ 1.5	$ 1.6	$ 1.6
Receivables	1.3	1.8	2.5
Inventories (at lower of cost or market)	1.3	2.6	4.0
Other	.4	.5	.4
Total current assets	$ 4.5	$ 6.5	$ 8.5
Fixed assets:			
Buildings (net)	2.0	1.9	1.8
Machinery and equipment (net)	7.0	6.5	6.0
Total fixed assets	$ 9.0	$ 8.4	$ 7.8
Other assets	1.0	.8	.6
Total assets	$14.5	$15.7	$16.9

San Jose Company balance sheet (in millions)

	19X1	19X2	19X3
Liabilities:			
Current liabilities:			
Notes payable (8½%)	$ 2.1	$ 3.1	$ 3.8
Trade payables	.2	.4	.9
Other payables	.2	.2	.2
Total	$ 2.5	$ 3.7	$ 4.9
Term loan (8½%)	4.0	3.0	2.0
Total	$ 6.5	$ 6.7	$ 6.9
Net worth			
Common stock	$ 5.0	$ 5.0	$ 5.0
Preferred stock (6½%)	1.0	1.0	1.0
Retained earnings	2.0	3.0	4.0
Total liabilities and net worth	$14.5	$15.7	$16.9

San Jose Company income statement (in millions)

	19X1	19X2	19X3
Net credit sales	$15.0	$15.8	$16.2
Cost of goods sold	11.3	12.1	13.0
Gross profit	$ 3.7	$ 3.7	$ 3.2
Operating expenses	1.1	1.2	1.2
Net profit before taxes	$ 2.6	$ 2.5	$ 2.0
Tax	1.3	1.2	1.0
Profit after taxes	$ 1.3	$ 1.3	$ 1.0
Dividends	.3	.3	.0
	$ 1.0	$ 1.0	$ 1.0

The San Jose Company has a Dun & Bradstreet rating of 4A-2. Inquiries into its banking disclosed balances generally in the low millions. Five suppliers to San Jose revealed that the firm takes its discounts from the three creditors offering of 2/10, net 30 terms, though it is about 15 days slow in paying the two firms offering terms of net 30.

Analyze the San Jose Company's application for credit.

7. Matlock Gauge Company makes wind and current gauges for pleasure boats. The gauges are sold throughout the Southeast to boat dealers, and the average order size is $50. The company sells to all registered dealers without a credit analysis. Terms are net 45 days, and the average collection period is 60 days, which is regarded as satisfactory. Jane Sullivan, vice-president—finance, is now uneasy about increasing bad-debt losses on new

orders. With credit ratings from local and regional credit agencies, she feels she would be able to classify new orders into one of three risk categories. Past experience shows the following:

	Order Category		
	Low risk	Medium risk	High risk
Bad-debt loss (percent)	3%	7%	24%
Percent of category orders to total orders	30%	50%	20%

The cost of producing and shipping the gauges and of carrying the receivables is 78 percent of sales. The cost of obtaining credit rating information and of evaluating it is $4 per order. Surprisingly, there does not appear to be any association between the risk category and the collection period; the average for each of the three risk categories is around 60 days. Based on this information, should the company obtain credit information on new orders instead of selling to all new accounts without credit analysis?

8. Vostick Filter Company is a distributor of air filters to retail stores. It buys its filters from several manufacturers. Filters are ordered in lot sizes of 1,000, and each order costs $40 to place. Demand from retail stores is 20,000 filters per month and the carrying cost is $0.10 a filter per month.

a) What is the optimal order quantity (in lot sizes)?

b) What would be the optimal order quantity if the carrying cost were $.05 a filter per month?

c) What would be the optimal order quantity if ordering costs were $10?

9. A college bookstore is attempting to determine the optimal order quantity for a popular book on psychology. The store sells 5,000 copies of this book a year at a retail price of $12.50, and the cost to the store is 20 percent less, which represents the discount from the publisher. The store figures that it costs $1 per year to carry a book in inventory and $100 to prepare an order for new books.

a) Determine the total costs associated with ordering 1, 2, 5, 10, and 20 times a year.

b) Determine the economic order quantity.

c) What implicit assumptions are being made about the annual sales rate?

10. A firm that sells 5,000 gidgets per month is trying to determine how many gidgets to keep in inventory. The financial manager has determined that it costs $200 to place an order. The cost of holding inventory is 4¢/month per average gidget in inventory. A 5-day lead time is required for delivery of goods ordered. (This lead time is known with certainty.)

a) Develop the algebraic expression for determining the total cost of holding and ordering inventory.

b) Plot the holding cost and the ordering cost on a graph where the abscissa represents size of order and the ordinate represents costs.

c) Determine the EOQ from the graph.

11. To reduce production start-up costs, Bodden Truck Company may manufacture longer runs of the same truck. Estimated savings from the increase in efficiency are $260,000 per year. However, inventory turnover will decrease from 8 times a year to 6 times a year. Costs of goods sold are $48 million on an annual basis. If the required rate of return on investment in inventories is 15 percent, should the company instigate the new production plan?

12. Fouchee Scents Inc. makes various scents for use in the manufacture of food products. Although the company does maintain a safety stock, it has a policy of "lean" inventories, with the result that customers sometimes must be turned away. In an analysis of the situation, the company has estimated the cost of being out of stock associated with various levels of safety stock:

	Level of safety stock (in gallons)	Annual cost of stockouts
Present safety-stock level	5,000	$26,000
New safety-stock level 1	7,500	14,000
New safety-stock level 2	10,000	7,000
New safety-stock level 3	12,500	3,000
New safety-stock level 4	15,000	1,000
New safety-stock level 5	17,500	0

Carrying costs are $.65 per gallon per year. What is the best level of safety stock for the company?

SELECTED REFERENCES

BARZMAN, SOL, *Everyday Credit Checking: A Practical Guide,* rev. ed. New York: National Association of Credit Management, 1980.

BIERMAN, HAROLD, JR., CHARLES P. BONINI, and WARREN H. HAUSMAN, *Quantitative Analysis for Business Decisions,* 5th ed., Chaps. 10–12, Homewood, Ill.: Irwin, 1977.

BROOKS, LEROY D., "Risk-Return Criteria and Optimal Inventory Stocks," *Engineering Economist,* 25 (Summer 1980), 275–99.

BROSKY, JOHN J., *The Implicit Cost of Trade Credit and Theory of Optimal Terms of Sale.* New York: Credit Research Foundation, 1969.

BUFFA, E. S., and W. H. TAUBERT, *Production-Inventory Systems: Planning and Control,* rev. ed. Homewood, Ill.: Irwin, 1972.

CARPENTER, MICHAEL D., and JACK E. MILLER, "A Reliable Framework for Monitoring Accounts Receivable," *Financial Management,* 8 (Winter, 1979), 37–40.

DYL, EDWARD A., "Another Look at the Evaluation of Investment in Accounts Receivable," *Financial Management,* 6 (Winter 1977), 67–70.

HALLOREN, JOHN A., and HOWARD P. LANSER, "The Credit Policy Decision in an Inflationary Environment," *Financial Management,* 10 (Winter 1981), 31–38.

HILL, NED C., and KENNETH D. RIENER, "Determining the Cash Discount in the Firm's Credit Policy," *Financial Management,* 8 (Spring 1979), 68–73.

KIM, YONG H. and JOSEPH C. ATKINS, "Evaluating Investments in Accounts Receivable: A Wealth Maximization Framework," *Journal of Finance,* 33 (May 1978), 403–12.

LEWELLEN, W. G., and R. O. EDMISTER, "A General Model for Accounts Receivable Analysis and Control," *Journal of Financial and Quantitative Analysis,* 8 (March 1973), 195–206.

LEWELLEN, W. G., and R. W. JOHNSON, "Better Way to Monitor Accounts Receivable," *Harvard Business Review,* (May–June 1972), 101–109.

LONG, MICHAEL S., "Credit Screening System Selection," *Journal of Financial and Quantitative Analysis,* 11 (June 1976), 313–28.

MAGEE, JOHN F., "Guides to Inventory Policy," I–III, *Harvard Business Review,* 34 (January–February 1956), 49–60; (March–April 1956), 103–16; and (May–June 1956), 57–70.

MARRAH, GEORGE L., "Managing Receivables," *Financial Executive,* 38 (July 1970), 40–44.

MEHTA, DILEEP, "The Formulation of Credit Policy Models," *Management Science,* 15 (October 1968), 30–50.

———, *Working Capital Management.* Englewood Cliffs, N.J.: Prentice-Hall, 1974, chaps. 1–5.

OH, JOHN S., "Opportunity Cost in the Evaluation of Investment in Accounts Receivable," *Financial Management,* 5 (Summer 1976), 32–36.

SACHDEVA, KANWAL S., "Accounts Receivable Decisions in a Capital Budgeting Framework," *Financial Management,* 10 (Winter 1981), 45–49.

SCHIFF, MICHAEL, "Credit and Inventory Management," *Financial Executive,* 40 (November 1972), 28–33.

SMITH, KEITH V., *Guide to Working Capital Management.* New York: McGraw-Hill, 1979, chaps. 5 and 6.

SNYDER, ARTHUR, "Principles of Inventory Management," *Financial Executive,* 32 (April 1964), 16–19.

STONE, BERNELL K., "The Payments-Pattern Approach to the Forecasting and Control of Accounts Receivable," *Financial Management,* 5 (Autumn 1976), 65–82.

WESTON, J. FRED, and PHAM D. TUAN, "Comment on Analysis of Credit Policy Changes," *Financial Management,* 9 (Winter 1980), 59–63.

Spontaneous financing 11

Short-term financing can be categorized according to whether or not the source is spontaneous. Accounts payable and accruals are classified as spontaneous because their magnitude is primarily a function of a company's level of operations. As operations expand, these liabilities typically increase and finance in part the buildup in assets. While both accounts payable and accruals behave in this manner, there still remains a degree of discretion on the part of a company as to their exact magnitude. In this chapter we consider these two methods of financing and how such discretion might be used. In the next chapter we examine the other major sources of short-term financing—money-market credit and short-term loans, the latter being either from banks or finance companies. Unlike the sources discussed in this chapter, such financing is not spontaneous or automatic. It must be arranged on a formal basis.

TRADE CREDIT FINANCING

Trade credit is a form of short-term financing common to almost all businesses. In fact, it is the largest source of short-term funds for business firms collectively. In an advanced economy, most buyers are not required to pay for goods upon deliver but are allowed a short deferment period before payment is due. During this period the seller of the goods extends credit to the buyer. Because suppliers generally are more liberal in the extension of credit than are financial institutions, small companies in particular rely on trade credit.

Of the three types of trade credit—open account, notes payable, and trade acceptances—by far the most common type is the open-account arrangement. The seller ships goods to the buyer and sends an invoice that specifies the goods shipped, the price, the total amount due, and the terms of the sale. Open-account credit derives its name from the fact that the buyer does not sign a formal debt instrument evidencing the amount owed the seller. The seller extends credit based upon a credit investigation of the buyer (see chapter 10).

In some situations promissory notes are employed instead of open-account credit. The buyer signs a note that evidences a debt to the seller. The note itself calls for the payment of the obligation at some specified future date. Promissory notes have been used in business such as those dealing in furs and jewelry. This arrangement is employed when the seller wants the buyer to recognize the debt formally. A seller might request a promissory note from a buyer if the buyer's open account became past due.

A trade acceptance is another arrangement by which the indebtedness of the buyer is formally recognized. Under this arrangement, the seller draws a draft on the buyer, ordering the buyer to pay the draft at some date in the future. The seller will not release the goods until the buyer accepts the time draft.[1] Accepting the draft, the buyer designates a bank at which the draft will be paid when it comes due. At that time, the draft becomes a trade acceptance, and depending upon the credit worthiness of the buyer, it may possess some degree of marketability. If the trade acceptance is marketable, the seller of the goods can sell it at a discount and receive immediate payment for the goods. At final maturity, the holder of the acceptance presents it to the designated bank for collection.

Terms of sale

Because the use of promissory notes and trade acceptances is rather limited, the subsequent discussion will be confined to open-account trade credit. The terms of sale make a great deal of difference in this type of credit. These terms, specified in the invoice, may be placed in several broad categories according to the net period within which payment is expected and according to the terms of the cash discount.

COD and CBD—no extension of credit.   COD terms mean *cash on delivery* of the goods. The only risk the seller undertakes is that the buyer may refuse the shipment. Under such circumstances, the seller will be stuck with the shipping costs. Occasionally a seller might ask for cash before delivery (CBD) to avoid all risk. Under either COD or CBD terms, the seller does not extend credit. CBD terms must be distinguished from progress payments, which are very common in certain industries. With progress payments, the buyer pays the manufacturer at various

---

[1]If the instrument is a sight draft, the buyer is ordered to pay the draft upon presentation. Under this arrangement, trade credit is not extended.

stages of production before the actual delivery of the finished product. Because large sums of money are tied up in work in progress, aircraft manufacturers request progress payments from airlines in advance of the actual delivery of aircraft.

Net period—no cash discount. When credit is extended, the seller specifies the period of time allowed for payment. The terms "net 30" indicate that the invoice or bill must be paid within 30 days. If the seller bills on a monthly basis, it might require such terms as "net 15 EOM," which means that all goods shipped before the end of the month must be paid for by the fifteenth of the following month.

Net period with cash discount. In addition to extending credit, the seller may offer a cash discount if the bill is paid during the early part of the net period. The terms "2/10, net 30" indicate that the seller offers a 2 percent discount if the bill is paid within 10 days; otherwise, the buyer must pay the full amount within 30 days. Usually, a cash discount is offered as an incentive to the buyer to pay early. In chapter 10, we discussed the optimal cash discount the seller might offer. A cash discount differs from a trade discount and from a quantity discount. A trade discount is greater for one class of customers (e.g., wholesalers) than for others (e.g., retailers). A quantity discount is offered on large shipments.

Datings. In a seasonal business, sellers frequently use datings to encourage customers to place their orders before a heavy selling period. A manufacturer of lawn mowers may give seasonal datings specifying that any shipment to a dealer in the winter or spring does not have to be paid for until summer. Earlier orders benefit the seller, who can gauge the demand more realistically and schedule production more efficiently. Also, the seller does not have to store certain finished-goods inventory. The buyer has the advantage of not having to pay for the goods until the height of the selling period. Under this arrangement, credit is extended for a longer-than-normal period of time.

Trade credit as a means of financing

We have seen that trade credit is a source of funds, because the buyer does not have to pay for goods until after they are delivered. If the firm automatically pays its bills a certain number of days after the date of invoice, trade credit becomes a built-in source of financing that varies with the production cycle. As the firm increases its production and corresponding purchases, accounts payable increase and provide part of the funds needed to finance the increase in production. As production decreases, accounts payable tend to decrease. Although the variation of accounts payable with production may not be directly proportional, because of shortages or gluts in inventory on hand, there is a strong degree of correspondence.

If a firm adheres strictly to the practice of paying its bills at a given time after invoice, trade credit is not a discretionary source of financing. It in entirely dependent upon the purchasing plans of the firm, which, in turn, are dependent upon its production cycle. In examining trade credit as a discretionary form of financing, we want to specifically consider situations in which (1) a firm does not take a cash discount but pays on the last day of the net period, and (2) a firm pays its bills beyond the net period.

Payment on the final due date

In this section we assume that the firm foregoes a cash discount but does pay its bill on the final due date of the net period. If no cash discount is offered, there is no cost for the use of credit during the net period. By the same token, if a firm takes the discount, there is no cost for the use of trade credit during the discount period. If a cash discount is offered but not taken, however, there is a definite opportunity cost. If the terms of sale are 2/10, net 30, the firm has the use of funds for an additional 20 days if it does not take the cash discount but pays on the final day of the net period. For a $100 invoice, it would have the use of $98 for 20 days. The annual interest cost is[2]

$$\frac{2}{98} \times \frac{360}{20} = 36.7 \text{ percent}$$

Thus, we see that trade credit can be a very expensive form of short-term financing when a cash discount is offered.

The cost of trade credit declines as the net period becomes longer in relation to the discount period. Had the terms in the above example been 2/10, net 60, the annual interest cost would have been

$$\frac{2}{98} \times \frac{360}{50} = 14.7 \text{ percent}$$

The relationship between the annual interest cost of trade credit and the number of days between the end of the discount period and the end of the net period is shown in Fig. 11-1. In the figure, we assume 2/10 discount terms. We see that the cost of trade credit decreases at a decreasing rate as the net period increases. The point is that if a firm does not take a cash discount, its cost of trade credit declines with the length of time it is able to postpone payment.

Stretching accounts payable

In the preceding section we assumed that payment was made at the end of the due period: however, a firm may postpone payment beyond this period. We shall call this postponement "stretching" accounts payable or "leaning on the trade." The cost of stretching accounts payable is twofold: the cost of the cash discount foregone and the possible deterioration in credit rating. In chapter 10 we discussed the rating system of credit agencies such as Dun & Bradstreet. If a firm stretches its payables excessively, so that trade payables are significantly delinquent, its credit rating will suffer. Suppliers will view the firm with apprehension and may insist upon rather strict terms of sale if, indeed, they sell at all. In assessing a company banks and other lenders do not favorably regard excessive

[2]For ease of calculation, 360 rather than 365 is used as the number of days in the year.

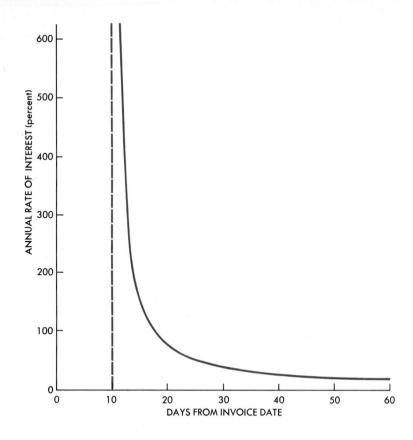

FIGURE 11-1
Annual rate of interest on accounts payable with terms of 2/10, net 30

slowness. Although it is difficult to measure, there is certainly an opportunity cost to a deterioration in a firm's credit reputation.

Notwithstanding the possibility of a deteriorating credit rating, it may be possible to postpone certain payables beyond the net period without severe consequences. Suppliers are in business to sell goods, and trade credit may increase sales. A supplier may be willing to go along with stretching payables, particularly if the risk of bad-debt loss is negligible. If the funds requirement of the firm is seasonal, suppliers may not view the stretching of payables in an unfavorable light during periods of peak requirements, provided that the firm is current in the trade during the rest of the year. There may be an indirect charge for this extension of credit, in the form of higher prices, a possibility that the firm should carefully consider in evaluating the cost of stretching accounts payable.

Periodic and reasonable stretching of payables is not necessarily bad per se. It should be evaluated objectively in relation to its cost and in relation to alternative sources of short-term credit. When a firm does stretch its payables, effort should be made to keep suppliers fully informed of its situation. A large number of suppliers will allow a firm to stretch payables if the firm is honest with the supplier and consistent in its payments. Sometimes a firm with seasonal funds requirements is able to obtain a dating from a supplier. When a firm obtains a dating, it does not stretch its payables; as long as it pays the bill by the final date, no deterioration in its credit rating is likely.

Advantages of trade credit

The firm must balance the advantages of trade credit as a discretionary source of financing against the cost of foregoing a cash discount, the opportunity cost associated with a possible deterioration in credit reputation if it stretches its payables, and the possible increase in selling price the seller imposes on the buyer. There are several advantages of trade credit as a form of short-term financing. Probably the major advantage is its ready availability. The accounts payable of most firms represent a continuous form of credit. There is no need to arrange financing formally; it is already there. If the firm is now taking cash discounts, additional credit is readily available by not paying existing accounts payable until the end of the net period. There is no need to negotiate with the supplier; the decision is entirely up to the firm. In stretching accounts payable, the firm will find it necessary, after a certain degree of postponement, to negotiate with the supplier.

In most other types of short-term financing, it is necessary to negotiate formally with the lender over the terms of the loan. The lender may impose restrictions on the firm and seek a secured position. Restrictions are possible with trade credit, but they are not nearly as likely. With other sources of short-term financing, there may be a lead time between the time the need for funds is recognized and the time the firm is able to borrow them. Trade credit is a more flexible means of financing. The firm does not have to sign a note, pledge collateral, or adhere to a strict payment schedule on the note. A supplier views an occasional delinquent payment with a far less critical eye than does a banker or other lender.

The advantages of using trade credit must be weighed against the cost. As we have seen, the cost may be very high when all factors are considered. Many firms utilize other sources of short-term financing in order to be able to take advantage of cash discounts. The savings in cost over other forms of short-term financing, however, must offset the loss of flexibility and convenience associated with trade credit. For certain firms, there are no alternative sources of short-term credit.

Who bears the cost?

We should recognize that trade credit involves a cost for the use of funds over time. In the previous sections, it was implied that there is no explicit cost to trade credit if the buyer pays the invoice during the discount period or, if no cash discount is given, during the net period. Although this supposition is valid from the standpoint of marginal analysis, it overlooks the fact that somebody must bear the cost of trade credit, for the use of funds over time is not free. The burden may fall on the supplier, the buyer, or both parties. The supplier may be able to pass the cost on to the buyer in the form of higher prices.

The supplier of a product for which demand is elastic, may be reluctant to increase prices and may end up absorbing most of the cost of trade credit. Under other circumstances the supplier is able to pass the cost on to the buyer. The buyer should determine who is bearing the cost of trade credit. A buyer who is bearing the cost may shop around for a better deal. The buyer should recognize that the cost of trade credit changes over time. In periods of rising interest rates and tight money, suppliers may raise the price of their products to take account of the rising cost of carrying receivables. This rise in price should not be confused with other rises caused by changing supply and demand conditions in the product markets.

ACCRUAL ACCOUNTS

Perhaps even more than accounts payable, accrual accounts represent a spontaneous source of financing. The most common accrual accounts are for wages and taxes. For both accounts, the expense is incurred or accrued but not paid. Usually a date is specified when the accrual must be paid. Income taxes are paid quarterly; property taxes are paid semiannually. Wages typically are paid weekly, every other week, bimonthly, or monthly. Like accounts payable, accruals tend to expand with the scope of the operation. As sales increase, labor costs usually increase; and with them, accrued wages increase. As profits increase, accrued taxes increase in almost direct proportion.

In a sense, accruals represent costless financing. Services are rendered for wages, but employees are not paid and do not expect to be paid until the end or after the end of the pay period. The lapse is established by the company, although unions and competing employers in the labor market influence its length. Similarly, taxes are not expected to be paid until their due date. Thus, accruals represent an interest-free source of financing.

Unfortunately for the company, they do not represent discretionary financing. For taxes, the government is the creditor, and it likes to be paid on time. A company in extreme financial difficulty can postpone tax payment for a short while but there is a penalty charge. It may also postpone payment of wages—at the expense of employees and hurt morale. Employees may respond with absenteeism, reduced efficiency or seek employment elsewhere. A company must be extremely careful in postponing wages. It must fully inform employees and set a firm date for payment. Such a measure is one of last resort; nevertheless, many a company on the precipice of cash-flow disaster finds itself having to postpone wages as well as all other payments.

Accrued wages are partially discretionary in that a company can change the frequency of wage payments and thereby affect the amount of financing. If the interval of time between the last working day of a pay period and pay day stays the same, the less frequent the paydays the more the financing. Suppose a company had a weekly payroll of $400,000 with an average amount accrued of $200,000. If the company were to increase its pay period from one to two weeks, the payroll at the end of the period would be $800,000. The average amount of accrued wages now would be $400,000 ($800,000 divided by two). Therefore, the company increases its interest-free financing by $200,000.

The longer the pay period, the greater the amount of accrued wage financing. This linear relationship is illustrated in Fig. 11-2 for $1 in weekly wages. (For a specific situation, one needs to multiply the amount of accrual shown on the vertical axis by the actual weekly payroll to determine the average amount accrued.) Obviously, it would be desirable from the standpoint of a company to have as long a pay period as possible, but union pressures and competition for labor from other employers limit the feasible range of options. Moreover, an increase in the pay period is usually "one-shot" in that it is not possible to repeat

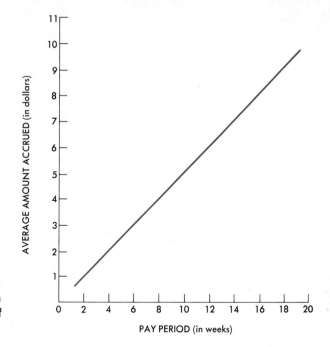

FIGURE 11-2
Relationship between average wages accrued and the length of the pay period for wages of $1 per week

with a subsequent increase. In most companies, the maximum pay period is no more than one month. In summary, then, accruals are a discretionary source of financing only within a very narrow range.

SUMMARY

Trade credit can be a significant source of short-term financing for the firm. It is a discretionary source of financing only if a firm does not have a strict policy regarding its promptness in paying bills. When a cash discount is offered but not taken, the cost of trade credit is the cash discount foregone. The longer the period between the end of the discount period and the time the bill is paid, the less the opportunity cost. "Stretching" accounts payable involves postponement of payment beyond the due period. The opportunity cost of stretching payables is the possible deterioration in the firm's credit rating. The firm must balance the costs of trade credit against its advantages and the costs of other short-term credit. The major advantage of trade credit is the flexibility it gives the firm.

Like accounts payable, accruals represent a spontaneous source of financing, albeit offering the firm even less discretion than it has with trade credit financing. The principal accrual items are wages and taxes, and both are expected to be paid on established dates. In the interim, interest-free financing is available to the company; and for an ongoing company, this financing is continuous. A company can increase the amount of its accrued wages by lessening the frequency of paydays within a narrow range. A company in dire financial straits will sometimes postpone tax and wage payments, but the consequences of such postponement can be severe.

QUESTIONS

1. Explain why trade credit is a "spontaneous source of funds."

2. Trade credit is a very costly source of funds when discounts are lost. Explain why many firms rely on this source of funds to finance their temporary working capital.

3. Stretching payables provides "free" funds to the customers for a short period. The supplier, however, can face serious financial problems if all of its customers stretch their accounts. Discuss the nature of the problems the supplier may face and suggest different approaches to cope with stretching.

4. What may be the impact of large-scale stretching on social welfare? Explain.

5. Suppose a firm elected to tighten its trade credit policy from 2/10, net 90 to 2/10, net 30. What effect could the firm expect this change to have on its liquidity?

6. Why do small firms in particular rely heavily on trade credit as a source of funds? Why will suppliers advance credit to firms when banks will not?

7. In what ways can accruals be varied to obtain more interest-free financing?

8. Why is the U.S. government an involuntary creditor with respect to accrued taxes?

9. Why are accruals a more spontaneous source of financing than trade credit?

10. What is to prevent a company from postponing payment on its accruals?

PROBLEMS

1. Determine the effective annual cost of capital for the following terms, assuming discounts are lost and a 360-day year.

   a)   1/10, n/30   e)   3/10, n/60
   b)   2/10, n/30   f)   2/10, n/90
   c)   3/10, n/30   g)   3/10, n/90
   d)   10/30, n/60   h)   5/10, n/100

2. The Dud Company purchases raw materials on terms of 2/10, net 30. A review of the company's records by the owner, Mr. Dud, revealed that payments are usually made 15 days after purchases are received. When asked why the firm did not take advantage of its discounts, the bookkeeper, Mr. Grind, replied that it cost only 2 percent for these funds, whereas a bank loan would cost the firm 12 percent.

   a)   What mistake is Grind making?
   b)   What is the real cost of not taking advantage of the discount?
   c)   If the firm could not borrow from the bank and were forced to resort to the use of trade credit funds, what suggestion might be made to Grind which would reduce the annual interest cost?

3. The manager of Wilstat Corporation envisions benefits in switching from cash purchase of merchandise to credit purchase on net-60-day terms. The manager feels that the increased liquidity of purchasing $5,000/month on 60-day terms will be reflected in the liquidity ratios. The present working-capital accounts of the corporation are as follows:

Cash	$15,000	Notes payable	$10,000
Receivables	25,000	Taxes payable	6,000
Inventories	40,000	Other accruals	4,000
	$80,000		$20,000

a) What effect would the purchase of $10,000 of merchandise on 60-day terms have on (1) the current ratio and (2) the quick ratio?

b) Do the ratios indicate increased liquidity? Explain.

4. Determine the annual percentage interest cost for each of the following terms of sale, assuming the firm does not take the cash discount but pays on the final day of the net period (assume a 360-day year):

a) 1/20, net 30 ($500 invoice)   c) 2/5, net 10 ($100 invoice)

b) 2/30, net 60 ($1,000 invoice)   d) 3/10, net 30 ($250 invoice)

5. Does the dollar size of the invoice affect the annual interest cost of not taking discounts? Illustrate with an example.

6. Recompute problem 4, assuming a 10-day stretching of the payment date.

7. On January 1, Faville Car Company, a large car dealer, gave its employees a 10 percent pay increase in view of the substantial profits the prior year. Before the increase, the weekly payroll was $50,000. Profits were $274,000 the previous year, but only $200,000 was previously used in estimating quarterly tax payments. The company is in the 46 percent marginal tax bracket and intends to pay the additional taxes on April 15. What is the combined effect of these two changes on accruals?

8. El Pedro Chili Company pays its employees weekly, and its payroll is $28,000. It plans to change this procedure so that it pays them every two weeks. Presently accrued wages are $14,000.

a) What is the effect of this change on accrued wages?

b) Suppose that the company also increases wages for all employees by 5 percent. Its opportunity cost of funds is 12 percent. Is the company better or worse off with these combined events (procedure change and wage increase)?

9. The Halow Harp and Chime Company is negotiating a new labor contract. Among other things, the union is demanding that the company pay its workers weekly as opposed to twice a month. The payroll currently is $260,000 per pay day and accrued wages average $130,000. What is the annual cost of the union's demand if the company's opportunity cost of funds is 9 percent?

SELECTED REFERENCES

BROSKY, JOHN J., *The Implicit Cost of Trade Credit and Theory of Optimal Terms of Sale.* New York: Credit Research Foundation, 1969.

SCHWARTZ, ROBERT A., "An Economic Model of Trade Credit," *Journal of Financial and Quantitative Analysis,* 9 (September 1974), 643–58.

SMITH, KEITH V., *Guide to Working Capital Management.* New York: McGraw-Hill, 1979, chaps. 7, 8.

Short-term borrowings 12

From trade credit and accruals, two of the main spontaneous sources of short-term financing, we turn to methods of external short-term financing in the public or private market. In the public market, various money-market instruments are sold to investors either directly by the issuer or indirectly through dealers. Short-term loans are placed privately, the principal sources being commercial banks and finance companies. With both money-market credit and short-term loans, financing must be arranged on a formal basis.

MONEY-MARKET CREDIT

Large, well-established companies sometimes borrow on a short-term basis through commercial paper and other money-market instruments. Commercial paper consists of unsecured short-term negotiable promissory notes sold in the money market. Because these notes are unsecured and are a money-market instrument, only the more credit-worthy companies are able to use commercial paper as a source of short-term financing.

Market for commercial paper

The commercial paper market is composed of two parts: the dealer market and the direct-placement market.[1] Industrial firms, utilities, and medium-sized finance companies sell commercial paper through dealers. The dealer organization is composed of a half-dozen major dealers who purchase commercial paper from the issuer and, in turn, sell it to investors. The typical commission a dealer earns is 1/8 percent, and maturities on dealer-placed paper generally range from one to six months. The market is a highly organized and sophisticated one; paper is sold in denominations ranging from $25,000 to several million dollars. Though the dealer market has been characterized in the past by a significant number of issuers who borrowed on a seasonal basis, the trend definitely is toward financing on a revolving or more permanent basis.

A number of large sales finance companies, such as General Motors Acceptance Corporation, bypass the dealer organization in favor of selling their paper directly to investors. These issuers tailor both the maturity and the amount of the note to the needs of investors, mostly large corporations with excess cash. Maturities on directly placed paper can range from as little as a few days up to nine months. Unlike many industrial issuers, finance companies use the commercial paper market as a permanent source of funds. With the development of the direct-placement market, pockets of idle investment funds have been tapped for short-term financing purposes. Directly placed paper has recently accounted for 60 to 80 percent of the total commercial paper outstanding.

Advantages to borrower.   The principal advantage of commercial paper as a source of short-term financing is that it is generally cheaper than a short-term business loan from a commercial bank. The rate on prime commercial paper is from 1 to 6 percent lower than the prime rate for bank loans to the highest quality borrower. Because the prime rate is more sluggish than money market rates, the differential tends to be greatest in a period of rapidly decreasing interest rates. It tends to be narrowest in a period of tight money when interest rates are high but stable. In assessing commercial paper as a means of financing, the firm should weigh relative cost and availability in comparison with alternative sources of funds. In this comparison, the cost of bank credit should be adjusted upward for compensating-balance requirements.

For most companies, commercial paper is a supplement to bank credit. In fact, commercial paper dealers require borrowers to maintain lines of credit at banks in order to backstop the use of commercial paper. This assures them that commercial paper borrowings can be paid off. Switching from commercial paper to bank borrowings and back again, depending on the interest rate differential, is feasible, but a company must be careful not to impair relations with its banks. The commercial paper market is highly impersonal. Interest rates fluctuate dramatically; and in times of great economic uncertainty, lesser quality companies are foreclosed from borrowing in this market. Therefore, it is important to maintain lines of credit and good relations with commercial banks, in order to protect against adverse money-market conditions.

[1]For a discussion of commercial paper from the standpoint of a short-term investor, see chapter 9.

Bankers' acceptances

For a company engaged in foreign trade, bankers' acceptances can be a meaningful source of financing. When an American company wishes to import $100,000 worth of electronic components from a company in Japan, the two companies agree that a 90-day time draft will be used in settlement of the trade. The American company arranges a letter of credit with its bank, whereby the bank agrees to honor drafts drawn on the company as presented through a Japanese bank. The Japanese company ships the goods and at the same time draws a draft ordering the American company to pay in 90 days. It then takes the draft to its Japanese bank. By prearrangement, the draft is sent to the American bank and accepted by that bank. At that time it becomes a bankers' acceptance. In essence, the bank accepts responsibility for payment, thereby substituting its credit-worthiness for that of the drawee, the American company.

If the bank is large and well known—and most banks accepting drafts are—the instrument becomes highly marketable upon acceptance. As a result the drawer, the Japanese company, does not have to hold the draft until the final due date; it can sell the draft in the market for less than its face value. The discount involved represents the interest payment to the investor. At the end of 90 days the investor presents the acceptance to the accepting bank for payment and receives $100,000. At this time the American company is obligated to have funds on deposit to cover the draft. Thus it has financed its import for a 90-day period. Presumably, the Japanese exporter would have charged a lower price if payment were to be made upon shipment. In this sense the American company is the borrower.

The presence of an active and viable bankers' acceptance market makes possible the financing of foreign trade at interest rates approximating those on commercial paper. Although the principles by which the acceptance is created are exactly the same for foreign and domestic trade, only a small portion of the total bankers' acceptances outstanding are domestic. In recent years, bankers' acceptances have greatly multiplied with the sharp growth in foreign trade, particularly with the Far East, and with more companies recognizing the usefulness of this form of financing.

UNSECURED BANK CREDIT

For expository purposes it is convenient to separate business loans into two categories: unsecured loans and secured loans. Almost without exception, finance companies do not offer unsecured loans, simply because a borrower who deserves unsecured credit can borrow at a lower cost from a commercial bank. Consequently, our discussion of unsecured loans will involve only commercial banks.

Short-term, unsecured bank loans typically are regarded as "self-liquidating" in that the assets purchased with the proceeds generate sufficient cash flows to pay the loan in less than a year. At one time, banks confined their lending almost exclusively to this type of loan. Fortunately, banks now provide a wide variety of business loans tailored to the specific needs of the borrower. Still, the short-term, self-liquidating loan is a popular source of business financing, particularly in financing seasonal buildups in accounts receivable and inventories. Unsecured short-term loans may be extended under a line of credit, under a revolving-credit agreement, or on a transaction basis. The debt itself is evidenced formally by a promissory note signed by the borrower, showing the time and amount of payment and the interest to be paid.

Line of credit

A line of credit is an arrangement between a bank and its customer, specifying the maximum amount of unsecured credit the bank will permit the firm to owe at any one time. Usually, credit lines are established for a one-year period and are subject to one-year renewals. Frequently, lines of credit are set for renewal after the bank receives the audited annual report and has had a chance to review the progress of the borrower. If the borrower's year-end statement date is December 31, a bank may set its line to expire sometime in March. At that time, the bank and the company would meet to discuss the credit needs of the firm for the coming year in light of its past year's performance. The amount of the line is based upon the bank's assessment of the credit worthiness and credit needs of the borrower. Depending upon changes in these conditions, a line of credit may be adjusted at the renewal date or before, if conditions necessitate a change.

The cash budget, perhaps, gives the best insight into the borrower's short-term credit needs. If maximum or peak borrowing needs over the forthcoming year are estimated at $800,000, a company might seek a line of credit of $1 million to give it a margin of safety. Whether the bank will go along with the request, of course, will depend upon its evaluation of the credit worthiness of the firm. If the bank agrees, the firm then may borrow on a short-term basis—usually 90 days—up to the full $1 million line. Because certain banks regard borrowing under lines of credit as seasonal or temporary financing, they may require that the borrower be out of bank debt at some time during the year. Frequently, the borrower will be required to clean up (pay off) bank debt for a period of time during the year. The cleanup itself is evidence to the bank that the loan is truly seasonal in nature and not a portion of the permanent financing of the firm.

Despite its many advantages to the borrower, a line of credit does not constitute a legal commitment on the part of the bank to extend credit. The borrower is usually informed of the line by means of a letter indicating that the bank is willing to extend credit up to a certain amount. An example of such a letter is shown in Fig. 12-1. This letter is not a legal obligation of the bank to extend credit. If the credit-worthiness of the borrower should deteriorate over the year, the bank might not want to extend credit and would not be required to do so. Under most circumstances, however, a bank feels bound to honor a line of credit.

Revolving-credit agreement

A revolving-credit agreement is a legal commitment by a bank to extend credit up to a maximum amount. While the commitment is in force, the bank must extend credit whenever the borrower wishes to borrow, provided total borrowings

March 23, 1980

Mr. Joseph A. Ralberg
Vice President & Treasurer
Barker Manufacturing Corporation
Palo Alto, California

Dear Mr. Ralberg:

Based upon our analysis of your year-end audited statements, we are pleased to renew your $1 million unsecured line of credit for the forthcoming year. Borrowings under this line will be at a rate of one-half percent (½%) over the prime rate.

This line is subject to only the understanding that your company will maintain its financial position and that it will be out of bank debt for at least 45 days during the fiscal year.

Yours very truly,

John D. Myers
Vice President

FIGURE 12-1
Sample letter extending line of credit

do not exceed the maximum amount specified. If the revolving credit is for $1 million, and $700,000 is already owing, the borrower can borrow an additional $300,000 at any time. For the privilege of having this formal commitment, the borrower usually is required to pay a commitment fee on the unused portion of the revolving credit. If the revolving credit is for $1 million, and borrowing for the year averages $400,000, the borrower will be required to pay a commitment fee on the $600,000 unused portion. If the fee is .5 percent, the cost of this privilege will be $3,000 for the year. Revolving-credit agreements frequently extend beyond one year. Because lending arrangements of more than a year must be regarded as intermediate rather than short-term credit, we shall examine revolving credits more extensively in chapter 21. The purpose of introducing them at this time is to illustrate the formal nature of the arrangement in contrast to the informality of a line of credit.

Transaction loans

Borrowing under a line of credit or under a revolving-credit arrangement is not appropriate when the firm needs short-term funds for only one purpose. A contractor may borrow from a bank in order to complete a job. When the contractor receives payment for the job, he pays the loan. For this type of loan, a bank evaluates each request by the borrower as a separate transaction. In these evaluations, the cash-flow ability of the borrower to pay the loan is usually of paramount importance.

Interest rates

Unlike interest rates on impersonal money-market instruments such as Treasury bills, bankers' acceptances, and commercial paper, most business loans are determined through personal negotiation between the borrower and the lender. In some measure, banks try to vary the interest rate charged according to the credit worthiness of the borrower; the lower the credit worthiness, the higher the interest rate. Interest rates charged also vary in keeping with money-market conditions. One measure that changes with underlying market conditions is the prime rate. The prime rate is the rate charged on business loans to financially sound companies. The rate itself is usually set by large money-market banks and is relatively uniform throughout the country. In the past, the rate changed only slowly over time in keeping with underlying changes in market conditions.

After the mid-1960s, the prime rate changed much more rapidly. Several factors were responsible. For one thing, there was a greater volatility in overall market rates of interest. Another factor was the cost of funds to banks. Over the years, time and other liabilities on which interest is paid have increased in relation to demand deposits. As a result, fluctuations in market rates of interest caused greater volatility in the cost of funds to banks than was true in earlier years. One way for banks to keep up with rapidly changing market rates of interest is simply to adjust the prime rate more frequently. Indeed this has happened in recent years, as evidenced in Fig. 12-2.

FIGURE 12-2
The prime rate on
commercial loans

Another means for coming to grips with volatile market conditions is with a floating prime rate. Initiated in 1971 by the First National City Bank of New York, the floating prime is geared to the rate on some money-market instrument. The rate might be established as 1 percent above the commercial paper rate, with adjustments occurring on a weekly basis. The differential between the floating prime and the money-market rate is periodically adjusted, depending on relative conditions in the money markets vis-à-vis the market for bank loans.

Differentials from prime. Despite the term *prime rate* implying the price a bank charges its most credit-worthy customers, this has not been the recent practice. With banks becoming more competitive for corporate customers and facing competition from the commercial paper market, the well-established, financially sound company often is able to borrow at a rate of interest below prime. The rate charged is based on the bank's marginal cost of funds, as typically reflected by the rate paid on money market certificates of deposit. An interest-rate margin is added to the cost of funds, and the sum becomes the rate charged the customer. This rate is changed daily in keeping with changes in money-market rates. Generally, the rate paid by the customer is one-quarter to one percent below the prime rate. The differential depends on competitive conditions and on the relative bargaining power of the borrower.

Other borrowers will pay either the prime rate or a rate above prime, the bank's pricing of the loan being relative to the prime rate. A bank might extend a line of credit to a company at a rate one-half percent above prime. If the prime rate is 14 percent, the borrower is charged an interest rate of 14.5 percent. If the prime rate changes to 10 percent, the borrower will pay 10.5 percent. Interest-rate differentials among the various customers of a bank supposedly should reflect only differences in credit worthiness.

Other factors, however, influence the differential. Among them are the balances maintained and other business the borrower has with a bank (such as trust business). A good customer who has maintained very attractive balances in the past may be able to obtain a more favorable interest rate than will a firm of equal credit worthiness that has carried rather meager balances. Also, the cost of servicing a loan is a factor determining the differential in rate from prime. Certain collateral loans are costly to administer, and this cost must be passed on to the borrower either in the interest rate charged or in a special fee.

Thus, the interest rate charged on a short-term loan will depend upon the prevailing cost of funds to banks, the existing prime rate, the credit worthiness of the borrower, the present and prospective relationship of the borrower with the bank, and sometimes upon other considerations. Because of the fixed costs involved in credit investigation and in the processing of a loan, we would expect the interest rate on small loans to be higher than the rate on large loans.

Methods of computing interest rates. There are three ways in which interest on a loan may be paid: on a collect basis; on a discount basis; and on an add-on basis. When paid on a collect basis, the interest is paid at the maturity of the note; when paid on a discount basis, interest is deducted from the initial loan. On a $10,000 loan at 12 percent interest for one year, the effective rate of interest on a collect note is

$$\frac{\$1,200}{\$10,000} = 12.00 \text{ percent}$$

On a discount basis, the effective rate of interest is not 12 percent but

$$\frac{\$1,200}{\$8,800} = 13.64 \text{ percent}$$

When we pay on a discount basis, we have the use of only $8,800 for the year but must pay back $10,000 at the end of that time. Thus, the effective rate of interest is higher on a discount note than on a collect note. We should point out that most bank business loans are on a collect note basis.

On installment loans, banks and other lenders usually charge interest on an *add-on* basis. This means that interest is added to the funds disbursed in order to determine the face value of the note. Suppose in our example that an installment loan were involved with 12 equal monthly installments and that the interest rate were 12 percent. The borrower would receive $10,000, and the face value of the note would be $11,200. Thus, $1,200 in interest is paid. However, the borrower has use of the full $10,000 for only one month and at the end of that month must pay 1/12th of $11,200 or $933.33. Installments in that amount are due at the end of each of the subsequent 11 months until the note is paid. For the full year, then, the borrower has use of only about one-half of the $10,000. Instead of a 12 percent rate, the effective rate is nearly double that, about 22 percent with monthly compounding. Thus, add-on interest is paid on the initial amount of the loan and not on the declining balance as is customary with other types of loans.

Compensating balances

In addition to charging interest on loans, commercial banks often require the borrower to maintain demand deposit balances at the bank in direct proportion to either the amount of funds borrowed or the amount of the commitment. These minimum balances are known as compensating balances. The amount required in the compensating balance varies according to competitive conditions in the market for loans and specific negotiations between the borrower and lender. Banks would like to obtain balances equal to 15 percent of a line of credit. If the line is $2 million, the borrower would be required to maintain average balances of at least $300,000 during the year. Another arrangement might be for the bank to require average balances of 10 percent of the line and 10 percent more on the amount owing when the line is in use. If a firm's line were $2 million and its borrowings were $600,000, it would be required to maintain $260,000 in compensating balances.

The effect of a compensating balance requirement is to raise the effective cost of borrowing if the borrower is required to maintain balances above the amount the firm would maintain ordinarily. If we borrow $1 million at 12 percent and are required to maintain $100,000 more in balances than we would ordinarily, we will then have use of only $900,000 of the $1 million loan. The effective annual interest cost is $120,000/$900,000 = 13.33 percent, rather than 12 percent. Compensating balance requirements may increase the liquidity position of the borrower from the bank's point of view. As a last resort, the bank can exercise its legal right of offset and apply the balances on deposit to pay off the loan or a portion of the loan.

The notion of compensating balances for loans may be weakening. Increasingly, banks are becoming profit- as opposed to deposit-oriented and, accordingly, are "fine-tuning" profitability analyses of customer relationships. With the rapid and significant fluctuations in the cost of funds to banks in recent years, as well as the accelerated competition among financial institutions, most banks make at least some loans without compensating balance requirements. The interest rate charged is in line with the bank's incremental cost of obtaining funds. The movement toward more sophisticated profitability analysis is likely to reduce further, though certainly not eliminate, the imposition of compensating balance requirements in connection with lending arrangements.

SECURED LENDING ARRANGEMENTS

Many firms cannot obtain credit on an unsecured basis, either because they are new and unproven or because bankers do not highly regard the firms' ability to service debt. In order to make a loan, lenders require security that will reduce their risk of loss. With security, lenders have two sources of loan payment: the cash-flow ability of the firm to service the debt and, if that source fails for some reason, the collateral value of the security. Most lenders will not make a loan unless the firm has sufficient expected cash flows to make proper servicing of debt highly probable. To reduce their risk further, they require security.

Collateral value

The excess of the market value of the security pledged over the amount of the loan determines the lender's margin of safety. If the borrower is unable to meet an obligation, the lender can sell the security to satisfy the claim. If the security is sold for an amount exceeding the amount of the loan and interest owed, the difference is remitted to the borrower. If the security is sold for less, the lender becomes a general, or unsecured, creditor for the amount of the difference. Because secured lenders do not wish to become general creditors, they usually seek security with a market value sufficiently above the amount of the loan to minimize the likelihood of their not being able to sell the security in full satisfaction of the loan. The degree of security protection a lender seeks varies with the credit worthiness of the borrower, the security the borrower has available, and the financial institution making the loan.

The value of the collateral to the lender varies according to several factors. Perhaps the most important is marketability. If the collateral can be sold quickly in an active market without depressing the price, the lender is likely to be willing to lend an amount which represents a fairly high percentage of the collateral's stated value. On the other hand, if the collateral is a special-purpose machine designed specifically for a company and has no viable secondary market, the lender may choose to lend nothing at all. The life of the collateral also matters. If the collateral has a life which parallels closely the life of the loan, it will be more valuable to the lender than collateral which is much longer-term in nature. As the collateral is liquidated into cash, the proceeds may be used to pay down the loan. Therefore, a lender will prefer short-term collateral for short-term loans and long-term collateral for long-term loans. Still another factor is the basic riskiness associated with the collateral. The greater the fluctuation in its market value or the more uncertain the lender is concerning market value, the less desirable the collateral from the standpoint of the lender. Thus, marketability, life, and riskiness determine the attractiveness of various types of collateral to a lender and, hence, the amount of financing available to a company. Before taking up specific short-term secured lending arrangements, we take a brief look at how lenders protect themselves under the Uniform Commercial Code.

Article 9 of the Code deals with security interests of lenders, the specific aspect with which we are concerned.[2] A lender who requires collateral of a borrower obtains a *security interest* in the collateral. The collateral may be accounts receivable, inventory, equipment, or other assets of the borrower. The security interest in the collateral is created by a *security agreement*, also known as a *security device*. This agreement is signed by the borrower and lender and contains a description of the collateral. In order to "perfect" a security interest in the collateral, the lender must file a copy of the security agreement or a financing statement with a public office of the state in which the collateral is located. Frequently, this office is that of the secretary of state. The filing gives public notice to other parties that the lender has a security interest in the collateral described. Before accepting collateral as security for a loan, a lender will search the public notices to see if the collateral has been pledged previously in connection with another loan. Only the lender with a valid security interest in the collateral has a prior claim on the assets and can sell the collateral in settlement of the loan.

RECEIVABLE LOANS

Assignment of accounts receivable

Accounts receivable are one of the most liquid assets of the firm; consequently, they make desirable security for a loan. From the standpoint of the lender, the major difficulties with this type of security are the cost of processing the collateral and the risk of fraud. To illustrate the nature of the arrangement, we trace through a typical assignment-of-accounts-receivable loan. A company may seek a receivable loan from either a commercial bank or a finance company. Because a bank usually charges a lower interest rate than a finance company does, the firm generally will try first to borrow from a bank.

[2]See Lester E. Denonn, "The Security Agreement," *Journal of Commercial Bank Lending*, 50 (February 1968), 32–40.

Quality and size of receivables. In evaluating the loan request, the lender will analyze the quality of the firm's receivables to determine how much to lend against them. The higher the quality of the accounts the firm maintains, the higher the percentage the lender is willing to advance against the face value of the receivables pledged. A lender does not have to accept all the borrower's accounts receivable; usually, accounts that have low credit ratings or that are unrated will be rejected. Also, government and foreign accounts usually are ineligible unless special arrangements are made. Depending upon the quality of the receivables accepted, a lender typically advances between 50 and 80 percent of their face value.

The lender is concerned not only with the quality of receivables but also with their size. The lender must keep records on each account receivable that is pledged; the smaller the average size of the accounts, the more it costs per dollar of loan to process them. Consequently, a firm that sells low-priced items on open account will generally be unable to obtain a receivable loan regardless of the quality of the accounts. The cost of processing the loan is simply too high. Occasionally a "bulk" assignment of receivables will be used to circumvent the problem. With a "bulk" assignment, the lender does not keep track of the individual accounts but records only the total amounts in the accounts assigned and the payments received. Because preventing fraud is difficult with a "bulk" assignment, the percentage advance against the face value of receivables is likely to be low—perhaps 25 percent.

Procedure. Suppose a lender has decided to extend a loan to a firm on the basis of a 75 percent advance against the face value of accounts receivable assigned. The firm then sends in a schedule of accounts showing the name of the account, the date of billings, and the amounts owed. Figure 12-3 shows an assignment schedule. The lender will sometimes require evidence of shipment, such as an invoice. Having received the schedule of accounts, the lender has the borrower sign a promissory note and a security agreement. The firm then receives 75 percent of the face value of the receivables shown on the schedule of accounts.

A receivable loan can be on either a nonnotification or a notification basis. Under the former arrangement, customers of the firm are not notified that their accounts have been pledged to the lender. When the firm receives payment on an account, it forwards this payment, together with other payments, to the lender. The lender checks the payments against its record of accounts outstanding, and reduces the amount the borrower owes by 75 percent of the total payments. The other 25 percent is credited to the borrower's account. With a nonnotification arrangement, the lender must take precautions to make sure the borrower does not withhold a payment check. With a notification arrangement, the account is notified of the assignment, and remittances are made directly to the lender. Under this arrangement, the borrower cannot withhold payments. Most firms naturally prefer to borrow on a nonnotification basis; however, the lender reserves the right to place the arrangement on a notification basis.

An accounts-receivable loan is a more or less continuous financing arrangement. As the firm generates new receivables that are acceptable to the lender, they are assigned, adding to the security base against which the firm is able to borrow.

SCHEDULE OF ACCOUNTS ASSIGNED

The undersigned hereby assigns to **WELLS FARGO BANK** the following accounts:

(LIST NAMES OR REFER TO ATTACHED)	GROSS AMOUNT	
Accounts receivable totalling_____		
evidenced by _____		
for (dates)_____		
Attached hereto and made a part hereof		
TOTAL		

The above accounts are assigned to **WELLS FARGO BANK** and a security interest is granted in accordance with the terms and conditions of the existing Continuing Security Agreement between undersigned and **WELLS FARGO BANK**, to which reference is made.

Signed _____

By: _____

Schedule No. S _____

**FIGURE 12-3
Accounts-receivable
assignment form**

Date _____

N503   —100/PAD—217—006

New receivables replace the old, and the security base and the amount of loan fluctuate accordingly. A receivable loan is a very flexible means of secured financing. As receivables build up, the firm is able to borrow additional funds to finance this buildup. Thus, it has access to "built-in" financing.

Factoring receivables

In the assignment of accounts receivable, the firm retains title to the receivables. When a firm *factors* its receivables, it actually sells them to a factor. The sale may be either with or without recourse, depending upon the type of arrangement negotiated. The factor maintains a credit department and makes credit checks on accounts. Based upon its credit investigation, the factor may refuse to buy certain accounts that it deems too risky. By factoring, a firm frequently relieves itself of the expense of maintaining a credit department and making collections. Any account that the factor is unwilling to buy is an unacceptable credit risk unless, of course, the firm wants to assume this risk on its own and ship the goods. Factoring arrangements are governed by a contract between the factor and the client. The contract frequently is for one year with an automatic provision for renewal and can be canceled only with prior notice of 30 to 60 days. Although it is customary in a factoring arrangement to notify customers that their accounts have been sold and that payments on the account should be sent directly to the factor, in many instances notification is not made. Customers continue to remit payments to the firm, which, in turn, endorses them to the factor. These endorsements frequently are camouflaged to prevent customers from learning that their accounts have been sold.

Factoring costs.   For bearing risk and servicing the receivables, the factor receives a commission, which typically is somewhat over one percent of the face value of the receivables. Commission varies according to the size of the individual accounts, the volume of receivables sold, and the quality of the accounts. Since receivables sold to the factor will not be collected from the various accounts for a period of time, the firm may wish to receive payment for the sale of its receivables before they are actually collected. On that advance, it must pay interest. Advancing payment is a lending function of the factor in addition to risk bearing and servicing the receivables. For this additional function, the factor requires compensation. If the receivables total $10,000 and the factoring fee is 2 percent, the factor will credit the firm's account with $9,800. If the firm wants to draw on this account before the receivables are collected, it will have to pay an interest charge—say $1\frac{1}{2}$ percent a month—for the use of the funds. If it wishes a cash advance of the full $9,800, and the receivables are collected, on the average, in one month, the interest cost will be approximately .015×9,800, or $147.[3] Thus, the total cost of factoring is composed of a factoring fee plus an interest charge if the firm draws upon its account before the receivables are collected. If the firm does not draw on its account until the receivables are collected, there is no interest charge. In a third alternative, the firm may leave its funds with the factor beyond the time when the receivables are collected, and it will receive interest on the account from the factor.

Flexibility.   The typical factoring arrangement is continuous. As new receivables are acquired, they are sold to the factor, and the firm's account is credited. The firm then draws upon this account as it needs funds. Sometimes the factor will allow the firm to overdraw its account during periods of peak needs and thereby borrow on an unsecured basis. Under other arrangements, the factor may withhold a reserve from the firm's account as a protection against losses. The principle sources of factoring are commercial banks, factoring subsidiaries of bank holding companies, and certain old-line factors. Originally, the business was confined to these old-line factors and to New York City. In the 1960s, the entry of banks expanded considerably the scope, reputation, and geography of the factoring business.

Factoring, like the assignment of accounts receivable, affords the firm flexibility in its financing. As sales increase and the firm needs funds, financing becomes available automatically. This eliminates the uncertainty associated with the collection cycle. Consequently, the cash flows of the firm are more predictable. Although some people attach a stigma to the company that factors, many others regard it as a perfectly acceptable method of financing. Its principal shortcoming is that it can be expensive. We must bear in mind, however, that the factor often relieves the firm of credit checkings, the cost of processing receivables, and collection expenses. For a small firm, the savings may be quite significant.

---

[3]The actual cash advance would be $9,800 less the interest cost, or $9,653.

Inventories also represent a reasonably liquid asset and are therefore suitable as security for a short-term loan. As with a receivable loan, the lender determines a percentage advance against the market value of the collateral. This percentage varies according to the quality of the inventory. Certain inventories, such as grains, are very marketable and when properly stored resist physical deterioration. The margin of safety required by the lender on a loan of this sort is fairly small, and the advance may be as high as 90 percent. On the other hand, the market for a highly specialized piece of equipment may be so narrow that a lender is unwilling to make any advance against its reported market value. Thus, not every kind of inventory can be pledged as security for a loan. The best collateral is inventory that is relatively standard and for which a ready market exists apart from the marketing organization of the borrower.

Lenders determine the percentage that they are willing to advance by considering marketability, perishability, market-price stability, and the difficulty and expense of selling the inventory to satisfy the loan. The cost of selling some inventory may be very high indeed. Lenders do not want to be in the business of liquidating collateral, but they do want to assure themselves that collateral has adequate value in case the borrower defaults in the payment of principal or interest. As is true with most secured loans, however, the actual decision to make the loan will depend upon the cash-flow ability of the borrower to service debt. There are a number of different ways a lender can obtain a secured interest in inventories, and we consider each in turn. In the first methods (floating lien, chattel mortgage, and trust receipt), the inventory remains in the possession of the borrower. In the last two methods (terminal warehouse and field warehouse receipts), the inventory is in the possession of a third party.

Floating lien

Under the Uniform Commercial Code, the borrower may pledge inventories "in general" without specifying the specific inventory involved. Under this arrangement, the lender obtains a floating lien on all inventory of the borrower. This lien is very general, and the lender may find it difficult to police. Frequently, a floating lien is requested only as additional protection and does not play a major role in determining whether or not the loan will be made. Even if the collateral is valuable, the lender usually is willing to make only a moderate advance because of the difficulty in exercising tight control over the collateral. The floating lien can be made to cover both receivables and inventories, as well as the collection of receivables. This modification gives the lender a lien on a major portion of a firm's current assets. In addition, the lien can be made to encompass almost any length of time so that it includes future as well as present inventory as security.

Chattel mortgage

With a chattel mortgage, inventories are identified specifically by serial number or by some other means. While the borrower holds title to the goods, the lender has a lien on inventory. This inventory cannot be sold unless the lender consents. Because of the rigorous identification requirements, chattel mortgages are ill suited for inventory with rapid turnover or inventory that is not easily identified because of size or other reasons. Chattel mortgages are well suited for certain capital assets such as machine tools.

Trust receipt loans

Under a trust receipt financing arrangement, the borrower holds in trust for the lender the inventory and proceeds from its sale. This type of lending arrangement, known also as floor planning, has been used extensively by automobile dealers, equipment dealers, and consumer durable goods dealers. An automobile manufacturer will ship cars to a dealer who, in turn, finances the payment for these cars through a finance company. The finance company pays the manufacturer for the cars shipped. The dealer signs a trust receipt security agreement, which specifies what can be done with the inventory. The car dealer is allowed to sell the cars but must turn the proceeds of the sale over to the lender, in payment of the loan. Inventory in trust, unlike inventory under a floating lien, is specifically identified by serial number or by other means. In our example, the finance company periodically audits the cars the dealer has on hand. The serial numbers of these cars are checked against those shown in the security agreement. The purpose of the audit is to see if the dealer has sold cars without remitting the proceeds of the sale to the finance company.

As the dealer buys new cars from the automobile manufacturer, a new trust receipt security agreement is signed taking account of the new inventory. The dealer then borrows against this new collateral, holding it in trust. Although there is tighter control over collateral with a trust receipt agreement than with a floating lien, there is still the risk of inventory's being sold without the proceeds being turned over to the lender. Consequently, the lender must exercise judgment in deciding to lend under this arrangement. A dishonest dealer can devise numerous ways to fool the lender.

Many durable-goods manufacturers finance the inventories of their distributors or dealers. Their purpose is to encourage dealers or distributors to carry reasonable stocks of goods. It is reasoned that the greater the stock, the more likely the dealer or distributor is to make a sale. Because the manufacturer is interested in selling its product, financing terms often are more attractive than they are with an "outside" lender.

Terminal warehouse receipt loans

A borrower secures a terminal warehouse receipt loan by storing inventory with a public, or terminal, warehousing company. The warehouse company issues a warehouse receipt, which evidences title to specified goods that are located in the warehouse. An example of a warehouse receipt is shown in Fig. 12-4. The warehouse receipt gives the lender a security interest in the goods, against which a loan can be made to the borrower. Under such an arrangement, the warehouseman can release the collateral to the borrower only when authorized to do

FIGURE 12-4 Warehouse receipt.

so by the lender. Consequently, the lender is able to maintain strict control over the collateral and will release collateral only when the borrower pays a portion of the loan. For protection, the lender usually requires the borrower to take out an insurance policy with a loss-payable clause in favor of the lender.

Warehouse receipts may be either nonnegotiable or negotiable. A nonnegotiable warehouse receipt is issued in favor of a specific party—in this case, the lender—who is given title to the goods and has sole authority to release them. A negotiable warehouse receipt can be transferred by endorsement. Before goods can be released, the negotiable receipt must be presented to the warehouseman. A negotiable receipt is useful when title to the goods is transferred from one party to another while the goods are in storage. With a nonnegotiable receipt, the release of goods can be authorized only in writing. Most lending arrangements are based upon nonnegotiable receipts.

Field warehouse receipt loans

In a terminal warehouse receipt loan, the goods are located in a public warehouse. Another arrangement, known as field warehousing, permits loans to be made against inventory that is located on the borrower's premises. Under this arrangement, a field warehousing company sets off a designated storage area on the borrower's premises for the inventory pledged as collateral. The field warehousing company has sole access to this area and is supposed to maintain strict control over it. (The goods that serve as collateral are segregated from the borrower's other inventory.) The field warehousing company issues a warehouse receipt as described in the preceding section, and the lender extends a loan based upon the collateral value of the inventory. The field warehouse arrangement is a useful means of financing when it is not desirable, either because of the expense or because of the inconvenience, to place the inventory in a public warehouse. Field warehouse receipt lending is particularly appropriate when a borrower must make frequent use of inventory. Because of the need to pay the field warehousing company's expenses, the cost of this method of financing can be relatively high.

The warehouse receipt, as evidence of collateral, is only as good as the issuing warehousing company. When administered properly, a warehouse receipt loan affords the lender a high degree of control over the collateral; however, sufficient examples of fraud show that the warehouse receipt does not always evidence actual value. The warehouseman must exercise strict control. A grain elevator that is alleged to be full may, in fact, be empty. Upon close examination, we may find that barrels reported to contain chemical concentrate actually contain water.[4]

COMPOSITION OF SHORT-TERM FINANCING

In this and the preceding chapter we considered various sources of short-term financing. Because the total amount of short-term financing was assumed to have been determined according to the framework presented in chapter 8, only determination of the best combination need be considered in this chapter. The appropriate mix, or the weighting, of alternative sources will depend upon considerations of cost, availability, timing, flexibility, and the degree to which the assets of the firm are encumbered. Central to any meaningful analysis of alternative sources of funds is a comparison of their costs, and inextricably related to the question of cost is the problem of timing. Differentials in cost between various alternatives are not necessarily constant over time. Indeed, they fluctuate in keeping with changing financial-market conditions. Thus, timing bears heavily on the question of the most appropriate mix of short-term financing.

Naturally, the availability of financing is important. If a firm cannot borrow through commercial paper or through a bank because of its low credit standing, it must turn to alternative sources. The lower the credit standing of the firm, of

---

[4]For a lively discussion of the various ways frauds have taken place against secured lenders, see Monroe R. Lazere, "Swinging Swindles and Creepy Frauds," *Journal of Commercial Bank Lending*, 60 (September 1977), 44–52.

course, the fewer the sources of short-term financing available to it. Flexibility with respect to short-term financing pertains to the ability of the firm to pay off a loan as well as to its ability to renew it or increase it. With factoring and also with a bank loan, the firm can pay off the loan when it has surplus funds and thereby reduce its overall interest costs. For commercial paper, the firm must wait until final maturity before paying off the loan.

Flexibility relates also to how easily the firm can increase its loan on short notice. With a line of credit or revolving credit at a commercial bank, it is an easy matter to increase borrowings, assuming the maximum has not been reached. With other forms of short-term financing, the firm is less flexible. Finally, the degree to which assets are encumbered bears on the decision. With secured loans, lenders obtain a lien on the assets of the firm. This secured position constrains the firm in future financing. Whereas receivables are actually sold under a factoring arrangement, the principle is the same. In this case, the firm sells one of its most liquid assets, thus reducing its credit worthiness in the minds of creditors.

All of these factors influence the firm in deciding upon the most appropriate mix of short-term financing. Because cost is perhaps the key factor, differences in other factors should be compared with differences in cost. What is the cheapest source of financing from the standpoint of explicit costs may not be the cheapest source when flexibility, timing, and the degree to which assets are encumbered are considered. Although it would be desirable to express sources of short-term financing in terms of both explicit and implicit costs, the latter are hard to quantify. A more practical approach is to list available sources according to their explicit costs and then consider the other factors to see if they change the ranking as it relates to total desirability. Because the financing needs of the firm change over time, multiple sources of short-term financing should be explored on a continuous basis.

SUMMARY

Commercial paper is used only by well established, high-quality companies. The evidence of debt is an unsecured short-term promissory note that is sold in the money market. Commercial paper is sold either through dealers or directly to investors. The direct method is used by large sales finance companies, and about two-thirds of commercial paper is placed in this manner. The principal advantage of commercial paper is that its yield is less than the rate of interest a company would have to pay on a bank loan. Bankers' acceptance financing is another type of money-market credit. Usually associated with a foreign trade transaction, the acceptance is highly marketable and can be a very desirable source of short-term funds.

Short-term loans can be divided into two types: unsecured and secured. Unsecured credit usually is confined to bank loans under a line of credit, under a revolving-credit agreement, or on a transaction basis. Typically, banks require balances to compensate for a lending arrangement. If the borrower is required to maintain balances above those that it would maintain ordinarily, the effective cost of borrowing is increased. Interest rates on business loans are a function of the cost of funds to banks, the existing prime rate, the credit worthiness of the borrower, and the profitability of the relationship for the bank.

Many firms unable to obtain unsecured credit are required by the lender to pledge security. In giving a secured loan, the lender looks first to the cash-flow ability of the company to service debt and, if this source of loan repayment might fail, to the collateral value of the security. To provide a margin of safety, a lender usually will advance somewhat less than the market value of the collateral. The percentage advance varies according to the quality of the collateral pledged and the control the lender has over this collateral.

Accounts receivable and inventory are the principal assets used to secure short-term business loans. Receivables may either be pledged to secure a loan or sold to a factor. Inventory loans can be under a general lien, under a trust receipt, or under terminal warehouse or field warehouse receipt arrangements. The most appropriate mix of short-term financing will depend upon consideration of relative cost, availability, flexibility, timing, and the degree to which the assets of the firm are encumbered.

QUESTIONS

1. Why is the rate on commercial paper usually less than the prime rate charged by bankers and more than the Treasury bill rate?

2. Why would a firm borrow bank funds at higher rates instead of issuing commercial paper?

3. Why would a firm invest its temporary excess liquidity in Treasury bills instead of buying higher-yielding commercial paper?

4. Who is able to issue commercial paper and for what purpose?

5. What determines whether a lending arrangement is unsecured or secured?

6. As a lender, how would you determine the percentage you are willing to advance against a particular type of collateral?

7. As a financial consultant to a company, how would you go about recommending whether to use an assignment of accounts receivable or a factoring arrangement?

8. Why might a company prefer an unsecured source of funds such as a line of credit or a revolving-credit agreement to some form of secured financing such as a receivable loan or chattel mortgage, even if the latter source is less expensive?

9. List assets that you would accept as collateral on a loan in your order of preference. Justify your priorities.

10. Inventory and accounts receivable are among the most liquid assets a firm owns. Does this liquidity make them the safest security available to the lender? Explain.

11. The settlements in the cases of Billie Sol Estes (the fertilizer scandal), Anthony DeAngelis (the salad oil scandal), and many other less notorious bankruptcies suggest that secured lenders are not really secure. Suggest methods of protecting the lender in short-term financing.

12. Which of the methods of short-term financing considered in this chapter would be most likely to be used by the following? Explain your reasoning.

a) A raw-material processor such as a mining or lumber company

b) A retail sales concern such as an appliance retailer or high-fidelity equipment dealer

c) An international company

d) A consumer durable dealer such as an automobile sales agency

13. What reaction might a firm expect from trade creditors when it pledges its receivables to secure a bank loan?

14. As the firm's financial manager, what factors would you consider in choosing a primary bank?

PROBLEMS

1. The Sphinx Supply Company needs to increase its working capital by $100,000. The following three alternatives of financing are available:

a) Forego cash discounts, granted on a basis of 3/10, net 30.

b) Borrow from the bank at 15 percent. This alternative would necessitate maintaining a 25 percent compensating balance.

c) Issue commercial paper at 14 percent. The cost of placing the issue would be $1,000 each six months.

Assuming the firm would prefer the flexibility of bank financing, provided the additional cost of this flexibility was no more than 2 percent per annum, which alternative should Sphinx select?

2. Bork Corporation wishes to borrow $100,000 for one year. It has the following alternatives available to it.

a) An 8 percent loan on a discount basis with 20 percent compensating balances required.

b) A 9 percent loan on a discount basis with 10 percent compensating balances required.

c) A 10½ percent loan on a collect basis with no compensating balance requirement.

Which alternative should Bork Corporation choose if it is concerned with the effective interest rate?

3. Commercial paper has no stipulated interest rate. It is sold on a discount basis, and the amount of the discount determines the interest cost to the issuer. On the basis of the following information, determine the percentage interest cost on an annual basis for each of the following issues (assume a 360-day year):

Issue	Face value	Price	Time to maturity
(a)	$25,000	$24,500	60 days
(b)	100,000	96,500	180 days
(c)	50,000	48,800	90 days
(d)	75,000	71,300	270 days
(e)	100,000	99,100	30 days

4. The Selby Gaming Manufacturing Company has experienced a severe cash squeeze and needs $200,000 over the next 90 days. The company already has pledged its receivables in support of a loan. However, it does have $570,000 in unencumbered inventories. Determine the best financing alternative from the following two that are available.

a) The Cody National Bank of Reno will lend against finished goods provided they are placed in a public warehouse under its control. As the finished goods are released for sale, the loan is reduced by the proceeds of the sale. The company currently has $300,000 in finished-goods inventory and would expect to replace finished goods that are sold out of the warehouse with new finished goods, so that it could borrow the full $200,000 for 90 days. The interest rate is 10 percent, and the company will pay warehousing costs of $3,000. Finally, it will experience a reduction in efficiency as a result of this arrangement. Management estimates that the lower efficiency will reduce before-tax profits by $5,000.

b) The Zarlotti Finance Company will lend the company the money under a floating lien on all of its inventories. The rate is 23 percent, but no additional expenses will be incurred.

5. The Bone Company has been factoring its accounts receivable for the past five years. The factor charges a fee of 2 percent and will lend up to 80 percent of the volume of receivables purchased for an additional 1.5 percent per month. The firm typically has sales of $500,000 per month, 70 percent of which are on credit. By using the factor, two savings are effected:

a) $2,000 per month that would be required to support a credit department

b) A bad-debt expense of 1 percent on credit sales.

The firm's bank has recently offered to lend the firm up to 80 percent of the face value of the receivables shown on the schedule of accounts. The bank would charge 15 percent per annum interest plus a 2 percent processing charge per dollar of receivables lending. The firm extends terms of net 30, and all customers who pay their bills do so by the thirtieth day. Should the firm discontinue its factoring arrangement in favor of the bank's offer if the firm borrows, on the average, $100,000 per month on its receivables?

6. The Barnes Corporation has just acquired a large account. As a result, it needs an additional $75,000 in working capital immediately. It has been determined that there are three feasible sources of funds:

a) Trade credit: the company buys about $50,000 of materials per month on terms of 2/30, net 90. Discounts are taken.

b) Bank loan: the firm's bank will loan $100,000 at 9 percent. A 20 percent compensating balance will be required.

c) A factor will buy the company's receivables ($100,000 per month), which have a collection period of 60 days. The factor will advance up to 75 percent of the face value of the receivables for an annual charge of 8 percent. The factor also will charge a 2 percent fee on all receivables purchased. It has been estimated that the factor's services will save the company a credit department expense and bad-debts expense of $1,500 per month.

Which alternative should Barnes select?

7. Vesco-Zultch Corporation is a chain of appliance stores in Chicago. It needs to finance all of its inventories which average the following during the four quarters of the year (in thousands):

Quarter	1	2	3	4
Inventory level (in thousands)	$1,600	$2,100	$1,500	$3,200

Vesco-Zultch presently utilizes a finance company loan secured by a floating lien. The interest rate is the prime rate plus 7½ percent, but no additional expenses are incurred. The Boundary Illinois National Bank of Chicago is bidding for the Vesco-Zultch business. It has proposed a trust receipt financing arrangement. The interest rate will be 2½ percent above the prime rate, with servicing costs of $20,000 each quarter. Should the company switch financing arrangements?

8. The Coral Machine Tool Company had the following balance sheet at the close of its fiscal year last month:

Cash	$ 14,000	Accounts payable	$240,000
Receivables	196,000	Bank loan	170,000
Inventories	170,000	Current liabilities	$410,000
Current assets	$380,000	Mortgage loan	240,000
Fixed assets	473,000	Common stock	50,000
		Retained earnings	153,000
	$853,000		$853,000

The company had the following income statement for the year:

Sales		$2,000,000
Cost of goods sold:		
Purchases	$960,000	
Wages	600,000	
Depreciation	60,000	1,620,000
Gross profit		$ 380,000
Expenses		310,000
Profit before taxes		$ 70,000
Taxes		33,000
Profit after taxes		$ 37,000

The company has approached the bank to increase its loan so that the company can become more current in the trade and avail itself of certain cash discounts. Suppliers are becoming very difficult. Paying higher prices and being unable to take cash discounts, Coral estimates that its costs are $40,000 more per year than they would be if its average payable were 30 days in length.

a) How much additional financing is necessary to bring the average payable collection period to 30 days?

b) What are some of the problems from the standpoint of the bank? Is it likely to extend the additional credit on an unsecured basis?

SELECTED REFERENCES

BARTLER, BRIT, JR., and RICHARD J. RENDLEMAN, JR., "Fee Based Pricing of Fixed Rate Bank Loan Commitments," *Financial Management,* 8 (Spring 1979), 13–20.

CAMPBELL, TIM S., "A Model of the Market for Lines of Credit," *Journal of Finance,* 33 (March 1978), 231–43.

CRANE, DWIGHT B., and WILLIAM L. WHITE, "Who Benefits from a Floating Prime Rate," *Harvard Business Review,* 50 (January–February 1972), 121–29.

CROSSE, HOWARD D., and GEORGE H. HEMPEL, *Management Policies for Commercial Banks,* 3rd ed. Englewood Cliffs, N.J.: Prentice-Hall, 1980.

DENONN, LESTER E., "The Security Agreement," *Journal of Commercial Bank Lending,* 50 (February 1968), 32–40.

LAZERE, MONROE R., "Swinging Swindles and Creepy Frauds," *Journal of Commercial Bank Lending,* 60 (September 1977), 44–52.

MANSFIELD, CHARLES F., JR., "The Function of Credit Analysis in a U.S. Commercial Bank," *Journal of Commercial Bank Lending,* 61 (September 1979), 21–34.

QUARLES, J. CARSON, "The Floating Lien," *Journal of Commercial Bank Lending,* 53 (November 1970), 51–58.

QUILL, GERALD D., JOHN C. CRESCI, and BRUCE D. SHUTER, "Some Considerations about Secured Lending," *Journal of Commercial Bank Lending,* 59 (April 1977), 41–56.

SCOTT, JAMES H., JR., "Bankruptcy, Secured Debt, and Optimal Capital Structure," *Journal of Finance,* 32 (March 1977), 1–19.

SMITH, KEITH V., *Guide to Working Capital Management.* New York: McGraw-Hill 1979, chaps. 7 and 8.

STONE, BERNELL K., "Allocating Credit Lines, Planned Borrowing, and Tangible Services over a Company's Banking System," *Financial Management,* 4 (Summer 1975), 65–78.

INVESTING
IN CAPITAL
ASSETS

V

Capital Budgeting 13

CAPITAL FORMATION

Capital expenditure decisions of corporations greatly influence the overall growth of the economy. A society's productive resources, such as land, machines, buildings, natural resources, and workers, are limited. These resources may all be devoted to producing goods and services for current consumption or a part of them may go toward things that will enhance the nation's ability to produce, and hence consume, in the future. This process might involve the production of machinery, the exploration for iron ore, or the training of workers in new technology. Capital formation can be defined as any investment that increases the productive capacity of society. If resources are fully employed, the only way to make such investments is to refrain from current consumption. If resources are less than fully employed, it is possible to have capital formation without necessarily foregoing current consumption.

Corporate capital expenditures for new plant and equipment have ranged from 7 to $8\frac{1}{2}$ percent of the gross national product in recent years. At the end of an economic downturn the percentage tends to be in the lower part of this range, and in periods of economic prosperity it tends to be in the upper part. In recent years, much of the growth in expenditures has been attributed to inflation as opposed to a growth in real outlays.

When a business firm makes a capital investment, it incurs a current cash outlay for future benefits. Usually, these benefits are expected beyond one year in the future. Examples include investment in assets such as equipment, buildings, and land, as well as the introduction of a new product, a new distribution system, or a new program for research and development. Thus, the firm's future success and profitability depends upon investment decisions made currently.

An investment proposal should be judged in relation to whether it provides a return equal to, or greater than, that required by investors.[1] To simplify our investigation of the methods of capital budgeting in this chapter, we assume the required rate of return is given and is the same for all investment projects. This assumption implies that the selection of any investment project does not alter the business-risk complexion of the firm as perceived by suppliers of capital. In chapter 15 we investigate how to determine the required rate of return, and in chapter 14 we allow for the fact that different investment projects have different degrees of business risk. As a result, the selection of an investment project may affect the business-risk complexion of the firm, which, in turn, may affect the rate of return required by investors. For purposes of introducing capital budgeting in this chapter, however, we hold risk constant.

INFORMATION REQUIRED

Capital budgeting involves

1. Generation of investment proposals
2. Estimate of cash flows for the proposals
3. Evaluation of cash flows
4. Selection of projects based upon an acceptance criterion
5. Continual reevaluation of investment projects after their acceptance

Starting with the first, investment proposals can emanate from a variety of sources. For purposes of analysis, projects may be classified into one of five categories:

1. New products or expansion of existing products
2. Replacement of equipment or buildings
3. Research and development
4. Exploration
5. Others

The fifth category comprises miscellaneous items such as the expenditure of funds to comply with certain health standards or the acquisition of a pollution-control

[1]The development of this chapter assumes the reader has covered chapter 4 on the mathematics of finance.

device. For a new product, the proposal usually originates in the marketing department. On the other hand, a proposal to replace a piece of equipment with a more sophisticated model usually emanates from the production area of the firm. In each case, efficient administrative procedures are needed for channeling investment requests.

Most firms screen proposals at multiple levels of authority. For a proposal originating in the production area, the hierarchy of authority might run from (1) section chiefs to (2) plant managers to (3) the vice-president for operations to (4) a capital-expenditures committee under the financial manager to (5) the president to (6) the board of directors. How high a proposal must go before it is finally approved usually depends upon its size. The greater the capital outlay, the greater the number of screens usually required. Plant managers may be able to approve moderate-sized projects on their own, but only higher levels of authority approve larger ones. Because the administrative procedures for screening investment proposals vary greatly from firm to firm, it is not possible to generalize. The best procedure will depend upon the circumstances. It is clear, however, that companies are becoming increasingly sophisticated in their approach to capital budgeting.[2]

Estimating cash flows

One of the most important tasks in capital budgeting is estimating future cash flows for a project. The final results we obtain are only as good as the accuracy of our estimates. Since cash, not income, is central to all decisions of the firm, we express whatever benefits we expect from a project in terms of cash flows rather than income. The firm invests cash now in the hope of receiving cash returns in a greater amount in the future. Only cash receipts can be reinvested in the firm or paid to stockholders in the form of dividends. In capital budgeting, good guys may get credit, but effective managers get cash.

For each investment proposal, we need to provide information on expected future cash flows on an after-tax basis. In addition, the information must be provided on an *incremental* basis, so that we analyze only the difference between the cash flows of the firm with and without the project. For example, if a firm contemplates a new product that is likely to compete with existing products, it is

[2]For surveys of the administrative practices of companies with respect to capital budgeting as well as of the evaluation techniques being used, see J. William Petty, David F. Scott, Jr., and Monroe M. Bird, "The Capital Expenditure Decision-Making Process of Large Corporations," *Engineering Economist*, 20 (Spring 1975), 159–72; Lawrence D. Schall, Gary L. Sundem, and William R. Geijsbeek, Jr., "Survey and Analysis of Capital Budgeting Methods," *Journal of Finance*, 33 (March 1978), 281–87; Lawrence J. Gitman and John R. Forrester, Jr., "Forecasting and Evaluation Practices and Performance: A Survey of Capital Budgeting Techniques Used by Major U.S. Firms," *Financial Management*, 6 (Fall 1977), 66–71; J. William Petty and Oswald D. Bowlin, "The Financial Manager and Quantitative Decision Models," *Financial Management*, 4 (Winter 1976), 32–41; Meir J. Rosenblatt, "A Survey and Analysis of Capital Budgeting Decision Process in Multi-Division Firms," *Engineering Economist*, 25 (Summer 1980), 259–73; and Suk H. Kim and Edward J. Farragher, "Current Capital Budgeting Practices," *Management Accounting*, 28 (June, 1981), 26–30.

See also James B. Weaver, "Organizing and Maintaining a Capital Expenditure Program," *Engineering Economist*, 20 (Fall 1974), 1–36; and E. Eugene Carter, "Designing the Capital Budgeting Process," *TIMS Studies in the Management Sciences*, 5 (1977), 25–42, for a discussion of administrative procedures. Finally, for a discussion of the importance of a post completion audit as well as of its form, see James. S. Schnell and Roy S. Nicolosi, "Capital Expenditure Feedback; Project Reappraisal," *Engineering Economist*, 19 (Summer 1974), 253–61.

not appropriate to express cash flows in terms of the estimated sales of the new product. We must take into account probable "cannibalization" of existing products, and we must make our cash-flow estimates on the basis of incremental sales. The key is to analyze the situation with and without the new investment. Only incremental cash flows matter.

In this regard, sunk costs must be ignored. One is concerned with incremental costs and benefits: and the recovery of past costs is irrelevant. They are bygones and should not enter into the decision process. Also, we must be mindful that certain costs do not necessarily involve a dollar outlay. If we have allocated plant space to a project and this space can be used for something else, its opportunity cost must be included in the project's evaluation. If a presently unused building can be sold for $300,000, that amount should be treated as a cash outlay at the outset of the project. Thus, in deriving cash flows we must consider appropriate opportunity costs.

To illustrate the information needed for a capital-budgeting decision, consider the following situation. A firm is considering the introduction of a new product. To launch the product, it will need to spend $150,000 for special equipment and the initial advertising campaign. The marketing department envisions the product life to be 6 years and expects incremental sales revenue to be

Year 1	Year 2	Year 3	Year 4	Year 5	Year 6
$60,000	$120,000	$160,000	$180,000	$110.000	$50,000

Cash outflows include labor and maintenance costs, material costs, and various other expenses associated with the product. As with sales, these costs must be estimated on an incremental basis. In addition to these outflows, the firm will need to pay higher taxes if the new product generates higher profits; and this incremental outlay must be included. Suppose that on the basis of these considerations the firm estimates total incremental cash outflows to be

Year 1	Year 2	Year 3	Year 4	Year 5	Year 6
$40,000	$70,000	$100,000	$100,000	$70,000	$40,000

Because depreciation is a noncash expense, it is not included in these outflows. The expected net cash flows from the project are

	Initial cost	Year 1	Year 2	Year 3	Year 4	Year 5	Year 6
Cash inflows		$60,000	$120,000	$160,000	$180,000	$110,000	$50,000
Cash outflows	$150,000	40,000	70,000	100,000	100,000	70,000	40,000
Net cash flows	−$150,000	$20,000	$ 50,000	$ 60,000	$ 80,000	$ 40,000	$10,000

Thus, for an initial cash outflow of $150,000, the firm expects to generate net cash flows of $20,000, $50,000, $60,000, $80,000, $40,000, and $10,000 over the next 6 years. These cash flows represent the relevant information we need in order to judge the attractiveness of the project.

Replacement decisions and depreciation.   To go to a somewhat more complicated replacement decision example involving taxes suppose that we are considering the purchase of a new machine to replace an old lathe and that we need to obtain cash-flow information in order to evaluate the attractiveness of this project. The purchase price of the new machine is $18,500; and it will require an additional $1,500 to install, bringing the total cost to $20,000. We can sell the old machine for its depreciated book value of $2,000. The initial net cash outflow for the investment project, therefore, is $18,000. The new machine should cut labor and maintenance costs and effect other cash savings totaling $7,600 a year before taxes for the next 5 years, after which it will probably not provide any savings, nor will it have a salvage value. These savings represent the net savings to the firm if it replaces the old machine with the new. In other words, we are concerned with the difference between the cash flows resulting from the two alternatives: continuing with the old machine or replacing it with a new one.

Because a machine of this sort has a useful life in excess of one year, we cannot charge its cost against income for tax purposes but must depreciate it. We then deduct depreciation from income in order to compute taxable income. As discussed in chapter 2, capital assets fall into defined cost recovery classes of 3, 5, 10, or 15 years, depending on their nature. The property class in which an asset falls determines its depreciable life for tax purposes. For ease of understanding, suppose for now that the machine we are considering falls into the 5-year property category and that the firm employs straight-line depreciation.

Later in the chapter we consider the exact depreciation that may be deducted under the accelerated cost recovery system (ACRS) of the 1981 Tax Act. For simplicity of illustration here, we assume that straight-line depreciation is employed. As a result, the annual depreciation charge is 20 percent of the total depreciable cost of $20,000, or $4,000 a year. Assume additionally that the corporate income tax rate is 50 percent. Moreover, assume that the old machine has

TABLE 13-1 ⟍ Determining the net cash flow

	Book account	Cash-flow account
Annual cash savings	$7,600	$7,600
Depreciation on new machine	4,000	
Less depreciation on old machine	400	
Additional depreciation charge	$3,600	
Additional income before taxes	4,000	
Income tax (50%)	2,000	2,000
Additional income after taxes	$2,000	
Annual net cash flow		$5,600

a remaining depreciable life of 5 years, that there is no expected salvage value at the end of this time, and that the machine also is subject to straight-line depreciation. Thus, the annual depreciation charge on the old machine is 20 percent of its depreciated book value of $2,000, or $400 a year. Because we are interested in the incremental impact of the project, we must subtract depreciation charges on the old machine from depreciation charges on the new one to obtain the incremental depreciation charges associated with the project. Given the information cited, we now are able to calculate the expected net cash flow (after taxes) resulting from the acceptance of the project. It is shown in Table 13-1.

In figuring the net cash flow, we simply deduct the additional cash outlay for federal income taxes from the annual cash savings. The expected annual net cash inflow for this replacement proposal is $5,600 for each of the next 5 years; this figure compares with additional income after taxes of $2,000 a year. The cash flow and net profit figures differ by the amount of additional depreciation. Because our concern is not with income, as such, but with cash flows, we are interested in the right-hand column. For an initial cash outlay of $18,000, then, we are able to replace an older machine with a new one that is expected to result in net cash savings of $5,600 a year over the next 5 years. As in the previous example, the relevant cash-flow information for capital-budgeting purposes is expressed on an incremental, after-tax basis.

METHODS FOR EVALUATING PROJECTS

Once we have collected the necessary information, we are able to evaluate the attractiveness of the various investment proposals under consideration. The investment decision will be either to accept or to reject the proposal. In this section, we evaluate four methods of capital budgeting:

poor
1. Average-rate-of-return
2. Payback
3. Internal rate of return
Good
4. Net present value
5. Profitability

The first two are approximate methods for assessing the economic worth of a project. For simplicity, we assume throughout that the expected cash flows are realized at the end of each year.

Average rate of return

This accounting method represents the ratio of the average annual profits after taxes to the average investment in the project. In our previous example, the average annual book earnings for the 5-year period are $2,000; and the average net investment in the project, assuming straight-line depreciation, is $18,000/2, or $9,000. Therefore,

$$\text{Average rate of return} = \frac{\$2,000}{\$9,000} = 22.22 \text{ percent} \qquad (13\text{-}1)$$

The average-rate-of-return method is sometimes based upon the original investment rather than upon the average investment. In the above example, the average rate of return would be $2,000/$18,000 = 11.11 percent under this version of the average-rate-of-return method. Once the average rate of return for a proposal has been calculated, it may be compared with a required rate of return to determine if a particular proposal should be accepted or rejected.

The principal virtue of the average-rate-of-return method is its simplicity; it makes use of readily available accounting information. Once the average rate of return for a proposal has been calculated, it may be compared with a required, or cutoff, rate of return to determine if a particular proposal should be accepted or rejected. The principal shortcomings of the method are that it is based upon accounting income rather than upon cash flows and that it fails to take account of the timing of cash inflows and outflows. The time value of money is ignored; benefits in the last year are valued the same as benefits in the first year.

Suppose that we have three investment proposals, each costing $9,000 and each having an economic and depreciable life of 3 years. Assume that these proposals are expected to provide the following book profits and cash flows over the next 3 years:

	Project A		Project B		Project C	
Period	Book Profit	Net Cash Flow	Book Profit	Net Cash Flow	Book Profit	Net Cash Flow
1	$3,000	$6,000	$2,000	$5,000	$1,000	$4,000
2	2,000	5,000	2,000	5,000	2,000	5,000
3	1,000	4,000	2,000	5,000	3,000	6,000

Each proposal will have the same average rate of return: $2,000/$4,500, or 44 percent; however, few, if any, firms would be equally favorable to all three projects. Most would prefer project A, which provides a larger portion of total cash benefits in the first year. For this reason, the average rate of return leaves much to be desired as a method for project selection.

Payback method

The payback period of an investment project tells us the number of years required to recover our initial cash investment. It is the ratio of the initial fixed investment over the annual cash inflows for the recovery period. For our example,

$$\text{Payback period} = \frac{\$18,000}{\$5,600} = 3.2 \text{ years} \tag{13-2}$$

If the annual cash inflows are not equal, the job of calculation is somewhat more difficult. Suppose that annual cash inflows are $4,000 in the first year, $6,000 in the second and third years, and $4,000 in the fourth and fifth years. In the first 3 years, $16,000 of the original investment will be recovered, followed by $4,000 in the fourth year. With an initial cash investment of $18,000, the payback period is 3 years + ($2,000/$4,000), or 3½ years.

If the payback period calculated is less than some maximum acceptable payback period, the proposal is accepted; if not, it is rejected. If the required payback period were 4 years, the project in our example would be accepted. The major shortcoming of the payback method is that it fails to consider cash flows after the payback period; consequently, it cannot be regarded as a measure of profitability. Two proposals costing $10,000 each would have the same payback period if they both had annual net cash inflows of $5,000 in the first two years; but one project might be expected to provide no cash flows after 2 years, whereas the other might be expected to provide cash flows of $5,000 in each of the next 3 years. Thus, the payback method can be deceptive as a yardstick of profitability. In addition to this shortcoming, the method does not take account of the magnitude or timing of cash flows during the payback period; it considers only the recovery period as a whole.

The method does give a rough indication of the liquidity of a project. Many managers use it also as a crude measure of risk; but as we shall see in the subsequent chapter, other analytical approaches do a much better job. While the payback method may provide useful insights, it is best employed as a supplement to the internal-rate-of return or net-present-value methods.

Internal-rate-of-return method

Because of the various shortcomings in the average-rate-of-return and payback methods, it generally is felt that discounted cash-flow methods provide a more objective basis for evaluating and selecting investment projects. These methods take account of both the magnitude and the timing of expected cash flows in each period of a project's life. In any economy in which capital has value, the time value of money is an important concept. Stockholders place a higher value on an investment project that promises returns over the next 5 years than on a project that promises identical returns for years 6 through 10. Consequently, the timing of expected future cash flows is extremely important in the investment decision.

Discounted cash-flow methods enable us to isolate differences in the timing of cash flows for various projects by discounting these cash flows to their present values. The two discounted cash-flow methods are the internal-rate-of-return method and the present-value method, and we consider each in turn. This presentation builds on the foundations established in chapter 4 when we covered the mathematics of finance and in chapter 5 when we took up the returns on common stocks.

The internal rate of return for an investment proposal is the discount rate that equates the present value of the expected cash outflows with the present value of the expected inflows. If the initial cash outlay or cost occurs at time 0, it is represented by that rate, r, such that

$$X_0 = \frac{X_1}{(1 + r)} + \frac{X_2}{(1 + r)^2} + \cdots + \frac{X_n}{(1 + r)^n} \qquad (13\text{-}3)$$

Thus, r is the rate that discounts the stream of future cash flows—X_1 through X_n—to equal in present value the initial outlay at time 0—X_0. For our example, the problem can be expressed as

$$\$18,000 = \frac{\$5,600}{(1 + r)} + \frac{\$5,600}{(1 + r)^2} + \frac{\$5,600}{(1 + r)^3} + \frac{\$5,600}{(1 + r)^4} + \frac{\$5,600}{(1 + r)^5} \quad \text{(13-4)}$$

Solving for the internal rate of return, r, sometimes involves a trial-and-error procedure using present-value tables. Fortunately, there are computer programs and special calculators for solving for the internal rate of return, and these eliminate the arduous computations involved in the trial-and-error procedure. Still, there are times when, by necessity, one must resort to the latter method. To illustrate it, consider again our example. The cash-flow stream is represented by an even series of cash flows of $5,600, to be received at the end of each of the next 5 years. We want to determine the discount factor that, when multiplied by $5,600, equals the cash outlay of $18,000 at time 0. Suppose that we start with the discount rates—14 percent, 16 percent, and 18 percent—and calculate the present value of the cash-flow stream. For the different discount rates, we find, using Table B in the Appendix at the end of the book,

Discount rate	Discount factor	Cash flow each year	Present value of stream
18%	3.1272	$5,600	$17,512.32
16	3.2743	5,600	18,336.08
14	3.4331	5,600	19,225.36

When we compare the present value of the stream with the initial outlay of $18,000, we see that the internal rate of return necessary to discount the stream to $18,000 falls between 16 and 18 percent, being closer to 16 than to 18 percent. To approximate the actual rate, we interpolate between 16 and 17 percent as follows:

	Discount rate	Present value
	16%	$18,336.08
	17	17,916.08
Difference	1%	$ 420.00
$\dfrac{336.08}{420.00} = .8$	16% + .8% = 16.8%	

Thus, the internal rate of return necessary to equate the present value of the cash inflows with the present value of the outflows is approximately 16.8 percent. Note that interpolation gives only an approximation of the exact percentage; the relationship between the two discount rates is not linear with respect to present value.

When, as above, the cash-flow stream is an even series, and the initial outlay occurs at time 0, there really is no need for trial and error. We simply divide the initial outlay by the cash flow and search for the nearest discount factor. Using our example, we divide $18,000 by $5,600, obtaining 3.214. The nearest discount factor on the 5-year row in Table B at the end of the book is 3.2743, and this figure corresponds to a discount rate of 16 percent. Inasmuch as 3.214 is less than 3.2743, we know that the actual rate lies between 16 and 17 percent, and we interpolate accordingly. When the cash-flow stream is an uneven series, the task is more difficult, and here we must resort to trial and error. With practice, a person can come surprisingly close in selecting discount rates from which to start.

In some circumstances, there will be more than one internal rate of return that equates the present value of the cash inflows with the present value of cash outflows. Although the existence of multiple internal rates of return is unusual, we do examine the problem in Appendix A to this chapter.

Acceptance criterion. The acceptance criterion generally employed with the internal-rate-of-return method is to compare the internal rate of return with a required rate of return, known also as the cutoff, or hurdle, rate. If the internal rate of return exceeds the required rate, the project is accepted; if not, it is rejected. If the required rate of return is 12 percent and this criterion is used, the investment proposal considered above will be accepted. If the required rate of return is the return investors expect the firm to earn on the project, accepting a project with an internal rate of return in excess of the required rate of return should result in an increase in the market price of the stock, because the firm accepts a project with a return greater than that required to maintain the present market price per share. Chapter 16 will say much more about relating the investment decision to the objective of the firm. We assume for now that the required rate of return is given.

Net present value method

Like the internal-rate-of-return method, the present-value method is a discounted cash-flow approach to capital budgeting. Recall from chapter 4 that with the present-value approach, all cash flows are discounted to present value, using the required rate of return. The net present value of an investment proposal is

$$NPV = X_0 + \frac{X_1}{(1 + k)} + \frac{X_2}{(1 + k)^2} + \cdots + \frac{X_n}{(1 + k)^n} \qquad (13\text{-}5)$$

where k is the required rate of return. If the sum of these discounted cash flows is zero or more, the proposal is accepted; if not, it is rejected. Another way to express the acceptance criterion is to say that the project will be accepted if the present value of cash inflows exceeds the present value of cash outflows. The rationale behind the acceptance criterion is the same as that behind the internal-rate-of-return method. If the required rate of return is the return investors expect the firm to earn on the investment proposal, and the firm accepts a proposal with a net present value greater than zero, the market price of the stock should rise. Again, the firm is taking on a project with a return greater than that necessary to leave the market price of the stock unchanged.

If we assume a required rate of return of 12 percent after taxes, the net present value of our example problem is

$$NPV = -\$18,000 + \frac{\$5,600}{(1.12)} + \frac{\$5,600}{(1.12)^2} + \frac{\$5,600}{(1.12)^3} + \frac{\$5,600}{(1.12)^4} + \frac{\$5,600}{(1.12)^5}$$

$$= -\$18,000 + \$20,187 = \$2,187 \tag{13-6}$$

An easier way to solve this problem, of course, is by direct reference to Table B at the end of the book, where we find the appropriate discount factor—3.6048—and multiply $5,600 by it to obtain $20,187. Subtracting the initial outlay of $18,000, we obtain $2,187. Inasmuch as the net present value of this proposal is greater than 0, the proposal should be accepted, using the present-value method.

With the internal-rate-of-return method, we are given the cash flows and we solve for the rate of discount that equates the present value of the cash inflows with the present value of outflows. We then compare the internal rate of return with the required rate of return to determine whether the proposal should be accepted. With the present-value method, we are given the cash flows and the required rate of return, and we solve for the net present value. The acceptability of the proposal depends on whether the net present value is zero or more.

Mutual exclusion and dependency

In evaluating a group of investment proposals, we have to determine whether they are independent of each other. A proposal is said to be *mutually exclusive* if the acceptance of it precludes the acceptance of one or more other proposals. For example, if the firm is considering investment in one of two temperature-control systems, acceptance of one system will rule out acceptance of the other. Two mutually exclusive proposals cannot both be accepted.

A *contingent* or *dependent* proposal is one whose acceptance depends upon the acceptance of one or more other proposals. The addition of a large machine may necessitate construction of a new wing to house it. Contingent proposals must be part of our thinking when we consider the original, dependent proposal. Recognizing the dependency, we can make investment decisions accordingly.

Profitability index

The profitability index, or benefit-cost ratio, of a project is the present value of future net cash flows over the initial cash outlay. It can be expressed as

$$PI = \frac{\sum_{t=1}^{n} \frac{X_t}{(1 + k)^t}}{X_o} \tag{13-7}$$

where the Greek sigma means the sum of discounted cash flows from period 1 through period n. For our example,

$$PI = \frac{\$20,187}{\$18,000} = 1.12 \qquad (13\text{-}8)$$

As long as the profitability index is 1.00 or greater, the investment proposal is acceptable. For any given project, the net-present-value method and the profitability index give the same accept-reject signals. If we must choose between mutually exclusive projects, the net-present-value measure is preferred because it expresses in absolute terms the expected economic contribution of the project. In contrast, the profitability index expresses only the relative profitability. To illustrate, consider the following mutually exclusive projects:

	Project A	Project B
Present value of net cash flows	$20,000	$8,000
Initial cash outlay	15,000	5,000
Net present value	$ 5,000	$3,000
Profitability index	1.33	1.60

According to the net-present-value method, project A would be preferred, whereas according to the profitability indexes, project B would be preferred. Because the net present value represents the expected economic contribution of a project, we should prefer A to B. Thus, the net-present-value method is the better of the two methods when we must choose between mutually exclusive projects that involve different initial cash outlays.[3]

COMPARISON OF PRESENT-VALUE AND INTERNAL-RATE-OF-RETURN METHODS

In general, the present-value and internal-rate-of-return methods lead to the same acceptance or rejection decision. In Fig. 13-1 we illustrate graphically the two methods applied to a typical investment project. The figure shows the relationship between the net present value of a project and the discount rate employed. When the discount rate is 0, net present value is simply the total cash inflows less the total cash outflows of the project. Assuming that total inflows exceed total outflows and that outflows are followed by inflows, the typical project will have the highest net present value when the discount rate is 0. As the discount rate increases, the present value of future cash inflows decreases relative to the present value of cash outflows. At the intercept, the net present value of the project is 0. The discount rate at that point represents the internal rate of return that

[3]See Bernhard Schwab and Peter Lusztig, "A Comparative Analysis of the Net-Present Value and the Benefit-Cost Ratio as Measures of the Economic Desirability of Investments," *Journal of Finance*, 24 (June 1969), 507–16.

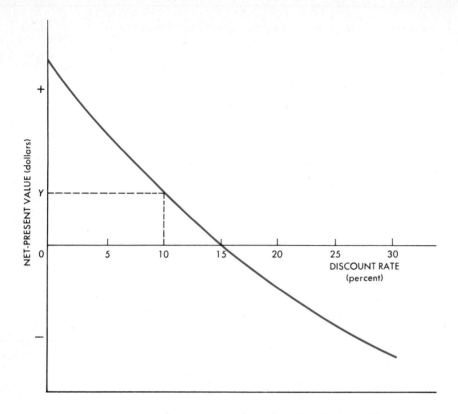

FIGURE 13-1
Relation between discount rate and net present value

equates the present value of cash inflows with the present value of cash outflows. For discount rates greater than the internal rate of return, the net present value of the project is negative.[4]

If the required rate of return is less than the internal rate of return, we would accept the project using either method. Suppose that the required rate were 10 percent. As seen in Fig. 13-1, the net present value of the project then would be Y. Inasmuch as Y is greater than 0, we would accept the project, using the present-value method. Similarly, we would accept the project using the internal-rate-of-return method because the internal rate exceeds the required rate. For required rates greater than the internal rate of return, we would reject the project under either method. Thus, we see that the internal-rate-of-return and present-value methods give us identical answers with respect to the acceptance or rejection of an investment project.

Differences between methods

We must identify important differences between the methods. When two investment proposals are mutually exclusive, so that we can select only one, the two methods may give contradictory results. To illustrate the nature of the prob-

---

[4]Again, we must recognize the possibility of multiple internal rates of return. See Appendix A to this chapter.

lem, suppose a firm had two mutually exclusive investment proposals that were expected to generate the following cash flows:

			Cash flows		
Year	0	1	2	3	4
Proposal A	−$23,616	$10,000	$10,000	$10,000	$10,000
Proposal B	− 23,616	0	5,000	10,000	32,675

Internal rates of return for proposals A and B are 25 percent and 22 percent, respectively. If the required rate of return is 10 percent, however, and we use this figure as our discount rate, the net present values of proposals A and B are $8,083 and $10,347, respectively. Thus, proposal A is preferred if we use the internal-rate-of-return method, whereas proposal B is preferred if we use the present-value method. If we can choose but one of these proposals, we obviously have a conflict.

Reinvestment rate. The conflict between these two methods is due to different assumptions with respect to the reinvestment rate on funds released from the proposals. The internal-rate-of-return method implies that funds are reinvested at the internal rate of return over the remaining life of the proposal. For proposal A, the assumption is that cash flows of $10,000 at the end of years 1, 2, and 3 can be reinvested to earn a return of 25 percent, compounded annually. The present-value method implies reinvestment at a rate equivalent to the required rate of return used as the discount rate. Because of these differing assumptions, the two methods can give different rankings of investment proposals, as we have seen.

To illustrate further the nature of the problem, consider two additional mutually exclusive proposals with the following cash flows:

		Cash flows		
Time	0	1	2	3
Proposal C	−$155.22	$100.00	0	$100.00
Proposal D	− 155.22	0	0	221.00

The net present value of each of these proposals is $10.82 if we assume a required rate of return of 10 percent. However, we would be indifferent between the two proposals only if the firm had opportunities for reinvestment at a rate of 10 percent. This concept is illustrated in Fig. 13-2, where the functional relationship between net present value and the discount rate is graphed for the two proposals. The intercepts on the 0 horizontal line represent the internal rates of return of the two proposals that equate their net present values with 0. For proposal C, the

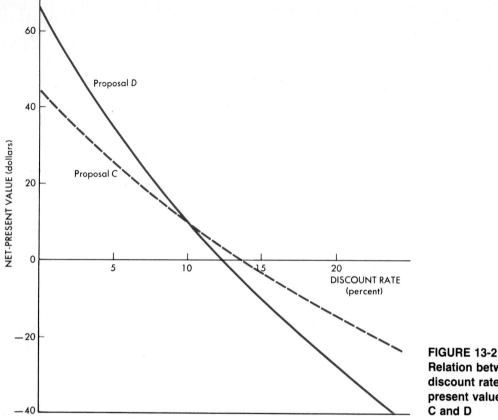

FIGURE 13-2
Relation between
discount rate and net
present values, proposals
C and D

internal rate of return is 14 percent; for proposal D, it is 12.5 percent. The intercepts on the vertical axis represent total cash inflows less total cash outflows for the two proposals, because the discount rate is 0. We see that proposal D ranks higher than proposal C if the reinvestment rate is below 10 percent and lower if it is above 10 percent. At the point of intersection, 10 percent, the proposals have identical net present values. This point represents the crossover rate. Given a reinvestment rate of 10 percent, then, the two proposals would have equal ranking. For reinvestment rates other than this percentage, we would prefer one proposal to the other. In a similar manner, other mutually exclusive investment proposals can be evaluated according to the intersections.

Scale of investment. In addition to the problem of different implicit compounding rates, a problem arises if the initial cash outlays are different for two mutually exclusive investment proposals. Because the results of the internal-rate-of-return method are expressed as a percent, the scale of investment is ignored. Without allowance for this factor, a 50 percent return on a $100 investment would always be preferred to a 25 percent return on a $500 investment. In contrast, the results of the present-value method are expressed in absolute terms. If the investment proposals above were each for one year, we would have the following, assuming a required rate of return of 10 percent:

	Cash Flows			
	Year 0	Year 1	IRR	NPV (10%)
Proposal X	−$100	$150	50%	$36.36
Proposal Y	− 500	625	25	68.18

With respect to absolute returns, the second proposal is superior, despite the fact that its internal rate of return is less. The reason is that the scale of investment is greater, affording a greater net present value.

We have seen that the present-value method always provides correct rankings of mutually exclusive investment projects, whereas the internal-rate-of-return method sometimes does not. With the IRR method, the implied reinvestment rate will differ depending upon the cash-flow stream for each investment proposal under consideration. For proposals with a high internal rate of return, a high reinvestment rate is assumed; for proposals with a low internal rate of return, a low reinvestment rate is assumed. Only rarely will the internal rate of return calculated represent the relevant rate for reinvestment of intermediate cash flows. With the present-value method, however, the implied reinvestment rate—namely, the required rate of return—is the same for each proposal. In essence, this reinvestment rate represents the minimum return on opportunities available to the firm. Not only is it consistently applied, but it is the only theoretically correct opportunity cost that can be employed if our objective is value maximization. In addition, the present-value method takes account of differences in the scale of investment, and for this reason it also is superior to the IRR method.

Many financial managers feel that, in practice, the internal rate of return is easier to visualize and to interpret than is the net-present-value. In addition, one does not have to specify a required rate of return in the calculations. To the extent that the required rate of return is but a rough estimate, the use of the internal-rate-of-return method may permit a more realistic comparison of projects. The principal shortcoming of the method is the possibility of multiple internal rates of return, a subject that we take up in Appendix A to this chapter.

ADDITIONAL FACTORS INFLUENCING CASH FLOWS

In our machine-replacement example we assumed straight-line depreciation, the depreciable life of the asset equaling its economic life, no investment tax credit, no salvage value, and no working-capital requirement. We wanted to keep the example simple so that we could analyze the methods for evaluating expected profitability. We need now to digress for a while in order to examine the effect of the above considerations on the magnitude and timing of cash flows. We also shall examine the question of mutually exclusive projects with different lives.

Accelerated depreciation

In our earlier example, the replacement of the old machine with a new one was expected to result in annual cash savings of $7,600 a year over the next 5 years. Straight-line depreciation charges on the new machine were $4,000 a year; and when we subtracted $400 annual depreciation charges on the old machine, we obtained incremental depreciation charges of $3,600 a year. Thus, the additional income before taxes was $4,000, resulting in additional taxes of $2,000 a year, assuming a 50 percent tax rate. When this $2,000 outlay was subtracted from the $7,600 cash savings, the net cash inflow became $5,600 a year. Consider now the modification of the example occasioned by accelerated depreciation.

As we know from chapter 2, the amount of accelerated depreciation is determined under the accelerated cost recovery system (ACRS) of the 1981 Tax Act. For the 5-year property class, allowable depreciation for assets placed in service through 1984 is 15 percent of the cost of the asset in the first year, 22 percent in the second year, followed by 21 percent in each of the next three years. Assuming a cost basis of $20,000 for our example project, and that it is placed in service sometime before 1985, depreciation charges on the new machine, additional depreciation above $400 a year on the old machine, and annual net cash flows (after taxes) would be

Year	(1) Depreciation on new machine	(2) Additional depreciation (1) − $400	(3) Net cash flow
1	$3,000	$2,600	$5,100
2	4,400	4,000	5,800
3	4,200	3,800	5,700
4	4,200	3,800	5,700
5	4,200	3,800	5,700
	$20,000	$18,000	$28,000

In the early years of a project's life, accelerated depreciation is generally more effective than straight-line depreciation in increasing depreciation charges, which result in lower taxes and higher cash flows. Our example is an exception because of the half-year convention for the first year, as well as the switch to straight-line depreciation. With the straight-line depreciation method illustrated earlier, net cash flows were $5,600 each year, compared with $5,100 the first year, followed by $5,800 the second year, and $5,700 in each of the next three years under ACRS.

Depreciable life shorter than economic life

The major advantage of ACRS is that in most cases the capital recovery (depreciation) period is shorter than the economic life of the asset. In addition, after 1984, multiples higher than 1.5 will be used in the declining-balance method.

To illustrate the former advantage, suppose in our previous example that the project had an economic life of eight years instead of five, and that annual cash savings were $5,500 instead of $7,600. For straight-line depreciation over the entire economic life of the project, annual depreciation on the new machine would be $20,000/8 = $2,500. Assume the old machine continues to have but five years of depreciable life remaining, involving $400 per year. As a result, the expected net cash flows (after taxes) are

| | Years 1–5 | | Years 6–8 | |
	Book account	Cash-flow account	Book account	Cash-flow account
Annual cash savings	$5,500	$5,500	$5,500	$5,500
Depreciation on new machine	2,500		2,500	
Less depreciation on old machine	400		—	
Additional depreciation charges	2,100		2,500	
Additional income before taxes	3,400		3,000	
Taxes (50%)	1,700	1,700	1,500	1,500
Additional income after taxes	$1,700		$1,500	
Net cash flow		$3,800		$4,000

With a 12 percent discount rate and an initial cash outflow of $18,000, the net present value of the project is $1,150; its internal rate of return is 13.8 percent.

Under ACRS, the project would fall in the 5-year property class. As we determined in the previous section, additional depreciation charges in the first five years are $2,600, $4,000, $3,800, $3,800, and $3,800, respectively. As a result, the expected net cash flows (after taxes) are

| | Year | | | |
	1	2	3–5	6–8
Annual cash savings	$5,500	$5,500	$5,500	$5,500
Additional depreciation charges	2,600	4,000	3,800	—
Additional income before taxes	2,900	1,500	1,700	5,500
Taxes (50%)	1,450	750	850	2,750
Annual net cash flow	$4,050	$4,750	$4,650	$2,750

We see that the tax shield occurs only in the first five years, which results in greater cash flows in those years that there would be with straight-line depreciation. In the last three years, there is no depreciation tax shield, so the full cash saving of $5,500 per year is subject to taxation. As a result, cash flows are lower. This shift in timing has a favorable present-value effect. The net present value of the project, assuming a required rate of return of 12 percent, is $2,054 compared with $1,150 before ACRS; and the internal rate of return is 15.5 percent compared with 13.8 percent before. In summary, it is the economic life, more than the depreciable life, that affects the timing of cash flows and the resulting attractiveness of the project.

Investment tax credit

The investment tax credit is available to companies and individuals who invest in capital assets. For the 3-year property class, the tax credit is 6 percent, and it is available at the time the asset is placed into service. For assets in the 5-year property class and for certain property in the 10-year class, 10 percent is applicable.

In our previous example, the new machine was assumed to fall into the 5-year property class, so the investment tax credit would be 10 percent of the total cost of purchase and installation (10 percent of $20,000 = $2,000). The company receives a tax credit of $2,000 when the machine is placed in service. For purposes of illustration, suppose this were at time 0. Assuming the company has sufficient taxable income to utilize the full tax credit, this reduces the initial net cash outflow in our previous example from $18,000 to $16,000.[5] This obviously enhances the profitability of the project. The net present value under ACRS becomes $2,000 + $2,054 = $4,054 compared with $2,054 without the tax credit. The internal rate of return becomes 19.6 percent, compared with 15.5 percent before.

Salvage value and taxes

The cash-flow pattern also will differ from that shown in the example if the new machine is expected to have a salvage, or scrap, value at the end of the project. As the machine will be fully depreciated at that time, the salvage value realized is subject to taxation at the ordinary income tax rate. If the expected salvage value of the machine at the end of its life were $2,000 and the corporate tax rate were 50 percent, the firm would realize cash proceeds of $1,000 at the end of the last year. This amount then would be added to the net cash inflow previously determined to give the total cash flow in the last year.

If the machine is sold before it is fully depreciated, the tax treatment is different. Suppose the machine were sold at the end of the second year for $17,000 and that $7,400 in depreciation were claimed during the first two years. Therefore, the depreciated book value of the machine is $20,000 − $7,400 = $12,600. The gain above the machine's depreciated book value, $17,000 − $12,600 = $4,400, is subject to taxation. If the tax rate were 50 percent, the firm would pay taxes of $2,200 on the gain and realize but $17,000 − $2,200 = $14,800 on the sale. As long as the gain is less than the total depreciation claimed in the past, it is subject to recapture of depreciation and taxed at the full corporate tax rate.

If the machine is sold for more than its cost, however, some of the gain is subject to the capital gains tax treatment, which usually is more favorable. Suppose the machine were sold for $23,000 at the end of the second year. The total gain would be $23,000−$12,600=$10,400. Of the total, the amount above cost, or $3,000, is treated as subject to the capital gains tax while the remainder, or $7,400, is taxed at the full corporate tax rate. If the capital gains tax rate were

[5]The investment tax credit does not alter the basis for depreciation; it remains at $20,000.

28 percent, there would be a tax of $840 on the $3,000 and a tax of $3,700 on the $7,400. In this case, the total cash proceeds realized from the sale of the machine would be $23,000−$840−$3,700=$18,460. If the machine is sold for less than its depreciated book value, the loss is deductible against ordinary income. Suppose in our example that the machine were sold for $10,000 at the end of the second year. The loss would be $12,600−$10,000=$2,600. This loss is used to offset other income of the company, so taxes are reduced by 50 percent of it, or by $1,300. Effectively, the $1,300 represents a cash inflow, as does the $10,000 sales price.

Working-capital requirement

In addition to the investment in a fixed asset—in our example, a machine—it sometimes is necessary to carry additional cash, receivables, or inventories. This investment in working capital is treated as a cash outflow at the time it occurs. For example, if $1,000 of additional inventory were required in connection with the new machine and the investment occurred at the outset, there would be an additional cash outflow of $1,000 at time 0, bringing the total outflow to $19,000. At the end of the project's life, the working-capital investment presumably is recaptured. Therefore, there would be a $1,000 additional cash inflow in year 5. As a result, the cash inflow in that year would be $6,600 instead of $5,600, using our original straight-line depreciation 5-year example.

If we solve for the net present value using a 12 percent discount rate, it is

$$NPV = -\$19,000 + \frac{\$5,600}{(1.12)} + \frac{\$5,600}{(1.12)^2} + \frac{\$5,600}{(1.12)^3} + \frac{\$5,600}{(1.12)^4} + \frac{\$6,600}{(1.12)^5}$$

$$= \$1,754$$

This compares with $2,187 before allowance for the working capital investment. The internal rate of return is 15.6 percent compared with 16.8 percent before. While the presence of a working-capital requirement does not affect the total cash flows, inasmuch as it is subtracted at the beginning and added at the end, it does affect the timing of cash flows and, hence, the net present value and the internal rate of return.

Projects with different lives

Sometimes a company is faced with having to choose between two mutually exclusive investment projects having different economic lives. We may be comparing two machines that will perform equally well. The Monarch machine sells for $30,000, lasts 4 years, and costs $5,000 per year to keep it running smoothly. The Regal machine's price is $20,000, but it lasts only 3 years and costs $7,000 a year to keep it up. The question is which machine should we choose?

If we need the services of the machine for only 3 years, we simply would compute the present values of cash outflows for both alternatives and pick the one with the lowest present value. If we need the services of such a machine into the foreseeable future, the situation is different. One way to look at the problem is to assume that we can replicate each machine at the end of its life. We might assume that we can replace the Regal machine at the end of year 3 with an identical machine costing $20,000 which will last another three years and cost $7,000 a year to keep up. The same type of replication could be assumed for the Monarch machine. If the two machines are replicated at constant scale forever, we can compare them because both would have an infinite life. The cash outflow streams (in thousands) would be

	0	1	2	3	4	5	6	7	8	...
Monarch	−$30	−$5	−$5	−$5	−$35	−$5	−$5	−$5	−$35	
Regal	− 20	− 7	− 7	−27	− 7	− 7	−27	− 7	− 7	

The calculation of the present value of a long stream of cash flows is arduous. A much simpler way to reach a decision is to calculate the present values of the cash outflows only for the original lives of the machines and then convert these present values into annual annuity payments. If the required return were 12 percent, the present values of the two cash flow streams would be

	Cash flows (in thousands)					
	0	1	2	3	4	Present value (12%)
Monarch	−$30	−$5	−$5	−$5	−$5	−$45,187
Regal	− 20	− 7	− 7	− 7		− 36,813

The next step is to divide these present values by the appropriate discount factor to determine the equivalent annual annuity amount. Turning to Table B at the back of the book, we see that the 12 percent discount factor for an even series of cash flows for three years is 2.4018 and for four years it is 3.0373. Therefore, we have the following annual annuity payments:

Monarch	−$45,187/3.0373 = −$14,877
Regal	−$36,813/2.4018 = −$15,327

The Monarch machine, having the lower annuity payment, would be preferred. Its longer life and lower running expenses more than offset the difference in initial cost. The procedure, then, is to convert costs that are spread over varying years into annual equivalent costs and then to compare these annual costs. The method is appropriate when the life of each machine is essentially infinite, owing to replication at a constant scale. When this is not the case and replication occurs not at all or at different assumed costs, we must calculate the present value of cash outflow for the entire stream.

CAPITAL RATIONING

Capital rationing occurs any time there is a budget ceiling, or constraint, on the amount of funds that can be invested during a specific period, such as a year. Such constraints are prevalent in a number of firms, particularly in those that have a policy of financing all capital expenditures internally. Another example of capital rationing occurs when a division of a large company is allowed to make capital expenditures only up to a specified budget ceiling, over which the division usually has no control. With a capital-rationing constraint, the firm attempts to select the combination of investment proposals that will provide the greatest profitability.

Your a firm may have the following investment opportunities, ranked in descending order of profitability indexes (the ratio of the present value of future net cash flows over the initial cash outlay):

Proposal	4	7	2	3	6	5	1
Profitability index	1.25	1.19	1.16	1.14	1.09	1.05	0.97
Initial outlay	$400,000	$100,000	$175,000	$125,000	$200,000	$100,000	$150,000

If the budget ceiling for initial outlays during the present period is $1 million, and the proposals are independent of each other, you would select proposals in descending order of profitability until the budget was exhausted. With capital rationing, you would accept the first five proposals, totaling $1 million in initial outlays. In other words, you do not necessarily invest in all proposals that increase the net present value of the firm; you invest in an acceptable proposal only if the budget constraint allows such an investment. You will not invest in proposal 5, even though the profitability index in excess of 1 would suggest its acceptance. The critical aspect of the capital-rationing constraint illustrated is that capital expenditures during a period are strictly limited by the budget ceiling, regardless of the number of attractive investment opportunities.

Opportunity costs and objections to capital rationing

A budget ceiling carries its cost, too, when it bars us from taking advantage of any opportunity beyond the cutoff. In our example, the opportunity foregone by the $1 million budget ceiling is proposal 5, which has a profitability index of 1.05. Although all cash flows are discounted at the required rate of return, we do not necessarily accept proposals that provide positive net present values. We see which proposals we can accept before we exhaust the budget; but even if we would not exhaust the budget, we would reject independent proposals yielding less than the required rate of return. However, we may reject projects that provide positive net present values, as was shown with proposal 5. Under capital rationing, the required rate of return is not the acceptance criterion. Should it then be used as the discount rate in present-value calculations, or should the opportunity cost be used? The implied discount rate in any budget period is the yield foregone on the most profitable investment opportunity rejected, or the required rate of return, whichever is the higher. This implied discount rate can vary significantly from period to period, depending upon variations in the total amount of investment projects from period to period and in the budget constraints.

Capital rationing usually results in an investment policy that is less than optimal. In some periods, the firm accepts projects down to its required rate of return; in others, it rejects projects that would provide returns substantially in excess of the required rate. If the firm actually can raise capital at that approximate real cost, should it not invest in all projects yielding more than the required rate of return? If it rations capital and does not invest in all projects yielding more than the required rate, is it not foregoing opportunities that would enhance the market price of its stock?

From a theoretical standpoint, a firm should accept all projects yielding more than the required rate of return.[6] By so doing, it will increase the market price per share, because it is taking on projects that will provide a return higher than that necessary to maintain the present market price per share. This proposition assumes that the firm actually can raise capital, within reasonable limits, at the required rate of return. Certainly, unlimited amounts of capital are not available at any one cost. However, most firms are involved in a more or less continual process of making decisions to undertake capital expenditures and to finance these expenditures. Given the assumptions above, the firm should accept all proposals yielding more than the required rate of return and raise capital to finance these proposals at that approximate real cost. Certainly, there are circumstances that complicate the use of this rule. In general, however, this policy should tend to maximize the market price of the stock over the long run. If the firm rations capital and rejects projects that yield more than the required rate of return, then the firm's investment policy, by definition, is less than optimal. Management could increase the value of the firm to the shareholders by accepting these projects.

SUMMARY

Capital budgeting involves the outlay of current funds in anticipation of cash-flow benefits. Capital-budgeting decisions by corporations have an important impact on capital formation and on a country's economic growth. In this chapter we first considered the collection of cash-flow information for the evaluation of investment proposals. The key is to measure incremental cash flows with and without the investment proposal being analyzed. Accelerated depreciation under ACRS, the depreciable life of an asset being shorter than its economic life, the investment tax credit, the presence of salvage value, and a working capital requirement all have significant effects on the pattern of cash flows and, hence, on present value. An additional refinement involves mutually exclusive projects with uneven economic lives.

[6]We shall examine the rationale for this criterion in Chapter 15.

Capital-budgeting methods, including the average-rate-of-return and pay-back methods, were evaluated under the assumption that the acceptance of any investment proposal does not change the total business-risk complexion of the firm. The two discounted cash-flow methods—internal rate of return and net present value—are the only appropriate means by which to judge the economic contribution of an investment proposal.

The important distinctions between the internal-rate-of-return method and the present-value method are the implied compounding rate, the scale of investment and the possibility of multiple internal rates of return. Depending upon the situation, contrary answers can be given with respect to the acceptance of mutually exclusive investment proposals. On theoretical grounds, a case can be made for the superiority of the present-value method. The problem of capital rationing was examined, and we concluded that such a policy is likely to result in investment decisions that are less than optimal.

APPENDIX A ╲ Multiple Internal Rates of Return

In a well-known article, Lorie and Savage pointed out that certain streams of cash flows may have more than one internal rate of return.[7] To illustrate the problem, suppose that we had the following stream of cash flows corresponding to the "pump" proposal of Lorie and Savage:

Year	0	1	2
Cash flow	−$1,600	$10,000	−$10,000

In this example, a new, more effective pump is substituted for an existing pump. On an incremental basis, there is an initial outlay followed by net cash inflows resulting from the increased efficiency of the new pump. If the quantity of oil, for example, is fixed, the new pump will exhaust this supply more quickly than the old pump would. Beyond this point of exhaustion, the new pump alternative would result in an incremental outflow, because the old pump would still be productive.

When we solve for the internal rate of return for the above cash-flow stream, we find that it is not one rate but two: 25 percent and 400 percent. This unusual situation is illustrated in Fig. 13-3, where the discount rate is plotted along the horizontal axis and net present value along the vertical axis. At a zero rate of discount, the net present value of the project is simply the sum of all the cash flows. It is − $1,600 because total cash outflows exceed total cash inflows. As the discount rate increases, the present value of the second-year outflow diminishes with respect to the first-year inflow, and the present value of the proposal becomes positive when the discount rate exceeds 25 percent. As the discount rate increases

[7]See James H. Lorie and Leonard J. Savage, "Three Problems in Rationing Capital," *Journal of Business*, 28 (October 1955), 229–39.

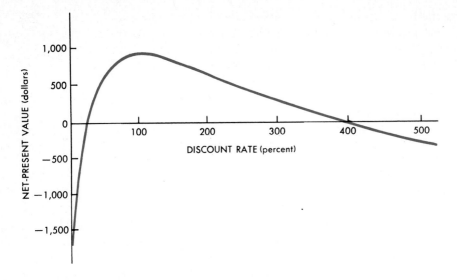

FIGURE 13-3
Dual rates of return

beyond 100 percent, the present value of all future cash flows (years 1 and 2) diminishes relative to the initial outflow of − $1,600. At 400 percent, the present value of all cash flows again becomes 0.

This type of proposal differs from the usual case, shown in Figure 13-1, in which net present value is a decreasing function of the discount rate, and in which there is but one internal rate of return that equates the present value of all inflows with the present value of all outflows. An investment proposal may have any number of internal rates of return, depending upon the cash-flow pattern. Consider the following series of cash flows:

Year	0	1	2	3
Cash flow	−$1,000	$6,000	−$11,000	$6,000

In this example, discount rates of 0, 100 percent, and 200 percent result in the net present value of all cash flows equaling 0.

The number of internal rates of return is limited to the number of reversals of sign in the cash-flow stream. In the above example, we have three reversals and three internal rates of return. Although a multiple reversal in signs is a necessary condition for multiple internal rates of return, it is not sufficient for such an occurrence. The occurrence of multiple internal rates of return also depends upon the magnitude of cash flows. For the following series of cash flows, there is but one internal rate of return (32.5 percent), despite two reversals of sign:

Year	0	1	2
Cash flow	−$1,000	$1,400	−$100

When confronted with a proposal having multiple rates of return, how does one decide which is the correct rate? In our dual-rate example, is the correct rate 25 percent or 400 percent? Actually, neither rate is correct, because neither is a measure of investment worth. In essence, the firm has "borrowed" $10,000 from the project at the end of the year 1 and will pay it back at the end of year 2. The relevant question is: what is it worth to the firm to have the use of $10,000 for one year? This question, in turn, depends upon the rate of return on investment opportunities available to the firm for that period of time. If the firm could earn 20 percent on the use of these funds and realize these earnings at the end of the period, the value of this opportunity would be $2,000, to be received at the end of year 2. This amount would then be compared with the initial outlay of $1,600 to determine whether the project is worthwhile. Similarly, other proposals can be evaluated in this manner to determine whether they are worthwhile.

In general, holding risk constant a company wishes to lend at as high a rate as possible and to borrow at as low a rate as possible. In the case of a project having multiple changes in signs, both lending and borrowing are involved. The best way to tackle the problem is to separate cash flows into their lending and borrowing components and then to use the net-present value approach. In this way, the appropriate minimum required rate of return can be used on the lending side and the appropriate borrowing rate on that side.

APPENDIX B \ Inflation and Capital Budgeting

In general, the presence of inflation in the economy distorts capital-budgeting decisions. The principal reason is that depreciation charges are based on original rather than replacement costs. As income grows with inflation, an increasing portion is taxed, with the result that real cash flows do not keep up with inflation. To illustrate, consider an investment proposal costing $24,000 under the assumptions that no inflation is expected, depreciation is straight line over four years, and the tax rate is 50 percent. The following cash flows are expected to occur:

Year	Cash savings	Depreciation	Taxes	Cash flow after taxes
1	$10,000	$6,000	$2,000	$8,000
2	10,000	6,000	2,000	8,000
3	10,000	6,000	2,000	8,000
4	10,000	6,000	2,000	8,000

Depreciation is deducted from cash savings to obtain taxable income, on which taxes of 50 percent are based.[8] Without inflation, depreciation charges represent the "cost" of replacing the investment as it wears out. Because nominal income on

---

[8]This example is similar to one in John A. Tatom and James. E. Turley, "Inflation and Taxes: Disincentives for Capital Formation," *Review of the Federal Reserve Bank of St. Louis*, 60 (January 1978), 2–8.

which taxes are paid represents real income, the last column represents real cash flows after taxes. The internal rate of return which equates the present value of the cash inflows with the cost of the project is 12.6 percent.

Consider now a situation in which inflation is at a rate of 7 percent per annum, and cash savings are expected to grow at this overall rate of inflation. The after-tax cash flows become

Year	Cash savings	Depreciation	Taxes	Cash flow after taxes
1	$10,700	$6,000	$2,350	$8,350
2	11,449	6,000	2,725	8,724
3	12,250	6,000	3,125	9,125
4	13,108	6,000	3,554	9,554

Although these cash flows are larger than before, they must be deflated by the inflation rate if one is concerned with the real as opposed to the nominal rate of return. Therefore, the last column becomes

	Year			
	1	2	3	4
Real after-tax cash flow	$7,804	$7,620	$7,449	$7,289

As we see, the real after-tax cash flows are less than before, and they decline steadily over time. The reason is that depreciation charges do not change in keeping with inflation, so that an increasing portion of the tax savings are subject to taxation. As taxes increase at a rate faster than inflation, real after-tax cash flows must decline. The internal rate of return based on real after-tax cash flows is 9.9 percent compared with 12.6 percent without inflation.

Therefore, the presence of inflation results in lower real rates of return. Consequently, there is less incentive for companies to undertake capital investments. While the cash-flow situation is improved with accelerated depreciation, the same unfavorable comparisons hold. There simply is a disincentive for companies to undertake capital expenditures, with the result that the amount invested typically is less than would be the case in the absence of inflation. It follows also that there will be an incentive to seek investments with faster paybacks (shorter economic lines) and that industry will become less capital intensive.[9]

[9]For an analysis of these points, see Charles R. Nelson, "Inflation and Capital Budgeting," *Journal of Finance*, 31 (June 1976), 923–31.

The bias in cash-flow estimates

In estimating cash flows, each company must take anticipated inflation into account. Often there is a tendency to assume that price levels will remain unchanged throughout the life of the project. Frequently, this assumption is imposed unknowingly: future cash flows are estimated on the basis of existing prices. However, a bias arises in the selection process, in that the required rate of return for the project usually is based on current capital costs, which in turn embody a premium for anticipated inflation.[10]

Assume a situation where the hurdle rate for a project is its required rate of return as perceived by investors and creditors. (The ways by which it is measured are taken up in chapter 15.) There is general agreement that security prices depend on anticipated changes in prices. In fact, over 80 years ago Irving Fisher expressed the nominal rate of interest on a financial instrument as the sum of the real rate and the rate of price change expected over the life of the instrument.[11] This observed phenomenon has come to be known as the *Fisher effect*.[12] It implies that the required rate of return for a project is

$$R_j = R_j^* + \rho \qquad\qquad (13B\text{-}1)$$

where R_j is the required rate of return in nominal terms, R_j^* is the required rate in real terms, and ρ is the weighted-average anticipated rate of inflation over the life of the project.

If anticipated inflation is embodied in the acceptance criterion, it is important that it be reflected in the estimated cash flows for the project as well. Anticipated inflation affects the expected cash flows of a project in several ways. If cash inflows ultimately arise from the sale of a product, expected future prices affect these inflows. As for cash outflows, inflation affects both expected future wages and material costs. Note that future inflation does not affect depreciation charges on existing assets. Once the asset is acquired, these charges are known with certainty. The effect of anticipated inflation on cash inflows and cash outflows will vary with the nature of the project. In some cases, cash inflows, through price increases, will rise faster than cash outflows; in other cases, the opposite will hold. No matter what the relationship, it is a vital part of the cash-flow estimates. Otherwise, a bias of the type described before arises.

Illustration of inflation bias. A project that cost $100,000 at time 0 was under consideration and was expected to provide cash-flow benefits over the next 5 years. Straight-line depreciation was $20,000 a year, and the corporate tax rate was 50 percent. Cash flows were estimated on the basis of price levels at time 0,

---

[10]This section is based on James C. Van Horne, "A Note on Biases in Capital Budgeting Introduced by Inflation," *Journal of Financial and Quantitative Analysis*, 6 (January 1971), 653–58.

[11]*Appreciation and Interest* (New York: Macmillan, 1896).

[12]Strictly speaking, $1 + R_j = (1 + R_j^*)(1 + \rho)$, so $R_j = R_j^* + \rho + R_j^*\rho$. Inasmuch as the cross-product, $R_j^*\rho$, term usually is small, it is conventional to drop it from consideration.

with no consideration to the effect of future inflation upon them, and these estimates were

	Period				
	1	2	3	4	5
Expected cash inflow, I_t	$30,000	$40,000	$50,000	$50,000	$30,000
Expected cash outflow, O_t	10,000	10,000	10,000	10,000	10,000
	$20,000	$30,000	$40,000	$40,000	$20,000
Times (1 − tax rate)	.50	.50	.50	.50	.50
	$10,000	$15,000	$20,000	$20,000	$10,000
Depreciation × Tax rate	10,000	10,000	10,000	10,000	10,000
Net cash flow	$20,000	$25,000	$30,000	$30,000	$20,000

If the project's required rate of return were 14 percent, the net present value of the
project would be −$14,821. As this figure is negative, the project would be re-
jected.

The results are biased in the sense that the discount rate embodies an
element attributable to anticipated future inflation, whereas the cash-flow estimates do not. Suppose that the existing rate of inflation, as measured by changes
in the price-level index, were 10 percent, and that this rate was expected to prevail
over the next 5 years. If both cash inflows and cash outflows were expected to
increase at this rate, the net present value of the project would be

$$NPV_0 = \sum_{t=1}^{5} \frac{[I_t(1.10)^t - O_t(1.10)^t][1 - .5] + 20,000_t[.5]}{(1.14)^t} - 100,000$$

$$= \$1,615 \tag{13B-2}$$

where I_t is the cash inflow in year t, O_t is the cash outflow in year t, and $20,000
is the annual depreciation in year t which is multiplied by the tax rate to give the
tax-shield cash savings. Because the net present value is positive, the project
would now be acceptable, whereas before it was not. To reject it under the previous method of estimating cash flows would result in an opportunity loss to
stockholders, for the project provides a return somewhat in excess of that required
by investors.

This example serves to illustrate the necessity of taking anticipated
inflation into account explicitly when estimating future cash flows. Too often,
there is a tendency not to consider its effect in these estimates. Because anticipated
inflation is embodied in the required rate of return, not to take account of it in the
cash-flow estimates will result in a biased appraisal of the project and, in turn, the
possibility of a less than optimal allocation of capital.

1. Explain what is meant by the time value of money. Why is a bird in the hand worth two (or so) in the bush? Which capital-budgeting approaches ignore this concept? Are they optimal?

2. In evaluating the return from investments, why is depreciation included in the cash flows from a project and not deducted as are other expenses such as wages and taxes?

3. In capital budgeting for a new machine, should the following be added or subtracted from the new machine's purchase price?

   a) The market value of the old machine is $500.

   b) An investment in inventory of $2,000 is required.

   c) The book value of the old machine is $1,000.

   d) $200 is required to ship the new machine to the plant site.

   e) A concrete foundation for the new machine will cost $250.

   f) Training of the machine operator will cost $300.

   g) There is an investment tax credit on the new machine.

4. Why does the payback period bias the process of asset selection toward shortlived assets?

5. Contrast the internal rate of return with the net present value. Why might these two time-value approaches to asset selection give conflicting decision rules?

6. Why is the rate of return in future periods important in selecting a measure with which to assign priorities to projects in the current period?

7. The payback period, although it is conceptually unsound, is very popular in business as a criterion for assigning priorities to investment projects. Why is it unsound, and why is it popular?

8. Why are capital-budgeting procedures not applied to working capital decisions?

9. Discuss the adjustments in the capital-budgeting decision one should make to compensate for expected inflation.

10. Discuss the relationship between the payback period of an annuity and its internal rate of return.

11. Is the economic efficiency of a country enhanced by the use of modern capital budgeting techniques? Why?

12. What is the purpose of requiring more levels of approval, the larger the capital expenditure? Is more information also required in support of the request?

13. If capital rationing is not optimal, why would any company use it?

14. The internal-rate-of-return method implies that intermediate cash flows are reinvested at the internal rate of return. Under what circumstances is this assumption likely to lead to a seriously biased measure of the economic return from the project?

15. What is the difference between a product expansion and an equipment replacement type of investment?

PROBLEMS

1. Lobears, Inc., has two investment proposals, which have the following characteristics:

		Project A			Project B	
Period	Cost	Profit after taxes	Net cash flow	Cost	Profit after taxes	Net cash flow
0	$9,000	–	–	$12,000	–	–
1		$1,000	$5,000		$1,000	$5,000
2		1,000	4,000		1,000	5,000
3		1,000	3,000		4,000	8,000

For each project, compute its average rate of return, its payback period, and its net present value, using a discount rate of 15 percent.

2. In problem 1, what criticisms may be offered against the average rate of return as a capital budgeting method? What criticisms may be offered against the payback method?

3. The following are exercises on internal rates of return:

   a) An investment of $1,000 today will return $2,000 at the end of 10 years. What is its IRR?

   b) An investment of $1,000 will return $500 at the end of each of the next 3 years. What is its IRR?

   c) An investment of $1,000 today will return $1,000 at the end of one year, $500 at the end of 2 years, and $100 at the end of 3 years. What is its IRR?

   d) An investment of $1,000 will return $60 per year forever. What is its IRR?

4. Two mutually exclusive projects have projected cash flows as follows:

Period	0	1	2	3	4
A	–$2,000	$1,000	$1,000	$1,000	$1,000
B	– 2,000	0	0	0	6,000

   a) Determine the internal rate of return for each project.

   b) Determine the net present value for each project at discount rates of 0, 5, 10, 20, 30, and 35 percent.

   c) Plot a graph of the net present value of each project at the different discount rates.

   d) Which project would you select? Why? What assumptions are inherent in your decision?

5. The Zwisp Corporation may purchase a machine to replace an existing machine that has a book value of $5,000 and can be sold for that amount. The old machine has a remaining

life of 5 years, at which time its salvage value is zero, and it is depreciated on a straight-line basis. The proposed machine will perform the same functions the old machine performs, but improvements will enable the firm to realize cash savings of $8,000 per year in labor and materials. The new machine costs $25,000, but an investment tax credit of 10 percent is available, so the effective cash outlay is reduced by $2,500. The new machine has a useful life of 5 years, no salvage value, and it falls in the 5-year class for depreciation purposes. Assuming straight-line depreciation, a 50 percent tax rate, and a required rate of return of 16 percent, what is the net present value of the machine replacement project?

6. Zaire Electronics can make either of two investments at time 0. Assuming a required rate of return of 14 percent, determine for each project: (a) the payback period; (b) the net present value; (c) the profitability index; and (d) the internal rate of return. Assume the accelerated cost recovery system (ACRS) for depreciation for a 5-year property class, that the project will be placed in service before 1985, that an investment tax credit of 10 percent is available at time 0, and the corporate tax rate is 50 percent.

Project	Investment	1	2	3	4	5	6	7
A	$28,000	$8,000	$8,000	$8,000	$8,000	$8,000	$8,000	$8,000
B	20,000	5,000	5,000	6,000	6,000	7,000	7,000	7,000

7. Hi Grade Distribution Company is faced with the prospect of having to replace a special-purpose tank car. Two cars currently being marketed will do the job satisfactorily. The Superior tank car costs $50,000 and will require cash operating expenses of $20,000 per year. The Peerless tank car costs $75,000, but operating expenses are only $15,000 per year. Both tank cars have a 10-year useful life with no salvage value and would be depreciated on a straight-line basis over the ten years. An investment tax credit is available at the time either machine is purchased and placed in service.

a) If the company pays taxes at a 50 percent rate and has a 12 percent after-tax required rate of return, which tank car should be purchased?

b) Would your answer be different if the required return were 8 percent?

8. Sea-Fly Developers needs a small computer and has found one that costs $60,000. The presence of this machine is expected to save one full-time worker at an annual savings of $20,000. The computer has a useful life of 5 years but falls in the 3-year property class for capital recovery (depreciation) purposes. Therefore, a 6 percent investment tax credit will be available when the computer is placed in service. The company's marginal tax rate is 40 percent, and the after-tax required rate of return on the project is 17 percent.

a) Using straight-line depreciation over 3 years, what is the project's net present value? Is it acceptable?

b) If the double declining balance method were used, what would be its net present value? (If profit after taxes on the project is negative in any year, the firm will receive a tax credit of 40 percent of the loss in that year.) Is the project acceptable? Why does your NPV answer to part b differ from that to part a?

c) If a working-capital requirement of $5,000 were required in addition to the cost of the computer and this additional requirement were needed over the life of the project, what would be the effect on net present value? (Assume straight-line depreciation.)

9. Truly Fair Clothes Company will choose one of two equally efficient spinning machines to perform a routine function. The Bob Bobber machine has an economic life of 2 years, upkeep expenses of $1,000 per year, and a price of $5,000. The Whip Willer machine costs $8,000 and will last 3 years with upkeep expenses of $500 per year. Under its production system, Truly Fair will need a spinning machine of this sort for many years to come. If its required rate of return is 15 percent, should it choose the Bob Bobber or the Whip Willer?

10. The Lake Tahoe Ski Resort is comparing a half-dozen capital-improvement projects. It has allocated $1 million for capital-budgeting purposes. The following proposals and associated profitability indexes have been determined. The projects themselves are independent of one another.

Project	Amount	Profitability index
1. Extend ski lift 3	$500,000	1.22
2. Build a new sports shop	150,000	.95
3. Extend ski lift 4	350,000	1.20
4. Build a new restaurant	450,000	1.18
5. Build addition to housing complex	200,000	1.20
6. Build an indoor skating rink	400,000	1.05

a) With strict capital rationing, which of the above investments should be undertaken?

b) Is this an optimal strategy?

11. The Platte River Perfect Cooker Company is evaluating 3 investment situations: (1) produce a new line of aluminum skillets; (2) expand its existing cooker line to include several new sizes; and (3) develop a new higher-quality line of cookers. If only the project in question is undertaken, the expected present values and the amounts of investment required after taking all investment tax credits are

Project	Investment required	Present value of future cash flows
1	$200,000	$290,000
2	115,000	185,000
3	270,000	400,000

If projects 1 and 2 are jointly undertaken, there will be no economies; the investment required and present values will be the sum of the parts. With projects 1 and 3, economies are possible in investment, because one of the machines acquired can be used in both production processes. The total investment required for projects 1 and 3 combined is $440,000. If projects 2 and 3 are undertaken, economies can be achieved in marketing and producing the products but not in investment. The expected present value of future cash flows for projects 2 and 3 is $620,000. If all three projects are undertaken simultaneously, the economies noted above will still hold. A $125,000 extension on the plant will be necessary, as space is not available for all three projects. Which project or projects should be chosen?

12. The City of San Jose must replace a number of its concrete mixer trucks with new trucks. It has received several bids and has evaluated closely the performance characteristics of the various trucks. The Patterbilt truck, which costs $74,000, is top-of-the-line equipment. The truck has a life of 8 years, assuming that the engine is rebuilt in the fifth year. Maintenance costs of $2,000 a year are expected in the first 4 years, followed by total maintenance and rebuilding costs of $13,000 in the fifth year. During the last 3 years, maintenance costs are expected to be $4,000 a year. At the end of 8 years the truck will have an estimated scrap value of $9,000.

A bid from Bulldog Trucks, Inc., is for $59,000 a truck. Maintenance costs for this truck will be higher. In the first year they are expected to be $3,000, and this amount is expected to increase by $1,500 a year through the eighth year. In year 4 the engine will need to be rebuilt, and this will cost the company $15,000 in addition to maintenance costs in that year. At the end of 8 years the Bulldog truck will have an estimated scrap value of $5,000.

The last bidder, Best Tractor and Trailer Company, has agreed to sell trucks at $44,000 each. Maintenance costs in the first 4 years are expected to be $4,000 the first year and to increase by $1,000 a year. For the city's purposes, the truck has a life of only 4 years. At that time it can be traded in for a new Best Truck, which is expected to cost $52,000. The likely trade-in value of the old truck is $15,000. During years 5 through 8 the second truck is expected to have maintenance costs of $5,000 in year 5, and these are expected to increase by $1,000 each year. At the end of 8 years the second truck is expected to have a resale or salvage value of $18,000.

a) If the City of San Jose's opportunity costs of funds is 8 percent, which bid should it accept? Ignore tax considerations, as the city pays no taxes

b) If its opportunity cost were 15 percent, would your answer change?

Appendix B problem

13. Rioka Corporation can invest in a project which costs $100,000 and has a useful life of 5 years. The expected cash flows from the project are

		Year		
1	2	3	4	5
$20,000	$40,000	$40,000	$30,000	$20,000

The company's tax rate is 50 percent, and its cost of capital based on present conditions in the financial markets is 12 percent. The company uses straight-line depreciation.

a) Compute the net present value of the project without the consideration of inflation.

b) If inflation of 7 percent per annum is expected over the life of the project and cash flows are adjusted upward, what is the project's net present value?

SELECTED REFERENCES

BACON, PETER W., "The Evaluation of Mutually Exclusive Investments," *Financial Management*, 6 (Summer 1977), 55–58.

BIERMAN, HAROLD, JR., and SEYMOUR SMIDT, *The Capital Budgeting Decision*. New York: Mac-millan, 1976.

CARTER, E. EUGENE, "Designing the Capital Budgeting Process," *TIMS Studies in the Management Sciences*, 5 (1977), 25–42.

GITMAN, LAWRENCE J., and JOHN R. FORRESTER, JR., "Forecasting and Evaluation Practices and Performance: A Survey of Capital Budgeting," *Financial Management*, 6 (Fall 1977), 66–71.

HASTIE, K. LARRY, "One Businessman's View of Capital Budgeting," *Financial Management*, 3 (Winter 1974), 36–44.

HERBST, ANTHONY, "The Unique, Real Internal Rate of Return: Caveat Emptor!" *Journal of Financial and Quantitative Analysis*, 13 (June 1978), 363–70.

HONG, HAI, "Inflation and the Market Value of the Firm: Theory and Tests," *Journal of Finance*, 32 (September 1977), 1031–48.

HOSKINS, COLIN G. and GLEN A. MUMEY, "Payback: A Maligned Method of Asset Ranking?" *Engineering Economist*, 25 (Fall 1979), 53–65.

KEANE, SIMON M., "The Internal Rate of Return and the Reinvestment Fallacy," *Journal of Accounting and Business Studies*, 15 (June 1979), 48–55.

KIM, SUK, H., and EDWARD J. FARRAGHER, "Current Capital Budgeting Practices," *Management Accounting*, 28 (June 1981), 26–30.

LORIE, JAMES H., and LEONARD J. SAVAGE, "Three Problems in Rationing Capital," Journal of Business, 28 (October 1955), 229–39.

NELSON, CHARLES R., "Inflation and Capital Budgeting," *Journal of Finance*, 31 (June 1976), 923–31.

PETTY, J. WILLIAM, and OSWALD D. BOWLIN, "The Financial Manager and Quantitative Decision Models," *Financial Management*, 4 (Winter 1976). 32–41.

PETTY, J. WILLIAM, DAVID F. SCOTT, JR., and MONROE M. BIRD, "The Capital Expenditure Decision-Making Process of Large Corporations," *Engineering Economist*, 20 (Spring 1975), 159–72.

QUIRIN, G. DAVID, and JOHN C. WIGINTON, *Analyzing Capital Expenditures* Homewood, Ill.: Irwin, 1981.

RAPPAPORT, ALFRED, and ROBERT A. TAGGART, JR., "Evaluation of Capital Expenditure Proposals under Inflation," *Financial Management,* 11 (Spring 1982), 5–13.

ROSENBLATT, MEIR J., "A Survey and Analysis of Capital Budgeting Decision Process in Multi-division Firms," *Engineering Economist*, 25 (Summer 1980), 259–73.

SCHALL, LAWRENCE D., GARY L. SUNDEM, and WILLIAM R. GEIJSBEEK, JR., "Survey and Analysis of Capital Budgeting Methods," *Journal of Finance*, 33 (March 1978), 281–87.

SCHNELL, JAMES S., and ROY S. NICOLOSI, "Capital Expenditure Feedback: Project Reappraisal," *Engineering Economist*, 19 (Summer 1974), 253–61.

SCHWAB, BERNHARD, and PETER LUSZTIG, "A Comparative Analysis of the Net-Present Value and the Benefit-Cost Ratios as Measures of the Economic Desirability of Investments," *Journal of Finance*, 24 (June 1969), 507–16.

TATOM, JOHN A., and JAMES E. TURLEY, "Inflation and Taxes: Disincentives for Capital Formation," *Review of the Federal Reserve Bank of St. Louis*, 60 (January 1978), 2–8.

VAN HORNE, JAMES C., "A Note on Biases in Capital Budgeting Introduced by Inflation," *Journal of Financial and Quantitative Analysis*, 6 (January 1971), 653–58.

——, "The Variation of Project Life as a Means for Adjusting for Risk," *Engineering Economist,* 21 (Spring 1976), 151–58.

WEAVER, JAMES B., "Organizing and Maintaining a Capital Expenditure Program," *Engineering Economist*, 20 (Fall 1974), 1–36.

WEINGARTNER, H. MARTIN, "Capital Rationing: *n* Authors in Search of a Plot," *Journal of Finance*, 32 (December 1977), 1403–31.

Risk and capital budgeting 14

In the preceding chapter we assumed that the acceptance of any investment proposal under consideration did not change the business-risk complexion of the firm as perceived by suppliers of capital. This assumption allowed us to hold risk constant and to base our analysis of an investment project on its expected future cash flows. When we relax this assumption, we must allow for the possibility of investment projects having different degrees of risk. Because suppliers of capital to the firm (investors and creditors) tend to be risk-averse, the acceptance of a project that changes the risk complexion of the firm may cause them to change their required rates of return for investing or extending credit.

When we allow for changes in risk, then, we must take into account possible changes in the firm's value. The project that is expected to provide a high return may be so risky that it causes a significant increase in the perceived risk of the firm. In turn, this may cause a decrease in the firm's value, despite the project's considerable potential.

In this chapter we consider various ways by which management can gauge the risk of a project or a group of projects. Our ultimate objective is to come to an understanding of how risk affects value. First, we must measure project risk under a variety of circumstances, and that is the purpose of this chapter. In this regard, certain elementary probability concepts will be employed in the treatment of risk.

Given information about the expected risk of an investment proposal or proposals, together with information about the expected return, management must then evaluate this information and reach a decision. As the decision to accept or reject an investment proposal depends on the risk-adjusted return required by suppliers of capital, we defer consideration of the evaluation of risky investments until we consider required rates of return in the next chapter. In this chapter we develop the information necessary to evaluate risky investments. In chapter 15 we examine the use of this information in reaching capital-budgeting decisions consistent with an objective of maximizing shareholder wealth. We begin this chapter with a discussion of the overall operating risk of the firm. We then move on to a general introduction to project risk, followed by the consideration of its specific measurement.

OPERATING LEVERAGE AND RISK

The overall business risk of a firm is related to its operating leverage. Operating leverage is simply the employment of an asset for which the firm pays a fixed cost. Expressed differently, operating leverage occurs any time a firm has fixed costs that must be met, regardless of volume. In the very long run, of course, all costs are variable. Consequently, our analysis necessarily involves the short run. We employ assets with a fixed cost in the hope that volume will produce revenues more than sufficient to cover all fixed and variable costs. One of the more dramatic examples of operating leverage is in the airline industry, where a large portion of total costs are fixed. Beyond a certain break-even load factor, each additional passenger represents essentially straight profit to the airline.

The essential thing is that fixed costs do not vary as volume changes. These costs include things such as depreciation of buildings and equipment, insurance, property taxes, part of the overall utility bills, and a portion of the cost of management. On the other hand, variable costs vary directly with the level of output. These costs include raw materials, direct labor costs, part of the overall utility bills, direct selling commissions, and certain parts of general and administrative expenses. With fixed costs, the percentage change in profits accompanying a change in volume is greater than the percentage change in volume. This phenomenon is known as operating leverage.

We should recognize that operating leverage is but one component of the overall business risk of the firm. The principal factors giving rise to business risk are variability or uncertainty of sales, and production costs. Operating leverage magnifies the impact of these factors on the variability of profits; however, operating leverage is not the source of the variability per se. Consequently, the degree of operating leverage of a firm should not be taken to represent its business risk. Because of the underlying variability of sales and costs, however, increases in operating leverage will increase the total variability of profits and, hence, magnify the company's business risk.

Analyzing operating leverage

Our firm produces a quality testing machine that sells for $50 a unit. We have annual fixed costs of $100,000, and variable costs of $25 a unit, regardless of

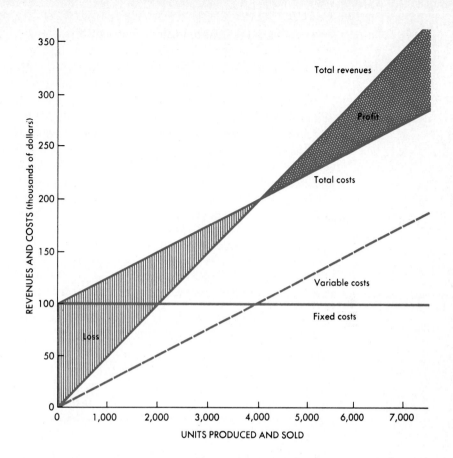

FIGURE 14-1
Break-even analysis:
original conditions

the volume sold. We wish to study the relationship between total costs and total revenues. One way to do that is shown in the break-even chart in Fig. 14-1, which depicts the relationship between profits, fixed costs, variable costs, and volume. By *profits*, we mean operating profits before taxes. This definition purposely excludes interest on debt and preferred-stock dividends. These costs are not part of the total fixed costs of the firm when it comes to analyzing operating leverage. They are taken into account when we analyze financial leverage in the next part.

The intersection of the total costs line with the total revenue line represents the break-even point. The fixed costs that must be recovered from the sales dollar after the deduction of variable costs determine the volume necessary to break even. In Fig. 14-1 this break-even point is 4,000 units of output. At the break-even point, variable costs plus fixed costs equal total revenue:

$$F + V(X) = P(X) \qquad \text{(14-1)}$$

where F = fixed costs

V = variable costs per unit

X = volume of output (in units)

P = price per unit.

299

Rearranging Eq.(14-1), the break-even point is

$$X = F/(P - V)$$
$$= 100,000/(50 - 25) = 4,000$$

For each additional increment of volume above the break-even point, there is increasing profit represented by the crosshatched area in the figure. Likewise, as volume falls below the break-even point, there are increasing losses, represented by the lined area. Table 14-1 shows the profit for various levels of volume. We see that the closer the volume to the break-even point, the greater the percentage change in profit in relation to a percentage change in volume. The fact that fixed costs equal variable costs at the break-even point is attributable to the nature of the example. Because price less variable costs equals $50 − $25 = $25, this amount is the same as variable costs per unit. As total price less variable costs must equal fixed costs at the break-even point, so, too, do total variable costs. As the example is changed in the subsequent section, this situation no longer holds.

TABLE 14-1 ⟍ **Relation between profit and volume—original case**

Volume (in thousand units)	0	1	2	3	4	5	6	7
Operating profit (in thousand dollars)	−$100	−$75	−$50	−$25	0	$25	$50	$75

Change in factors. A break-even chart, like that in Fig. 14-1, tells us the relationship between operating profits and volume. The greater the ratio of price to variable costs per unit, the greater the absolute sensitivity of profits to volume and the greater the degree of operating leverage for all levels of output. A change in volume is not the only factor that affects profits, however; a change in selling price, in variable cost per unit, or in fixed costs also affects profits. In the light of Fig. 14-1, we examine a favorable change in each of these factors, all other factors held constant.

An increase in price lowers the break-even point. For example, an increase in price from $50 to $65 per unit would result in the following break-even point (in units)

$$X = 100,000/(65 - 25) = 2,500$$

Table 14-2 shows the relationship between profits and volume for 5 levels of output. The original situation is shown in the second column; the situation with a $65 price is in the third column. Profits, of course, are $15 per unit greater for each level of volume.

A decrease in fixed costs also lowers the break-even point; indeed, that is the whole idea behind operating leverage. If fixed costs were lowered from

TABLE 14-2 ╲ **Relation between profits and volume—changing assumptions**

Volume (in units)	Profits (in thousands)				
	Original case	Price ($65)	Fixed costs ($50,000)	Variable costs ($20)	All three
0	−$100	−$100	−$ 50	−$100	−$ 50
2,000	− 50	− 20	0	− 40	40
4,000	0	60	50	20	130
6,000	50	140	100	80	220
8,000	100	220	150	140	310

$100,000 to $50,000, the break-even point would be

$$X = 50,000/(50 - 25) = 2,000$$

With this change, profits for various levels of volume are shown in the fourth column of Table 14-2.

Finally, a decrease in variable costs again lowers the break-even point. If the change were from $25 to $20 per unit, the break-even point would be

$$X = 100,000/(50 - 20) = 3,333$$

Profits are $5 per unit greater, and the relationship of profits with volume is shown in column 5 of Table 14-2.

The last column of the table shows the relationship between profits and volume if all three of the above changes occur simultaneously. Although we have considered only a favorable change in each case, it should be clear that a decrease in price, an increase in fixed costs, and an increase in variable costs will result in a higher break-even point and lower profits. In both directions, the closer the volume to the break-even point, the greater the percentage change in profit for a percentage change in volume.

Thus, operating leverage magnifies the overall risk of the firm. It is not the underlying cause of risk, for that depends on the variability of demand for the product plus the variability of various costs. However, increases in operating leverage increase the variability of profits that accompany the underlying fluctuations mentioned above. With this in mind, we turn now to the measurement of risk for investment projects.

THE PROBLEM OF PROJECT RISK

We define the riskiness of an investment project as the variability of its cash flows from those that are expected. The greater the variability, the riskier the project is said to be. For each project under consideration, we can make estimates of the future cash flows. Rather than estimate only the most likely cash-flow outcome for each year in the future as we did in chapter 4, we estimate a number of possible outcomes. In this way we are able to consider the range of possible cash flows for a particular future period rather than just the most likely cash flow.

An illustration

To illustrate the formulation of multiple cash-flow forecasts for a future period, suppose we had two investment proposals under consideration. Suppose further that we were interested in making forecasts for the following states of the economy: normal, deep recession, mild recession, major boom, and minor boom. After assessing the future under each of these possible states, we estimate the following cash flows for the next year:

	Annual Cash Flows	
State	Proposal A	Proposal B
Deep recession	$3,000	$2,000
Mild recession	3,500	3,000
Normal	4,000	4,000
Minor boom	4,500	5,000
Major boom	5,000	6,000

We see that the dispersion of possible cash flows for proposal B is greater than that for proposal A; therefore, we could say that it was riskier. In order to quantify our analysis of risk, however, we need additional information. More specifically, we need to know the likelihood of the various states of the economy occurring. Suppose our estimate of the odds for a deep recession is 10 percent, of a mild recession 20 percent, of a normal economy 40 percent, of a minor economic boom 20 percent, and of a major economic boom 10 percent. Given this information, we now are able to formulate a probability distribution of possible cash flows for proposals A and B:

Proposal A		Proposal B	
Probability	Cash Flow	Probability	Cash Flow
.10	$3,000	.10	$2,000
.20	3,500	.20	3,000
.40	4,000	.40	4,000
.20	4,500	.20	5,000
.10	5,000	.10	6,000

FIGURE 14-2
Comparison of
two proposals

We can graph these probability distributions, and the results are shown in Fig. 14-2. As we see, the dispersion of cash flows is greater for proposal B than it is for proposal A, despite the fact that the most likely outcome is the same for both investment proposals: $4,000. According to the discussion in chapter 13, the firm would rank the proposals equally. The critical question is whether dispersion should be considered. If risk is associated with the probability distribution of possible cash flows, such that the greater the dispersion the greater the risk, proposal B would be the riskier investment. If management, stockholders, and creditors are averse to risk, proposal A then would be preferred to proposal B.

Measurement of dispersion

Rather than always having to resort to graph paper, we need a measure of the dispersion of a probability distribution. The tighter the distribution, the lower this measure should be; the wider the distribution, the greater it should be. The conventional measure of dispersion is the *standard deviation*, which will be presented first mathematically and then illustrated with the previous example. The *standard deviation* can be expressed mathematically as

$$\sigma = \sqrt{\sum_{x=1}^{n} (A_x - \overline{A})^2 P_x} \qquad (14\text{-}2)$$

303

where A_x is the cash flow for the xth possibility, P_x is the probability of occurrence of that cash flow, and $\overline{A}$ is the *expected value* of cash flows, to be defined in Eq. (14-3). The Greek sigma, Σ, means the sum of the bracketed amounts from possibility 1 through possibility n. In other words, n is the total number of possibilities—five in our example. The square-root sign, $\sqrt{\ }$, indicates that we take the square root of the calculated amount. While all of this seems rather formidable, in fact the standard deviation can be computed rather easily with the aid of a calculator. The *expected value*, $\overline{A}$, of a probability distribution is defined as

$$\overline{A} = \sum_{x=1}^{n} A_x P_x \qquad (14\text{-}3)$$

It is simply a weighted average of the possible cash flows, with the weights being the probabilities of occurrence.

The standard deviation is simply a measure of the tightness of a probability distribution. For a normal, bell-shaped distribution, approximately 68 percent of the total area of the distribution falls within one standard deviation on either side of the expected value. This means that there is only a 32 percent chance that the actual outcome will be more than one standard deviation from the mean. The probability that the actual outcome will fall within two standard deviations of the expected value of the distribution is approximately 95 percent, and the probability that it will fall within three standard deviations is over 99 percent. A table showing the area of a normal distribution that is so many standard deviations to the right or left of the expected value is given in Appendix B to this chapter. As we shall see later in the chapter, the standard deviation is used to assess the likelihood of an event's occurring.

An illustration. To illustrate the derivation of the expected value and standard deviation of a probability distribution of possible cash flows, consider again our previous example. The expected value of the distribution for proposal A is

$$\overline{A}_a = .10(3{,}000) + .20(3{,}500) + .40(4{,}000) + .20(4{,}500) + .10(5{,}000) = 4{,}000$$

which is the same as that for proposal B:

$$\overline{A}_b = .10(2{,}000) + .20(3{,}000) + .40(4{,}000) + .20(5{,}000) + .10(6{,}000) = 4{,}000$$

However, the standard deviation for proposal A is

$$\sigma_a = [.10(3{,}000 - 4{,}000)^2 + .20(3{,}500 - 4{,}000)^2 + .40(4{,}000 - 4{,}000)^2$$
$$+ .20(4{,}500 - 4{,}000)^2 + .10(5{,}000 - 4{,}000)^2]^{1/2} = [300{,}000]^{1/2} = 548$$

where $[\ ]^{1/2}$ is simply the square root, the same as $\sqrt{\ }$. Note also that when we square a minus number, such as $(3{,}000 - 4{,}000)^2$, it becomes positive. The standard deviation for proposal B is

$$\sigma_b = [.10(2{,}000 - 4{,}000)^2 + .20(3{,}000 - 4{,}000)^2 + .40(4{,}000 - 4{,}000)^2$$
$$+ .20(5{,}000 - 4{,}000)^2 + .10(6{,}000 - 4{,}000)^2]^{1/2} = [1{,}200{,}000]^{1/2} = 1{,}095$$

Thus, proposal B has a higher standard deviation, indicating a greater dispersion of possible outcomes, and so we would say it had greater risk.

Coefficient of variation. A measure of relative dispersion is the coefficient of variation, which simply is the standard deviation of a probability distribution over its expected value. For proposal A, the coefficient of variation is

$$CV_a = 548/4{,}000 = .14$$

while that for proposal B is

$$CV_b = 1{,}095/4{,}000 = .27$$

Because the coefficient of variation for proposal B exceeds that for proposal A, we would say that it had a greater degree of risk. One might question the use of the coefficient of variation when in our example it was obvious that proposal B had greater risk owing to its larger standard deviation. In our example, however, the expected values of the probability distributions of possible cash flows for the two proposals were the same. What if they were different? Here we need a measure of relative dispersion, and the coefficient of variation is such a measure. Frequent reference to the expected value, standard deviation, and coefficient of variation will be made in the remainder of this chapter.[1]

RISK FOR THE INDIVIDUAL PROJECT

If investors and creditors are risk-averse—and all available evidence suggests that they are, it behooves management to incorporate the risk of an investment proposal into its analysis of the proposal's worth. Otherwise, capital-budgeting decisions are unlikely to be in accord with an objective of maximizing share price. Having established the need for taking risk into account, we proceed to measure it for individual investment proposals. But remember that the riskiness of a stream of cash flows for a project can, and usually does, change with the length of time in the future. In other words, the probability distributions are not necessarily the same from one period to the next.

---

[1] We assume that risk can be judged solely in relation to the expected value and standard deviation of a probability distribution. Implied is that the shape of the distribution is unimportant. This holds when the distribution is relatively symmetric or "bell-shaped." However, if it is significantly skewed to the right or left, management may wish to take account of this fact as well. Although it is possible to incorporate a skewness measure into our analysis of risk, it is difficult mathematically to do so. For simplicity, we shall deal with only the expected value and standard deviation of a normal probability distribution.

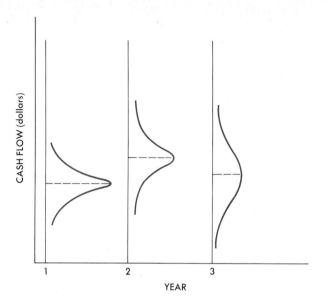

FIGURE 14-3
Changing risk
over time

This notion is illustrated in Fig. 14-3 for a hypothetical investment project. The distributions are like those shown in Fig. 14-2 except that they are continuous instead of being discrete bars. This means that a cash-flow outcome is assigned to each possible state of the economy, and a continuous line is drawn. As before, the tighter and more peaked the distribution, the less the risk. The expected value of each of the distributions is depicted by the horizontal dashed line. We see that both the expected value of cash flow and the dispersion of the probability distribution change over time. We must come to grips with this factor so that we can quantify the risk of a prospective investment proposal.

Use of a probability tree

One way of approaching the problem is with a probability tree. Here we specify the likely future cash flows of a project as they relate to the outcomes in previous periods. If a project turns out to be good in the first period, it may well turn out to be good in subsequent periods. While there frequently is a link between what happens in one period and what happens in the next, this is not always the case. If cash flows are believed to be independent from period to period, we simply specify a probability distribution of cash-flow outcomes for each period. If there is a link, we should take this dependence into account.

With a probability tree we attempt to unfold future events as they might occur. Fig. 14-4 shows a probability tree for a three-period case. Here we see that if the outcome in period 1 is the upper branch, it results in a different set of possible outcomes in period 2 than if the lower branch occurred in period 1. The same thing applies to going from period 2 to period 3. Therefore, at time 0 the probability tree represents our best estimate of what is likely to occur in the future, contingent upon what occurs before. For each of the branches in the figure, a cash flow as well as a probability is attached.

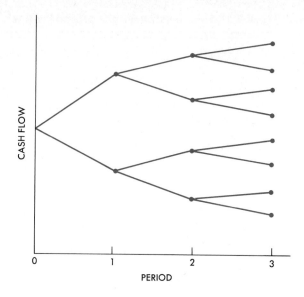

FIGURE 14-4
A probability tree

For the first period, the cash-flow outcome does not depend on what happened before. Therefore, the probabilities associated with the two branches are said to be *initial probabilities*. For the second and third periods, however, cash-flow outcomes depend on what happened before. Therefore, the probabilities involved in these periods are said to be *conditional probabilities*. Finally, the *joint probability* is the probability that a particular sequence of cash flows might occur. For example, one sequence is the top branches in each of the three periods. The joint probability is the product of the initial probability and the two conditional probabilities for the top branches. Rather than continue to discuss probability trees in the abstract, let us proceed to an example.

An illustration for a project

Suppose that we were considering the investment in a project costing $240 at time 0 that was expected to generate the possible cash flows shown in Table 14-3. Given a cash flow of −$100 in period 1, the probability is .40 that this negative flow will become −$400 in period 2, .40 that it will remain at −$100, and .20 that it will be $200. The joint probability that a −$100 cash flow in period 1 will be followed by a −$400 cash flow in period 2 is simply the product of the initial probability and the conditional probability, or .25 × .40 = .10.

Similarly, the joint probability that a cash flow of −$100 in period 1 will be followed by a cash flow of −$100 in period 2 is .25 × .40 = .10, and the probability that a −$100 cash flow in period 1 will be followed by a $200 cash flow in period 2 is .25 × .20 = .05. If the cash flow in period 1 turns out to be $200, there is a .20 probability it will become −$100 in period 2; .60 it will remain at $200 in period 2, and .20 it will become $500. In the same manner as before, we can calculate the joint probabilities for this branch, and they are found to be .10, .30, and .10, respectively. Similarly, the joint probabilities for the last branch, where a $500 net cash flow in period 1 occurs, can be determined.

TABLE 14-3 \ Illustration of a probability tree

Period 1		Period 2		
Initial probability P(1)	Net cash flow	Conditional probability P(2 | 1)	Net cash flow	Joint probability P(1, 2)
.25	−$100	.40	−$400	.10
		.40	− 100	.10
		.20	200	.05
.50	200	.20	− 100	.10
		.60	200	.30
		.20	500	.10
.25	500	.20	200	.05
		.40	500	.10
		.40	800	.10

Initial investment at time 0 = $240.

Discounting to present value. In discounting the various cash flows to their present value, one should employ the risk-free rate. This rate is used because we attempt to isolate the time value of money by discounting, and then we analyze risk separately. To include a premium for risk in the discount rate would result in double counting with respect to our evaluation. We would compensate for risk in the discounting process and then again in our analysis of the dispersion of the distribution of possible net present values. For this reason, we use the risk-free rate for discounting purposes.

For our example problem, the expected value of the probability distribution of possible net present values is

$$\overline{NPV} = -\$240 + \sum_{x=1}^{z} NPV_x P_x \qquad (14\text{-}4)$$

where NPV_x is the net present value for series X of net cash flows, covering all periods, P_x is the probability of occurrence of that series, and z is the total number of cash-flow series. For our example, there are 9 possible series of net cash-flows, so z = 9. The first series is represented by a cash flow of −$100 in period 1, followed by a −$400 cash flow in period 2. The probability of occurrence of that cash flow is .10. If the risk-free rate used as the discount rate is 8 percent, the net present value of this series is

$$NPV_1 = -240 - \frac{100}{(1.08)} - \frac{400}{(1.08)^2} = -\$676$$

The second cash-flow series is represented by a cash flow of −$100 in period 1, followed by a −$100 cash flow in period 2. The net present value of this series is

$$NPV_2 = -240 - \frac{100}{(1.08)} - \frac{100}{(1.08)^2} = -\$418$$

In the same manner, the net present values for the seven other cash-flow series can be determined. When these values are multiplied by their respective probabilities of occurrence (the last column in Table 14-3) and summed, we obtain the expected value of net present value of the probability distribution of possible net present values (rounded to the nearest dollar). The calculations are shown in Table 14-4, and we see that the expected value of net present value is $116.

TABLE 14-4 ⟍ Calculation of expected value of net present value for example problem

(1) Cash-flow series	(2) Net present value	(3) Probability of occurrence	(4) (2) × (3)
1	−$676	.10	−$68
2	− 418	.10	− 42
3	− 161	.05	− 8
4	− 141	.10	− 14
5	117	.30	35
6	374	.10	37
7	394	.05	20
8	652	.10	65
9	909	.10	91
Weighted average			$116

The standard deviation of the probability distribution of possible net present values can be determined by

$$\sigma = \sqrt{\sum_{x=1}^{z} (NPV_x - \overline{NPV})^2 P_x} \qquad (14\text{-}5)$$

where the symbols are the same as for Eq.(14-4). The standard deviation for our example problem is

$$\sigma = [.10(-676 - 116)^2 + .10(-418 - 116)^2$$
$$+ .05(-161 - 116)^2 + .10(-141 - 116)^2$$
$$+ .30(117 - 116)^2 + .10(374 - 116)^2$$
$$+ .05(394 - 116)^2 + .10(652 - 116)^2$$
$$+ .10(909 - 116)^2]^{1/2} = [197,277]^{1/2} = \$444$$

Rounding to the nearest dollar, the project has an expected value of net present value of $116 and a standard deviation of $444. Although the mathematical calculation of the standard deviation is feasible for simple cases, it is not for complex situations. Here, one should resort to simulation to approximate the standard deviation. The technique is explained in Appendix A to this chapter, where the Hertz model for evaluating risky investments is considered.

Use of information

The expected value and the standard deviation of the probability distribution of possible net present values, whether derived by a probability tree or some other means, give us a considerable amount of information by which to evaluate the risk of the investment proposal. If the probability distribution is approximately normal, we are able to calculate the probability of the proposal's providing a net present value of less or more than a specified amount. The probability is found by determining the area under the curve to the left or to the right of a particular point of interest. To go on with our previous illustration, suppose we wish to determine the probability that the net present value will be zero or less. To determine this probability, we first calculate the difference between 0 and the expected value of net present value for the project.

In our example, this difference is − $116. We then standardize this difference by dividing it by the standard deviation of possible net present values. The formula is

$$S = \frac{X - \overline{NPV}}{\sigma} \tag{14-6}$$

where X is the outcome in which we are interested, $\overline{NPV}$ is the expected value of net present value, and σ is the standard deviation of the probability distribution. In our case,

$$S = \frac{0 - 116}{444} = -.26$$

This figure tells us that a net present value of 0 lies .26 standard deviations to the left of the expected value of the probability distribution of possible net present values.

To determine the probability that the net present value of the project will be 0 or less, we consult a normal probability distribution table found in most statistics texts or in Appendix B at the end of this chapter. We find that for the normal distribution, there is a .4013 probability that an observation will be less than −.25 standard deviations from the expected value of that distribution and a .3821 probability that it will be less than −.30 standard deviations from the expected value. Interpolating, we find that there is approximately a 40 percent probability that the net present value of the proposal will be zero or less. We know also that there is a 60 percent probability that the net present value of the project will be greater than zero. With a normal distribution, .68 of the distribution falls

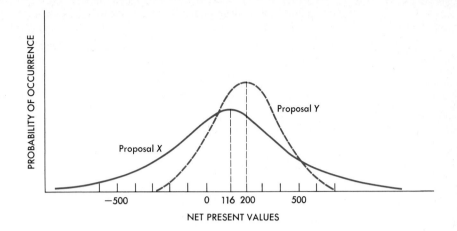

FIGURE 14-5
Probability distributions
of net present values
for two projects

within one standard deviation on either side of the expected value. We know then that there is approximately a two-thirds probability that the net present value of the proposal will be between $116 − $444 = −$328 and $116 + $444 = $560. By expressing differences from the expected value in terms of standard deviations, we are able to determine the probability that the net present value for an investment proposal will be greater or less than a particular amount.[2]

The information above tells us that the dispersion of possible outcomes for the project is rather wide. There is a 40 percent probability that the net present value will be zero or less and about a one-sixth probability that it will be −$328 or worse. (The latter is simply the area of a curve that is greater than one standard deviation to the left of the expected value.)

Knowledge of these probabilites is fundamental for a realistic assessment of risk. Suppose that the firm is considering another investment proposal, call it Y. The probability distribution for this proposal is shown in Fig. 14-5, as is that for our example problem, which we call proposal X. We see that the expected value of net present value for proposal Y is $200, which is higher than that for proposal X, $116. Moreover, there is less dispersion with proposal Y than there is with proposal X. Therefore, we would say that proposal Y dominates proposal X on the basis of both risk and return. Whether proposal Y or both projects should be accepted depends on the risk tolerances of management. We address ourselves to this question in the next chapter. In this chapter we want to learn how to measure risk.

RISK IN A PORTFOLIO SENSE

In the last section we measured risk for a single investment proposal. When multiple investment projects are involved and we have a combined risk, the measurement procedure differs from that for a single project. The approach we

[2]In the examples above we have assumed normal probability distributions. Although this property is very desirable for purposes of calculation, it is not necessary for use of the above approach. Even when the distribution is not normal, we usually are able to make relatively strong probability statements by using Chebyshev's inequality.

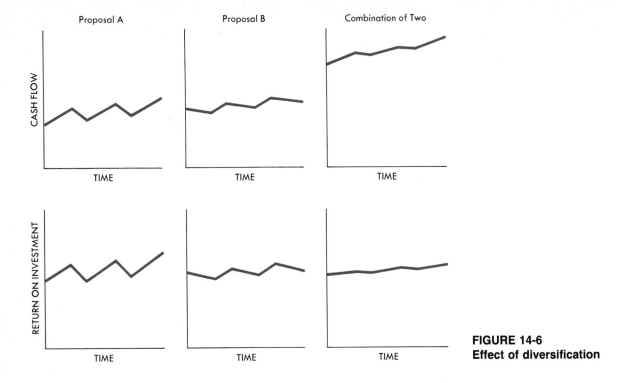

FIGURE 14-6
Effect of diversification

take corresponds to the portfolio approach in security analysis. Portfolio theory was discussed in chapter 5; here we apply the approach to capital-investment projects. The circumstances under which the approach is feasible are taken up in chapter 15, when we examine the acceptance criteria for risky investments. Our purpose here is only to show how to measure risk for combinations of risky investments, assuming that such a measure is desired.

If a firm adds a project whose future cash flows are likely to be highly correlated with those of existing assets, the total risk of the firm will increase more than if it adds a project that has a low degree of correlation with existing assets. The idea is that projects can be combined to reduce relative risk.

Fig. 14-6 shows the expected cash-flow patterns for two projects over time. Proposal A is cyclical, while proposal B is mildly countercyclical. By combining the two projects, we see that total cash-flow dispersion is reduced, and the dispersion of the return on investment is reduced even more. The combination of projects to reduce risk is known as diversification, and the principle is the same as diversification in securities. One attempts to reduce deviations in return from the expected value of return.

Measurement of portfolio risk

The standard deviation of the probability distribution of possible net present values is more difficult to calculate for a portfolio than for a single investment. It is not the summation of the standard deviations of the individual projects making up the portfolio, but

$$\sigma = \sqrt{\sum_{j=1}^{m}\sum_{k=1}^{m} \sigma_{jk}} \qquad (14\text{-}7)$$

where j refers to project j; k to project k; m is the total number of projects in the portfolio, and σ_{jk} is the covariance between possible net present values for projects j and k. (This rather formidable expression will be illustrated shortly.)
The covariance term in Eq. (14-7) is

$$\sigma_{jk} = r_{jk}\sigma_j\sigma_k \qquad (14\text{-}8)$$

where r_{jk} is the expected correlation between possible net present values for projects j and k; σ_j is the standard deviation for project j, and σ_k is the standard deviation for project k. The standard deviations of the probability distributions of possible net present values for projects j and k are determined by the methods taken up in the previous section. When $j = k$ in Eq. (14-8), the correlation coefficient is 1.0, and $\sigma_j\sigma_k$ becomes σ_j^2 (that is, the standard deviation squared of the probability distribution of possible net present values for investment project j).

An illustration

To illustrate these concepts, suppose that a firm has a single existing investment project, 1, and that it is considering investing in an additional project, 2. Assume further that the projects have the following expected values of net present value, standard deviations, and correlation coefficients:

	Expected value of net present value	Standard deviation	Correlation coefficient
Project 1	$12,000	$14,000	1.00
Project 2	8,000	6,000	1.00
Projects 1 and 2			.40

The expected value of the net present value of the combination of projects is simply the sum of the two separate net present values.

$$\text{NPV} = \$12{,}000 + \$8{,}000 = \$20{,}000$$

The standard deviation for the combination, using Eqs. (14-7) and (14-8), is

$$\sigma = \sqrt{r_{11}\sigma_1^2 + 2r_{12}\sigma_1\sigma_2 + r_{22}\sigma_2^2}$$

$$= \sqrt{(1.00)(14{,}000)^2 + (2)(.40)(14{,}000)(6{,}000) + (1.00)(6{,}000)^2}$$

$$= \$17{,}297$$

Thus, the expected value of net present value of the firm increases from $12,000 to $20,000 and the standard deviation of possible net present values from $14,000 to $17,297 with the acceptance of project 2. The coefficient of variation (standard deviation over expected value of net present value) is 14,000/12,000 = 1.17 without project 2 and 17,297/20,000 = .86 with the project. If we employ the coefficient of variation as a measure of relative business risk, we conclude that acceptance of project 2 would lower the business risk of the firm.

By accepting projects with relatively low degrees of correlation with existing projects, a firm diversifies and in so doing may be able to lower its overall business risk. We note above that the lower the degree of positive correlation, r_{12}, the lower the standard deviation of possible net present values, all other things being equal. Whether the coefficient of variation declines when an investment project is added depends also upon the expected value of net present value for the project.

Correlation between projects

Estimating the correlation between possible net present values for two projects in Eq. (14-8) is the key ingredient in analyzing risk in a portfolio context. When two projects are similar to projects with which the company has had experience, it may be feasible to compute the correlation coefficients using historical data. For other investments, estimates of the correlation coefficients must be based solely upon an assessment of the future.

Management might have reason to expect only slight correlation between investment projects involving research and development for an electronic tester and a new consumer product. On the other hand, it might expect high positive correlation between investments in a milling machine and a turret lathe if both machines were used in the production of industrial lift trucks. The profit from a machine to be used in a production line will be highly, if not completely, correlated with the profit for the production line itself.

The correlation between expected net present values of various investments may be positive, negative, or 0, depending upon the nature of the association. A correlation coefficient of 1.00 indicates that the net present values of two investment proposals vary directly in exactly the same proportional manner; a correlation coefficient of −1.00 indicates that they vary inversely in exactly the same proportional manner; and a 0 correlation coefficient indicates that they are independent or unrelated. For most pairs of investments, the correlation coefficient lies between 0 and 1.00. The reason for the lack of negatively correlated investment projects is that most investments are correlated positively with the economy.

Estimates of the correlation coefficients must be as objective as possible if the total standard deviation figure obtained in Eq. (14-7) is to be realistic. It is not unreasonable to expect management to make fairly accurate estimates of these coefficients. When actual correlation differs from expected correlation, the situation can be a learning process, and estimates on other projects can be revised.

Combinations of risky investments

We now have a procedure for determining the total expected value and the standard deviation of a probability distribution of possible net present values for a combination of investments. For our purposes, we define a *combination* as including all existing investment projects and one or more proposals under consideration. We assume, then, that the firm has existing investment projects and that these projects are expected to generate future cash flows. Thus, existing projects constitute a subset that is included in all combinations. We denote this portfolio of projects by the italic letter E.

A firm has under consideration four investment proposals, which are independent of one another; that is, they are not contingent or mutually exclusive. If these proposals are labeled 1, 2, 3, and 4, we have the following possible combinations of risky investments:

E	E,1	E,1,2	E,1,2,3	E,1,2,3,4
	E,2	E,1,3	E,1,2,4	
	E,3	E,1,4	E,1,3,4	
	E,4	E,2,3	E,2,3,4	
		E,2,4		
		E,3,4		

Thus, 16 combinations of projects are possible, with one possibility being the rejection of all of the proposals under consideration, so that the firm is left with only its existing projects, E. The expected value of net present value and standard deviation for each of these combinations can be computed in the manner described previously. The results can then be graphed.

Fig. 14-7 is a scatter diagram of the 16 possible combinations. Here the expected value of net present value is along the horizontal axis, and the standard

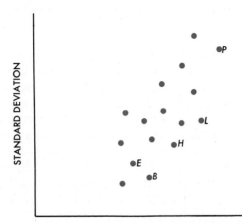

**FIGURE 14-7
Opportunity set of
combinations of
projects**

deviation is on the vertical axis. Each dot represents a combination. Collectively, these dots constitute the total set of feasible combinations of investment opportunities available to the firm.

We see that certain dots dominate others in the sense that they represent a higher expected value of net present value and the same standard deviation, a lower standard deviation and the same expected value of net present value, or both a higher expected value and a lower standard deviation. The dominating dots are those that are farthest to the right in the figure. Four of them have been identified specifically—combinations B, H, L, and P. (The dot E represents all existing investment projects.)

Although the selection process itself is deferred until chapter 15, we observe here that the combination ultimately chosen determines the new investment proposal or proposals that will be accepted. If combination H were selected and it consisted of E, 1, and 4, investment proposals 1 and 4 would be accepted. Those investment proposals not in the combination finally selected would be rejected. In our case, they would be proposals 2 and 3. If the combination finally selected consisted of only existing investment projects, E, all investment proposals under consideration would be rejected. The selection of any other combination implies the acceptance of one or more of the investment proposals under consideration.

The incremental expected value of net present value and standard deviation can be determined by measuring on the horizontal and vertical axes the distance from dot E to the dot representing the combination finally selected. These distances can be thought of as the incremental contribution of expected value of net present value and standard deviation to the firm as a whole. In chapter 15, we explore how the actual selection can be made and under what circumstances this approach is appropriate. Our purpose here has been to measure risk for combinations of risky investments in order to provide management with such information.

SUMMARY

Operating leverage may be defined as the employment of an asset with a fixed cost in the hope that sufficient revenue will be generated to cover all fixed and variable costs. We study the operating leverage of a firm by using a break-even graph, which enables us to analyze the relationship among profits, volume, fixed costs, variable costs, and prices. By varying these factors, management may determine the sensitivity of profits and, in so doing, obtain a better understanding of the operating risk of the firm.

The risk of an investment project can be defined as the deviation in actual cash flows from those that were expected. Expressing the future in terms of probability distributions of possible cash flows, we can express risk quantitatively as the standard deviation of the distribution. The coefficient of variation is simply the standard deviation of a probability distribution over its expected value, and it serves as a relative measure of risk. Business risk is the risk associated with the operations of the firm, and it can be expressed in terms of the coefficient of variation.

One approach to the evaluation of risky investments is the direct analysis of the probability distribution of possible net present values of a project. Given the expected value and standard deviation of the distribution, management can determine the probability that the actual net present value will be lower than some amount such as zero. This type of information is extremely valuable in judging the risk of a project. The use of a probability tree was illustrated for taking account of changing risk over time.

Investment projects also can be judged with respect to their portfolio risk. Here we are concerned with the marginal risk of a project to the firm as a whole. By diversifying into projects not having high degrees of correlation with existing assets, a firm is able to reduce the standard deviation of its probability distribution of possible net present values relative to the expected value of the distribution. The likely degree of correlation between projects is the key to measuring portfolio risk.

Our purpose in this chapter has been to explore the means by which risk can be quantified for investment proposals and combinations of proposals. With this information, together with information about the expected profitability of the investment, we should reach much more informed, better decisions. In chapter 15 we consider how this information can be employed in the decision process.

APPENDIX A \ Simulation Approach to Risky Investments

In considering risky investments, we can use simulation to approximate the expected return and dispersion about the expected return for an investment proposal. By *simulation*, we mean testing the results of an investment decision before it actually occurs. The testing itself is based on a model coupled with probabilistic information. A simulation model proposed by Hertz considers the following factors in deriving a project's earnings stream:

Market analysis

1. Market size
2. Selling price
3. Market growth rate
4. Share of market (which results in physical sales volume)

Investment Cost Analysis

5. Investment required
6. Residual value of investment

Operating and Fixed Costs

7. Operating costs
8. Fixed costs
9. Useful life of facilities[3]

---

[3]David B. Hertz, "Risk Analysis in Capital Investment," *Harvard Business Review*, 42 (January–February 1964), 95–106.

Probability distributions are assigned to each of these factors, based upon management's assessment of the probable outcomes. Thus, the possible outcomes are charted for each factor according to their probability of occurrence; examples of these probability distributions are shown in Fig. 14-8.

Once the probability distributions are determined, the next step is to determine the average rate of return that will result from a random combination of the nine factors listed above. To illustrate the simulation process, assume that the market-size factor had the following probability distribution:

Market size (in thousand units)	450	500	550	600	650	700	750
Probability	.05	.10	.20	.30	.20	.10	.05

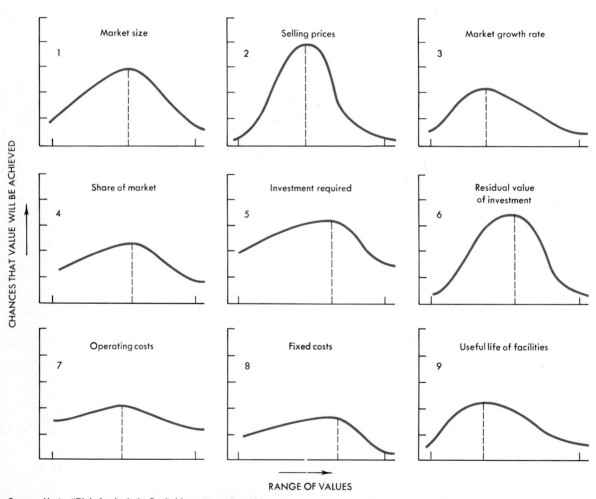

Source: Hertz, "Risk Analysis in Capital Investment," p. 102.

FIGURE 14-8 Probability distributions of nine key factors

Now suppose that we have a roulette wheel with 100 numbers, on which numbers 1 to 5 represent a market size of 450,000 units, 6 to 15 represent a market size of 500,000; 16 to 35, a market size of 550,000 units, and so on through 100. As in roulette, we spin the wheel, and the ball falls in one of the 100 slots: number 26. For this trial, then, we simulate a market size of 550,000 units. Fortunately, we do not need a roulette wheel to undertake a simulation; the same type of operation can be carried out on a computer in a much more efficient manner.

Simulation trials are undertaken for each of the other eight factors. The first four factors (market analysis) give us the annual sales per year; factors 7 and 8 give us the operating costs and fixed costs per year. Together, these six factors enable us to calculate the annual earnings per year. When trial values for these six factors are combined with trial values for the required investment, the useful life, and the residual value of the project, we have sufficient information to calculate the return on investment for that trial run. Thus, the computer simulates trial values for each of the nine factors and then calculates the return on investment based upon the values simulated. The process is repeated a number of times: each time we obtain a combination of values for the nine factors and the return on investment for that combination. When the trial is repeated often enough, the rates of return can be plotted in a frequency distribution like that shown in Fig. 14-9.

From this frequency distribution we are able to evaluate the expected return and the dispersion about this expected return, or risk, in the same manner as before; in other words, we can determine the probability that an investment will provide a return greater or less than a certain amount. By comparing the probability distribution of rates of return for one proposal with the probability distribution of rates of return for another, management is able to evaluate the respective merits of different risky investments.

Two points should be mentioned with respect to Hertz's simulation method. Although it computes the average rate of return on investment, the method could easily be modified to calculate the internal rate of return, the net present value, or the profitability index. In addition, although Hertz allows for dependency among the nine factors, the model presented treats the factors as though they were independent. To the extent that dependency exists among factors, it must be taken into account in determining the probability distributions. For example, there is likely to be significant correlation between the market size and

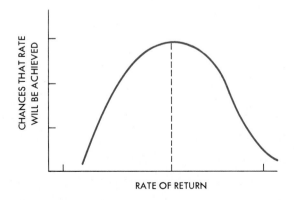

FIGURE 14-9
Probability distribution
for rate of return

the selling price. These interrelationships add considerable complexity to the estimating procedure. Notwithstanding the added complexity of estimating and specifying in the model the relationships among factors, it must be done if the model is to provide realistic results. These estimates may be based upon empirical testing when such testing is feasible. Once the relationships are incorporated in the model, those factors that are correlated would then be simulated jointly. Rates of return for the simulated trials would be calculated and a frequency distribution of simulated trials formed in the same manner as before.

APPENDIX B ╲ Normal Probability Distribution Table

Table 14B-1 shows the area of the normal distribution that is X standard deviations to the left or to the right of the mean. The test is "one-tail" in the sense that we are concerned with one side of the distribution or the other. If we wished to know the area of the curve, or probability, that was 1.5 standard deviations or more from the arithmetic mean on the right, it would be depicted by the colored area in Fig. 14-10. In Table 14B-1 we see that this corresponds to 6.68 percent of the total area of the normal distribution. Thus, we would say that there was a 6.68 percent probability that the actual outcome would exceed the mean by 1.5 standard deviations. In a similar manner, the table can be used to determine the probability associated with other distances from the mean.

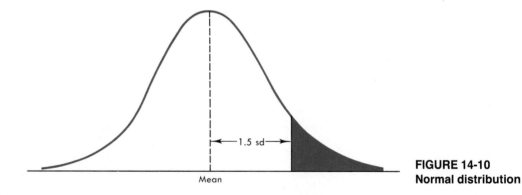

FIGURE 14-10
Normal distribution

QUESTIONS

1. The literature on finance assumes that the risk associated with an investment is a measurable phenomenon equivalent to the variability of returns on an investment. In your opinion, is this definition of risk adequate for asset selection by average investors? Explain.

2. Define the concept of *operating leverage*.

3. Classify the following short-run manufacturing costs as either typically fixed or typically variable. Which costs are variable at management's discretion? Are any of these costs "fixed" in the long run?

TABLE 14B-1 ╲ **Area of normal distribution that is _X_ standard deviations to the left or right of the mean**

Number of standard deviations from mean (X)	Area to the left or right (one tail)	Number of standard deviations from mean (X)	Area to the left or right (one tail)
.00	.5000	1.55	.0606
.05	.4801	1.60	.0548
.10	.4602	1.65	.0495
.15	.4404	1.70	.0446
.20	.4207	1.75	.0401
.25	.4013	1.80	.0359
.30	.3821	1.85	.0322
.35	.3632	1.90	.0287
.40	.3446	1.95	.0256
.45	.3264	2.00	.0228
.50	.3085	2.05	.0202
.55	.2912	2.10	.0179
.60	.2743	2.15	.0158
.65	.2578	2.20	.0139
.70	.2420	2.25	.0122
.75	.2264	2.30	.0107
.80	.2119	2.35	.0094
.85	.1977	2.40	.0082
.90	.1841	2.45	.0071
.95	.1711	2.50	.0062
1.00	.1577	2.55	.0054
1.05	.1469	2.60	.0047
1.10	.1357	2.65	.0040
1.15	.1251	2.70	.0035
1.20	.1151	2.75	.0030
1.25	.1056	2.80	.0026
1.30	.0968	2.85	.0022
1.35	.0885	2.90	.0019
1.40	.0808	2.95	.0016
1.45	.0735	3.00	.0013
1.50	.0668		

a)	Insurance	e)	R & D	i)	Depletion
b)	Direct labor	f)	Advertising	j)	Depreciation
c)	Property taxes	g)	Raw materials	k)	Maintenance
d)	Interest expense	h)	Bad-debt loss		

4. What would be the effect on the break-even point of the following?

a) Increased selling price

b) Increase in the minimum wage

c) Change from straight-line to accelerated depreciation

d) Increased sales

e) A 5-percent surtax on corporate profits

f) A liberalized credit policy

5. Discuss the importance of correlation among the expected returns of different projects.

6. Contrast uncertainty with risk as you perceive the terms. Is there a difference?

7. Risk in capital budgeting can be judged by analyzing the probability distribution of possible returns. What shape distribution would you expect to find for a safe project whose returns were absolutely certain? For a very risky project?

8. If project A has an expected value of net present value of $200 and a standard deviation of $400, is it more risky than project B whose expected value is $140 and standard deviation is $300?

9. What are the benefits of using simulation to evaluate capital-investment projects?

10. Is the standard deviation an adequate measure of risk? Can you think of a better measure?

11. Is there any business that is risk free?

PROBLEMS

1. R.A. Rice, Inc., can invest in one of two mutually exclusive projects. The two proposals have the following discrete probability distributions of net cash flows for period p:

	A		B	
Probability	Cash flow	Probability	Cash flow
.20	$2,000	.10	$2,000
.30	4,000	.40	4,000
.30	6,000	.40	6,000
.20	8,000	.10	8,000

a) Without calculating a mean and a coefficient of variation, can you select the better proposal, assuming a risk-averse management?

b)   Verify your intuitive determination.

2. The Madison Company earns monthly, after taxes, $2,400 on sales of $88,000. The average tax rate of the company is 40 percent. The company's only product sells for $20, of which $15 is variable cost.

a)   What is the monthly fixed cost of the Madison Company?

b)   What is its break-even point in units? In dollars?

3. What would be the effect of the following on the break-even point of the Madison Company (problem 2)?

a)   An increase in price of $5 per unit (assume that volume is constant)

b)   A decrease in fixed costs of $2,000

c)   A decrease in variable costs of $1 per unit and an increase in fixed costs of $6,000

4. The D.T. Crazy Horse Hotel has a capacity to stable 50 horses. The fee for stabling a horse is $100 per month. Maintenance, depreciation, property taxes, and other fixed costs total $1,200 per month. Variable costs per horse are $12 per month for hay and bedding and $8 per month for grain. Income is taxed at a 40 percent rate.

a)   Determine the break-even point.

b)   Compute the monthly profits after taxes if an average of 40 horses are stabled.

5. The Hume Corporation is faced with several possible investment projects. For each, the total cash outflow required will occur in the initial period. The cash outflows, expected net present values, and standard deviations are given in the following table. All projects have been discounted at the risk-free rate, and it is assumed that the distributions of their possible net present values are normal.

Project	Cost	Net present value	Standard deviation
A	$100,000	$10,000	$20,000
B	50,000	10,000	30,000
C	200,000	25,000	10,000
D	10,000	5,000	10,000
E	500,000	75,000	75,000

a)   Ignoring size problems, are there some projects that are clearly dominated by others with respect to the coefficient of variation?

b)   May size problems be ignored?

c)   What is the probability that each of the projects will have a net present value greater than or equal to zero?

6. The probability distribution of possible net present values for project X has an expected value of $20,000 and a standard deviation of $10,000. Assuming a normal distribution, calculate the probability that the net present value will be zero or less; that it will be greater than $30,000; and that it will be less than $5,000.

7. Xonics Graphics Inc. is evaluating a new technology for its reproduction equipment. The technology will have a 3-year life; it will cost $1,000, and its impact on cash flows is subject to risk. Management estimates that there is a 50-50 chance that the technology will either save the company $1,000 in the first year or save it nothing at all. If nothing at all, savings in the last 2 years would be zero as well. Even here there is some possibility that in the second year an additional outlay of $300 would be required to convert back to the original process, for the new technology may decrease efficiency. Management attaches a 40 percent probability to this occurrence if the new technology "bombs out" in the first year. If the technology proves itself, it is felt that second-year cash flows will be $1,800, $1,400 or $1,000, with probabilities of .20, .60, and .20, respectively. In the third year, cash flows are expected to be $200 greater or $200 less than the cash flow in period 2, with an equal chance of occurrence. (Again, these cash flows depend on the cash flow in period 1 being $1,000.)

a) Set up a probability tree to depict the above cash-flow possibilities.

b) Calculate a weighted net present value for each 3-year possibility, using a risk-free rate of 5 percent.

c) What is the risk of the project?

8. The Windrop Company will invest in two of three possible proposals, the cash flows of which are normally distributed. The expected net present value (discounted at the risk-free rate) and the standard deviation for each proposal are given as follows:

	1	2	3
Expected net present value	$10,000	$8,000	$6,000
Standard deviation	4,000	3,000	4,000

Assuming the following correlation coefficients for each possible combination, which combination dominates the others?

Proposals	Correlation coefficients
1	1.00
2	1.00
3	1.00
1 and 2	.60
1 and 3	.40
2 and 3	.50

9. The Plaza Corporation is confronted with various combinations of risky investments.

Combination	Net present value	Standard deviation
A	$100,000	$200,000
B	20,000	80,000
C	75,000	100,000
D	60,000	150,000
E	50,000	20,000
F	40,000	60,000
G	120,000	170,000
H	90,000	70,000
I	50,000	100,000
J	75,000	30,000

a) Plot the above portfolios.

b) Which combinations dominate the others?

Appendix A problem

10. The Bertz Company uses a simulation approach to judge investment projects. Three factors are employed: market demand, in units; price per unit minus cost per unit; and investment required at time 0. These factors are felt to be independent of one another. In analyzing a new consumer product, Bertz estimates the following probability distributions:

Annual Demand		Price Minus Cost per Unit		Investment Required	
Prob.	Units	Prob.	Dollars	Prob.	Dollars
.05	10,000	.10	$3.00	.30	$1,800,000
.10	20,000	.20	4.50	.40	2,000,000
.20	30,000	.40	6.00	.30	2,300,000
.30	45,000	.20	7.00		
.20	60,000	.10	8.00		
.10	75,000				
.05	90,000				

a) Using a random number table or some other random process, simulate 20 or more trials for these three factors and compute the return on investment for each trial. (*Note:* return = profit/investment.)

b) Approximately what is the most likely return? How risky is the project?

SELECTED REFERENCES

BEY, ROGER P., and J. CLAYTON SINGLETON, "Autocorrelated Cash Flows and the Selection of a Portfolio of Capital Assets," *Decision Sciences,* 8 (October 1978), 640–57.

BIERMAN, HAROLD, JR., and VITHALA R. RAO, "Investment Decisions with Sampling," *Financial Management,* 7 (Autumn 1978), 19–24.

COZZOLINA, JOHN M., "A New Method of Risk Analysis," *Sloan Management Review,* 20 (Spring 1979), 53–65.

HAYES, ROBERT H., "Incorporating Risk Aversion into Risk Analysis," *Engineering Economist,* 20 (Winter 1975), 99–121.

HERTZ, DAVID B., "Investment Policies That Pay Off," *Harvard Business Review,* 46 (January–February 1968), 96–108.

———, "Risk Analysis in Capital Investment," *Harvard Business Review,* 42 (January–February 1964), 95–106.

HESPOS, RICHARD F., and PAUL A. STRASSMANN, "Stochastic Decision Trees for the Analysis of Investment Decisions," *Management Science,* 11 (August 1965), 244–59.

HILLIER, FREDERICK S., "A Basic Model for Capital Budgeting of Risky Interrelated Projects," *Engineering Economist,* 17 (Fall 1971), 1–30.

———, "The Derivation of Probabilistic Information for the Evaluation of Risky Investments," *Management Science,* 9 (April 1963), 443–57.

LESSARD, DONALD R., and RICHARD S. BOWER, "Risk-Screening in Capital Budgeting," *Journal of Finance,* 28 (May 1973).

LEVY, HAIM, and MARSHALL SARNAT, *Capital Investment and Financial Decisions.* Englewood Cliffs, N.J.: Prentice-Hall, 1978.

LEWELLEN, WILBER G., and MICHAEL S. LONG, "Simulation versus Single-Value Estimates in Capital Expenditure Analysis," *Decision Sciences* 3 (1972), 19–33.

MAGEE, J.F., "How to Use Decision Trees in Capital Investment," *Harvard Business Review,* 42 (September–October 1964), 79–96.

QUIRIN, G. DAVID and JOHN C. WIGINTON, *Analyzing Capital Expenditures.* Homewood, Ill: Irwin, 1981.

ROBICHEK, ALEXANDER A., "Interpreting the Results of Risk Analysis," *Journal of Finance,* 30 (December 1975), 1384–86.

ROBICHEK, ALEXANDER A., and JAMES VAN HORNE, "Abandonment Value and Capital Budgeting," *Journal of Finance,* 22 (December 1967), 577–89; EDWARD A. DYL and HUGH W. LONG, "Comment," *Journal of Finance,* 24 (March 1969), 88–95; and ROBICHEK and VAN HORNE, "Reply," *ibid.,* 96–97.

SCHALL, LAWRENCE D., and GARY L. SUNDEM, "Capital Budgeting Methods and Risk: A Further Analysis," *Financial Management,* 9 (Spring 1980), 7–11.

SPAHR, RONALD W., and STANLEY A. MARTIN, "Project Pricing in Limited Diversification Portfolios," *Engineering Economist,* 26 (Spring 1981), 207–22.

VAN HORNE, JAMES C., "The Analysis of Uncertainty Resolution in Capital Budgeting for New Products," *Management Science,* 15 (April 1969), 376–86.

———, "Capital-Budgeting Decisions Involving Combinations of Risky Investments," *Management Science,* 13 (October 1966), 84–92.

———, "Capital Budgeting under Conditions of Uncertainty as to Project Life," *Engineering Economist,* 17 (Spring 1972), 189–99.

———, "Variation of Project Life as a Means for Adjusting for Risk," *Engineering Economist,* 21 (Summer 1976).

Required returns on capital investments

15

The acceptance criterion for capital investments is perhaps the most difficult and controversial topic in finance. We know in theory that it should be the rate of return on a project that will leave the market price of the company's stock unchanged. The difficulty is in determining this rate in practice. Because predicting the effect of decisions on stock prices is an inexact science (some would call it an art form), estimating the appropriate required rate of return is inexact as well. Rather than skirt the issue, we address it head on and propose a general framework for measuring the required rate of return. We begin with the required rate of return for the company as a whole and then move on to consider the required rate of return for individual projects and for various subsets of an enterprise such as divisions.

OVERALL COST OF CAPITAL OF THE FIRM

For a company as a whole, there is an aggregation of assets. As a result, the use of an overall cost of capital as the acceptance criterion for investment decisions is appropriate only under certain circumstances. These circumstances are that the assets of the firm are homogeneous with respect to risk and that investment proposals under consideration are of the same character. If investment proposals vary widely with respect to risk, the required rate of return for the company as a whole is not appropriate as an acceptance criterion. The advantage of using it is, of course, its simplicity. Once it is computed, projects can be evaluated using a single rate that does not change unless underlying conditions

327

change. This avoids the problem of computing individual required rates of return for each investment proposal. However, it is important that if the firm's overall required rate of return is used as an acceptance criterion, projects correspond in general to the above conditions. Otherwise, one should determine an acceptance criterion for each project, a topic we take up in the latter part of this chapter.

The overall cost of capital of a firm is comprised of the costs of the various components of financing. The cost of equity capital is the most difficult to measure, and it will occupy most of our attention. We consider also the costs of debt and preferred stock. Our concern throughout will be with the *marginal* cost of a specific source of financing. The use of marginal costs follows from the fact that we use the cost of capital to decide whether to invest in new projects. Past costs of financing have no bearing on this decision. All costs will be expressed on an after-tax basis, to conform to the expression of investment project cash flows on an after-tax basis. Once we have examined the explicit costs of various sources of financing, we shall combine these costs to obtain an overall cost of capital to the firm. We assume in the development of this chapter that the reader has covered the foundation materials in chapters 4 and 5 on the mathematics of finance and on valuation.

Cost of debt

Although debt can be both current and long-term, our concern is only with the long term. The assumption is that the firm will finance a capital project, whose benefits extend over a number of years, with long-term financing.

The explicit cost of debt can be derived by solving for the discount rate, k, that equates the net proceeds of the debt issue with the present value of interest plus principal payments, then adjusting the explicit cost obtained for the tax effect. The discount rate, k, which also is known as the yield, is solved with the following formula:

$$P_0 = \sum_{t=1}^{n} \frac{I_t + P_t}{(1 + k)^t} \qquad (15\text{-}1)$$

where P_0 is the initial cash inflow to the firm, the capital Greek sigma denotes the summation for periods 1 through n, the final maturity, I_t is the interest payment in period t, and P_t is the payment of principal in period t. If principal payments occur only at final maturity, only P_n will appear. By solving for k, the rate of discount that equates the present value of cash outflows with the initial cash inflow, we obtain the before-tax cost of debt. The after-tax cost, which we denote by k_i, can be approximated by

$$k_i = k(1 - t) \qquad (15\text{-}2)$$

where k is the internal rate of return or yield, and t is the marginal tax rate. Because interest charges are tax deductible, the after-tax cost of debt is substantially less than the before-tax cost. If the before-tax cost, k, in Eq. (15-1) were found to be 15 percent and the tax rate were 50 percent,

$$k_i = 15.00(1 - .50) = 7.50 \text{ percent}$$

We note that the 7.50 percent after-tax cost in our example represents the marginal, or incremental, cost of additional debt. It does not represent the cost of debt funds already employed.

The explicit cost of debt is considerably cheaper than the cost of another source of financing having the same k but where the financial charges are not deductible for tax purposes. Implied in the calculation of an after-tax cost of debt is the fact that the firm is profitable. Otherwise, it does not gain the tax benefit associated with interest payments. The explicit cost of debt for an unprofitable firm is the before-tax cost, k.

Cost of preferred stock

The cost of preferred stock is a function of its stated dividend. As we discuss in chapter 22, this dividend is not a contractual obligation of the firm but is payable at the discretion of the board of directors. Consequently, unlike debt, it does not create a risk of legal bankruptcy. To holders of common stock, however, preferred stock is a security interest that takes priority over theirs. Most corporations that issue preferred stock intend to pay the stated dividend. As preferred stock has no maturity date, its cost may be represented as

$$k_p = \frac{D}{I_0} \qquad (15\text{-}3)$$

where D is the stated annual dividend and I_0 represents the net proceeds of the preferred-stock issue. If a company were able to sell a 14 percent preferred-stock issue ($100 par value) and realize net proceeds of $98 ½ a share, the cost of the preferred stock would be $14/98.5 = 14.21$ percent. Note that this cost is not adjusted for taxes, because the preferred-stock dividend is paid after taxes. Thus, the explicit cost of preferred stock is substantially greater than that for debt.

Cost of equity capital

The cost of equity capital is by far the most difficult cost to measure. In theory, it may be defined as the minimum rate of return that the company must earn on the equity-financed portion of an investment project in order to leave unchanged the market price of the stock. If the firm invests in projects having an expected return less than this required return, the market price of the stock over the long run will suffer.

In the context of the dividend-capitalization model presented in chapter 5, the cost of equity capital can be thought of as the rate of discount that equates the present value of all expected future dividends per share, as perceived by investors at the margin, with the current market price per share. Recall from chapter 5 that

$$P_0 = \frac{D_1}{(1 + k_e)} + \frac{D_2}{(1 + k_e)^2} + \ldots + \frac{D_\infty}{(1 + k_e)^\infty}$$

$$P_0 = \sum_{t=1}^{\infty} \frac{D_t}{(1 + k_e)^t} \qquad (15\text{-}4)$$

where P_0 is the value of a share of stock at time 0; D_t is the dividend per share expected to be paid in period t; k_e is the appropriate rate of discount, and the capital Greek sigma represents the sum of discounted expected future dividends from period 1 through infinity, where infinity is depicted by the symbol ∞.

Estimating future dividends.   If we can successfully estimate the stream of future dividends that the market expects, it is an easy matter to solve for the rate of discount that equates this stream with the current market price of the stock. Because expected future dividends are not directly observable, they must be estimated. Herein lies the major difficulty in estimating the cost of equity capital. For reasonably stable patterns of past growth, one might project this trend into the future. However, we must temper the projection to take account of current market sentiment. Insight into such sentiment can come from reviewing various analyses about the company in financial newspapers and magazines.

On the basis of the long-range plans of the company, the financial manager can make internal estimates of the expected future growth in earnings per share and in dividends per share. These estimates should take account of economic and other factors that bear on the firm's future operating performance. With access to a great deal of relevant information, the financial manager's estimates of future earnings may be the most accurate of all, but it is important that investors also expect these earnings. There is an obvious bias if the financial manager's estimate of growth used to solve for k_e differs significantly from that of the market. The important question is, What growth in dividends are investors at the margin expecting when they pay x dollars for a share of stock? Every effort should be made to get as accurate a handle as possible on this expected growth pattern. Thus, in estimating future dividends for the company, the financial manager must think as investors do.

If, for example, dividends were expected to grow at an 8 percent annual rate into the foreseeable future, the perpetual growth model presented in chapter 5 might be used to determine the required rate of return. If the expected dividend in the first year were $2 and the present market price per share were $27, we would have

$$k = \frac{\$2}{\$27} + .08 = .154 = 15.4 \text{ percent.}$$

This rate then would be used as an estimate of the firm's required return on equity capital. If the growth in dividends is expected to taper off in the future, another growth model explained in chapter 5 must be used.

Capital-asset pricing model approach to the cost of equity.   Rather than estimating the future dividend stream of the firm and then solving for the cost of equity capital, one may approach the problem directly by estimating the required rate of return on the company's equity. From our discussion of the capital-asset pricing model in chapter 5, we know that it implies the following required rate of return for a stock:

$$R_j = i + (\overline{R}_m - i)\beta_j \tag{15-5}$$

where i is the risk-free rate, $\overline{R}_m$ is the expected return for the market portfolio, and $\overline{\beta}_j$ is the beta coefficient for stock j.

Recall from chapter 5 that beta is a measure of the responsiveness of the excess returns for security j (in excess of the risk-free rate) to those of the market, using some broad-based market index such as Standard & Poor's 500-stock index as a surrogate for the market portfolio. If the historical relationship between security returns and those for the market portfolio is believed to be a reasonable proxy for the future, one can use past returns to compute the beta for a stock. This was illustrated in chapter 5, where a characteristic line was fitted to the relationship between returns in excess of risk-free rate for the stock and those for the market index. *Beta* is defined as the slope of this line. To free us of the need to calculate beta information directly, several services provide historical beta information on a large number of publicly traded stocks. These services allow one to obtain the beta for a stock with ease, thereby facilitating greatly the calculation of the cost of equity capital.

Again, if the past is thought to be a good proxy for the future, one can use Eq. (15-5) to compute the cost of equity capital for a company. To illustrate, suppose that the beta for the Silva-Chin Company were found to be 1.20, based on monthly excess return data over the last five years. This coefficient tells us that the stock's excess return goes up or down by a somewhat greater percentage than does the excess return for the market. (A beta of 1.00 means that excess returns for the stock vary proportionally with excess returns for the market portfolio.) Thus, the stock of Silva-Chin Company has more unavoidable, or systematic, risk than does the market as a whole. But management believes that this past relationship is likely to hold in the future. Furthermore, a rate of return of about 17 percent on stocks in general is expected to prevail and a risk-free rate of 12 percent is expected.

This is all the information we need in order to compute the required rate of return on equity for Silva-Chin Company. Using Eq. (15-5), the cost of equity capital would be

$$R_j = .12 + (.17 - .12)1.20 = 18 \text{ percent}$$

Thus, the estimated required rate of return on equity for Silva-Chin Company is approximately 18 percent. In essence, we are saying that this is the rate of return that investors expect the company to earn on its equity.

If measurement were exact and certain assumptions held,[1] the cost of equity capital determined by this method would be the same as that provided by a

---

[1]As discussed in chapter 5, the capital-asset pricing model assumes the presence of perfect capital markets. When this assumption is relaxed to take account of real-world conditions, the residual risk of a stock may take on a degree of importance. We know that the total risk of a security is comprised of its systematic as well as its residual risk. The assumption of the capital-asset pricing model is that residual risk can be completely diversified away, leaving us with only systematic risk.

If imperfections exist in the capital markets, these may impede efficient diversification by investors. (One example of an imperfection is the presence of significant bankruptcy costs.) The greater the imperfections that are believed to exist, the greater the allowance that must be made for residual risk. As a result, it will be necessary to adjust upward the required rate of return. For amplification of this point, see James C. Van Horne, *Financial Management and Policy*, 6th ed. (Englewood Cliffs, N.J.: Prentice-Hall, 1983), chaps. 7–8.

dividend capitalization model. Recall that the latter estimate is the rate of discount that equates the present value of the stream of expected future dividends with the current market price of the stock. By now it should be apparent that we can hope only to approximate the cost of equity capital. We believe that the methods suggested above enable such an approximation more or less accurately, depending on the situation. For a large company whose stock is actively traded on the New York Stock Exchange and whose systematic risk is close to that of the market as a whole, we can usually estimate more confidently than we can for a moderate-sized company whose stock is inactively traded in the over-the-counter market and whose systematic risk is very large. We must live with the inexactness involved in the measurement process and try to do as good a job as possible.

Debt cost as the base. Rather than estimate the required return in this manner, some people use the company's debt cost as a basis for estimating its equity cost. A firm's cost of debt will exceed the risk-free rate by a risk premium. The greater the risk of the firm, the greater this premium and the more interest the firm must pay in order to borrow. The relationship is illustrated in Fig. 15-1. On the horizontal axis, the firm's debt is shown to have systematic risk equal to β_i. As a result, its required return is k_i, which exceeds the risk-free rate of i.

In addition to this risk premium, the common stock of a company must provide a higher expected return than the debt of the same company. The reason is that there is more systematic risk involved. This phenomenon also is illustrated in the figure. We see that for a beta of β_s, an expected return of k_s is required and that this percentage exceeds the company's cost of debt, k_i. The historical risk premium in expected return for stocks over bonds has been around 4 percent. If this seemed reasonable for a particular company, one could use the firm's cost of debt as a base and add to it a premium of around 4 percent to estimate its cost of equity capital. To illustrate, suppose Valkury Corporation's bonds sell in the market to yield 15 percent. Using the approach outlined above, its approximate cost of equity would be

$$k_e = k_i + \frac{\text{stock over debt}}{\text{risk premium}} = 15\% + 4\% = 19 \text{ percent}$$

FIGURE 15-1

The security market line
with debt and stock

This percentage then would be used as the cost of equity capital. The advantage of the approach is that one does not have to use beta information and make the calculation involved in Eq. (15-5). The disadvantage is that it does not allow for changing risk premiums over time; and because the 4 percent is for companies overall, the approach is not as accurate as the direct estimate of the required return on equity capital for a specific company. However, it does offer an alternative method of estimating the cost of equity capital within the overall framework of the capital-asset pricing model

Weighted-average cost of capital

Once we have computed costs of individual components of the capital structure,[2] we may weigh them according to some standard and calculate a weighted-average cost of capital. The firm's overall cost of capital may be expressed as

$$\text{Cost of capital} = \sum_{x=1}^{j} k_x w_x \qquad (15\text{-}6)$$

where k_x is the after-tax cost of the xth method of financing, w_x is the weight given to that method as a percentage of the firm's total financing, and the capital Greek sigma denotes the summation for financing methods 1 through j. To illustrate the calculations involved, suppose that a firm had the following capital structure at the latest statement date, where the amounts shown represent market values:

	Amount	Proportion
Debt	$ 30 million	30%
Preferred stock	10 million	10%
Common-stock equity	60 million	60%
	$100 million	100%

Common-stock equity includes both common-stock issues and retained earnings. In calculating proportions, it is important that we use market-value as opposed to book-value weights. Because we are trying to maximize the value of the firm to its shareholders, only market-value weights are consistent with our objective. Market values are used in the calculation of the costs of the various components of financing, so market-value weights should be used in determining the weighted average cost of capital.

[2]While equity, debt, and preferred stock are the major types of financing, there are other types. These include leasing, convertible securities, warrants, and other options. Because determining the costs of these methods of financing involves some special and rather complex valuation issues, we treat them in individual chapters where we are able to give such issues proper attention. For our purposes in this chapter, knowing the costs of equity, debt, and preferred-stock financing is sufficient for illustrating the overall cost of capital of a company. When costs are determined for other types of financing, they can be inserted in the weighting scheme to be discussed now.

To continue with our illustration, suppose that the firm computed the following after-tax costs for the component methods of financing:

	Cost
Debt	7.5%
Preferred stock	14.0
Common-stock equity	18.0

Therefore, the weighted-average cost of capital for this example problem is

	(1) Proportion	(2) Cost	(3) Weighted Cost (1) × (2)
Debt	30%	7.5%	2.25%
Preferred stock	10	14.0	1.40
Common-stock equity	60	18.0	10.80
			14.45%

Thus, with the assumptions of this example, 14.45 percent represents the weighted-average cost of the component methods of financing, where each component is weighted according to market-value proportions.

With the calculation of a weighted-average cost of capital, the critical question is whether the figure represents the firm's real cost of capital. The answer depends upon how accurately we have measured the individual marginal costs, upon the weighting system, and upon certain other assumptions. Assume for now that we are able to measure accurately the marginal costs of the individual sources of financing, and let us examine the importance of the weighting system.

Weighting system. The critical assumption in any weighting system is that the firm will in fact raise capital in the proportions specified. Because the firm raises capital *marginally* to make a *marginal* investment in new projects, we need to work with the marginal cost of capital to the firm as a whole. This rate depends upon the package of funds employed to finance investment projects. In other words, our concern is with new or incremental capital, not with capital raised in the past. In order for the weighted-average cost of capital to represent a marginal cost, the weights employed must be marginal; that is, the weights must correspond to the proportions of financing inputs the firm intends to employ.

If they do not, capital is raised on a marginal basis in proportions other than those used to calculate this cost. As a result, the real weighted-average cost of capital will differ from that calculated and used for capital-investment decisions. An obvious bias results. If the real cost is greater than that which is measured, certain investment projects will be accepted that will leave investors worse off than before. On the other hand, if the real cost is less than the measured cost, projects will be rejected that could increase shareholder wealth. Therefore, the 14.45 percent weighted-average cost of capital computed in our example is realistic only if the firm intends to finance in the future in the same proportions as its existing capital structure.

Raising capital is "lumpy," and strict proportions cannot be maintained. For example, a firm would have difficulty financing each project with 30 percent debt, 10 percent preferred stock, and 60 percent retained earnings. In practice, it may finance with debt in one instance and with preferred stock or retained earnings in another. Over time, most firms are able to finance in roughly a proportional manner. It is in this sense that we try to measure the marginal cost of capital for the package of financing employed.

Flotation costs. Flotation costs involved in the sale of common stock, preferred stock, or a debt instrument affect the profitability of a firm's investments. In many cases, the new issue must be priced below the market price of existing financing; in addition, there are out-of-pocket flotation costs. Owing to flotation costs, the amount of funds the firm receives is less than the price at which the issue is sold. The presence of flotation costs in financing requires an adjustment be made in the evaluation of investment proposals.

That adjustment is made by adding flotation costs of financing to the project's initial cash outlay. Suppose that an investment proposal costs $100,000 and that to finance the project the company must raise $60,000 externally. Both debt and common stock are involved, and flotation costs come to $4,000. Therefore, $4,000 should be added to $100,000, bringing the total initial outlay to $104,000. In this way, the proposal is properly "penalized" for the flotation costs associated with its financing. The expected future cash flows associated with the project are discounted at the weighted-average cost of capital. If the project were expected to provide annual cash inflows of $24,000 forever and the weighted-average cost of capital were 20 percent, the project's net present value would be:

$$\text{NPV} = \frac{\$24,000}{.20} - \$104,000 = \$16,000$$

This amount contrasts with a net present value of $20,000 if no adjustment is made for flotation costs.

Thus, the adjustment for flotation costs is made in the project's cash flows and not in the cost of capital.[3] To adjust the cost of capital results in an excessive "penalty" whenever the net present value of the project is positive. In our previous example, $4,000 in flotation costs represents 4 percent of the $100,000 investment, so the "adjusted" cost of capital would be 20 percent/(1 − .04) = 20.83 percent.

[3]For a defense of the procedure, see Simon E. Keane, "The Investment Discount Rate—In Defense of the Market Rate of Interest," *Accounting and Business Research*, Summer 1976, 234; and John R. Ezzell and R. Burr Porter, "Flotation Costs and the Weighted Average Cost of Capital," *Journal of Financial and Quantitative Analysis*, 11 (September 1976), 403–13.

Therefore, the net present value of the project would be

$$NPV = \frac{\$24,000}{.2083} - \$100,000 = \$15,218$$

As we see, the use of an adjusted cost of capital results in a biased, low estimate of the net present value of a project whenever this value is positive. The appropriate procedure is to adjust the project's initial cash outlay and to use the weighted-average "unadjusted" cost of capital as the discount rate.

Rationale for weighted-average cost

The rationale behind the use of a weighted-average cost of capital is that by financing in the proportions specified and accepting projects yielding more than the weighted-average cost, the firm is able to increase the market price of its stock. This increase occurs because investment projects accepted are expected to yield more on their equity-financed portions than the cost of equity capital, k_e. Once these expectations are apparent to the marketplace, the market price of the stock should rise, all other things the same, because expected future earnings per share (and dividends per share) are higher than those expected before the projects were accepted. The firm has accepted projects that are expected to provide a return greater than that required by investors at the margin, based on the risk involved.

We must return to the critical assumption that over time the firm finances in the proportions specified. If it does so, the financial risk of the company remains roughly unchanged. As we shall see in chapter 17, the "implicit" costs of financing are embodied in the weighted-average cost of capital by virtue of the fact that a firm has to supplement nonequity financing with equity financing. It does not raise capital continually with supposedly cheaper debt funds without increasing its equity base. The firm's capital structure need not be optimal for the firm to employ the weighted-average cost of capital for capital-budgeting purposes. The important consideration is that the weights used be based upon the future financing plans of the company. If they are not, the weighted-average cost of capital calculated does not correspond to the actual cost of funds obtained; as a result, capital-budgeting decisions are likely to be suboptimal.

The use of a weighted-average cost of capital figure must be qualified also for the points raised earlier. It assumes that the investment proposals being considered do not differ in systematic, or unavoidable, risk from that of the firm and that the residual risk of the proposals does not provide any diversification benefits to the firm. Only under these circumstances is the cost-of-capital figure obtained appropriate as an acceptance criterion. These assumptions are extremely binding. They imply that the projects of a firm are completely homogeneous with respect to risk and that only projects of the same risk will be considered.

In practice, of course, the issue is one of degree. If the conditions above are approximately met, then the company's weighted-average cost of capital may be used as the acceptance criterion. If a firm produced only one product and all proposals considered were in conjunction with the marketing and production of that product, the use of the firm's overall cost of capital as the acceptance criterion probably would be appropriate. (Even here, however, there may be significant enough differences in risk among investment proposals to warrant separate consideration.) For a multiproduct firm with investment proposals of varying risk, the use of an overall required rate of return is inappropriate. Here the required rate of return for the specific proposal should be used, as determined with the methods proposed in the next section. The key, then, is the homogeneity with respect to risk of existing investment projects and investment proposals under consideration.

THE CAPM: PROJECT-SPECIFIC AND GROUP-SPECIFIC REQUIRED RETURNS

When the existing investment projects of the firm and investment proposals under consideration are not homogeneous with respect to risk, the use of the firm's cost of capital as an acceptance criterion will not do. In these cases, we must formulate a specific acceptance criterion for the particular project involved. One means for doing so is with the capital-asset pricing model, and this approach is described in this section.

Capital-asset pricing model approach to projects

Essentially, the capital-asset pricing model approach is the same as that for determining the cost of equity capital of the firm. However, instead of the expected relation between excess returns for the stock (returns in excess of the risk-free rate) and those for the market portfolio, one is concerned with the expected relation of excess returns for the project and those for the market portfolio. The required return for an equity-financed project would be

$$R_k = i + (\overline{R}_m - i)\beta_k \qquad (15\text{-}7)$$

where β_k is the slope of the characteristic line that describes the relationship between excess returns for project k and those for the market portfolio. As can be seen, this equation is identical to Eq. (15-5) except for the substitution of the project return and its beta for those of the stock

Assume that the firm intends to finance a project entirely with equity. The acceptance criterion then would be to invest in the project if its expected return exceeded the required return, R_k, as determined with Eq. (15-7). Recall from chapter 5 that the market-determined relationship between systematic risk, as described by beta, and the required rate of return is depicted by the security market line. To illustrate the acceptance criterion for projects using this concept, we turn to Fig. 15-2. All projects with internal rates of return lying on or above the line should be accepted, for they provide expected excess returns. Acceptable projects are depicted by x's. All projects lying below the line, shown by the o's, would be rejected. Note that the greater the systematic risk of a project, the greater the return that is required. If the project had no risk, only the risk-free rate would be required. For projects with more risk, however, a risk premium is demanded, and it increases with the degree of systematic risk of the project. The goal of the firm in this context is to search for investment opportunities lying above the line.

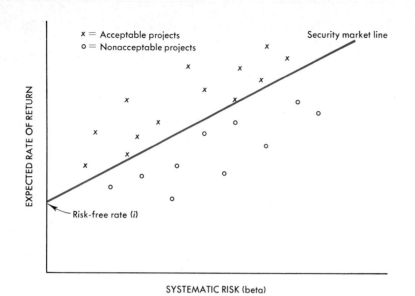

EXPECTED RATE OF RETURN

x = Acceptable projects
o = Nonacceptable projects

Security market line

Risk-free rate (*i*)

SYSTEMATIC RISK (beta)

FIGURE 15-2
The security market line as
applied to risky investment

Application of the model—the use of proxy companies. The difficulty in applying this approach is in estimating the beta for a project. Recall from chapter 5 that derivation of the characteristic line is based on changes in market value for a stock and those for the market portfolio. It is therefore necessary to estimate changes in the market value of the project over time in relation to changes in value for the market portfolio. Estimation of the former represents unfamiliar ground for most people accustomed to thinking in terms of net present values and internal rates of return.

In many cases, the project is sufficiently similar to a company whose stock is publicly held so that we can use that company's beta in deriving the required rate of return on equity for the project. For large projects, such as new products, one frequently can identify publicly traded companies that are engaged entirely, or almost entirely, in the same type of operation. The important thing is to identify a company or companies with systematic risk characteristics similar to those of the project in question.

Suppose that a steel company is considering the formation of a real estate subsidiary. As there are a number of real estate companies with publicly traded stocks, one simply could determine the beta for one of those companies or a group of them and use it in Eq. (15-5) to derive the required rate of return for the project. Note that the relevant required rate of return is not that for the steel company, but that for other real estate firms. Stated differently, the market views the steel company's venture in the same way it views other firms engaged solely in real estate. By concentrating on companies in the same line as the firm desires to enter, we can find surrogates that approximate the systematic risk of the project. An exact duplication of the project's risk is unlikely, but reasonable approximations frequently are possible.

To illustrate the calculations, suppose that the average beta for a sample of real estate companies whose stocks were publicly traded and whose basic businesses were similar to the venture contemplated by the steel company was 1.6. We can use this beta as a surrogate for the beta of the project. If we expect the average return on the market portfolio of stocks to be 17 percent and the risk-free rate to be 12 percent, the required return on equity for the project would be

$$R_k = .12 = (.17 - .12)1.6 = 20 \text{ percent}$$

Therefore, 20 percent would be used as the required equity return for the project.

When there are no companies whose stocks are publicly traded, so we cannot find proxies for the project, the task becomes much more difficult. Even here, however, there sometimes exists information on the market value of the project in question. For machine tools, a secondary market of sorts exists, where prices are established for used machines of various ages. Other assets have similar markets where prices can be determined. Given these prices, we can measure the market return for a particular period and then use such information to derive an estimate of beta for the project.[4] The approach is hampered however, by a number of measurement problems. Unless one is able to use a company or companies whose stock is publicly traded as a proxy for the project, the derivation of a beta for a specific project is a difficult matter. For this reason we will restrict our attention to the use of proxy company information.

The required return with leverage

If the firm consistently finances projects with equity, one would use R_k as the required rate of return for the project. If some debt financing is employed, however, we need to determine a weighted-average required return. Here the weighting system is the same as that illustrated earlier for the firm's overall cost of capital. Rather than vary the proportion of debt financing project by project, a more consistent approach is to apply the same weights to all projects. Presumably these weights will correspond to the proportions with which the firm intends to finance over time. If the firm intends to finance with one part debt for every two parts equity, and the after-tax cost of debt is 7.50 percent while the required return on equity for the project is 20 percent, the overall required return for the project is

$$R_k = .075(1/3) + .200(2/3) = 15.83 \text{ percent}$$

If the project were expected to provide an internal rate of return in excess or equal to this rate, the project would be accepted. If not, it would be rejected. Thus, the acceptance criterion is specifically related to the systematic risk of the project through the cost of equity capital.

Group-specific required returns

Rather than determine project-specific required returns, some companies categorize projects into roughly homogeneous groups and then apply the same required return to all projects emanating from that group. One advantage is that it

[4]For such an example, see Van Horne, *Financial Management and Policy*, 6th ed., chap. 7.

**FIGURE 15-3
Group-specific required
returns**

is not as time consuming as computing required returns for each project. Another is that it often is easier to find proxy companies for a group than it is for an individual project. By group, we mean some subunit of the company that carries on a set of activities that can be differentiated from the other activities of the firm. Usually these activities are differentiated along product or service lines as well as along management lines. Frequently the subunits are divisions or subsidiaries of the company, though a group is not restricted to this definition.

If the products or services of the group are homogeneous with respect to risk, and new proposals are of the same sort, a group-specific required return is an appropriate acceptance criterion. It represents the transfer price of capital from the company to the group. Stated differently, it is the rate of return the company expects the group to earn on its capital investments. The greater the systematic risk of the group, the greater its required return.

The computation of the required rate of return is the same as that for the specific project. For each group, proxy companies whose stocks are publicly traded are identified. On the basis of these surrogates, betas are derived for each group and from these a required return on equity capital is calculated.[5] If debt is used, a weighted average required return for the group is derived in the same manner as in the previous section. Once group specific required returns are computed, capital is allocated, or transferred, throughout the firm on a risk-adjusted return basis. The approach provides a consistent framework for allocating capital among groups with greatly different risks.

The approach is illustrated in Fig. 15-3. Here, the bars represent the required returns for four groups. The weighted average cost of capital for the firm as a whole is depicted by the dashed line. Projects providing expected returns above

[5]For an illustration of this approach, which was used by an actual company, see James C. Van Horne, "An Application of the Capital Asset Pricing Model to Divisional Required Returns," *Financial Management*, 9 (Spring 1980), 14–19. Russell J. Fuller and Halbert S. Kerr, "Estimating the Divisional Cost of Capital: An Analysis of the Pure-Play Technique," *Journal of Finance*, 36 (December 1981), 997–1009, collected proxy company betas for the various divisions of some sixty multi-division firms. The authors found that an appropriately weighted average of the betas of the proxy firms closely approximated the beta of the multi-division firm. Although an adjustment for leverage was made, the results here did not provide as good an estimate of the multi-division firm beta as the unadjusted betas.

the bars should be accepted; those below the bars rejected. Note that this criterion means that for the two "safer" groups, some accepted projects may provide expected returns below the firm's overall cost of capital but above the required return for the group. For the two "riskier" groups, rejected projects may have provided returns greater than the overall cost of capital but less than the group's required return. Indeed, capital is allocated on a risk-return basis specific to the systematic risk of the group.

Some qualifications. Whether the required returns be project specific or group specific, there are certain problems in the application of the capital-asset pricing model. For one thing, the amount of nonequity financing that is assigned to a project is an important consideration. For the above procedure to hold, it should approximate the same relative amount as that used by the proxy company. In other words, the proportion of nonequity financing allocated to a project should not be significantly out of line with that for the proxy company being used. Otherwise, one will not get a reasonable proxy for the systematic risk of the project. Where the proportions are not nearly the same, the proxy company's beta should be adjusted before it is used as the cost of equity capital for the project. A procedure for adjusting the beta is presented in the Appendix to this chapter. Using this procedure, one can approximate the beta for the proxy company, assuming it had the same relative proportion of nonequity financing as that contemplated for the project. The cost of equity capital for the project can then be determined in the same manner as before.

In addition to the practical problems, there is an underlying assumption in the capital-asset pricing model approach which must be questioned. As we know, this assumption is that only the systematic risk of the firm is important. However, the probability of a firm's becoming insolvent depends on its total risk, not just its systematic risk. When insolvency or bankruptcy costs are significant, investors may be served by the firm's paying attention to the impact of a project on the total risk of the firm. The total risk is comprised of both systematic and residual risk. Systematic risk means more to investors; but residual risk may be a factor,[6] and the greater its weight, the less relevant is the capital-asset pricing model approach to risky investments.

EVALUATION OF PROJECTS ON THE BASIS OF THEIR TOTAL RISK

When for either theoretical or practical reasons it is not appropriate to compute a required rate of return for a project or group using the capital-asset pricing model, we must turn to more subjective means for evaluating risky investments. In fact, most firms approach the problem in this manner. Many, of course, deal with risky investments in informal ways. Decision makers simply try

---

[6]When there are significant bankruptcy costs, these work to the detriment of stockholders as residual owners of the company. It therefore may be important for the firm to keep the probability of becoming bankrupt within reasonable bounds. To do so, it must consider the impact of the project on the firm's total risk (systematic and residual). This approach is taken up in the last section of the chapter.

to incorporate risk into their judgment on the basis of their "feel" for the projects being evaluated. This "feel" can be improved upon by discussions with others familiar with the proposals and the risks inherent in them. Frequently, such discussions center around "what if" types of questions. In a general way, then, an allowance can be made for risk in capital-expenditure decisions. The problem with informal approaches to risk, of course, is that the information developed usually is sketchy, and the treatment of it is not consistent from project to project or over time.

We know from our discussion in chapter 14 that expected return and risk can be quantified in a consistent manner. Given this information, the question is whether a project should be accepted or rejected. We will begin by examining how management might evaluate a single investment proposal and then move on to combinations of risky investments. These methods are firm-risk oriented in the sense that management does not consider explicitly the effect of the project on investors' portfolios. The focus is on total risk, the sum of systematic and residual risk. Management assesses the likely effect of the project on the variability of cash flows and earnings of the firm. From this assessment, it then can estimate the likely effect on share price. The critical factor from the standpoint of valuation is how accurately management is able to link share price with risk-profitability information for an investment proposal. As we shall see, the linkage tends to be subjective, which detracts from the accuracy of the approaches.

Evaluation of a proposal

You will recall from chapter 14 that the information generated for an investment proposal was the probability distribution of possible net present values. We saw also that by standardizing the dispersion in terms of so many standard deviations from the expected value of the distribution, we can determine the probability that the net present value of the project will be zero or less. In the evaluation of a single proposal, it is unlikely that management would accept an investment proposal having an expected value of net present value of zero unless the probability distribution had no dispersion. In this special case the proposal, by definition, would be riskless. For risky investments, the net present value would have to exceed zero. How much it would have to exceed zero before acceptance were warranted depends upon the amount of dispersion of the probability distribution and the utility preferences of management with respect to risk.

In order to facilitate project selection as well as to make it consistent over time, management may wish to formulate maximum risk profiles. To express the probability distributions in relative instead of absolute terms, we can convert the net present value probability distribution into a distribution of possible profitability indexes. (Recall that the profitability index is simply the present value of future net cash flows over the initial cash outlay.) Suppose we had a proposal costing $10,000 where the expected value of the probability distribution of possible net present values was $1,200. The profitability index for this expected value would be ($1,200 + $10,000)/$10,000 = 1.12. The profitability index for zero net present value is (0 + $10,000)/$10,000 = 1.00. Similarly, we can convert the entire distribution of possible profitability indexes. An example of such distribution is shown in Fig. 15-4.

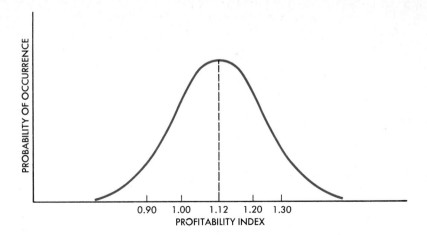

FIGURE 15-4
Probability distribution of profitability indexes, proposal X

If management has specified maximum risk profiles for various expected values of profitability indexes, one would simply compare the proposal shown in Fig. 15-4 with the maximum risk profile for an expected value of profitability index of 1.12. If the dispersion of the proposal is less than that for the risk profile, the proposal will be accepted. If not, it will be rejected. The maximum level of dispersion permitted, as depicted by the risk profile, will increase with the expected value of profitability index. For a profitability index of 1.02, the dispersion of the maximum risk profile will be narrower than that for a profitability index of 1.10. Some hypothetical risk profiles are shown in Fig. 15-5. We note that the greater the expected value of profitability index, the greater the dispersion that is tolerable to management. To illustrate their application, compare the probability distribution in Fig. 15-4 with that shown in the third row, first column, of Fig. 15-5. The latter is for a profitability index of 1.12. We see that the dispersion of the probability distribution for the hypothetical project (Fig. 15-4) is somewhat wider than the dispersion tolerable to management for that level of expected profitability. Therefore, the proposal would be rejected according to this method.

Some qualifications. The real problem with this approach is that the link with share price is not direct. Management is presented with information about the expected return and risk of a project; and on the basis of this information it reaches a decision. However, there is no direct link to the likely reaction of well-diversified investors. This link depends entirely upon the perceptiveness of management in judging investors' tradeoff between profitability and risk. Moreover, there is no analysis of the impact of the project on the overall risk of the firm; as we know, this factor becomes important if capital markets are less than perfect. In essence, the project is evaluated in isolation of investors and of existing investment projects.

For these reasons, the approach leaves much to be desired. Still, we must recognize that in practice most investment decisions are made by management in this or some similar way. By providing management with information about the dispersion of possible outcomes, more informed decisions are possible than in the conventional capital-budgeting analysis, which considers only the expected values of cash flows.

343

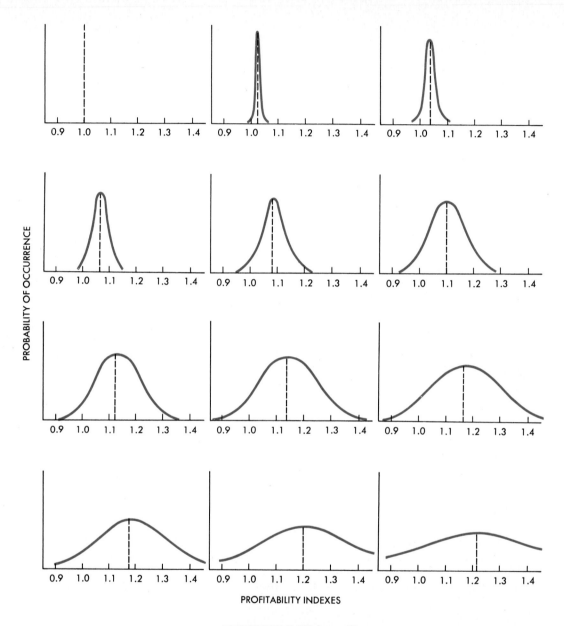

FIGURE 15-5 Risk profiles

Combinations of risky investments

From chapter 14 we know that the marginal risk of an individual proposal to the firm as a whole depends upon its correlation with existing projects as well as its correlation with proposals under consideration that might be accepted. The appropriate information is the standard deviation and expected value of the proba-

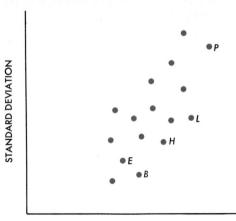

**FIGURE 15-6
Opportunity set of
combinations of
projects**

STANDARD DEVIATION

NET PRESENT VALUE

bility distribution of possible net present values for all feasible combinations of existing projects and investment proposals under consideration. Assume for now that management is interested only in the marginal impact of an investment proposal on the risk complexion of the firm as a whole.

The selection of the most desirable combination of investments will depend upon management's risk preferences with respect to net present value and variance, or standard deviation. Fig. 15-6 shows various combinations of risky investments available to the firm. This figure is the same as Fig. 14-7 in chapter 14. Each dot represents a combination of proposals under consideration and existing investment projects for the firm. We see that certain dots dominate others in the sense that they represent a higher expected value of net present value and the same standard deviation, a lower standard deviation and the same expected value of net present value, or both a higher expected value and a lower standard deviation. The dots that dominate others are those that are farthest to the right. With information of this sort before it, management can eliminate most combinations of risky investments simply because they are dominated by other combinations.

In this case, management would probably consider only four combinations of risky investments—B, H, L, and P. From these it would choose the one that it felt offered the best combination of expected return and risk. If it were moderately averse to risk, it might choose combination L. While combination P provides a somewhat higher expected value of net present value, it also has a much higher standard deviation. Combinations B and H have lower risk, but also lower expected values of net present values. If management were fairly averse to risk, one of these two combinations might be chosen.

As discussed in chapter 14, the final selection determines the new investment proposal or proposals that will be accepted. An exception would occur only when the combination selected was comprised of existing projects. In this situation, no investment proposals under consideration would be accepted. If the portfolio of existing projects were represented by combination E in the figure, the selection of any of the four outlying combinations would imply the acceptance of one or more new investment proposals. Investment proposals under consideration that were not in the combination finally selected would, of course, be rejected.

Conceptual implications

On the basis of the information presented, management determines which investment proposals under consideration offer the best marginal contribution of expected value of net present value and standard deviation to the firm as a whole. In determining the standard deviation for a combination, management must consider the correlation between an investment proposal and existing and other proposed investments. This evaluation suggests that the total risk of the firm is what is important; investment decisions are made in light of their marginal impact on total risk.

This approach implies that from the standpoint of stockholders, management should be concerned with the firm's solvency. As discussed, such solvency depends on the total risk of the firm. Owing to less-than-perfect correlation with each other, certain projects have diversification properties. As a result, the total risk of the firm will be less than the sum of the parts. Management presumably will endeavor to accept investment proposals in a way that will keep the probability of insolvency within reasonable bounds while maximizing net present value.

As indicated before, the problem with this approach is that it ignores the fact that investors can diversify the portfolios of common stocks they hold. They are not dependent on the firm to diversify away risk. Therefore, diversification by the firm may not be a thing of value in the sense of doing something for investors that they cannot do for themselves. To the extent that investors are concerned only with the unavoidable or systematic risk of a project, the capital-asset pricing model approach illustrated earlier should be used.

It may be reasonable to use both approaches. The capital-asset pricing model approach might serve as the foundation for judging the valuation implications of an investment project. To the extent the possibility of insolvency exists and the bankruptcy costs which result are considerable, the project also would be judged in a total firm-risk context. If both approaches give clear accept or reject signals, those signals should be followed. The obvious problem occurs if one approach gives an accept signal while the other gives a reject signal. In this case, management should place more weight on one or the other signal, depending on which approach is more applicable.

If the stock of a large company is publicly held, and if the possibility of insolvency is remote, a strong case can be made for using the signal given by the capital-asset pricing model. If the stock is traded in a market with high transaction and information costs, if the possibility of insolvency is significant, and if the expression of project returns in terms of market-based returns is crude, greater reliance should be placed on the total firm-risk approach. Even here, one should recognize that a portion of the residual risk can be diversified away.

SUMMARY

In theory, the required rate of return for an investment project should be the rate that leaves the market price of the stock unchanged. If existing investment projects and investment proposals under consideration are homogeneous with respect to risk, it is appropriate to use the overall cost of capital of a company as the acceptance criterion. This can be a weighted-average cost of the various instruments with which the company intends to finance. By far the most difficult cost to measure is the cost of equity capital. Using a dividend-capitalization model, this cost is the rate of discount that equates the present value of the stream of expected future dividends with the market price of the stock. The key ingredient in the formula is the accuracy of estimates of expected future dividends. Approaching the problem directly, we can estimate the cost of equity capital with the capital-asset pricing model. The model itself was presented in chapter 5, and its application to determining equity costs was illustrated in this chapter.

Given the measurement of marginal costs of debt, preferred stock, and equity, a weighted-average cost of capital can be computed. The weights employed should correspond to the proportions with which the firm intends to finance. Once computed, the weighted-average cost is used as a basis for accepting or rejecting investment proposals. The rationale for its use was discussed, as were certain qualifications. When investment projects, both existing and new, are widely variant with respect to risk, use of the company's overall cost of capital as an acceptance criterion is not appropriate.

In such cases, we should determine an acceptance criterion for each investment project or group of projects under consideration. One means for computing a risk-adjusted required rate of return for a proposal is with the capital-asset pricing model. One relates excess returns (in excess of the risk-free rate) for the project to excess returns for the market portfolio. Once a beta is computed, the required rate of return on equity can easily be determined. The key to this approach is to find a company whose stock is publicly traded and whose business closely corresponds to the investment proposal being contemplated. This company's stock is then used as a surrogate for the proposal in computing beta. If debt financing is employed, a weighted average required return for the project is calculated, based on the proportions the firm uses in its financing. In the same manner, a group-specific required return may be determined for a division, a subsidiary, or some other subunit of the firm. On a theoretical level, the capital-asset pricing model assumes that the only risk that is relevant is the systematic risk of the firm, an assumption that may not be appropriate in some situations.

A practical means for evaluating risky investments is to analyze the expected value and standard deviation of the probability distribution of possible returns for an investment proposal and, on the basis of this information, reach a decision. The greater the dispersion of the distribution, the greater the expected value that presumably would be required by management. The problem with this approach is that the link between the investment decision and share price is not direct. It depends on the perceptions of management with respect to likely investor reaction.

Finally, we examined the marginal impact of an investment project on the total risk of the firm. This becomes a concern if there is a possibility of insolvency. By analyzing the expected return and risk of various possible combinations of existing projects and investment proposals under consideration, management is able to select the best one, usually on the basis of dominance. The selection itself determines which proposals will be accepted and which will be rejected. With this approach, the diversification properties of a project are recognized in the computation of the standard deviation for a combination. Again, this is important if one is concerned with the impact of investment proposals accepted on the total risk of the firm as opposed to only its systematic risk.

APPENDIX ⟍ Adjusting the Beta for Leverage

The systematic risk of a stock is due to both the business and the financial risk of the company. In the calculation of a project's or group's cost of equity capital, the external company used as a proxy for the business risk of the project or group will sometimes have a significantly different proportion of debt than that used by the firm. As a result, it may be desirable to adjust the beta of the proxy company for this difference in relative debt. In what follows, we present a procedure for making such an adjustment under the assumptions of the capital-asset pricing model. In the end, we will qualify the results for the considerations to be taken up in chapter 17.

With corporate income taxes, interest payments are deductible for tax purposes. Under these circumstances, Hamada, as well as others, has demonstrated that the required rate of return for a stock is[7]

$$R_j = i + \left(\frac{R_m - i}{\sigma_m^2}\right)(r_{ju,m}\sigma_{ju}\sigma_m)\left[1 + \frac{B}{S}(1 - T)\right] \qquad (15A\text{-}1)$$

where i = risk-free rate

R_m = the expected return on the market portfolio

σ_m = standard deviation of the probability distribution of possible market returns

σ_{ju} = standard deviation of the probability distribution of possible returns for security j *in the absence of leverage*

$r_{ju,m}$ = correlation coefficient between returns for security j *in the absence of leverage* and the market portfolio

B/S = the debt-to-equity ratio in market value terms

T = corporate tax rate

The important thing to note is that the covariance between returns, which is the second bracketed term in the equation, is as if the company had an all-equity capital structure.

Equation (15A-1) can be expressed in terms of the more familiar beta:

$$R_j = i + (R_m - i)\beta_{ju}\left[1 + \frac{B}{S}(1 - T)\right] \qquad (15A\text{-}2)$$

---

[7]Robert S. Hamada, "Portfolio Analysis, Market Equilibrium and Corporation Finance," *Journal of Finance*, 24 (March 1969), 19–30.

where β_{ju} is the beta measuring the responsiveness of the excess return for the security *in the absence of leverage* to the excess return for the market portfolio. Thus the overall required rate of return is comprised of the risk-free rate, i, plus a premium for business risk, $(R_m - i)\beta_{ju}$, and a premium for financial risk,

$$(R_m - i)\beta_{ju} \left[\frac{B}{S}(1 - T) \right]$$

The measured beta for the stock, β_j, embodies both risks and it is simply

$$\beta_j = \beta_{ju} \left[1 + \frac{B}{S}(1 - T) \right] \qquad \text{(15A-3)}$$

Rearranging, the beta for the stock *in the absence of leverage* is

$$\beta_{ju} = \frac{\beta_j}{\left[1 + \dfrac{B}{S}(1 - T) \right]} \qquad \text{(15A-4)}$$

Given these expressions, we are able to derive the beta *in the absence of leverage* for a particular stock. Suppose the measured beta, β_j, for security j were 1.4; the debt-to-equity ratio, B/S, were 0.6; and the tax rate were 50 percent. Therefore the beta *in the absence of leverage* would be

$$\beta_{ju} = \frac{1.4}{[1 + 0.6(0.5)]} = 1.08$$

If we now wished to determine the beta for a different amount of leverage, we would use Eq. (15A-3). Suppose that we were interested in using security j as a proxy for the systematic risk of our project or group. However, we employ a debt-to-equity ratio of 0.3 as opposed to the 0.6 for security j. Therefore the adjusted beta would be

$$\text{Adjusted } \beta_j = 1.08[1 + 0.3(0.5)] = 1.24$$

This beta contrasts with 1.08 for security j *in the absence of leverage*, and with 1.40 for security j with a debt-to-equity ratio of 0.6.

In summary, we are able to derive an adjusted beta for a security under the assumption of a different proportion of debt than what occurs. We first estimate the beta for the stock *in the absence of leverage* and then adjust this figure for the proportion of leverage we wish to employ. The final result is an approximation of the beta that would prevail if the external company were to employ the desired proportion of debt.

Note that the adjustment procedure assumes that all the tenets of the capital-asset pricing model hold. One of these is that in the absence of taxes, changes in the capital structure of a firm do not affect its valuation. With taxes, value increases in a linear manner with leverage. Chapter 17, which follows, analyzes this proposition in depth. The adjustment procedure presented provides an approximate beta when the proportion of debt is varied, but it is only an approximation.

QUESTIONS

1. Why is it important to use marginal weights in calculating a weighted-average cost of capital?

2. Under what circumstances is it appropriate to use the weighted-average cost of capital as an acceptance criterion?

3. Do the funds provided by sources such as accounts payable and accruals have a cost of capital? Explain.

4. What is the critical assumption inherent in the capital-asset pricing model as it relates to the acceptance criterion for risky investments?

5. What is the distinction between evaluating the expected value and standard deviation for an individual investment project and for a group or combination of projects?

6. If management of a company has significant holdings of stock in the company, with little in the way of "outside" wealth, how is this likely to affect its behavior with respect to risky investment decisions? Is this in the shareholders' best interests?

7. Trace the effects of the following on the cost of capital.

    a) The Federal Reserve increases the money supply by buying bonds from the public.

    b) The public decides to save a larger proportion of its income.

    c) The capital-gains tax rate is lowered.

    d) Major economic depressions are eliminated.

    e) The corporation income tax rate is lowered.

8. Is it possible to find projects that consistently provide returns in excess of those required? What if the product markets are competitive and highly efficient?

9. Should companies in the same industry have approximately the same required rates of return on investment projects? Why or why not?

10. If you use debt funds to finance a project, why is not their cost the required return for the project? As long as the project earns more than enough to pay interest and service the principal, does it not benefit the firm?

11. If the cost of bankruptcy proceedings (attorney fees, trustee fees, delays, inefficiencies, and so on) were to rise substantially, would this occurrence have an effect on a company's required rate of return and on the way it looks at investment opportunities?

12. Should a company with multiple divisions establish separate required rates of return, or costs of capital, for each division as opposed to using the company's overall cost of capital?

1. Zapata Enterprises is financed by two sources of funds: bonds and common stock. The cost of capital for funds provided by bonds is K_i while K_e is the cost of capital for equity funds. The capital structure consists of amount B of bonds and S of stock. Compute the weighted-average of cost of capital, K_o.

2. Assume B (problem 1) is $3 million and S is $7 million. The bonds have a 14 percent cost, and the stock is expected to pay $500,000 in dividends this year. The growth rate of dividends has been 11 percent and is expected to continue at the same rate. Find the cost of capital if the corporate tax rate on income is 40 percent.

3. On March 10, International Copy Machines (ICOM), one of the favorites of the stock market, was priced at $300 per share. This price was based on an expected annual growth rate of at least 20 percent for quite some time in the future. In July, economic indicators turned down, and investors revised downward to 15 percent their estimate for future growth of ICOM. What should happen to the price of the stock? Assume the following:

   a) A perpetual-growth valuation model is a reasonable representation of the way the market values ICOM.

   b) The measured cost of equity capital to the firm is the true cost.

   c) The firm does not change its dividend, the risk complexion of its assets, or its degree of financial leverage.

   d) The expected dividend in the first year is $3 per share.

4. K-Far Stores has launched an expansion program, which should result in the saturation of the Bay Area marketing region of California in 6 years. As a result, the company is predicting a growth in earnings of 12 percent for 3 years, 6 percent for years 4 through 6, after which it expects constant earnings forever. The company expects to increase its dividends per share, now $2 in keeping with this growth pattern. Currently, the market price of the stock is $25 per share. Estimate the company's cost of equity capital.

5. The Manx Company was recently formed to manufacture a new product. It has the following capital structure in market value terms:

13% Debentures of 2005	$ 6,000,000
12% Preferred stock	2,000,000
Common stock (320,000 shares)	8,000,000
	$16,000,000

The common stock sells for $25 a share, and the company has a marginal tax rate of 50 percent. A study of publicly held companies in this line of business suggests that the required return on equity is about 17 percent for a company of this sort. (The capital-asset pricing model approach was used to determine the required rate of return.) Compute the firm's present weighted-average cost of capital.

6. The Tumble Down D Ranch in Montana would like a new mechanized barn, which will cost $600,000. The new barn is expected to provide annual cash savings of $90,000 indefinitely

(for practical purposes of computation, forever). The ranch, which is incorporated and has a public market for its stock, has a weighted-average cost of capital of 14.5 percent. For this project, Howard Kelsey, the president, intends to use $200,000 in retained earnings and to finance the balance half with debt and half with a new issue of common stock.

Flotation costs on the debt issue amount to 2 percent of the total debt raised, whereas flotation costs on the new common-stock issue come to 15 percent of the issue. What is the net present value of the project after allowance for flotation costs? Should the ranch invest in the new barn?

7. Cohn and Sitwell, Inc., may begin to manufacture special drill bits and other equipment for oil rigs. This is currently regarded as a "hot" area, and the company has certain expertise by virtue of its having a large mechanical-engineering staff. Because of the large outlays required to get into the business, management is concerned that Cohn and Sitwell earn a proper return. Since the new venture is believed to be sufficiently different from the company's existing operations, management feels that a required rate of return other than the company's present one should be employed.

The financial manager's staff has identified several companies engaged solely in the manufacture and sale of oil-drilling equipment whose stocks are publicly traded. Over the last 5 years, the average beta for these companies has been 1.28. The staff believes that 18 percent is a reasonable estimate of the average return on stocks in general for the foreseeable future and that the risk-free rate will be around 12 percent. In financing projects, Sitwell and Cohn uses 40 percent debt and 60 percent equity. The after-tax cost of debt is 8 percent.

a) On the basis of this information, determine a required rate of return for the project, using the capital-asset pricing-model approach.

b) Is the figure obtained likely to be a realistic estimate of the required rate of return on the project?

8. Acosta Sugar Company has estimated that the overall return for Standard & Poor's 500-stock index will be 15 percent the next ten years. The company also feels that the interest rate on Treasury bills will average 10 percent over this interval. The company is thinking of expanding into a new product line: almonds. It has no experience in this line but has been able to obtain information on various companies involved in producing and processing nuts. Although no company examined produces only almonds, Acosta's management feels that the beta for such a company would be 1.10, once the almond operation was ongoing. There is some uncertainty about the beta that will actually prevail. Management has attached the following probabilities to possible outcomes:

Probability	.2	.3	.2	.2	.1
Beta	1.00	1.10	1.20	1.30	1.40

a) What is the required rate of return for the project using the mode beta of 1.10?

b) What is the range of required rates of return?

c) What is the expected value of required rate of return?

9. George and Yuji Tanaka, who are brothers, own a small motel on the island of Maui in Hawaii. There are no loans against their property. Because of its location, they have been offered $500,000 for the property. If they were to sell, they feel they could obtain a return of $100,000 a year before taxes in alternative investments of comparable risk. The other option is to expand and modernize the motel and install a swimming pool. The total cost would be $300,000. Knowing the value of fee-simple land (owned land) on Maui, a savings and loan association is willing to make a long-term mortgage loan for the full cost at an interest rate of 15 percent.

a) What should be the lowest acceptable rate of return to George and Yuji on the improvement project?

b) What incremental annual profits before taxes must the new project earn in order to provide George and Yuji with exactly their minimum required return?

10. After a careful study of the risk preferences of its management, the Henken Aviation Company has determined certain risk profiles for investment projects. These risk profiles depict the maximum standard deviation of profitability index that is tolerable for a particular expected value of profitability index. (The profitability index is the present value of future cash flows of a project divided by the initial cash outlay.) The risk profiles for various profitability indexes are as follows:

Expected profitability index	1.00	1.05	1.10	1.15	1.20	1.25
Maximum standard deviation	0	.04	.10	.15	.21	.26

The company is considering two new investment proposals, which are expected to have the following characteristics:

Proposal X Cost = $2 million		Proposal Y Cost = $5 million	
Net present value	Probability of occurrence	Net present value	Probability of occurrence
−$ .5 million	.10	−$ .4 million	.10
0	.20	.1 million	.15
.5 million	.40	.5 million	.50
1.0 million	.20	.9 million	.15
1.5 million	.10	1.4 million	.10

Given the risk profiles of the company, should either or both of the two proposals be accepted?

11. Benzo Tube Company wishes to evaluate three new investment proposals. It is concerned with the impact of the proposals on its total risk. Consequently, it has determined expected values and standard deviations of the probability distributions of possible net present

values for the possible combinations of existing projects, *E,* and investment proposals under consideration:

Combination	Expected value of net present value (in thousands)	Standard deviation (in thousands)
E	$6,500	$5,250
E,1	6,800	5,000
E,2	7,600	8,000
E,3	7,200	6,500
E,1,2	7,900	7,500
E,1,3	7,500	5,600
E,2,3	8,300	8,500
E,1,2,3	8,600	9,000

Which combination do you feel is most desirable? Which proposals should be accepted? Which should be rejected?

Appendix Problem

12. Willie Sutton Bank Vault Company has a debt-to-equity ratio (market value) of 0.75. Its present cost of debt funds is 15 percent, and it has a marginal tax rate of 40 percent. Willie Sutton Bank Vault is eyeing the automated bank teller business, a field that involves electronics and is considerably different from its own, so the company is looking for a benchmark or proxy company. The Peerless Machine Company, whose stock is publicly traded, produces only automated teller equipment. Peerless has a debt-to-equity ratio of 0.25, a beta of 1.15, and an effective tax rate of 0.40.

   a) If Willie Sutton Bank Vault Company wishes to enter the automated bank teller business, what systematic risk (beta) is involved if it intends to employ the same amount of leverage in the new venture as it presently employs?

   b) If the risk-free rate presently is 13 percent and the expected return on the market portfolio is 17 percent, what return should the company require for the project if it uses a capital-asset pricing model approach?

SELECTED REFERENCES

AIVAZIAN, VAROUJ, and JEFFREY L. CALLEN, "Investment, Market Structure, and the Cost of Capital," *Journal of Finance,* 34 (March 1979), 85–92.

ALBERTS, W.W., and S.H. ARCHER, "Some Evidence on the Effect of Company Size on the Cost of Equity Capital," *Journal of Financial and Quantitative Analysis,* 8 (March 1973), 229–42.

ARDITTI, FRED D., and HAIM LEVY, "The Weighted Average Cost of Capital as a Cutoff Rate: A Critical Analysis of the Classical Textbook Weighted Average," *Financial Management,* 6 (Fall 1977), 24–34.

BERANEK, WILLIAM, "The Weighted Average Cost of Capital and Shareholder Wealth Maximization," *Journal of Financial and Quantitative Analysis,* 12 (March 1977), 17–32.

ELLIOTT, J. WALTER, "The Cost of Capital and U.S. Investment," *Journal of Finance*, 35 (September 1980), 981–1000.

EZZELL, JOHN R., and R. BURR PORTER, "Flotation Costs and the Weighted Average Cost of Capital," *Journal of Financial and Quantitative Analysis*, 11 (September 1976), 403–13.

FAMA, EUGENE F., "Risk-Adjusted Discount Rates and Capital Budgeting under Uncertainty," *Journal of Financial Economics*, 5 (1977), 3–24.

FINDLAY, M. CHAPMAN, III, ARTHUR E. GOODING, and WALLACE Q. WEAVER, JR., "On the Relevant Risk for Determining Capital Expenditure Hurdle Rates," *Financial Management*, 5 (Winter 1976), 9–16.

FULLER, RUSSELL J., and HALBERT S. KERR, "Estimating the Divisional Cost of Capital: An Analysis of the Pure-Play Technique," *Journal of Finance*, 36 (December 1981), 997–1009.

GALLINGER, GEORGE W., and GLENN V. HENDERSON, JR., "The SML and the Cost of Capital," Research Paper, Arizona State University, 1981.

GUP, BENTON E., and SAMUEL W. NORWOOD III, "Divisional Cost of Capital: A Practical Approach," *Financial Management*, 11 (Spring 1982), 20–24.

KEANE, SIMON E., "The Investment Discount Rate—In Defence of the Market Rate of Interest," *Accounting and Business Research*, Summer 1976, 228–36.

LESSARD, DONALD R., and RICHARD S. BOWER, "An Operational Approach to Risk Screening," *Journal of Finance*, 27 (May 1973), 321–38.

MILES, JAMES A., and JOHN R. EZZELL, "The Weighted Average Cost of Capital, Perfect Capital Markets, and Project Life: A Clarification," *Journal of Financial and Quantitative Analysis*, 15 (September 1980), 719–30.

MYERS, STEWART C., and STUART M. TURNBULL, "Capital Budgeting and the Capital Asset Pricing Model: Good News and Bad News," *Journal of Finance*, 32 (May 1977), 321–32.

NANTELL, TIMOTHY J. and C. ROBERT CARLSON, "The Cost of Capital as a Weighted Average," *Journal of Finance*, 30 (December 1975), 1343–55.

REILLY, RAYMOND R., and WILLIAM E. WECKER, "On the Weighted Average Cost of Capital," *Journal of Financial and Quantitative Analysis*, 8 (January 1973), 123–26.

SCOTT, DAVID F., JR., "Determining the Cost of Common Equity Capital: The Direct Method," *Journal of Business Research*, 8 (March 1980), 89–103.

VAN HORNE, JAMES C., "An Application of the Capital Asset Pricing Model to Divisional Required Returns," *Financial Management*, 9 (Spring 1980), 14–19.

CAPITAL STRUCTURE AND DIVIDEND POLICIES

VI

Leveraging the firm

16

Financial leverage involves the use of funds for which the firm pays a fixed cost in the hope of increasing the return to its common stockholders. Since increases in leverage also increase the risk of the earnings stream to common stockholders, however, we face the familiar tradeoff between risk and expected return. Higher expected return leads to higher stock prices, all other things being the same. Greater risk results in lower stock prices, again holding all else constant. With respect to financial leverage, the goal is to strike a happy balance between risk and expected return, maximizing the market price of the firm's stock.

In this chapter we are going to explore ways a company may evaluate the impact of leverage on expected return and risk. Our purpose here is to show how we might approach the problem in practice. In the next chapter, we shall explore the conceptual underpinnings to the problem. The additional discussion in that chapter will provide a richer insight into the problem and reinforce the presentation in this chapter. Thus, the two chapters are closely related. Before proceeding further, however, let us take a moment to define financial risk.

FINANCIAL RISK

Broadly speaking, financial risk encompasses both the risk of possible insolvency and the variability in earnings available to common stockholders. As a firm increases the proportion of debt, lease financing, and preferred stock in its capital structure, fixed charges increase. As a result, the probability of cash insolvency increases. To illustrate this notion, suppose that two firms have different degrees of leverage but are identical in every other respect. Each has expected annual cash earnings of $80,000 before interest and taxes. Firm A has no debt; Firm B has $300,000 worth of 10% perpetual bonds outstanding. Thus, the total annual financial charges for Firm B are $30,000, whereas Firm A has no financial charges. If cash earnings for both firms happen to be 75 percent lower than expected—namely, $20,000—Firm B will be unable to cover its financial charges with cash earnings. We see, then, that the probability of cash insolvency increases with the financial charges incurred by the firm.

The second aspect of financial risk involves the relative dispersion of income available to common stockholders. Suppose that the expected future annual operating incomes over the next 5 years for Firms A and B were subjective random variables where the expected values of the probability distributions were each $80,000 and the standard deviations, $40,000. As before, assume that Firm A has no debt, while Firm B has $300,000 in 10% bonds. If, for simplicity, we neglect federal income taxes, the expected value of earnings available to common stockholders would be $80,000 for Firm A and $50,000 for Firm B. Because the standard deviation about the expected values is the same for both firms, the relative dispersion of expected earnings available to common stockholders is greater for Firm B than for Firm A. For Firm A the coefficient of variation, which is simply the standard deviation divided by the expected value, is

$$\text{Coefficient of variation} = \frac{\$40,000}{\$80,000} = .50$$

while for Firm B it is

$$\text{Coefficient of variation} = \frac{\$40,000}{\$50,000} = .80$$

Graphically, the relationship is shown in Fig. 16-1. We see that the degree of dispersion from the expected value of earnings available to common stockholders is the same for both firms, but the expected value of these earnings is greater for Firm A than for Firm B. As a result, the relative dispersion, as measured by the coefficient of variation, is less for Firm A.

The dispersion in earnings available to common stockholders is to be distinguished from the dispersion of operating income, known as business risk. In our example above, both firms had the same degree of business risk, as defined, because the coefficient of variation of expected future operating income was the same

$$\text{Coefficient of variation} = \frac{\$40,000}{\$80,000} = .50$$

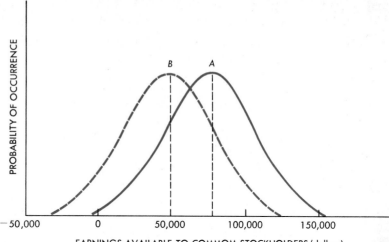

FIGURE 16-1
Probability distribution of earnings available to common stockholders

PROBABILITY OF OCCURRENCE

−50,000   0   50,000   100,000   150,000

EARNINGS AVAILABLE TO COMMOM STOCKHOLDERS (dollars)

Only in the degree of financial risk did the two firms differ. In summary, we regard financial risk as encompassing the volatility of earnings available to common stockholders as well as the probability of insolvency. Both aspects are related directly to the dispersion of expected operating income, or the business risk, of the firm.

EBIT-EPS RELATIONSHIPS

To analyze the appropriate degree of financial leverage for a firm, we need among other things to understand the sensitivity of earnings per share (EPS) to earnings before interest and taxes (EBIT) for various financing alternatives. EBIT does not depend on financial leverage, but rather is a result of the operations and the business risk of the firm. We must know what happens to a firm's earnings per share under various financing options as changes in EBIT occur.

Calculation of earnings per share

To illustrate an EBIT-EPS analysis of leverage, suppose Cherokee Tire Company with long-term capitalization of $10 million, consisting entirely of common stock, wishes to raise another $5 million for expansion through one of three possible financing plans. The company may finance with (1) all common stock, (2) all debt at 12 percent interest, or (3) all preferred stock with an 11 percent dividend. Present annual earnings before interest and taxes (EBIT) are $2 million, the income tax rate is 50 percent, and 200,000 shares of stock are now outstanding. Common stock can be sold at $50 per share under financing option 1, or 100,000 additional shares of stock.

In order to determine the EBIT break-even, or indifference, points between the various financing alternatives, we begin by calculating earnings per share for some hypothetical level of EBIT. Suppose we wished to know what earnings per share would be under the three financing plans if EBIT were $2.4 million. The calculations are shown in Table 16-1. We note that interest on debt is deducted before taxes, while preferred-stock dividends are deducted after taxes. As a result, earnings available to common stockholders are higher under the debt alternative than they are under the preferred-stock alternative, despite the fact that the interest rate on debt is higher than the preferred-stock dividend rate.

Break-even, or indifference, analysis

Given the information in Table 16-1, we are able to construct a "break-even" or indifference chart similar to what we did for operating leverage. On the horizontal axis we plot earnings before interest and taxes (EBIT) and on the vertical axis, earnings per share (EPS). For each financing alternative, we must draw a straight line to reflect EPS for all possible levels of EBIT. To do so, we need two datum points for each alternative. The first is the EPS calculated for some hypothetical level of EBIT. For $2.4 million in EBIT, we see in Table 16-1 that earnings per share are $4.00, $4.50, and $3.25 for the common, debt, and preferred-stock financing alternatives. We simply plot these earnings per share at the $2.4 million mark in EBIT. Note that it does not matter which hypothetical level of EBIT we choose for calculating EPS. On good graph paper, one level is as good as the next.

The second datum point is simply the EBIT necessary to cover all fixed financial costs for a particular financing plan, and it is plotted on the horizontal axis. For the common-stock alternative, there are no fixed costs, so the intercept on the horizontal axis is zero. For the debt alternative, we must have EBIT of $600,000 to cover interest charges; so $600,000 becomes the horizontal axis intercept. For the preferred-stock alternative, we must divide total annual dividends by one minus the tax rate in order to obtain the EBIT necessary to cover these dividends. Thus we need $1.1 million in EBIT to cover $550,000 in preferred-stock dividends, assuming a 50 percent tax rate. Again, preferred dividends are de-

TABLE 16-1 \ **Calculations of earnings per share under three financing alternatives**

	All common	All debt	All preferred
Earnings before interest and taxes (hypothetical)	$2,400,000	$2,400,000	$2,400,000
Interest	–	600,000	–
Earnings before taxes	2,400,000	1,800,000	2,400,000
Income taxes	1,200,000	900,000	1,200,000
Earnings after taxes	1,200,000	900,000	1,200,000
Preferred stock dividend	–	–	550,000
Earnings available to common stockholders	$1,200,000	$ 900,000	$ 650,000
Number of shares	300,000	200,000	200,000
Earnings per share	$4.00	$4.50	$3.25

EPS = (after tax − Dividend)

Range of Earnings Chart

FIGURE 16-2
Indifference chart for three financing alternatives

ducted after taxes, so it takes more in before-tax earnings to cover them than it does to cover interest. Given the horizontal axis intercepts and earnings per share for some hypothetical level of EBIT, we draw a straight line through the two sets of points. The break-even or indifference chart for Cherokee Tire Company is shown in Fig. 16-2.

We see from the figure that the earnings-per-share indifference point between the debt and common-stock financing alternatives is $1,800,000 in EBIT. If EBIT is below that point, the common-stock alternative will provide higher earnings per share; above that point the debt alternative is best. The indifference point between the preferred-stock and the common-stock alternative is $3,300,000 in EBIT. Above it, the preferred-stock alternative is favored with respect to earnings per share; below it, the common-stock alternative is best. We note that there is no indifference point between the debt and preferred-stock alternatives. The debt alternative dominates for all levels of EBIT and by a constant amount of earnings per share, namely $1.25.

Indifference point mathematically. The indifference point between two methods of financing can be determined mathematically by

$$\frac{(EBIT^* - C_1)(1 - t)}{S_1} = \frac{(EBIT^* - C_2)(1 - t)}{S_2} \qquad (16\text{-}1)$$

where EBIT* = the EBIT indifference point between the two methods of financing for which we solve

C_1, C_2 = annual interest expenses or preferred-stock dividends on a before-tax basis for financing methods 1 and 2

t = corporate tax rate

S_1, S_2 = number of shares of common stock to be outstanding after financing for methods 1 and 2

Suppose we wished to determine the indifference point between the common-stock and the debt-financing alternative in our example. We would have

$$\frac{(\text{EBIT}^* - 0)(0.5)}{300,000} = \frac{(\text{EBIT}^* - 600,000)(0.5)}{200,000} \tag{16-2}$$

Rearranging, we obtain

$$0.5(\text{EBIT}^*)(200,000) = 0.5(\text{EBIT}^*)(300,000)$$
$$- 0.5(600,000)(300,000)$$

$$50,000 \ \text{EBIT}^* = 90,000,000,000$$
$$\text{EBIT}^* = \$1,800,000$$

The indifference point in EBIT, where earnings per share for the two methods of financing are the same, is $1.8 million. This amount can be verified graphically in Fig. 16-2. Thus, indifference points for financial leverage can be determined either graphically or mathematically.

Effect on risk

So far our concern has been only with what happens to the return to common stockholders. We have seen in our example that if EBIT is above $1.8 million, debt financing is the preferred alternative from the standpoint of earnings per share. We know from our earlier discussion, however, that the impact on expected return is only one side of the coin. The other side is the effect of leverage on risk. An EBIT-EPS chart does not permit a precise answer to this question; nevertheless, certain generalizations are possible. For one thing, the financial manager should compare the indifference point between debt and common-stock financing with the most likely level of EBIT. The higher the level of EBIT, assuming it exceeds the indifference point, the stronger the case that can be made for debt financing, all other things the same.

In addition, the financial manager should assess the likelihood of EBIT's falling below the indifference point. Suppose that the EBIT in our example is $3 million. Given the business risk of the company and the resulting possible fluctuations in EBIT, the financial manager should assess the probability of EBIT's falling below $1.8 million. If the probability is negligible, the use of the debt alternative will be supported. On the other hand, if EBIT presently is only slightly above the indifference point and the probability of EBIT's falling below this point is high, the financial manager may conclude that the debt alternative is too risky. This notion is illustrated in Fig. 16-3, where two probability distributions of possible EBIT's are superimposed on the indifference chart shown in Fig. 16-2. In Fig. 16-3, however, we focus on only the debt and common-stock alternatives. For the "safe" distribution, there is virtually no probability that EBIT will fall below the indifference point. Therefore, we might conclude that debt should be

FIGURE 16-3
Indifference chart with EBIT probability distributions

used, because the effect on shareholder return is substantial, whereas risk is negligible. For the "risky" distribution, there is a significant probability that EBIT will fall below the indifference point. In this case, the financial manager may conclude that the debt alternative is too risky.

In summary, the greater the level of EBIT above the indifference point and the lower the probability of downside fluctuation, the stronger the case that can be made for the use of debt financing. EBIT–EPS analysis is but one of several methods for determining the appropriate amount of debt a firm might carry. No one method of analysis is satisfactory by itself. When several methods are undertaken simultaneously, however, generalizations are possible. Let us examine the other methods for analyzing the appropriate degree of financial leverage for a firm.

CASH-FLOW ABILITY TO SERVICE DEBT

When considering the appropriate capital structure, it is necessary to analyze the cash-flow ability of the firm to service fixed charges. The greater the dollar amount of senior securities the firm issues and the shorter their maturity, the greater the fixed charges of the firm. These charges include principal and interest payments on debt, lease payments, and preferred-stock dividends. Before assuming additional fixed charges, the firm should analyze its expected future cash flows, for fixed charges must be met with cash. The inability to meet these charges, with the exception of preferred-stock dividends, may result in financial insolvency. The greater and more stable the expected future cash flows of the firm, the greater the debt capacity of the company.

Coverage ratios

Among the ways we can gain insight into the debt capacity of a firm is through the use of coverage ratios. In the computation of these ratios, one typically uses earnings before interest and taxes as a rough measure of the cash flow available to cover debt-servicing obligations. Perhaps the most widely used coverage ratio is *times interest earned*, which is simply

$$\text{Times interest earned} = \frac{\text{EBIT}}{\text{Interest on debt}} \qquad (16\text{-}3)$$

Suppose that the most recent annual earnings before interest and taxes for a company were $6 million, and interest payments on all debt obligations were $1.5 million. Therefore, times interest earned would be four times. This tells us that EBIT can drop by as much as 75 percent and the firm still will be able to cover its interest payments out of earnings.

A coverage ratio of only one indicates that earnings are *just* sufficient to satisfy the interest burden. Although generalizations about what is an appropriate interest coverage ratio are difficult, one usually is concerned when the ratio gets much below 3 : 1. Circumstances differ however. In a highly stable industry, a relatively low times-interest-earned ratio may be appropriate, whereas it is not appropriate in a highly cyclical industry.

Note that the times-interest-earned ratio tells us nothing about the firm's ability to meet principal payments on its debt. The inability to meet a principal payment constitutes the same legal default as failure to meet an interest payment. Therefore, it is useful to compute the coverage ratio for the full debt-service burden. This ratio is

$$\text{Debt-service coverage} = \frac{\text{EBIT}}{\text{Interest} + \dfrac{\text{Principal payments}}{1 - \text{Tax rate}}} \qquad (16\text{-}4)$$

Here principal payments are adjusted upward for the tax effect. The reason is that EBIT represents earnings before taxes. Because principal payments are not deductible for tax purposes, they must be paid out of after-tax earnings. Therefore, we must adjust principal payments so that they are consistent with EBIT. If principal payments in our previous example were $1 million per annum and the tax rate were 40 percent, the debt-service coverage ratio would be

$$\text{Debt-service coverage} = \frac{\$6 \text{ million}}{\$1.5 \text{ million} + \dfrac{\$1 \text{ million}}{1 - .4}} = 1.26$$

A coverage ratio of 1.26 means that EBIT can fall by only 21 percent before earnings coverage is insufficient to service the debt.[1] Obviously, the closer the ratio

[1] This percent is determined by $1 - (1/1.26) = .21$.

is to 1.0, the worse things are, all other things the same. However, even with the coverage ratio of less than one, a company may still meet its obligations if it can renew some of its debt when it comes due.

The financial risk associated with leverage should be analyzed on the basis of the firm's ability to service total fixed charges. While lease financing is not debt per se, its impact on cash flows is exactly the same as the payment of interest and principal on a debt obligation. (See chapter 20 for an analysis of lease financing.) Annual lease payments, therefore, should be added to the numerator and denominator of Eq. (16-4) in order to properly reflect the total cash-flow burden associated with financing.

As with the times-interest-earned ratio, exact rules of thumb are lacking for what constitutes a good or bad debt-service ratio. It varies according to the business risk of the firm. This is illustrated in Fig. 16-4, which shows the probability distributions of EBIT for two hypothetical companies. The expected value of EBIT is the same for both companies, as is the debt-service burden as described by the denominator in Eq. (16-4). Therefore, the debt-service coverage ratios also are the same, $100/$60 = 1.67. Company A, however, has much more business risk. The probability that EBIT will fall below the debt-service burden is depicted by the shaded areas in the figure. We see that this probability is much greater for Company A than it is for Company B. While a debt-service coverage ratio of 1.67 may be appropriate for Company B, it may not be appropriate for Company A. Simply put, a company with stable cash flows is able to take on relatively more fixed charges. This explains why electric utility companies have low coverage ratios when compared with manufacturing companies.

As discussed in chapter 6 on financial ratios, two comparisons should be undertaken with a coverage ratio. First, it should be compared with past and expected future ratios of the same company. Called trend analysis, the comparison determines if there has been an improvement or deterioration in coverage over time. The second comparison is with similar companies, perhaps in the same

**FIGURE 16-4
Possible EBIT in
relation to
debt-service
burden**

industry. The idea here is to try to isolate business risk as nearly as possible by comparing like companies. Sources of data and types of analysis possible are described in chapter 6, so we do not dwell on them here.

Ultimately, one wants to make generalizations about the appropriate amount of debt (and leases) for a firm to have in its capital structure. It is clear that over the long run the wherewithal to service debt for the going concern is earnings. Therefore, coverage ratios are an important tool of analysis. However, they are but one tool by which a person is able to reach conclusions with respect to appropriate capital structure for the firm. Coverage ratios are subject to certain limitations and, consequently, cannot be used as a sole means for determining a capital structure. For one thing, the fact that EBIT falls below the debt-service burden does not spell immediate doom for the company. Often alternative sources of funds, including renewal of the loan, are available, and these sources must be considered.

Probability of cash insolvency

The vital question for the firm is not so much whether a coverage ratio will fall below one, but what are the chances of insolvency? The answer depends on whether all sources of payment—EBIT, cash, a new financing arrangement, or the sale of assets—are collectively deficient. A coverage ratio tells only part of the story. In order to address the broader question of cash insolvency, we must obtain information on the possible deviation of actual cash flows from those which are expected. As we discussed in chapter 7, cash budgets can be prepared for a range of possible outcomes, with a probability attached to each. This information is extremely valuable to the financial manager in evaluating the ability of the firm to meet fixed obligations. Not only expected earnings are taken into account in determining this ability, but other factors as well: the purchase or sale of assets, the liquidity of the firm, dividends, seasonal patterns, and any other factors impacting on cash flows. Given the probabilities of particular cash-flow sequences, the financial manager is able to determine the amount of fixed charges and debt the company can undertake while still remaining within insolvency limits tolerable to management.

Management may feel that a 5 percent probability of being out of cash is the maximum it can tolerate, and that this probability corresponds to a cash budget prepared under pessimistic assumptions. In this case, debt might be undertaken up to the point where the cash balance under the pessimistic cash budget is just sufficient to cover the fixed charges associated with the debt. In other words, debt would be increased to the point at which the additional cash drain would cause the probability of cash insolvency to equal the risk tolerance specified by management. Note that the method of analysis simply provides a means for assessing the effect of increases in debt on the risk of cash insolvency. On the basis of this information, management would arrive at the most appropriate level of debt.

Donaldson has proposed a similar type of analysis.[2] He suggests that the ultimate concern of a company is whether cash balances during some future

[2]Gordon Donaldson, *Corporate Debt Capacity* (Boston: Division of Research, Harvard Business School, 1961). See also Donaldson, "Strategy for Financial Emergencies," *Harvard Business Review*, 47 (November-December 1969), 67–79.

period will be involuntarily reduced below zero. Therefore, he advocates examining the cash flows of the company under the most adverse circumstances; that is, in his definition, under recession conditions. These conditions may or may not be the most adverse; however, in keeping with the spirit of his proposal, the firm should evaluate its cash flows under adverse circumstances. Donaldson defines the net cash balance during a recession as

$$CB_r = CB_o + NCF_r \qquad\qquad (16\text{-}5)$$

where CB_o = cash balance at start of recession
NCF_r = net cash flows during recession.

Donaldson then calculates a probability distribution of expected net cash flows,[3] and analyzes the cash-flow behavior of a firm during a recession. Combining the beginning cash balances, CB_o, with the probability distribution of recession cash flows, NCF_r, he prepares a probability distribution of cash balances during the recession—CB_r.

To ascertain its debt capacity, a firm first would calculate the fixed charges associated with additional increments of debt. For each addition, the firm then would determine the probability of being out of cash. As before, management could set tolerance limits on the probability of being out of cash. Suppose the firm were considering issuing $20 million in additional debt and that the annual fixed charges were $4 million. By subtracting $4 million from the expected cash balances shown for the probability distribution of CB_r, we obtain the probability distribution of CB_r with the addition of $20 million in debt. If the probability of being out of cash with this increment of debt is negligible, Donaldson would contend that the company has unused debt capacity. Therefore, it would be possible to increase the amount of debt until the probability of being out of cash equaled the risk tolerance of management.

Donaldson extends his analysis to calculate the probability of cash inadequacy. Our discussion before was in terms of cash insolvency, which is defined as lack of cash after all nonessential expenditures have been cut. Cash inadequacy is said to occur if the firm is out of cash after making certain desired expenditures such as dividends, R & D expenditures, and capital expenditures. Thus, cash insolvency is the extreme form of cash inadequacy.

The analysis of the cash-flow ability of the firm to service fixed charges is perhaps the best way to analyze financial risk, but there is some question as to whether the external market analyzes a company in this manner. Sophisticated lenders and institutional investors certainly analyze the amount of fixed charges and evaluate financial risk in keeping with the ability of the firm to service these charges, but individual investors may judge financial risk more by the book-value proportions of debt to equity. There may or may not be a reasonable correspondence between the ratio of debt to equity and the amount of fixed charges relative

---

[3]The determinants of net cash flows with which he works are sales collections, other cash receipts, payroll expenditures, raw-material expenditures, and nondiscretionary cash expenditures. By analyzing each of these determinants, he determines the range and probability of recession net cash flows.

to the firm's cash-flow ability to service these charges. Some firms may have relatively high ratios of debt to equity but substantial cash-flow ability to service debt. Consequently, the analysis of debt-to-equity ratios alone can be deceiving, and an analysis of the magnitude and stability of cash flows relative to fixed charges is extremely important in determining the appropriate capital structure for the firm.

OTHER METHODS OF ANALYSIS

Comparison of capital structure ratios

Another method of analyzing the appropriate capital structures for a company is to evaluate the capital structure of other companies having similar business risk. Companies used in this comparison may be those in the same industry. If the firm is contemplating a capital structure significantly out of line with that of similar companies, it is conspicuous in the marketplace. This is not to say that the firm is wrong. Other companies in the industry may be too conservative in their use of debt. The optimal capital structure for all companies in the industry might call for a higher proportion of debt to equity than the industry average. As a result, the firm may well be able to justify more debt than the industry average. If the firm is noticeably out of line in either direction, it should be prepared to justify its position, because investment analysts and creditors tend to evaluate companies by industry.

There are wide variations in the use of financial leverage among business firms. A good deal of the variation is removed if one goes to industry classifications, because there is a tendency for the firms in an industry to cluster when it comes to debt ratios. For selected industries, the total liabilities-to-net-worth ratios are as follows.[4]

Industry	Debt to net worth
General building contractors	5.3
Dairy products	1.1
Air transportation	2.1
Drugs	0.8
Motor vehicles and equipment	1.6
General merchandise stores	1.7
Real estate investment trusts	3.4
Newspapers	0.6

Whereas general contractors make extensive use of debt in financing projects, drug companies and newspapers do not employ much leverage. Compare apples with

[4]These data come from Leo Troy, *Almanac of Business and Industrial Financial Ratios* (Englewood Cliffs, N.J.: Prentice-Hall, 1981).

apples as opposed to apples with oranges. Look at other companies in the same industry.

Surveying analysts and investors

The firm may profit also by talking with investment analysts, institutional investors, and investment houses to obtain their views on the appropriate amount of leverage. These analysts examine many companies and are in the business of recommending stocks. They therefore have an influence upon the market, and their judgments with respect to how the market evaluates leverage may be very worthwhile. Similarly, a firm may wish to interview lenders to see how much debt it can undertake before the cost of borrowing is likely to rise. Finally, the management of a company may develop a "feel" for what has happened to the market price of the stock when they have issued debt.

The methods described above for analyzing the appropriate amount of leverage do not give an exact answer. Nevertheless, by undertaking a variety of analyses, the financial manager should be able to determine, within some range, the appropriate capital structure. By necessity, the final decision has to be somewhat subjective, but it can be based upon the best information available. In this way, the firm is able to obtain the capital structure most appropriate for its situation—the one it hopes will tend to maximize the market price of the stock, all other factors held constant.

SUMMARY

Financial leverage involves the use of funds for which the firms agrees to pay a fixed charge. The greater the financial leverage of a firm, the greater the fluctuation in earnings available to common stockholders, all other things the same. Therefore, the advantage of higher expected returns to common stockholders must be balanced against the risks to them.

By using an indifference chart, we can study the relationship between earnings before interest and taxes (EBIT) and earnings per share under alternative methods of financing. The degree of sensitivity of earnings per share to EBIT depends upon the explicit cost of the method of financing, the number of shares of common stock to be issued, and the nearness to the indifference point. It is important in this analysis to evaluate the indifference point in relation to the level of EBIT as well as likely fluctuations in EBIT.

In addition, the cash-flow ability of the firm to service debt should be evaluated. The firm's debt capacity can be assessed by analyzing coverage ratios and the probability of cash insolvency under various levels of debt. Other methods of analysis include a comparison with capital-structure ratios of like companies, such as those within the same industry, and discussions with investment analysts, investment bankers, and lenders. In deciding upon an appropriate capital structure, all of these factors should be considered. In addition, certain concepts involving valuation should guide the decision. These concepts are discussed in the next chapter.

QUESTIONS

1. Define the concept of *financial leverage.*

2. Discuss the similarities and differences of financial and operating leverage.

3. Can the concept of financial leverage be analyzed quantitatively? Explain.

4. The EBIT-EPS chart suggests that the higher the debt ratio, the higher the earnings per share for any level of EBIT above the indifference point. Why do firms choose financing alternatives that do not maximize EPS?

5. Why is the percentage of debt for an electric utility higher than that for the typical manu-facturing company?

6. Is the debt/equity ratio a good proxy for financial risk as represented by the cash-flow ability of a company to service debt? Why or why not?

7. How can a company determine in practice if it has too much debt? Too little debt?

8. How can coverage ratios be used to determine an appropriate amount of debt to employ? Are there any shortcomings to the use of these ratios?

9. In financial leverage, why not simply increase leverage as long as the firm is able to earn more on the employment of the funds than they cost? Would not earnings per share increase?

PROBLEMS

1. The Lemaster Company is a new firm that wishes to determine an appropriate capital structure. It can issue 16 percent debt or 15 percent preferred stock. The total capitalization of the company will be $5 million, and common will be sold at $20 per share. The company is expected to have a 50 percent tax rate. The possible capital structures are

Plan	Debt	Preferred	Equity
1	0%	0%	100%
2	30	0	70
3	50	0	50
4	50	20	30

a) Construct an EBIT-EPS chart for the four plans.

b) Determine the relevant indifference points.

c) Using Eq. (16-1), verify the indifference points on your graph for the dominant plans.

d) What plan is best?

2. Hi Grade Regulator Company currently has 100,000 shares of common stock outstanding with a market price of $60 per share. It also has $2 million in 6 percent bonds. The company is considering a $3 million expansion program that it can finance with either (1) all common

stock at $60 a share, (2) straight bonds at 8 percent interest, (3) preferred stock at 7 percent, (4) half common stock at $60 per share and half 8 percent bonds.

a) For a hypothetical EBIT level of $1 million after the expansion program, calculate the earnings per share for each of the alternative methods of financing. Assume a corporate tax rate of 50 percent.

b) Construct an EBIT-EPS chart. What are the indifference points between alternatives? What is your interpretation of them?

3. Hi Grade Regulator Company (see problem 2) expects the EBIT level after the expansion program to be $1 million, with a two-thirds probability that it will be between $600,000 and $1,400,000.

a) Which financing alternative do you prefer? Why?

b) Suppose the expected EBIT level were $1.5 million and there were a two-thirds probability that it would be between $1.3 million and $1.7 million. Which financing alternative would you prefer? Why?

4. Tahoe Power and Light Company currently has the following long-term capitalization:

	Amount	Average before-tax cost
Debt	$ 80 million	9.50%
Preferred stock	10 million	8.00%
Common stock (1 million shares)	5 million	
Retained earnings	65 million	
	$160 million	

Earnings before interest and taxes (EBIT) are presently $16 million. Because Tahoe services a recreational area, however, its revenues are more volatile that those of most public utilities.

The company needs to undertake a $20 million plant expansion program in order to keep up with growing demand. Management estimates the following EBIT possibilities for the near future if the expansion program is undertaken:

EBIT ($ millions)	$17	$18	$19	$20	$21	$22	$23	$24
Probability of occurrence	5%	5%	10%	20%	25%	20%	10%	5%

The bonds of the company currently are rated A by Moody's, and the tax rate is 50 percent. To finance the expansion program, common stock could be sold at a price which would result in net proceeds to the company of $33 ⅓ per share. If debt financing were used, the company's bond rating would be lowered to Baa, and the interest rate would be 10 ½% on the new debt.

a) What are present earnings per share?

b) What are the earnings per share for the various possible levels of EBIT if common stock is used to finance the expansion program?

c) What are earnings per share if debt is used?

d) Which method of financing would you recommend? Is there adequate information? Does the use of debt affect the value of existing debt and equity?

5. Cornwell Real Estate Speculators, Inc., and the Northern California Electric Utility Company have the following EBIT and debt-servicing burden:

	Cornwell	Northern California
Expected EBIT	$5,000,000	$100,000,000
Annual interest	1,600,000	45,000,000
Annual principal payments on debt	2,000,000	35,000,000

The tax rate for Cornwell is 40 percent; for Northern California Electric Utility, 50 percent. Compute the times-interest-earned ratio and the debt-service coverage ratio for the two companies. With which company would you feel more comfortable if you were a lender? Why?

6. Gamma Tube Company plans to undertake a $7.5 million capital improvement program and is considering how much debt to use. It feels that it could obtain debt financing at the following interest rates (assume that this debt is perpetual):

Amounts (in millions)	First $3	Next $2	Next $1.5	Next $1
Interest cost	10%	11%	12%	13%

The company has made projections of its net cash flows (exclusive of new financing) during a period of adversity such as a recession. In a recession, it expects a net cash flow of $3 million with a standard deviation of $2 million (assume a normal distribution). Its beginning cash balance is $1 million. If the company is willing to tolerate only a 5 percent probability of running out of cash during a recession, what is the maximum proportion of the $7.5 million capital improvement program that can be financed with debt? (Use the probability concepts discussed in chapter 14 and the table in Appendix B to that chapter.)

7. The debt ratios of four companies are shown below:

Company	Total debt/ Total assets	Long-term debt/ Total capitalization
A	0.56	0.43
B	0.64	0.66
C	0.47	0.08
D	0.42	0.26

The companies are part of the following industries: supermarket, chemical, apparel making, and airline (not in order). Match the company with the industry.

SELECTED REFERENCES

CRITTA, RICHARD D., "The Effect of Financial Leverage on Air Carrier Earnings: A Break-Even Analysis," *Financial Management,* 8 (Summer 1979), 53–60.

DONALDSON, GORDON, *Corporate Debt Capacity.* Boston: Division of Research, Harvard Business School, 1961.

———, "Strategy for Financial Emergencies," *Harvard Business Review,* 47 (November-December 1969), 67–79.

FERRI, MICHAEL G., and WESLEY H. JONES, "Determinants of Financial Structure: a New Methodological Approach," *Journal of Finance,* 34 (June 1979), 631–44.

HANDORF, WILLIAM C., "Flexible Debt Financing," *Financial Management,* 3 (Summer 1974), 17–23.

HELFERT, ERICH A., *Techniques of Financial Analysis,* 5th ed., Homewood, Ill.: Irwin, 1981, chap. 2.

HONG, HAI, and ALFRED RAPPAPORT, "Debt Capacity, Optimal Capital Structure, and Capital Budgeting," *Financial Management,* 7 (Autumn 1978), 7–11.

LITZENBERGER, ROBERT H., and HOWARD B. SOSIN, "A Comparison of Capital Structure Decisions of Regulated and Non-regulated Firms," *Financial Management,* 8 (Autumn 1979), 17–21.

MARSH, PAUL, "The Choice Between Equity and Debt: An Empirical Study," *Journal of Finance,* 37 (March 1982), 121–44.

SCOTT, DAVID R., JR., and JOHN D. MARTIN, "Industry Influence on Financial Structure," *Financial Management,* (Spring 1975), 67–73.

SHALIT, SOL S., "On the Mathematics of Financial Leverage," *Financial Management,* 4 (Spring 1975), 57–66.

Conceptual aspects of capital structure 17

We have just observed a company approaching the question of how much debt it should have in its capital structure. The incremental expected return and risk to common stockholders are very much a part of the answer. Now we explore the valuation underpinnings to the question of capital structure. As we shall see, much controversy surrounds the issue. Despite the unsettled nature of the matter, we hope that this presentation will provide the conceptual backdrop necessary to guide the financial manager in capital-structure decisions.

Throughout our discussion, we assume that the investment and dividend decisions of the firm are held constant. We wish to determine the effect of a change in financing mix on share price. The focus is different from before in that we are concerned with how security prices are determined in the overall financial markets. That is, how do suppliers of capital value a company in relation to other companies when it changes its capital structure? We shall see that financial market imperfections play a major role. For simplicity, we consider only debt-versus-equity financing, though the principles taken up apply to preferred-stock financing as well.

The key question with which we are concerned is whether a firm can affect its total valuation (debt plus equity) and its cost of capital by changing its financing mix. Changes in the financing mix are assumed to occur by issuing debt and repurchasing stock or by issuing stock and retiring debt. In what follows, our attention is directed to what happens to the total valuation of the firm and to its cost of capital when the ratio of debt to equity, or degree of leverage, is varied.

For ease of illustration, let us assume that we are concerned with a company whose operating earnings are not expected to grow and which pays out all of its earnings to stockholders in the form of dividends. Moreover, suppose that we live in a world where, happily, there are no income taxes. Later this assumption will be relaxed to consider the issue in the real, and perhaps cruel, world of taxes. For now, the issue can be best understood if we assume no taxes and later treat taxes as a market imperfection.

In the subsequent discussion we are concerned with the three different rates of return. The first is

$$k_i = \frac{F}{B} = \frac{\text{Annual interest charges}}{\text{Market value of debt outstanding}} \qquad (17\text{-}1)$$

In this equation, k_i is the yield on the company's debt, assuming this debt to be perpetual. The second rate of return with which we are concerned is

$$k_e = \frac{E}{S} = \frac{\text{Earnings available to common stockholders}}{\text{Market value of stock outstanding}} \qquad (17\text{-}2)$$

With our assumptions of a firm whose earnings are not expected to grow and that has a 100 percent dividend-payout ratio, the earnings/price ratio represents the market rate of discount that equates the present value of the stream of expected future dividends with the current market price of the stock.[1] This is not to say that it should be used as a general rule to depict the cost of equity capital. (See chapter 15.) We use it only because of its simplicity in illustrating the theory of capital structure. The final rate we consider is

$$k_o = \frac{O}{V} = \frac{\text{Net operating earnings}}{\text{Total market value of the firm}} \qquad (17\text{-}3)$$

where $V = B + S$. Here, k_o is an overall capitalization rate for the firm. It is defined as the weighted-average cost of capital, and may also be expressed as

$$k_o = k_i\left(\frac{B}{B + S}\right) + k_e\left(\frac{S}{B + S}\right) \qquad (17\text{-}4)$$

---

[1] In chapter 5 we saw that the price of a security that is expected to pay a fixed payment of C forever is $P = C/k$, where k is the yield required on a perpetual investment. Rearranging, we have $k = C/P$, which is the same as Eq. (17-2) above.

We want to know what happens to k_i, k_e, and k_o when the degree of leverage, as denoted by the ratio B/S, increases.

THE BOUNDARIES TO VALUATION

It is useful to consider the two extremes to the valuation of a company when debt is employed in the capital structure. These extremes or boundaries are definitional only. That is, we do not attach any behavioral or economic meaning to them. They merely provide the basis for further discussion of the issue, at which time we will consider their validity. Therefore, the reader should not accept either position as necessarily true, but reserve judgment until we cover additional ground. The two extremes to the valuation of the earnings of a company are the *net income approach* and the *net operating income approach*, and we consider each in turn.[2]

Net income approach

This approach can best be presented with an illustration. Assume that a company has $1,000 in perpetual debt at 15 percent interest, or $150 in interest per annum. Moreover, the annual net operating earnings of the company now and in the future are $1,000; that is, no growth is expected. Net operating earnings are simply earnings before interest payments. Finally, suppose the required return on equity of the company, k_e, is 20 percent. With this information and according to the net income approach, the value of the firm is

O	Net operating earnings	$1,000
F	Interest	150
E	Earnings available to common stockholders	$ 850
k_e	Equity-capitalization rate (divide by)	0.20
S	Market value of stock	$4,250
B	Market value of debt	1,000
V	Total value of firm	$5,250

With the net income approach, earnings available to common stockholders are capitalized at a constant rate, k_e. The implied overall capitalization rate in the above example is

$$k_o = \frac{O}{V} = \frac{\$1,000}{\$5,250} = 19.05 \text{ percent}$$

[2]These approaches were originally considered by David Durand. "The Cost of Debt and Equity Funds for Business," in *The Management of Corporate Capital*, Ezra Solomon, ed. (New York: Free Press, 1959), pp. 91–116.

Here the rate calculated is merely the result of dividing the net operating earnings of the firm by the total value of the firm which is derived. Therefore, the k_o is an implied rate of return as opposed to being given.

Assume now that the firm increases its debt from $1,000 to $3,000 and uses the proceeds of the debt issue to repurchase stock. The interest rate on debt remains unchanged at 15 percent. The value of the firm then is

O	Net operating earnings	$1,000
F	Interest	450
E	Earnings available to common stockholders	$ 550
k_e	Equity-capitalization rate (divide by)	0.20
S	Market value of stock	$2,750
B	Market value of debt	3,000
V	Total value of firm	$5,750

The implied overall capitalization rate now is

$$k_o = \frac{O}{V} = \frac{\$1,000}{\$5,750} = 17.39 \text{ percent}$$

According to the net income approach, the firm is able to increase its total valuation, V, and lower its cost of capital, k_o, as it increases the degree of leverage. As a result, the market price per share increases. To illustrate, assume in our example that the firm with $1,000 in debt has 425 shares of common stock outstanding. Thus, the market price per share is $10 a share ($4,250/425). The firm issues $2,000 in additional debt and at the same time repurchases $2,000 of stock at $10 a share, or 200 shares in total. It then has 225 shares outstanding. We saw in the example that the total market value of the firm's stock after the change in capital structure is $2,750. Therefore, the market price per share is $2,750/225 = $12.22, whereas before it was $10 a share.

Graphically, the approach is illustrated in Fig. 17-1. The degree of leverage, B/S, is plotted along the horizontal axis, while the percentage rate for k_i, k_e, and

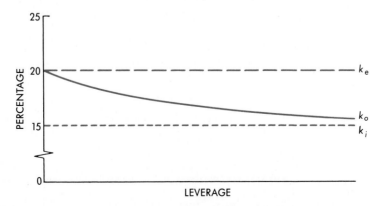

**FIGURE 17-1
Capital costs:
net income
approach**

k_o is on the vertical axis. This graph can be constructed based upon the hypothetical examples we have shown. As can be seen, the critical assumptions of the net-income approach are that k_i and more particularly k_e remain unchanged as the degree of leverage increases. As the proportion of cheaper debt funds in the capital structure is increased, the weighted-average cost of capital, k_o, decreases and approaches the cost of debt, k_i. The significance of this approach is that a firm can lower its cost of capital continually and increase its total valuation by the use of debt funds.

Net operating income approach

We turn now to the net operating income approach. The assumption here is that the overall capitalization rate of the firm, k_o, is constant for all degrees of leverage. Assume the same example as before but with k_o equal to 20 percent. In other words, we are given the overall capitalization rate as opposed to the equity-capitalization rate. For $1,000 in debt, we have

O	Net operating income	$1,000
k_o	Overall capitalization rate (divide by)	0.20
V	Total value of firm	$5,000
B	Market value of debt	1,000
S	Market value of stock	$4,000

The implied equity-capitalization rate in this case is

$$k_e = \frac{E}{S} = \frac{\$850}{\$4,000} = 21.25 \text{ percent}$$

With this approach, net operating income is capitalized at an overall capitalization rate to obtain the total market value of the firm. The market value of the debt then is deducted from the total market value to obtain the market value of the stock.

Suppose, as before, that the firm increases the amount of debt from $1,000 to $3,000 and uses the proceeds of the debt issue to repurchase stock. The valuation of the firm then is

O	Net operating income	$1,000
k_o	Overall capitalization rate (divide by)	0.20
V	Total value of firm	$5,000
B	Market value of debt	3,000
S	Market value of stock	$2,000

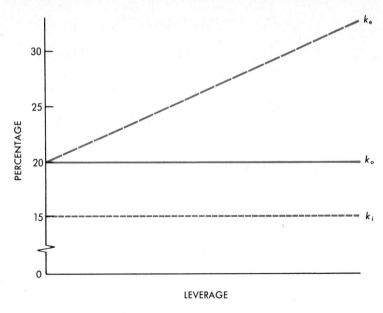

FIGURE 17-2
Capital costs: net operating income approach

The implied equity-capitalization rate is

$$k_e = \frac{E}{S} = \frac{\$550}{\$2,000} = 27.50 \text{ percent}$$

We see that the equity-capitalization rate, k_e, rises with the degree of leverage. This approach implies that the total valuation of the firm is unaffected by its capital structure. Figure 17-2 shows the approach graphically.

The critical assumption with this approach is that k_o is constant regardless of the degree of leverage. The market capitalizes the value of the firm as a whole; as a result, the breakdown between debt and equity is unimportant. An increase in the use of supposedly "cheaper" debt funds is offset exactly by the increase in the equity-capitalization rate, k_e. Thus, the weighted average of k_e and k_i remains unchanged for all degrees of leverage. As the firm increases its degree of leverage, it becomes increasingly more risky; and investors penalize the stock by raising the equity-capitalization rate (lowering the P/E ratio) directly in keeping with the increase in the debt-to-equity ratio. As long as k_i remains constant, k_e is a constant linear function of the debt-to-equity ratio. Because the cost of capital of the firm, k_o, cannot be altered through leverage, the net operating income approach implies that there is no one optimal capital structure.

So far, our discussion of the net operating income approach has been purely definitional; it lacks behavioral significance. Modigliani and Miller offered behavioral support for the independence of the total valuation and the cost of capital of the firm from its capital structure.[3] Before taking up the implications of their position, however, we examine the traditional approach to valuation.

[3]Franco Modigliani and Merton H. Miller, "The Cost of Capital, Corporation Finance and the Theory of Investment," *American Economic Review*, 48 (June 1958), 261–97.

Traditional approach

The traditional approach to valuation and leverage assumes that there is an optimal capital structure and that the firm can increase the total value of the firm through the judicious use of leverage. Actually, this approach encompasses all the ground between the net income approach and the net operating income approach. The traditional approach suggests that the firm initially can lower its cost of capital and raise its total value through leverage. Although investors raise the equity-capitalization rate, the increase in k_e does not offset entirely the benefit of using "cheaper" debt funds. As more leverage occurs, investors increasingly penalize the firm's equity capitalization rate until eventually this effect more than offsets the use of "cheaper" debt funds.

In one variation of the traditional approach, shown in Fig. 17-3, k_e is assumed to rise at an increasing rate with leverage, whereas k_i is assumed to rise only after significant leverage has occurred. At first, the weighted-average cost of capital declines with leverage because the rise in k_e does not offset entirely the use of cheaper debt funds. As a result, the weighted-average cost of capital, k_o, declines with moderate use of leverage. After a point, however, the increase in k_e more than offsets the use of cheaper debt funds in the capital structure, and k_o begins to rise. The rise in k_o is supported further once k_i begins to rise. The optimal capital structure is the point at which k_o bottoms out. In the figure, this optimal capital structure is point X.

Thus, the traditional position implies that the cost of capital is not independent of the capital structure of the firm and that there is an optimal capital structure. At that optimal structure, the marginal true cost of debt is the same as the marginal true cost of equity. For degrees of leverage before that point, the

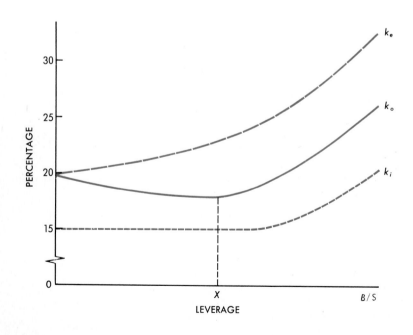

FIGURE 17-3
Traditional approach

marginal true cost of debt exceeds that of equity. There are wide variations in the traditional approach. As we mentioned earlier, the approach falls somewhere between the extremes of the net income approach and the net operating income approach.

TOTAL-VALUE PRINCIPLE

Modigliani and Miller (MM) advocate that the relationship between leverage and the cost of capital is explained by the net operating income approach. They make a formidable attack on the traditional position by offering behavioral justification for having the cost of capital, k_o, remain constant throughout all degrees of leverage.

MM argue that the total risk for all security holders of a firm is not altered by changes in its capital structure. Therefore, the total value of the firm must be the same, regardless of its financing mix. Simply put, the Modigliani-Miller position is based on the idea that no matter how you divide up the capital structure of a firm among debt, equity, and other claims, there is a conservation of investment value.[4] That is, because the total investment value of a corporation depends upon its underlying profitability and risk, it is invariant with respect to relative changes in the firm's financial capitalization. Thus, the total pie does not change as it is divided into debt, equity, and other securities. The sum of the parts must equal the whole; so regardless of financing mix, the total value of the firm stays the same, according to MM.

The support for this position rests on the idea that investors are able to substitute personal for corporate leverage, thereby replicating any capital structure the firm might undertake. Because the firm is unable to do something for its stockholders (leverage) that they cannot do for themselves, capital structure changes are not a thing of value in the perfect capital market world that MM assume. Therefore, two firms alike in every respect except for capital structure must have the same total value. If not, arbitrage will be possible, and its occurrence will cause the two firms to sell in the market at the same total value. In other words, arbitrage precludes perfect substitutes from selling at different prices in the same market.

Arbitrage support illustrated

Consider two firms identical in every respect except that Company A is not levered, while Company B has $30,000 of 12 percent bonds outstanding. According to the traditional position, Company B may have a higher total value and lower average cost of capital than Company A. The valuation of the two firms is assumed to be the following:

---

[4]This idea was first espoused by John Burr Williams, *The Theory of Investment Value* (Amsterdam: North-Holland Publishing Co., 1938), pp. 72–73.

		Company A	Company B
O	Net operating income	$10,000	$10,000
F	Interest on debt		3,600
E	Earnings available to common stockholders	$10,000	$ 6,400
k_e	Equity-capitalization rate (divide by)	0.15	0.16
S	Market value of stock	$66,667	$40,000
B	Market value of debt		30,000
V	Total value of firm	$66,667	$70,000
k_o	Implied overall capitalization rate	15%	14.3%
B/S	Debt-to-equity ratio	0	75.0%

MM maintain that this situation cannot continue, for arbitrage will drive the total values of the two firms together. Company B cannot command a higher total value simply because it has a financing mix different from Company A's. MM argue that by investing in Company A, investors in Company B are able to obtain the same dollar return with no increase in financial risk. Moreover, they are able to do so with a smaller investment outlay.[5] Because investors would be better off with the investment requiring the lesser outlay, they would sell their shares in Company B and buy shares in Company A. These arbitrage transactions would continue until Company B's shares declined in price and Company A's shares increased in price enough to make the total value of the two firms identical.

If you are a rational investor who owns 1 percent of the stock of Company B, the levered firm, worth $400 (market value), you should

1. sell the stock in Company B for $400.
2. borrow $300 at 12 percent interest. This personal debt is equal to 1 percent of the debt of Company B, your previous proportional ownership of the company.
3. buy 1 percent of the shares of Company A, the unlevered firm, for $666.67.

Prior to this series of transactions, your expected return on investment in Company B's stock was 16 percent on a $400 investment, or $64. Your expected return on investment in Company A is 15 percent on a $666.67 investment, or $100. From this return, you must deduct the interest charges on your personal borrowings, so your net dollar return is

Return on investment in Company A	$100
Less interest ($300 × .12)	36
Net return	$ 64

[5]This arbitrage proof appears in Franco Modigliani and Merton H. Miller, "Reply to Heins and Sprenkle," *American Economic Review,* 59 (September 1969), 592–95.

Your net dollar return, $64, is the same as it was for your investment in Company B; however, your cash outlay of $366.67 ($666.67 less personal borrowings of $300) is less than the $400 investment in Company B, the levered firm. Because of the lower investment, you would prefer to invest in Company A under the conditions described. In essence, you "lever" the stock of the unlevered firm by taking on personal debt.

The action of a number of investors undertaking similar arbitrage transactions will tend to drive up the price of Company A shares, and lower its k_e, drive down the price of Company B, and increase its k_e. This arbitrage process will continue until there is no further opportunity for reducing one's investment outlay and achieving the same dollar return. At this equilibrium, the total value of the two firms must be the same. As a result, their average costs of capital, k_o, also must be the same.

The important thing is the presence of rational investors in the market who are willing to substitute personal, or "homemade," leverage for corporate leverage. The analysis can be extended further to cross risk classes and include general equilibrium in the capital markets. Here, however, we must take account of differences in business-risk premiums. On the basis of the arbitrage process illustrated, MM conclude that a firm cannot change its total value or its weighted-average cost of capital by leverage. Consequently, the financing decision does not matter from the standpoint of our objective of maximizing market price per share. One capital structure is as suitable as the next.

Presence of market imperfections

With perfect capital markets, the arbitrage argument assures the validity of MM's thesis that the cost of capital and total valuation of a firm are independent of its capital structure. To dispute the MM position, we need to look for reasons why the arbitrage process may not work perfectly. If perfect capital markets do not exist in practice, opponents of the MM position are able to contest its behavioral support and argue that the cost of capital can decline with the appropriate use of leverage. The following are the major arguments against the MM arbitrage process.

Bankruptcy costs. If there is a possibility of bankruptcy, and if administrative and other costs associated with bankruptcy are significant, the levered firm may be less attractive to investors than the unlevered one. With perfect capital markets, zero bankruptcy costs are assumed. If the firm goes bankrupt, assets presumably can be sold at their economic values with no liquidating or legal costs involved. Proceeds from the sale are distributed according to the priority of claims on assets described in chapter 27. If capital markets are less than perfect, however, there may be administrative costs, and assets may have to be liquidated at less than their economic values. These costs and the "shortfall" in liquidating value from economic value represent a drain in the system from the standpoint of debt and equityholders.

In the event of bankruptcy, securityholders as a whole receive less than they would in the absence of bankruptcy costs. To the extent the levered firm has a greater possibility of bankruptcy than the unlevered one, it would be a less attrac-

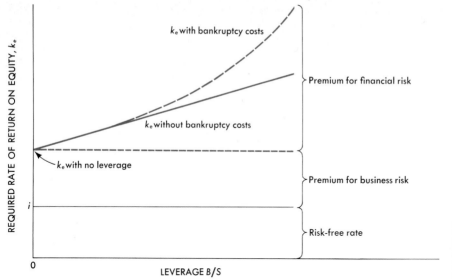

FIGURE 17-4
Required rate of return for equity capital when bankruptcy costs exist

tive investment, all other things the same. The possibility of bankruptcy is not a linear function of the debt/equity ratio but increases at an increasing rate beyond some threshold. As a result, the expected cost of bankruptcy increases in this manner and would be expected to have a corresponding negative effect upon the value of the firm.

Put another way, investors are likely to penalize the price of the stock as leverage increases. The nature of the penalty is illustrated in Fig. 17-4 for the case of a no-tax world. Here the required rate of return for investors, k_e, is broken down into its component parts. There is the risk-free rate, i, plus a premium for business risk. This premium is depicted on the vertical axis by the difference between the required rate of return for an all-equity capital structure and the risk-free rate. As debt is added, the required rate of return rises, and this increment represents a financial-risk premium. In the absence of bankruptcy costs, the required return would rise in a linear manner according to Modigliani-Miller, and this relationship is shown. However, with bankruptcy costs and an increasing probability of bankruptcy with leverage, the required rate of return would be expected to rise at an increasing rate beyond some point. At first there might be a negligible probability of bankruptcy, so there would be little or no penalty. As leverage increases, so does the penalty; for extreme leverage, the penalty becomes very substantial indeed.

Differences in corporate and personal leverage. The perceived risks of personal leverage and corporate leverage may differ. Despite the implication in the MM analysis that personal and corporate leverage are perfect substitutes, in the case of corporate borrowings the individual has only limited liability. If the levered company goes bankrupt, the investors' losses are limited to their investments in the stock. They are not liable for the debts of the company. If they borrow personally and default, lenders can claim assets in addition to the stock. Therefore their total risk exposure is greater with personal leverage and investment in the unlevered company than it is with a straight investment in the levered company.

In addition to greater risk, there are other reasons why investors may have a greater aversion to personal leverage than they do to corporate leverage. If investors borrow personally and pledge their stock as collateral, they are subject to possible margin calls. Many investors view this possibility with considerable alarm. Moreover, personal leverage involves a certain amount of inconvenience for investors, which they do not experience with corporate leverage. For these reasons, personal leverage may not be a perfect substitute for corporate leverage in the minds of many investors. Owing to market imperfections, the risk-adjusted cost of borrowing may be higher for the individual than for the corporation. If so, the levered company could have a somewhat greater total value than the unlevered firm for this reason alone.

Institutional restrictions.   Restrictions on investment behavior may retard the arbitrage process. Many institutional investors, such as pension funds and life insurance companies, are not allowed to engage in the "homemade" leverage that was described. Regulatory bodies often restrict stock and bond investments to a list of companies meeting certain quality standards such as only a "safe" amount of leverage. If a company breaches that amount, it may be removed from the acceptable list, thereby precluding certain institutions from investing in it. This reduction in investor demand can have an adverse effect on the market value of the company's financial instruments. Moreover, if there are enough restrictions on lenders, a firm may find that credit is unavailable to it beyond a certain degree of leverage.

Transaction costs.   Transaction costs tend to restrict the arbitrage process. Arbitrage will take place only up to the limits imposed by transaction costs, after which it is no longer profitable. As a result, the levered firm could have a slightly higher or slightly lower total value. The direction of the net effect of this imperfection is not predictable.

All of the factors listed above impede the effectiveness of the arbitrage process. If the arbitrage process is less than perfectly effective, a firm may be able to increase its total valuation and lower its cost of capital with an appropriate amount of leverage. As a result, the financing decision would matter, for it could affect the market value of the stock. In other words, the irrelevance-of-capital-structure argument depends on an equilibration in financial markets among security prices according to their respective risks and expected returns. If market imperfections systematically affect the arbitrage process, then capital-structure decisions would matter. To develop a complete picture, we must include the important role of taxes, to which we now turn.

THE EFFECT OF TAXES

When we allow for taxes, most would agree that the use of leverage can have a favorable impact on a company's total valuation if used judiciously. We must consider two taxes—corporate and personal—and because their effects are very different, we take them up separately. In the end, we will draw together their separate effects along with those of the market imperfections previously considered. For now, we assume that there are no market imperfections other than the presence of corporate taxes.

Corporate taxes

The advantage of debt in a world of corporate taxes is that interest payments are deductible as an expense. They elude taxation at the corporate level, whereas dividends or retained earnings associated with stock are not deductible by the corporation for tax purposes. Consequently, the total amount of payments available both for debtholders and stockholders is greater if debt is employed.

To illustrate, suppose that the earnings before interest and taxes are $2,000 for companies X and Y, and they are alike in every respect except in leverage. Company Y has $5,000 in debt at 12 percent interest, whereas Company X has no debt. If the tax rate (federal and state) is 50 percent for each company, we have

	Company X	Company Y
Earnings before interest and taxes	$2,000	$2,000
Interest—income to debtholders	0	600
Profit before taxes	2,000	1,400
Taxes	1,000	700
Income available to stockholders	$1,000	$700
Income to debtholders plus income to stockholders	$1,000	$1,300

Thus, total income both to debtholders and stockholders is larger for levered Company Y than it is for unlevered Company X. The reason is that debtholders receive interest payments without the deduction of taxes at the corporate level, whereas income to stockholders is after corporate taxes have been paid. In essence, the government pays a subsidy to the levered company for the use of debt. Total income to all investors increases by the interest payment times the tax rate. In our example, this amounts to $600 \times 0.50 = \$300$. This figure represents a tax shield that the government provides the levered company. If the debt employed by a company is permanent, the present value of the tax shield using the perpetuity formula is

$$\text{Present value of tax shield} = \frac{t_c r B}{r} = t_c B \qquad (17\text{-}5)$$

where t_c is the corporate tax rate, r is the interest rate on the debt, and B is the market value of the debt. For Company Y in our example,

$$\text{Present value of tax shield} = 0.50(\$5,000) = \$2,500.$$

What we are saying is that the tax shield is a thing of value and that the overall value of the company will be $2,500 more if debt is employed than if the company has no debt. This increased valuation occurs because the stream of income to all investors is $300 per year greater. The present value of $300 per year discounted at 12 percent is $300/0.12 = $2,500. Implied is that the risk associated with the tax shield is that of the stream of interest payments, so the appropriate discount rate is the interest rate on the debt. Thus, the value of the firm is

$$\text{Value of firm} = \frac{\text{Value if}}{\text{unlevered}} + \frac{\text{Value of}}{\text{tax shield}} \qquad (17\text{-}6)$$

For our example, suppose that the equity capitalization rate for Company A, which has no debt, is 16 percent. Therefore, the value of the firm if it were unlevered would be $1,000/0.16 = $6,250. The value of the tax shield is $2,500, so the total value of Company B, the levered firm, is $8,750.

We see in Eqs. (17-5) and (17-6) that the greater the amount of debt, the greater the tax shield and the greater value of the firm, all other things the same. By the same token, the greater the leverage, the lower the cost of capital of the firm. Thus, the original MM proposition as subsequently adjusted for corporate taxes suggests that an optimal strategy is to take on a maximum amount of leverage.[6] This implies a capital structure consisting almost entirely of debt. Since this is not consistent with the behavior of corporations, we must seek alternative explanations.

Personal taxes

The presence of taxes on personal income may reduce the corporate tax advantage associated with debt financing. With the combination of corporate taxes and personal taxes on both debt and stock income, the present value of the corporate tax shield shown in Eq. (17-5) may change. The equation becomes[7]

$$\text{Present value of tax shield} = \left[1 - \frac{(1 - t_c)(1 - t_{ps})}{1 - t_{pd}} \right] B \qquad (17\text{-}7)$$

where t_{ps} is the personal income tax rate applicable to common-stock income to the investor; t_{pd} is the personal tax rate applicable to income from the company's debt; and B is the market value of the firm's debt. We see that as long as t_{pd} is greater than t_{ps}, the tax advantage of debt is less that t_cB, which we determined to be the advantage in a world of corporate but not personal taxes.

If the income from holding a common stock consists only of dividends and if dividends and interest both are taxed as ordinary income, t_{ps} would equal t_{pd}. As a result, the tax advantage in Eq. (17-7) would reduce to t_cB, which is the same as

---

[6]Modigliani and Miller, "Corporate Income Taxes and the Cost of Capital: A Correction," *American Economic Review*, 64 (June 1963), 433–42.

[7]Merton H. Miller, "Debt and Taxes," *Journal of Finance*, 32 (May 1977), 266–68. See also Donald E. Farrar and Lee L. Selwyn, "Taxes, Corporate Financial Policies and Returns to Investors," *National Tax Journal*, 20 (December 1967), 444–54; and M. J. Brennan, "Taxes, Market Valuation and Corporate Financial Policy," *National Tax Journal*, 23 (December 1970), 417–27.

appears in Eq. (17-5) for the valuation of a levered firm with corporate income taxes but no personal income taxes. Suppose, however, that part of the income from holding a stock consists of capital gains. Assuming the tax rate on capital gains is less than that on ordinary income, t_{pd} would be greater than t_{ps}. As a result, the tax advantage associated with leverage would be less than $t_c B$. In other words, investors overall must hold both a company's common stock and its debt instruments. If the tax on debt income is greater than that on common-stock income, increases in a company's debt ratio result in an increase in the personal income taxes that must be paid. Therefore the existence of personal income taxes, differential tax rates on ordinary income and capital gains, and share repurchase will reduce but probably not eliminate the corporate income tax advantage associated with leverage.[8]

Suppose that the corporate tax rate is 0.46, the effective personal tax rate on debt income 0.40, and the market value of DSS Corporation's perpetual debt is $1 million. If the effective tax rate on stock income is 0.40, the present value of the tax shield is

$$\text{Present value of tax shield} = \left[1 - \frac{(1 - .46)(1 - .40)}{(1 - .40)} \right] \$1 \text{ million}$$
$$= [.46] \$1 \text{ million} = \$460,000$$

which, of course, is the straight corporate tax shield. If the effective personal tax rate on stock income is 0.20 instead of 0.40, we have

$$\text{Present value of tax shield} = \left[1 - \frac{(1 - .46)(1 - .20)}{(1 - .40)} \right] \$1 \text{ million}$$
$$= [.28] \$1 \text{ million} = \$280,000$$

Thus, the tax advantage associated with debt is less if the effective personal tax rate on debt income exceeds that on stock income. Moreover, the greater the personal tax on debt income relative to stock income, the lower the corporate tax shield.

The magnitude of net tax shield is an empirical question. Perhaps the only evidence that bears directly upon the issue comes from the study of changes in value when companies significantly recapitalize their capital structures. These changes occur when a company exchanges one type of security for another. Unfortunately, there have been few such studies, and the evidence from them is

---

[8]Miller, "Debt and Taxes," 261–75, argues that the tax advantage of corporate debt is eliminated in market equilibrium. If this were the case, the value of the firm and its cost of capital would be independent of its capital structure even with taxes. Essentially his argument is based on corporations adjusting the supply of corporate debt to take advantage of clienteles of investors with different tax brackets. In market equilibrium, Miller claims that $(1 - t_c)(1 - t_{ps}) = (1 - t_{pd})$, so that the term in brackets in Eq. (17-7) is zero. This provocative claim has been challenged by a number of authors who argue that the tax on stock income is positive, empirical relationships between market instruments are inconsistent with the claim, and that Miller's position is deficient theoretically. Space does not permit a review of these articles, but the reader should appreciate the controversy generated by Miller's position.

fragmentary.[9] Those available show that the net tax shield is less than the corporate tax rate, namely t_cB. These as well as certain indirect tax-effect studies imply that the net tax effect associated with debt may be in the neighborhood of .20.[10] That is, if there is a $1 increment in corporate debt, the net tax advantage is roughly 20¢. Again, such estimates must be taken as crude.

The tax advantage associated with leverage is reduced but not eliminated when we allow for different personal tax rates. As a result, an optimal leverage strategy would still call for the corporation to have a large proportion of debt. As this is not true for corporations overall, we must search for other factors affecting the valuation of the corporation when it alters the proportion of debt in its capital structure.

TAXES AND MARKET IMPERFECTIONS COMBINED

This statement brings us back to the influence of the various market imperfections considered earlier. Only if in some way they restrict the use of debt financing can the observed capital structure behavior of corporations be explained.

Bankruptcy costs and taxes

If one allows for bankruptcy costs, and if the probability of bankruptcy increases at an increasing rate with the degree of leverage, extreme leverage is likely to be penalized by investors. (As discussed earlier, bankruptcy costs represent a drain on the system to securityholders.) In a world of both taxes and bankruptcy costs, there would likely be an optimal capital structure even if all of the other behavioral tenets of the MM position held. The cost of capital of a firm would decline as leverage was first employed because of the net tax advantage of debt (corporate less personal). Gradually, however, the prospect of bankruptcy would become increasingly important, causing the cost of capital to decrease at a decreasing rate as leverage increased. As leverage became extreme, the bankruptcy effect might more than offset the tax effect, causing the cost of capital of the firm to rise. By definition, this would be the point at which the capital structure of the firm was optimal. The joint effect of taxes and bankruptcy is illustrated in Fig. 17-5 for a hypothetical firm.

Impact of additional imperfections

If other imperfections and behavioral factors dilute the MM position further, the point at which the cost-of-capital line turns up would be earlier than that

---

[9]Ronald W. Masulis, "The Effects of Capital Structure Change on Security Prices: A Study of Exchange Offers," *Journal of Financial Economics*, 8 (June 1980), 139–78; and J. J. McConnell and R. Schlarbaum, "Evidence on the Impact of Exchange Offers on Security Prices: The Case of Income Bonds," *Journal of Business*, 54 (January 1981), 65–85.

[10]For an indirect study of the effect, see David Flath and Charles R. Knoeber, "Taxes, Failure Costs, and Optimal Industry Capital Structure," *Journal of Finance*, 35 (March 1980), 99–117.

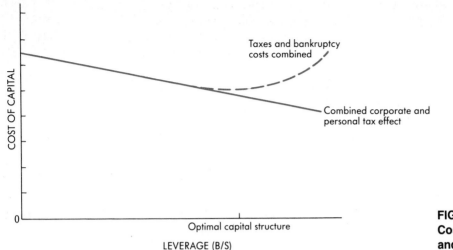

FIGURE 17-5
**Cost of capital with taxes
and bankruptcy costs**

depicted in the figure. Consider now the cost of borrowing. After some point of leverage, the interest rate charged by creditors usually rises. The greater the leverage, of course, the higher the interest rate charged. As a result, the cost of debt would turn up after a point. This phenomenon was illustrated earlier in Fig. 17-3. In turn, this factor exerts upward influence on the overall cost-of-capital line. Institutional restrictions on lenders also might cause the cost-of-capital line to turn up sooner than it does in Fig. 17-5. If, because of extreme leverage, a company no longer is able to sell debt securities to institutions, it must seek out unrestricted investors, and they will demand even higher interest rates. If institutional imperfections are serious enough, debt funds may not be available beyond a point of leverage, in which case there would be a discontinuity in Fig. 17-5.

Other capital-market imperfections work to hamper the arbitrage process so that "homemade" leverage is not a perfect substitute for corporate leverage. Recall that these imperfections include transaction costs, higher costs of borrowing for individuals than for corporations and imperfections in information. The greater the importance one attaches to these factors, the less effective the arbitrage process becomes, and the stronger the case that can be made for an optimal capital structure.

In conclusion, there are a number of reasons for believing that an optimal capital structure exists in theory. Depending upon one's view as to the strengths of the various capital-market and behavioral imperfections, the expected optimal capital structure may occur earlier or later along the scale of possible leverage.

SUMMARY

Much controversy has developed over whether the capital structure of a firm, as determined by its financing decision, affects its cost of capital. Traditionalists argue that the firm can lower its cost of capital and increase market value per share by the judicious use of leverage. Modigliani and Miller, on the other hand, argue that in the absence of taxes and other market imperfections, the total value of the firm and its cost of capital are independent of capital structure. This position, which is the same as the net operating income approach, is based on the notion that there is a conservation of investment value. No matter how you divide the pie between debt and equity claims, the total pie or investment value of the firm stays the same. Therefore, leverage is said to be irrelevant. We saw that behavioral support for the MM position was based upon the arbitrage process.

In a world of corporate income taxes, there is a substantial advantage to the use of debt, and we can measure the present value of the tax shield. When we allow for personal income taxes and a higher personal tax rate on debt income than on stock income, we find the tax advantage of debt to be lower. Bankruptcy costs work to the disadvantage of leverage, particularly extreme leverage. A combination of net tax effect with bankruptcy costs will result in an optimal capital structure. Other market imperfections—such as differences between corporate and "homemade" leverage and institutional restrictions on lender and stock investor behavior—impede the equilibration of security prices according to expected return and risk. As a result, leverage may affect the value of the firm because of these reasons.

In order for the financial manager to make proper capital structure decisions, these decisions must be rooted in theory. Every effort should be made to judge an alternative with respect to the imperfections described. In practice, such analysis can be accomplished with the tools taken up in the preceding chapter.

QUESTIONS

1. Contrast the net operating income approach with the Modigliani-Miller approach to the theory of the capital structure.

2. As a financial manager who believes the cost of capital to the firm can be minimized by using moderate amounts of debt, you have been asked to defend your proposal to change the debt/equity proportions of the firm to the board of directors. The majority stockholder argues that the cost of capital to the firm is his return. Because you work for him, the majority stockholder wants your resignation unless you can defend wanting to minimize his return. Discuss your rebuttal.

3. Why might you suspect that the optimal capital structure would differ significantly from one industry to another? Would the same factors produce differing optimal capital structures within all industry groupings?

4. What factors determine the interest rate a firm must pay for debt funds? Is it reasonable to expect this rate to rise with an increasing debt/equity ratio? Why?

5. Explain why the following three firms with similar asset structures and growth rates sell at different market prices. Are any of the firms overlevered? Explain carefully.

	Firm A	Firm B	Firm C
Dividend/share	$ 4	$ 3	$ 2
Market price	18	20	15

6. If there were not imperfections in financial markets, what capital structure should the firm seek? Why are market imperfections important in finance? Which imperfections are most important?

7. Why do the effects of corporate taxes and personal taxes tend to be in opposite directions when it comes to the capital structure issue?

8. Suppose a company has a large tax-loss carryforward and then goes bankrupt. If there are no out-of-pocket costs involved in bankruptcy proceedings, is there a cost of bankruptcy?

9. There are frequent complaints that debt funds are not available for capital-formation purposes, particularly for small and medium-sized firms. Is there any truth to this assertion?

10. If the corporate tax rate were cut in half, what would be the effect on debt financing?

11. Dividends presently are taxed twice. The corporation must pay taxes on its earnings and then stockholders must pay taxes on the dividends distributed. What would be the effect on corporate financing if this double taxation were eliminated by permitting companies to deduct dividend payments as an expense?

PROBLEMS

1. The E. W. Lambert Company has net operating earnings of $10 million and $20 million of debt with a 7 percent interest charge. In all cases, assume no taxes.

a) Using the net income approach and an equity capitalization rate of $12\frac{1}{2}$ percent, compute the total value of the firm and the implied overall capitalization rate.

b) Next, assume that the firm issues an additional $10 million in debt and uses the proceeds to retire stock; the interest rate and equity capitalization rate remain the same. Compute the new total value of the firm and overall capitalization rate.

c) Using the net operating income approach and an overall capitalization rate of 11 percent, compute the total market value, the stock market value, and the implied equity-capitalization rate for the E. W. Lambert Company prior to the sale of additional debt.

d) Determine the answers to part c if the company were to sell the additional $10 million in debt.

2. Abacus Calculation Company and Zoom Calculators, Inc., are identical except for capital structures. Abacus has 50 percent debt and 50 percent equity, while Zoom has 20 percent debt and 80 percent equity. (All percentages are in market value terms.) The borrowing rate for both companies is 13 percent, we live in a no-tax world, and capital markets are assumed to be perfect.

a) If you own 2 percent of the stock of Abacus, what is your dollar return if the company has net operating income of $360,000 and the overall capitalization rate of the company, k_o, is 18 percent? What is the implied equity capitalization rate?

b) What would be your dollar return if you invested the same amount of money in Zoom? (Zoom has the same net operating income as Abacus.) What percentage of the total stock of Zoom would you own? What is the implied equity capitalization rate of Zoom? Why does it differ from that of Abacus?

3. The Kelly Company and the Green Company are identical in every respect except that the Kelly Company is not levered, while the Green Company has $2 million in 12 percent bonds outstanding. There are no taxes, and capital markets are assumed to be perfect. The valuation of the two firms is the following:

	Kelly	Green
Net operating income	$ 600,000	$ 600,000
Interest on debt	0	240,000
Earnings to common	$ 600,000	$ 360,000
Equity capitalization rate	.15	.16
Market value of stock	$4,000,000	$2,250,000
Market value of debt	0	2,000,000
Total value of firm	$4,000,000	$4,250,000
Implied overall capitalization rate, k_o	15.00%	14.12%
Debt/equity ratio, B/S	0	0.89

a) You own $22,500 worth of Green stock. Show the process and the amount by which you could reduce your outlay through the use of arbitrage.

b) When will this arbitrage process cease?

4. The C. T. Carlisle Corporation has a $1 million capital structure and will always maintain this book-value amount. Carlisle currently earns $250,000 per year before taxes of 50 percent, has as all-equity capital structure of 100,000 shares, and pays all earnings in dividends. The company is considering issuing debt in order to retire stock. The cost of the debt and the price of the stock at various levels of debt are given in the following table. It is assumed that the new capital structure would be reached all at once by purchasing stock at the current price. In other words, the table is a schedule at a point in time.

Amount of debt	Average pre-tax cost of debt	Price of stock
$ 0	—	$10.00
100,000	10.0%	10.00
200,000	10.0	10.50
300,000	10.5	10.75
400,000	11.0	11.00
500,000	12.0	10.50
600,000	14.0	9.50

a) By observation, what do you think is the optimal capital structure?

b) Construct a graph in terms of k_e, k_i, and k_o based upon the above data.

c) Are your calculations in part a confirmed?

5. Zapatta Cottonseed Oil Company has $1 million in earnings before interest and taxes. Currently it is all equity financed. It may issue $3 million in perpetual debt at 15 percent interest in order to repurchase stock, thereby recapitalizing the corporation. There are no personal taxes.

   a) If the corporate tax rate is 46 percent, what is the income to all security holders if the company remains all equity financed? If it is recapitalized?

   b) What is the present value of the debt tax shield?

   c) The equity capitalization rate for the company's stock is 20 percent while it remains all equity financed. What is the value of the firm? What is the value if it is recapitalized?

6. Petroles Vintage Wine Company is presently family owned and has no debt. The Petroles family is considering going public by selling some of their stock in the company. Investment bankers tell them the total market value of the company is $10 million if no debt is employed. In addition to selling stock, the family wishes to consider issuing debt that, for computational purposes, would be perpetual. The debt then would be used to purchase stock, so the size of the company would stay the same. Based upon various valuation studies, the present value of tax shield is estimated at 22 percent of the amount borrowed when both corporate and personal taxes are taken into account. The investment banker has estimated the following present values for bankruptcy costs associated with various levels of debt:

Debt (in millions)	Present value of bankruptcy costs
$1	0
2	$ 50,000
3	100,000
4	200,000
5	400,000
6	700,000
7	1,100,000
8	1,600,000

Given this information, what amount of debt should the family choose?

7. Acme-Menderhall Corporation is trying to determine an appropriate capital structure. It knows that as its leverage increases, its cost of borrowing will eventually increase as will the required rate of return on its common stock. The company has made the following estimates for various leverage ratios.

Debt/(Debt + Equity)	Interest rate on borrowings	Required Rate of Return on Equity	
		Without bankruptcy costs	With bankruptcy costs
0	—	10 %	10 %
.10	8 %	10½	10½
.20	8	11	11¼
.30	8½	11½	12
.40	9	12¼	13
.50	10	13¼	14½
.60	11	14½	16¼
.70	12½	16	18½
.80	15	18	21

a)   At a tax rate of 50 percent, what is the weighted average cost of capital of the company at various leverage ratios in the absence of bankruptcy costs? What is the optimal capital structure?

b)   With bankruptcy costs, what is the optimal capital structure?

SELECTED REFERENCES

ARDITTI, FRED D., "The Weighted Average Cost of Capital: Some Questions on its Definition, Interpretation and Use," *Journal of Finance,* 28 (September 1973), 1001–9.

———, and JOHN M. PINKERTON, "The Valuation and Cost of Capital of the Levered Firm with Growth Opportunities," *Journal of Finance,* 33 (March 1978), 65–73.

BARNEA, AMIR, ROBERT A. HAUGEN, and LEMMA W. SENBET, "Market Imperfections, Agency Problems, and Capital Structure: A Review," *Financial Management,* 10 (Summer 1981), 7–22.

BAXTER, NEVINS D., "Leverage, Risk of Ruin, and the Cost of Capital," *Journal of Finance,* 22 (September 1967), 395–404.

CHEN, ANDREW H., and E. HAN KIM, "Theories of Corporate Debt Policy: A Synthesis," *Journal of Finance,* 34 (May 1979), 371–84.

DEANGELO, HARRY, and RONALD W. MASULIS, "Optimal Capital Structure under Corporate and Personal Taxation," *Journal of Financial Economics,* 8 (March 1980), 3–29.

DURAND, DAVID, "Costs of Debt and Equity Funds for Business: Trends and Problems of Measurement," reprinted in *The Management of Corporate Capital,* ed. Ezra Solomon. New York: Free Press, 1959, pp. 91–116.

FAMA, EUGENE F., and MERTON H. MILLER, *The Theory of Finance.* New York: Holt, 1972, chap. 4.

FLATH, DAVID, and CHARLES R. KNOEBER, "Taxes, Failure Costs, and Optimal Industry Capital Structure: An Empirical Test," *Journal of Finance,* 35 (March 1980), 99–117.

GLENN, DAVID W., "Super Premium Security Prices and Optimal Corporate Financing Decisions," *Journal of Finance,* 31 (May 1976).

GORDON, MYRON J., and CLARENCE C.Y. KWAN, "Debt Maturity, Default Risk, and Capital Structure," *Journal of Banking and Finance,* 3 (December 1979), 313–29.

HAMADA, ROBERT S., "The Effect of the Firm's Capital Structure on the Systematic Risk of Common Stocks," *Journal of Finance,* 27 (May 1972), 435–52.

HAUGEN, ROBERT A., and LEMMA W. SENBET, "The Irrelevance of Bankruptcy Costs to the Theory of Optimal Capital Structure," *Journal of Finance,* 33 (June 1978), 383–94.

HEINS, A. JAMES, and CASE M. SPRENKLE, "A Comment on the Modigliani-Miller Cost of Capital Thesis," *American Economic Review,* 59 (September 1969), 590–92.

HELLWIG, MARTIN F., "Bankruptcy, Limited Liability, and the Modigliani-Miller Theorem," *American Economic Review,* 71 (March 1981), 155–70.

HONG, HAI, and ALFRED RAPPAPORT, "Debt Capacity, Optimal Capital Structure, and Capital Budgeting," *Financial Management,* 7 (Autumn 1978), 7–11.

JENSEN, MICHAEL C., and WILLIAM E. MECKLING, "Theory of the Firm: Managerial Behavior, Agency Cost and Ownership Structure," *Journal of Financial Economics,* 3 (October 1976), 305–60.

LITZENBERGER, ROBERT H., and JAMES C. VAN HORNE, "Elimination of the Double Taxation of Dividends and Corporate Financial Policy," *Journal of Finance,* 33 (June 1978).

MILLER, MERTON H., "Debt and Taxes," *Journal of Finance,* 32 (May 1977), 266–68.

MODIGLIANI, FRANCO, and M. H. MILLER, "The Cost of Capital, Corporate Finance, and the Theory of Investment," *American Economic Review,* 48 (June 1958), 261–97.

————,"The Cost of Capital Corporation Finance, and the Theory of Investment: Reply," *American Economic Review,* 51 (September 1959), 655–69; "Taxes and the Cost of Capital: A Correction," *ibid.,* 53 (June 1963), 433–43; "Reply," *ibid.,* 55 (June 1965), 524–27; "Reply to Heins and Sprenkle," *ibid.,* 59 (September 1969), 592–95.

NANTELL, TIMOTHY J., and C. ROBERT CARLSON, "The Cost of Capital as a Weighted Average," *Journal of Finance,* 30 (December 1975), 1343–55.

RENDLEMAN, RICHARD J., "The Effects of Default Risk on the Firm's Investment and Financing Decision," *Financial Management,* 7 (Spring 1978), 45–53.

SCOTT, JAMES H., JR., "Bankruptcy, Secured Debt, and Optimal Capital Structure," *Journal of Finance,* 32 (March 1977), 1–20.

SCHALL, LAWRENCE D., "Firm Financial Structure and Investment," *Journal of Financial and Quantitative Analysis,* 6 (June 1971), 925–42.

SMITH, CLIFFORD W. JR., and JEROLD B. WARNER, "On Financial Contracting: An Analysis of Bond Covenants," *Journal of Financial Economics,* 7 (June 1979), 117–61.

VAN HORNE, JAMES C., "Optimal Initiation of Bankruptcy Proceedings by Debt Holders," *Journal of Finance,* 31 (June 1976), 897–910.

Dividend policy and retained earnings

18

Over the years, business corporations have relied heavily on retained earnings as a source of financing. Since the dividend-payout ratio, the percentage of earnings paid to stockholders in cash, reduces the amount of earnings the firm retains, a dividend decision is a financing decision. The dividend-payout ratio is a major aspect of the dividend policy of the firm, which affects the value of the firm to the stockholder. But other aspects also affect valuation: stability of dividends, certain factors that influence the payout ratio from the standpoint of the firm, stock dividends and stock splits, the repurchase of stock, and the procedural and legal elements of dividend policy. We are going to turn to these now.

DIVIDEND-PAYOUT RATIO

The first questions before us are whether the payment of cash dividends can affect shareholder wealth and, if it can, what dividend-payout ratio will maximize shareholder wealth. Again, we assume that business risk is held constant. In order to evaluate the question of whether the dividend-payout ratio affects shareholder wealth, it is necessary to examine first the firm's policy solely as a financing decision involving the retention of earnings. Consider the situation in which the use of funds from earnings, and the dividend policy that results, is strictly a financing decision. As long as the firm's investment projects have returns that exceed the required return, it will use retained earnings—and the amount of senior securities the increase in equity base will support—to finance these projects. If the firm has retained earnings left over after financing all acceptable investment opportunities, these earnings will be distributed to stockholders in the form of cash dividends. If not, there will be no dividends. If the number of acceptable investment opportunities involves a total dollar amount that exceeds the amount of retained earnings plus the senior securities these retained earnings will support, the firm will finance the excess with a combination of a new equity issue and senior securities.

When we treat dividend policy strictly as a financing decision, the payment of cash dividends is a passive residual. The amount of dividend payout will fluctuate from period to period in keeping with fluctuations in the amount of acceptable investment opportunities available to the firm. If these opportunities abound, the percentage of dividend payout is likely to be zero. On the other hand, if the firm is unable to find profitable investment opportunities, dividend payout will be 100 percent. For situations between these two extremes, the payout will be a fraction between 0 and 1.

Walter's formula

To illustrate dividend policy as a financing decision determined solely by the profitability of investment opportunities available, let us examine Walter's formula.[1] His model was one of the earlier dividend models, and certain later models correspond to this one. His formula is

$$P = \frac{D + \frac{r}{\rho}(E - D)}{\rho} \tag{18-1}$$

where P = market price per share of common stock
D = dividends per share
E = earnings per share
r = return on investment
ρ = market capitalization rate

Suppose that r = 24 percent, ρ = 20 percent, E = \$4, and D = \$2. The market price per share would be

$$P = \frac{2 + (.24/.20)(4 - 2)}{.20} = \$22$$

The optimal dividend-payout ratio is determined by varying D until you obtain the the maximum market price per share. Under a strict interpretation of the

---

[1]James E. Walter, "Dividend Policies and Common Stock Prices," *Journal of Finance*, 11 (March 1956), 29–41.

Walter formula, the optimal dividend-payout ratio should be 0 if r is greater than ρ. Thus, in our example,

$$P = \frac{0 + (.24/.20)(4 - 0)}{.20} = \$24$$

With a payout ratio of 0, market price per share is maximized. Similarly, if r is less than ρ, the optimal payout ratio should be 100 percent. Suppose that $r = .16$ percent, $\rho = .20$ percent, $E = \$4$, and $D = \$2$. The market price per share then would be

$$P = \frac{2 + (.16/.20)(4 - 2)}{.20} = \$18$$

However, with a dividend-payout ratio of 100 percent,

$$P = \frac{4 + (.16/.20)(4 - 4)}{.20} = \$20$$

Thus, market price per share can be maximized with a complete distribution of earnings. If $r = \rho$, market price per share is insensitive to the payout ratio.

The Walter formula implies that the optimal dividend payout should be determined solely by the profitability of investments. If the firm has an abundance of profitable investment opportunities, there should be no cash dividends, for the earnings are needed to finance these opportunities. On the other hand, if the firm has no profitable investment opportunities, all earnings should be distributed to stockholders in the form of dividends. In this case, the funds are not needed for financing.

Dividends as a passive residual

The treatment of dividend policy as a passive residual determined solely by the availability of acceptable investment proposals implies that dividends are irrelevant; investors are indifferent between dividends and retention by the firm. If investment opportunities promise a return greater than their required return, investors would prefer to have the company retain earnings. If the return is equal to the required return, they would be indifferent between retention and dividends. Contrarily, if the return were less than the required return, they would prefer dividends. Supposedly, if the firm can earn more on projects than the required return, investors are perfectly happy to let the firm retain as much in earnings as it needs to finance the investments. With irrelevance, the required return is invariant with respect to changes in dividend payout. Are dividends more than just a means of distributing unused funds? Should dividend policy in any way be an active decision variable? To answer these questions, we must examine more thoroughly the argument that dividends are irrelevant, so that changes in the payout ratio (holding investment opportunities constant) do not affect shareholder wealth.

Irrelevance of dividends

Modigliani and Miller's 1961 article[2] is the most comprehensive argument for the irrelevance of dividends. They assert that, given the investment decision of the firm, the dividend payout ratio is a mere detail. It does not affect the wealth of shareholders. MM argue that the value of the firm is determined solely by the earning power of the firm's assets, or its investment policy, and that the manner in which the earnings stream is split between dividends and retained earnings does not affect this value. As in the previous chapter, when we considered the capital-structure decision, MM assume perfect capital markets where there are no transaction costs, no flotation costs to companies issuing securities, and no taxes. Moreover, the future profits of the firm are assumed to be known with certainty. (Later this assumption is removed.)

Dividends versus terminal value. The crux of MM's position is that the effect of dividend payments on shareholder wealth is offset exactly by other means of financing. Consider first selling additional stock in lieu of retaining earnings. When the firm has made its investment decision, it must decide whether to retain earnings, or to pay dividends and sell new stock in the amount of these dividends in order to finance the investments. MM suggest that the sum of the discounted value per share after financing and dividends paid is equal to the market value per share before the payment of dividends. In other words, the stock's decline in market price because of the dilution caused by external financing offsets exactly the payment of the dividend. Thus, the stockholder is said to be indifferent between dividends and the retention of earnings.

One might ask: how does this correspond to our earlier chapters, when we said that dividends are the foundation for the valuation of common stocks? Although it is true that the market value of a share of stock is the present value of all expected future dividends, the timing of the dividends can vary. The irrelevance position simply argues that the present value of future dividends remains unchanged even though dividend policy changes their timing. It does not argue that dividends, including liquidating dividends, are never paid, only that their postponement is a matter of indifference when it comes to market price per share.

Conservation of value. Given MM's assumptions of perfect certainty as well as their other assumptions, the irrelevance of dividends follows. As with our example for corporate leverage in the previous chapter, the conservation-of-value principle assures that the sum of market value plus current dividends of two firms identical in all respects other than dividend-payout ratios will be the same.

Investors are able to replicate any dividend stream the corporation might pay. If dividends are less than desired, investors can sell portions of their stock to obtain the desired cash distribution. If dividends are more than desired, investors can use dividends to purchase additional shares in the company. Thus, investors are able to manufacture "homemade" dividends in the same way they devise "homemade" leverage in capital-structure decisions. In order for a corporate deci-

---

[2]Merton H. Miller and Franco Modigliani, "Dividend Policy, Growth, and the Valuation of Shares," *Journal of Business*, 34 (October 1961), 411–33.

sion to be a thing of value, the company must be able to do something for stock-holders that they cannot do for themselves. Because investors can manufacture "homemade" dividends, which are perfect substitutes for corporate dividends under the above assumptions, dividend policy is irrelevant. As a result, one dividend policy is as good as the next. The firm is unable to create value simply by altering the mix of dividends and retained earnings. As in capital structure theory, there is a conservation of value so that the sum of the parts is always the same. The total size of the pie is what will be eaten, and it is unchanged in the slicing.

Arguments for relevance

A number of arguments have been advanced in support of the contrary position; namely, that dividends are relevant under conditions of uncertainty. In other words, investors are not indifferent to whether they receive their returns on investment in dividend income or stock-price appreciation. We shall examine these arguments under conditions of uncertainty.

Preference for dividends. Certain investors in the market may have a preference for dividends over capital gains. The payment of dividends may re-solve uncertainty in their minds. It might be argued that because dividends are received on a current, on-going basis, whereas the prospect of capital gains is off in the future, investors in a dividend-paying company resolve their uncertainty earlier than do those investing in a nondividend paying company. To the extent investors prefer the early resolution of uncertainty, they may be willing to pay a higher price for the stock that offers the greater current dividend, all other things held constant. If in fact investors can manufacture "homemade" dividends, such a preference is irrational. Nonetheless, sufficient statements from investors make it difficult to dismiss the argument. Perhaps, for either psychological or incon-venience reasons, investors prefer not to manufacture "homemade" dividends but to get the "real thing" directly from the company.

Informational content of dividends. This argument implies that divi-dends have an impact on share price because they communicate information to investors about the firm's profitability. When a firm has a target payout ratio that is stable over time, and it changes this ratio, investors may believe that manage-ment is announcing a change in the expected future profitability of the firm. Accordingly, the price of the stock may react to this change in dividend. Dividends may offer proof of a company's ability to generate cash, whereas management's words about the bright prospects of the company and the potential for capital gains are far less clear. MM do not deny the possibility of this effect but continue to maintain that present and expected future earnings are what determine value. They assert that dividends are merely a reflection of these factors and do not in themselves determine value; therefore, the irrelevance proposition holds.[3] Thus, dividends are said to be used by investors as predictors of the firm's future per-formance; they convey management's expectation of the future.

[3] Miller and Modigliani, "Dividend Policy," pp. 429–30.

Taxes on the investor.   When we allow for taxes, there are a variety of effects. On the surface there appears to be a strong advantage to the retention of earnings, because capital gains are taxed at a much lower rate than dividends. Presently, 60 percent of any capital gain realized from selling a security held 12 or more months is exempt from taxation. Thus, only 40 percent of a capital gain is subject to taxation, in contrast to 100 percent of any dividend. For most individual investors, a much higher tax is associated with a dollar of dividends than with a dollar of capital gains. Moreover, the capital gains tax is deferred until investors actually sell their stock.

There are exceptions. Individuals are able to exclude the first $100 of dividends from taxable income. Presumably, this provision creates a preference for current dividends on the part of small investors. For corporate investors, intercompany dividends are taxed at a rate below that applicable to capital gains. For example, if Laurel Corporation owns 100 shares of Hardy Corporation, which pays $1 per share dividend, 85 percent of the dividend income is tax exempt. In other words, Laurel Corporation would pay taxes on $15 of dividend income at the corporate tax rate. The overall tax effect will be less than if Hardy Corporation had share appreciation of $100 and all of this were taxed at the capital gains rate. Accordingly, there may be a preference for current dividends on the part of corporate investors. Finally, there are a growing number of tax-free institutional investors. Despite these exceptions, for the majority of investors there exists a differential in taxes between a dollar of dividends and a dollar of capital gains.

Flotation costs.   The irrelevance of dividend payout is based upon the idea that in accordance with the investment policy of the firm, funds paid out of the firm must be replaced by funds acquired through external financing. The introduction of flotation costs favors the retention of earnings in the firm. For each dollar paid out in dividends, the firm nets less than a dollar after flotation costs per dollar of external financing.

Transaction costs and divisibility of securities.   Transaction costs involved in the sale of securities tend to restrict the arbitrage process in the same manner as that described for debt. Stockholders who desire current income must pay brokerage fees on the sale of portions of their stocks if the dividend paid is not sufficient to satisfy their current desire for income. This fee varies inversely, per dollar of stock sold, with the size of the sale. For a small sale, the brokerage fee can be rather significant. As a result of this fee, stockholders with consumption desires in excess of current dividends will prefer the company to pay additional dividends. Perfect capital markets also assume that securities are infinitely divisible. The fact that the smallest integer is one share may result in "lumpiness" with respect to selling shares for current income. This, too, acts as a deterrent to the sale of stock in lieu of dividends. On the other hand, stockholders not desiring dividends for current consumption purposes will need to reinvest their dividends. Here again, transaction costs and divisibility problems work to the disadvantage of the stockholder, although in the opposite direction. Thus, transaction costs and divisibility problems cut both ways.

Institutional restrictions. The law limits the types of common stock that certain institutional investors may buy. The prescribed list of eligible securities is determined in part by the duration over which dividends have been paid. If a company does not pay dividends or has not paid them over a sufficiently long period, certain institutional investors are not permitted to invest in the stock.

Universities, on the other hand, sometimes have restrictions on the expenditure of capital gains from their endowment. Also, a number of trusts have a prohibition against the liquidation of principal. In the case of common stocks, the beneficiary in entitled to the dividend income, but not to the proceeds from the sale of stock. As a result of this stipulation, the trustee who manages the investments may feel constrained to pay particular attention to dividend yield and seek stocks paying reasonable dividends. Though the two influences described are small in aggregate, they work in the direction of a preference for dividends as opposed to retention and capital gains.

A summing up

A company should endeavor to establish a dividend policy that will maximize shareholder wealth. Most everyone agrees that if a company does not have sufficiently profitable investment opportunities, it should distribute any excess funds to its stockholders. The firm need not pay out the exact unused portion of earnings every period. Indeed, it may wish to stabilize the absolute amount of dividends paid from period to period. But over the longer run the total earnings retained, plus the senior securities the increasing equity base will support, will correspond to the amount of profitable investment opportunities. Dividend policy still would be a passive residual determined by the amount of investment opportunities.

For the firm to be justified in paying a dividend larger than that dictated by the amount left over after profitable investment opportunities, there must be a net preference for dividends in the market. It is very difficult to "net out" the arguments discussed above in order to arrive at the bottomline. Only institutional restrictions and some investors' preference for dividends, for tax and other reasons, argue strongly for dividends. The other arguments suggest either a neutral effect or a systematic bias favoring retention. Empirical evidence concerning the effect of dividends on the market price of a stock is far from clear. There does appear to be some positive value associated with a modest dividend as opposed to none at all. This occurrence may be due to institutional restrictions and a signaling effect. Beyond that, the picture is very cloudy, and some argue that even a modest dividend has no effect on valuation.

Despite the unsettled nature of the issue, we should point out that many companies behave as if dividends are relevant. A number of growth companies, which expand at a rate faster than their growth in earnings, pay small dividends. If these companies believed dividend policy were irrelevant, they would retain all their earnings. A number of companies pay significant dividends and go to the capital markets for additional equity capital, rather than retain a greater portion of earnings. Examples include public utilities and airlines. Whereas these actions do not support the idea that dividends are relevant, they do indicate that many

companies behave as though they are. The dividend payout ratio that these firms
believe is optimal is greater than that dictated by investment opportunities alone.

MANAGERIAL CONSIDERATIONS IN DETERMINING A DIVIDEND PAYOUT

So far we have discussed only the theoretical aspects of dividend policy.
Yet when a company establishes a dividend policy it looks at a number of things.
These considerations should be related back to the theory of dividend payout and
the valuation of the firm. In what follows, we take up various factors that firms in
practice can and should analyze when approaching a dividend decision.

Funds needs of the firm

Perhaps the place to begin is with an assessment of the funds needs of the
firm. In this regard, cash budgets and projected source-and-use-of-funds statements (topics taken up in chapter 7) are of particular use. The expected operating
cash flows of the firm, expected future capital expenditures, any likely buildups
in receivables and inventories, scheduled reductions in debt, and any other thing
that affects the cash position of the firm should be taken into account. The key is
to determine the likely cash flows and cash position of the company in the absence
of a change in dividend. In addition to looking at expected outcomes, we should
factor in business risk, so that we may obtain a range of possible cash flow outcomes, a procedure spelled out in chapter 7.

In keeping with our earlier discussion of the theory of dividend payout, the
firm wishes to determine if anything is left over after servicing its funds needs,
including profitable investment projects. In this regard, the firm should look at its
situation over a reasonable number of future years, to iron out fluctuations. The
likely ability of the firm to sustain a dividend should be analyzed relative to the
probability distributions of possible future cash flows and cash positions. On the
basis of this analysis, the firm can determine its likely future residual funds.

Liquidity

The liquidity of a company is a prime consideration in many dividend
decisions. Because dividends represent a cash outflow, the greater the cash position and overall liquidity of a company, the greater its ability to pay a dividend.
A company that is growing and profitable may not be liquid, for its funds may go
into fixed assets and permanent working capital. Because the management of such
a company usually desires to maintain some liquidity cushion to give it flexibility
and a protection against uncertainty, it may be reluctant to jeopardize this position
in order to pay a large dividend. The liquidity of the company, of course, is
determined by the firm's investment and financing decisions. The investment
decision determines the rate of asset expansion and the firm's need for funds; and
the financing decision determines the way in which this need will be financed.

Ability to borrow

A liquid position is not the only way to provide for flexibility and thereby protect against uncertainty. If a firm has the ability to borrow on comparatively short notice, it may be relatively flexible. This ability to borrow can be in the form of a line of credit or a revolving credit from a bank, or simply the informal willingness of a financial institution to extend credit. In addition, flexibility can come from the ability of a firm to go to the capital markets with a bond issue. The larger and more established a company, the better its access to the capital markets. The greater the ability of the firm to borrow, the greater its flexibility, and the greater its ability to pay a cash dividend. With ready access to debt funds, management should be less concerned with the effect that a cash dividend has upon its liquidity.

Assessment of any valuation information

To the extent there are insights into the effect of a dividend on valuation, they should be gathered. Regression analysis involving similar companies may give some indication, even though studies of this sort have statistical problems in addition to the troublesome job of trying to hold all else constant. As a result, it usually is difficult to make company-specific generalizations concerning the effect of dividends on valuation. Most companies look at the dividend payout ratios of other companies in the industry, particularly those having about the same growth. It may not matter that a company is out of line with similar companies, but it will be conspicuous and usually a company will want to justify its position. Finally, a company should judge the informational effect of a dividend. What do investors expect? Here security analysts and security reports are useful. The company should ask itself what information it is conveying with its present dividend and what it would convey with a possible change in dividend.

Control

If a company pays substantial dividends, it may need to raise capital at a later time through the sale of stock in order to finance profitable investment opportunities. Under such circumstances, the controlling interest of the company may be diluted if controlling stockholders do not or cannot subscribe for additional shares. These stockholders may prefer a low dividend payout and the financing of investment needs with retained earnings. Such a dividend policy may not maximize overall shareholder wealth, but it still may be in the best interests of those in control.

Control can work two ways, however. When a company is being sought by another company or by individuals, a low dividend payout may work to the advantage of the "outsiders" seeking control. The outsiders may be able to convince stockholders that the company is not maximizing shareholder wealth and that they (the outsiders) can do a better job. Consequently, companies in danger of being acquired may establish a high dividend payout in order to please stockholders.

Restrictions in bond indenture or loan agreement

The protective covenants in a bond indenture or loan agreement often include a restriction on the payment of dividends. This restriction is employed by the lenders to preserve the company's ability to service debt. Usually, it is expressed as a maximum percentage of cumulative earnings. When such a restriction is in force, it naturally influences the firm's dividend policy. Sometimes the management of a company welcomes a dividend restriction imposed by lenders, because then it does not have to justify to stockholders the retention of earnings. It need only point to the restriction.

A final observation

In determining a dividend payout, the typical company will analyze a number of the factors described above. These factors largely dictate the boundaries within which a dividend can be paid. When a company pays a dividend in excess of its residual funds, it implies that management and the board of directors believe the payment has a favorable effect on shareholder wealth. The frustrating thing is that we have so little in the way of clear generalizations from the empirical evidence. The lack of firm footing for predicting the long-run effect of a specific dividend policy on valuation makes the dividend decision more difficult in many ways than either the investment or financing decisions. Considerations taken up in this section allow a company to determine with reasonable accuracy what would be an appropriate passive dividend strategy. An active dividend policy involves an act of faith, because it demands that a portion of the cumulative dividends ultimately be replaced with common-stock financing. Such a strategy may enhance shareholder wealth, but it is undertaken in a foggy area where nobody can have much confidence in predicting the results.

DIVIDEND STABILITY

In addition to the percentage of dividend payout, stability is attractive to investors. By stability, we mean maintaining its position in relation to a trend line, preferably one that is upward sloping. All other things the same, a stock may be higher in price if it pays a stable dividend over time than if it pays out a fixed percentage of earnings. Suppose Company A has a long-run dividend payout ratio of 50 percent of earnings. It pays out this percentage every year, despite the fact that its earnings are cyclical. The dividends of Company A are shown in Fig. 18-1. Company B, on the other hand, has exactly the same earnings and a long-run dividend payout ratio of 50 percent, but it maintains a relatively stable dividend over time. It changes the absolute amount of dividend only in keeping with the underlying trend of earnings. The dividends of Company B are shown in Fig. 18-2.

Over the long run, the total amount of dividends paid by these two firms is the same; however, the market price per share of Company B may be higher than that of Company A, all other things being the same. Investors may well place a positive utility on dividend stability and pay a premium for the company that offers it. To the extent that investors value dividend stability, the overall dividend policy of Company B would be better than that of Company A. This policy in-

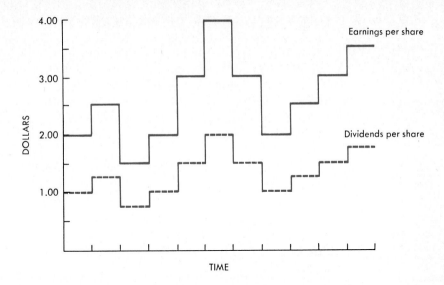

FIGURE 18-1
Hypothetical dividend
policy of Company A

cludes not only the percentage of dividend payout in relation to earnings but also the manner in which the actual dividends are paid. Rather than vary dividends directly with changes in earnings per share, Company B raises the dividend only when reasonably confident a higher dividend can be maintained.

Valuation of stability

Investors are willing to pay a premium for stable dividends because of the informational content of dividends, the desire of investors for current income, and certain legal considerations.

Informational content. When earnings drop and a company does not cut its dividend, the market may have more confidence in the stock than it would have

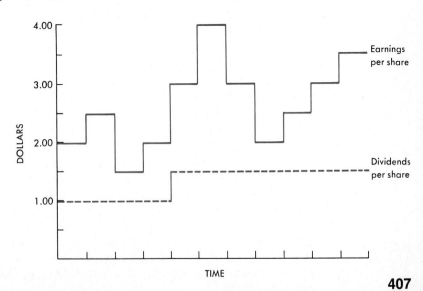

FIGURE 18-2
Hypothetical dividend
policy of Company B

407

if the dividend were cut. The stable dividend may convey management's view that the future of the company is better than the drop in earnings suggests. Thus, management may be able to affect the expectations of investors through the informational content of dividends. Management will not be able to fool the market permanently. If there is a downward trend in earnings, a stable dividend will not convey forever an impression of a rosy future. Moreover, if a firm is in an unstable business with wide swings in earnings, a stable dividend cannot give the illusion of underlying stability.

Current income desires.   A second factor may favor stable dividends. Investors who desire a specific periodic income will prefer a company with stable dividends to one with unstable dividends, even though both companies may have the same pattern of earnings and long-run dividend payout. Although investors can always sell a portion of their stock for income when the dividend is not sufficient to meet their current needs, many investors have an aversion to dipping into principal. Moreover, when a company reduces its dividend, earnings usually are down and the market price of the stock depressed. Overall, income conscious investors place a positive utility on stable dividends, even though they can always sell a few shares of stock for income.

Legal considerations.   A stable dividend may be advantageous from the legal standpoint of permitting certain institutional investors to buy the stock. Various governmental bodies prepare legal lists of securities in which pension funds, savings banks, trustees, insurance companies, and others may invest. In order to qualify, a company must have an uninterrupted pattern of dividends. A cut in the dividend may result in the removal of a company from these legal lists.

The arguments presented in support of the notion that stable dividends have a positive effect upon the market price of the stock are only suggestive. Little empirical evidence sheds light on the question. Although studies of individual stocks often suggest that stable dividends buffer the market price of the stock when earnings turn down, there have been no comprehensive studies of a large sample of stocks dealing with the relationship between dividend stability and valuation. Nevertheless, most companies strive for stability in their dividend payments. This occurrence is illustrated in Fig. 18-3, showing total corporate dividends and profits after taxes and adjustments for inventory valuation and depreciation in the post-World War II period.[4] Overall, corporations behave in a manner consistent with a belief that stable dividends have a positive effect on value.

Target payout ratios

A number of companies appear to follow the policy of a target dividend payout ratio over the long run. Lintner contends that dividends are adjusted to changes in earnings, but only with a lag.[5] When earnings increase to a new level, a company increases dividends only when it feels it can maintain the increase in earnings. Companies are also reluctant to cut the absolute amount of their cash dividend. Both of these factors explain the lag in dividend changes behind

---

[4] Source: *Economic Report of the President.*

[5] See John Lintner, "Distribution of Income of Corporations," *American Economic Review,* 46 (May 1956), 97–113.

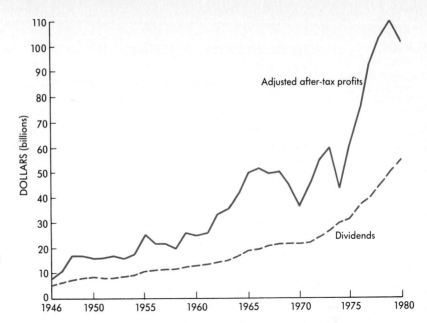

FIGURE 18-3
Corporate profits after tax with inventory valuation and capital consumption adjustments and corporate dividends.

changes in earnings. In an economic upturn, the lag relationship becomes visible when retained earnings increase in relation to dividends. In a contraction, retained earnings will decrease relative to dividends.

The case of Coleman Company illustrates the use of a target payout ratio and stable dividends. Coleman makes outdoor recreation equipment and central heating and air-conditioning units. Business is somewhat cyclical, with resulting swings in earnings, but the company maintained stable and increasing dividends over time; it raises dividends when management and the board of directors are confident that earnings can be sustained. The dividends per share and earnings per share for the company are shown in Fig. 18-4.

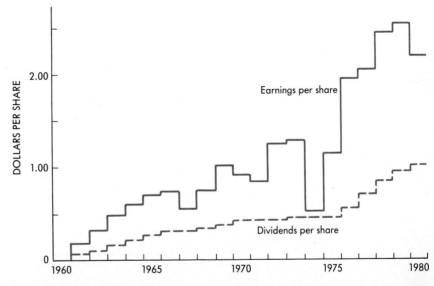

FIGURE 18-4
Coleman Company dividends and earnings per share

Regular and extra dividends

One way for a company to increase its cash distribution in periods of prosperity is to declare an *extra* dividend in addition to the *regular* quarterly or semiannual dividend. By declaring an extra dividend, the company warns investors that the dividend is not an increase in the established dividend rate. The declaration of an extra dividend is suitable particularly for companies with fluctuating earnings. General Motors, for example, has declared extra dividends in good years. The use of the extra dividend enables the company to maintain a stable record of regular dividends but also to distribute to stockholders some of the rewards of prosperity. If a company pays extra dividends continuously, it defeats its purpose. The extra becomes the expected.

STOCK DIVIDENDS AND STOCK SPLITS

Stock dividends and stock splits typically are used for different purposes; nevertheless, in an economic sense the two are very similar. Only from an accounting standpoint is there a significant difference.

Stock dividends

A stock dividend is simply the payment of additional stock to stockholders. It represents nothing more than a recapitalization of the company; a stockholder's proportional ownership remains unchanged. Chen Industries had the following capital structure before issuing a stock dividend:

Common stock ($5 par, 400,000 shares)	$ 2,000,000
Paid-in capital	1,000,000
Retained earnings	7,000,000
Net worth	$10,000,000

Chen pays a 5 percent stock dividend, amounting to 20,000 additional shares of stock. The fair market value of the stock is $40 a share. For each 20 shares of stock owned, the stockholder receives an additional share. The balance sheet of the company after the stock dividend would be

Common stock ($5 par, 420,000 shares)	$ 2,100,000
Paid-in capital	1,700,000
Retained earnings	6,200,000
Net worth	$10,000,000

With a stock dividend, $800,000 is transferred ($40 × 20,000 shares) from retained earnings to the common-stock and paid-in capital accounts. Because the par value stays the same, the increase in number of shares is reflected in a $100,000 increase in the common-stock account ($5 × 20,000 shares). The residual of $700,000 goes into the paid-in capital account. The net worth of the company remains the same.

Because the number of shares of stock outstanding is increased by 5 percent, earnings per share of the company are reduced proportionately. Total net profit after taxes is $1 million. Before the stock dividend, earnings per share were $2.50 ($1 million/400,000). After the stock dividend, earnings per share would be $2.38 ($1 million/420,000). Thus, stockholders have more shares of stock but lower earnings per share. Their proportion of total earnings available to common stockholders remains unchanged.

Value to investor. If the company pays no cash dividend, what do stockholders receive with a stock dividend? In theory, nothing but an additional stock certificate. Their proportionate ownership of the company is unchanged. Presumably, the market price of the stock will drop, all other things being equal, so that the total market value of their holdings stays the same. If you had held 100 shares of stock previously, and market price per share were $40, the total value of your holdings would be $4,000. After the stock dividend, the price of the stock should drop by $40(1 − 1.00/1.05), or by $1.90. The total value of your holdings then would be $38.10 × 105, or $4,000. Under these conditions, the stock dividend does not represent a thing of value to you. You merely have an additional stock certificate evidencing ownership.

To the extent that the investor wishes to sell a few shares of stock for income, the stock dividend may make it easier to do so. Without the stock dividend, of course, stockholders also could sell a few shares of their original holdings for income. In either case, the sale of stock represents the sale of principal and is subject to the capital-gains tax. It is probable that certain investors do not look at the sale of a stock dividend as a sale of principal. To them, the stock dividend represents a windfall gain; they can sell it and still retain their original holdings. The stock dividend may have a favorable psychological effect on these stockholders.

The stock dividend can also be a thing of value to the investor if the cash dividend per share remains the same after the stock dividend. Suppose an investor owns 100 shares of a company paying a $1 dividend. The company declares a 10 percent stock dividend and, at the same time, announces that the cash dividend per share will remain unchanged. The investor then will have 110 shares; and total cash dividends will be $110 rather than $100, as before. In this case, a stock dividend increases the total cash dividends. Whether this increase in cash dividend has a positive effect upon shareholder wealth will depend upon the tradeoff between current dividends and retained earnings, which we discussed earlier. Clearly, the stock dividend in this case represents a decision by the firm to increase modestly the amount of cash dividends.

Use of the stock dividend may convey some information. Stock dividends typically are associated with growth companies. The dividend may connote to investors that management expects earnings to continue to grow and to more than offset the dilution in earnings per share because there are more shares. The underlying cause for the rise in value is the company's growth, however, not the stock dividend itself.

Possible advantages to company. Frequently, a stock dividend is employed to conserve cash. Instead of increasing the cash dividend as earnings rise, a company may desire to retain a greater portion of its earnings and declare a stock dividend. The decision then is to lower the dividend payout ratio; for as earnings rise and the dividend remains the same, the payout ratio will decline. Whether shareholder wealth is increased by this action will depend upon considerations discussed previously. The decision to retain a higher proportion of earnings, of course, could be accomplished without a stock dividend. However, the stock dividend may tend to please certain investors by virtue of its informational content as well as its psychological impact. In addition, if the cash dividend per share is kept the same, total cash dividends will increase slowly in keeping with the increase in the number of shares.

A firm may also use a stock dividend to keep the market price of the stock within a desired trading range. Some companies do not like to see the market price of their stocks above a certain amount—say $60 a share—because a high price will not appeal to small investors. Consequently, they endeavor to keep the price below a desired ceiling either by using stock dividends or, more commonly, by means of stock splits. Increasing the total number of shares outstanding may increase the total number of stockholders, resulting in greater overall popularity for the stock. The principal disadvantage of stock dividends is that they are much more costly to administer than cash dividends.

Stock splits

With a stock split, the number of shares is increased through a proportional reduction in the par value of the stock. A lumber company has the following capital structure before a two-for-one stock split:

Common stock ($5 par, 400,000 shares)	$ 2,000,000
Paid-in capital	1,000,000
Retained earnings	7,000,000
Net worth	$10,000,000

After the split, the capital structure is

Common stock ($2.50 par, 800,000 shares)	$ 2,000,000
Paid-in capital	1,000,000
Retained earnings	7,000,000
Net worth	$10,000,000

With a stock dividend, the par value is not reduced, whereas with a split, it is. As a result, the common-stock, paid-in capital, and retained-earnings accounts remain unchanged. The net worth, of course, also stays the same; the only change is in the par value of the stock. Except in accounting treatment, the stock dividend and stock split are very similar. A stock split, however, is usually reserved for occasions when a company wishes to achieve a substantial reduction in the market price per share. The principal purpose of a split is to place the stock in a more popular trading range, thereby attracting more buyers.[6] One might expect that the increased shares would provide a better market for trading. However, in an empirical study by Thomas E. Copeland, market liquidity of a stock, as measured by the relative volume of trading and transaction costs, was found to decline following a stock split.[7]

Like the stock dividend, the stock split does not represent a thing of value to investors. They have more shares than before, but their proportional ownership of the company remains unchanged. The market price of the stock should decline proportionately, so that the total value of their holdings stays the same. Again, however, the split may have a favorable informational content. The announcement of the split may indicate to investors that management believes that earnings will continue to grow. As a result, the market price per share may increase upon the announcement or rumor of the split, and it may remain higher. The underlying cause for the increase in market price, again, is growth and not the split itself.

Very seldom will a company maintain the same cash dividends per share before and after a split, but it might increase the effective dividends to stockholders. A company may split its stock two-for-one and establish a dividend rate of $1.20 a share; whereas before, the rate was $2 a share. A stockholder owning 100 shares before the split would receive $200 in cash dividends per annum. After the split, the stockholder would own 200 shares and would receive $240 in dividends. The market price of the stock (on an after-split basis) may react favorably to the increase in cash dividends.

Reverse split. Rather than increase the number of shares of stock outstanding, a company may want to reduce the number. It can accomplish this with a *reverse split.* In our example above, had there been a one-to-four reverse split instead of the two-for-one straight stock split, for each four shares held, the stockholder would receive one share in exchange. The par value per share would become $20, and there would be 100,000 shares outstanding rather than 400,000. Reverse stock splits are employed to increase the market price per share when the stock is considered to be selling at too low a price. Many companies have an aversion to seeing their stock fall significantly below $10 per share. If financial difficulty or some other depressant lowers the price into this range, it can be increased with a reverse split. The reverse split is regarded by many as an admission by the company that it is in financial difficulty, although that is not always the reason for the split. The stock market's reaction to it depends primarily upon the company's past and expected earnings.

---

[6]For a survey of opinions of financial officers regarding stock splits, see H. Kent Baker and Patricia L. Gallagher, "Management's View of Stock Splits," *Financial Management,* 9 (Summer 1980), 73–77.

[7]"Liquidity Following Stock Splits," *Journal of Finance,* 34 (March 1979), 115–41.

REPURCHASE OF STOCK

In recent years a number of companies have repurchased a portion of their outstanding common stock. Some companies repurchase stock in order to have it available for stock options. In this way, the total number of shares is not increased with the exercise of the options. Another reason for repurchase is to have shares available for the acquisition of other companies. In certain cases, companies no longer wishing to be publicly owned "go private" by purchasing all of the stock of the outside stockholders. In still other situations, stock is repurchased with the full intention of retiring it. Under these circumstances, repurchase of stock may be treated as a part of the firm's dividend decision.

Repurchasing as part of a dividend decision

If a firm has excess cash and insufficient profitable investment opportunities to justify the use of these funds, it may be in the shareholders' interests to distribute the funds. The distribution can be accomplished either by the repurchase of stock or by paying the funds out in increased dividends. In the absence of personal income taxes and transaction costs, the two alternatives, theoretically, should make no difference to stockholders. With repurchase, fewer shares remain outstanding, and earnings per share rise. As a result, the market price per share should rise as well. In theory, the capital gain arising from repurchase should equal the dividend that otherwise would have been paid.

A hardware company has the following earnings and market price per share:

Net profit after taxes	$2,000,000
Number of shares outstanding	500,000
Earnings per share	$4
Market price per share, after distribution	$60
Price/earnings ratio	15

The company is considering the distribution of $1.5 million, either in cash dividends or in the repurchase of its own stock. If investors are expecting the cash dividend, the value of a share of stock before the dividend is paid will be $63; that is, $3 a share in expected dividends ($1.5 million/500,000) plus the $60 market price. The firm chooses to repurchase its stock, however, and makes a tender offer to stockholders at $63 a share. It then will be able to repurchase $1.5 million/$63, or 23,810 shares. Earnings per share will be

$$EPS = \$2,000,000/476,190 = \$4.20$$

If the price/earnings ratio stays at 15, the total market price per share will be $63 (4.20 × 15), the same total value as under the dividend alternative. Thus, the amount of distribution to stockholders is $3 per share, whether dividends or repurchase of stock (and subsequent capital gain) is used.

With a differential tax rate on dividends and capital gains, repurchase of stock offers a tax advantage over payment of dividends to the taxable investor. The market-price increase resulting from a repurchase of stock is subject to the capital-gains tax, whereas dividends are taxed at the higher ordinary income tax rate.[8] The repurchase of stock seems particularly appropriate when the firm has a large amount of unused funds to distribute. To pay the funds out through an extra dividend would result in a substantial tax to stockholders. The tax effect could be alleviated somewhat by paying the funds out as extra dividends over a period of time, but this action might result in investors' counting on the extra dividend. The firm must be careful not to undertake a steady program of repurchase in lieu of paying dividends. The Internal Revenue Service is likely to regard such a program an as attempt to allow stockholders to avoid the payment of taxes on dividends. Accordingly, it may impose a penalty.[9] Hence, it is important that the repurchase of stock be a "one-shot" transaction and not be used as a substitute for regular dividends or even for recurring extra dividends.

Investment or financing decision?

Some regard the repurchase of stock as an investment decision instead of a dividend decision. Indeed, in a strict sense, it is, even though stock held in the treasury does not provide an expected return as other investments do. No company can exist by investing only in its own stock. The decision to repurchase should involve distribution of unused funds when the firm's investment opportunities are not sufficiently attractive to employ those funds, either now or in the foreseeable future. The repurchase of stock cannot be treated as an investment decision as we define the term. In some cases the repurchase of stock occurs because management believes its stock is undervalued. Whether there is a signaling effect over and above what could be accomplished through other information channels is unclear.

Repurchase may be regarded as a financing decision, however, provided its purpose is to alter the capital-structure proportions of the firm. By issuing debt and repurchasing stock, a firm can immediately change its debt-to-equity ratio toward a greater proportion of debt. In this case, the repurchase of stock is a financing decision, because the alternative is to not pay out dividends. Only when there is excess cash can the repurchase of stock be treated as a dividend decision.

Method of repurchase

The two most common methods of repurchase are through a tender offer and through the purchase of stock in the marketplace. With a tender offer, the

[8]See Edwin J. Elton and Martin J. Gruber, "The Effect of Share Repurchases on the Value of the Firm," *Journal of Finance*, 23 (March 1968), 135–50.

[9]The tax consequences involved in the repurchase of stock are complex and, in places, ambiguous. In most cases, the monies received by stockholders who tender their shares are subject to the capital-gains tax. Under certain circumstances, however, the distribtuion can be treated as ordinary income to the redeeming stockholder. If the stockholders' percentage of ownership of the company after the tender is greater than .80 of their percentage prior to the tender, the repurchase can be treated as ordinary income by the Internal Revenue Service. This problem can be avoided if the company obtains an advance ruling from the IRS that the repurchase of stock is not equivalent to a dividend.

company makes a formal offer to stockholders to purchase so many shares, typically at a set price. This bid price is above the current market price; stockholders
can elect either to sell their stock at the specified price or to continue to hold it.
Typically the tender-offer period is between two and three weeks. If stockholders
tender more shares than originally sought by the company, the company may elect
to purchase all or part of the excess. It is under no obligation to do so. In general,
the transaction costs to the firm in making a tender offer are higher than those
incurred in the purchase of stock in the open market. The principal costs involve
the fee paid to the investment banker who manages the repurchase and the fees
paid to soliciting dealers.

In open-market purchases, a company buys its stock as any other investor
does—through a brokerage house. Usually, the brokerage fee is negotiated. Certain
Security and Exchange Commission rules restrict the manner in which a company
bids for its shares. As a result, it takes an extended period of time for a company
to accumulate a relatively large block of stock. For this reason, the tender offer is
more suitable when the company seeks a large amount of stock.

Before the company repurchases stock, stockholders must be informed of
the company's intentions. In a tender offer, these intentions are announced by the
offer itself. Even here, the company must not withhold other information. It would
be unethical for a mining company, for example, to withhold information of a
substantial ore discovery while making a tender offer to repurchase shares.

In open-market purchases, especially, it is necessary to disclose the company's repurchase intentions. Otherwise, stockholders may sell their stock not
knowing about a repurchase program that will increase earnings per share. Given
full information about the amount of repurchase and the objective of the company,
the stockholders can sell their stock if they so choose. Without proper disclosure,
the selling stockholder may be penalized. When the amount of stock repurchased
is substantial, a tender offer is particularly suitable, for it gives all stockholders
equal treatment.

ADDITIONAL CONSIDERATIONS

Procedural aspects

When the board of directors of a corporation declares a cash dividend, it
specifies a *date of record*. At the close of business that day, a list of stockholders
is drawn up from the stock transfer books of the company. Stockholders on the list
are entitled to the dividend, whereas stockholders who come on the books after the
date of record are not entitled to the dividend. When the board of directors of
United Chemical Company met on May 8, it declared a dividend of 25 cents a
share payable June 15 to stockholders of record on May 31. Jennifer Doakes owned
the stock on May 31, so she is entitled to the dividend even though she might sell
her stock prior to the dividend actually being paid on June 15.

A problem can develop in the sale of stock in the days immediately prior
to the date of record. The buyer and the seller of the stock have several days to
settle; that is, to pay for the stock or to deliver it, in the case of the seller. As a

result, the company may not be notified of the stock transfer in sufficient time. For this reason, the brokerage community has a rule whereby new stockholders are entitled to dividends only if they purchase the stock ~~four~~ *five* business days prior to the date of record. If the stock is purchased after that time, the stockholder is not entitled to the dividend. The date itself is known as the *ex-dividend date*. In our example, the date of record was May 31. If this were a Friday, four business days before would be May 27, and this would be the ex-dividend date. In order to receive the dividend, a new stockholder must purchase the stock on May 26 or before. If purchased on May 27 or after, the stock is said to be ex-dividend. That is, it is without the 25-cent dividend.

On the ex-dividend date, the market price of the stock should decline by approximately the amount of the dividend. Suppose the stock of United Chemical Company in our example were selling for $20 a share on May 26. If nothing else changed, the stock should sell for approximately $19.75 on May 27 because the purchaser on that date is not entitled to the 25-cent dividend. Because other factors influence the market price of the stock, this effect is sometimes difficult to measure. For one thing, taxable investors may prefer to buy the stock after it goes ex-dividend, so that they will not have to pay ordinary income taxes on the dividend. If enough of them do so, the stock price will fall by less than 25 cents. Once a dividend is declared, stockholders become creditors of the company until the dividend is actually paid; the declared but unpaid dividend is a current liability of the company.

Automatic dividend reinvestment plans. In recent years, a number of large companies have instigated automatic dividend reinvestment plans (ADR plans). Under these plans, stockholders can reinvest the dividends that they would receive in the stock of the company. The stock involved can be either existing stock or newly issued stock. If it is existing stock, a bank acting as trustee accumulates funds from all stockholders wishing to reinvest and then purchases shares in the open market. The stockholder must bear the brokerage costs, but these costs are relatively low because the trustee buys stock in volume.

Some plans provide for purchase at a discount from the current market price of the stock. Normally the discount is 5 percent, and it serves as an inducement for reinvestment. Even though reinvested, the dividend is taxable to the stockholder as ordinary income, and this is a major disadvantage to the taxable stockholder. (The exception is public utilities stocks, where reinvested dividends are not immediately taxed.) Companies offering such plans have found that shareholder participation is around 20 percent. The number of companies using dividend reinvestment plans has increased steadily from their origination in the early 1970s. Utilities are the dominant user, followed by banks. Industrial companies have made only limited use of such plans.

Legal restrictions

Capital restriction. Although state laws vary considerably, most states prohibit the payment of dividends if these dividends impair capital. *Capital* is defined in some states as the par value of the common stock. If a firm had one million shares outstanding with a $2 par value, total capital would be $2 million. If the net worth of a company were $2.1 million, the company could not pay a cash dividend totaling $200,000 without impairing capital.

Other states define *capital* to include not only the par value of the common stock but also the paid-in capital. Under such statutes, dividends can be paid only out of retained earnings. The purpose of the capital-impairment laws is to protect creditors of a corporation, and they may have some effect when a corporation is relatively new. With established companies that have been profitable in the past and have built up retained earnings, substantial losses will usually have been incurred before the restriction has an effect. By this time, the situation may be sufficiently hopeless that the restriction gives creditors little protection.

Insolvency.   Some states prohibit the payment of cash dividends if the company is insolvent. *Insolvency* is defined either in a legal sense, as liabilities exceeding assets, or in a technical sense, as the firm's being unable to pay its creditors as obligations come due. As the ability of the firm to pay its obligations is dependent upon its liquidity rather than upon its capital, the technical-insolvency restriction gives creditors a good deal of protection. When cash is limited, a company is restricted from favoring stockholders to the detriment of creditors.

— only applys to small closely held companies

Excess accumulation of cash.   The Internal Revenue Code prohibits the undue retention of earnings. Although *undue retention* is defined vaguely, it usually is thought to be retention significantly in excess of the present and future investment needs of the company. The purpose of the law is to prevent companies from retaining earnings for the sake of avoiding taxes. For example, a company might retain all its earnings and build up a substantial cash and marketable-securities position. The entire company then could be sold, and stockholders would be subject only to a capital-gains tax. If the excess earnings were distributed as dividends, the dividends would be taxed as ordinary income. If the IRS can prove unjustified retention, it can impose penalty tax rates on the accumulation. Whenever a company does build up a substantial liquid position, it has to be sure that it can justify the retention of these funds to the IRS. Otherwise, it may be in order to pay the excess funds out to stockholders as dividends.

SUMMARY

The critical question in dividend policy is whether dividends have an influence upon the value of the firm, given its investment decision. If dividends are irrelevant, as Modigliani and Miller believe, the firm should retain earnings only in keeping with its investment opportunities. If there are not sufficient investment opportunities to provide expected returns in excess of those required, the unused funds should be paid out as dividends. The key issue is whether dividends are more than just a means of distributing unused funds. With perfect capital markets and an absence of taxes, stockholders can manufacture "homemade" dividends, making dividend payout irrelevant. With differential taxes on dividends and capital gains, there seemingly is a bias in favor of retention.

Small investors and tax free institutions, however, are not affected in this way. The market imperfection of flotation costs biases things in favor of retention because retention is less expensive than the common-stock financing used to replace the dividend. Restrictions on the investment behavior of financial institutions work in the direction of a preference for dividends. Other imperfections also are part of the picture.

Unfortunately, empirical evidence on the relevance of dividends in a world with market imperfections is conflicting. In final analysis, we are not able to state whether or not the dividend payout of the firm should be more than a passive decision variable. While many companies behave as if dividend policy is relevant, the case for it is not conclusive.

When a company is faced with a dividend decision, managerial considerations include the funds needs of the firm, business risk, liquidity, ability to borrow, assessment of any valuation information, control, and restrictions in a bond indenture or loan agreement. Many people feel that the stability of dividends has a positive effect upon the market price of the stock. Stable dividends may tend to resolve uncertainty in the minds of investors, particularly when earnings per share drop. Stable dividends also may have a positive utility to investors interested in current periodic income. Many companies appear to follow the policy of a target dividend payout ratio, increasing dividends only when they feel that an increase in earnings can be sustained. The use of an extra dividend permits a cyclical company to maintain a stable record of regular dividends while paying additional dividends whenever earnings are unusually high.

A stock dividend pays additional stock to stockholders. It is used frequently to conserve cash and to reduce the cash dividend payout ratio of the firm. Theoretically, the stock dividend is not a thing of value to the stockholder unless cash dividends per share remain unchanged or are increased. A much more effective device for reducing market price per share is a stock split. With a split, the number of shares is increased by the terms of the split; for example, a three-for-one split means that the number of shares is tripled.

A company's repurchase of its own stock should be treated as a dividend decision when the firm has funds in excess of present and foreseeable future investment needs. It may distribute these funds either as dividends or by the repurchase of stock. In the absence of a tax differential between dividends and capital gains, the monetary value of the two alternatives should be about the same. With the tax differential, there is a tax advantage to the repurchase of stock. Because of objections by the Internal Revenue Service, repurchase of stock cannot be used in lieu of regular dividends. Finally, we examined various procedural aspects associated with paying dividends as well as certain legal restrictions.

QUESTIONS

1. Justify borrowing money in order to have liquidity with which to pay dividends on common stock.

2. What is the impact of a stock dividend on the wealth of stockholders? Is the answer different for a stock split?

3. The performance of some institutional investors (some pension funds, for example) is measured on the basis of income yield, recognizing capital gains or losses only if the securities are sold. Does this method of measuring performance have an impact on corporate dividend policy? Discuss the wisdom of this method of measuring performance.

4. Discuss the factors that would tend to bias dividend policy toward a high payout.

5. Discuss the factors that would tend to bias dividend policy toward a zero payout.

6. What effect would you expect on the firm's optimal dividend policy if the federal government began taxing all capital gains at the ordinary income tax rate?

7. What weakness do you see in the Walter formula as the indicator of an optimal dividend policy? Consider carefully the firm's investment opportunities and optimal capital structure before you answer.

8. As the firm's financial manager, would you recommend to the board of directors that the firm adopt as policy a stable dividend payment per share or a stable payout ratio? What are the disadvantages of each? Would the firm's industry influence your decision? Why?

9. As an investor, would you prefer the firm to repurchase its stock by means of a tender offer or through open market operations? Why?

10. Why do companies with high growth rates tend to have low dividend-payout ratios, and companies with low growth rates high payout ratios?

11. Are regular stock dividends valuable to investors? Why or why not?

12. How does an investor manufacture "homemade" dividends? What is the effect of the actions of a number of investors doing so, all other things held constant?

13. When earnings turn bad, why are boards of directors of companies reluctant to reduce the dividend?

14. Why do lenders frequently place a formal restriction in the loan agreement or the indenture on the amount of dividends that can be paid?

15. Is the dividend decision really a financing decision in disguise?

PROBLEMS

1. The Peters Company's equity account (book value) is as follows:

The Peters Company Equity Accounts December 31, 19X8

Common stock ($5 par, 1,000,000 shares)	$ 5,000,000
Paid-in capital	5,000,000
Retained earnings	15,000,000
	$25,000,000

Currently, Peters is under pressure from stockholders to pay some dividends. Peters's cash balance is $500,000, all of which is needed for transactions purposes. The stock is trading for $7 a share.

a) What is the legal limit that can be paid in cash dividends?

b) Compute the equity account if the company pays a 20 percent stock dividend.

c) Compute the equity account if the company declares a 6-for-5 stock split.

d) Discuss the stock price movements that should occur after parts (b) and (c) above.

2. The Beta-Alpha Company expects with some degree of certainty to generate the following net income and to have the following capital expenditures during the next five years (in thousands):

Year	1	2	3	4	5
Net income	$2,000	$1,500	$2,500	$2,300	$1,800
Capital expenditures	1,000	1,500	2,000	1,500	2,000

Presently the company has one million shares of common stock outstanding and pays dividends of $1 per share.

a) Determine dividends per share if dividend policy is treated as a residual decision.

b) Determine the amounts of external financing that will be necessary if the present dividend per share is maintained.

c) Determine dividends per share and the amounts of external financing that will be necessary if a dividend payout ratio of 50 percent is maintained.

d) Under which of the three dividend policies are aggregate dividends maximized? Under which of them is external financing minimized?

3. The Axalt Corporation and the Baxalt Corporation have had remarkably similar earnings patterns over the last five years. In fact, both firms have had identical earnings per share. Further, both firms are in the same industry, produce the same product, and face the same business and financial risks. In short, these firms are carbon copies of each other in every respect but one: Axalt paid out a constant percentage of its earnings (50 percent) in dividends, while Baxalt has paid a constant cash dividend. The financial manager of the Axalt Corporation has been puzzled by the fact that the price of his firm's stock has been generally lower than the price of Baxalt's stock, even though in some years Axalt's dividend was substantially larger than Baxalt's.

a) What might account for the condition that has been puzzling the financial manager of Axalt?

b) What might be done by both companies to increase the market prices of their stock?

	Axalt			Baxalt		
Years	EPS	Div.	Mkt. price	EPS	Div.	Mkt. price
1	$1.00	.50	$6	$1.00	.23	$4⅞
2	.50	.25	4	.50	.23	4⅜
3	−.25	nil	2	−.25	.23	4
4	.30	.15	3	.30	.23	4¼
5	.50	.25	3½	.50	.23	4½

4. Malkor Instruments Company treats dividends as a residual decision. It expects to gener-
    ate $2 million in net earnings after taxes in the coming year. The company has an all-equity
    capital structure, and its cost of equity capital is 15 percent. The company treats this cost
    as the opportunity cost of retained earnings. Because of flotation costs and underpricing,
    the cost of common-stock financing is higher. It is 16 percent.

    a) How much in dividends (out of the $2 million in earnings) should be paid if the
        company has $1.5 million in projects whose expected returns exceed 15 percent?

    b) How much in dividends should be paid if it has $2 million in projects whose expected
        returns exceed 15 percent?

    c) How much in dividends should be paid if it has $3 million in projects whose expected
        returns exceed 16 percent? What else should be done?

5. The Mann Company belongs to a risk class for which the appropriate capitalization rate is
    15 percent. It currently has outstanding 100,000 shares selling at $100 each. The firm is
    contemplating the declaration of a $5 dividend at the end of the current fiscal year, which
    just began. Answer the following questions based on the Modigliani and Miller model and
    the assumption of no taxes.

    a) What will be the price of the stock at the end of the year if a dividend is not declared?
        What will it be if one is?

    b) Assuming that the firm pays the dividend, has net income of $1 million, and makes new
        investments of $2 million during the period, how many new shares must be issued?

    c) Is the MM model realistic with respect to valuation? What factors might mar its validity?

6. Forte Papers Corporation and Great Southern Paper Company are in the same industry,
    both are publicly held with a large number of stockholders, and they have the following
    characteristics:

	Forte	Great Southern
Expected annual cash flow (in thousands)	$ 50,000	$35,000
Standard deviation of cash flows (in thousands)	30,000	25,000
Annual capital expenditures (in thousands)	42,000	40,000
Cash and marketable securities (in thousands)	5,000	7,000
Existing long-term debt (in thousands)	100,000	85,000
Unused short-term line of credit (in thousands)	25,000	10,000
Flotation costs and underpricing on common stock issues as a percent of proceeds	.05	.08
Present annual inflation rate	.13	.13

On the basis of this information, which company is likely to have the higher dividend payout
ratio? Why?

7. The Canales Copper Company declared a 25 percent stock dividend on March 10 to
    stockholders of record on April 1. The market price of the stock is $50 per share. You own
    160 shares of the stock.

a) If you sold your stock on March 20, what would be the price per share, all other things the same?

b) After the stock dividend is paid, how many shares of stock will you own?

c) At what price would you expect the stock to sell on April 2, all other things the same?

d) What will be the total value of your holdings before and after the stock dividend, all other things the same?

8.   The Sherill Corporation capital structure December 30, 19X3

Common stock ($1 par, 1,000,000 shares)	$1,000,000
Paid-in capital	300,000
Retained earnings	1,700,000
Net worth	$3,000,000

The firm earned $300,000 after taxes in 19X3 and paid out 50 percent of these earnings as cash dividends. The price of the firm's stock on December 30 was $5.

a) If the firm declared a stock dividend of 3 percent on December 31, what would the reformulated capital structure be?

b) Assuming the firm paid no stock dividend, how much would earnings per share for 19X3 be? Dividends per share?

c) Assuming a 3 percent stock dividend, what would happen to EPS and DPS for 19X3?

d) What would the price of the stock be after the 3 percent stock dividend?

9. The T. N. Cox Company is owned by several wealthy Texans. The firm earned $3,500,000 after taxes this year. With one million shares outstanding, earnings per share were $3.50. The stock recently has traded at $72 per share, among the current stockholders. Two dollars of this value is accounted for by investor anticipation of a cash dividend. As financial manager of T. N. Cox, you have contemplated the alternative of repurchasing the company stock by means of a tender offer at $72 per share.

a) How much stock could the firm repurchase if this alternative were selected?

b) Ignoring taxes, which alternative should be selected?

c) Considering taxes, which alternative should be selected?

10. On February 2, 1983, the board of directors of International Zinc and Iron Corporation met and declared a 20 cent per share cash dividend payable March 20 to stockholders of record on March 1.

a) If you wished to buy the stock before it went ex-dividend, by what date would you need to make your purchase?

b) If you already own the stock but the company declares bankruptcy on March 10, what happens to your dividend?

SELECTED REFERENCES

BAKER, H. KENT, and PATRICIA L. GALLAGHER, "Management's View of Stock Splits," *Financial Management,* 9 (Summer 1980), 73–77.

424

PART VII

Longer-term
financing—
instruments
and markets

BAR-YOSEF, SASSON, and LAWRENCE D. BROWN, "A Reexamination of Stock Splits Using Moving Averages," *Journal of Finance,* 32 (September 1977), 1069–80.

BIERMAN, HAROLD, JR., and RICHARD WEST, "The Acquisition of Common Stock by the Corporate Issuer," *Journal of Finance,* 21 (December 1966), 687–96.

BLACK, FISCHER, and MYRON SCHOLES, "The Effects of Dividend Yield and Dividend Policy on Common Stock Prices and Returns," *Journal of Financial Economics,* 1 (May 1974), 1–22.

BRITTAIN, JOHN A., *Corporate Dividend Policy.* Washington, D.C.: Brookings Institution, 1966.

CHAREST, GUY, "Split Information, Stock Returns and Market Efficiency," *Journal of Financial Economics,* 6 (June-September 1978), 265–96.

DIELMAN, TERRY, TIMOTHY J. NANTELL, and ROGER L. WRIGHT, "Price Effects of Stock Repurchasing: A Random Coefficient Regression Approach," *Journal of Financial and Quantitative Analysis,* 15 (March 1980), 175–89.

ELTON, EDWIN J., and MARTIN J. GRUBER, "The Cost of Retained Earnings—Implications of Share Repurchase," *Industrial Management Review,* 9 (Spring 1968), 87–104.

FERRIS, KENNETH R., ARIE MELNIK, and ALFRED RAPPAPORT, "Factors Influencing the Pricing of Stock Repurchase Tenders," *Quarterly Review of Economics and Business,* 18 (Spring 1978), 31–39.

HIGGINS, ROBERT C., "The Corporate Dividend-Saving Decision," *Journal of Financial and Quantitative Analysis,* 7 (March 1972), 1527–41.

KWAN, CLARENCE C. Y., "Efficient Market Tests of the Informational Content of Announcements: Critique and Extension," *Journal of Financial and Quantitative Analysis,* 16 (June 1981), 193–206.

LINTNER, JOHN, "Distribution of Income of Corporations among Dividends, Retained Earnings, and Taxes," *American Economic Review,* 46 (May 1956), 97–113.

———, "Dividends, Earnings, Leverage, Stock Prices and the Supply of Capital to Corporations," *Review of Economics and Statistics,* 44 (August 1962), 243–69.

LITZENBERGER, ROBERT H., and KRISHNA RAMISWAMY, "Dividends, Short Selling Restrictions, Tax Induced Investor Clienteles and Market Equilibrium," *Journal of Finance,* 35 (May 1980), 469–82.

MILLAR, JAMES A., "Split or Dividend: Do the Words Really Matter?" *Accounting Review,* 52 (January 1977), 52–55.

MILLER, MERTON H., and FRANCO MODIGLIANI, "Dividend Policy, Growth, and the Valuation of Shares," *Journal of Business,* 34 (October 1961), 411–33.

PALMON, DAN, and UZI YAARI, "Retention and Tax Avoidance: A Clarification," *Financial Management,* 10 (Spring 1981), 29–35.

PETTIT, R. RICHARDSON, "The Impact of Dividend and Earnings Announcements: A Reconciliation," *Journal of Business,* 49 (January 1976), 86–96. Watts, Ross, "Comments," *Journal of Business,* 49 (January 1976), 97–106.

PETTWAY, RICHARD H., and R. PHIL MALONE, "Automatic Dividend Reinvestment Plans for Nonfinancial Corporations," *Financial Management,* 2 (Winter 1973), 11–18.

REILLY, FRANK K., and EUGENE F. DRZYCIMSKI, "Short-Run Profits from Stock Splits," *Financial Management,* 10 (Summer 1981), 64–74.

SHILLER, ROBERT H., "Do Stock Prices Move Too Much to be Justified by Subsequent Changes in Dividends?" *American Economic Review,* 71 (June 1981), 421–36.

STEWART, SAMUEL S., JR., "Should a Corporation Repurchase its Own Stock?" *Journal of Finance,* 31 (June 1976), 911–21.

VAN HORNE, JAMES C., and JOHN G. McDONALD, "Dividend Policy and New Equity Financing," *Journal of Finance,* 26 (May 1971), 507–19.

WALTER, JAMES E., "Dividend Policies and Common Stock Prices," *Journal of Finance,* 11 (March 1956), 29–41.

LONGER-TERM FINANCING— INSTRUMENTS AND MARKETS

VII

Interface with suppliers of capital

19

In part VI we studied how business firms arrange their long-term capitalization and how they finance internally through retained earnings. We need now to find out how firms raise long-term funds externally. More specifically, the purpose of this chapter is to observe the ways in which bond and stock issues are sold. We shall see issues to the public placed through investment bankers, privileged subscriptions to the company's own stockholders, and direct placements by the firm to institutional investors.

OFFERINGS THROUGH INVESTMENT BANKERS

When a company issues securities to the public, it frequently avails itself of the services of an investment banker. The principal function of the investment banker is to buy the securities from the company and then resell them to investors. For this service, investment bankers receive the difference, or spread, between the price they pay for the security and the price at which the securities are resold to the public. Because most companies make only occasional trips to the capital market, they are not specialists in the distribution of securities. To sell securities on their own would be both costly and risky. On the other hand, investment banking firms have the expertise, the contacts, and the sales organization necessary to do an efficient job of marketing securities to investors. Because they are continually in the business of buying securities from companies and selling them to investors, investment bankers can perform this service at a lower cost than can the individual firm.

Competitive bidding versus negotiated offering

A security offering through an investment banker to investors other than the firm's own stockholders (known as a public offering) can be either on a competitive-bid basis or on a negotiated basis. When new securities are sold by competitive bidding, the company issuing the securities invites bids from investment bankers. Frequently, two or more investment banking firms join together to bid on a security issue; the combination is known as a syndicate. The purpose underlying formation of a syndicate is to spread the risk and to obtain a larger overall selling organization. The issuing company specifies the date that sealed bids will be received, and competing syndicates submit bids at the specified time and place. The syndicate with the highest bid wins the security issue. At that time, it pays the company the difference between its good-faith deposit and the bid price; then it attempts to resell the issue at a higher price to investors.

With a negotiated offering, the company issuing the securities selects an investment banking firm and works directly with that firm in determining the essential features of the issue. Together they discuss and negotiate a price for the security and the timing of the issue. Depending upon the size of the issue, the investment banker may invite other firms to join it in sharing the risk and selling the issue. If a company has satisfactory experience with an investment banking firm, it usually will use the same firm for subsequent security issues.

From the standpoint of the issuing company, the key consideration in deciding between a competitive and a negotiated offering is the price it is likely to get. Advocates of a competitive offering argue that the competition between bidding syndicates results in a higher price to the company and a lower profit spread to the investment banker than does a negotiated offering. For this reason, certain types of companies are required to issue securities on a competitive-bid basis. The Public Utility Holding Company Act of 1935 mandates that registered utility holding companies receive at least two bids. (Because of depressed markets in recent years, the Securities and Exchange Commission has granted a number of exemptions to this rule.) In addition to federal regulations, many state public utility commissions require that public utilities in their states issue securities by competitive bidding, unless an exemption is sought by the utility and approved by the commission.

Advocates of negotiated offerings argue that such underwritings allow the investment banker more time to locate investors and to place the issue, which in turn results in a more favorable price than is possible under a competitive-bidding situation. In particular, this is said to be important in times of "demoralized" markets when security prices are falling, or when the issue is very large. In a "demoralized" market, certain investment bankers may refuse to enter into a competitive-bid syndicate. Their absence, together with the reluctance of others to

428

PART VII

Longer-term
financing—
instruments
and markets

bid aggressively, could result in a lower net price to the company than would be the case with a negotiated offering.

Underwriting function

One of the key functions the investment banker performs is that of bearing risk. An investment banker or group of investment bankers buying a security issue *underwrites* the sale of the issue by giving the company a check for the purchase price. At that time, the company is relieved of the risk of not being able to sell the issue at the established price. If the issue does not sell well, either because of an adverse turn in the market or because it is overpriced, the underwriter, not the company, takes the loss. Thus, the investment banker insures, or underwrites, the risk of adverse market price fluctuations during the period of distribution.

Typically, the investment banking institution with whom a company discusses the offering does not handle the underwriting alone. In order to spread risk and obtain better distribution, it invites other investment bankers to participate in the offering. The originating house usually is the manager and has the largest participation. Other investment bankers are invited into the syndicate, and their participations are determined primarily on the basis of their ability to sell securities. For the risk-bearing function of the offering, these investment bankers are compensated by an underwriting profit.

Underwriting commission.   To illustrate the compensations of investment bankers, we turn to an example. Figure 19-1 shows the cover of the prospectus for a $300 million issue of 13¼ percent debentures of Conoco, Inc. The issue was on a negotiated basis with Morgan Stanley & Co. as manager putting together a syndicate of some 140 investment banking firms. Morgan Stanley's participation was by far the largest, being $65.1 million. Other participations ranged from $10 million down to $150,000. We see in the figure that the syndicate bought the debentures from the company for $297,375,000, or $991.25 a bond. In turn, it priced the bonds to the public at $1,000 per bond, or $300 million in total. The spread of $8.75 per bond, or $2,625,000 in total, represents the gross commission to the syndicate for underwriting the issue, for selling it, and for covering the various expenses incurred.

Of the total spread of $8.75 per bond, $3.75, or 43 percent, is the gross underwriting profit. The remaining 57 percent is the selling concession, which we will discuss shortly. This breakdown between underwriting and selling profits is typical for corporate bonds. A portion of the gross underwriting profit goes to the originating house as manager of the offering. Though this figure is not given for the issue, the typical fee is 15 to 20 percent of the total spread. After the bonds are sold, total underwriting profits less expenses and managers' fee are distributed to members of the syndicate on the basis of their percentage participation. It should be noted that the amount of underwriting profit to a member of a syndicate after expenses and the managers' fee is not large. In our example, it probably is less than $2 a bond. The principal reward from participation comes from selling the securities.

With respect to underwriter risk, each member is liable for its percentage participation in the unsold securities of the syndicate, regardless of the number of

FIGURE 19-1
A prospectus

securities the individual member sells. If a member of a syndicate had a 20 percent participation in an offering involving a total of 40,000 bonds, and 10,000 remained unsold at the termination of the syndicate, the member would be responsible for 2,000 of the remaining bonds. Its liability would be the same, regardless of the number of bonds the member previously sold.

430

PART VII

Longer-term
financing—
instruments
and markets

Best-efforts offering.   Instead of underwriting a security issue, investment bankers may sell the issue on a *best-efforts* basis. Under this arrangement, the investment bankers agree to sell only as many securities as they can at an established price. They have no responsibility for securities that are unsold. In other words, they bear no risk. Investment bankers frequently are unwilling to underwrite a security issue of a small company. For these companies, the only feasible means by which to place securities may be through a best-efforts offering.

Making a market.   On occasion, the underwriter will make a market for a security after it is issued. In the first public offering of common stock, making a market is extremely important to investors. In making a market, the underwriter maintains a position in the stock, quotes bid and asked prices, and stands ready to buy and sell it at those prices. These quotations are based upon underlying supply and demand conditions. With a secondary market, the stock has greater liquidity to investors; this appeal enhances the success of the original offering.

Selling the securities

The second major function of the investment banker is that of selling the securities to investors. As we discussed earlier, investment bankers are invited into syndicates, and their participations are determined primarily on the basis of their ability to distribute securities. For this function, an investment banker is rewarded by a selling concession of so many dollars a bond. In the Conoco offering, the selling concession was $5 per bond, or 57 percent of the total spread of $8.75. The ultimate seller can be either a member of the underwriting syndicate or a qualified outside security dealer. In order to earn the full concession, however, the seller must be a member of the syndicate. An outside security dealer must purchase bonds from a member and will obtain only a dealer concession, which is less than the full selling concession. In our example, the outside dealer concession was $2.50 per bond out of a total selling concession of $5.

In a negotiated offering, the underwriters begin to line up prospective buyers before the actual offering date. A preliminary prospectus stating certain facts about the issue and the company is printed and given to interested investors. At this time, a price has not been established for the securities; the prospectus is known as a "red herring" because it contains, printed in red, a statement to the effect that a registration statement has been filed with the Securities and Exchange Commission but that it has not as yet been approved. Upon approval of the registration, the offering price to the public is established, and a final prospectus is printed. At that time, security sales representatives seek orders from investors. If the issue is priced fairly, it will be sold within a day or two or perhaps even within a few hours. Sometimes "hot" issues are sold out in advance to preorder subscribers. Upon the sale of all the securities, the underwriting syndicate is dissolved.

Advising

In a negotiated offering such as our example, the originating house is able to advise the company on a wide variety of matters pertinent to the success of the offering. To a company that makes infrequent trips to the capital markets, this advice can be valuable, for the matters considered include the timing of the issue, its pricing, and features that are desirable to assure a successful sale. When the sale of securities is by competitive bid, the issuer does not receive the benefit of this advice because the underwriter enters the picture only after the bid is accepted and the price determined. Advice from investment bankers may be of a continuing nature, with the company consulting a certain investment banker or a group of bankers regularly.

Pricing the issue

The issuing company and the investment banker determine the price in a negotiated offering. Investment bankers like to see a price low enough to assure a successful sale, but they are aware that if the price is too low, the issuing company will be dissatisfied. An investment banker can ill afford dissatisfied customers, for news of such dissatisfaction spreads quickly in the financial community. Moreover, the issuing company must agree to the price recommended by the underwriter. Otherwise, of course, there can be no offering.

A bond issue will be priced in relation to the price of other new issues of the same grade. If the bond being issued is rated Baa, comparisons will be made with other Baa new issues. The underwriter and the issuing company must assess the tone of the market with respect to expectations of future interest rates. In addition to recent interest-rate movements in the money and capital markets, they consider the forthcoming supply of new issues, the expected future of the economy, and expectations of monetary and fiscal policy. Typically, a new issue will have to be sold at a lower price and higher yield to maturity than a seasoned issue of the same maturity and grade. In a competitive-bidding situation, the syndicate will consider these same factors in determining the bid it will submit. The syndicate wants to submit a bid high enough to win the issue but low enough to be able to sell the issue readily to investors. For the negotiated issue, the underwriter wants a price that is high enough to satisfy the issuer but still low enough to increase the probability of a successful sale to investors.

The problem of pricing a common-stock issue is perhaps more difficult because of the greater volatility of the stock market. When a company already has stock outstanding, held by the public, the principal factor that governs the price of any new issue is the market price of the existing stock. The new issue will need to be underpriced in order to sell. The degree of underpricing will depend upon the volatility of the stock and the tone of the market. When it becomes known in the marketplace that a company is going to offer new stock, downward pressure usually is exerted on the market price of the outstanding stock. Pressure usually develops on the day the new issue is announced, or before, if rumors of the new issue are out. This pressure contributes to the problem of underpricing the issue. For a negotiated offering by a company whose stock is already held by the public, the price usually is not established until the night before the offering.

If a company is issuing stock to the public for the first time, the pricing problem is much more difficult because there is no current market price to serve as a benchmark. For privately held companies that are going public, a comparison with similar companies usually is made to determine the appropriate

432

PART VII

Longer-term
financing—
instruments
and markets

price/earnings ratio. Some companies, so specialized that comparison with other companies is very difficult, consider essentials such as present earnings, the growth rate, and the volatility of earnings. For a company going public for the first time, the underwriter and company may agree on a price well before the offering. Because there is no secondary market for existing shares, it is not necessary to delay pricing to the last minute.

Flotation costs.   The flotation costs of a new issue of securities tend to vary with the size and the type of the issue. These costs include the underwriting spread, registration expenses, and other out-of-pocket expenses. In general, the larger the issue, the lower the cost of flotation as a percentage of gross proceeds. Because certain company expenses—printing and legal fees in particular— essentially are fixed, the larger the issue, the lower their percentage cost. The underwriter also has certain "fixed" expenses. Thus, the larger the issue, the smaller the percentage of underwriting expense. Additionally and more significantly, there usually is a direct relationship between the size of an issue and the quality of the issuing company. Also, the relative cost of flotation tends to be highest for a common-stock issue and lowest for a debt issue—a fact not surprising in view of the differences in underwriting risk.

For a large issue, say over $50 million, of a high quality company, the total cost of a debt issue (underwriting and other expenses) will be around 1 percent of the gross proceeds. This percentage compares with about 1½ percent for a preferred stock issue and around 4 percent for a common stock issue. For a smaller issue, say $5 million, the percentages will be much higher. Here percentage costs of around 3 percent, 4 percent, and 8 percent, respectively, are likely to be incurred.

RIGHTS OFFERINGS

Instead of selling a security issue to the general public, many firms offer the securities first to existing shareholders on a privileged-subscription basis. This type of offering is known as a rights offering. Frequently, the corporate charter requires that a new issue of common stock or an issue of securities convertible into common be offered first to existing shareholders because of their preemptive right.

Preemptive right

Under a preemptive right, existing common stockholders have the right to preserve their proportionate ownership in the corporation. If the corporation issues additional common stock, they must be given the right to subscribe to the new stock so that they maintain their pro-rata interest in the company. You may own 100 shares of a corporation that decides to make a new common-stock offering for the purpose of increasing outstanding shares by 10 percent. If you have a preemptive right, you must be given the option to buy 10 additional shares so that you can preserve your proportionate ownership in the company. Various states have different laws regarding preemptive rights, but most of them provide that a stockholder has a preemptive right unless the corporate charter otherwise denies it.

Terms of offering

When a company offers its securities for sale by privileged subscription, it mails to its stockholders one right for each share of stock they hold. With a common-stock offering, the rights give stockholders the option to purchase additional shares according to the terms of the offering. The terms specify the number of rights required to subscribe for an additional share of stock, the subscription price per share, and the expiration date of the offering. The holder of rights has three choices: (1) exercise them and subscribe for additional shares; (2) sell them, because they are transferable; or (3) do nothing and let them expire. The last usually occurs only if the value of a right is negligible or if the stockholder owns but a few shares of stock. Generally, the subscription period is 3 weeks or less. A stockholder who wishes to buy a share of additional stock but does not have the necessary number of rights may purchase additional rights. If you now own 85 shares of stock in a company, and the number of rights required to purchase one additional share is 10, your 85 rights would allow you to purchase only 8 full shares of stock. If you would like to buy the ninth share, you may do so by purchasing an additional 5 rights.

In a rights offering, the board of directors establishes a date of record. Investors who buy the stock prior to that date receive the right to subscribe to the new issue. The stock is said to sell with *rights on* prior to the date of record. After the date of record, the stock is said to sell *ex-rights*; that is, the stock is traded without the rights attached. An investor who buys the stock after this date does not receive the right to subscribe to additional stock.

Value of rights

The market value of a right is a function of the present market price of the stock, the subscription price, and the number of rights required to purchase an additional share of stock. The theoretical market value of one right after the offering is announced but while the stock is still selling rights-on is

$$R_o = \frac{P_o - S}{N + 1} \tag{19-1}$$

where R_o = market value of one right when stock is selling rights-on
$\quad P_o$ = market value of a share of stock selling rights-on
$\quad S$ = subscription price per share
$\quad N$ = number of rights required to purchase one share of stock.

If the market price of a stock is $100 a share, the subscription price is $90 a share, and it takes 4 rights to buy an additional share of stock, the theoretical value of a right when the stock is selling rights-on is

$$R_o = \frac{100 - 90}{4 + 1} = \$2 \tag{19-2}$$

We note that the market value of the stock with rights on contains the value of one right.

434

PART VII

Longer-term
financing—
instruments
and markets

When the stock goes ex-rights, the market price theoretically declines, for investors no longer receive the right to subscribe to additional shares. The theoretical value of one share of stock when it goes ex-rights is

$$P_x = \frac{(P_o \times N) + S}{N + 1} \qquad (19\text{-}3)$$

where P_x = market price of stock when it goes ex-rights. For our example,

$$P_x = \frac{(100 \times 4) + 90}{4 + 1} = \$98$$

From this example, we see that, theoretically, the right does not represent a thing of value to the stockholder, whose stock is worth $100 before the date of record; after the date of record, it is worth $98 a share. The decline in market price is offset exactly by the value of the right. Thus, theoretically, the stockholder does not benefit from a rights offering; the right represents merely a return of capital.

The theoretical value of a right when the stock sells ex-rights is

$$R_x = \frac{P_x - S}{N} \qquad (19\text{-}4)$$

where R_x = the market value of one right when the stock is selling ex-rights. If, in our example, the market price of the stock is $98 when it goes ex-rights,

$$R_x = \frac{98 - 90}{4} = \$2$$

or the same value as before.

We should be aware that the actual value of a right may differ somewhat from its theoretical value on account of transaction costs, speculation, and the irregular exercise and sale of rights over the subscription period. However, arbitrage limits the deviation of actual value from theoretical value. If the price of a right is significantly higher than its theoretical value, stockholders will sell their rights and purchase the stock in the market. Such action will exert downward pressure on the market price of the right and upward pressure on its theoretical value. The latter occurs because of the upward pressure on the market price of the stock. If the price of the right is significantly lower than its theoretical value, arbitragers will buy the rights, exercise their option to buy stock, and then sell the stock in the market. This occurrence will exert upward pressure on the market price of the right and downward pressure on its theoretical value. These arbitrage actions will continue as long as they are profitable.

Success of the offering

One of the most important aspects of a successful rights offering is the subscription price. If the market price of the stock should fall below the subscription price, stockholders obviously will not subscribe to the stock, for they can buy it in the market at a lower price. Consequently, a company will set the subscription price at a value lower than the current market price to reduce the risk of the market price's falling below it. We know that the stock should fall in price when it goes ex-rights. Its new theoretical value is determined by Eq. (19-3); and we see that it strongly depends upon N, the number of rights required to purchase one share of stock. The greater the N, the less the theoretical price decline when the stock goes ex-rights. Thus, the risk that the market price will fall below the subscription price is inversely related to N.[1] To illustrate, suppose the following were true:

	Company A	Company B
Market value per share rights-on, P_o	$60.00	$60.00
Subscription price, S	$46.00	$46.00
Number of rights needed to purchase one share, N	1	10
Theoretical value of one share ex-rights, P_x	$53.00	$58.73

We see that Company A will have a greater decline in value per share when its stock goes ex-rights than will Company B. All other things the same, there is a greater probability, or risk, that Company A's stock will fall below the subscription price of $46 than there is that Company B's stock will fall below it.

Apart from the number of rights required to purchase one share, the risk that the market price of a stock will fall below the subscription price is a function of the volatility of the company's stock, the tone of the market, expectations of earnings, and other factors. To avoid all risk, a company can set the subscription price so far below the market price that there is virtually no possibility that the market price will fall below it. The greater the discount from the current market price, the greater the value of the right, and the greater the probability of a successful sale of stock. As long as stockholders do not allow their rights to expire, theoretically they neither gain nor lose by the offering. Therefore, it might seem feasible to set the subscription price at a substantial discount in order to assure a successful sale.

The greater the discount, however, the more shares that will have to be issued to raise a given amount of money, and the greater the dilution in earnings per share. This dilution may be of practical concern, for the investment community analyzes closely the growth trend in earnings per share. Significant underpricing of the new issue will dampen the growth trend in earnings per share. Although theoretically the stockholders should be equally well off regardless of the subscription price set, in practice the market value of their stock holdings may suffer if investors are fooled by the dilution in reported earnings per share and they lower the stock's price/earnings ratio. Obviously this would be an imperfection in

[1] See Haim Levy and Marshall Sarnat, "Risk, Dividend Policy, and the Optimal Pricing of a Rights Offering," *Journal of Money, Credit, and Banking*, 3 (November 1971), 840–49.

436

PART VII

Longer-term
financing—
instruments
and markets

the market, but imperfections on occasion can make a difference. There is no empirical evidence, however, to support the view that the amount of dilution in a rights offering matters.

If the firm wishes to maintain the same dividend per share, underpricing, which will result in more shares issued, will increase the total amount of dividends the company will need to pay and lower its coverage ratio. The disadvantages of underpricing must be balanced against the risk of the market price's falling below the subscription price. The primary consideration in setting the subscription price is to reduce the probability of this occurrence to a tolerable level. If, then, the subscription price appears to result in excessive dilution and this dilution seems to matter, the company should consider a public issue, wherein the amount of underpricing usually is less. For most rights offerings, the subscription-price discount from the current market price ranges between 10 and 20 percent.

Standby arrangement and oversubscriptions

A company can insure the complete success of a rights offering by having an investment banker or group of investment bankers "stand by" to underwrite the unsold portion of the issue. For this standby commitment, the underwriter charges a fee that varies with the risk involved in the offering. Often the fee consists of two parts: a flat fee and an additional fee for each unsold share of stock that the underwriter has to buy. From the standpoint of the company issuing the stock, the greater the risk of an unsuccessful sale, the more desirable a standby arrangement, although it also is more costly.

Another means to increase the probability that the entire issue will be sold is through oversubscriptions. This device gives stockholders not only the right to subscribe for their proportional share of the total offering, but also the right to oversubscribe for any unsold shares. Oversubscriptions are then awarded on a pro-rata basis relative to the number of unsold shares. Stockholders may subscribe to 460,000 shares of a 500,000-share rights offering. Perhaps some of them would like to purchase more shares, and their oversubscriptions total 100,000 shares. As a result, each stockholder oversubscribing is awarded $\frac{4}{10}$ of a share for each share oversubscribed. This results in the entire issue being sold. Although the use of oversubscriptions increases the chances that the issue will be entirely sold, it does not assure this occurrence, as does the standby agreement. It is possible that the combination of subscriptions and oversubscriptions will fall short of the amount of stock the company desires to sell.

Privileged subscription versus public issue

By offering stock first to existing stockholders, the company taps investors who are familiar with its operations. As a result, a successful sale is more probable. The principal sales tool is the discount from the current market price, whereas with a public issue, the major selling tool is the investment banking organization. Because the issue is not underwritten, the flotation costs of a rights offering are lower than the costs of an offering to the general public. Moreover, many stockholders feel that they should be given the first opportunity to buy new common shares.

Offsetting these advantages to some degree, perhaps, a rights offering will have to be sold at a lower price than will an issue to the general public. If a company goes to the equity market with reasonable frequency, this means that there will be somewhat more dilution with rights offerings than there will be with public issues. Even though this consideration is not relevant theoretically, many companies wish to minimize dilution and will choose the public offering. To the extent that there are information, legal, and institutional imperfections which influence this choice, existing shareholder wealth may be enhanced by a decision to go the public-issue route. Examples of imperfections include financial reporting that masks the "true" trend in earnings per share, restraints on a company's issuing stock at below its book value, and possible institutional incentives for a company to sell stock at as high a price per share as possible. Although these factors may have an effect on shareholder wealth, we would expect their effect to be slight. Still, these factors may loom important in the minds of management and favor a public issue.

REGULATION OF SECURITY OFFERINGS

Both the federal and state governments regulate the sale of new securities to the public, but federal authority is far more encompassing in its influence.

Federal regulation

With the collapse of the stock market in 1929 and the subsequent Depression, there came a cry to protect investors from misinformation and fraud. Congress undertook extensive investigations and proposed federal regulation of the securities industry. The *Securities Act of 1933* dealt with the sale of new securities and required the full disclosure of information to investors. The *Securities Exchange Act of 1934* dealt with the regulation of securities already outstanding. Moreover, it created the Securities and Exchange Commission to enforce the two acts.

Most corporations selling securities to the public must register the issue with the SEC. Certain types of corporations, such as railroads, are exempt because they are regulated by other authorities. In addition, a corporation selling $1.5 million or less in new securities is required to file only a limited amount of information with the SEC under Regulation A. Also, if the issue is entirely sold to citizens of a single state, it does not necessarily fall under the SEC. Other corporations, however, must file a detailed registration statement, which contains information such as the nature and history of the company, the use of the proceeds of the security issue, financial statements, the management and directors and their security holdings, competitive conditions and risks, legal opinions, and a description of the security being issued. Along with the registration statement, the corporation must file a copy of the *prospectus* (see Fig. 19-1), which is a summary of the essential information in the registration statement. The prospectus must be available to prospective investors and others who request it.

The SEC reviews the registration statement and the prospectus to see that all the required information is presented and that it is not misleading. If the SEC

438

PART VII
Longer-term
financing—
instruments
and markets

is satisfied with the information, it approves the registration, and the company is then able to issue a final prospectus and sell the securities. If not, the SEC issues a *stop order*, which prevents the sale of the securities. Most deficiencies can be corrected by the company, and approval will usually be given eventually, except in cases of fraud or misrepresentation. For serious violations of the 1933 Securities Act, the SEC is empowered to go to court and seek an injunction. It should be pointed out that the SEC is not concerned with the investment value of the securities being issued, only with the presentation of complete and accurate information. Investors must make their own decisions based upon that information. The security being issued may well be a highly speculative one subject to considerable risk. As long as the information is correct, the SEC will not prevent its sale.

The minimum period required between the time a registration statement is filed and the time it becomes effective is 20 days. The usual time lapse, however, is around 40 days. During this time, sometimes known as a cooling-off period, investors can evaluate the information in the prospectus and reach a decision.

The SEC regulates the sale of securities in the secondary markets in addition to the sale of new issues. In this regard, it regulates the activities of the security exchanges, the over-the-counter market, investment bankers and brokers, the National Association of Security Dealers, and investment companies. In its regulatory capacity, the SEC seeks to prevent manipulative practices by investment dealers and by officers and directors of the company, abuses by insiders (officers and directors) in transactions involving the company's stock, fraud by any party, and other abuses affecting the investing public.

State regulation. Individual states have security commissions that regulate the issuance of new securities in their states. Like the SEC, these commissions seek to prevent the fraudulent sale of securities. The laws providing for state regulation of securities are known as blue-sky laws, because they attempt to prevent the false promotion and sale of securities representing nothing more than blue sky. State regulations are particularly important when a security issue is sold entirely to people within the state and is not subject to SEC scrutiny. In addition, it can be important when the amount of the issue is less than $1.5 million and subject to only limited SEC scrutiny. Unfortunately, the laws of the individual states vary greatly in their effectiveness. Some states are strict, others are fairly permissive, with the result that misrepresentative promotion can thrive.

PRIVATE PLACEMENTS

Rather than sell securities to the public or to existing stockholders through a privileged subscription, a corporation can sell the entire issue to a single institutional investor or a small group of such investors. This type of sale is known as a private or direct placement, for the company negotiates directly with the investor over the terms of the offering, eliminating the function of the underwriter. Some issues of common stock are placed privately, but the vast majority of private placements involve debt issues, which we shall discuss. In recent years, private placements have accounted for approximately one-third of the net issuance of bonds by corporations.

Features

One of the more frequently mentioned advantages of a private placement is the speed of the commitment. A public issue must be registered with the SEC, documents must be prepared and printed, and extensive negotiations undertaken; all this requires lead time. In addition, the public issue always involves risks with respect to timing. With a private placement, the terms can be tailored to the needs of the borrower, and the financing can be consummated much more quickly. Because the issue is negotiated, the exact timing in the market is not a critical problem. The fact that there is but a single investor or small group of investors is attractive if it becomes necessary to change any of the terms of the issue. It is much easier to deal with a single investor than with a large group of public securityholders. A possible disadvantage in this regard, however, is that a single investor may monitor the company's operations in much greater detail than will a trustee for the purchasers of a public issue.

Another advantage of a privately placed debt issue is that the actual borrowing does not necessarily have to take place all at once. The company can enter into an arrangement whereby it can borrow up to a fixed amount over a period of time. For this nonrevolving credit arrangement, the borrower usually will pay a commitment fee. This type of arrangement gives the company flexibility, allowing it to borrow only when it needs the funds. With a public issue, it is necessary to sell the entire issue at one time. Because the private placement does not have to be registered with the SEC, the company avoids making available to the public the detailed information required by the SEC.

Private placements allow medium-sized and sometimes small companies to sell a bond issue that they could not sell by public offering because flotation costs would be prohibitive. Institutional investors are willing to invest in bonds of these smaller companies, provided the company is credit-worthy. It is doubtful that institutional investors would seek an issue of less than $250,000 (and many insist upon a higher minimum), but we must remember that a $10 million bond issue is considered small as a public offering. The dominant lender in the private placement market is the life insurance category, though private and public pension funds are active as well.

Cost of issue

There are two costs to consider in comparing a private placement of debt with a public offering: the initial costs and the interest cost. As the negotiations usually are direct, private placement involves no underwriting or selling expenses, except, perhaps, for services of an investment banker, whom companies frequently consult about planning and negotiating the issue. Investment bankers have become increasingly involved as agents in private placements, thus offsetting to a certain degree the loss of underwriting and selling business. Nevertheless, the initial total cost of a private placement is usually significantly less than that of a public offering.

The second aspect of the cost of a private placement of debt is the interest cost. Fragmentary evidence here indicates that the yield on private placements is above that on public offerings. In addition to interest costs, institutional investors

440

PART VII
Longer-term
financing—
instruments
and markets

sometimes will request an equity "sweetener," such as warrants, to entice them to invest in the debt issue of a company. While the exact cost of this "sweetener" is difficult to measure, it certainly adds to the total cost of a private placement. Some contend that the private placement market is segmented and that the yield differential between a private placement and a public offering varies inversely with the flow of funds to life insurance companies and to other private placement lenders. Furthermore, it is suggested that with direct contact markets, such as the private placement market, nonprice factors are used to allocate credit. Owing to credit rationing and to the alleged aversion of lenders to sharp changes in rates, a lag is felt to exist between changes in public market rates and changes in private placement rates. Burton Zwick tested these notions and found little support for the segmented market effect but did find strong indication of a lag of approximately a quarter between changes in public rates and changes in private placement rates.[2]

In summary, it appears that the initial cost of a private placement of debt is less than that of a public offering; however, the interest cost and any additional compensation appear to be higher. For a long-term debt issue, the total cost is likely to be somewhat higher for a private placement than for a public offering. Moreover, the difference in cost will vary somewhat over time as interest rates, in general, change. The difference in cost between the private placement and the public markets must be balanced against the advantages of the private placement.

SUMMARY

When companies finance their long-term needs externally, they may obtain funds from the capital markets or directly from a single institutional investor or a small group of them. If the financing involves a public offering, the company will usually use the services of an investment banking firm. The investment banker's principal functions are risk-bearing, or underwriting, and selling the securities. For these functions, the investment banking firm is compensated by the spread between the price it pays for the securities and the price at which it resells the securities to investors. With a negotiated offering, the investment banker provides an additional service in advising the company on pricing and timing the issue and on procedures and features involved in the issue. With an offering on a competitive-bid basis, the issue is sold to the investment banker or syndicate of investment bankers that submits the highest bid.

A company may give its existing stockholders the first opportunity to purchase a new security issue on a privileged-subscription basis. This type of issue is known as a rights offering, because existing stockholders receive one right for each share of stock they hold. A right represents an option to buy the new security at the subscription price; and it takes a specified number of rights to purchase the security. Depending upon the relationship between the current market price of the stock and the subscription price, a right will usually have a market value. Security offerings to the general public and offerings on a privileged-subscription basis

[2] "Yields on Privately Placed Corporate Bonds," *Journal of Finance*, 35 (March 1980), 23–29.

must comply with federal and state regulations. The enforcement agency for the federal government is the Securities and Exchange Commission, whose authority encompasses both the sale of new securities and the trading of existing securities in the secondary market.

Rather than offering securities to existing stockholders or the general public, a company may place them privately with an institutional investor. With a private placement, the company negotiates directly with the investor; there is no underwriting and no registration of the issue with the SEC. The private placement has the virtue of flexibility and affords the medium-sized and even the small company the opportunity to sell its securities.

QUESTIONS

1. If competitive bidding, as opposed to negotiated offerings, were required for all security sales, would business firms benefit in higher prices for their securities?

2. How does the brokerage function of buying and selling securities differ from the underwriting function for an investment banker?

3. The financial manager handling a stock issue must choose between going directly or going through the intermediary, the investment banker, to the ultimate investor. Discuss the advantages and disadvantages of each alternative.

4. In issuing a new bond issue, the firm may decide to sell the bonds through a private placement or through a public issue. Evaluate these two alternatives.

5. There exists an inverse relationship between flotation costs and the size of the issue being sold. Explain the economic forces that cause this relationship.

6. For all sizes of issues, flotation costs for common stock are higher than those for preferred stock, and flotation costs for common stock are higher than those for bonds. Explain this cost structure.

7. What factors enable the investment banker to continue to earn a profit on the underwriting and sale of securities? Are the banker's profits in the best interests of society as a whole? Why?

8. Many major U.S. corporations, notably Exxon and American Telephone and Telegraph, have extensively used rights offerings in the past decade. Why do you feel these corporations have chosen to raise funds with a rights offering rather than a new equity issue, especially when a fair percentage of the rights (2%–5%) are never exercised?

9. Which of the following companies would you expect to use a private placement of long-term debt as opposed to a public offering?

   a) An electric utility serving Chicago

   b) A $13 million annual volume maker of electronic components

   c) A consortium of oil companies to finance an oil discovery in the Arctic

   d) A tennis-shoe retreading company serving northern California

10. Should the preemptive right be required of all companies that issue common stock or securities convertible into common?

PROBLEMS

1. Caldacci Copper Company needs to raise $75 million in long-term debt funds. The company is negotiating the offering through First Columbia Corporation. First Columbia believes it can bring together a syndicate of investment bankers to underwrite and sell the issue. The bonds will be given a coupon rate so that they may be priced to the public at their face value of $1,000. The selling concession will be $6 per bond; in addition, administrative expenses of $115,000 will be incurred. Typically, First Columbia requires a managers' fee of 15 percent of the total spread. To sell this issue, it feels that the underwriting commission, net of expenses and management fees must be 25 percent of the total spread.

   a) What will be the total spread? the total spread per bond?

   b) What will be the net proceeds of the issue to Caldacci Copper?

   c) What is the selling concession as a percent of the total spread?

   d) What are the total costs of issuing the securities as a percent of the net proceeds to the company?

2. The Ville Platte Artists School will issue 200,000 shares of common stock at $40 per share through a subscription issue. The 800,000 shares of stock currently outstanding have a market price of $50 per share.

   a) Compute the number of rights required to buy a share of stock at $40.

   b) Compute the value of a right.

   c) Compute the value of the stock ex-rights.

3. The stock of the American Corporation is selling for $50 per share. The company then issues rights to subscribe for one new share at $40 for each 5 shares held.

   a) What is the theoretical value of a right if the stock is selling rights-on?

   b) What is the theoretical value of one share of stock when it goes ex-rights?

   c) What is the theoretical value of a right when the stock sells ex-rights at $50?

4. The stock of the Dunbar Company is selling for $150 per share. If the company were to issue rights to subscribe for one additional share of stock at $125 a share for each 9 held, compute the following:

   a) The theoretical value of a right when the stock is selling rights-on

   b) The theoretical value of one share of stock when it goes ex-rights

   c) The theoretical value of a right when the stock sells ex-rights and the actual market price goes to $143 per share

5. Two different companies are considering rights offerings. The current market price per share is $48 in both cases. In order to allow for fluctuations in market price, Company X wants to set a subscription price of $42 while Company Y feels a subscription price of $41½ is in order. The number of rights necessary to purchase an additional share is 14 in the case of Company X and 4 in the case of Company Y.

   a) Which company has the larger stock issue relatively? Is it the larger stock issue in absolute terms?

   b) In which case is there less risk that the market price will fall below the subscription price?

6. The Balboa Diving Company wishes to sell a preferred-stock issue. Flotation costs are expected to be 8.5 percent of the gross proceeds. Moreover, the company feels that the stock will need to provide a yield of 9 percent to investors in order to find acceptance in the marketplace. Assuming the issue is perpetual, what is the effective cost of the preferred-stock issue to the company?

7. Obtain a prospectus on a recent security issue of a corporation. Analyze it according to

   a) The type of security being offered. Are there any special features? If a bond, is it secured? How is it secured?

   b) The size of the issue and the type of company involved. How sound is the company financially? How stable are its earnings? What is the growth potential? Is the size of the issue appropriate?

   c) The flotation cost. What is the underwriter spread? Is it too high a percentage of gross proceeds? What portion of the spread is in support of underwriting? in support of selling? What is the dealer concession? Under what conditions may it be earned?

   d) The underwriting syndicate. How many underwriters are there? What is the maximum participation? the minimum participation? Who is the manager? Are there provisions made for support of the price during the distribution period?

   e) The pricing. Is the issue priced properly from the standpoint of the company? Of the investor? Of the underwriter? How successful was the issue?

SELECTED REFERENCES

BACON, PETER W., "The Subscription Price in Rights Offerings," *Financial Management,* 1 (Summer 1972), 59–64.

BLOCH, ERNEST, "Pricing a Corporate Bond Issue: A Look behind the Scenes," *Essays in Money and Credit,* pp. 72–76. New York: Federal Reserve Bank of New York, 1964.

BLOCK, STANLEY, and MARJORIE STANLEY, "The Financial Characteristics and Price Movement Patterns of Companies Approaching the Unseasoned Securities Market in the Late 1970s," *Financial Management,* 9 (Winter 1980), 30–36.

DIPCHAND, CECIL R., "The Canadian Experience with Inherent Stock Splits of Rights Issues," *Financial Management,* 6 (Summer 1977), 34–41.

EDERINGTON, LOUIS H., "Negotiated Versus Competitive Underwritings of Corporate Bonds," *Journal of Finance,* 30 (September 1975), 1129–33.

———, "Uncertainty, Competition, and Costs in Corporate Bond Underwriting," *Journal of Financial Economics,* 2 (March 1975), 71–94.

EVANS, G. H., JR., "The Theoretical Value of a Stock Right," *Journal of Finance,* 10 (March 1955), 55–61.

HAYES, SAMUEL L., III, "The Transformation of Investment Banking," *Harvard Business Review,* 57 (January-February 1979), 153–70.

———, "Investment Banking: Power Structure in Flux," *Harvard Business Review,* 49 (March-April 1971), 136–52.

HUNTSMAN, BLAIN, and JAMES P. HOBAN, JR., "Investment in New Enterprise: Some Empirical Observations on Risk, Return, and Market Structure," *Financial Management,* 9 (Summer 1980), 44–51.

JOHNSON, KEITH B., T. GREGORY MORTON, and M. CHAPMAN FINDLAY, III, "An Empirical Analysis of the Flotation Cost of Corporate Securities, 1971–1972," *Journal of Finance,* 30 (September 1975), 1129–33.

KEANE, SIMON M., "The Significance of the Issue Price in Rights Issues," *Journal of Business Finance,* 4, No. 3 (1972), 40–45.

444

PART VII

Longer-term
financing—
instruments
and markets

LEVY, HAIM, and MARSHALL SARNAT, "Risk, Dividend Policy, and the Optimal Pricing of a Rights Offering," *Journal of Money, Credit and Banking,* 3 (November 1971), 840–49.

LOGUE, DENNIS E., and ROBERT A. JARROW, "Negotiation vs. Competitive Bidding in the Sale of Securities by Public Utilities," *Financial Management,* 7 (Autumn 1978), 31–39.

LOGUE, DENNIS E., and JOHN R. LINDVALL, "The Behavior of Investment Bankers: An Econometric Investigation," *Journal of Finance,* 29 (March 1974), 203–16.

LOGUE, DENNIS E., and RICHARD J. ROGALSKI, "Does It Pay to Shop for Your Bond Underwriter?" *Harvard Business Review,* 57 (July-August 1979), 111–17.

PARKER, GEORGE G. C., and DANIEL COOPERMAN, "Competitive Bidding in the Underwriting of Public Utilities Securities," *Journal of Financial and Quantitative Analysis.* 13 (December 1978), 885–902.

SHAPIRO, ELI, and CHARLES R. WOLF, *The Role of Private Placements in Corporate Finance.* Boston: Division of Research, Graduate School of Business Administration, Harvard University, 1972.

SMITH, CLIFFORD W., JR., "Alternative Methods for Raising Capital," *Journal of Financial Economics,* 5 (November 1977), 273–307.

TALLMAN, GARY D., DAVID F. RUSH and RONALD W. MELICHER, "Competitive versus Negotiated Underwriting Costs for Regulated Industries," *Financial Management,* 3 (Summer 1974), 49–55.

VAN HORNE, JAMES C., *Financial Market Rates and Flows.* Englewood Cliffs, N.J.: Prentice-Hall, 1978.

——, "Implied Fixed Costs in Long-Term Debt Issues," *Journal of Financial and Quantitative Analysis,* 8 (December 1973).

WHITE, R. W., and P. A. LUSZTIG, "The Price Effects of Rights Offerings," *Journal of Financial and Quantitative Analysis,* 15 (March 1980), 25–40.

ZWICK, BURTON, "Yields on Privately Placed Corporate Bonds," *Journal of Finance,* 35 (March 1980), 23–29.

Term and lease financing | 20

The principal characteristic of short-term loans is that they are self-liquidating in less than a year. Frequently, they finance seasonal and temporary funds requirements. Term financing, on the other hand, finances more permanent funds requirements, such as fixed assets and underlying buildups in receivables and inventories. The loan is usually paid with the generation of cash flows over a period of years. As a result, most of these loans are paid in regular, periodic installments. We regard term financing as involving final maturities of one to seven years. These boundaries are arbitrary, although the one-year boundary is rather commonly accepted. In this chapter we examine various types of term debt as well as lease financing.

TERM LOANS

Commercial banks have become increasingly involved in providing term financing to industry. Two features of a bank term loan distinguish it from other types of business loans. First, it has a final maturity of more than one year; second, it most often represents credit extended under a formal loan agreement. For the most part, these loans are repayable in periodic installments: quarterly, semi-

446

PART VII

Longer-term
financing—
instruments
and markets

annually, or annually. The payment schedule of the loan usually is geared to the borrower's cash-flow ability to service the debt. Typically, this schedule calls for equal periodic installments, but it may specify irregular amounts or repayment in a lump sum at final maturity. Sometimes the loan is amortized in equal periodic installments except for the final payment, known as a "balloon" payment, which is larger than any of the others.

Most bank term loans are written with original maturities in the 3-to-7-year range. Some banks are willing to make longer term loans, but only rarely will a bank make a term loan with a final maturity of more than 10 years. The final maturity of a term loan does not always convey the length of time the loan is likely to remain outstanding. In some cases the bank and the company expect the loan to be renewed successively with maturity. These evergreen loans are typically characterized by credits to companies in growth phases. Despite the expectation of evergreen refunding upon maturity, the bank is not legally obligated to extend the loan. As a result, most requests for extensions and additional credit are analyzed afresh based on changed conditions from the time of the original loan. What was thought to be an evergreen loan may turn out to be a "deciduous" one if the financial condition and performance of the borrower deteriorates.

Costs and benefits

Generally, the interest rate on a term loan is higher than the rate on a short-term loan to the same borrower. If a firm could borrow at the prime rate on a short-term basis, it might pay .25 percent to .50 percent more on a term loan. The interest rate on a term loan can be set in one of two ways: (1) a fixed rate which is effective over the life of the loan may be established at the outset, or (2) a variable rate may be set, to be adjusted in keeping with changes in the prime rate. Sometimes a ceiling or a floor rate is established, limiting the range within which the rate may fluctuate.

In addition to interest costs, the borrower is required to pay the legal expenses that the bank incurs in drawing up the loan agreement. Also, a commitment fee may be charged for the time during the commitment period when the loan is not taken down. For an ordinary term loan, these additional costs usually are rather small in relation to the total interest cost of the loan. A typical fee on the unused portion of a commitment is $\frac{1}{2}$ percent, with a range of $\frac{1}{4}$ percent to $\frac{3}{4}$ percent. This means that if the commitment fee were $\frac{1}{2}$ percent on a commitment of $1 million, and the company took down all of the loan 3 months after the commitment, it would owe the bank $1 million $\times$ .005 $\times$ $\frac{3}{12}$ = $1,250. In addition to the commitment fee, the need to maintain compensating balances, discussed in chapter 12, is an indirect cost to the borrower.

The principal advantage of an ordinary bank term loan is flexibility. The borrower deals directly with the lender, and the loan can be tailored to the borrower's needs through direct negotiation. The bank usually has had previous experience with the borrower, so it is familiar with the company's situation. Should the firm's requirements change, the terms and conditions of the loan may be revised. It is considerably more convenient to negotiate with a single lender or a reasonably small group of lenders than with a large number of public security holders, who are involved with a bond issue. The borrower can deal confidentially with a bank or, for that matter, with any private lending institution and does not have to reveal certain financial information to the public.

In many instances, bank term loans are made to small businesses that do not have access to the capital markets and cannot readily float a public issue. The ability to sell a public issue varies over time in keeping with the tone of the capital markets, whereas access to term loan financing is more dependable. Even large companies which are able to go to the public market may find it quicker and more convenient to seek a bank term loan than to float a public issue. A term loan can be arranged in several weeks, whereas a public issue takes much longer.

Revolving credits

As we said in chapter 12, a revolving credit is a formal commitment by a bank to lend up to a certain amount of money to a company over a specified period of time. The actual notes evidencing debt are short-term, usually 90 days; but the company may renew them or borrow additionally, up to the specified maximum, throughout the duration of the commitment. Many revolving-credit commitments are for 3 years, although it is possible for a firm to obtain a shorter commitment. As with an ordinary term loan, the interest rate is usually .25 to .50 percent higher than the rate at which the firm could borrow on a short-term basis under a line of credit. When a bank makes a revolving-credit commitment, it is legally bound under the loan agreement to have funds available whenever the company wants to borrow. The borrower usually must pay for this availability in the form of a commitment fee, perhaps ½ percent per annum, on the difference between the amount borrowed and the specified maximum.

This borrowing arrangement is particularly useful at times when the firm is uncertain about its funds requirements. The borrower has flexible access to funds over a period of uncertainty and can make more definite credit arrangements when the uncertainty is resolved. Revolving-credit agreements can be set up so that at the maturity of the commitment, borrowings then owing can be converted into a term loan at the option of the borrower. Someday your company may introduce a new product and face a period of uncertainty over the next several years. To provide maximum financial flexibility, you might arrange a 3-year revolving credit that is convertible into a 5-year term loan at the expiration of the revolving-credit commitment. At the end of 3 years, the company should know its funds requirements better. If these requirements are permanent, or nearly so, the firm might wish to exercise its option and take down the term loan.

Insurance company term loans

In addition to banks, life insurance companies lend money on a term basis, but with important differences in the maturity of the loan extended and in the interest rate charged. In general, life insurance companies are interested in term loans with final maturities in excess of 7 years. Because these companies do not have the benefit of compensating balances or other business from the borrower, and because their loans usually have a longer maturity than bank term loans,

448

PART VII
Longer-term
financing—
instruments
and markets

typically, the rate of interest is higher. To the insurance company, the term loan represents an investment and must yield a return commensurate with the costs involved in making the loan, the risk, the maturity, and prevailing yields on alternative investments. Because an insurance company is interested in keeping its funds employed without interruption, it normally has a prepayment penalty, whereas usually the bank does not.

Insurance company term loans generally are not competitive with bank term loans. Indeed, they are complementary, for they serve different maturity ranges. Sometimes a bank and an insurance company will participate in the same loan. The bank may take the early maturities, perhaps the first five years, with the insurance company taking the remaining maturities. Including an insurance company in the credit permits a longer maturity range than the bank can provide, and the bank can offer a lower interest rate on the early maturities. A term loan of this sort may serve both the intermediate- and long-term funds requirements of the firm.

LOAN AGREEMENTS

When a lender makes a term loan or revolving-credit commitment, it provides the borrower with available funds for an extended period. Much can happen to the financial condition of the borrower during that period. In order to safeguard itself, the lender requires the borrower to maintain its financial condition and, in particular, its current position at a level at least as favorable as when the commitment was made. The provisions for protection contained in a loan agreement are known as protective covenants.

The loan agreement itself simply gives the lender legal authority to step in should the borrower default under any of the provisions. Otherwise, the lender would be locked into a commitment and would have to wait until maturity before being able to effect corrective measures. The borrower who suffers losses or other adverse developments will default under a well-written loan agreement; the lender then will be able to act. The action usually takes the form of working with the company to straighten out its problems. Seldom will a lender demand immediate payment, despite the legal right to do so in cases of default. More typically, the condition under which the borrower defaults is waived or the loan agreement is amended. The point is that the lender has the authority to act, even though negotiation with the borrower may be instituted to resolve the problem.

Formulation of provisions

The formulation of the different restrictive provisions should be tailored to the specific loan situation. The lender fashions these provisions for the overall protection of the loan. No one provision is able by itself to provide the necessary safeguards; but together with the other provisions, it is designed to assure overall liquidity and ability to pay a loan. The important protective covenants of a loan agreement may be classified as follows: (1) general provisions used in most loan agreements, which are variable to fit the situation; (2) routine provisions used in most agreements, which usually are not variable; and (3) specific provisions that are used according to the situation. Although we focus on a loan agreement, the protective covenants used and the philosophy underlying their use are the same for a bond indenture, which is described in chapter 21.

General provisions. The *working-capital requirement* probably is the most commonly used and most comprehensive provision in a loan agreement. Its purpose is to preserve the company's current position and ability to pay the loan. Frequently, a straight dollar amount, such as $6 million, is set as the minimum working capital the company must maintain during the duration of the commitment. When the lender feels that it is desirable for a specific company to build working capital, it may increase the minimum working-capital requirement throughout the duration of the loan. The establishment of a working-capital minimum normally is based upon the amounts of present working capital and projected working capital, allowing for seasonal fluctuations. The requirement should not restrict the company unduly in the ordinary generation of profit. Should the borrower incur sharp losses or spend too much for fixed assets, purchase of stock, dividends, redemption of long-term debt, and so forth, it would probably breach the working-capital requirement.

The *cash-dividend and repurchase-of-stock restriction* is another major restriction in this category. Its purpose is to limit cash going outside the business, thus preserving the liquidity of the company. Most often, cash dividends and repurchase of stock are limited to a percentage of net profits on a cumulative basis after a certain base date, frequently the last fiscal year-end prior to the date of the term-loan agreement. A less flexible method is to restrict dividends and repurchase of stock to an absolute dollar amount each year. In most cases the prospective borrower must be willing to undergo a cash-dividend and repurchase-of-stock restriction. If tied to earnings, this restriction still will allow adequate dividends as long as the company is able to generate satisfactory profits.

The *capital-expenditures limitation* is third in the category of general provisions. Capital expenditures may be limited to a fixed dollar amount yearly or, probably more commonly, either to depreciation or to a percentage thereof. The capital-expenditures limitation is another tool the lender uses to assure the maintenance of the borrower's current position. By limiting capital expenditures directly, the bank can be surer that it will not have to look to liquidation of fixed assets for payment of its loan. Again, the provision should not be so restrictive that it prevents the adequate maintenance and improvement of facilities.

A *limitation on other indebtedness* is the last general provision. This limitation may take a number of forms, depending upon the circumstances. Frequently, a loan agreement will prohibit a company from incurring any other long-term debt. This provision protects the lender, inasmuch as it prevents future lenders from obtaining a prior claim on the borrower's assets. Usually a company is permitted to borrow within reasonable limits for seasonal and other short-term purposes arising in the ordinary course of business.

Routine provisions. The second category of restrictions includes routine, usually invariable provisions found in most loan agreements. Ordinarily, the loan

450

PART VII

Longer-term
financing—
instruments
and markets

agreement requires the borrower to furnish the bank with financial statements and to maintain adequate insurance. Additionally, the borrower normally must not sell a significant portion of its assets but must pay, when due, all taxes and other liabilities, except those it contests in good faith. A provision forbidding the pledging or mortgaging of any of the borrower's assets is almost always included in a loan agreement; this important provision is known as a negative pledge clause.

Ordinarily, the company is required not to discount or sell its receivables. Moreover, the borrower generally is prohibited from entering into any leasing arrangement of property, except up to a certain dollar amount of annual rental. The purpose of this provision is to prevent the borrower from taking on a substantial lease liability, which might endanger its ability to pay the loan. A lease restriction also prevents the firm from leasing property instead of purchasing it and thereby getting around the limitations on capital expenditures and debt. Usually, too, there is a restriction on other contingent liabilities. The provisions in this category appear as a matter of routine in most loan agreements. Although somewhat mechanical, they close many loopholes and provide a tight, comprehensive loan agreement.

Special provisions. In specific loan agreements, the bank uses special provisions to achieve a desired total protection of its loan. A loan agreement may contain a definite understanding regarding the use of the loan proceeds, so that there will be no diversion of funds to purposes other than those contemplated when the loan was negotiated. A provision for limiting loans and advances often is found in a bank term-loan agreement. Closely allied to this restriction is a limitation on investments, which is used to safeguard liquidity by preventing certain nonliquid investments.

If one or more executives are essential to a firm's effective operation, a bank may insist that the company carry life insurance on them. Proceeds of the insurance may be payable to the company or directly to the bank, to be applied to the loan. An agreement may also contain a management clause, under which certain key individuals must remain actively employed in the company during the time the loan is owing. Aggregate executive salaries and bonuses sometimes are limited in the loan agreement, to prevent excessive compensation of executives, which might reduce profits. This provision closes another loophole; it prevents large stockholders who are officers of the company from increasing their own salaries in lieu of paying higher dividends, which are limited under the agreement.

Negotiation of restrictions

The provisions described above represent the most frequently used protective covenants in a loan agreement. From the standpoint of the lender, the aggregate impact of these provisions should be to safeguard the financial position of the borrower and its ability to pay the loan. Under a well-written agreement, a borrower cannot get into serious financial difficulty without defaulting under an agreement, thereby giving the lender legal authority to take action. Although the lender is instrumental in establishing the restrictions, the restrictiveness of protective covenants is subject to negotiation between borrower and lender. The final result will depend upon the relative bargaining power of each of the parties involved.[1]

EQUIPMENT FINANCING

Equipment represents another asset of the firm that may be pledged to secure a loan. If the firm either has equipment that is marketable or is purchasing such equipment, it is usually able to obtain some sort of secured financing. Because such loans usually are for more than a year, we classify them in this chapter rather than under short-term secured loans. As with other secured loans, the lender evaluates the marketability of the collateral and will advance a percentage of the market value, depending upon the quality of the equipment. Frequently, the repayment schedule for the loan is set in keeping with the economic depreciation schedule of the equipment. A trucking company usually will depreciate its tractors over 3 years and its trailers over 5 years. A lender might set a 3-year installment payment schedule for a loan secured by tractors and a 5-year schedule for a loan secured by trailers. In setting the repayment schedule, the lender wants to be sure that the market value of the tractor or trailer always exceeds the balance of the loan.

The excess of the expected market value of the equipment over the amount of the loan is the margin of safety, which will vary according to the specific situation. The rolling stock of a trucking company is movable collateral and reasonably marketable. As a result, the advance may be as high as 80 percent. Less-marketable equipment, such as that with a limited use, will not command as high an advance. A certain type of lathe may have a thin market; and a lender might not be willing to advance more than 50 percent of its reported market value. Some equipment is so specialized that it has no value as collateral. Frequently, the lender either will have its own appraiser or will hire an appraiser to estimate the approximate value of a piece of equipment if it has to be sold. As with other collateral, the lender must know not only the estimated market price of the equipment but also the cost of selling it.

Sources of equipment financing

Commercial banks, finance companies, and the sellers of equipment are among the sources of equipment financing. Because the interest charged by a finance company on an equipment loan usually is higher than that charged by a commercial bank, a firm will turn to a finance company only if it is unable to obtain the loan from a bank. The seller of the equipment may finance the purchase either by holding the secured note itself of by selling the note to its captive finance subsidiary. The interest charge will depend upon the extent to which the seller uses financing as a sales tool. The seller who uses financing extensively may

[1]For a linear-programming approach for evaluating the opportunity costs of the protective-covenant restrictions, see James C. Van Horne, "A Linear-Programming Approach to Evaluating Restrictions under a Bond Indenture or Loan Agreement," *Journal of Financial and Quantitative Analysis*, 1 (June 1966), 68–83.

452

PART VII
Longer-term
financing—
instruments
and markets

charge only a moderate interest rate, but may make up for part of the cost of carrying the notes by charging higher prices for the equipment. The borrower must consider this possibility in judging the true cost of financing. Equipment loans may be secured either by a chattel mortgage or by a conditional sales contract arrangement.

Chattel mortgage

A chattel mortgage is a lien on property other than real property. The borrower signs a security agreement that gives the lender a lien on the equipment specified in the agreement. In order to perfect the lien, the lender files a copy of the security agreement or a financing statement with a public office of the state in which the equipment is located. Given a valid lien, the lender can sell the equipment if the borrower defaults in the payment of principal or interest on the loan.

Conditional sales contract

With a conditional sales contract arrangement, the seller of the equipment retains title to it until the purchaser has satisfied all the terms of the contract. The buyer signs a conditional sales contract security agreement to make periodic installment payments to the seller over a specified period of time. These payments usually are monthly or quarterly. Until the terms of the contract are satisfied completely, the seller retains title to the equipment. Thus, the seller receives a down payment and a promissory note for the balance of the purchase price upon the sale of the equipment. The note is secured by the contract, which gives the seller the authority to repossess the equipment if the buyer does not meet all the terms of the contract.

The seller may either hold the contract himself or sell it, simply by endorsing it, to a commercial bank or finance company. The bank or finance company then becomes the lender and assumes the security interest in the equipment. If the buyer should default under the terms of the contract, the bank or finance company could repossess the equipment and sell it in satisfaction of its loan. Often, the vendor will sell the contract to a bank or finance company with recourse. Under this arrangement, the lender has the additional protection of recourse to the seller in case the buyer defaults.

LEASE FINANCING

A lease is a contract whereby the owner of an asset (the lessor) grants to another party (the lessee) the exclusive right to use the asset, usually for an agreed period of time, in return for the payment of rent. Most of us are familiar with leases of houses, apartments, offices, or telephones. Recent decades have seen an enormous growth in the leasing of business assets such as cars and trucks, computers, and manufacturing plants. An obvious advantage to the lessee is the use of an asset without having to buy it. Along with the right of usage, a lease contract may also transfer to the lessee some of the burdens and risks of ownership. It may provide that the lessee is responsible for the repair and maintenance of the asset or for insuring it against accidental damage or loss. The owner of an asset usually carries the risk of obsolescence, a serious one, because changes in technology or in consumer tastes may lower the asset's value, sometimes dramatically. The extent to which this risk is transferred to the lessee depends on the terms of the lease agreement.

Our focus in this chapter is on the financial lease, a noncancellable contract in which a lessee agrees to make a series of payments to a lessor for the use of an asset. The lessee acquires most of the economic values associated with outright ownership of the asset, even though the lessor retains title to it. With a financial lease, the total payments the lessee agrees to make must exceed the purchase price of the asset.

In lease financing, the obligations of the lessor and the lessee are specified in the lease contract. This contract contains

1. The basic lease period, during which the lease is noncancellable.
2. The timing and amounts of periodic rental payments during the basic lease period.
3. Any option to renew the lease or to purchase the asset at the end of the basic period.
4. Provision for the payment of the costs of maintenance and repairs, taxes, insurance, and other expenses. With a "net lease," the lessee pays all of these costs. Under a "maintenance lease," the lessor maintains the asset and pays the insurance.

Forms of lease financing

Virtually all lease-financing arrangements fall into one of three main types of lease financing: a sale and leaseback arrangement, the direct acquisition of an asset under a lease, and leveraged leasing. In this section we briefly describe these categories, and in the subsequent section we present a framework for the analysis of lease financing.

Sale and leaseback. Under a sale and leaseback arrangement a firm sells an asset to another party, and this party leases it back to the firm. Usually, the asset is sold at approximately its market value. The firm receives the sales price in cash and the economic use of the asset during the basic lease period. In turn, it contracts to make periodic lease payments and give up title to the asset. As a result, the lessor realizes any residual value the asset might have at the end of the lease period; whereas before, this value would have been realized by the firm. Lessors engaged in sale and leaseback arrangements include insurance companies, other institutional investors, finance companies, and independent leasing companies.

Direct leasing. Under direct leasing, a company acquires the use of an asset it did not own previously. A firm may lease an asset from the manufacturer: IBM leases computers; Xerox Corporation leases copiers. Indeed, capital goods are abundantly available today on a lease-financed basis. A wide variety of direct leasing arrangements meet various needs of firms. The major types of lessors are

454

PART VII

Longer-term
financing—
instruments
and markets

manufacturers, finance companies, banks, independent leasing companies, special-purpose leasing companies, and partnerships. For leasing arrangements involving all but manufacturers, the vendor sells the asset to the lessor who, in turn, leases it to the lessee. As in any lease arrangement, the lessee has use of the asset, along with a contractual obligation to make lease payments to the lessor.

Since 1963, commercial banks have been allowed to engage in direct leasing and they have become highly active in the leasing industry. Independent leasing companies finance the purchase of a wide variety of equipment. In doing so, they frequently borrow from banks, securing the loan with the assignment of the lease payments. Special-purpose leasing companies confine their operations to certain types of assets; computer leasing companies, for example, lease mainly computer hardware and peripheral equipment. In recent years, individuals in high tax brackets have formed partnerships for the purpose of purchasing equipment and leasing it to companies. The tax shield afforded by the investment tax credit, accelerated depreciation charges, and interest paid on borrowings may be more valuable to them than to a corporation. As a result, both the lessor and the lessee may benefit.

Leveraged leasing. A special form of leasing has recently developed in conjunction with the financing of assets requiring large capital outlays. This new device is known as *leveraged leasing*. In contrast to the two parties involved in the forms of leasing previously described, there are three parties involved in leveraged leasing: (1) the lessee, (2) the lessor, or equity participant, and (3) the lender. We examine each in turn.

From the standpoint of the lessee, there is no difference between a leveraged lease and any other type of lease. The lessee contracts to make periodic payments over the basic lease period and, in return, is entitled to the use of the asset over that period of time. The role of the lessor, however, is changed. The lessor acquires the asset in keeping with the terms of the lease arrangement and finances the acquisition in part by an equity investment of, say, 20 percent (hence the name *equity participant*). The remaining 80 percent is provided by a long-term lender or lenders. Usually, the loan is secured by a mortgage on the asset, as well as by the assignment of the lease and lease payments. The lessor is the borrower.

As owner of the asset, the lessor is entitled to deduct all depreciation charges associated with the asset, as well as utilize the entire investment tax credit. The cash-flow pattern for the lessor typically involves (1) a cash outflow at the time the asset is acquired, which represents its equity participation less the investment tax credit; (2) a period of cash inflows represented by lease payments and tax benefits, less payments of the debt (principal and interest); and (3) a period of net cash outflows during which, because of declining tax benefits, the sum of lease payments and tax benefits falls below the debt payments due. If there is any residual value at the end of the lease period, this of course represents a cash inflow to the lessor. Although the leveraged lease may seem the most complicated of the three forms of leasing we have described, it reduces to certain basic concepts. From the standpoint of the lessee, which is our stance, the leveraged lease can be analyzed in the same manner as any other lease. Therefore, we will not treat it separately in the rest of this chapter.

Accounting treatment

Accounting for leases has changed dramatically in recent years. A number of years ago lease financing was attractive to some because the obligation did not appear on the company's financial statements. As a result, leasing was regarded as a "hidden" or "off balance sheet" method of financing. However, accounting requirements have changed so that now many leases must be shown on the balance sheet as a capitalized asset with the associated liability being shown as well. For these leases, the reporting of earnings is affected. Other leases must be fully disclosed in footnotes to the financial statement. As the accounting treatment of leases is involved, we discuss it in the Appendix to this chapter, in order to maintain the chapter's continuity. The main point is that it no longer is possible for a firm to "fool" investors and creditors by using lease as opposed to debt financing. The full impact of the lease obligation is apparent to any supplier of capital who takes the effort to read the financial statements.

Tax treatment and considerations

For tax purposes, the lessee can deduct the full amount of the lease payment. The Internal Revenue Service wants to be sure that the lease contract truly represents a lease and not an installment purchase of the asset. To assure itself that a "true" lease in fact is involved, it may check on whether there is a meaningful residual value at the end of the lease term. Usually this is construed to mean that the term of the lease cannot exceed 90 percent of the useful life of the asset. In addition to this criterion, the lessee must not be given an option to purchase the asset or to release it at a nominal price at the end of the lease period. Any option must be based on fair market value at the lease's expiration.

In essence, the IRS wants to assure itself that the lease contract is not, in effect, a purchase of the asset, for which payments are much more rapid than would be allowed with depreciation. As lease payments are deductible for tax purposes, such a contract would allow the lessor effectively to "depreciate" the asset more quickly than allowed under a straight purchase. The lessor must have a meaningful investment stake in the asset at all times—10 percent or more. With the Tax Act of 1981, the faster depreciation allowed the owner of an asset largely mitigates the problem of lease payments being regarded as too rapid. If the lease contract meets the conditions described above, the full lease payment is deductible for tax purposes.

With leasing, the cost of any land is amortized in the lease payments. By deducting the lease payments as an expense for federal income tax purposes, in essence, the lessee is able to write off the original cost of the land. If the land is purchased, the firm cannot depreciate it for tax purposes. When the value of land represents a significant portion of the asset acquired, lease financing can offer a tax advantage to the firm. Offsetting this tax advantage is the likely residual value of land at the end of the basic lease period. The firm also may gain certain tax advantages in a sale and leaseback arrangement when the assets are sold for less than their depreciated value.

456

PART VII

Longer-term
financing—
instruments
and markets

An important tax consideration is the investment tax credit, which is available to corporations and individuals who invest in certain types of assets. This credit was described in chapter 2, and we know that it is available at the time the asset is placed in service. When the lessor takes the tax credit, lease payments generally are lower than they would be in the absence of the credit. This reduction is occasioned by the forces of competition among lessors. The exact amount by which lease payments are lowered depends upon negotiations between the lessor and the lessee.

When the lessee is unable to utilize the full tax credit because of an insufficient tax liability, but the lessor is able to use it, both parties tend to gain. The lessee realizes a significant part of the tax credit through lease payments that are lower than they would otherwise be. In turn, the lessor is able to use the full tax credit. Perhaps the most striking illustration of this arrangement is the lease financing of jet airplanes by airlines. Often the profits of airline companies are not sufficient to utilize the full tax credit available on a significant purchase of aircraft. Through a lease arrangement, the airline is able to avail itself of a greater portion of the benefits than it could with a straight purchase.

EVALUATING LEASE FINANCING IN RELATION TO DEBT FINANCING

To evaluate whether or not a lease financing proposal is a good thing, compare it with financing the asset with debt. Whether leasing or borrowing is best will depend upon the patterns of cash outflows for each financing method and upon the opportunity cost of funds. To illustrate a method of analysis, we compare lease financing with debt financing, using a hypothetical example. We assume that the firm has decided to invest in a project on the basis of considerations that were discussed in part IV. In other words, the investment worthiness of the project is evaluated separately from the specific method of financing to be employed. We assume also that the firm has determined an appropriate capital structure and has decided to finance the project with a fixed-income type of instrument—either debt or lease financing. We turn now to examining the two alternatives.

Leasing

Suppose a firm has decided to acquire an asset costing $200,000 and having an expected economic life of five years, after which the asset is not expected to have any residual value. Once the investment decision is made, the question becomes, Is it better to finance the asset by leasing or by borrowing? If leasing is used, the lessor requires that the cost of the asset be completely amortized over the ten-year period and that it yield a 14 percent return. As is customary, lease payments are to be made in advance—that is, at the end of the year prior to each of the five years. The amount of annual lease payment may be calculated by solving the following equation for x:

$$\$200,000 = \sum_{t=0}^{4} \frac{x}{(1.14)^t}$$

$$\$200,000 = x + 2.9137x \qquad (20\text{-}1)$$

$$x = \frac{\$200,000}{3.9137}$$

$$x = \$51,103$$

Because lease payments are made in advance, we solve for the annual lease payment which equates the cost of the asset, $200,000, with the present value of one lease payment at time 0, plus the present value of nine lease payments at the end of each of the next four years. Because the discount rate is 14 percent, we look in Table B at the end of the book to find the present-value discount factor for an even stream of cash flows for four years, discounted at 14 percent; its value is 2.9137. Therefore, the annual lease payment necessary to amortize the cost of the asset completely and to return the lessor 14 percent is $51,103.

From our previous discussion, we know that the firm will make annual lease payments of $51,103 if the asset is leased. Because these payments are an expense, they are deductible for tax purposes, but only in the year for which the payment applies. The $51,103 payment at the end of year 0 represents a prepaid expense and is not deductible for tax purposes until year 1. Similarly, the other four payments are not deductible until the following year. If we assume an income tax rate of 46 percent, cash outflows after taxes each year would be those in column 3 of Table 20-1. Suppose that the appropriate opportunity cost of funds on an essentially risk-free investment is 10 percent. The reason for using this rate as our discount rate is that the difference in cash flows between lease financing and debt financing involves little or no risk. Therefore, it is not appropriate to use the cost of capital, which embodies a risk premium for the firm as a whole, as the discount rate.

Given the information in the paragraph above, we are able to compute the present value of cash outflows. The computations are shown in the last column of Table 20-1. We see that the present value of the total cash outflows under the

TABLE 20-1 \\ **Schedule of cash outflows: leasing alternative**

End of year	(1) Lease payment	(2) Tax shield (1) × (.46)	(3) Cash outflow after taxes (1) − (2)	(4) Present value of cash outflows (10%)
0	$51,103	—	$51,103	$ 51,103
1–4	51,103	$23,507	27,596	81,477
5	—	23,507	−23,507	−14,596
				$123,984

458

PART VII
Longer-term
financing—
instruments
and markets

leasing alternative is $123,984. This figure, then must be compared with the present value of cash outflows under the borrowing alternative.

Borrowing

If the asset is purchased, the firm is assumed to finance it entirely with a 16 percent unsecured term loan. For tax purposes, the firm is able to deduct depreciation charges as well as avail itself of the investment tax credit. We assume that the asset falls into the 5-year property category for cost recovery (depreciation) purposes. Although a firm usually will want to use accelerated depreciation, for ease of understanding we assume for now that straight-line depreciation is employed. As a result, annual depreciation charges are $40,000, assuming as before a $200,000 purchase price. The investment tax credit is available at the time the asset is placed in service. We assume this is at time 0 and that the applicable credit is 10 percent. This deduction effectively lowers the purchase price by $20,000 to $180,000 if the asset is purchased. A loan of this amount is assumed to be taken out at time 0 and is payable over 5 years in equal payments of $54,974, annually.[2] The proportion of interest in each payment depends upon the unpaid balance of the principal amount owing during the year. For example, the principal amount owing during year 1 is $180,000; therefore, the annual interest for that year is $28,800. Table 20-2 shows the schedule of debt payments.

TABLE 20-2 \\ **Schedule of debt payments**

End of year	Interest plus principal payments	Principal amount owing at end of year	Annual interest
0	$ —	$180,000	$ —
1	54,974	153,826	28,800
2	54,974	123,464	24,612
3	54,974	88,244	19,754
4	54,974	47,389	14,119
5	54,971	—	7,582

Given annual interest and depreciation, we are able to compute the cash outflows after taxes for the borrowing alternative; these outflows are shown in Table 20-3. Because both depreciation and interest are deductible for tax purposes, they provide a tax shield equal to their sum times the tax rate. When this shield is deducted from the total payment, we obtain the cash outflow after taxes at the end of each year. Finally, we compute the present value of these outflows and find that the total is $103,527. According to this analysis, the firm should acquire the asset through debt financing, because the present value of cash outflows with borrowing, $103,527, is less than that with leasing, $123,984.

---

[2] This amount is computed in the same manner as in Eq. (20-1) with the exception that time goes from $t = 1$ through 5 instead of $t = 0$ through 4. Because of rounding to the nearest dollar, the payment in year 5 is slightly lower.

TABLE 20-3 \ **Schedule of cash outflows: borrowing alternative**

End of year	(1) Loan payment	(2) Interest	(3) Depreciation	(4) Tax shield $[(2) + (3)].46$	(5) Cash outflow after taxes $(1) - (4)$	(6) Present value of cash outflows (10%)
1	$54,974	$28,800	$40,000	$31,648	$23,326	$ 21,205
2	54,974	24,612	40,000	29,722	25,252	20,870
3	54,974	19,754	40,000	27,867	27,107	20,366
4	54,974	14,119	40,000	24,895	30,079	20,544
5	54,971	7,582	40,000	21,888	33,083	20,542
						$103,527

This conclusion arises despite the fact that the implied interest rate embodied in the lease payments, 14 percent, is less than the explicit interest rate on the debt, 16 percent. The major relative advantage of purchasing the asset and financing it with debt is the realization of the investment tax credit at the outset. This credit effectively reduces the purchase price and the amount of debt to be incurred. In the case of the lease, the lessor is entitled to the investment tax credit. This advantage may be passed off in part to the lessee in the form of lease payments lower than would otherwise be the case. While the lower interest rate embodied in the lease payments in our example reflects this occurrence, it is not sufficient to cause the lease alternative to be more attractive. Another factor that favors the debt alternative is the deductibility of interest payments for tax purposes. Because the amount of interest embodied in a "mortgage-type" debt payment is high at first and declines with successive payments, the tax benefits associated with these payments follow the same pattern over time. From a present-value standpoint, this pattern benefits the firm relative to a pattern of lease payments, which are constant over time.

Other considerations

The decision to borrow rests upon the relative timing and magnitude of cash flows under the two financing alternatives as well as upon the discount rate employed. If the asset has a residual value at the end of the lease period, the results of our calculations will be changed. Suppose that the asset has a market value of $40,000 at the end of the fifth year. If we assume a capital-gains tax of 28 percent, the tax on this capital gain will be $11,200. Therefore, a net cash flow of $40,000 − $11,200 = $28,800 is realized at the end of the fifth year.[3] The present value of $28,800 at the end of year 5 discounted at 10 percent is $17,882. When this value is subtracted from the present value of cash outflows after taxes, the total present value under the borrowing alternative becomes $85,645. Thus, if an asset has a residual value, borrowing becomes relatively more attractive.

[3] For simplicity, we assume that the depreciation schedule is the same as before. If the depreciable life is longer than before, total tax payments during the five years will be greater, and net cash flows after taxes smaller.

460

PART VII

Longer-term
financing—
instruments
and markets

In our example above, we assumed straight-line depreciation. If the company uses accelerated depreciation, it obtains a greater tax shield in the early years and a lower one in later years. As a result, cash outflows after taxes in the early years are reduced relative to cash outflows in later years, and the present value of these outflows under the borrowing alternative is decreased. Thus, accelerated depreciation makes borrowing more attractive than it is with straight-line depreciation.

If the discussion so far seems strongly to suggest the borrowing alternative, this is not always the case. A company that has operating losses is unable to avail itself of the tax benefits associated with owning the asset. As a result, the effective cash outlay at time 0 would be $200,000 instead of the $180,000 shown in our example, for the investment tax credit would not be available. Also, such a firm may be unable to use as a tax shield all of the interest and depreciation charges shown in Table 20-3. Leasing may be advantageous to such a company, for the lessor may reduce the lease payments as a way of passing off to the lessee a goodly portion of the tax benefits associated with ownership. As the firm is unable to realize these tax benefits on its own, lease financing may well be the preferred alternative.

As we can see, deciding between leasing and borrowing can involve some rather extensive calculations. Each situation requires a separate analysis. The analysis is complicated if the two alternatives involve different amounts of financing. If we finance less than the total cost of the asset by borrowing, but finance 100 percent of the cost by leasing, we must consider the difference in the amount of financing both from the standpoint of explicit as well as implicit costs. These considerations and the others mentioned throughout this chapter can make the evaluation of lease financing rather detailed.

SUMMARY

Term financing generally is thought to include maturities of one to seven years. There are a number of sources of such financing. Commercial banks, insurance companies, and other institutional investors make term loans to business firms. Banks also provide financing under a revolving-credit arrangement, which represents a formal commitment on the part of the bank to lend up to a certain amount of money over a specified period of time. Lenders who offer unsecured credit usually impose restrictions on the borrower. These restrictions are called protective covenants and are contained in a loan agreement. If the borrower defaults under any of the provisions of the loan agreement, the lender may initiate immediate corrective measures. On a secured basis, firms can obtain intermediate-term financing by pledging equipment that they own or are purchasing. Banks, finance companies, and sellers of the equipment are active in providing this type of secured financing.

In lease financing, the lessee agrees to pay the lessor, periodically, for economic use of the lessor's asset. Because of this contractual obligation, leasing is regarded as a method of financing similar to borrowing. Leasing can involve the direct acquisition of an asset under a lease, a sale and leaseback arrangement, or a leveraged lease. The accounting treatment of leases and the tax implications were discussed.

One of the principal economic reasons for leasing is the inability of a firm to utilize all the tax benefits associated with ownership of an asset (depreciation and the investment tax credit). This can arise not only because of unprofitable operations but because earnings are not of sufficient size to effectively utilize all of the possible tax benefits. One means for analyzing lease financing in relation to debt financing is to discount to present value the net cash outflows after taxes under each alternative, using the risk-free rate as the discount rate. The preferred alternative is the one that provides the lower present value.

APPENDIX ∖ Accounting Treatment of Leases

The accounting treatment of leases has undergone sweeping change over the past two decades. Where once leases were not disclosed, gradually disclosure was required in the footnotes to the financial statement. With only minimal disclosure, leasing was attractive to certain firms as an "off balance sheet" method of financing. There was no evidence that such financing had a favorable effect on valuation, all other things the same; nevertheless, many a company proceeded on the assumption that "off balance sheet" financing was a good thing. Then came the Financial Accounting Standards Board Statement No. 13 in 1976 with an explicit ruling which called for the capitalization on the balance sheet of certain types of leases.[4] In essence, this statement says that if the lessee acquires essentially all of the economic benefits and risks of the leased property, then the value of the asset along with the corresponding lease liability must be shown on the balance sheet.

Capital and operating leases

Leases that conform in principle to this definition are called *capital leases*. More specifically, a lease is regarded as a capital lease if it meets any one of the following conditions:

1. The lease transfers title to the asset to the lessee by the end of the lease period.
2. The lease contains an option to purchase the asset at a bargain price.
3. The lease period is equal to or greater than 75 percent of the estimated economic life of the asset.
4. At the beginning of the lease the present value of the minimum lease payments equals or exceeds 90 percent of the fair value of the leased property to the lessor (minus any investment tax credit realized by the lessor).

If any of these conditions is met, the lessee is said to have acquired most of the economic benefits and risks associated with the leased property; therefore, a cap-

---

[4] *Statement of Financial Accounting Standards No. 13, Accounting for Leases* (Stamford, Conn.: Financial Accounting Standards Board, November 1976).

462

PART VII

Longer-term
financing—
instruments
and markets

ital lease is involved. If a lease does not meet one of these conditions, it is classified as an *operating lease*. Essentially, operating leases give the lessee the right to use the leased property over a period of time but they do not give the lessee all of the benefits and risks that are associated with the asset.

Determining the value of a capital lease. With a capital lease, the lessee must report the value of the leased property on the asset side of the balance sheet. The amount reflected is the present value of the minimum lease payments over the lease period. If executory costs, such as insurance, maintenance, and taxes are a part of the total lease payment, these are deducted and only the remainder is used for purposes of calculating the present value. As required by the accounting rules, the discount rate employed is the lower of (1) the lessee's incremental borrowing rate or (2) the lessor's implicit interest rate, if that rate can be determined.

These computations, for a company that wishes to lease a stamping machine, are illustrated in what follows. Lease payments of $15,336 are due at the beginning of each of the next 8 years. (The lease payments are due in advance.) The company's incremental borrowing rate is 8 percent. The cost of the machine to the lessor is $100,000, and the machine is not expected to have any residual value at the end of the lease period. The lessor will avail itself of the 10 percent investment tax credit and thereby realize $10,000 in tax savings at the time the asset is placed in service. The lessor's out-of-pocket cost is therefore $90,000. The implicit interest rate realized by the lessor can be determined by solving the following equation for r:

$$\$90,000 = \sum_{t=0}^{7} \frac{\$15,336}{(1 + r)^t} \qquad \text{(21A-1)}$$

Because lease payments are made in advance, the first payment can be thought of as being due at time 0 with 7 other payments due in yearly intervals. As a result, we turn to Table B at the end of the book for the present-value discount factors for an even stream of cash flows over 7 years. To the discount factor, we must add 1 because the payment at time 0 is not discounted. For an interest rate of 9 percent, we see that the discount factor shown in Table B is 5.0329, to which we add 1 to obtain a discount factor of 6.0329. Dividing $90,000 by 6.0329, we obtain $14,918. As this amount is less than the lease payment, we know the implicit interest rate must be higher. For 10 percent, the discount factor is 4.8684, to which we add 1 to obtain 5.8684. Dividing $90,000 by 5.8684, we obtain $15,336, exactly the lease payment. The lessor's implicit interest rate is 10 percent. By trial and error, then, we can determine the lessor's implied interest rate, provided we know the purchase price of the asset and certain other information.

As the lessor's implicit interest rate for our example is higher than the lessee's incremental borrowing rate of 8 percent, the latter would be used in determining the capitalized value of the lease. In most instances this will be the case. Insofar as is practical, the lessee must try to determine the lessor's implicit interest rate. When the implicit rate is less than the lessee's incremental borrowing rate, it must be used as the discount rate.

Given the amount of the lease payments and the discount rate to employ, one can easily determine the amount that should be recorded on the balance sheet for a capital lease. For our example, the present value at time 0, after the initial lease payment, is

$15,336 for seven years at 8% (5.2064 discount factor) = $79,845

Recording the capital lease on the balance sheet. This amount should be recorded as an asset on the lessee's balance sheet. (If the fair value of the leased property is lower than the present value of the minimum lease payments, then the fair value would be shown.) The associated lease obligation would be shown on the liability side of the balance sheet, with the present value of payments due within one year being reflected as current liabilities and the present value of payments due after one year being shown as noncurrent liabilities. The leased property may be combined with similar information on assets which are owned, but there must be a disclosure in a footnote with respect to the value of the leased property and its amortization. A hypothetical balance sheet might look like the following:

Assets		Liabilities	
Gross fixed assets*	$3,000,000	Current:	
Less accumulated depreciation and amortization	1,000,000	Obligations under capital leases	$ 90,000
Net fixed assets	$2,000,000	Noncurrent:	
		Obligations under capital assets	$270,000

*Gross fixed assets include leased property of $500,000. Accumulated depreciation and amortization includes $140,000 in amortization associated with such property.

In addition to this information, more details are required in footnotes. Relevant information here includes: the gross amounts of leased property by major property categories (these can be combined with categories of owned assets), the total future minimum lease payments, a schedule by years of future lease payments required over the next 5 years, the total minimum sublease rentals to be received, the existence and terms of purchase or renewal options and escalation clauses, rentals which are contingent on some factor other than the passage of time, and any restrictions imposed in the lease agreement.

Disclosure of operating leases. For operating leases, as for capital leases, some of the same disclosure is required, but it can be in footnotes. For non-cancellable leases having remaining terms in excess of one year, the lessee must disclose total future minimum lease payments, a schedule by year for the next 5 years, the total sublease rentals to be received, the basis for contingent rental payments, the existence and terms of purchase and renewal options and escalation clauses, and any lease agreement restrictions. The last two categories are included in a general description of the leasing arrangement.

464

PART VII

Longer-term
financing—
instruments
and markets

Amortizing the capital lease and reducing the obligation

A capital lease must be amortized and the liability reduced over the lease period. The method of amortization can be the lessee's usual depreciation method for assets which are owned. In our example, if the firm normally depreciates its assets on a straight-line basis, the annual amortization over the 8-year lease period would be ($79,845 + $15,336)/8 = $11,898. The $79,845 represents the present value of 7 future lease payments, whereas the $15,336 represents the initial lease payment at the outset. The amortization of $11,898 annually means that at the beginning of year 2, the value of the leased property is shown as $79,845 − $11,898 = $67,947, at the beginning of year 3 as $67,947 − $11,898 = $56,049, and so on. It should be pointed out that the period of amortization is always the lease term even if the economic life of the asset is longer. If the latter occurs, the asset has an expected residual value, which will go to the lessor.

FASB No. 13 also requires that the capital lease obligation be reduced over the lease period by the "interest" method. Under this method, each lease payment is separated into two components: the payment of principal and the payment of interest. The obligation is reduced by the amount of the principal payment. In our example, the firm had the obligation to pay $15,336 at the beginning of each year. Its incremental borrowing rate was 8 percent, and this rate is used as the discount rate.[5] Table 20A-1 shows the calculation of interest and principal payments. At the beginning of year 1, which represents the beginning of the lease period, the lease payment is represented entirely by a payment of principal. After that, interest is involved, but the proportional amount declines over the lease period.

TABLE 20A-1 ╲ **Illustration of the "interest" method to reduce the lease obligation**

Beginning of year	Lease payment	Principal payment	Principal amount owing at beginning of year	Annual interest at 8%
1	$15,336	$15,336	$79,845	0
2	15,336	8,949	70,896	$6,387
3	15,336	9,664	61,232	5,672
4	15,336	10,438	50,794	4,898
5	15,336	11,272	39,522	4,064
6	15,336	12,174	27,348	3,162
7	15,336	13,148	14,200	2,188
8	15,336	14,200	0	1,136

The reporting of earnings. For income tax reporting purposes, FASB No. 13 requires that both the amortization of the leased property and the annual interest embodied in the lease payment be treated as an expense. This expense

---

[5] If the fair value of the leased property is less than the present value of the net lease payments, using the incremental borrowing rate as the discount rate, then the interest rate used for amortization purposes is the rate of discount that equates the present value of the minimum lease payments with the fair value.

then is deducted in the same way that any expense is, to obtain net income. For our example, we would have the following lease expense at the end of each of the eight years (as opposed to the beginning):

End of year	Amortization of asset (straight line)	Annual interest (from Table 20A-1)	Annual lease expense
1	$11,898	$6,387	$18,285
2	11,898	5,672	17,570
3	11,898	4,898	16,796
4	11,898	4,064	15,962
5	11,898	3,162	15,060
6	11,897	2,188	14,085
7	11,897	1,136	13,033
8	11,897	0	11,897

This treatment differs from that for the operating lease, for which only the lease payment itself is deductible as an expense. It also differs from the way all leases were treated prior to FASB No. 13, when only the lease payment was deductible.

QUESTIONS

1. What reasons can you cite for the firm's use of intermediate-term debt? Why isn't long-term debt substituted in its place? Short-term debt?

2. Why do insurance companies not compete more actively with banks for short- and intermediate-term financing?

3. What is the purpose of protective covenants in a term-loan agreement?

4. How does a revolving credit agreement differ from a line of credit?

5. How should a lender go about setting the working-capital protective covenant in a loan agreement? the capital-expenditure covenant?

6. As a borrower, how would you negotiate over the working-capital and capital-expenditure restrictions a lender wished to impose?

7. What are the key financial institutions providing intermediate-term financing to business firms?

8. Chapter 1 suggests that the decision-making processes of investing funds (buying assets) and of raising funds (financing assets) are two separate and distinct functions of the financial manager. This chapter suggests that, at least in the case of leasing, the decision-making processes cannot be separated. Discuss the problems raised by this sort of situation and prepare your analytical method for making decisions in this situation.

9. Explain the concept of sale and leaseback. Compare this arrangement with a mortgage loan on the leased asset.

466

PART VII

Longer-term
financing—
instruments
and markets

10. Discuss the probable impact that a sale and leaseback arrangement will have on

   a)   Liquidity ratios

   b)   Return on investment

   c)   Return on equity

   d)   The risk class of the corporation's stock

   e)   The price of the stock

11. Some businesspeople consider that the risk of obsolescence and inflexibility is being transferred from the lessee to the lessor. How is the lessor induced to accept higher risk and greater inflexibility?

12. In your opinion, would the following factors tend to favor borrowing or leasing as a financing alternative? Why?

   a)   Increased corporate tax rate

   b)   Accelerated depreciation

   c)   Rising price level

   d)   Increased residual value of the leased asset

   e)   An increase in the risk-free interest rate

13. The Economic Recovery Tax Act of 1981 provided for a much quicker recovery period for depreciation. Does the faster write-off of capital investments make lease financing more attractive or less attractive than debt financing?

PROBLEMS

1. Zenda Fashions Corporation wishes to borrow $600,000 on a 5-year term basis. Oysterman's National Bank is willing to make such a loan at a 14 percent rate, provided the loan is completely amortized over the 5-year period. Payments are due at the end of each of the five years. Set up an amortization schedule of equal annual loan payments that will satisfy the above. Be sure to show both the principal and interest components of each of the overall payments.

2. On January 1, Sharpe Razor Corporation is contemplating a 4-year, $3 million term loan from the Fidelity First National Bank. The loan is payable at the end of the fourth year and would involve a loan agreement that would contain a number of protective covenants. Among these restrictions are that the company must maintain working capital of $3 million at all times, that it cannot take on any more long-term debt, that its total liabilities cannot be more than .6 of its total assets, and that capital expenditures in any year are limited to depreciation plus $3 million. The company's balance sheet at December 31, before the term loan, is

Current assets	$ 7 million	Current liabilities	$ 3 million
Net fixed assets	10 million	Long-term debt (due in 5 years)	5 million
		Net worth	9 million
	$17 million		$17 million

The proceeds of the term loan will be used to increase Sharpe's investment in inventories and receivables in response to introducing a new "closer-to-the-face" razor blade. The company anticipates a subsequent need to grow at a rate of 24 percent a year, equally divided between current assets and net fixed assets. Profits after taxes of $1.5 million are expected this year, and these profits are expected to grow by $250,000 per year over the subsequent three years. The company pays no dividends and does not intend to pay any over the next four years. Depreciation in the past year was $2.5 million, and this is predicted to grow over the next four years at the same rate as the increase in net fixed assets.

Under the loan agreement, will the company be able to achieve its growth objective?

3. Given the following information, compute the annual lease payment (paid in advance) that a lessor will require:

   a) Purchase price of $260,000, interest rate of 13 percent, 5-year lease period, and no residual value

   b) Purchase price of $138,000, interest rate of 6 percent, 9-year lease period, and a near-certain residual value of $20,000

   c) Purchase price of $773,000, interest rate of 9 percent, 10-year lease period, and no residual value

4. Bork Electronics Company is considering leasing one of its products in addition to selling it outright to customers. The product, the Zeus Tester, sells for $18,600 and has an economic life of 8 years.

   a) In order to earn 12 percent interest, what annual lease payment must Bork require as lessor? (Assume lease payments are payable in advance.)

   b) If the product has a salvage value (known with certainty) of $4,000 at the end of 8 years, what annual lease payment will be required?

5. The Baker Tool Company, which has a 40 percent tax rate, wishes to acquire a $100,000 stamping machine. This machine would be depreciated on a straight-line basis with a 5-year life but no salvage value. An investment tax credit of 10 percent is available to the company at the time the machine is placed into service. The company can lease the machine for $21,500 per year, payable in advance. It also can purchase the asset and borrow the $100,000 less the tax credit, or $90,000, at 15 percent; this would require annual debt payments of $26,848 the first four payments and $26,850 the last. Which is the superior method of financing if the risk-free rate is 10 percent?

6. In problem 6, which would be the superior method of financing if Baker Tool Company used sum-of-the-years'-digits depreciation with all other conditions the same? (See chapter 2 for an explanation of how to compute depreciation using the sum-of-the-years'-digits method.)

APPENDIX PROBLEM

7. Conrad Reduction Company has just leased a press that calls for annual lease payments of $40,000 payable in advance. The lease period is 9 years, and the leased property is classified as a capital lease. The company's incremental borrowing rate is 7 percent, whereas the lessor's implied interest rate is 12 percent. The company depreciates all of its owned assets on a straight-line basis. On the basis of this information, compute

   a) The value of the leased property to be shown on the balance sheet after the initial lease payment.

   b) The annual lease expense in each year as it will appear on the accounting income statement.

SELECTED REFERENCES

ANDERSON, PAUL F., and JOHN D. MARTIN, "Lease vs. Purchase Decisions: A Survey of Current Practice," *Financial Management,* 6 (Spring 1977), 41–47.

BOWER, RICHARD S., "Issues in Lease Financing," *Financial Management,* 2 (Winter 1973), 25–34.

——, FRANK C. HERRINGER, and J. PETER WILLIAMSON, "Lease Evaluation," *Accounting Review,* 41 (April 1966), 257–65.

BOWER, RICHARD S., and GEORGE S. OLDFIELD, JR., "Of Lessees, Lessors, and Discount Rates and Whether Pigs Have Wings," *Journal of Business Research,* 9 (March 1981), 29–38.

BREALEY, R. A., and C. M. YOUNG, "Debt, Taxes and Leasing—A Note," *Journal of Finance,* 35 (December 1980), 1245–50.

CAPETTINI, ROBERT, and HOWARD TOOLE, "Designing Leveraged Leases: A Mixed Integer Linear Programming Approach," *Financial Management,* 10 (Autumn 1981), 15–23.

CRAWFORD, PEGGY J., CHARLES P. HARPER, and JOHN J. McCONNELL, "Further Evidence on the Terms of Financial Leases," *Financial Management,* 10 (Autumn 1981), 7–14.

DYL, EDWARD A., and STANLEY A. MARTIN, JR., "Setting Terms for Leveraged Leasing," *Financial Management,* 6 (Winter 1977), 20–27.

FINDLAY, M. CHAPMAN, III, "A Sensitivity Analysis of IRR Leasing Models," *Engineering Economist,* 20 (Summer 1975), 231–42.

GAUMNITZ, JACK E., and ALLEN FORD, "The Lease or Sell Decision," *Financial Manager,* 7 (Winter 1978), 69–74.

GILL, RICHARD C., "Term Loan Agreements," *Journal of Commercial Bank Lending,* 62 (February 1980), 22–27.

GORDON, MYRON J., "A General Solution to the Buy or Lease Decision: A Pedagogical Note," *Journal of Finance,* 29 (March 1974).

IDOL, CHARLES R., "A Note on Specifying Debt Displacement and Tax Shield Borrowing Opportunities in Financial Lease Valuation Models," *Financial Management,* 9 (Summer 1980), 24–29.

JOHNSON, ROBERT W., and WILBUR G. LEWELLEN, "Analysis of the Lease-or-Buy Decision," *Journal of Finance,* 27 (September 1972), 815–23.

KIM, E. HAN, WILBUR G. LEWELLEN, and JOHN J. McCONNELL, "Sale and Leaseback Agreements and Enterprise Valuation," *Journal of Financial and Quantitative Analysis,* 13 (December, 1978), 871–84.

LEWELLEN, WILBUR G., and DOUGLAS R. EMERY, "On the Matter of Parity Among Financial Obligations," *Journal of Finance,* 36 (March 1981), 97–111.

LEWELLEN, WILBUR G., MICHAEL S. LONG, and JOHN J. McCONNELL, "Asset Leasing in Competitive Capital Markets," *Journal of Finance,* 31 (June 1976), 787–98.

LONG, MICHAEL S., "Leasing and the Cost of Capital," *Journal of Financial and Quantitative Analysis,* 12 (November 1977), 579–86.

MIDDLETON, J. WILLIAM, "Term Lending—Practical and Profitable," *Journal of Commercial Bank Lending,* 50 (August 1968), 31–43.

MILLER, MERTON H., and CHARLES W. UPTON, "Leasing, Buying, and the Cost of Capital Services," *Journal of Finance,* 31 (June 1976), 787–98.

MOYER, R. CHARLES, "Lease Financing and the Investment Tax Credit: A Framework for Analysis," *Financial Management,* 4 (Summer 1975), 39–44.

MYERS, STEWART C., DAVID A. DILL, and ALBERTO J. BAUTISTA, "Valuation of Financial Lease Contracts," *Journal of Finance,* 31 (June 1976), 799–820.

OFFER, AHARON R., "The Evaluation of the Lease versus Purchase Alternatives," *Financial Management,* 5 (Summer 1976), 67–74.

PACKHAM, E. RICHARD, "An Analysis of the Risks of Leveraged Leasing," *Journal of Commercial Bank Lending,* 57 (March 1975), 2–29.

ROENFELDT, RODNEY L., and JEROME S. OSTERYOUNG, "Analysis of Financial Leases," *Financial Management,* 2 (Spring 1973), 74–87.

SCHALL, LAWRENCE D., "The Lease-or-Buy and Asset Acquisition Decisions," *Journal of Finance,* 29 (September 1974), 1203–14.

SMITH, CLIFFORD W., JR., and JEROLD B. WARNER, "On Financial Contracting: An Analysis of Bond Covenants," *Journal of Financial Economics,* 7 (June 1980), 117–61.

SORENSEN, IVAR W., and RAMON E. JOHNSON, "Equipment Financial Leasing Practices and Costs: An Empirical Study," *Financial Management,* 6 (Spring 1977), 33–40.

VANCIL, RICHARD F., "Lease or Borrow: New Method of Analysis," *Harvard Business Review,* 39 (September–October 1961),122–36.

VAN HORNE, JAMES, "A Linear-Programming Approach to Evaluating Restrictions under a Bond Indenture or Loan Agreement," *Journal of Financial and Quantitative Analysis,* 1 (June 1966), 68–83.

———, "The Cost of Leasing with Capital Market Imperfections," *Engineering Economist,* 23 (Fall 1977), 1–12.

———, "Optimal Initiation of Bankruptcy Proceedings by Debtholders," *Journal of Finance,* 31 (June 1976), 897–910.

WIAR, ROBERT C., "Economic Implications of Multiple Rates of Return in the Leverage Lease Contest," *Journal of Finance,* 28 (December 1973), 1275–86.

ZIMMERMAN, CHARLES S., "An Approach to Writing Loan Agreement Covenants," *Journal of Commercial Bank Lending,* 58 (November 1975), 2–17.

Long-term debt

21

As we look into long-term debt issues having an original maturity of more than 10 years, we first take up their features, move on to various types of instruments, and then explore the nature of the call provision. Finally, we shall analyze the profitability of refunding an existing bond issue.

FEATURES OF DEBT

The fixed return of a long-term debt instrument is denoted by the *coupon rate*. A 13 percent debenture indicates that the issuer will pay bondholders $130 per annum for every $1,000-face-value bond they hold. The *yield to maturity* on a bond is determined by solving for the rate of discount that equates the present value of principal and interest payments with the current market price of the bond. (See chapter 4 for the mathematics of bond interest.)

A company issuing bonds to the public designates a qualified *trustee* to represent the interests of the bondholders. The obligations of a trustee are specified in the Trust Indenture Act of 1939, administered by the Securities and Exchange Commission. The trustee's responsibilities are to authenticate the bond issue's legality at the time of issuance, to watch over the financial condition and behavior of the borrower to make sure all contractual obligations are carried out, and to initiate appropriate actions if the borrower does not meet any of these obligations. The trustee is compensated directly by the corporation, a compensation that adds to the costs of borrowing.

The legal agreement between the corporation issuing the bonds and the trustee, who represents the boldholders, is defined in the *indenture*. The indenture contains the terms of the bond issue as well as the restrictions placed upon the company. These restrictions, known as *protective covenants*, are very similar to those contained in a term-loan agreement. Because we analyzed protective covenants in chapter 20, it is not necessary to describe them here. The terms contained in the indenture are established jointly by the borrower and trustee. If the issue is a negotiated underwriting, the underwriter also will be involved. If the corporation defaults under any of the provisions of the indenture, the trustee, on behalf of the bondholders, can take action to correct the situation. If not satisfied, the trustee then can call for the immediate payment of all outstanding bonds.

Retirement

The retirement of bonds may be accomplished in a number of ways: by payment at final maturity, by conversion if the bonds are convertible, by calling the bonds if there is a call feature, or by periodic repayment. Periodic repayment of the debt is possible with either a sinking-fund issue or a serial bond issue. Conversion is discussed in chapter 23, and calling is examined later in this chapter, so let us turn now to sinking-fund and serial bonds.

Sinking funds.   The majority of corporate bond issues carry a provision for a sinking fund which requires the corporation to make periodic sinking-fund payments to a trustee, in order to retire a specified face amount of bonds each period. Payments can be cash or bonds that the company purchases in the open market. The trustee uses cash to call bonds for redemption. Usually, bonds are called on a lottery basis by their serial numbers, which are published in *The Wall Street Journal* and other papers. The corporation should purchase the bonds in the open market as long as the market price is less than the call price; when the market price exceeds the call price, it should make cash payments to the trustee.

Because of the orderly retirement of debt as well as the liquidity provided by the regular purchase activity, many investors find the sinking-fund provision valuable. In general, sinking-fund bonds yield less than comparable bond issues that have no sinking-fund provision,[1] partly because of the shorter duration. Many sinking funds begin not at the time of issuance of the bond, but after a period of 5 or 10 years. Also, sinking-fund payments do not necessarily retire the bond issue. There can be a "balloon" payment at final maturity.

Some corporations, in purchasing bonds for sinking-fund payment, find that *accumulators* have got there first. Accumulators are institutional or other investors who buy bonds in advance of the corporation going into the market to acquire them for sinking funds. If supply is sufficiently restricted, the corporation

---

[1] For empirical support of this phenomenon, see Edward A. Dyl and Michael D. Joehnk, "Sinking Funds and the Cost of Corporate Debt," *Journal of Finance*, 34 (September 1979), 887–93.

472

PART VII
Longer-term
financing—
instruments
and markets

will be able to purchase bonds only by bidding up the price. In this way, the accumulator hopes to sell the bonds at an inflated price, knowing the corporation must purchase them in order to satisfy the sinking-fund requirement. Though perfectly legal, accumulators are not looked upon with great favor by financial managers. Only when the bonds sell at a discount from the sinking-fund call price, of course, does accumulation occur. Otherwise, the corporation will make a cash payment to the trustee, who will purchase bonds at the call price.

The amount of required sinking-fund payment may be either fixed or variable, depending upon the terms in the indenture. Under the fixed arrangement, the corporation retires a fixed face amount of bonds each period. Variable periodic sinking-fund payments are those that are not equal in amount. These payments may be tied to the earnings of the corporation, so that the greater the earnings, the greater the sinking-fund payment. This variability obviously is appealing to a company and its stockholders. In periods of poor earnings, the company is not constrained by the need to make a fixed sinking-fund payment. Bondholders, of course, would prefer fixed payments, because they assure a steady reduction of the debt. A borrower who cannot meet these payments is in clear default under the terms of the indenture. This default enables the trustee to take corrective actions. The amount of sinking-fund payment may vary also with the number of years to final maturity. For some bond issues the amount of sinking-fund payment may increase over the years; for others it may decrease. Overall, variable sinking-fund payments are employed far less often than are fixed payments.

Serial bonds.   All sinking-fund bonds in an issue mature on the same date, although specific bonds are retired before that date. Serial bonds mature periodically until final maturity; a $20 million issue of serial bonds might have $1 million of the bonds maturing each year for 20 years. Giving investors a choice of maturity that best suits their needs, a serial bond issue appeals to a larger group of investors than does an issue in which all the bonds have the same maturity. However, serial bonds are seldom used by corporations. Their principal use is found in the municipal bond market.

TYPES OF DEBT INSTRUMENTS

Debentures

The word *debenture* usually applies to the unsecured bonds of a corporation. Investors look to the earning power of the corporation as their security. Because these general credit bonds are not secured by specific property, in the event of liquidation the holder becomes a general creditor. Although the bonds are unsecured, debenture holders are protected by the restrictions imposed in the indenture, particularly the negative pledge clause, which precludes the corporation from pledging its assets to other creditors. This provision safeguards the investor in that the borrower's assets will not be impaired in the future. Because debenture holders must look to the general credit of the borrower to meet principal and interest payments, only well-established and credit-worthy companies are able to issue debentures.

Subordinated debentures

Subordinated debentures represent debt that ranks behind debt senior to these debentures with respect to the claim on assets. In the event of liquidation, subordinated debenture holders receive settlement only if all senior creditors are paid the full amount owed them. These holders still would rank ahead of preferred and common stockholders in the event of liquidation. The existence of subordinated debentures works to the advantage of senior bondholders, because senior holders are able to assume the claims of the subordinated debenture holders. To illustrate: a corporation is liquidated for $600,000. It had $400,000 in straight debentures outstanding, $400,000 in subordinated debentures outstanding, and $400,000 in obligations owed to general creditors. One might suppose that the straight debenture holders and the general creditors would have an equal and prior claim in liquidation, that each would receive $300,000. The fact is, the straight debenture holders are entitled to the subordinated debenture holders' claims, giving them $800,000 in total claims. As a result, they are entitled to two-thirds of the liquidating value, or $400,000; whereas general creditors are entitled to only one-third or $200,000.

Because subordinated debentures are subordinate to all existing and future debt, senior creditors regard them as equity when evaluating the financial condition of the company. In fact, subordinated debt usually is employed to increase the equity base and support further borrowing. The popularity of the instrument stems in part from the fact that interest payments are deductible for tax purposes, whereas dividends on preferred stock, the closest substitute method of financing, are not.

Because of the nature of the claim, a straight subordinated debenture issue has to provide a yield significantly higher than a regular debenture issue in order to be attractive to investors. Frequently, subordinated debentures are convertible into common stock and therefore may sell at a yield that actually is less than what the company would have to pay on an ordinary debenture. From the standpoint of a creditor, the equity base of the firm is the same whether the issue remains as subordinated debentures or is converted into common stock.

Mortgage bonds

A mortgage bond issue is secured by a lien on specific assets of the corporation—usually fixed assets. The specific property securing the bonds is described in detail in the mortgage, which is the legal document giving the bondholder a lien on the property. As with other secured lending arrangements, the market value of the collateral should exceed the amount of the bond issue by a reasonable margin of safety. If the corporation defaults in any of the provisions of the bond indenture, the trustee, on behalf of the bondholders, has the power to foreclose. In a foreclosure, the trustee takes over the property and sells it, using the proceeds to pay the bonds. If the proceeds are less than the amount of the issue outstanding, the bondholders become general creditors for the residual amount.

A company may have more than one bond issue secured by the same property. A bond issue may be secured by a *second mortgage* on property already used to secure another bond issue under a *first mortgage*. In the event of fore-

474

PART VII

Longer-term
financing—
instruments
and markets

closure, the first-mortgage bondholders must be paid the full amount owed them before there can be any distribution to the second-mortgage bondholders. For the obvious reason of lack of appeal to investors, second-mortgage bonds seldom are used.

Income bonds

A company is obligated to pay interest on an income bond only when it is earned. There may be a cumulative feature in the issue where unpaid interest in a particular year accumulates. If the company does generate earnings, it will have to pay the cumulative interest to the extent that earnings permit. However, the cumulative obligation usually is limited to no more than 3 years. As should be evident, this type of security offers the investor a rather weak promise of a fixed return. Nevertheless, the income bond is still senior to preferred and common stock, as well as to any subordinated debt. Unlike preferred-stock dividends, the interest payment is deductible for tax purposes. Because income bonds are not popular with investors, they have been used principally in reorganizations.[2]

Equipment trust certificates

Although equipment trust financing is a form of lease financing, the certificates themselves represent an intermediate- to long-term fixed-income investment. This method of financing is used by railroads to finance the acquisition of rolling stock. Under this method, the railroad arranges with a trustee to purchase equipment from a manufacturer. The railroad signs a contract with the manufacturer for the construction of specific equipment. When the equipment is delivered, equipment trust certificates are sold to investors. The proceeds of this sale, together with the down payment by the railroad, are used to pay the manufacturer. Title to the equipment is held by the trustee, who in turn leases the equipment to the railroad. Lease payments are used by the trustee to pay a fixed return on the certificates outstanding—actually a dividend—and to retire a specified portion of the certificates at regular intervals. Upon the final lease payment by the railroad, the last of the certificates is retired, and title to the equipment passes to the railroad.

The duration of the lease varies according to the equipment involved, but 15 years is rather common. Because rolling stock is essential to the operation of a railroad and has a ready market value, equipment trust certificates enjoy a very high standing as fixed-income investments. As a result, railroads are able to acquire cars and locomotives on favorable financing terms. Airlines, too, use a form of equipment trust certificate to finance jet aircraft. Though these certificates are usually sold to institutional investors, some issues are sold to the public.

Industrial development and pollution control bonds

With industrial development and pollution control bonds, a local government establishes an agency for a project. In the case of the former type of bond, the

---

[2] For an extensive analysis of income bonds, see John J. McConnell and Gary G. Schlarbaum, "Returns, Risks, and Pricing of Income Bonds," *Journal of Business*, 54 (January 1981), 33–57.

project usually is the construction of a plant. The purpose of the local government is to attract industry to the area and thereby increase employment. In the case of the latter type of bond, the project usually is the addition of pollution control equipment to an existing plant. For example, such equipment might be a "scrubber" for the smoke generated by an electric utility. If the project conforms to federal regulations, the agency is empowered to issue municipal securities whose interest is tax exempt to finance the project. The agency leases the plant or equipment to the corporation. The bonds issued are backed by the lease payments, and, hence, by the credit worthiness of the company involved, but not by the general taxing power of the municipality.

The advantage of this arrangement to the company is that the borrowing rate is lower (because interest payments on the bonds are tax exempt) than it would be if the company borrowed directly to finance the project. Most of the savings in borrowing costs are passed on to the company through lower lease payments. The company therefore enjoys lower financing costs than it would with direct financing. Despite this attraction, in recent years the U.S. Department of Treasury has taken steps to curtail this type of financing. Clearly, the ultimate intention is to eliminate such financing altogether. It represents borrowing by corporations, not by municipalities, for whom the tax-exempt feature was intended.

Project financing

The term *project financing* describes various financing arrangements for large, individual investment projects. Often a separate legal entity is formed to own the project. Suppliers of capital then look to the earnings stream of the project for repayment of their loan or for the return on their equity investment. With the energy problems of recent years, there has come the need to finance not only large explorations of gas, oil, and coal but also tankers, port facilities, refineries, and pipelines. Other projects include alumina plants, fertilizer plants, and nuclear plants. These projects require huge amounts of capital, which a single company cannot usually supply. Many times a consortium of companies is formed to spread risk and to finance the project. Part of the funds come from equity participations by the companies, and the rest come from lenders or lessors.

If the loan or lease is on a nonrecourse basis, the lender or lessor pays exclusive attention to the size of the equity participation and to the economic feasibility of the project. In other words, the lender or lessor can look only to the project for payout, so the larger the equity cushion and the more confidence that can be placed in the projections, the better the project. Sometimes the project's sponsors will write "comfort" letters giving general assurance that they will do their best to make the project a success. The letters are not legally binding, although they do represent a moral commitment.

One risk is that the project will be seriously delayed, pushing the completion date and the start of cash flows far into the future. For this reason, the project's sponsors sometimes are required to guarantee its timely completion with suitable remedies to the lender or lessor if such does not occur. After its completion, suppliers of capital are on their own. Repayment must come from the project's earnings, so the economic feasibility of the project continues to be of

476

PART VII
Longer-term
financing—
instruments
and markets

major concern.[3] In still another type of arrangement, each sponsor may guarantee its share of the project's obligations. Under these circumstances, the lender or lessor places emphasis on the credit worthiness of the sponsors as well as upon the economic feasibility of the project.

For the sponsors of the project, there are several types of sharing rules. In a "take-or-pay" type of arrangement, each sponsor agrees to purchase a specific percentage of the ouput of the project and to pay that percentage of the operating costs of the project plus debt-servicing charges. In a "through put" arrangement, which frequently involves pipelines, each sponsor is required to ship through the facility a certain amount, or percentage, of product. If the total shipped is insufficient to cover the expenses of running the facility, sponsors are assessed additional amounts to cover the shortfall. The amount of assessment is proportional to their participation. The maturity of the loan or lease corresponds to the likely ability of the project to generate cash over time. While the financing need not be long-term, in most cases it extends over 8 or more years.

Actually, the term *project financing* conveys nothing more than the financing of a large project. The methods of financing are no different from those we have studied. They include debt and lease financing. What is different is the size and complexity of the financing. It is tailored to the needs of the sponsors as well as to the needs of potential suppliers of capital. Tax considerations rank very high in tailoring the financing to the best advantage of all parties. The key is that the project stands alone in the sense that the sponsoring companies are liable for no more than their equity participations and their obligations under a "through put" arrangement if such exists.

CALL PROVISION

Nearly all corporate bond issues provide for a call feature, which gives the corporation the option to buy back the bonds at a stated price before their maturity. The call price usually is above the par value of the bond and decreases over time. A bond with 20 years to maturity might be callable at $110 ($1,100 per $1,000-face-value bond) the next two years, $109 the following two years, and so on until the final two years, when it is callable at $101. Frequently, the call price in the first year is established at one year's interest above the face value of the bond. If the coupon rate is 14 percent, the initial call price may be $114 ($1,140 per $1,000 face value).

There are two types of call provision, according to when they can be exercised. The security may be immediately callable, which simply means that the instrument may be bought back by the issuer at the call price at any time. Rather than being immediately callable, the call provision may be deferred for a period of time. The most widely used deferred call periods are five years for public utility bonds and ten years for industrial bonds. During this deferment period, the investor is protected from a call by the issuer. In recent years, virtually all issues of

---

[3] For further discussion of these two kinds of arrangements, see Grover R. Castle, "Project Financing—Guidelines for the Commercial Banker," *Journal of Commercial Bank Lending*, 57 (April 1975), 14–30.

corporate bonds have involved a deferred-call as opposed to an immediate-call feature.

The call provision gives the company flexibility in its financing. If interest rates should decline significantly, it can call the bonds and refinance the issue at a lower interest cost. Thus, the company does not have to wait until the final maturity to refinance. In addition, the provision may be advantageous to the company if it finds any of the protective covenants in the bond indenture to be unduly restrictive. By calling the bonds before maturity, the company can eliminate these restrictions. Of course, if the issue is refinanced with bonds, similar restrictions may be imposed.

Value of call privilege

Although the call privilege is beneficial to the issuing corporation, it works to the detriment of investors. If interest rates fall and the bond issue is called, they can invest in other bonds only at a sacrifice in yield to maturity. Consequently, the call privilege usually does not come free to the borrower. Its cost, or value, is measured at the time of issuance by the difference in yield on the callable bond and the yield that would be necessary if the security were noncallable. This value is determined by supply and demand forces in the market for callable securities.

When interest rates are high and expected to fall, the call feature is likely to have significant value. Investors are unwilling to invest in callable bonds unless such bonds yield more than bonds that are noncallable, all other things the same. In other words, they must be compensated for assuming the risk that the bonds might be called. On the other hand, borrowers are willing to pay a premium in yield for the call privilege in the belief that yields will fall and that it will be advantageous to refund the bonds.

When interest rates are low and expected to rise, the call privilege may have a negligible value in that the company might pay the same yield if there were no call privilege. For the privilege to have value, interest rate expectations must make it seem possible that the issue will be called. If interest rates are low and not expected to fall further, there is little probability that the bonds will be called. The key factor is that the borrower has to be able to refund the issue at a profit; and that cannot be done unless interest rates drop significantly, for the issuer must pay the call price—which is usually at a premium above par value—as well as the flotation costs involved in refinancing. If there is no probability that the borrower can refund the issue at a profit, the call privilege is unlikely to have a value.

REFUNDING A BOND ISSUE

In this section, we analyze the profitability of a company's refunding a bond issue before its maturity. By *refunding* we mean calling the issue and replacing it with a new issue of bonds. In this regard, we focus our attention on only one reason for refunding—profitability—which, in turn, is due to interest rates' having declined since the bonds were issued. Occasionally, other reasons prompt companies to refund outstanding bonds. Sometimes a company will refund a bond issue

478

PART VII

Longer-term
financing—
instruments
and markets

simply to eliminate overly restrictive protective covenants in the bond indenture. This assumes, of course, that the protective covenants in the new bond indenture will be less onerous.

Another reason, and usually an unfortunate one, is to show higher reported profits in an accounting sense. The difference between the purchase price of the old bonds and their book value is treated as income in the year in which the bonds are called. If a bond had a book value of $1,000 and interest rates rose so that it could be acquired in the market at a discount, say at $900, the reported income on the transaction would be $100. Since the bond needs to be replaced with one which bears a higher interest rate, the present value of interest payments will be higher, and the company generally will be worse off in an economic sense because of transaction costs. Presumably, the motivation is to "fool the market" in the short run at the expense of higher interest costs in the long run. It is doubtful that even in the short run the market is fooled, so let us spend our time on the economic motivation for refunding.

A refunding example

The refunding decision can be regarded as a form of capital budgeting: there is an initial cash outlay followed by future interest savings. These savings are represented by the difference between the annual net cash outflow required under the old bonds and the net cash outflow required on the new, or refunding, bonds. Calculating the initial cash outlay is more complex. Consequently, it is best to show an example of this method of evaluation.[4]

A company currently has a $20 million, 12 percent debenture issue outstanding, and the issue still has 20 years to final maturity. Because interest rates are significantly lower than at the time of the original offering, the company can now sell a $20 million issue of 20-year bonds at a coupon rate of 10 percent that will net it $19,600,000 after the underwriting spread.

For federal income tax purposes, the unamortized issuing expense of the old bonds, the call premium, and the unamortized discount of the old bonds, if they were sold at a discount, are deductible as expenses in the year of the refunding. The old bonds were sold 5 years ago at a $250,000 discount from par value, so that the unamortized portion now is $200,000. Moreover, the legal fees and other issuing expenses involved with the old bonds have an unamortized balance of $100,000. The call price on the old bonds is $109, issuing expenses on the new bonds are $150,000, the income tax rate is 50 percent, and there is a 30-day period of overlap. The period of overlap is the lag between the time the new bonds are sold and the time the old bonds are called. This lag occurs because most companies wish to have the proceeds from the new issue in hand before they call the old issue. Otherwise, there is a certain amount of risk associated with calling the old issue and being at the "mercy" of the bond market in raising new funds. During the period of overlap, the company pays interest on both bond issues.

---

[4] This section draws upon Oswald D. Bowlin, "The Refunding Decision: Another Special Case in Capital Budgeting," *Journal of Finance,* 21 (March 1966), 55–68. Its development assumes the reader has covered chapter 13.

Framework for analysis.   With this rather involved background information in mind, we can calculate the initial cash outflow and the future cash benefits. The net cash outflow at the time of the refunding is as follows:

Cost of calling old bonds (call price $109)		$21,800,000
Net proceeds of new bond issue		19,600,000
Difference		$ 2,200,000
Expenses:		
Issuing expense of new bonds	$ 150,000	
Interest expense on old bonds during overlap period	200,000	350,000
Gross cash outlay		$ 2,550,000
Less tax savings:		
Interest expense on old bonds during overlap period	200,000	
Call premium	1,800,000	
Unamortized discount on old bonds	200,000	
Unamortized issuing expenses on old bonds	100,000	
Total	$2,300,000	
Tax savings (50% of amount above)		1,150,000
Net cash outflow		$ 1,400,000

The annual net cash benefits may be determined by calculating the difference between the net cash outflow required on the old bonds and the net cash outflow required on the new or refunding bonds. We assume for simplicity that interest is paid but once a year, at year end. The annual net cash outflow on the old bonds is

Interest expense 12%		$2,400,000
Less tax savings:		
Interest expense	$2,400,000	
Amortization of bond discount ($200,000/20)	10,000	
Amortization of issuing costs ($100,000/20)	5,000	
Total	$2,415,000	
Tax savings (50% of amount above)		$1,207,500
Annual net cash outflow—old bonds		$1,192,500

For the new bonds, the bond discount as well as the issuing costs may be amortized for tax purposes in the same manner as were the old bonds. The annual net cash outflow on the new bonds is shown in the table on the next page.

480

PART VII

Longer-term
financing—
instruments
and markets

Interest expense 10%		$2,000,000
Less tax savings:		
Interest expense	$2,000,000	
Amortization of bond discount ($400,000/20)	20,000	
Amortization of issuing costs ($150,000/20)	7,500	
Total	$2,027,500	
Tax savings (50% of amount above)		1,013,750
Annual net cash outflow—new bonds		$ 986,250
Difference between annual net cash outflows ($1,192,500–$986,250)		$ 206,250

Discounting. Thus, for an initial net cash outflow of $1.4 million, the company can achieve annual net cash benefits of $206,250 over the next 20 years. Because the net cash benefits occur in the future, they must be discounted back to present value. But what discount rate should be used? Certain authors advocate the use of the cost of capital. However, a refunding operation differs from other investment proposals. Once the new bonds are sold, the net cash benefits are known with certainty. From the standpoint of the corporation, the refunding operation is essentially a riskless investment project. The only risk associated with the cash flows is that of the firm's defaulting in the payment of principal or interest. Because a premium for default risk is embodied in the market rate of interest the firm pays, the appropriate discount rate might be the after-tax cost of borrowing on the refunding bonds. Using this cost, 10% (1 − 0.50) = 5 percent, as our discount factor, the refunding operation would be worthwhile if the net present value were positive.[5] For our example, the net present value is $1,170,328, indicating that the refunding operation is worthwhile. The internal rate of return is 13.58 percent, indicating again that the refunding is worthwhile, because the internal rate of return exceeds the required rate of 5 percent.

Other considerations

Just because a refunding operation is found to be worthwhile, it should not necessarily be undertaken right away. If interest rates are declining, and this decline is expected to continue, management may prefer to delay the refunding. At a later date, the refunding bonds can be sold at an even lower rate of interest, making the refunding operation even more worthwhile. The decision concerning timing must be based upon expectations of future interest rates.

Finally, two points should be raised with respect to the calculations in our example. First, most firms refund an existing issue with a new bond issue of a longer maturity. In our example, we assumed that the new bond issue had the same maturity as that of the old bond issue. Our analysis needs to be modified slightly when the maturity dates are different. The usual procedure is to consider only the net cash benefits up to the maturity of the old bonds. A second assump-

---

[5] We recall from chapter 13 that the net present value is the present value of net cash benefits less the initial cash outflow.

bonds. If either issue calls for periodic reduction of the debt, we must adjust our procedure for determining future net cash benefits.

SUMMARY

The principal features of debt include the fixed return, the priority of claim on assets, the call privilege, and the method of retirement of the debt. Periodic reduction of the debt can be accomplished by issuing either sinking-fund bonds or serial bonds. Types of debt financing include debentures, subordinated debentures, mortgage bonds, collateral trust bonds, income bonds, equipment trust certificates, and project financing.

In financing with long-term debt, the company must bargain with investors over the terms of the debt instrument. If the company wishes to include terms that are not beneficial to investors, it must be prepared to pay a higher yield in order to sell the instrument. If debentures are subordinated, investors will demand a higher yield than if the issue involves straight debentures. Another interesting aspect of the bargaining process between the borrower and the investors relates to the call privilege. If interest-rate expectations in the market lead investors to think that the issue may be called, the company will have to pay a higher yield for the privilege of being able to call it.

In the last section of the chapter, a method was proposed for analyzing the refunding of an existing bond issue before maturity. This method treats the refunding operation as a riskless capital-budgeting project.

QUESTIONS

1. Contrast serial bonds and bonds requiring a sinking fund.

2. In the refunding decision, differential cash flows are discounted at the after-tax cost of debt. Explain why these cash flows are not discounted at the average cost of capital.

3. Explain why a commercial bank loan officer would be particularly concerned with subordinating debt owed to the principal stockholders or officers of a company.

4. Which of the principal features of bond issues would you seek as a borrower and avoid as a lender under the following circumstances?

   a) A continuing period of inflation

   b) A period of declining interest rates

   c) Considerable short-term borrowing projected in the near future

   d) Cash inflows exceeding cash outflows for the foreseeable future

5. Why would a corporation ever issue bonds that were immediately callable if the interest rate were higher than that for a deferred callable bond?

6. In issuing long-term debt, which types of instruments would be most used by railroads? By public utilities? By industrial firms?

7. Why would you expect very long-term bonds (30–50 years) to be *unsecured*? If the

482

PART VII
Longer-term
financing—
instruments
and markets

earning power of a secured bond's collateral were in doubt, would the collateral have any value to a bondholder?

8. With the tax deductibility of interest payments, why should a company ever finance with preferred stock when it could finance with income bonds?

9. Why do callable bonds typically have a higher yield to maturity than noncallable bonds, holding all other things constant? Is the yield differential likely to be constant over time? If not, why not?

10. There are two ways in which sinking-fund payments may be used by the trustee. What are the benefits and drawbacks of each to the bondholders and the company?

PROBLEMS

1. The Hirsch Corporation is in bankruptcy. Mortgaged assets have been sold for $5 million and other assets have yielded $10 million. Hirsch has $10 million in mortgage bonds, $5 million in subordinated (to the mortgage bonds) debentures, $15 million owed to general creditors, and $10 million par value of common stock. How would distribution in bankruptcy be made?

2. Five years ago, Zapada International issued $50 million of 10 percent, 25-year debentures at a price of $990 per bond. The call price was originally $1,100 per bond the first year after issuance, and this price declined by $10 each subsequent year. Zapada now is calling the bonds in order to refund them at a lower interest rate.

   a) Ignoring taxes, what is the bondholder's return on investment for the five years? (Assume that interest is paid once a year and that the investor owns one bond.)

   b) If the bondholder now can invest $1,000 in a 20-year bond of equivalent risk that provides 8 percent interest, what is his overall return over the 25-year holding period? How does this compare with the return on the Zapada bonds had they not been called? (Assume again that interest is paid once a year. Both rates of return can be approximated using the present-value tables at the end of the book.)

3. The U.S. Zither Corporation has $50 million of 10 percent debentures outstanding, which are due in 25 years. USZ could refund these bonds in the current market with new 25-year bonds, sold to the public at par ($1,000) with a 9 percent coupon; total gross spread would be 2½ percent of the issue. The old bonds have an unamortized discount of $1 million, unamortized legal fees and other expenses of $100,000, and a call price of $107. The tax rate is 50 percent. There is a 2-month overlap, and issuing expenses are $200,000. Compute the present value of the refunding, using the after-tax rate on the new bonds. Is the refunding worthwhile?

4. Northern California Public Service Company is considering refunding its preferred stock. The dividend rate on this stock is $6 and it has a par value of $50 a share. The call price is $52 a share, and 500,000 shares are outstanding. George Arroya, vice-president, finance, feels the company can issue new preferred stock in the current market at an interest rate of 11 percent. With this rate, the new issue could be sold at par; the total par value of the issue would be $25 million. Flotation costs of $780,000 are tax deductible, but the call premium is not tax deductible; the company's marginal tax rate is 50 percent. A 90-day period of overlap is expected between the time the new preferred stock is issued and the time the old preferred stock is retired. Should the company refund its preferred stock? (Preferred stock dividends are assumed to be paid forever unless the issue is called. The problem may be set up in the same way as a bond refunding, except for the qualifications noted above.)

5. The Lemand Corporation has $8 million of 10 percent mortgage bonds outstanding under an open-end indenture. The indenture allows additional bonds to be issued as long as all of the following conditions are met.

   a) Pretax interest coverage [(income before taxes + bond interest)/bond interest] remains greater than 4.

   b) Net depreciated value of mortgaged assets remains twice the amount of mortgage debt.

   c) Debt/equity ratio remains below 0.5.

   The Lemand Corporation has net income of $2 million and a 50 percent tax rate, $40 million in equity, and $30 million in depreciated assets, covered by the mortgage. Assuming that 50 percent of the proceeds of a new issue would be added to the base of mortgaged assets and that the company has no sinking-fund payments until next year, how much more 10 percent debt could be sold?

6. Crakow Machine Company wishes to borrow $10 million for 10 years. It can issue either a noncallable bond at 11.40 percent interest or a bond callable at the end of 5 years for 12 percent. For simplicity, we assume that the bond will be called only at the end of year 5. The interest rate that is likely to prevail 5 years hence for a 5-year straight bond can be described by the following probability distribution:

Interest rate	9%	10%	11%	12%	13%
Probability	0.1	0.2	0.4	0.2	0.1

   Issuing and other costs involved in selling a bond issue five years hence will total $200,000. The call price is assumed to be par.

   a) What is the total absolute amount of interest payments for the noncallable issue over the ten years? (Do not discount.) What is the expected value of total interest payments and other costs if the company issues callable bonds? (Assume the company calls the bonds and issues new ones only if there is a savings in interest costs after issuing expenses.) On the basis of total costs, should the company issue noncallable or callable bonds?

   b) What would be the outcome if the probability distribution of interest rates 5 years hence were the following?

Interest rate	7%	9%	11%	13%	15%
Probability	0.2	0.2	0.2	0.2	0.2

   Assume all other conditions stay the same.

7. Reserach project: Obtain copies of several bond indentures. Pay particular attention to the restrictive covenants concerning things such as dividends, working capital, additional debt, and nature of the business. Try to relate the cost of debt to the firm to the relative restrictiveness of these provisions. Does management pay extra for discretion? If it does, can these covenants truly be said to be nonquantifiable? How would you go about finding a measure of the degree of restriction so that tradeoffs with interest could be made?

SELECTED REFERENCES

AGMON, T., A. R. OFER, and A. TAMIR, "Variable Rate Debt Instruments and Corporate Debt Policy," *Journal of Finance,* 36 (March 1981), 113–26.

ANG, JAMES S., "The Two Faces of Bond Refunding," *Journal of Finance,* 30 (June 1975), 869–74.

BOWLIN, OSWALD D., "The Refunding Decision: Another Special Case in Capital Budgeting," *Journal of Finance,* 21 (March 1966), 55–68.

DYL, EDWARD A., and WILLIAM J. SAWAYA, "The Bond Issue Size Decision Revisited," *Financial Management,* 8 (Winter 1979), 60–67.

DYL, EDWARD A., and MICHAEL D. JOEHNK, "Sinking Funds and the Cost of Corporate Debt," *Journal of Finance,* 34 (September 1979), 887–94.

EMERY, DOUGLAS R., "Overlapping Interest in Bond Refunding: A Reconsideration," *Financial Management,* 7 (Summer 1978), 19–20.

EVERETT, EDWARD, "Subordinated Debt—Nature and Enforcement," *Business Lawyer,* 20 (July 1965), 953–87.

HARRIS, ROBERT S., "The Refunding of Discounted Debt: An Adjusted Present Value Analysis," *Financial Management,* 9 (Winter 1980), 7–12.

JEN, FRANK C., and JAMES E. WERT, "The Deferred Call Provision and Corporate Bond Yields," *Journal of Financial and Quantitative Analysis,* 3 (June 1968), 157–69.

KALOTAY, A. J., "On the Advanced Refunding of Discounted Debt," *Financial Management,* 7 (Summer 1978), 14–18.

———, "Sinking Funds and the Realized Cost of Debt," *Financial Management,* 11 (Spring 1982), 43–54.

KALOTAY, ANDREW J., "On the Management of Sinking Funds," *Financial Management,* 10 (Summer 1981), 34–40.

LABER, GENE, "Repurchases of Bonds through Tender Offers: Implications for Shareholder Wealth," *Financial Management,* 7 (Summer 1978), 7–13.

LOGUE, DENNIS E., and RICHARD J. ROGALSKI, "Does It Pay to Shop for Your Bond Underwriter?" *Harvard Business Review,* 57 (July–August 1979), 111–17.

MARSHALL, WILLIAM J., and JESS B. YAWITZ, "Optimal Terms of the Call Provision on a Corporate Bond," *Journal of Financial Research,* 2 (Fall 1980), 203–11.

McCONNELL, JOHN J., and GARY G. SCHLARBAUM, "Returns, Risks, and Pricing of Income Bonds, 1956–76," *Journal of Business,* 54 (January 1981), 33–57.

McENALLY, RICHARD W., and MICHAEL L. RICE, "Hedging Possibilities in the Flotation of Debt Securities," *Financial Management,* 8 (Winter 1979), 12–18.

NEVITT, PETER K., *Project Financing,* 2nd ed. San Francisco: Advanced Management Research, 1979.

OFER, AHARON R., and ROBERT A. TAGGART, JR., "Bond Refunding: A Clarifying Analysis," *Journal of Finance,* 32 (March 1977), 21–30.

PINCHES, GEORGE E., and KENT A. MINGO, "The Role of Subordinate and Industrial Bond Ratings," *Journal of Finance,* 30 (March 1975), 201–6.

RIENER, KENNETH D., "Financial Structure Effects on Bond Refunding," *Financial Management,* 9 (Summer 1980), 18–23.

SMITH, CLIFFORD W., JR., and JEROLD B. WARNER, "On Financial Contracting; An Analysis of Bond Covenants," *Journal of Financial Economics,* 7 (June 1979), 117–61.

VAN HORNE, JAMES C., "Called Bonds: How Does the Investor Fare?" *Journal of Portfolio Management,* 6 (Summer 1980), 58–61.

———, *Financial Market Rates and Flows.* Englewood Cliffs, N.J.: Prentice-Hall, 1978, chaps. 6 and 7.

———, "Implied Fixed Costs in Long-Term Debt Issues," *Journal of Financial and Quantitative Analysis,* 8 (December 1973).

YAWITZ, JESS B., and JAMES A. ANDERSON, "The Effect of Bond Refunding on Shareholder Wealth," *Journal of Finance,* 32 (December 1977), 1738–46.

Preferred stock and common stock 22

In this chapter we take up two forms of equity financing—preferred stock and common stock. Although they both fall under the same general heading, their differences are far more pronounced than their similarities. From the standpoint of the ultimate owners of the corporation—namely, the common stockholders—preferred stock is a form of leverage to be evaluated much like debt. Because the theory behind the use of these securities was discussed in chapter 18, this chapter is devoted primarily to examining their features.

PREFERRED STOCK AND ITS FEATURES

Preferred stock is a hybrid form of financing, combining features of debt and common stock. In the event of liquidation, a preferred stockholder's claim on assets comes after that of creditors but before that of common stockholders. Usually, this claim is restricted to the par value of the stock. If the par value of a share of preferred stock is $100, the investor will be entitled to a maximum of $100 in settlement of the principal amount. Although preferred stock carries a stipulated dividend, the actual payment of a dividend is a discretionary rather than a fixed obligation of the company. The omission of a dividend will not result in a default of the obligation or insolvency of the company. The board of directors has full power to omit a preferred-stock dividend if it so chooses.

The maximum return to preferred stockholders usually is limited to the specified dividend, and these stockholders ordinarily do not share in the residual earnings of the company. Thus, if you own 100 shares of 10½ percent preferred stock, $100 par value, the maximum return you can expect in any one year is

486

PART VII

Longer-term
financing—
instruments
and markets

$1,050; and this return is at the discretion of the board of directors. The corporation cannot deduct this dividend on its tax return; this fact is the principal shortcoming of preferred stock as a means of financing. In view of the fact that interest payments on debt are deductible for tax purposes, the company that treats a preferred-stock dividend as a fixed obligation finds the explicit cost to be rather high.

Cumulative feature

Almost all preferred stocks have a cumulative feature, providing for unpaid dividends in any one year to be carried forward. Before the company can pay a dividend on its common stock, it must pay the dividends *in arrears* on its preferred stock. A board of directors may omit the preferred-stock dividend on a company's 8 percent cumulative preferred stock for 3 consecutive years. If the stock has a $100 par value, the company is $24 per share in arrears on its preferred stock. Before it can pay a dividend to its common stockholders, it must pay preferred stockholders $24 for each share of preferred stock held. It should be emphasized that just because preferred-stock dividends are in arrears, there is no guarantee that they ever will be paid. If the corporation has no intention of paying a common-stock dividend, there is no need to clear up the arrearage on the preferred. The preferred-stock dividend typically is omitted for lack of earnings, but the corporation does not have to pay a dividend if earnings are restored.

If the preferred-stock dividends are in arrears, and the company wishes to pay a common-stock dividend, it may choose not to clear up the arrearage but to make an exchange offering to preferred stockholders. Say that the dividend arrearages on an issue of $100 par value preferred stock are $56 and that the market price of the stock is $38 a share. The company might offer preferred stockholders common stock in the company, valued at $90, for each share of preferred stock held. Although theoretically the preferred stockholders are asked to give up $156 ($100 par value plus $56 dividend arrearages), the exchange offering promises them $90 relative to a current preferred-stock market value of only $38 per share. In order to eliminate the preferred stock, the company must obtain the approval of a required percentage of the stock outstanding, often two-thirds. Consequently, it probably will make its exchange offering contingent upon obtaining the required acceptance.

If a preferred stock is noncumulative, dividends not paid in one year do not carry forward. As a result, a company can pay a common-stock dividend without regard to any dividends it did not pay in the past on its preferred stock. From the standpoint of an investor, a noncumulative preferred stock is little more than an income bond. In fact, there is somewhat less uncertainty with income bonds, for the conditions under which interest will be paid are specified clearly, and bondholders have a prior claim on assets. Because of the obvious disadvantage to investors, noncumulative preferred-stock issues are rare, although they may be used in reorganizations.

Participating feature

A participating feature allows preferred stockholders to participate in the residual earnings of the corporation according to some specified formula. The preferred stockholder might be entitled to share equally with common stock-holders in any common-stock dividend beyond a certain amount. Suppose that a 6 percent preferred stock ($100 par value) were participating, so that the holders were entitled to share equally in any common-stock dividends in excess of $6 a share. If the common-stock dividend is $7, the preferred stockholder will receive $1 in extra dividends for each share of stock owned. The formula for participation can vary greatly. The essential feature is that preferred stockholders have a prior claim on income and an opportunity for additional return if the dividends to common stockholders exceed a certain amount. Unfortunately for the investor, practically all preferred-stock issues are nonparticipating, with the maximum return limited to the specified dividend rate.

Voting power

Because of their prior claim on assets and income, preferred stockholders normally are not given a voice in management unless the company is unable to pay preferred-stock dividends during a specified period. Arrearages on four quarterly dividend payments might constitute such a default; under such circumstances, preferred stockholders as a class would be entitled to elect a specific number of directors. Usually, the number of directors is rather small in relation to the total; and, by the time the preferred stockholders obtain a voice in management, the company probably is in considerable financial difficulty. Consequently, the voting power that preferred stockholders are granted may be virtually meaningless.

Depending upon the agreement between the preferred stockholders and the company, they may obtain voting power under other conditions as well. The company may default under restrictions in the agreement that are similar to those found in a loan agreement or a bond indenture. One of the more frequently imposed restrictions is that dividends on common stock are prohibited if the company does not satisfy certain financial ratios. We note, however, that default under any of the provisions of the agreement between the corporation and its preferred stockholders does not result in the obligation's becoming immediately payable, as does default under a loan agreement or bond indenture. The preferred stockholders merely are given a voice in management and assurance that common-stock dividends will not be paid during the period of default. Thus, preferred stockholders do not have nearly the same legal power in default as do debtholders.

Retirement of preferred stock

The fact that preferred stock, like common stock, has no maturity does not mean that most preferred-stock issues are regarded as a means of perpetual financing, because provision for retirement of the stock invariably is made.

Call feature. Almost all preferred-stock issues have a stated call price, which is above the original issuance price and may decrease over time. Like the call feature on bonds, the call feature on preferred stock affords the company flexibility. Because the market price of a straight preferred stock tends to fluctuate in keeping with interest rate cycles, the value of the preferred-stock call feature is determined by the same considerations as is the call feature for bonds, which we

488

PART VII

Longer-term
financing—
instruments
and markets

discussed in chapter 21. Long-term debt, unlike preferred stock, has a final maturity that assures the eventual retirement of the issue. Without a call feature on preferred stock, the corporation would be able to retire the issue only by the more expensive and less efficient methods of purchasing the stock in the open market, inviting *tenders* of the stock from preferred stockholders at a price above the market price, or offering the preferred stockholders another security in its place.

Sinking fund. Many preferred-stock issues provide for a sinking fund, which partially assures an orderly retirement of the stock. Like bond issues, a preferred-stock sinking fund is advantageous to investors because the retirement process exerts upward pressure on the market price of the remaining shares. Also, the coverage ratio on the preferred-stock dividend is improved as the number of shares outstanding is reduced. Overall, sinking funds are used much less with preferred stock than with bonds.

Use in financing

Nonconvertible preferred stock is not used extensively in financing; only public utilities employ it with any degree of regularity. One of the principal drawbacks to its use is the fact that the preferred dividend is not tax deductible. With a 46 percent corporate tax rate, the explicit cost of preferred stock is about twice that of bonds. To corporate investors, preferred stock may be more attractive than bonds because 85 percent of the dividends received by the corporation is not subject to taxation. As a result, many preferred stocks sell at a lower yield than do the bonds of the same issuing company, despite their lower priority of claim.

The advantage of preferred-stock financing is that it is a flexible financing arrangement; the dividend is not a legal obligation of the corporation issuing the securities. If earnings turn bad and the financial condition of the company deteriorates, the dividend can be omitted. With debt financing, interest must be paid regardless of whether earnings are good or bad. To be sure, companies that are accustomed to paying dividends on their common stock certainly regard the preferred dividend as a fixed obligation. Nevertheless, under dire circumstances, a company that omits its common-stock dividend also can omit its preferred dividend.

Another advantage of a straight preferred-stock issue is that it has no final maturity; in essence, it is a perpetual loan. Also, the majority of preferred-stock issues do not require sinking-fund payments. Thus, a preferred-stock issue gives a corporation flexibility by allowing it not to make principal payments or plan for refinancing. Moreover, from the standpoint of creditors, preferred stock adds to the equity base of the company and thereby strengthens its financial condition. The additional equity base enhances the ability of the company to borrow in the future. Although the explicit cost of preferred stock is considerably higher than that of bonds, the implied benefits discussed above may offset this cost. In addition, the implicit cost of preferred-stock financing, from the standpoint of investors' penalizing the price/earnings ratio of the common stock, may be somewhat less than that of debt financing.[1] To the extent that investors are apprehen-

---

[1]Gordon Donaldson, in "In Defense of Preferred Stock," *Harvard Business Review,* 40 (July–August 1962), 123–36, defends rigorously the use of preferred stock as a means of financing

sive over legal bankruptcy, they would regard debt as a riskier form of leverage. Unlike creditors, preferred stockholders cannot force a company into legal bankruptcy.

COMMON STOCK AND ITS FEATURES

The common stockholders of a corporation are its residual owners; collectively, they own the company and assume the ultimate risk associated with ownership. Their liability, however, is restricted to the amount of their investment. In the event of liquidation, these stockholders have a residual claim on the assets of the company after the claims of all creditors and preferred stockholders are settled in full. Common stock, like preferred stock, has no maturity date; and holders can liquidate their investments by selling their stocks in the secondary market.

Authorized, issued, and outstanding shares

The corporate charter of a company specifies the number of *authorized* shares of common stock, the maximum that the company can issue without amending its charter. Although amending the charter is not a difficult procedure, it does require the approval of existing stockholders, which takes time. For this reason, a company usually likes to have a certain number of shares that are authorized but unissued. These unissued shares allow flexibility in granting stock options, pursuing mergers, and splitting the stock. When authorized shares of common stock are sold, they become *issued* stock. *Outstanding* stock is the number of shares issued and actually held by the public; the corporation can buy back part of its issued stock and hold it as *treasury* stock.

Par value

A share of common stock can be authorized either with or without par value. The par value of a stock is merely a stated figure in the corporate charter and is of little economic significance. A company should not issue stock at a price less than par value, because stockholders who bought stock for less than par would be liable to creditors for the difference between the price they paid and the par value. Consequently, the par values of most stocks are set at fairly low figures relative to their market values. Suppose a company sold 10,000 shares of new common stock at $45 a share and that the par value of the stock was $5 per share. The equity portion of the balance sheet would be

Common stock ($5 par value)	$ 50,000
Paid-in capital	400,000
Net worth	$450,000

under certain circumstances. He argues that when a company has utilized its debt capacity, it may be able to finance further with preferred stock because the preferred-stock capacity of a company is distinct from its debt capacity.

490

PART VII

Longer-term
financing—
instruments
and markets

Stock can be authorized without par value and carried on the books at the market price or some stated value. The difference between the issuing price and the stated value is reflected as paid-in capital.

Book value and liquidating value

The book value of a share of stock is the net worth of a corporation less the par value of preferred stock outstanding, divided by the number of shares outstanding. Suppose the equity portion of the balance sheet of a company is as follows

Preferred stock ($100 par value)	$10,000,000
Common stock ($5 par value)	5,000,000
Paid-in capital	10,000,000
Retained earnings	16,000,000
Net worth	$41,000,000

The book value of a share of common stock is $31 million/1 million shares = $31 per share. Although one might expect the book value of a share of stock to correspond to the liquidating value of the company, this situation seldom occurs. Only if the assets of a corporation can be liquidated for the book values shown on the financial statement will book value per share correspond to the liquidating value per share. Even then, if liquidating costs are high, the liquidating value per share will be less than book value per share. For most companies, the liquidating value per share is less than book value per share because many of the assets can be liquidated only at distress prices. The books of some companies, however, carry certain assets—notably land and mineral rights—at values that are modest in relation to market value. For these companies, the liquidating value per share may be significantly higher than the book value.

Market value

Market value per share is the current price at which the stock is traded. For actively traded stocks, market-price quotations are readily available. For the many inactive stocks that have thin markets, prices are difficult to obtain. Even when obtainable, the information may reflect only the sale of a few shares of stock and not typify the market value of the firm as a whole. For companies of this sort, care must be taken in interpreting market-price information.

The market value of a share of common stock usually will differ from its book value and its liquidating value. It is a function of the current and expected future dividends of the company and the perceived risk of the stock on the part of investors. Because these factors bear only a partial relationship to the book value and liquidating value of the company, the market value per share may not be tied closely to these values.

Typically, the shares of a newer company are traded in the *over-the-counter* market, where one or more security dealers maintain an inventory in the stock and buy and sell it at bid and ask prices they quote. As a company grows in financial stature, number of stockholders, and volume of transactions, it may qualify for *listing* on a stock exchange. In contrast to the over-the-counter market, an *exchange* represents an auction market where buy and sell orders are matched. The listing requirements of the New York Stock Exchange are more stringent than those of the American Stock Exchange or of the regional stock exchanges, such as the Pacific Stock Exchange.

RIGHTS OF STOCKHOLDERS

Right to income

Common stockholders are entitled to share in the earnings of the company only if cash dividends are paid. Stockholders prosper from the market-value appreciation of their stock, but they are entirely dependent upon the board of directors for the declaration of dividends that give them income from the company. Thus, we see that the position of a common stockholder differs markedly from that of a creditor. If the company fails to pay contractual interest and principal payments to creditors, the creditors are able to take legal action to assure that payment is made or the company is liquidated. Stockholders, on the other hand, have no legal recourse to a company for not distributing profits. Only if management, the board of directors, or both, are engaged in fraud may stockholders take their case to court and possibly force the company to pay dividends.

Voting power

Inasmuch as the common stockholders of a company are its owners, they are entitled to elect a board of directors. In a large corporation, stockholders usually exercise only indirect control through the board of directors they elect. The board, in turn, selects the management, and management actually controls the operations of the company. In a proprietorship, partnership, or small corporation, the owners usually control the operations of the business directly. In a large corporation, there may be times when the goals of management differ from those of the common stockholders. The only recourse of a stockholder to management is through the board of directors.

Because common stockholders often are widely dispersed geographically and therefore disorganized, management can often exercise effective control of a large corporation if it controls only a small percentage of the stock outstanding. By proposing a slate of directors that is favorable to its own interests, management is able to maintain control. Outside stockholders have the right to expect that the directors will administer the affairs of the corporation properly in their behalf. If the directors act in a manner that results in personal gain, a stockholder can sue to recover. These *derivative suits* are infrequent, partly because many states require that a stockholder who loses the suit must bear the legal expenses of the corporation.

492

PART VII

Longer-term
financing—
instruments
and markets

Proxies

Common stockholders are entitled to one vote for each share of stock they own. Because most stockholders do not attend the annual meeting, they may vote by proxy, a form by which stockholders assign their right to vote to another person. The SEC regulates the solicitation of proxies and also requires companies to disseminate information to its stockholders through proxy mailings. Prior to the annual meeting, management solicits proxies from stockholders to vote for the recommended slate of directors and for any other proposals requiring stockholder approval. If stockholders are satisfied with the company, they generally sign the proxy in favor of management, giving written authorization to management to vote their shares. If some stockholders do not vote their shares, the number of shares voted at the meeting and the number needed to constitute a majority are lower. Because of the proxy system and the fact that management is able to mail information to stockholders at the company's expense, management has a distinct advantage in the voting process. As a result, it usually is able to perpetuate existing practices if it so chooses.

But the fortress is not invulnerable. Outsiders can seize control of a company through a proxy contest. Obviously, they would not attempt a takeover if management controlled a large percentage of shares outstanding. When an outside group undertakes a proxy raid, it is required to register its proxy statement with the Securities and Exchange Commission to prevent the presentation of misleading or false information.

Voting procedures

Depending upon the corporate charter, the board of directors is elected either under a *majority voting system* or under a *cumulative voting system*. Under the majority system, stockholders have one vote for each share of stock they own, and they must vote for each director position that is open. A stockholder who owns 100 shares will be able to cast 100 votes for each director's position open. Because each person seeking a position on the board must win a majority of the total votes cast for that position, the system precludes minority interests from electing directors. If management can obtain proxies for over 50 percent of the shares voted, it can select the entire board.

Under a cumulative voting system, a stockholder is able to accumulate votes and cast them for less than the total number of directors being elected. The total number of votes is the number of shares the stockholder owns times the number of directors being elected. If you are a stockholder who owns 100 shares, and 12 directors are to be elected, you may cast 1,200 votes for whatever number of directors you choose, the maximum being 1,200 votes for one director.

A cumulative voting system, in contrast to the majority system, permits minority interests to elect a certain number of directors. The minimum number of shares necessary to elect a specific number of directors is determined by

$$\frac{\text{Total shares outstanding times specific number of directors sought}}{\text{Total number of directors to be elected plus one}} + 1 \qquad (22\text{-}1)$$

If there are 3 million shares outstanding, the total number of directors to be elected is 14, and a minority group wishes to elect two directors, it will need at least the following number of shares:

$$\frac{3,000,000 \times 2}{14 + 1} + 1 = 400,001$$

Cumulative voting gives minority interests a better opportunity to be represented on the board of directors of a corporation. Because the system is more democratic, a number of states require that companies in the state elect directors in this way. Even with cumulative voting, however, management can reduce the number of directors and sometimes preclude minority interests from obtaining a seat on the board. Suppose the minority group above actually owns 400,001 shares. With 14 directors to be elected, the group can elect 2 directors. If the board is reduced to 6 members, the minority group can elect no directors because the minimum number of shares needed to elect a single director is

$$\frac{3,000,000 \times 1}{6 + 1} + 1 = 428,572$$

Another method of thwarting a minority interest from obtaining representation is to stagger the terms of the directors so that only a portion are elected each year. If a firm has 12 directors and the term is 4 years, only 3 are elected each year. As a result, a minority group needs considerably more shares voted in its favor to elect a director than it would need if all 12 directors came up for election each year.

Preemptive right

A preemptive right (see chapter 19) entitles common stockholders to maintain their proportional ownership in the corporation. Stockholders are given the first opportunity to purchase, on a pro-rata basis, any new stock being offered or any new securities that are convertible into common.

Right to examine books

A stockholder legally is entitled to inspect the books and records of a corporation. This access is limited, for most corporations feel that the audited financial statement is sufficient to satisfy the requirement. The stockholder may have to go to court to prove the necessity of obtaining more specific information. Stockholders are also entitled to a list of the stockholders of the corporation and their addresses. The list is vital to an insurgent group in a proxy contest, and management may engage in delaying tactics by contending that the stockholder list will be misused. Here, too, the stockholder may have to go to court and demonstrate sufficient cause for obtaining the information. Upon a court order, management is required to provide the list.

CLASSIFIED COMMON STOCK

A company may have more than one class of common stock. Its common stock can be classified according to the claim on income and voting power. Class A common of a company may have no voting privilege but may be entitled to a prior claim to dividends, while the Class B common has voting rights but a lower claim to dividends. Usually, the promoters of a corporation and its management will hold the Class B common stock, whereas the Class A Common is sold to the public. Actually, the Class A shares in this example are no more than a form of preferred stock. Usually, Class A stock is given some voting power but not as much as the Class B stock per dollar of investment.

Suppose that the Class A and Class B common stockholders of a company are entitled to one vote per share, but that the Class A stock is issued at an initial price of $20 a share. If $2 million is raised in the original offering through the issuance of 80,000 shares of Class A common for $1.6 million and 200,000 shares of Class B common for $400,000, the Class B stockholders will have over twice as many votes as Class A holders have, although their original investment is only one-quarter as large. Thus, the Class B holders have effective control of the company. Indeed, this is the purpose of classified stock.

For this control, the Class B holders must be willing to give up something in order to make Class A stock attractive to investors. Usually, they take a lower claim both to dividends and assets. An appropriate balance must be struck between voting power and the claim to dividends and assets if the company is to bargain effectively for Class A equity funds. Sometimes, the Class B common simply is given to the promoters of a corporation without any cash investment on their part.

Ford Motor Company

Perhaps the most famous example of a company with classified common stock is the Ford Motor Company. On December 31, 1980, the issued shares of capital stock for the company were:

	Shares Issued
Class B	13,935,719
Common stock	106,592,461
	120,528,180

The Class B common is owned by members of the Ford family and constitutes 40 percent of the total voting power of the company. The common is held by the general public and has 60 percent of the voting power of the company. The common stock was owned originally by the Ford Foundation but later sold to the general public. Those who own it are entitled to one vote for each share they own. A holder of Class B common is entitled to that number of votes per share that will make the voting power of the Class B common 40 percent of the total voting power of the corporation. At December 31, 1980, this number was

$$\frac{106,592,461}{13,935,719} \times \frac{.40}{.60} = 5.1 \text{ votes}$$

Each shareholder of Class B stock was entitled to 5.1 votes per share at the end of 1980. Thus, members of the Ford family retain substantial voting power in the company, even though they hold far fewer shares than does the general public. All shares of common and Class B stock share equally in dividends and equally in their claim on assets in the event of liquidation.[2] The use of classified capital stock in this case affects only the voting power.

SUMMARY

Preferred stock is a hybrid form of security having characteristics both of debt and common stock. The payment of dividends is not a legal but a discretionary obligation, although many companies regard the obligation as fixed. Preferred stockholders' claims on assets and income come after those of creditors but before those of common stockholders. The return on their investment is almost always limited to the specified dividend; very seldom do preferred stockholders participate in the residual earnings of the company. Although they may have some voting power, this power generally is restricted to situations in which the company has evolved itself into financial difficulty.

Because preferred stock has no final maturity, almost all issues have call features that give the corporation financial flexibility. Retirement of the preferred stock can be accomplished also by a sinking fund, convertibility, or an exchange offering. The principal disadvantage of preferred stock is that the dividend is not tax deductible. Implicit benefits associated with debt capacity and financial flexibility offset in some measure the difference between explicit after-tax costs of preferred-stock and debt financing. Despite these implicit benefits, preferred stock is used only moderately as a method of financing.

The common stockholders of a corporation are its owners. As such, they are entitled to share in the residual earnings of the company if cash dividends are paid. As owners, however, they have only a residual claim on assets in the event of liquidation. Common stockholders are also entitled to a voice in management through the board of directors they elect. These directors can be elected under a majority voting system or a cumulative voting system. The cumulative system allows minority interests to obtain representation on the board of directors. Differences between authorized, issued, and outstanding shares were explained as were differences in par value, book value, liquidating value, and market value. The use of different classes of common stock allows the promoters and management of a corporation to retain voting control without having to make a large capital contribution.

[2]*Annual Report*, Ford Motor Company, 1980; and *Prospectus to Ford Motor Company Stock*, November 20, 1963.

QUESTIONS

1. Because the dividend payments on preferred stock are not a tax-deductible expense, the explicit cost of this form of financing is high. What are some of the offsetting advantages to the firm and to the investor that enable this type of security to be sold? Can you explain why the utilities are the principal preferred-stock issuers?

2. Why would a preferred stockholder suffer a loss on those dividend payments in arrears even if the arrearage were ultimately paid up?

3. Why do you suppose Congress allows 85 percent of intercorporate preferred dividends to remain untaxed? Would a decrease in the percentage exemption raise or lower the amount of preferred stock issued? Why?

4. Preferred stock is said to combine the worst features of both common stock and debt. Do you agree with the contention? From whose point of view does it make sense?

5. Why do most preferred stock issues have a cumulative feature? Would not the company be better off with a noncumulative feature?

6. If not otherwise stated, what would you assume as usual with respect to the following features for a preferred stock: cumulative, participation, voting power, call feature, and claim on assets?

7. What advantages to the firm are there from broad share distribution? Is the preemptive right in conflict with an objective of broad share distribution?

8. Why would a company ever wish to use classified common stock in its financing instead of straight common stock?

9. Why does most common stock have a low par value in relation to its market value?

10. Why does book value per share of common stock change over time?

11. The common stockholder is considered the residual owner of a corporation. What does this mean in terms of risk and return?

12. Why does the number of authorized shares usually exceed the number that are actually outstanding?

13. In any proxy attempt by an outside group to gain control of a company, the advantage lies with management. What are the reasons for this advantage?

14. If Congress were to eliminate the double taxation of dividends so that a company could deduct dividend payments in the same way it does interest payments for tax purposes, what would be the effect on preferred-stock and common-stock financing?

PROBLEMS

1. The Riting Railroad needs to raise $9.5 million for capital improvements. One possibility is a new preferred-stock issue: 8%, $100 par value stock that would yield 9 percent to investors. Flotation costs for an issue this size amount to 5 percent of the total amount of preferred stock sold; these costs are deducted from gross proceeds in determining the net proceeds to the company. (Ignore any tax considerations.)

a) At what price per share will the preferred stock be offered to investors? (Assume the issue never will be called.)

b) How many shares must be issued to raise $9.5 million for Riting Railroad?

2. Lost Horizon Silver Mining Company has 200,000 shares of $7 cumulative preferred stock outstanding, $100 par value. The preferred stock has a participating feature. If dividends on the common stock exceed $1 per share, preferred stockholders receive additional dividends per share equal to one-half of the excess. In other words, if the common stock dividend were $2, preferred stockholders would receive an additional dividend of $.50. The company has 1 million shares of common outstanding. What would dividends per share be on the preferred stock and on the common stock if earnings available for dividends in three successive years were (a) $1,000,000; $600,000; and $3,000,000; (b) $2,000,000; $2,400,000; and $4,600,000; and (c) $1,000,000; $2,500,000; and $5,700,000. (Assume all of the available earnings are paid in dividends, but nothing more is paid.)

3. D. Sent, a disgruntled stockholder of the Zebec Corporation, desires representation on the board. The Zebec Corporation, which has 10 directors, has 1 million shares outstanding.

a) How many shares would Sent have to control to be assured of one directorship under a majority voting system?

b) Recompute part a, assuming a cumulative voting system.

c) Recompute parts a and b, assuming the number of directors was reduced to 5.

4. The Berkeley Brass Company has a 9-person board and has 2 million shares of common stock outstanding. It is chartered with a cumulative voting rule. Jane Irwin, a granddaughter of the founder, controls directly or indirectly 482,000 shares. As she disagrees with present management, she wants a slate of her own directors on the board.

a) If all directors are elected once a year, how many directors can she elect?

b) If director terms are staggered so that only 3 are elected each year, how many can she elect?

5. The stock of the Moribund Corporation is currently selling in the market for $45 per share, yet it has a liquidation value of $70 per share. The Raid Corporation has decided to make a tender offer for the shares of Moribund. Raid feels that it must obtain at least 50 percent of the shares in order to effect the liquidation. Assuming Raid makes its tender offer on the expected relationship shown in the following table, at what price should the tender be made?

Price per share	Expected percentage of shares tendered
$55	50%
57	60
59	70
62	80
67	90
72	100

498

PART VII

Longer-term
financing—
instruments
and markets

6. At last year-end, the long-term capitalization of Belgravia Furniture Company consisted of the following:

Long-term bonds, 9%	$ 3,400,000
Preferred stock, 8%, $50 par value	2,000,000
Common stock, $5 par value	1,000,000
Paid-in capital	500,000
Retained earnings	4,000,000
	$10,900,000

During the current year the company earned $2.5 million before interest and taxes. Its dividend payout rate with respect to profits after taxes was 40 percent, and the company's marginal tax rate is 46 percent. At the current year-end, it issues 50,000 additional shares of common stock at a price to the public of $38 per share. The underwriters' spread is $3 a share. What is the long-term capitalization of the company at the current year-end?

SELECTED REFERENCES

BEAR, ROBERT M., and ANTHONY J. CURLEY, "Unseasoned Equity Financing," *Journal of Financial and Quantitative Analysis,* 10 (June 1975), 311–26.

BILDERSEE, JOHN S., "Some Aspects of the Performance of Non-Convertible Preferred Stocks," *Journal of Finance,* 28 (December 1973), 1187–1202.

BLOCK, STANLEY, and MARJORIE STANLEY, "The Financial Characteristics and Price Movement Patterns of Companies Approaching the Unseasoned Securities Market in the Late 1970s," *Financial Management,* 9 (Winter 1980), 30–36.

DONALDSON, GORDON, "Financial Goals: Management vs. Stockholders," *Harvard Business Review,* 41 (May–June 1963), 116–29.

———, "In Defense of Preferred Stock," *Harvard Business Review,* 40 (July–August 1962), reprinted in *Foundations for Financial Management,* ed. James Van Horne, pp. 194–218. Homewood, Ill.: Irwin, 1966.

EIBOTT, PETER, "Trends in the Value of Individual Stockholdings," *Journal of Business,* 47 (July 1974), 339–48.

HAYES, SAMUEL L., III, "The Transformation of Investment Banking," *Harvard Business Review,* 57 (January–February 1979), 153–70.

SOLDOFSKY, ROBERT M., "Classified Common Stock," *Business Lawyer* (April 1968), 899–902.

VAN HORNE, JAMES C., "New Listings and Their Price Behavior," *Journal of Finance,* 25 (September 1970), 783–94.

WHITE, R. W., and P. A. LUSZTIG, "The Price Effects of Rights Offerings," *Journal of Financial and Quantitative Analysis,* 15 (March 1980), 25–40.

YOUNG, ALAN, and WAYNE MARSHALL, "Controlling Shareholder Servicing Costs," *Harvard Business Review,* 49 (January–February 1971), 71–78.

Convertible securities and warrants

23

In addition to straight debt and equity instruments, a company may finance with an option, a contract giving its holder the right to buy common stock or to exchange something for it within a specific period of time. As a result, the value of the option instrument is strongly influenced by changes in value of the stock. In this chapter, we consider two specific types of options frequently employed by business firms in their financing: the convertible security and the warrant. In the Appendix to this chapter, a more detailed discussion of option pricing theory appears.

CONVERTIBLE-SECURITY FEATURES

A convertible security is a bond or a share of preferred stock that can be converted at the option of the holder into common stock of the same corporation. Once converted into common stock, the stock cannot be exchanged again for bonds or preferred stock. The ratio of exchange between the convertible security and the common stock can be stated in terms of either a *conversion price* or a *conversion ratio*. Foremost-McKesson 9¾ percent convertible subordinated debentures ($1,000 face value), issued in June 1981, have a conversion price of $43.75, meaning that each debenture is convertible into 22.86 shares of common stock. We simply divide the face value of the security by the conversion price to obtain the conversion ratio, $1,000/$43.75 = 22.86 shares. The conversion privilege can be stated in terms of either the conversion price or the conversion ratio.

499

500

PART VII
Longer-term
financing—
instruments
and markets

The conversion terms are not necessarily constant over time. Many convertible issues provide for increases or "step-ups" in the conversion price at periodic intervals. For example, a $1,000-face-value bond might have a conversion price of $100 a share for the first five years, $110 a share for the second five years, $120 for the third five, and so on. In this way, the bond converts into fewer shares of common stock as time goes by. Usually, the conversion price is adjusted for any stock splits or stock dividends that occur after the securities are sold. If the common stock were split two for one, the conversion price would be halved. This provision protects the convertible bondholder and is known as an antidilution clause.

Conversion value and premium

The *conversion value* of a convertible security is the conversion ratio of the security times the market price per share of the common stock. If Foremost-McKesson stock were selling for $50, the conversion value of one convertible subordinated debenture would be 22.86 × $50, or $1,143.

The convertible security provides the investor with a fixed return from a bond or with a specified dividend from preferred stock. In addition, the investor receives an option to convert the security into common stock and thereby participates in the possibility of capital gains associated with being a residual owner of the corporation. Because of this option, the company usually is able to sell the convertible security at a lower yield than it would have to pay on a straight bond or preferred-stock issue. At the time of issuance, the convertible security will be priced higher than its conversion value. The differential is known as the *conversion premium*. The Foremost-McKesson convertible subordinated debentures were sold to the public for $1,000 a bond. The market price of the common stock at the time of issuance of the convertibles was approximately $38½ per share. Therefore the conversion value of each bond was 22.86 × $38½ = $880, and the differential of $120 between this value and the issuing price represented the conversion premium. Frequently, this premium is expressed as a percentage; in our example the conversion premium is $120/$880 = 13.6 percent.

Almost without exception, convertible securities provide for a *call price*. As was true with the straight bond or preferred stock, the call feature enables the corporation to call the security for redemption. Few convertible securities, however, are ever redeemed. Instead, the purpose of the call usually is to force conversion when the conversion value of the security is significantly above its call price.

Other features

Almost all convertible bond issues are subordinated to other creditors. That fact permits the lender to treat convertible subordinated debt or convertible preferred stock as a part of the equity base when evaluating the financial condition of the issuer. In the event of liquidation, it makes no difference to the creditor if the issue is actually converted; in either case, the lender has a prior claim. The situation is different with a convertible bond that is not subordinate. As long as the bond is not converted, its holder would be a general creditor in the event of liquidation. Consequently, creditors tend to regard the convertible bond as debt until actual conversion takes place. For this reason, there is a strong incentive for the company to make the issue subordinated.

Investors in a company's common stock tend to recognize the potential dilution in their position before actual conversion takes place. For accounting reporting purposes, a company with convertible securities or warrants outstanding is required to report earnings per share in such a way that the reader of the financial statement can visualize the potential dilution. More specifically, it must report earnings per share on two bases. The first is *primary* earnings per share, which are simply earnings available to common stockholders divided by the actual number of shares outstanding. The second is *fully diluted* earnings per share, which are earnings available to common stockholders divided by the total number of shares outstanding plus the number of shares that would be added if all warrants were exercised and all convertible securities were converted. For companies with sizable financing with convertibles and warrants, the difference between the two earnings-per-share figures can be substantial.

USE OF CONVERTIBLES

Convertible securities, in most cases, are employed as deferred common-stock financing. Technically these securities represent debt or preferred stock, but in essence they are delayed common stock. Companies that issue convertibles expect them to be converted in the future. By selling a convertible security instead of common stock, they create less dilution in earnings per share, both now and in the future. The reason is that the conversion price on a convertible security is higher than the issuing price on a new issue of common stock.

The current market price of the common stock of the mythical ABC Corporation is $40 per share. If the company raises capital with an issue of common stock, it will have to underprice the issue in order to sell it in the market, but it can sell the stock through underwriters and realize net proceeds of $36 per share. If the company wishes to raise $18 million, the issue will involve 500,000 shares of additional stock. On the other hand, if ABC Corporation sells a convertible issue, it is able to set the conversion price above the current market price per share. If the conversion premium is 15 percent, the conversion price will be $46 per share. Assuming an $18 million issue of convertibles, the number of shares of additional stock after conversion will be

$$\frac{\$18 \text{ million}}{\$46} = 391,305$$

We see that potential dilution with a convertible issue is less than that with a common issue because fewer shares are being added.

As a financing strategy, management may wish to finance with convertible securities as opposed to common stock when its estimates of the firm's future are more favorable than those of the market. By so doing, it obtains lesser dilution for

502

PART VII

Longer-term
financing—
instruments
and markets

existing stockholders than it would if it financed with common stock. Once management's expectations are realized, the stock presumably will rise in price. Of course, the merit of such a strategy depends upon management's estimating the future more accurately than the market does. When the stock is depressed in price, however, it may be wise to avoid both common stock and convertible financing. This situation will be discussed later in the chapter when we consider the timing of a convertible issue.

Another advantage to the company in using convertible securities is that the interest rate or preferred-dividend rate typically is lower than the rate the company would have to pay on a straight bond or a straight preferred-stock issue. The conversion feature makes the issue more attractive to investors. The greater the value of the conversion feature to investors, the lower the yield the company will have to pay in order to sell the issue. Companies with relatively low credit ratings but good prospects for growth may find it extremely difficult to sell a straight issue of bonds or preferred stock. The market may respond more favorably to a convertible issue of these companies, not because of its quality as a bond or as preferred stock but because of its quality as common stock.

Forcing or stimulating conversion

Companies usually issue convertible securities with the full expectation that these securities will be converted within a certain length of time. Investors can exercise their options voluntarily at any time and exchange the convertible security for common stock; however, they may prefer to hold the security, for its price will increase as the price of the common stock increases. During this time, also, they receive regular interest payments or preferred-stock dividends. For the security convertible to common stock that pays no dividend, it is to the holder's advantage never to convert voluntarily . In other words, the investor should delay conversion as long as possible. (When a company pays a common-stock dividend, it may be in the interest of the convertible security holder to convert voluntarily.) On the other hand, it is in the company's interest, in behalf of existing stockholders, to force conversion as soon as possible. In this way, the cost of paying interest on the convertible debenture, or dividends on the convertible preferred stock, can be avoided.

In order to force conversion, companies issuing convertible securities usually must call the issue. If the call is to succeed, the market price of the security must be significantly higher than the call price, so that investors will convert rather than accept the lower call price. Many companies regard a 20 percent premium of conversion value over call price as a sufficient cushion for possible declines in market price and for enticing investors to convert their securities. The conversion price of a convertible debenture ($1,000 face value) might be $50 and the call price $1,080. For the conversion value of the bond to equal the call price, the market price of the stock must be $1,080/20, or $54 a share. If the bonds are called when the market price is $54, many investors might choose to accept the call price rather than convert. The company then would have to redeem many of the bonds for cash, in part defeating the purpose of the original financing. In order to assure almost complete conversion, it might wait to call the debentures until the conversion value of the bond was 20 percent above the call price, a value that corresponds to a common-stock market price of approximately $65 a share. At this price, the investor who accepts the call price suffers a significant opportunity loss.[1] Studies show that companies tend to call their convertibles after a period of rise in their common stock price relative to the market.[2] As a result, the opportunity loss to the holder for not converting is pronounced.

Other means are available to a company for "stimulating," as opposed to "forcing," conversion. By establishing an acceleration or "step-up" in the conversion price at steady intervals in the future, there is persistent pressure on bondholders to convert, assuming the conversion value of the security is relatively high. If the conversion price is scheduled to increase from $50 to $56 at the end of next month, convertible bondholders have an incentive to convert prior to that time, all other things the same. If the holders wait, they receive fewer shares of stock. The "step-up" provision must be established at the time the convertible issue is sold; it cannot be used for purposes of stimulating conversion at a particular moment.

Another means for stimulating conversion is to increase the dividend on the common stock, thereby making the common more attractive. In certain cases, the dividend income available on the common may exceed interest income on the convertible security. Although the two stimulants discussed above enhance conversion, invariably a portion of the convertible bondholders will not convert, owing to the downside protection of the bond, the superior legal claim on assets, and other reasons. Consequently, calling the issue may be the only means for assuring that the issue will be substantially converted.

Overhanging issue. If a company is unable to force or stimulate conversion because the market price of the stock has not risen sufficiently to entice the investor to convert, the issue is said to be overhanging. With an overhanging issue, the company is said to be constrained in its ability to obtain new financing. It is difficult to sell another convertible-security issue until the present one is converted. The overhanging issue creates apprehension in the market over the investment worthiness of any new issue of convertibles and may even create apprehension over the worthiness of a nonconvertible security offering.

The chance of an overhanging issue and the loss of flexibility associated with such an issue may offset, at least in part, the advantage in issuing price of the convertible security over a common-stock offering. With a common-stock offering, the firm obtains equity capital now. With a convertible-security issue, it is uncertain when, if ever, the security will convert and the company will obtain equity capital.

Conversion premiums

For most issues of convertibles, the conversion premium ranges from 10 to 20 percent. Remember that this premium is the percentage by which the issuing price of the convertible exceeds its conversion value. If a convertible bond is sold

---

[1]For a discussion of ways a company can notify bondholders of the call and to assure that a very high percentage exercise their option, see Alexander B. Miller, "How to Call Your Convertibles," *Harvard Business Review*, 49 (May–June 1971), 66–70.

[2]Gordon J. Alexander and Roger D. Stover, "The Effect of Forced Conversions on Common Stock Prices," *Financial Management*, 9 (Spring 1980), 39–45.

504

PART VII

Longer-term
financing—
instruments
and markets

for $1,000 with a conversion price of $50, and if the market price of common at the time of issuance is $43 a share, the conversion premium will be $7/$43, or 16.3 percent. For a growth company, the conversion premium can be in the upper part of the 10 to 20 percent range, or perhaps even higher in the case of a supergrowth stock. For companies with more moderate growth, the conversion premium may be closer to 10 percent. The range itself is established mainly by market tradition, in keeping with the idea that the stock should be expected to rise in price so that it exceeds the conversion price within a reasonable period of time. The greater the growth in market price per share, the more quickly will the market price exceed the conversion price, all other things the same. Thus, the supergrowth company is able to command a higher conversion premium in the market than is a company with only moderate growth potential.

The higher the conversion premium, of course, the lower the dilution. If the company sets too high a conversion price, the issue will have to be sold as essentially a fixed-income security with a yield commensurate with what the company would pay on a straight debt or preferred-stock issue. Under such circumstances, the issue cannot be considered delayed equity financing; the ability of the firm to force conversion is too uncertain. For this reason, there are practical limits to how high a conversion premium can be set. For most situations, it is 20 percent or less.

VALUE OF CONVERTIBLE SECURITIES

The value of a convertible security to an investor is twofold: its value as a bond or preferred stock and its potential value as common stock. (Because the principles of valuation of a convertible bond and a convertible preferred stock are nearly the same, our subsequent discussion will refer to convertible bonds.) Investors obtain a hedge when they purchase a convertible bond. If the market price of the stock rises, the value of the convertible is determined largely by its conversion value. If the market for the stock turns down, the investor still holds a bond whose value provides a floor below which the price of the convertible is unlikely to fall.

Bond value

The bond value of a convertible security is the price at which a straight bond of the same company would sell in the open market. It can be determined by solving the following equation for B:

$$B = \sum_{t=1}^{2n} \frac{I}{(1 + \frac{i}{2})^t} + \frac{F}{(1 + \frac{i}{2})^n} \tag{23-1}$$

where B = straight bond value of the convertible

I = semiannual interest payments determined by the coupon rate

F = face value of the bond

n = years to final maturity

i = market yield to maturity on a straight bond of the same company.

In the equation, we assume semiannual interest payments, which are typical with corporate bonds, so the total number of interest payments is two times the years to maturity, n, and the semiannual interest rate on a straight bond is i divided by 2.

Amos White Company has outstanding a 9 percent convertible debenture with a final maturity 20 years hence. If the company is to sell a straight 20-year debenture in the current market, the yield will have to be 11 percent to be attractive to investors. For a 20-year bond with a 9 percent coupon to yield 11 percent to maturity, the bond has to sell at a discount. Using the above equation and rounding, we have

$$B = \sum_{t=1}^{40} \frac{\$4.50}{(1.055)^t} + \frac{\$1,000}{(1.055)^{40}} = \$839$$

Although it is possible to solve this equation by hand, using present-value tables, we need only consult a bond table to determine the market price. Thus the bond-value floor of Amos White Company's convertible bonds would be $839. This floor suggests that if the price of the common stock were to fall sharply so that the conversion feature had negligible value, the price of the convertible would fall only to $839. At that price, the security would sell as a straight bond in keeping with prevailing bond yields for that grade of security.

The bond-value floor of a convertible is not constant over time. It varies with (1) interest-rate movements in the capital market and (2) changes in the financial risk of the company involved. If interest rates in general rise, the bond value of a convertible will decline. If the yield to maturity on a straight bond in our example increases from 11 to 12 percent, the bond value of the convertible will drop from $839 to $774. Moreover, the company's credit rating can either improve or deteriorate over time. If it improves, and the company is able to sell a straight bond at a lower yield to maturity, the bond value of the convertible security will increase, all other things held constant. If the company's credit standing deteriorates, and the yield on a straight bond increases, the bond-value floor will decline. Unfortunately for the investor, when the market price of the stock falls because of poor earnings, the company may have financial difficulty, in which case its credit standing will suffer. As a result, the straight bond value of the convertible may decline along with the decline in its conversion value, giving investors less downside protection than they might have expected originally.[3]

Premiums

Convertible securities usually sell at premiums over both their bond value and their conversion value. Recall that the conversion value of a convertible is simply the current market price per share of the company's common stock times

---

[3]Mathematically, the straight bond value of a convertible will rise over time, all other things held constant, if the face value of the convertible is above the straight bond value at the time of issuance. At final maturity the straight bond value will equal the face value of the convertible, assuming the company is not in default.

506

PART VII
Longer-term
financing—
instruments
and markets

the number of shares into which the security is convertible. The fact that the convertible bond provides the investor with a degree of downside protection, given the qualifications mentioned above, often results in its selling at a market price somewhat higher than its conversion value. In general, the more volatile the price movements of the stock, the more valuable is the downside protection afforded by the bond-value floor. For this reason as well as for additional reasons discussed later, the market price of a convertible security frequently is above its conversion value. The difference is known as the *premium-over-conversion value*.

Moreover, a convertible bond typically will sell at a *premium-over-bond value*, primarily because of the conversion feature. Unless the market price of the stock is very low relative to the conversion price, the conversion feature usually will have value, in that investors may eventually find it profitable to convert the securities. To the extent that the conversion feature does have value, the convertible will sell at a premium over its straight bond value. The higher the market price of the common relative to the conversion price, the greater this premium.

The tradeoff between the two premiums depicts the value of the option to investors and is illustrated in Fig. 23-1. The market price of the common is on the horizontal axis; the value of the convertible security is on the vertical. It should be pointed out that the two axes are on different scales. If the conversion ratio were 20 to 1, the horizontal axis might be in units of $10, while the vertical axis would be in units of $200. The diagonal line, which starts at the origin, represents the conversion value of the bond. It is linear, as the conversion ratio is invariant with respect to the market price of the stock. The bond value line, however, is related to the market price of the common. If a company is doing badly financially, the prices of both its common stock and its bonds are likely to be low. At the extreme, if the total value of the company were zero, both the bonds and the stock would have a value of zero. As the company becomes sounder financially and the com-

FIGURE 23-1
Relation between bond value and conversion value premiums

mon stock increases in price, bond value increases but at a decreasing rate. After a point, the bond value line becomes flat, and further increases in common stock price are unrelated to it. At this point, the bond value floor is determined by what other high grade bonds sell for in the market. The upper curved line represents the market price of the convertible security. The distance between this line and the bond-value line is the premium over bond value, while the distance between the market-value line and the conversion-value line represents the premium over conversion value.

We see that at relatively high common-stock price levels, the value of the convertible as a bond is insignificant. Consequently, its premium-over-bond value is high, whereas its premium-over-conversion value is negligible. The security sells mainly for its stock equivalent. Investors are unwilling to pay a significant premium-over-conversion value for the following reasons. First, the greater the premium of market price of the convertible over its bond value, the less valuable the bond-value protection is to the investor. Second, when the conversion value is high, the convertible may be called; if it is, the investor will want to convert rather than redeem the bond for the call price. Upon conversion, of course, the bond is worth only its conversion value.

On the other hand, when the market value of the convertible is close to its straight bond value, the conversion feature has little value. At this level, the convertible security is valued primarily as a straight bond. Under these circumstances, the market price of the convertible is likely to exceed its conversion value by a significant premium.

The principal reason for premiums in market price over both conversion value and bond value is the unusual appeal of a convertible as both a bond and a common stock. It offers the holder partial protection on the downside together with participation in upward movements in stock price. Thus the distribution of possible outcomes is skewed to the right, and this characteristic finds favor with investors.

WARRANTS AND THEIR VALUATION

A warrant is an option to purchase a specified number of shares of common stock at a stated price. When holders exercise options, they surrender the warrants. Warrants often are employed as "sweeteners" to a public issue of bonds or debt that is privately placed. The investor obtains not only the fixed return associated with debt but also an option to purchase common stock at a stated price. If the market price of the stock should rise, this option can be valuable. As a result, the corporation should be able to obtain a lower interest rate than it would otherwise. For companies that are marginal credit risks, the use of warrants may spell the difference between being able and not being able to raise funds through a debt issue. In addition to being a "sweetener" to debt financing, warrants are used in the origination of a company as compensation to underwriters and venture capitalists.

Features

The warrant itself contains the provisions of the option. It states the number of shares the holder can buy for each warrant. Eastern Airlines warrants provide

508

PART VII

Longer-term
financing—
instruments
and markets

an option to purchase one share of common stock for each warrant held; Tri-Continental warrants provide for the purchase of 4.34 shares for each warrant held. Another important provision is the price at which the warrant is exercisable. Eastern Airlines warrants are exercisable at $10 a share. The exercise price can be either fixed or "stepped up" over time. The Textron Inc., warrants were exercisable at $10 a share until May 1, 1979; since then they have been exercisable at $11.25.

The warrant must specify the date the option expires unless it is perpetual, having no expiration date, such as warrants of Allegheny Corporation. Warrants may be nondetachable or detachable (sold separately from the bond), so that bondholders do not have to exercise their options in order to obtain the value of the warrant. They can sell only the warrants in the marketplace. Many detachable warrants are listed on the American Stock Exchange, the Chicago Board Options Exchange, and regional exchanges. A nondetachable warrant cannot be sold separately from the bond; it can be detached only when the bondholders exercise their options and purchase stock.

Because a warrant is only an option to purchase stock, warrant holders are not entitled to any cash dividends paid on the common stock, nor do they have voting power. If the common stock is split or a stock dividend is declared, the option price of the warrant usually is adjusted to take this change into account.

Exercise of warrants

When warrants are exercised, the common stock of the company is increased. Moreover, the debt which was issued in conjunction with the warrants remains outstanding, assuming the warrants are detachable. At the time of the issue of the warrants, the exercise price usually is set in excess of the market price of the common stock. The premium often is 15 percent or so above the stock's value. If the share price is $40, this translates into an exercise price of $46.

To see how new capital can be infused with the exercise of warrants, let us take a company we shall call Westman Bodac. It has just raised $25 million in debt funds with warrants attached. The debentures carry a 12 percent coupon rate; and with each debenture ($1,000 face value) investors receive one warrant entitling them to purchase 4 shares of common stock at $30 a share. The capitalization of the company before financing, after financing, and after complete exercise of the options are as follows (in millions):

	Before financing	After financing	After exercise
Debentures		$25	$25
Common stock ($10 par value)	$10	10	11
Paid-in capital			2
Retained earnings	40	40	40
Net worth	$50	$50	$53
Total capitalization	$50	$75	$78

The retained earnings of the company remain unchanged, and the debenture issue has neither matured nor been called. Exercising their options, the warrant holders purchase 100,000 shares of stock at $30 a share, or $3 million in total. Consequently, the total capitalization of the company is increased by that amount.

A company cannot force the exercise of the warrant option as it can force the exercise of the conversion option by calling a convertible security. Consequently, it is unable to control when, if ever, the warrant will be exercised and there will be an infusion of new equity capital into the corporation. Only the expiration date sets a limit on how long the warrants can remain outstanding and unexercised. As with convertibles, it is necessary for companies to report earnings per share on a fully diluted basis. Full dilution means the maximum possible dilution if all convertible securities were converted into common stock and all warrants or options to purchase common stock were exercised. As a result of this requirement, the common-stock investor is not likely to overlook the potential dilution inherent in a company's financing with convertible securities and warrants.

Valuation of warrants

The theoretical value of a warrant can be determined by

$$NP_s - E \qquad (23\text{-}2)$$

where N = the number of shares that can be purchased with one warrant
P_s = the market price of one share of stock
E = the exercise price associated with the purchase of N shares.

The theoretical value of a warrant is the lowest level at which the warrant will generally sell. If, for some reason, the market price of a warrant were to go lower than its theoretical value, arbitragers would eliminate the differential by buying the warrants, exercising them, and selling the stock. A warrant is unlikely to sell below its theoretical value, and many warrants sell above that value.

Premium over theoretical value. The primary reason that a warrant sells at a price higher than its theoretical value is the opportunity for leverage. To illustrate the concept of leverage, consider the Textron warrants. For each warrant held, one share of common stock can be purchased, and the exercise price is $10. If the stock were selling at $12 a share, the theoretical value of the warrant would be $2. Suppose, however, that the common stock increased by 25 percent in price to $15 a share. The theoretical value of the warrant would go from $2 to $5, a gain of 150 percent.

The opportunity for increased gain is attractive to investors when the common stock is selling near its exercise price. For a particular investment, the investor can buy more warrants than common stock. If the stock moves up in price the investor will make more money on the warrants than on an equal investment in common stock. Of course, leverage works both ways; the percentage change can be almost as pronounced on the downside. However, there is a limit to how far the warrant can fall in price because it is bounded at zero. Moreover, in order for the

510
PART VII

Longer-term
financing—
instruments
and markets

market price to drop to zero, there would have to be no probability that the market price of the stock would exceed the exercise price during the exercise period. Usually there is some probability.

The market prices of many warrants are in excess of their theoretical values because of the potential for upside movements in the value of the warrant while, at the same time, downside movements are cushioned. In particular, this event occurs when the market price of the associated common stock is near the exercise price of the warrant.

The typical relationship between the market value of a warrant and the value of the associated common stock is shown in Fig. 23-2. The theoretical value of the warrant is represented by the solid line in the figure, and the actual market value by the dashed line. When the market value of the associated stock is less than the exercise price, the theoretical value of the warrant is zero. When the value of the associated common stock is greater than the exercise price, the theoretical value of the warrant is positive, as depicted by the solid, diagonal line.

One might think of the theoretical value line as representing the values a warrant might take with only a moment to expiration. When there is a reasonable amount of time to expiration of the warrant, the relationship between warrant value and stock value is better depicted by the dashed line in Fig. 23-2. The greater the length of time to expiration, the more time the investor has in which to exercise the warrant and the more valuable it becomes. As a result, the further in the future the expiration date of the warrant, the higher the market-value line tends to be in relation to the theoretical-value line.

We note in the figure that when the market value of the associated common stock is low in relation to the exercise price, the actual market value of a warrant exceeds its theoretical value. As the market value of the associated stock rises, the market value of the warrant usually approaches its theoretical value. This simply suggests that a warrant has the greatest value, relative to its theoretical value, when

**FIGURE 23-2
Relation between
theoretical and actual values
of a warrant**

it has the greatest potential percentagewise for upside movements and where the amount of funds invested is not all that great. The valuation of options, of which warrants are one form, is explored in more depth in the Appendix to this chapter.

511
CHAPTER 23
Convertible
securities and
warrants

SUMMARY

Convertible securities and warrants are two types of options under which the holder can obtain common stock. The conversion feature enables the investor to convert a debt instrument or preferred stock into common stock, whereas a warrant enables the holder to purchase a specified number of shares of common stock at a specified price. With a warrant, the exercise of the option does not result in the elimination of the bonds. Convertibles are used more than warrants in financing.

The value of the convertible in the market place is determined by its value as a straight bond or preferred stock and its conversion value as common stock. For the corporation, convertibles represent delayed common-stock financing, and the timing of a convertible issue must be analyzed by the company in relation to the market for its common stock. For a given amount of financing, there will be less dilution with a convertible issue than with a common-stock issue, assuming, of course, that the issue eventually converts. This advantage is offset somewhat by the risk of an "overhanging" issue, which occurs when the company is unable to force conversion. A firm encounters this difficulty when the market price of a stock does not go high enough to raise the conversion value of the security significantly above the call price. An overhanging issue results in less financing flexibility for the issuer.

Normally, warrants are employed as a "sweetener" for a public or private issue of debt. The market value of a warrant usually is higher than its theoretical value when the market value of the stock is close to the exercise price, because this situation gives the investor an opportunity for favorable leverage. When the market price of the stock is high relative to the exercise price, warrants tend to sell at about their theoretical values.

APPENDIX A ⟍ Option Pricing

An option is simply a contract that gives the holder the right to buy or sell the common stock of a company at some specified price. Among a variety of option contracts, the most prevalent are the *call option* and the *put option*. The call option gives the holder the right to buy a share of stock at a specified price, known as the exercise price. We might have a call option to buy one share of ABC Corporation's common stock at $10 through December 31, which is the expiration date. The party who provides the option is known as the *writer*. In the case of a call option, the writer must deliver stock to the optionholder when the latter exercises the option.

As evident from our discussions in the chapter, a warrant is a form of call option, as is the convertible security, in that it gives the holder an option on the company's stock. In contrast to a call option, a put option gives the holder the right

512

PART VII

Longer-term
financing—
instruments
and markets

to sell a share of stock at a specified price up to the expiration date. It is the mirror image of a call option. In what follows, we will focus only on the valuation of call options.

Valuation on expiration date

Suppose that we were concerned with the value of a call option, (hereafter simply called an option) on its expiration date. The value of the option is simply

$$V_o = \text{Max}(V_s - E, 0) \tag{23A-1}$$

where V_s is the market price of one share of stock, E is the exercise price of the option, and Max means the maximum value of $V_s - E$ or zero, whichever is greater. To illustrate the formula, suppose one share of Selby Corporation's stock is $25 at the expiration date and that the exercise price of an option is $15. The value of the option would be $25 − $15 = $10. Note that the value of the option is determined solely by the value of the stock less the exercise price; however, the option cannot have a negative value. When the exercise price exceeds the value of the stock, the value of the option becomes zero.

This notion is illustrated graphically in Fig. 23-2, where the theoretical value of a warrant is shown. The expiration value of the option lies along the theoretical-value line; the horizontal axis represents the price of a share of stock at the expiration date.

Consider now the value of an option with one period to expiration. For simplicity, let us assume that it can be exercised only on the expiration date. The value of stock at the expiration date is not known, but rather is subject to probabilistic beliefs. As long as there is some time to expiration, it is possible for the market value of the option to be greater than its theoretical value. The reason is that the option *may* have value in the future. This was discussed for the warrant, so further discussion is not necessary. The actual value of the option might be described by the dashed line in Fig. 23-2.

The effect of time to expiration. In general, the longer the period of time to expiration, the greater the value of the option relative to its theoretical value. This makes sense in that there is more time in which the option may have value. Moreover, the further in the future one pays the exercise price, the lower its present value, and this too enhances the option's value. As the expiration date of an option approaches, the relationship between the option value and the stock value becomes more convex. This is illustrated in Fig. 23-A-1. Line 1 represents an option with a shorter time to expiration than that for line 2, and line 2 represents an option with a shorter time to expiration than that for line 3.

The influence of volatility. Usually the most important factor in the valuation of options is the price volatility of the associated stock. More specifically, the

FIGURE 23A-1
Relation between stock price and option price for various expiration dates

greater the possibility of extreme outcomes, the greater the value of the option to the holder, all other things the same. We may, at the beginning of a period, be considering options on two stocks that have the following probability distributions of possible values at the expiration of the option:

Probability of occurrence	Price of Stock A	Price of Stock B
.10	$30	$20
.25	36	30
.30	40	40
.25	44	50
.10	50	60

The expected stock price at the end of the period is the same for both stocks: $40. For Stock B, however, there is a much larger dispersion of possible outcomes. Suppose that the exercise prices of options to purchase Stock A and Stock B at the end of the period are also the same, say $38. Thus, the two stocks have the same expected values at the end of the period, and the options have the same exercise price. The expected value of the option for Stock A at the end of the period, however, is

$$\text{Option A} = 0(.10) + 0(.25) + (\$40 - \$38)(.30)$$
$$+ (\$44 - \$38)(.25) + (\$50 - \$38)(.10) = \$3.30$$

514

PART VII
Longer-term
financing—
instruments
and markets

whereas that for Stock B is

$$\text{Option } B = 0(.10) + 0(.25) + (\$40 - \$38)(.30)$$
$$+ (\$50 - \$38)(.25) + (\$60 - \$38)(.10) = \$5.80$$

Thus, the greater dispersion of possible outcomes for Stock B leads to a greater expected value of option price on the expiration date. The reason is that values for the option cannot be negative. As a result, the greater the dispersion, the greater the magnitude of favorable outcomes as measured by the stock price minus the exercise price. Increases in the volatility of the stock therefore increase the magnitude of favorable outcomes for the option buyer and, hence, increase the value of the option.

Hedging with options

Having two related financial assets—a stock and an option on that stock—we can set up a risk-free hedged position. Price movements in one of the financial assets will be offset by opposite price movements in the other. A hedged position can be established by buying the stock (holding it long) and by writing options. If the stock goes up in price, we gain in our long position; that is, in the stock we hold. We lose in the options we have written, because the price we must pay for the stock in order to deliver to the person exercising the option is higher than it was when the option was written. If the stock goes down in price, the opposite occurs. We lose on our long position, but gain on the options we have written.

Thus, when one holds a combination of stock and options written, movements upward or downward in the price of the stock are offset by opposite movements in the value of the option position written. If one does this properly, the overall position (long in stock, options written) can be made approximately risk-free. In market equilibrium, one would expect to earn only the risk-free rate on a perfectly hedged position.

Black-Scholes option model

In a seminal paper, Fischer Black and Myron Scholes developed a precise model for determining the equilibrium value of an option.[4] This model is based on the hedging notion discussed above. Black-Scholes assume an option that can be exercised only at maturity, no transaction costs or market imperfections, a stock that pays no dividend, a known short-term interest rate at which market participants can both borrow and lend, and, finally, stock price movements that follow a random pattern.

Given these assumptions, we can determine the equilibrium value of an option. Should the actual price of the option differ from that given by the model, we could establish a riskless hedged position and earn a return in excess of the short-term interest rate. As arbitragers entered the scene, the excess return would

---

[4]"The Pricing of Options and Corporate Liabilities," *Journal of Political Economy*, 81 (May–June 1973), 637–54.

FIGURE 23A-2
**Relation between the option
price and the stock price
for XYZ Corporation**

eventually be driven out and the price of the option would equal that value given by the model.

To illustrate a hedged position, suppose that the appropriate relationship between the option and the stock of XYZ Corporation were that shown in Fig. 23A-2. Suppose further that the current market price of the stock were $20 and the price of the option $7. At $20 a share, the slope of the line in Fig. 23A-2 is one-half. A hedged position could be undertaken by buying a share of stock for $20 and writing two options at $7 each. The "net money" invested in this position would be $20 − 2($7) = $6.

This combination of holding one share of stock long and two options short leaves us essentially hedged with respect to risk. If the stock drops slightly in value, the value of the short position goes up by approximately an equal amount. We say *approximately* because with changes in the price of the common and with changes in time, the ideal hedge ratio changes. With a stock price increase, for example, the slope of the line in Fig. 23A-2 increases. Therefore, fewer options would need to be written. If the stock price declines, the slope decreases and more options would need to be written to maintain a hedge. In addition, the line itself will shift downward as time goes on and the expiration date approaches. This was illustrated in Fig. 23A-1. The downward shift due to the passage of time causes the line to be more convex and, therefore, its slope to be affected.

Thus, one's short position in options must be continually adjusted for changes in the stock price and for changes in time if a riskless hedged position is to be maintained. The assumptions of the model make this possible; but in the real world, transaction costs make it impractical to adjust one's short position continuously. Even here, however, the risk that will appear as a result of moderate changes in stock price or of the passage of time will be small. Moreover, it can be diversified away. For practical purposes, then, it is possible to maintain a hedged position that is approximately risk-free. Arbitrage will assure that the return on this position is approximately the short-term, risk-free rate.

516

PART VII

Longer-term
financing—
instruments
and markets

If the price of the option got out of line with that of the stock, it would be possible for a person to earn more than the short-term rate on a hedged position. In the example above, the "net money" invested in the position was $6 [$20 − 2($7)]. As the total hedged position is riskless, the "net money" invested should provide a return equal only to the short-term rate. If for some reason the prices on the two instruments got out of line with each other, it would be possible to earn a return on the total position in excess of the short-term rate times the "net money" invested. In other words, excess returns would be possible on a position perfectly hedged for risk.

As a result, arbitragers would enter the picture and would borrow large sums of money, establish hedged positions, and reap the excess returns available. This action would continue until the buying or selling pressure on the prices of the stock and the option drove such prices into "equilibrium" with each other. At such time, the return on the "net money" invested in a fully hedged position would once again be the short-term rate. Thus, there are equilibrating forces that cause a riskless hedge to provide a return equal to the short-term rate.

The exact formula and implications. In this context, the equilibrium value of an option that entitles the holder to buy one share of stock is shown by Black and Scholes to be

$$V_o = V_s N(d_1) - \left(\frac{E}{e^{rt}}\right)N(d_2) \tag{23A-2}$$

where V_s = the current price of the stock
E = the exercise price of the option
e = 2.71828
r = the short-term interest rate continuously compounded
t = the length of time in years to the expiration of the option
$N(d)$ = the value of the cumulative normal density function
$d_1 = \dfrac{\ln(V_s/E + (r + 1/2\sigma^2)t}{\sigma\sqrt{t}}$
$d_2 = \dfrac{\ln(V_s/E) + (r - 1/2\sigma^2)t}{\sigma\sqrt{t}}$
$\ln$ = the natural logarithm
σ = the standard deviation of the annual rate of return on the stock continuously compounded

The important implication of this formula is that the value of the option is a function of the short-term interest rate, of the time to expiration, and of the variance rate of return on the stock, but it is not a function of the expected return on the stock. The value of the option in Eq. (23A-2) increases with the increase of the duration to expiration, t, the standard deviation, σ, and the short-term interest rate, r.

The reason for the first two relationships with option values is obvious from our earlier discussion. The last is not so obvious. Recall that a person is able to take a position in options that will provide the same dollar movements as the associated stock, but with a lower net investment. The "difference" in net money in the option relative to the stock may be invested in short-term market instruments. The greater the return on these investments, therefore, the greater the attraction of the option relative to the stock, and the greater its value. Another way to look at the matter is that the greater the interest rate, the lower the present value of exercise price that will need to be paid in the future if the option is exercised, and the greater the value of the option. Of the three factors affecting the value of the option, however, the short-term interest rate has the least impact.

In solving the formula, we know the current stock price, the time to expiration, the exercise price, and the short-term interest rate. The key unknown, then, is the standard deviation. This must be estimated. The usual approach is to use the past volatility of the stock's return as a proxy for the future. Black and Scholes as well as others have tested the model using standard deviations estimated from past data with some degree of success. Given the valuation equation for options, Black and Scholes derive the ratio of shares of stock to options necessary to maintain a fully hedged position. It is shown to be $N(d_1)$, which was defined earlier. Thus, the Black-Scholes model permits the quantification of the various factors that affect the value of an option. As we saw, the key factor is estimating the future volatility of the stock.

A summing up

In summary, it is possible to establish a riskless hedged position by buying a stock and by writing options. The hedge ratio determines the portion of stock held long in relation to the options that are written. In efficient financial markets, the rate of return on a perfectly hedged position would be the risk-free rate. If this is the case, it is possible to determine the appropriate value of the option at the beginning of the period. If the actual value is above or below this value, arbitrage should drive the price of the option toward the correct price.

The Black-Scholes option-pricing model provides an exact formula for determining the value of an option based on the volatility of the stock, the price of the stock, the exercise price of the option, the time to expiration of the option, and the short-term interest rate. The model is based on the notion that investors are able to maintain reasonably hedged positions over time and that arbitrage will drive the return on such positions to the risk-free rate. As a result, the option price will bear a precise relationship to the stock price. The Black-Scholes model provides considerable insight into the valuation of contingent claims.

QUESTIONS

1. Because the interest on convertible bonds is tax deductible, but the dividend on a convertible preferred is not, would a company be more inclined to force or stimulate conversion of a convertible preferred than it would a convertible bond?

2. This chapter has argued that convertibles are a form of delayed equity financing allowing the sale of equity at a 10 to 20 percent premium over current market price. Yet most convertibles are finally called only if the current market price is well in excess of the

518

PART VII
Longer-term
financing—
instruments
and markets

conversion price. Would not the firm have been better off to wait and sell the common stock? Explain your position.

3. If convertible securities can be issued at a lower effective interest rate than long-term bonds, why would a company ever issue straight debt?

4. Why do warrants whose theoretical value is zero sell for positive prices?

5. Suppose you are the financial manager of a rather closely held small electronics firm. You have a favorable investment opportunity and are considering raising funds to finance it, using subordinated convertible debentures or straight bonds with warrants attached. Equity funds are not a possibility, as you feel the current stock price has been unnecessarily penalized for recent start-up expenses and the firm's high debt ratio (relative to the industry). If you expect additional large future funds requirements, which financing alternative would you adopt? Why?

6. Why might a convertible bondholder elect to convert voluntarily?

7. What reasons can you offer for the use of warrants by small, rapidly growing companies?

8. Why does the market price of an option such as a warrant usually exceed its value as common stock?

9. When a convertible security is converted into common stock, there is dilution in earnings per share. Would you expect the market price of the stock to decline as a result of this dilution?

10. If the desire of a company in selling convertible securities is delayed equity financing, would not it be wise to establish at the time the security is sold a "step-up" in conversion price every few years?

11. Why would an investor want to invest in warrants as opposed to common stock?

12. As a lender, how attractive are warrants to you as a "sweetener"? Will you give terms more favorable than you otherwise would?

PROBLEMS

1. The Charrier Boat Company has current earnings of $3 a share with 500,000 shares outstanding. The company plans to issue 40,000 shares of 7%, $50-par-value convertible preferred stock at par. The preferred stock is convertible into two shares of common for each preferred share held. The common stock has a current market price of $21 per share.

   a) What is the preferred stock's conversion value?

   b) What is its conversion premium?

   c) Assuming that total earnings stay the same, what will be the effect of the issue on earnings per share before conversion? after full conversion?

   d) If profits after taxes increase by $1 million, what will be earnings per share before conversion? after full conversion?

2. The common stock of the Davidson Corporation earns $2.50 per share, has a 60 percent dividend payout, and sells at a P/E ratio of 10. Davidson wishes to offer $10 million of 9

percent, 20-year convertible debentures with an initial conversion premium of 20 percent and a call price of $105. Davidson currently has 1 million common shares outstanding and has a 50 percent tax rate.

a) What is the conversion price?

b) What is the conversion ratio per $1,000 debenture?

c) What is the initial conversion value of each debenture?

d) How many new shares of common must be issued if all debentures are converted?

e) If Davidson can increase operating earnings (before taxes) by $1 million per year with the proceeds of the debenture issue, compute the new earnings per share and earnings retained before and after conversion.

3. Assume that the Davidson Corporation (in problem 2) raised the $10 million through an issue of stock (total spread and expenses = 10 percent of gross proceeds of issue). How many new shares would have to be issued? If operating earnings were increased by $1 million through the use of the proceeds, compute the new earnings per share and earnings retention. Compare your answers with those obtained in 2(e) above.

4. Assume that the Davidson Corporation (in problem 2) could sell $10 million in straight debt at 12 percent as an alternative to the convertible issue. Compute the earnings per share and earnings retained after issuance of the straight debt under the assumption of a $1 million increase in operating earnings and compare your answers with those obtained in 2(e) above.

5. The Beruth Company needs to raise $10 million by means of a debt issue. It has the following alternatives:

a) A 20-year, 8 percent convertible debenture issue with a $50 conversion price and $1,000 face value, or

b) A 20-year, 12 percent straight debt issue. Each $1,000 bond has a detachable warrant to purchase 4 shares of stock for a total of $200.

The company has a 50 percent tax rate, and its stock is currently selling at $40 per share. Its net income before interest and taxes is a constant 20 percent of its total capitalization, which currently appears as follows:

Common stock (par $5)	$ 5,000,000
Paid-in capital	10,000,000
Retained earnings	15,000,000
Total	$30,000,000

1) Show the capitalizations resulting from each alternative, both before and after conversion or exercise (a total of four capitalizations).

2) Compute earnings per share currently and under each of the four capitalizations determined in part a.

3) If the price of Beruth stock went to $75, determine the theoretical value of each warrant issued under alternative b above.

6. Using Eq. (23-2), compute the theoretical value of each of the following warrants:

520

PART VII
Longer-term
financing—
instruments
and markets

Warrant	N	P_s	E
(a)	5	$100	$400
(b)	10	10	60
(c)	2.3	4	10
(d)	3.54	27⅛	35.40

7. Stanley Zinc Company called its 7 percent convertible subordinated debentures for redemption on March 25, 1983. The call price was $106. A holder of a $1,000 bond was
entitled to convert into 34.7 shares of stock. At the time of the call announcement, the
common stock of Stanley Zinc was selling at $43 per share.

a) What is the approximate market price at which the debentures would be selling at the
time of the announcement?

b) By what percentage would market price per share need to drop before bondholders
would rationally accept the call price?

8. Max Murphy Inc. has warrants outstanding which allow the holder to purchase 3 shares
of stock for a total $60 for each warrant that is held. Currently, the market price per share
of Max Murphy common is $18. However, investors hold the following probabilistic beliefs
about the stock six months hence.

Market price per share	$16	$18	$20	$22	$24
Probability	.15	.20	.30	.20	.15

a) What is the present theoretical value of the warrant?

b) What is the expected value of stock price 6 months hence?

c) What is the expected theoretical value of the warrant 6 months hence?

d) Would you expect the present market price of the warrant to equal its theoretical value?
If not, why not?

9. Suppose you have just bought a warrant which entitles you to purchase two shares of
stock for $45. The market price of the stock is $26 per share, whereas the market price
of the warrant is $10 in excess of its theoretical value. One year later the stock has risen
in price to $50 per share. The warrant now sells for $2 more than its theoretical value.

a) If the common stock paid $1 in dividends for the year, what is the return on investment
in the common?

b) What is the return on investment in the warrant?

c) Why do the two rates of return differ?

10. Sadfield Manufacturing Company plans to issue $10 million in 7½ percent convertible
subordinated debentures. Currently, the stock price is $36 per share, and the company
believes it could obtain a conversion premium (issuing price in excess of conversion
value) of approximately 12 percent. The call price of the debenture in the first ten years
is $1,060 per bond, after which it drops to $1,030 in the next ten years and to $1,000 in
the last ten years. To allow for fluctuations in the market price of the stock, the company

does not want to call the debentures until their conversion value is at least 15 percent in excess of the call price. Earnings per share are expected to grow at an 8 percent compound annual rate for the foreseeable future, and the company envisions no change in its price/earnings ratio.

a) Determine the expected length of time that must elapse before the company is in a position to force conversion.

b) Is the issuance of a convertible security a good idea for the company?

SELECTED REFERENCES

ALEXANDER, GORDON J., and ROGER D. STOVER, "The Effect of Forced Conversion on Common Stock Prices," *Financial Management*, 9 (Spring 1980), 39–45.

———, and DAVID B. KUHNAU, "Market Timing Strategies in Convertible Debt Financing," *Journal of Finance*, 34 (March 1979), 143–56.

BACON, PETER W., and EDWARD L. WINN, JR., "The Impact of Forced Conversion on Stock Prices," *Journal of Finance*, 24 (December 1969), 871–74.

BLACK, FISCHER, and MYRON SCHOLES, "The Pricing of Options and Corporate Liabilities," *Journal of Political Economy*, 81 (May–June 1973), 637–54.

———, "The Valuation of Option Contracts and a Test of Market Efficiency," *Journal of Finance*, 27 (May 1972), 399–417.

BRENNAN, MICHAEL J., and EDUARDO S. SCHWARTZ, "Analyzing Convertible Bonds," *Journal of Financial and Quantitative Analysis*, 15 (November 1980), 907–29.

———, "Convertible Bonds: Valuation and Optimal Strategies for Call and Conversion," *Journal of Finance,* 32 (December 1977), 1699–1715.

BRIGHAM, EUGENE F., "An Analysis of Convertible Debentures: Theory and Some Empirical Evidence," *Journal of Finance*, 21 (March 1966), 35–54.

FRANK, WERNER G., and CHARLES O. KRONCKE, "Classifying Conversions of Convertible Debentures over Four Years," *Financial Management*, 3 (Summer 1974). 33–42.

JENNINGS, EDWARD H., "An Estimate of Convertible Bond Premiums," *Journal of Financial and Quantitative Analysis,* 9 (January 1974), 33–56.

LEWELLEN, WILBUR G., and GEORGE A. RACETTE, "Convertible Debt Financing," *Journal of Financial and Quantitative Analysis*, 7 (December 1973), 777–92.

MERTON, ROBERT C., "On the Pricing of Corporate Debt," *Journal of Finance*, 29 (May 1974), 449–70.

MILLER, ALEXANDER B., "How to Call Your Convertible," *Harvard Business Review*, 49 (May–June 1971), 66–70.

NOREEN, ERIC, and MARK WOLFSON, "Equilibrium Warrant Pricing Models and Accounting for Executive Stock Options," *Journal of Accounting Research*, forthcoming.

PIPER, THOMAS R., and JASPER H. ARNOLD, III, "Warrants and Convertible Debt as Financing Vehicles in the Private Placement Market," *Explorations in Economic Research of the National Bureau of Economic Research* 4 (Spring 1977), 277–302.

RUBINSTEIN, MARK, and JOHN C. COX, *Option Markets*. Englewood Cliffs, N.J.: Prentice-Hall, 1982.

RUSH, DAVID F., and RONALD W. MELICHER, "An Empirical Examination of Factors Which Influence Warrant Prices," *Journal of Finance*, 29 (December 1974), 1449–66.

SHARPE, WILLIAM F., *Investments,* 2d. ed. Englewood Cliffs, N.J.: Prentice-Hall, 1981, chap. 16.

SMITH, CLIFFORD W., JR., "Option Pricing: A Review," *Journal of Financial Economics* 3 (January–March 1976), 3–51.

STONE, BERNELL K., "Warrant Financing," *Journal of Financial and Quantitative Analysis*, 11 (March 1976), 143–54.

VAN HORNE, JAMES C., "Warrant Valuation in Relation to Volatility and Opportunity Costs," *Industrial Management Review*, 10 (Spring 1969), 19–32.

SPECIAL AREAS OF FINANCIAL MANAGEMENT

VIII

Mergers and acquisitions

24

Growth is an essential ingredient to the success and vitality of many a company. Without it, a company has difficulty generating dedication of purpose and attracting first-rate managers. Growth can be either internal or external. Up to now, we have considered only internal growth: a firm acquires specific assets and finances them by the retention of earnings or external financing. External growth, on the other hand, involves the acquisition of another company. In principle, growth by acquiring another company is little different from growth by acquiring a specific asset. Each requires an initial outlay, which is expected to be followed by future benefits. The objective of either type of acquisition is to maximize the value of the firm to existing shareholders.

By way of definition, a *statutory merger* is a combination of two corporations wherein one loses its corporate existence. The surviving company acquires both the assets and the liabilities of the merged company. A merger must be distinguished from a *statutory consolidation,* which is a combination of two companies, whereby an entirely new corporation is formed. Both the old companies cease to exist, and shares of their common stock are exchanged for shares in the new company. When two companies of about the same size combine, they usually consolidate. When the two companies differ significantly in size, they usually merge. Though it is necessary to understand the distinction, the words *merger* and *consolidation* tend to be used interchangeably to describe the combination of two companies.

REASONS FOR COMBINATION

The reasons for a combination are many and complex. Moreover, they are not mutually exclusive; more than one reason usually is involved in a combination. In this section we consider various reasons for combinations but recognize that they must be taken collectively.

Operating economies and economies of scale

Often, operating economies can be achieved through a combination of companies. Duplicate facilities can be eliminated; marketing, accounting, purchasing, and other operations can be consolidated. The sales force may be reduced to avoid duplication of effort in a particular territory. In a railroad merger, the principal objective is to realize economies of operation through elimination of duplicate facilities and runs. When industrial companies merge, a firm with a product that complements an existing product line may fill out that line and increase the total demand for products of the acquiring company. The realization of such economies is known as *synergism*; the fused company is of greater value than the sum of the parts; that is, $2 + 2 = 5$.

In addition to operating economies, economies of scale may be possible with a merger of two companies. Economies of scale occur when average cost declines with increases in volume. Usually we think of economies of scale in production, and overlook their possibilities in marketing, purchasing, distribution, accounting, and even finance. The idea is to concentrate a greater volume of activity into a given facility, into a given number of people, into a given distribution system, and so on. In other words, increases in volume permit a more efficient utilization of resources. Like anything else, it has limits. Beyond a point, increases in volume may cause more problems than they remedy, and a company actually may become less efficient. Economists speak of an "envelope curve" with economies of scale possible up to some optimal point, after which diseconomies occur.

Economies can best be realized with a *horizontal merger*, combining two companies in the same line of business. The economies achieved by this means result primarily from eliminating duplicate facilities and offering a broader product line in the hope of increasing total demand. A *vertical merger*, whereby a company expands either forward toward the ultimate consumer or backward toward the source of raw material, may also bring about economies. This type of merger gives a company more control over its distribution and purchasing. There are few operating economies in a *conglomerate merger*, combining two companies in unrelated lines of business.

Management acquisition

Closely related to economies is the acquisition of management. If a firm finds that it is unable to hire top-quality management and that it has no one coming up through the ranks, it may seek a combination with another company having aggressive and competent management. The choice may be between gradual stagnation with an existing organization or combination with another company in order to obtain competent management. To foster the long-run wealth of stockholders, the combination may be the only realistic alternative.

Growth

A company may not be able to grow at a fast or balanced enough rate by internal expansion and may find that its only way of achieving a desired growth rate is by acquiring other companies. Growth by acquisition may well be cheaper than internal growth; the numerous costs and risks involved in developing and embarking upon a new-product line or a new facility may be avoided through acquisition of a going concern. It usually is quicker to acquire new products and facilities through mergers than through internal development. External growth may demand acquisition of research capabilities of another firm. Because research tends to be individually oriented, the acquiring company may be unable to develop such capabilities on its own. Closely related to research is the possession of basic patents. A company having certain patent rights may be extremely valuable for this reason alone. Finally, it may be that a company is able to acquire needed physical assets of another firm less expensively than it could obtain similar assets by direct purchase.

Although these factors may lead to higher future earnings and growth, the critical factor is the price paid for the acquisition. If the company to be acquired is priced rationally in the market (that is, it is not undervalued or overvalued), its acquisition is unlikely to increase share price *unless* there is synergism. Increased growth in *total* earnings is not the important thing—it is increased growth in earnings *per share,* all other things the same. Unfortunately, in certain cases growth in sales, assets, and total earnings appears to have supplanted maximization of shareholder wealth as the primary goal of the firm.

Tax loss carry forward

A factor in some mergers is the presence of a tax loss carry forward. A company with cumulative tax losses may have little prospect of earning enough in the future to utilize fully its tax loss carry forward.[1] By merging with a profitable company, it may be possible for the surviving company to fully utilize the carry forward. Therefore, there is an economic gain—at the expense of the government—which cannot be realized by either company separately.

[1] A loss is carried back three years and forward fifteen years to offset taxable income in those years. It first must be applied to the earliest preceding year and then to the next two years in order. If the loss is not entirely offset by earnings in the three prior years, the residual is carried forward sequentially to reduce future profits, and taxes, in each of the next fifteen years.

Diversification

Diversification is the motive in some mergers. By acquiring a firm in a different line of business, a company may be able to reduce cyclical instability in earnings. Although it is virtually impossible to find two companies with negative correlation in earnings, it is possible to find situations in which there is only moderate correlation. Related to the argument for diversification is the notion of spreading risk. To the extent that investors in a company's stock are averse to risk and are concerned only with the total risk of the firm, a reduction in earnings instability would have a favorable impact upon share price.

This argument assumes that investors evaluate risk solely in relation to the *total* risk of the firm. We know from chapters 5 and 15, however, that investors are able to diversify risk on their own. If they evaluate risk in an overall market context, they will diversify at least as effectively on their own as the firm is able to do for them. Particularly when the stock of the company being acquired is publicly traded, there is no reason to believe that investors are not able to diversify their portfolios efficiently. Because the firm is unable to do something for them that they cannot do for themselves, diversification as a reason for merging usually is not a thing of value. Consequently, it would not lead to an increase in share price. For the most part, the prospect for synergism is what is valuable when it comes to a merger.

Personal reasons

In a tightly held company, the individuals who have controlling interest may want their company acquired by another company that has an established market for its stock. For estate tax purposes, it may be desirable for these individuals to hold shares of stock that are readily marketable and for which market-price quotations are available. The owners of a tightly held company may have too much of their wealth tied up in the company. By merging with a publicly held company, they obtain a marked improvement in their liquidity, enabling them to sell some of their stock and diversify their investments.

IMPACT OF TERMS OF MERGER

When two companies are combined, a ratio of exchange occurs, denoting the relative weighting of the firms. In this section we consider the ratio of exchange with respect to the earnings, the market prices, and the book values of the stocks of the two companies involved. We assume that the combination is consummated in stock rather than in cash or debt. The objective in any merger should be to maximize the long-run wealth of existing stockholders. A successful merger, then, would be one that increased the market price of the firm's stock over the price it would have brought if the combination had not taken place.

Earnings impact

In evaluating a possible acquisition, the acquiring firm must consider the effect the merger will have on the earnings per share of the surviving corporation.

Company A is considering the acquisition, by stock, of Company B. The financial data on the acquisition at the time it is being considered are as follows:

	Company A	Company B
Present earnings	$20,000,000	$5,000,000
Shares	5,000,000	2,000,000
Earnings per share	$ 4.00	$ 2.50
Price per stock	$64.00	$30.00
Price/earnings ratio	16	12

Company B has agreed to an offer of $35 a share to be paid in Company A's stock. The exchange ratio, then, is $35/$64, or about .547 shares of Company A's stock for each share of Company B's stock. In total 1,093,750 shares of Company A will need to be issued in order to acquire Company B. Assuming that the earnings of the component companies stay the same after the acquisition, earnings per share of the surviving company would be:

	Surviving Company A
Earnings	$25,000,000
Shares	6,093,750
Earnings per share	$4.10

Thus, there is an immediate improvement in earnings per share for Company A as a result of the merger. Company B's former stockholders experience a reduction in earnings per share, however. For each share of B's stock they had held, they now hold .547 shares of A. Thus, the earnings per share on each share of Company B's stock they held is (.547)(4.10), or $2.24, compared with $2.50 before.

Suppose now that the price agreed upon for Company B's stock is $45 instead of $35 a share. The ratio of exchange, then, would be $45/$64, or about .703 shares of A for each share of B. In total, 1,406,250 shares would have to be issued, and earnings per share after the merger would be

	Surviving Company A
Earnings	$25,000,000
Shares	6,406,250
Earnings per share	$3.90

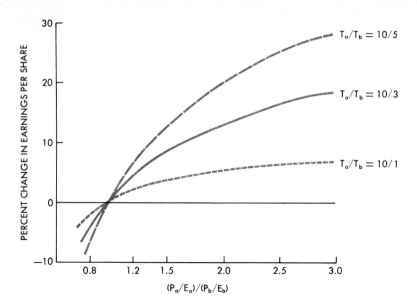

FIGURE 24-1
Relationship between
earnings-per-share change
and the price/earnings
ratio differential and
relative earnings

In this case, there is initial dilution in Company A's earnings per share on account of the acquisition of Company B.[2] Dilution in earnings per share will occur anytime the price/earnings ratio paid for a company exceeds the price/earnings ratio of the company doing the acquiring. In our example, the price/earnings ratio in the first case was $35/$2.50, or 14, and in the second case it was $45/$2.50, or 18. Because the price/earnings ratio of Company A was 16, there was an increase in earnings per share in the first case and a decrease in the second.

Thus, initial increases and decreases in earnings per share are both possible. The *amount* of increase or decrease is a function of (1) the differential in price/earnings ratios, and (2) the relative size of the two firms as measured by total earnings.[3] The higher the price/earnings ratio of the acquiring company in relation to that of the company being acquired, and the larger the earnings of the acquired company in relation to those of the acquiring company, the greater the increase in earnings per share of the acquiring company. These relationships are illustrated in Fig. 24-1 for three different earnings relationships. The a subscript for total earnings, T_a, and for price/earnings ratio, P_a/E_a, denotes the acquiring company, while the b subscript for T_b and P_b/E_b denotes the company being acquired.

Future earnings. If the decision to acquire another company were based solely upon the initial impact on earnings per share, an initial dilution in earnings per share would stop any company from acquiring another. This type of analysis, however, does not take into account the possibility of a future growth in earnings owing to the merger. This growth may be due to the expected growth in earnings of the acquired company as an independent entity and to any synergistic effects that result from the fusion of the two companies. If the earnings of Company B are

[2]Company B's former stockholders obtain an improvement in earnings per share. Earnings per share on each share of stock they had held are $2.74.

[3]See Walter J. Mead, "Instantaneous Merger Profit as a Conglomerate Merger Motive," *Western Economics Review*, 7 (December 1969), 295–306.

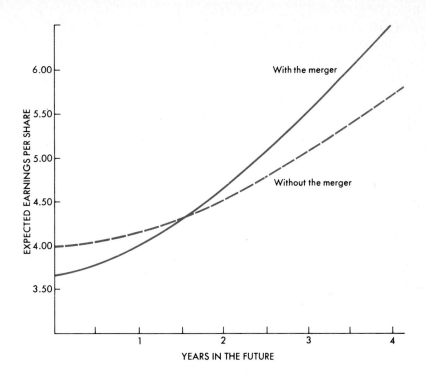

FIGURE 24-2
Expected earnings per share with and without the merger

Chart labels: Y-axis: EXPECTED EARNINGS PER SHARE (values 3.50, 4.00, 4.50, 5.00, 5.50, 6.00). X-axis: YEARS IN THE FUTURE (1, 2, 3, 4). Curves labeled "With the merger" and "Without the merger".

expected to grow at a faster rate than those of Company A or if there is expected synergy, a high ratio of exchange for the stock may be justified, even though there is initial dilution in earnings per share for stockholders of Company A. The superior growth in earnings of the acquired company may result eventually in higher earnings per share for these stockholders relative to earnings per share without the merger.

It is useful to graph likely future earnings per share with and without the acquisition. Figure 24-2 shows this for a hypothetical merger. The graph tells us how long it will take for the dilution in earnings per share to be eliminated, and for an accretion to take place. In this example, it is one and one-half years; earnings per share drop $.30 initially, but this relative dilution is eliminated by the middle of the second year. The greater the duration of dilution, the less desirable the acquisition is said to be from the standpoint of the acquiring company. Some companies set a ceiling on the number of years dilution will be tolerated, and this ceiling serves as a constraint in establishing the exchange ratio to be paid in the acquisition. When an acquisition is being considered, graphs should be prepared under differing assumptions of the exchange ratio. They also should be made under differing earnings assumptions for the combination; preparing such multiple graphs gives management greater information on which to base negotiations.

Market-value impact

The major emphasis in the bargaining process is on the ratio of exchange of market prices per share. Judging the intrinsic value of a company, investors focus on the market price of its stock. That price reflects the earnings potential of the

company, dividends, business risk, capital structure, asset values, and other factors that bear upon valuation. The ratio of exchange of market prices is simply

$$\frac{\text{Market price per share of acquiring company} \times \text{Number of shares offered}}{\text{Market price per share of acquired company}}$$

If the market price of Acquiring Company is $60 per share and that of Bought
Company is $30, and Acquiring Company offers a half share of its stock for each
share of Bought Company, the ratio of exchange will be

$$\frac{\$60 \times .5}{\$30} = 1.00$$

In other words, the stocks of the two companies will be exchanged on a one-to-one
market-price basis. If the market price of the surviving company is relatively stable
at $60 a share, stockholders of both companies are as well off as before with respect
to market value. The company being acquired finds little enticement to accept a
one-to-one market-value ratio of exchange, however. The acquiring company usually must offer a price in excess of the current market price per share of the
company it wishes to acquire. Instead of a half share of stock, Acquiring Company
might have to offer .667 shares, or $40 a share in current market value.

Bootstrapping earnings per share.   In the absence of synergism or of the
underpricing of Bought Company's stock in an inefficient market, we would not
expect it to be in the interest of Acquiring's stockholders to offer a price in excess
of Bought Company's current market price. Acquiring stockholders could be better
off if their company's price/earnings ratio is higher than Bought Company's and if
somehow the surviving company is able to keep that same higher price/earnings
ratio after the merger. Perhaps the potential acquiree has a price/earnings ratio of
10. The potential acquirer, on the other hand, has a price/earnings ratio of 18.
Assume the following financial information:

	Company A	Company B
Present earnings	$20,000,000	$6,000,000
Shares	6,000,000	2,000,000
Earnings per share	$ 3.33	$ 3.00
Market price per share	$60.00	$30.00
Price/earnings ratio	18	10

With an offer of .667 shares of Acquiring Company for each share of Bought
Company, or $40 a share in value, the market-price exchange ratio for Bought
Company is

$$\frac{\$60 \times .667}{\$30} = 1.33$$

Stockholders of Bought Company are being offered a stock with a market value of $40 for each share of stock they own. Obviously, they benefit from the acquisition with respect to market price, because their stock was formerly worth $30 a share. Stockholders of Acquiring Company also stand to benefit, if the price/earnings of the surviving company stays at 18. The market price per share of the surviving company after the acquisition, all other things held constant, would be

	Surviving company
Total earnings	$26,000,000
Number of shares	7,333,333
Earnings per share	$3.55
Price/earnings ratio	18
Market price per share	$63.90

The reason for this apparent bit of magic whereby the stockholders of both companies benefit is the difference in price/earnings ratios.

Thus, companies with high price/earnings ratios supposedly would be able to acquire companies with lower price/earnings ratios and obtain an immediate increase in earnings per share, despite the fact that they pay a premium with respect to the market-value exchange ratio. The key factor is what happens to the price/earnings ratio after the merger. If it stays the same, the market price of the stock will increase. As a result, an acquiring company would be able to show a steady growth in earnings per share if it acquired a sufficient number of companies over time in this manner. This increase is not the result of operating economies or underlying growth but is due to the "bootstrap" increase in earnings per share through acquisitions. As long as the marketplace values this illusory growth, a company presumably could increase shareholder wealth through acquisitions alone.

In reasonably efficient capital markets, it seems unlikely that the market will hold constant the price/earnings ratio of a company that cannot demonstrate growth potential in ways other than acquiring companies with lower price/earnings ratios. The acquiring company must be able to manage the companies it acquires and show some degree of synergism if the benefit of acquisitions is to be lasting. If the market is relatively free from imperfections and if synergism is not anticipated, we would expect the price/earnings ratio of the surviving firm to approach a weighted average of the two previous price/earnings ratios. Under these circumstances, the acquisition of companies with lower price/earnings ratios would not enhance shareholder wealth. For the acquiring company, share price would actually decline if the market value exchange ratio were more than 1.00. If synergism were expected, however, shareholder wealth could be increased through the acquisition.

Empirical evidence

In the numerous empirical studies of how mergers affect the valuation of the merged companies, differences in samples, sample periods, and research methods have rendered much of the evidence ambiguous.[4] From the more recent studies, certain generalizations seem possible. In almost all cases, the selling company's stockholders received a premium over the market price of their stock before negotiations took place. Otherwise, there would be little reason to consider a merger, unless it were a financial bailout. The size of the premium ranged from 15 percent to 50 percent in different studies. The premium itself began to be reflected in market price increases once information of merger negotiations became available. The typical time here was 7 to 10 months in advance of the actual merger.[5] Paying a premium for an acquisition was consistent with expected synergy or more efficient management of the resources of the acquired company. Indeed, many acquired companies were characterized by relatively low returns prior to merging.

For the buying company, the evidence is less clear. Several studies show that share price relative to similar risk stocks increased moderately for several years up to roughly the time of the merger, after which there was no noticeable effect.[6] Estimates of the improvement in share price are in the neighborhood of 5 to 10 percent; however, it cannot be said that the merger caused the increase in share price. The fact that share price performs well relative to the market may be a reason for a company to expand through acquisition.

The general nature of the share price effects found in various empirical studies is illustrated in Fig. 24-3. In summary, the empirical evidence gives indication that the selling company's stockholders reap significant gains from a merger. Although there appears to be a pre-merger share price improvement for buying companies in the aggregate, the effect is far less than that for selling companies, and it begins earlier. Since the share price increase may be the cause of the merger, rather than the result, it is not clear that, on average, buying companies gain from mergers. They do not lose, however, a result implying expected synergism that offsets the premium paid for the acquired company.

ACQUISITIONS AND CAPITAL BUDGETING

From the standpoint of the buying corporation, acquisitions can be treated as another aspect of capital budgeting. In principle, the prospective acquisition may be evaluated in much the same manner as any capital-budgeting project.

[4]For a comprehensive review of the empirical literature on mergers, see Dennis C. Mueller, "The Effects of Conglomerate Mergers," *Journal of Banking and Finance*, 1 (December 1977), 315–47. See also Pieter T. Elgers and John J. Clark, "Merger Types and Shareholder Returns: Additional Evidence," *Financial Management*, 9 (Summer 1980), 66–72.

[5]See Gershon Mendelker, "Risk and Return: The Case of Merging Firms," *Journal of Financial Economics*, 1 (December 1974), 303–35.

[6]Mendelker, "Risk and Return: The Case of Merging Firms;" James C. Ellert, "Mergers, Antitrust Law Enforcement and Stockholder Returns," *Journal of Finance*, 31 (May 1976), 715–32; and Elgers and Clark, "Merger Types and Shareholder Returns: Additional Evidence."

CUMULATIVE AVERAGE RETURN

Selling companies

Buying companies

Date of merger

TIME (in months)

FIGURE 24-3
Typical average relative stock returns before and after merging

There is an initial outlay and expected future benefits. Whether the outlay is cash or stock, the firm should attempt to allocate capital optimally in order to increase shareholder wealth over the long run. The only difference is that, with acquisitions, the initial cost may not be established; indeed, it usually is subject to bargaining. If it can be assumed that the acquiring company intends to maintain its existing capital structure over the long run, it is appropriate to evaluate the prospective acquisition without reference to the way it is financed.

In evaluating the prospective acquisition, the buying company should estimate the future cash income that the acquisition is expected to add after taxes, net of any new investment. The estimates should include consideration of any synergistic effects, for we are interested in the marginal impact of the acquisition. Moreover, the cash-flow estimates should be before any financial charges. The idea is to divorce the prospective acquisition's financial structure from its overall worth as an investment. Our concern is with operating cash flows that arise from operating the acquired company, not with prospective net income after financial charges. On the basis of these considerations, suppose the following incremental cash flows are expected from a prospective acquisition:

	Average for Years (in thousands)				
	1–5	*6–10*	*11–15*	*16–20*	*21–25*
Annual cash income after taxes from acquisition	$2,000	$1,800	$1,400	$800	$200
Net investment	600	300	—	—	—
Cash flow after taxes	$1,400	$1,500	$1,400	$800	$200

If the acquisition is not expected to increase or decrease the business-risk complexion of the firm as perceived by suppliers of capital, the appropriate discount rate would be the cost of capital. If this rate were 15 percent after taxes, the present value of the expected net cash flows shown above would be $8,724,000. If the prospective acquisition has no debt, this figure suggests that the company can pay a maximum price of $8,724,000 for the acquisition and still be acting in the best interests of the company's stockholders. The actual price paid will be subject to negotiation. However, the present value of the prospective acquisition should represent an upper boundary for the acquiring company. Any price up to this amount should result in a worthwhile investment for the company. As a result, the market price per share of the firm's stock should increase over the long run. If the price paid is in excess of the acquisition's present value, this suggests that capital is less than optimally allocated.

Estimating cash flows

In an acquisition, there are the usual problems with estimating future cash flows. The process may be somewhat easier than for a capital-budgeting proposal because the company being acquired is a going concern. The acquiring company buys more than assets; it buys experience, an organization, and proven performance. The estimates of sales and costs are based upon past results; consequently, they are likely to be more accurate than the estimates for a new investment proposal. Less uncertainty involved in the estimates means less dispersion of expected outcomes and lower risk, all other things held constant. An additional problem, however, is introduced when the acquisition is to be integrated into the acquiring company. Under these circumstances, the acquisition cannot be evaluated as a separate operation; the synergistic effects must be considered. Estimates of these effects are difficult, particularly if the organization that results from the acquisition is complex.

Cash-flow versus the earnings-per-share approach

The analysis of an acquisition on a cash-flow basis differs from that on an earnings-per-share basis. With an earnings-per-share approach, the question was whether there would be an earnings-per-share improvement now or in the future. In the cash-flow approach, the question is whether the expected net cash flows have a present value in excess of the acquisition's cost.

In general, the cash-flow approach looks at the valuation of an acquisition over the long run, whereas the earnings-per-share approach focuses on the short run. If a prospective acquisition does not result in a positive increment in earnings per share within a few years, it usually is ruled out if one relies only on the earnings-per-share approach. In contrast, the cash-flow approach looks at incremental cash flows likely to be generated from the acquisition for many years in the future. Thus, the earnings-per-share approach tends to bias the selection process in favor of companies with immediate growth prospects, but not necessarily long-term ones. Neither approach embodies in it a consideration for changes in business risk; however, this dimension can be incorporated into either method of analysis using the techniques discussed in chapter 14.

Aside from risk, the question is which method—the cash-flow or the earnings-per-share method—should be used? Probably the best answer is that both methods should be employed. The cash-flow method is the more comprehensive with respect to the economic worth of an acquisition over the long run. If management is concerned with near-term growth in earnings per share and believes that this is what the market values, then a strong case can be made for the earnings-per-share method. In practice, it is difficult to imagine management ignoring the effect of an acquisition on earnings per share, no matter how sound the cash-flow approach is conceptually. By the same token, an earnings-per-share approach by itself may be too shortsighted and may bias things away from solid long-term growth prospects. Therefore, a strong case can be made for using a cash-flow method of analysis *in addition to* an earnings-per-share one.

HOLDING COMPANIES

Instead of actually acquiring another company, a firm may purchase a portion of its stock and act as a holding company. By definition, a *holding company* owns sufficient voting stock to have a controlling interest in one or more other corporations. A holding company does not necessarily have to own 51 percent of the stock of another company in order to have control. For a widely held corporation, ownership of 20 percent or as little as 10 percent of the stock outstanding may constitute effective working control. The holding company had its origin in the latter part of the nineteenth century when the state of New Jersey first permitted corporations to exist for the sole purpose of owning stocks of other corporations.

Advantages

One of the advantages of a holding company is that it allows a company to acquire control of another company by investing much less than would be necessary for a merger. Moreover, by acquiring only a portion of the stock, the holding company usually does not have to pay as high a price per share as it would if it sought to purchase all the stock. It may purchase the stock gradually without undue upward pressure on the market price of the stock. Another advantage is that formal approval from stockholders of the acquiring company is not required. It is an informal arrangement. A further advantage of a holding company is the possibility that, although limited, operating economies can be achieved through centralized management.

Disadvantages

One of the principal disadvantages of the holding company is that 15 percent of the dividends paid to it by the subsidiary is subject to taxation.[7] Thus, the holding company must pay a partial tax on dividends, and stockholders of the holding company also must pay a tax on dividends they receive. The partial tax

---

[7]If the holding company owns 80 percent or more of the voting stock of the subsidiary, the dividend is not subject to taxation.

could be avoided, of course, if the stockholders owned the operating companies directly.

Through pyramiding a series of holding companies, it is possible to obtain considerable leverage with respect to assets controlled and earnings. Suppose Holding Company A owns 20 percent of Holding Companies B, C, and D, which, in turn, own 20 percent controlling interest in 9 operating companies. Thus, for every dollar of capital in each of the operating companies—$9 in all—Company A is able to control them with an investment of $.36, (.20 × .20 × $9), or 4 percent of the total capital of the operating companies. As long as the operating companies are profitable and able to pay dividends to the holding companies, all may go well. In the 1920s there tended to be excessive pyramiding of holding companies, particularly in public utilities. In the 1930s, the leverage of these companies magnified the losses, and a number of the pyramids crumbled. Because of the many abuses of holding companies, the Public Utility Holding Company Act of 1935 was passed to restrict the operation of holding companies in the public utility field.

BRINGING THE MERGER TO FRUITION

A merger or consolidation often begins with negotiations between the management of the two companies. Usually, the boards of directors of the companies are kept up to date on the negotiations. The acquirer evaluates many facets of a target company, as the rather exhaustive checklist shows in Fig. 24-4. Terms are agreed upon, initially, ratified by the respective boards, then approved by the common stockholders of both companies. Depending upon the corporate charter, an established majority—usually two-thirds—of the total shares is required. After approval by the common stockholders, the merger or consolidation can take place once the necessary papers are filed with the states in which the companies are incorporated.

One hurdle remains. The Antitrust Division of the Department of Justice or the Federal Trade Commission could bring suit to block the combination. In order to block a merger or consolidation, the government, under Section 7 of the Clayton Act, must prove that a "substantial lessening of competition" might occur on account of it. Usually restraint of competition is interpreted as applying to either a geographical area, such as food stores in New Orleans, or to a line of commerce, such as aluminum ingot production. Broader interpretations are possible, and the combination of two large companies in unrelated lines of business and geographic areas is suspect simply because of "largeness," per se. Because the costs in executive time, legal expenses, and other expenses of waging an antitrust battle are so great, most companies, before going ahead with a combination, want to be reasonably sure that they will not be challenged.

Accounting treatment

From an accounting standpoint, a combination of two companies is treated either as a *purchase* or as a *pooling of interests*. In a purchase, the buyer treats the acquired company as an investment. If the buyer pays a premium above the fair

General Information

☐ Exact corporate name
☐ Address
☐ Date and state of incorporation
☐ States in which the company is qualified to do business
☐ Location of minute books, by-laws, and certificate of incorporation
☐ History
☐ Description of products
☐ Fiscal year
☐ Capitalization
☐ Rights of each class of stock and other securities
☐ Stockholders' agreements and terms thereof
☐ Names of stockholders and holdings
☐ Bank depositaries and average bank balances
☐ Bank references
☐ Credit rating
☐ Location of company records
☐ Accountants: Name, address, and reputation
☐ Attorneys: Name and address

Personnel

☐ Directors and their affiliations
☐ Officers: For each — position, duties, age, health, salary, service, experience, personal plans for the future, other interests (including time devoted thereto), and stockholdings
☐ Organization chart
☐ Employee contracts: Terms, expiration date(s)
☐ Number of employees in production, sales, administration, etc.
☐ Union contracts: Terms, expiration dates
☐ Strike record, labor morale, handling of labor relations
☐ Labor market
☐ Pension, profit sharing, insurance, stock bonus, deferred compensation, and severance plans
☐ Comparison with industry as to number of employees, hours per week, and wage rates for the past five years and for the past twelve months

Operations

☐ Description, including significant changes in the past few years
    1. Capacity and per cent of utilization
    2. Production controls (scheduling and inventories)
    3. Shipping and receiving controls
    4. Accounting controls
☐ Principal suppliers and terms
☐ Distribution methods and terms (also, brokers or agents and compensation arrangements)
☐ Branch offices and their operations
☐ Subsidiaries, their operations and inter-company dealings
☐ Government contracts and subcontracts
☐ Seasonal factors
☐ Public and stockholder relations

Sales

☐ Description of market
☐ Number of customers and names of principal customers
☐ Gross and net sales for the past five years and for the past twelve months
    1. Penetration of market by product
    2. Possibilities of increase through existing lines and by diversification
☐ Sales comparison with the industry for the past five years and for the past twelve months
☐ Sales backlog, accounts receivable activity, customer continuity
☐ Sales correspondence
☐ Sales policies and method of compensation of sales personnel
☐ Pricing policies and fluctuations in the past five years
☐ Principal competitors
☐ Relative size in the industry
☐ Comparative advantages and disadvantages
☐ Anything significant in lines produced in the past few years
☐ Any nonrelated activities
☐ Missing product lines
☐ Advertising and other sales promotion programs: Cost and effectiveness in the past five years
☐ Research program: Cost, history, scope, potential, results, work by outsiders
☐ New developments
☐ Industry trends
☐ Current and future prospects

Earnings and Dividends

☐ Earnings record and budget for the past five years and the last twelve months, break-even point, gross profit margins and reasons for variations, nonrecurring income and expenses, changes in overabsorbed and underabsorbed burden
☐ Earnings comparison with the industry for the past five years
☐ Dividend and earnings record for the past five years in total and per share
☐ Potential economies
☐ Current and future prospects
☐ Analysis of selling and general and administrative expenses
☐ Contribution of company's effort to profit

Plant Facilities

☐ Location
☐ Shipping facilities
☐ Real estate taxes
☐ Land
    1. Acreage
    2. Cost
    3. Assessed value
    4. Fair market value

FIGURE 24-4   Acquisition evaluation checklist

☐ Buildings
1. Description, including pictures, if available
2. Age and condition
3. Area
4. Depreciation: Reserves, methods, rates, policies
5. Assessed value
6. Fair market value (recent appraisals)
7. Fire insurance
☐ Title to realty and title policy
☐ Machinery and equipment
1. Description
2. Age, condition, efficiency, insurance coverage
3. Depreciation: Reserves, methods, rates, policies
4. Total acquisitions during the past five years
5. Analysis of most recent additions
☐ Future plant, machinery, and equipment requirements
☐ Capitalization versus repair policies
☐ Capital expenditures and repairs for the past five years
☐ Percentage relationship of production costs and comparison with the industry
☐ Efficiency of operations
☐ Subcontracting done by others
☐ Certificates of necessity
☐ Facility contracts or leases
☐ Surplus or idle buildings or equipment

Assets
☐ Relationship of cash to current liabilities
☐ Age and number of accounts receivable (latest accounts receivable aging)
☐ Provision for bad debts
☐ Inventories for the past five years
1. Relationship of inventories to current assets
2. Location
3. Finished goods by product
4. Work in process by product
5. Raw materials by product
6. Pricing methods
7. Accounting procedures and practices
8. Provision for obsolete or slow-moving stock (latest inventory aging)
☐ Analysis of notes receivable
☐ Analysis of investments
☐ Subsidiaries
1. Treatment on parent company's balance sheet
2. Analysis (per check list) of significant items
☐ Analysis of other assets
☐ Patents held

Liabilities
☐ Renegotiable business
☐ Renegotiation status
☐ Current federal and state tax status and tax payments for the past three years
☐ Commitments for new buildings, machinery, inventories
☐ Long-term loans outstanding and terms
☐ Debentures outstanding and terms

☐ Dividend and interest arrearages
☐ Leases: Locations, areas, terms
☐ Insurance coverage, fidelity bonds, and amounts
☐ Pensions, etc.
☐ Contingent liabilities: Warranties; patent, etc., infringements; loss contracts; compensation for services
☐ Litigation record and present status

Financial Data
☐ Annual statements and audit reports for the past five years
☐ Tax returns for the past five years
☐ Surplus statements
☐ Disposition of funds statements
☐ Reports to Securities and Exchange Commission
☐ Explanation of how consolidations, if any, were effected and separate statement for each company involved
☐ Chart of accounts
☐ Book, net quick, liquidating, and market values for the past five years
☐ Working capital for the past five years and normal requirements based on trade practices, credit terms to customers, consignments, finished inventory, and raw inventory
☐ Net working capital ratios for the past five years
☐ Net quick position for the past five years
☐ Annual depreciation compared with capital additions for the past five years
☐ Inventory turnover for the past five years
☐ Cash, inventory, and working capital requirements for the past two years
☐ Interest charges for the past five years
☐ Exchange, if any, on which the company's stock is traded
☐ Recent stock sales and prices paid

Comparison with Comparable Companies
The following ratios for the subject company should be compared with those of comparable companies for the past five years and, if data are available, by quarters for the current year:
☐ Price to earnings
☐ Price to book value
☐ Sales to accounts receivable
☐ Sales to inventories
☐ Sales to fixed assets
☐ Earnings to book value

Terms of Acquisition
☐ Reasons for sale
☐ Price to be paid
☐ Terms of payment
☐ Financing
☐ Brokerage fees
☐ Tax considerations

Projected Financial Data
☐ Pro forma balance sheet
☐ Earnings forecast

FIGURE 24-4 (cont.)

market value of the assets, this premium must be reflected as goodwill on the buyer's balance sheet. Moreover, goodwill must be written off against future income, the logic being that it will be reflected in such income. An estimate must be made of the life of goodwill, as of any asset; and goodwill is amortized over this period, which cannot exceed 40 years. Thus, accounting earnings are reduced by the amount of the charge. Note that goodwill charges are not deductible for tax purposes. Therefore, the acquiring firm generally views as a disadvantage the reduction of reported future earnings associated with this accounting treatment.

In a pooling of interests, the balance sheets of the two companies are combined, with assets and liabilities simply being added together. As a result, goodwill is not reflected in the combination, and there is no charge against future income. Because reported earnings will be higher with the pooling-of-interests accounting treatment than they will be with the purchase treatment, many acquiring companies prefer it when the goodwill being acquired is substantial.

The choice of accounting treatment does not rest entirely with the acquiring company, but rather is governed by the circumstances of the merger and the rules of the accounting profession. Only under the following rather restricted conditions can a merger be treated as a pooling of interests.[8]

> Each of the combined companies must be autonomous for at least two years prior to the pooling and independent of the others in the sense that no more than 10 percent of the stock is owned.
>
> The combination must be consummated in a single transaction *or* in accordance with a specific plan within one year after the plan is initiated. In this regard, no contingent payments are permitted.
>
> The acquiring corporation can issue only common stock, with rights identical to those of the majority of outstanding voting stock, in exchange for *substantially* all of the voting common stock of another company. Here, "substantially" means 90 percent or more.
>
> The surviving corporation must not later retire or reacquire common stock issued in connection with the combination, must not enter into an arrangement for the benefit of former stockholders, and must not dispose of a significant portion of the assets of the combining companies for at least 2 years.

The most limiting condition is number 3, which states that common must be exchanged for common. The next most limiting condition is the prohibition of contingent payments. The result of these conditions is a significant constraint on the number of poolings of interest.

ABC Company acquired XYZ Company in an exchange of stock valued at $2 million. XYZ Company had debt of $1 million and a net worth of $1.2 million prior to the merger, the net book value of its assets being $2.2 million. On the other hand, ABC Company, the acquirer, had a net worth of $10 million, debt of $5 million, and assets having a net book value of $15 million prior to the merger. The effects of the merger under the purchase and the pooling-of-interests methods of accounting treatment are as follows (in thousands):

[8]*Opinions of the Accounting Principles Board,* No. 16 (New York: American Institute of Certified Public Accountants, August 1970).

	Before Merger		After Merger	
	ABC Company	*XYZ Company*	*Purchase*	*Pooling*
Net tangible assets	$15,000	$2,200	$17,200	$17,200
Goodwill	0	0	800	0
Total assets	$15,000	$2,200	$18,000	$17,200
Debt	$ 5,000	$1,000	$ 6,000	$ 6,000
Net worth	10,000	1,200	12,000	11,200
Total liabilities and net worth	$15,000	$2,200	$18,000	$17,200

With the purchase method, the total assets of the acquired company are written up by $800,000, which is the price paid in excess of book value. Moreover, this amount is reflected as goodwill and must be amortized in the manner described before. Under the pooling-of-interests accounting treatment, the assets shown for the surviving company are simply the sum of the book values of assets shown for the two companies before the merger.

So far we have considered only a case in which the acquiring company pays a price in excess of the book value of the assets. In many situations, the fair market value of the assets of the acquired company exceeds the book value of those assets. Under the purchase method of accounting, the tangible assets of the acquired amount of goodwill. In our example, had the fair market value of the assets of the acquired company been $2.5 million instead of $2.2 million, net tangible assets of the surviving company would have been $17.5 million instead of $17.2 million, and goodwill would have been $500,000 instead of $800,000. If the purchase transaction is taxable, as defined in the previous section, the surviving company can claim a larger depreciation expense for tax purposes which, in turn, enhances cash flows. This represents an advantage for purchase over pooling if the objective of the firm is to maximize the present value of after-tax cash flows. To the extent that the objective is maximizing accounting earnings, however, the purchase method loses its appeal as a greater amount of goodwill must be recorded.

Purchase of assets or purchase of stock

A company may be acquired either by the purchase of its assets or common stock. The buying company may purchase all or a portion of the assets of another company and pay for them in cash or with its own stock. Frequently, the buyer acquires only the assets of the other company and does not assume its liabilities. If all the assets are purchased, the selling company is but a corporate shell. After the sale, its assets are composed entirely of cash or the stock of the buying company. The selling company can either hold the cash or stock or distribute it to its stockholders as a liquidating dividend, after which the company is dissolved.

Thus, when its assets are purchased, the selling company can continue to exist if it holds the cash or stock arising from the sale. If it has cash, it may invest in other assets, such as a division of another company. Obviously, if only a portion of its assets are sold, the selling company will continue as a corporate entity. When an acquiring company purchases the stock of another company, the latter is merged into the acquiring company. The company that is acquired ceases to exist, and the surviving company assumes all its assets and liabilities. As with a purchase of assets, the means of payment to the stockholders of the company being acquired can be either cash or stock. A purchase of assets is easier to effect than a purchase of stock, for all that is needed on the part of the buying company is approval by the board of directors. The selling company, however, needs the approval of its stockholders.

Taxable or tax-free transaction

If the acquisition is made with cash or with a debt instrument, the transaction is taxable to the selling company or to its stockholders at that time. This means that they must recognize any capital gain or loss on the sale of the assets or the sale of the stock at the time of the sale. If payment is made with voting preferred or common stock, the transaction is not taxable at the time of the sale. The capital gain or loss is recognized only when the stock is sold. In addition to the requirement of voting stock, in order for a combination to be tax free it must have a business purpose. In other words, it cannot be entirely for tax reasons. Moreover, in a purchase of assets the acquisition must involve substantially all of the assets of the selling company, and no less than 80 percent of those assets must be paid for with voting stock. In a purchase of stock, the buying company must own at least 80 percent of the selling company's stock immediately after the transaction.

In most cases, a tax free transaction is preferred by the selling company and its stockholders because a postponable capital gain is involved. A tax free combination allows the selling company—in a purchase of assets—or its stockholders—in a purchase of stock—to postpone taking the gain and paying taxes on it until it is desirable to do so.

Another consideration is that with a taxable transaction the buying company is able to write up the value of the assets if their fair market value exceeds their book value. For example, Sanchez Metal Company acquires Baker Worm Gear, Inc., which has $800,000 in assets at book value. In market value terms, these assets are worth $1 million. If Sanchez acquires the company through a taxable transaction, it is able to write up the assets to $1 million. The advantage, of course, is that Sanchez will be able to claim a higher depreciation expense for tax purposes. By paying lower taxes, greater after-tax cash flows occur—a desirable outcome. If the acquisition is a tax free transaction, Sanchez is unable to write up the value of the assets and claim the higher depreciation charges. Therefore, this consideration may make a taxable transaction more desirable from the standpoint of the buying company and cause it to pay a higher price than otherwise would be the case. Whether this factor significantly offsets the usual advantage to the seller of a tax free transaction depends on the individual circumstances.

Although a combination generally depends only upon the approval of a required majority of the total number of shares outstanding, minority stockholders can contest the price paid for their stock. If a dissenting stockholder and the company fail to agree on a just settlement, the stockholder can take the case to court and demand an appraisal of his shares and a settlement in cash. After a "fair market price" has been established by the court, the dissenting stockholder receives payment in cash for his shares. A large number of dissenting stockholders can cause considerable trouble. If the transaction is in stock, their demands for cash payments may put a severe financial strain on the combination. Thus, most combinations depend not only upon obtaining approval of a required majority of stockholders but also upon minimizing the number of dissenting stockholders by making the offer attractive to all. Dissenting stockholders may be able to block the combination if they suspect that fraud is involved, even though the required majority of stockholders has approved it.

Tender offers

In our hypothetical examples, negotiations were confined to the managements and boards of directors of the companies involved. However, the acquiring company can make a tender offer directly to stockholders of the company it wishes to acquire. A tender offer is an offer to purchase shares of stock of another company at a fixed price per share from any stockholders who "tender" their shares. The tender price usually is set significantly above the present market price, as an incentive. Use of the tender offer allows the acquiring company to bypass the management of the company it wishes to acquire and, therefore, serves as a threat in any negotiations with that management. If management holds out for too high a price or otherwise balks at the offer, the acquiring company can always make a tender offer.

The tender offer can be used also when there are no negotiations but when one company simply wants to acquire another. It no longer is possible to surprise another company, because the Securities and Exchange Commission requires rather extensive disclosure. In both cash and stock tenders, the primary selling tool is the premium that is offered over the existing market price of the stock. As a rule of thumb, a premium of at least 20 percent usually is required, which may be adjusted up depending upon the circumstances. In addition, brokers are often given attractive commissions for shares tendered through them. The tender offer itself is usually communicated through financial newspapers. Direct mailings are made to the stockholders of the company being bid for if the bidder is able to obtain a list of stockholders. Although a company is legally obligated to provide such a list, it usually is able to delay delivery long enough to frustrate the bidder.

The company being bid for may use a number of defensive tactics. Management may try to persuade stockholders that the offer is not in their best interests. Usually, the argument is that the bid is too low in relation to the true, long-run value of the firm. Hearing that, stockholders may look at an attractive premium and find the long run too long. Some companies raise the cash dividend or declare

A bidder takes pains to keep his intentions secret until the last minute.
"Claude; Courtesy of *Fortune Magazine.*"

Management often seeks to foil a bidder by quickly arranging a merger with another company.
"Claude; Courtesy of *Fortune Magazine.*"

Determined management opposition can usually fend off an unwanted take-over bid.
"Claude; Courtesy of *Fortune Magazine.*"

FIGURE 24-5
Tender offers

a stock split in hopes of gaining stockholder support. Legal actions are often undertaken, more to delay and frustrate the bidder than with the expectation of winning. When the two firms are competitors, an antitrust suit may prove a powerful deterrent to the bidder. As a last resort, management of the company being bid for may seek a merger with a "friendly" company.[9] Some of the strategies involved in tender offers are depicted in Fig. 24-5.

[9]For an extended discussion of these and other issues involving tender-offer takeovers, see "Corporate Takeovers—The Unfriendly Tender Offer and the Minority Stockholder Freezeout," Special Issue of *The Business Lawyer,* 32 (May 1977).

SUMMARY

A company may grow internally, or it may grow externally through acquisitions. The objective of the firm in either case is to maximize existing shareholder wealth. Both types of expansion can be regarded as capital-budgeting decisions. The criteria for acceptance are essentially the same: capital should be allocated to increase shareholder wealth. In this regard, a cash-flow method of analysis was presented. When two companies combine and one loses its corporate existence, the combination is known as a merger. If two companies combine and form a new corporation, the combination is known as a consolidation. Rather than acquiring another company in its entirety, a company can acquire working control and act as a holding company. There are a number of reasons for merging, all relating to expected return and risk. Among the reasons are economies, acquisition of management, growth potential, tax advantages, diversification, and personal motives of the owners.

Whenever two companies exchange stock, certain financial relationships come into prominence. Many companies focus on the impact on earnings per share. When the price/earnings ratio of the company being acquired is lower than the price/earnings ratio of the acquiring company, there is an initial improvement in earnings per share of the latter company; a dilution occurs when the price/earnings ratio is higher. Instead of looking only at the effect on initial earnings per share, it is desirable to look at the effect on expected future earnings per share as well. In efficient financial markets and in the absence of synergism, we would expect the price/earnings ratio of the surviving company to be a weighted average of the price/earnings ratio of the two premerger companies. For the most part, wealth cannot be created simply by merging with companies with low price/earnings ratios. Certain empirical evidence indicates substantial excess returns to the stockholders of the selling company and little excess returns to those of the buying company, both of which were reflected in share price improvements before the actual merger.

Once sufficient financial information is developed, management of the acquiring company usually negotiates directly with management of the prospective acquisition. The acquiring company can, however, make its appeal directly to the stockholders of the prospective acquisition through a tender offer to purchase their shares. Another company can be acquired through the purchase of either its assets or its stock. In turn, the means of payment can be cash or stock. Accounting considerations come into play in that the merger must be treated either as a purchase or as a pooling of interests. With a purchase, any goodwill arising from the merger must be amortized against future earnings. The accounting method used depends on the circumstances of the merger and the constraints imposed by rules of the accounting profession. Whether a combination is taxable or tax free is highly consequential to the selling company and its stockholders and, sometimes, to the buying company.

QUESTIONS

1. Explain the concept of *synergism*.

2. Illustrate and explain how the ratio of P/E multiples for two stocks affects the growth rate of reported earnings.

3. Why is the book value of a firm important in determining the exchange ratio of stock in a merger?

4. Some argue that the method of payment in a merger (stock-for-stock transaction at one end of the spectrum and cash-for-stock at the other, with various combinations of bonds, convertibles, etc., for stock in between the two extremes) is the principal factor in determining the price of the acquired firm. Explain this position.

5. Explain the concept of instantaneous merger profit. What assumptions are made about economies of scale in explaining the concept?

6. It has been noted that the number of mergers tends to vary directly with the level of relative business activity. Why would this be?

7. Can a merger with a large, stable company serve as an effective way to raise capital for a growth-oriented smaller company?

8. Company X and Company Y both have considerable variability in their earnings, but they are in unrelated industries. Could a merger of the two companies reduce the risk for stockholders of both companies? Could investors lower the risk on their own?

9. Many a corporate merger is made with the motive of increasing growth. What does this mean? Can you increase growth without increasing the overall risk of the surviving company?

10. Why is it that so many acquisition opportunities look good before the merger but later prove to be "dogs"?

11. Is an acquisition-minded company consistently able to find bargains? If so, why is it that other companies do not discover these bargains?

12. When evaluating a potential acquisition's future, why penalize the prospect by deducting the capital expenditures that will need to be made? Are not future earnings what really matter?

13. No merger is going to be attractive to all the acquired company's stockholders. Why should a company be concerned with dissenting stockholders as long as the majority favor the merger?

PROBLEMS

1. The following data are pertinent for Companies A and B:

	Company A	Company B
Present earnings (in millions)	$20	$ 4
Shares (in millions)	10	1
Price/earnings ratio	18	10

a) If the two companies were to merge and the exchange ratio were one share of Company A for each share of Company B, what would be the initial impact on earnings per share of the two companies? What is the market-value exchange ratio? Is a merger likely to take place?

b) If the exchange ratio were two shares of Company A for each share of Company B, what would happen with respect to the above?

c) If the exchange ratio were 1.5 shares of Company A for each share of Company B, what would happen?

d) What exchange ratio would you suggest?

2.

	Expected earnings	Number of shares	Market price per share	Tax rate
Hargrave Company	$5,000,000	1,000,000	$100	50%
Hooper Company	3,000,000	500,000	60	50%

The Hargrave Company wishes to acquire the Hooper Company. If the merger were effected through an exchange of stock, Hargrave would be willing to pay a 25 percent premium for the Hooper shares. If done for cash, the terms would have to be as favorable to the Hooper shareholders; to obtain the cash, Hargrave would have to sell its own stock in the market.

a) Compute the exchange ratio and the combined expected earnings per share for an exchange of stock.

b) If we assume that all Hooper shareholders have held their stock for more than one year, have a 20 percent marginal capital-gains tax rate, and paid an average of $14 for their shares, what cash price would have to be offered to be as attractive as the terms in part a?

3. Assume the exchange of Hargrave shares for Hooper shares as outlined in problem 2.

a) What is the ratio of exchange?

b) Compare the earnings per Hooper share before and after the merger. Compare the earnings per Hargrave share. On this basis alone, which group fared better? Why?

c) Why do you imagine that Hargrave commanded a higher P/E than Hooper? What should be the change in P/E ratio resulting from the merger? Does this conflict with your previous one? Why?

d) If the Hargrave Company were in a high-technology growth industry and Hooper made cement, would you revise your answers?

e) In determining the appropriate P/E ratio for Hargrave, should the increase in earnings resulting from this merger be added as a growth factor?

4. Three years and 20 mergers later, Hargrave (see problems 2 and 3), under pressure to report earnings growth, is looking at a proposed merger.

	Expected earnings	Number of shares	Market price
Hargrave	$35,000,000	3,500,000	$200
Fontenot	3,000,000	500,000	90

Assume the merger is consummated under the same terms as in problem 2.

a) Compute the exchange ratio and the combined expected earnings per share if an exchange of stock were accomplished.

b) What do you think will happen to the P/E ratio?

5. Copper Tube Company presently has annual earnings of $10 million with 4 million shares of common stock outstanding and a market price per share of $30. In the absence of any mergers, Copper Tube's annual earnings are expected to grow at a compound rate of 5 percent per annum. Brass Fitting Company, whom Copper Tube is seeking to acquire, has present annual earnings of $2 million, 1 million shares of common outstanding, and a market price per share of $36. Its annual earnings are expected to grow at a compound annual rate of 10 percent per annum. Copper Tube will offer 1.2 shares of its stock for each share of Brass Fitting Company.

a) What is the immediate effect on the surviving company's earnings per share?

b) Would you want to acquire Brass Fitting Company? If it is not attractive now, when will it be attractive from the standpoint of earnings per share?

6. The Resin Corporation, which has a 16 percent after-tax cost of capital, is considering the acquisition of the Smythe Company, which has about the same degree of systematic risk. If the merger were effected, the incremental cash flows would be as follows:

	Average for Years (in millions)			
	1–5	6–10	11–15	16–20
Annual cash income attributable to Smythe	$10	$15	$20	$15
Required new investment	2	5	10	10
Net after-tax cash flow	$ 8	$10	$10	$ 5

What is the maximum price that Resin should pay for Smythe?

7. Cougar Pipe and Brass Company is considering the cash acquisition of Red Wilson Rod Inc. for $750,000. The acquisition is expected to result in incremental cash flows of $100,000 in the first year, and this amount is expected to grow at a 6 percent compound rate. In the absence of the acquisition, Cougar expects net cash flows (after capital expenditures) of $600,000 this year, and these are expected to grow at a 6 percent compound rate forever. Presently, suppliers of capital require a 14 percent overall rate of return for Cougar Pipe and Brass Company. However, Red Wilson Rod is much more risky, and the acquisition of it will raise the company's overall required return to 15 percent.

a) Should Cougar Pipe and Brass Company acquire Red Wilson Rod Inc.?

b) Would your answer be the same if the overall required rate of return stayed the same?

c) Would your answer be the same if the acquisition increased the surviving company's growth rate to 8 percent forever?

8. Let it be assumed that a holding company can always be set up with 50 percent debt at 12 percent and 20 percent preferred stock at 10 percent. Further assume that all companies pay a tax rate of 50 percent, that the 85 percent intercorporate dividend exclusion applies in all cases, and that ownership of 40 percent of the stock of another company constitutes control. The shares of the Target Company can be obtained at their book value.

Target Company

Total assets	$25,000,000	Debt (12%)	$15,000,000
		Common	10,000,000
			$25,000,000

a) A group of investors has set up Holding Company A to acquire control of the Target Company. If the group holds all the equity of Holding Company A, how much money must it put up? If Target has operating earnings equal to 20 percent of total assets and pays all earnings in dividends, what return on investment will the group earn?

b) Suppose the group sets up Holding Company B to acquire control of Holding Company A. If the group holds all the equity of B, how much money must it put up? If A pays all earnings in dividends, what return on investment will the group earn? How many dollars of operating assets does the group control per dollar of its own investment?

c) How would your answers change if Target had operating earnings equal to 15 percent of total assets?

9. Toranaga Chemical Company, which is in a 46 percent tax bracket, has a chance to acquire Barro Liner Company, owned entirely by Antonio Barro. The price being discussed is $5 million. The company's buildings and equipment have a book value of $2 million but a current market value of $3.2 million. The remaining average depreciable life of these assets is 8 years, and depreciation is straight line. Mr. Barro acquired the business some ten years ago for $2 million, after which he renamed it. He is in a 20 percent capital gains tax bracket.

a) What are the consequences for Mr. Barro if the purchase is in cash? For Toranaga Chemical Company with respect to the buildings and equipment?

b) What are the consequences for both parties if the acquisition is with Toranaga common stock?

10. Biggo Stores, Inc. (BSI) has acquired the Nail It, Glue It and Screw It Hardware Company (NGS) for $4 million in stock and the assumption of $2 million in NGS liabilities. The balance sheets of the two companies before the merger were

	BSI	NGS
Tangible and total assets	$10.0 million	$5.0 million
Liabilities	4.0	2.0
Net worth	6.0	3.0

Determine the balance sheet of the combined company after the merger under the purchase and pooling of interests methods of accounting.

SELECTED REFERENCES

ALBERTS, WILLIAM W., and JOEL E. SEGALL, eds., *The Corporate Merger*. Chicago: University of Chicago Press, 1966.

APPLEYARD, A. R. and G. K. YARROW, "The Relationship Between Take-over Activity and Share Valuation," *Journal of Finance,* 30 (December 1975), 1239–50.

AUSTIN, DOUGLAS V., "The Financial Management of Tender Offer Takeovers," *Financial Management,* 3 (Spring 1974), 37–43.

"Corporate Takeovers—The Unfriendly Tender Offer and the Minority Stockholder Freezeout," Special Issue of *The Business Lawyer,* 32 (May 1977).

DODD, PETER, and RICHARD RUBACK, "Tender Offers and Stockholder Returns," *Journal of Financial Economics,* 5 (November 1977), 351–73.

ELGERS, PIETER T., and JOHN J. CLARK, "Merger Types and Shareholder Returns: Additional Evidence," *Financial Management,* 9 (Summer 1980), 66–72.

ELLERT, JAMES C., "Mergers, Antitrust Law Enforcement and Stockholder Returns," *Journal of Finance,* 31 (May 1976), 715–32.

GAHLON, JAMES M., and ROGER D. STOVER, "Diversification, Financial Leverage, and Conglomerate Systematic Risk," *Journal of Financial and Quantitative Analysis,* 14 (December 1979), 999–1014.

HAUGEN, ROBERT A., and TERENCE C. LANGETIEG, "An Empirical Test for Synergism in Merger," *Journal of Finance,* 30 (September 1975), 1003–14.

HIGGINS, ROBERT C., and LAWRENCE D. SCHALL, "Corporate Bankruptcy and Conglomerate Merger," *Journal of Finance,* 30 (March 1975), 93–114.

HOFFMEISTER, J. RONALD, and EDWARD A. DYL, "Predicting Outcomes of Cash Tender Offers," *Financial Management,* 10 (Winter 1981), 50–58.

HONG, H., G. MANDELKER, and R. S. KAPLAN, "Pooling vs. Purchase: The Effects of Accounting for Mergers on Stock Prices," *Accounting Review,* 53 (January 1978), 31–47.

KEOWN, ARTHUR J., and JOHN M. PINKERTON, "Merger Announcements and Insider Trading Activity: An Empirical Investigation," *Journal of Finance,* 36 (September 1981), 855–70.

KUMMER, DONALD R., and J. RONALD HOFFMEISTER, "Valuation Consequences of Cash Tender Offers," *Journal of Finance,* 33 (May 1978), 505–16.

LANGETIEG, TERENCE C., ROBERT A. HAUGEN and DEAN W. WICHERN, "Merger and Stockholder Wealth," *Journal of Financial and Quantitative Analysis,* 15 (September 1980), 689–717.

LARSON, KERMIT D., and NICHOLAS J. GONEDES, "Business Combinations: An Exchange-Ratio Determination Model," *Accounting Review,* 44 (October 1969), 720–28.

MEAD, WALTER J., "Instantaneous Merger Profit as a Conglomerate Merger Motive," *Western Economic Review,* 7 (December 1969), 295–306.

MELICHER, RONALD W., and THOMAS R. HARTER, "Stock Price Movements of Firms Engaging in Large Acquisitions," *Journal of Financial and Quantitative Analysis,* 7 (March 1972), 1469–75.

———, and DAVID F. RUSH, "Evidence on the Acquisition-Related Performance of Conglomerate Firms," *Journal of Finance,* 29 (March 1974), 141–50.

MENDELKER, GERSHON, "Risk and Return: The Case of Merging Firms," *Journal of Financial Economics,* 1 (December 1974), 303–35.

MUELLER, DENNIS C., "The Effects of Conglomerate Mergers," *Journal of Banking and Finance,* 1 (December 1977), 315–47.

NEILSEN, JAMES F., and RONALD W. MELICHER, "A Financial Analysis of Acquisition and Merger Premiums," *Journal of Financial and Quantitative Analysis,* 8 (March 1973), 139–48.

SALTER, MALCOLM S., and WOLF A. WEINHOLD, "Diversification via Acquisition: Creating Value," *Harvard Business Review,* (July–August 1978), 166–76.

SCOTT, JAMES H., JR., "On the Theory of Conglomerate Mergers," *Journal of Finance,* 32 (September 1977), 1235–50.

SHICK, RICHARD A., and FRANK C. JEN, "Merger Benefits to Shareholders of Acquiring Firms," *Financial Management,* 3 (Winter 1974), 45–53.

SMALTER, DONALD J., and RODERIC C. LANCEY, "P/E Analysis in Acquisition Strategy," *Harvard Business Review,* 44 (November–December 1966), 85–95.

SMILEY, ROBERT, "Tender Offers, Transactions Costs and the Firm," *Review of Economics and Statistics,* 58 (February 1976), 22–32.

International financial management

25

In recent years, international trade has grown to become a major portion of the total activity of many business firms. In the wake of this surge has come the development of the multinational enterprise. By definition, a *multinational business* is one with investment and sales in two or more countries. For some companies, foreign sales are only a small portion of total revenues, and we would not regard these companies as multinational in any real sense. However, companies such as IBM, Gillette, Pfizer, and American Smelting and Refining derive over half their profits from international operations. As a result of the rapidly changing international scene, many a financial manager has had to keep abreast of fluctuating exchange rates, changing political and economic structures, the flow of petrodollars to and from oil-producing countries, changing financing methods and rates, and a host of other developments.

How does financial management in a multinational enterprise differ from that in a domestic business firm? In principle, the concepts of efficient allocation of funds among assets and the raising of funds on as favorable terms as possible are the same for both types of companies. It is the environment in which these decisions are made that is different. In this chapter we shall see the institutional factors that make investing and financing for a multinational company somewhat different from that for a domestic company. We shall take a look at the tax environment, political risks, foreign exchange risk, investment constraints imposed by the government, financing instruments, and certain specialized documents used in foreign trade. Our purpose is not an in-depth understanding but rather an exposure to those factors that influence the basic decisions of the firm in an international setting.

INVESTING ABROAD

The decision to invest capital in a project abroad should be based upon considerations of expected return and risk, the same as any investment proposal. Quantifying these parameters is complicated by disparities in currency exchange rates, differences in taxes, differences in accounting practices, and differences in factors affecting risk; but once expected return and risk are quantified, the evaluation of the project itself is the same whether it be domestic or foreign in origin.[1] Consequently, we shall concentrate on the various factors that make foreign investment unique rather than on the evaluation process itself. That process was taken up earlier in the book and has not changed.

Reasons for foreign investment

Risk considerations. International diversification is often more effective than domestic diversification in reducing a company's risk in relation to expected return. You will recall from our discussion of portfolio risk in chapter 14 that the key element was the correlation among projects in the asset portfolio. By combining projects with low degrees of correlation with each other, a firm is able to reduce risk in relation to expected return. Since domestic investment projects tend to be correlated with each other, most being highly dependent on the state of the economy, foreign investments have an advantage. The economic cycles of different countries do not tend to be completely synchronized, so it is possible to reduce risk relative to expected return by investing across countries.

If a company in the machine tool business invested in another plant domestically, the return would likely be highly correlated with the return from existing assets. Consequently, there would be little reduction in relative risk. If it invested in a plant to market machine tools in a country whose economy was not highly correlated with the domestic economy, the project's return would not likely be so highly correlated with the return from existing assets. Consequently, it may be possible to reduce risk relative to expected return by investing in the same industry internationally. The idea is simply that returns on investment projects tend to be less correlated among countries than they are in any one particular country.

Whether foreign diversification by a company benefits its stockholders depends on whether or not capital markets between countries are segmented. If they

---

[1] For a survey of capital budgeting techniques employed by multinational companies, see David J. Oblak and Roy J. Helm, Jr., "Survey and Analysis of Capital Budgeting Methods used by Multinationals," *Financial Management,* 9 (Winter 1980), 37–41. The authors found that a large number of the companies surveyed used discounted cash flow methods and adjusted for risk.

are not, there is little reason to believe that foreign diversification by a company will increase its value. This notion is the same as that for diversification of assets involving domestic projects, which was discussed earlier. If capital markets are perfect, investors can effectively replicate any asset diversification by the firm. Therefore, such diversification adds nothing at the margin to shareholder wealth. If currency restrictions, investment barriers, legal restrictions, lack of information, and other capital-market imperfections of this sort exist, capital markets between countries may be segmented. Under these circumstances, foreign diversification may enhance shareholder wealth. In general, studies of common-stock investments across countries have supported the diversification potential of international investments, though there is disagreement on the degree of capital-market segmentation.

The concept of diversification is applicable also to the acquisition of foreign companies. To the extent again that market imperfections result in segmentation among international capital markets, the diversification properties associated with a foreign acquisition may be of value. We know from chapters 15 and 24 that domestic acquisitions are a thing of value only if the acquiring company can do something for its investors that they cannot do for themselves. In the case of a company with a publicly traded stock, there was little reason to believe that stockholders could not achieve the same diversification on their own by investing directly in the company involved. Making foreign acquisitions, however, the acquiring company may be able to do something for investors that they cannot do for themselves if specific international capital markets are segmented. As a result, the risk-reduction properties associated with the foreign acquisition may be a thing of value.

Return considerations. The other reason for investing abroad is the expectation of a higher return for a given level of risk. Within a firm's particular expertise, there may be gaps in markets abroad where excess returns can be earned. Domestically, competitive pressures may be such that only a normal rate of return can be earned. Although expansion into foreign markets is the reason for most investment abroad, there are other reasons. Some firms invest in order to produce more efficiently. In another country, where labor or other costs are less, a company may seek foreign production facilities simply to operate at a lower cost. The electronics industry has moved toward foreign production facilities for saving. Finally, some companies invest abroad to secure necessary raw materials. Oil companies and mining companies in particular invest abroad for this reason. All of these pursuits—markets, production facilities, and raw materials—are in keeping with an objective of securing a higher rate of return than is possible through domestic operations alone.

As we observed earlier, among the factors that make investment abroad different from investment at home are tax differences and political and foreign exchange risk. Before taking up each in turn, we should point out that there is more risk to a foreign investment than simply the political and foreign exchange risks. Frequently, the predominant risk is business risk in the country itself. We discussed methods for analyzing this risk in chapters 14 and 15.

Taxation

Owing to different tax laws and different treatments of foreign investment, the taxation of a multinational firm is extremely complex. Our purpose is to discuss some of the salient aspects of the problem, and we begin with the way the United States government taxes a company with foreign operations. Then we can move on to taxation by foreign countries.

Taxation by U.S. government. If a U.S. corporation carries on business abroad through a branch or division, the income from that operation is reported on the company's U.S. tax form and taxed in the same way as domestic income. If business is carried on through a foreign subsidiary, the income normally is not taxed in the U.S. until it is distributed to the parent in the form of dividends. The advantage here, of course, is that the tax is deferred until the parent receives a cash return. In the meantime, earnings are reinvested in the subsidiary to finance expansion. Unlike dividends from a domestic corporation (85 percent exempt), dividends received by a U.S. corporation from a foreign subsidiary are fully taxable.

In certain cases, income of a foreign subsidiary is subject to U.S. taxation prior to its actual remission in the form of dividends. In order to prevent tax havens, where U.S. taxes are deferred through transfer price and other arrangements between a U.S. company and its foreign subsidiary, Subpart F of the Revenue Act of 1962 was instigated. Its purpose is simply to prevent the excessive accumulation of earnings in the tax havens and the resulting deferral of U.S. taxes.[2] Under this provision, a U.S. stockholder owning more than 10 percent of a foreign company is taxed on certain types of income from that company. The provision is complicated, and presentation of the types of income subject to taxation is beyond the scope of this book.

Taxation by foreign governments. Every country taxes income of foreign companies doing business in that country. The type of tax imposed varies, but most of the larger industrial countries tax corporate income at roughly the corporate rate in the U.S. Some of these countries differentiate between income distributed to stockholders and undistributed income, with a lower tax on distributed income. Less-developed countries frequently have lower taxes and provide certain other tax incentives to encourage foreign investment. One method of taxation that has been prominent in Europe is the value-added tax, in essence a sales tax on each stage of production, which is taxed on the value added. It works this way: an aluminum fabricator buys aluminum sheets for $1,000, cuts, shapes, and otherwise works them into doors, which are sold for $1,800. The value added is $800, and the fabricator is taxed on this amount. If the fabricator sold its doors to a wholesaler who, in turn, sold them to retailers for $2,000, the value added would be $200 and taxed accordingly.

---

[2] Also in the Revenue Act of 1962 is a provision dealing with the liquidation of a foreign subsidiary. The capital gain is largely treated as dividend income and not subject to the more favorable capital-gains tax.

The taxation policies of foreign governments are not only varied but also highly complex. The definition of what constitutes taxable income is different for different countries, and the tax rate varies among countries. Certain nations, such as Luxembourg, Panama, and the Bahamas, have low tax rates on corporate profits in order to encourage foreign investment, whereas the tax rates in most advanced industrial countries are high. The picture is complicated further by the numerous tax treaties that the United States has with other nations. Although the U.S. government restricts use of a low-tax country as a tax haven, enough latitude remains so that companies still devise complicated legal structures in order to take advantage of such havens.

In order to avoid double taxation, the U.S. gives a federal income tax credit for foreign taxes paid by a U.S. corporation. If a foreign country has a tax rate of less than 46 percent, the U.S. corporation pays combined taxes at the 46 percent rate. Part of the taxes are paid to the foreign government, the other part to the U.S. A foreign branch of a U.S. corporation may operate in a country where the income tax rate is 35 percent. The branch earns $100,000 and pays $35,000 in taxes. The $100,000 earnings are subject to a 46 percent rate domestically, or $46,000 in taxes. The company receives a tax credit of $35,000; thus, it pays only $11,000 in U.S. taxes on the earnings of its foreign branch. If the foreign tax rate were 55 percent, the company would pay $55,000 in foreign taxes, nothing in U.S. taxes. Here, total taxes paid are obviously higher. The parent U.S. company does not receive a refund from the Internal Revenue Service for these extra taxes paid. The same tax credit arrangement applies to dividends received from a foreign subsidiary.

Note carefully that the foreign tax credit provision applies only to income taxes paid in a foreign country. It does not apply to sales taxes, value added taxes, property taxes, or other taxes. Often a sizable portion of the total foreign taxes paid will not be eligible for a U.S. tax credit.

In addition to these considerations, there are special tax incentives for doing business in less-developed countries (LDC's). In particular, the dividends paid by an LDC subsidiary to the U.S. parent are subject to more favorable tax treatment than that for dividends paid by a non-LDC subsidiary. As a result, the parent usually is able to keep a greater portion of its repatriated income.

Political risk

A multinational company faces political risks ranging from mild interference to complete confiscation of all assets. Interference includes laws that specify a minimum percentage of nationals who must be employed in various positions, required investment in environmental and social projects, and restrictions on the convertibility of currencies. The ultimate political risk is expropriation, such as that which occurred in Chile in 1971, when the country took over the copper companies. Between mild interference and outright expropriation, there are discriminatory practices such as higher taxes, higher utility charges, and the requirement to pay higher wages than a national company. In essence, they place the foreign operation of the U.S. company at a competitive disadvantage.

Because political risk has a serious influence upon the overall risk of an investment project, it must be assessed realistically. Essentially, the job is one of forecasting political instability. How stable is the government involved? What are the prevailing political winds? What is likely to be a new government's view of foreign investment? How efficient is the government in processing requests? How much inflation and economic stability is there? How strong and equitable are the courts? Answers to these questions should give considerable insight into the political risk involved in an investment. Some companies have categorized countries according to their political risk. If a country is classified in the undesirable category, probably no investment will be permitted no matter how high its expected return.

Once a company decides to invest, it should take steps to protect itself. By cooperating with the host country in hiring nationals, making the "right" types of investment, and in other ways being desirable, political risk can be reduced. A joint venture with a company in the host country can improve the public image of the operation. Indeed, in some countries a joint venture may be the only way to do business, because direct ownership, particularly of manufacturing, is prohibited. Though every effort should be made to protect an investment once it is made, often when sharp political changes occur nothing can be done. The time to look hardest at political risk is before the investment is made.

The Overseas Private Investment Corporation insures projects in some less-developed countries. The OPIC is government owned and insures against inconvertibility into dollars as well as against loss due to expropriation. It also insures against normal business losses. Where uncertainty is great, this insurance makes a good deal of sense for the investing company.

CURRENCY EXPOSURE MANAGEMENT

Foreign exchange risk

An exchange rate represents the number of units of the currency of one country that can be exchanged for another. The currencies of the major countries are traded in an active market, where rates are determined by the forces of supply and demand. The market itself is known as the *spot market*, as currencies are traded currently or on the spot.

Foreign exchange risk is the risk that the currency of a country in which a U.S. firm does business will decline in value relative to the dollar or that its convertibility into dollars will be restricted. (If the dollar declines in value relative to the currency in question, this works to the advantage of the company.) When a currency declines in value relative to the dollar, the U.S. company suffers a loss on the currency and on the assets payable in currency it holds. Say the British pound is worth $2. If XYZ Multinational Company held currency and receivables amounting to 500,000 pounds and the pound dropped in value by 10 percent, XYZ would suffer a loss in dollar terms of $100,000. Thus a significant devaluation or drop in price of a currency can be very costly to the multinational company. Another risk is that a country may block its currency so that it cannot be converted into other currencies.

Accounting for gains and losses. With the accounting rules in effect in late 1981 when this chapter was completed, changes in exchange rates affected the balance sheet and income of the company with a foreign subsidiary, often quite dramatically. A company that we shall call Richmond Precision Instruments has a subsidiary in West Germany with current assets (exclusive of inventories) of 480,000 Deutsche marks (DM) and current liabilities of 240,000 DM. If the exchange rate were 2.40 DM to the dollar, the implied dollar value of the current assets would be $200,000 and the current liabilities, $100,000. This suggests that if the current position of the subsidiary were to be liquidated, the current assets (exclusive of inventories) would produce 480,000 DM from which would be subtracted 240,000 DM in the settlement of current liabilities, leaving 240,000 DM in net-current-asset position. This amount then could be converted into $100,000. However, if the dollar were to depreciate in terms of the Deutsche mark to, say, 2.00 DM to the dollar, the dollar value of the current assets would increase from $200,000 to $240,000. However, it also would cost more dollars to pay off the current liabilities, $120,000 as compared with $100,000 before. Because the subsidiary's current assets exceed its current liabilities, the dollar value of the net-current-asset position increases from $100,000 to $120,000

Thus, when the dollar falls in relation to a foreign currency, current assets increase in dollar value, as do current liabilities. If the subsidiary is a net monetary creditor, the dollar value of its net current asset position increases. On the other hand, if it is a net monetary debtor, the dollar value of its net current asset position (deficit) deteriorates. Contrarily, when the dollar rises relative to a foreign currency, the current assets of a foreign subsidiary decline in dollar value, as do the current liabilities. If the subsidiary is a net monetary creditor, the dollar value of its net-current-asset position declines, while if it is a net monetary debtor, its net-current-asset position increases in dollar value.

Thus, changes in exchange rates cause changes in the dollar value of a foreign subsidiary's net current asset position. These translation gains or losses had to be reported on the parent company's consolidated statement of income each quarter according to the Financial Accounting Standards Board rules (FASB No. 8) in effect in late 1981.[3] Because of this requirement, multinational companies were very sensitive to exchange rate fluctuations. Because the net current asset position of a foreign subsidiary is what determined the magnitude and direction of risk exposure, and because translation gains and losses could result in sharp swings in reported earnings per share, the financial manager devoted considerable—and in my judgment excessive—attention to these matters. At the time of this writing, a great deal of discussion was going on concerning the accounting rules. Pressure from corporations, as a result of the swings in reported earnings, coupled with concern by the FASB will surely result in a change. The exact nature of the change is unclear from all the controversy. I would expect that there will be some kind of deferral of translation gains and losses and that such

---

[3] Fixed assets, long-term debt, and equity were not reported on the income statement. They were recorded on the balance sheet at the exchange rate applicable when the investment was made, the loan was received, or the equity was contributed. Similarly, inventories were recorded at historic as opposed to current translation rates.

adjustments will not affect the income statement, but rather the statement of retained earnings.

Exposure more broadly defined

The exchange-risk exposure of a company is not confined to changes in the value of monetary assets. It encompasses all factors that give rise to the foreign operation's cash flows. When a devaluation or sharp drop in currency value occurs, it may affect future sales, costs, and remittances. This effect often influences total value to a greater extent than does the immediate effect on the operation's monetary position. The long-run effects of a currency value change on cash flows and value are difficult to quantify and certainly important, but beyond the scope of this book. We shall concentrate on the way a change in currency value affects the monetary assets and liabilities of a company.

If a company believed that the currency of a country is going to drop sharply in value, it makes sense to reduce monetary assets in that currency to as low a figure as possible and to borrow extensively in that currency. As we have discussed, the drop in the value of a currency works to the advantage of a net debtor and to the disadvantage of a net creditor. In order to protect itself against adverse exchange-rate fluctuations, a multinational company can hedge its monetary position. By hedging, we mean offsetting monetary assets—such as cash, marketable securities, and receivables—with monetary liabilities, such as payables and loans, of the same amount. If a change in currency value occurs, monetary assets and liabilities will be equally affected and the company will suffer neither a gain nor a loss. Its net monetary position (assets less liabilities) is zero before and after the change in currency value.

If a company knew a currency were going to fall in value, it would want to do a number of things. First of all, it should reduce its cash to a minimum by purchasing inventories or other real assets. Moreover, the company should try to avoid extended trade credit. As quick a turnover as possible of receivables into cash is desirable. In contrast, it should try to obtain extended terms on its accounts payable. It may also want to borrow in the local currency to replace advances made by the U.S. parent. The last step will depend on relative interest rates. If the currency were going to appreciate in value, opposite steps should be undertaken. Without knowledge of the future direction of currency value movements, aggressive policies in either direction are inappropriate. Under most circumstances we are unable to predict the future, so the best policy may be one of balancing monetary assets against monetary liabilities in order to neutralize the effect of exchange-rate fluctuations.

Forward market

In addition to the above, a company can protect itself against exchange-rate fluctuations by use of the forward, or futures, market. In this market, one buys a futures contract for the exchange of one currency for another at a specific future date and at a specific exchange ratio. A futures contract is assurance of being able to obtain conversion into the desired currency at a specific exchange ratio.

The Xicon Electronics Company is hedging through the futures market. It sold equipment to a French customer through its Paris branch for 1 million francs with terms of 90 days. Upon payment, Xicon intends to convert the francs into dollars. The spot and 90-day future rates of French francs in terms of dollars were the following:

Spot rate	$0.160
Ninety-day future	0.158

The spot rate is simply the current market-determined exchange rate for French francs. In our example, one franc is worth 16¢, and $1 will buy $1.00/.16 = 6.25$ francs.

If Xicon wishes to avoid foreign exchange risk, it should sell 1 million francs forward ninety days. When it delivers the francs 90 days hence, it will receive $158,000 (1 million francs times the 90-day futures price of $0.158). If the spot rate stays at $0.160, of course, Xicon would be better off not having sold francs forward. It could sell 1 million francs in the spot market for $160,000. Thus, Xicon pays $0.002 per franc, or $2,000 in total, to insure its ability to convert French francs to dollars. On an annualized basis, the cost of this protection is

$$\left(\frac{.002}{.160}\right)\left(\frac{360}{90}\right) = 5 \text{ percent}$$

For stable pairs of currencies, the discount or premium of the forward rate over the spot rate varies from zero to 3 percent on an annualized basis. For somewhat less stable currencies, the discount or premium will be higher. For an unstable currency, the discount may go as high as 20 percent. Much beyond this point of instability, the forward market for the currency ceases to exist. In summary, the forward exchange market allows a company to insure against devaluation or market-determined declines in value.

Quotations on selected foreign exchange as of June 2, 1981 are shown in Table 25-1. The spot rates reported in the first column indicate the conversion rates into dollars. The Austrian schilling is seen to be worth $0.06, or $1/.06 = 16.67$ schillings to the U.S. dollar. Future rates for 30, 90, and 180 days are shown for the British pound, the Canadian dollar, the French franc, the Japanese yen, the Swiss franc, and the German mark. Note that the Canadian dollar and French franc decline in U.S. dollar value with the length of time in the future while the British pound, the Japanese yen, the Swiss franc, and the Deutsche mark increase in U.S. dollar value. These relationships imply that at the time the market regarded French francs and Canadian dollars as a more risky currency than the U.S. dollar. The pound, yen, Swiss franc and mark were regarded as less risky. Through the use of the forward market for these currencies as well as for other currencies not shown here, transactions are undertaken to blunt the effect of foreign exchange fluctuations.

TABLE 25-1 \ Foreign exchange rates, June 2, 1981

	U.S. dollars required to buy one unit	Units required to buy one U.S. dollar
Australia (dollar)	1.1373	0.8793
Austria (schilling)	.0600	16.67
Brazil (cruzeiro)	.01167	85.69
Britain (pound)	2.0420	0.4897
30-day future	2.0536	0.4869
90-day future	2.0730	0.4824
180-day future	2.0890	0.4787
Canada (dollar)	.8279	1.2080
30-day future	.8273	1.2088
90-day future	.8254	1.2115
180-day future	.8245	1.2129
France (franc)	.1791	5.584
30-day future	.1780	5.617
90-day future	.1772	5.642
180-day future	.1765	5.665
Hong Kong (dollar)	.1825	5.480
Italy (lira)	.000853	1,172.33
Japan (yen)	.00448	223.20
30-day future	.00453	220.95
90-day future	.00461	217.15
180-day future	.00469	213.05
Mexico (peso)	.0413	24.20
Netherlands (guilder)	.3824	2.615
Saudi Arabia (rial)	.2950	3.390
Singapore (dollar)	.4636	2.157
Spain (peseta)	.0107	93.51
Sweden (krona)	.1996	5.010
Switzerland (franc)	.4778	2.093
30-day future	.4818	2.075
90-day future	.4882	2.048
180-day future	.4943	2.023
West Germany (mark)	.4234	2.362
30-day future	.4256	2.349
90-day future	.4293	2.329
180-day future	.4320	2.315

Inflation, interest rates, and exchange rates

If product and financial markets are efficient internationally, we would expect certain consistent relationships to hold. From chapter 3, where we discussed inflation and interest rates, we know the Fisher effect implies that the nominal rate of interest is comprised of the real rate plus the rate of inflation expected to prevail over the life of the instrument. If the real rate of interest were 3 percent and inflation of 10 percent were expected, the current nominal rate of interest would be 13 percent. When inflation expectations change so, too, does the nominal rate of interest. Thus, the Fisher effect suggests that the expected inflation for a country has a powerful effect on interest rates in that country.

Interest-rate parity theorem. The interest-rate parity theorem states that there is an orderly relationship between forward and spot currency exchange rates and nominal interest rates for two countries. Expressing the relationship between the U.S. dollar ($) and the British pound (£) both now and 90 days in the future, the theorem suggests that

$$\frac{F_£}{S_£} = \frac{1 + r_£}{1 + r_\$} \tag{25-1}$$

where $F_£$ = Current 90-day forward exchange rate in pounds per dollar
$S_£$ = Current spot exchange rate in pounds per dollar
$r_£$ = Nominal interest rate on risk-free 90-day British securities, expressed in terms of the 90-day return
$r_\$$ = Nominal interest rate on risk-free 90-day U.S. securities, expressed in terms of the 90-day return

If the nominal interest rate in Britain were 16 percent and the nominal U.S. rate 12 percent, these annualized rates translate into 90-day rates of 4 percent and 3 percent, respectively. If the current spot rate were 0.50 pounds per dollar, we would have

$$\frac{F_£}{0.50} = \frac{1.04}{1.03}$$

Solving for the implied forward rate

$$1.03F_£ = 0.52$$

$$F_£ = 0.50485$$

Thus, the implied forward rate is 0.50485 British pounds per U.S. dollar. The British pound forward rate is at a discount from the spot rate of 0.50 pounds to the dollar. That is, a pound is worth less in terms of dollars in the forward market, $1/.50485 = \$1.98079$, than it is in the spot market, $1/.50 = \$2.00$. The discount is equal to $(.50485 - .50)/.50 = .0097$. With interest-rate parity, the discount must equal the relative difference in interest rates and, indeed, this is the case, for $(1.04/1.03)/1.03 = .0097$. If the interest rate in Britain were less than that in the United States, the implied forward rate in our example would be less than the spot rate. In this case, the British pound forward rate would be at a premium above the spot rate. For example, if the U.S. interest rate (annualized) were 16 percent and the British rate 12 percent, the implied 90-day forward rate for British pounds would be

$$\frac{F_£}{0.50} = \frac{1.03}{1.04}$$

Solving for $F_£$, we have

$$1.04F_£ = 0.515$$

$$F_£ = .49519$$

Therefore, the forward rate is at a premium in the sense that it is worth more in terms of dollars than in the spot market.

If interest-rate parity did not occur, presumably arbitragers would be alert to the opportunity for profit. Their actions to exploit profit opportunities would continue until interest-rate parity was established. Does this mean that interest-rate parity prevails between all sets of currencies at all times? For European and other currencies where there is largely an absence of imperfections, interest-rate parity generally holds within the limits of transaction costs. Where government restrictions on exchange and tax imperfections occur, interest-rate parity is not expected. With reasonable adherence to interest-rate parity, one is able to determine the cost in dollars of a foreign sale or purchase where a future receipt or payment is involved.

In summary, the forward exchange market permits a multinational company to protect itself against foreign exchange risk. This risk embodies both devaluation, where a sharp decline in value occurs, and downside fluctuations in the spot rate. For this protection there is a cost, determined by the relationship between the forward rate and the future spot rate. Whether or not one wishes to use the forward market depends upon one's view of the future and one's risk aversion. The greater the possibility of currency value changes and the greater the risk aversion, the greater the case that can be made for use of the forward market. If others feel the same way, unfortunately, the cost of this insurance will rise.

Foreign currency swap

Yet another means for hedging against foreign exchange risk is a swap arrangement, an agreement between two parties to exchange one currency for another at a specific future date and at a specified exchange ratio. In effect, the swap is a simultaneous spot and forward transaction, with the forward transaction reversing the original swap transaction. A U.S. parent company might wish to transfer funds temporarily abroad to a foreign subsidiary with the understanding that the funds would be returned in 120 days. In order to protect itself against exchange risk, it might enter into a swap arrangement with a private trader or commercial bank. This arrangement assures the company that it will be able to get dollars back 120 days hence. The cost of the arrangement is the difference in exchange ratios at the time of the initial swap and at reversion 120 days later.

Because the latter exchange ratio is set in advance, the cost can be determined in the same way as the cost of a forward transaction.

Swap arrangements are made available also by foreign governments and central banks in an effort to encourage international trade and investment. When economic conditions are volatile and the currency markets unsettled because of the possibility of devaluation, the government often is the only party that can effectively underwrite exchange risk. From time to time central banks are active in currency swaps as a means for stabilizing their own currencies. These swaps, of course, do not involve companies; they are directly between central banks. They do protect the firm against devaluation, particularly in transactions with countries whose currency is soft and where viable forward exchange markets are lacking.

Adjustment of intracompany accounts

Finally, a company with multiple foreign operations can protect itself against foreign exchange risks by adjusting transfer-of-funds commitments between countries. You may hold a high position in such a company at a time when you think the German mark will soon be revalued upward, but the French franc will hold steady. Your company has foreign subsidiaries in both countries. The French subsidiary purchases approximately $100,000 of goods each month from the German subsidiary. Normal billing calls for payment three months after delivery of the goods. Instead of this arrangement, you instruct the French subsidiary to pay for the goods on delivery, in view of the likely revaluation upward of the German mark.

In addition to these arrangements, the multinational company also can adjust intercompany dividends and royalty payments. Sometimes the currency in which a sale is billed is varied in keeping with anticipated foreign exchange movements. In all of these cases as well as others, intercompany payments are arranged so that they fit into the company's overall management of its currency exposure.

MULTINATIONAL FINANCING

Another major facet of financial management is raising funds on as favorable terms as possible. In a multinational company, this involves raising funds from either internal or external sources to finance a foreign affiliate. Internal funds are comprised of equity investment and loans from the U.S. parent, retained earnings, and depreciation and depletion allowances. Recently, internal sources of funds have accounted for somewhat over 70 percent of the total financing of U.S.-owned foreign affiliates.

External financing

Although the major sources of funds for a foreign affiliate are internal, external sources are often used, particularly for temporary requirements. A wide variety of sources of external financing is available to the foreign affiliate. These range from commercial bank loans within the host country to loans from international lending agencies. In this section we consider the chief sources of external financing.

Commercial bank loans and trade bills. One of the major sources of financing abroad, commercial banks perform essentially the same financing function as domestic banks—a topic discussed in chapter 10. One subtle difference is that banking practices in Europe allow longer-term loans than are available in the United States. Another is that loans tend to be on an overdraft basis. That is, a company writes a check that overdraws its account and is charged interest on the overdraft. Many of these banks are known as merchant banks, which simply means that they offer a full menu of financial services to business firms. Corresponding to the growth in multinational companies, international banking operations of U.S. banks have increased. All the principal cities of the free world have branches or offices of a U.S. bank. Under the Edge Act, American banks may act as holding companies and own stock in foreign banks. These banks may be either wholly owned subsidiaries or owned in part by nationals. Thus, U.S. banks are able to provide, directly or indirectly, banking arrangements for foreign affiliates in almost any country. Foreign affiliates sometimes bypass them, nevertheless, in favor of local banks, where they can make contacts and become familiar with local practices.

In addition to commercial bank loans, the discounting of trade bills is a common method of short-term financing. Although this method of financing is not used extensively in the United States, it is widely used in Europe to finance both domestic and international trade. More will be said about the instruments involved later in the chapter.

Eurodollar and Eurobond financing. A *Eurodollar* is defined as a dollar deposit held in a bank outside the United States. Since the late 1950s an active market has developed for these deposits. Foreign banks and foreign branches of U.S. banks, mostly in Europe, bid actively for Eurodollar deposits, paying interest rates that fluctuate in keeping with supply and demand. The deposits are in large denominations, frequently $100,000 or more, and the banks use them to make dollar loans to quality borrowers. The loans are made at a rate in excess of the deposit rate; the differential varies according to the relative risk of the borrower. All loans are unsecured. Essentially, borrowing and lending Eurodollars is a wholesale operation, with far fewer costs than are usually associated with banking.

The Eurodollar market is a major source of short-term financing for the working-capital requirements of the multinational company. Many American firms arrange for lines of credit and revolving credits from Eurodollar banks. For the revolving credit arrangement, the firm pays a commitment fee the same as it does for a domestic revolving credit. The interest rate on loans is based upon the Eurodollar deposit rate and bears only an indirect relationship to the prime rate. Typically, rates on loans are quoted in terms of the London interbank offering rate, commonly called LIBOR. The greater the risk, the greater the spread above LIBOR. A prime borrower will pay about one-half percent over LIBOR for an intermediate-term loan. One should realize that LIBOR usually is more volatile than the U.S. prime rate, owing to the sensitive nature of supply and demand for Eurodollar deposits. Consequently, it is more difficult to project the cost of a Eurodollar loan than that of a domestic loan. Nevertheless, no compensating balances are required, thus enhancing the attractiveness of this kind of financing.

The Eurobond market developed in the late 1960s into a highly regarded source of long-term funds for the multinational company. A *Eurobond* is a long-term security issued by an internationally known borrower in several countries simultaneously. The currencies in which the bonds are denominated usually are actively traded and strong. Most bonds are straight, fixed-income bonds; some are convertible into common stock, others are floating-rate bonds.[4] The market for Eurobonds is truly international; investment banking syndicates are comprised of bankers from a number of countries, and the securities are placed all over the world. Like the Eurodollar market, it is free of government regulation. Somewhat over half of its total volume of funds raised is in dollars. Still, its volume is only a fraction of that which occurs in the United States bond market.

Development banks.   Many countries have development banks that make intermediate- and long-term loans. The purpose of these loans is to support economic development within the country. If the investment project or international transaction qualifies, financing through a development bank may be a viable financing alternative. The bank itself can be either a governmental agency or one that is run privately. To understand their operation, we shall discuss briefly several of the larger development banks.

The *Export-Import Bank* is an independent agency of the U.S. government. Known as the Exim Bank, it was established in 1934 to facilitate the financing of exports from the United States. It accomplishes this purpose in several ways. Its major program is making long-term loans to foreigners, enabling them to purchase U.S. goods and services. The Exim Bank tries to supplement, rather than compete with, private capital. It will participate with private lenders in extending credit, and this arrangement has been used successfully. The bank also guarantees payment of medium-term financing incurred in the export of U.S. goods and services.

The *Agency for International Development* (AID) was established in 1961 to carry out U.S. foreign assistance programs. One aspect of its program is development loans to friendly governments and private enterprises. The effort here is to stimulate investment in underdeveloped countries. The *Inter-American Development Bank* was formed in 1959 by a number of Latin American countries together with the United States. It is an example of a regional development bank that makes both public and private loans for purposes of enhancing economic development in the member countries. The development banks of individual countries are too numerous to list. To mention only a few of the larger ones there are the *Industrial Reorganization Corporation* in Britain, *National Financiera, S.A.,* in Mexico, *Credit National* in France, *Kreditanstalt für Wiederaufbau* in

---

[4]For a study of the behavior of interest rates in this market, see Joseph E. Finnerty, Thomas Schneeweis, and Shantaram P. Hegde, "Interest Rates in the Eurobond Market," *Journal of Financial and Quantitative Analysis,* 15 (September 1980), 743–55.

West Germany, and *Instituto Mobiliare Italiano* in Italy. *Adela* is an example of a privately owned development bank. It makes private investments in Latin American firms, usually in participation with other investors.

FINANCING INTERNATIONAL TRADE

Foreign trade differs from domestic trade with respect to the instruments and documents employed. Most domestic sales are an open-account credit; the customer is billed and has so many days to pay. In international trade, sellers are seldom able to obtain as accurate or as thorough credit information on potential buyers as domestic sales. Communication is more cumbersome and transportation of the goods slower and less certain. Moreover, the channels for legal settlement in cases of default are more complicated and more costly to pursue. For these reasons, procedures for international trade differ from those for domestic trade. There are three key documents: an order to pay, or draft; a bill of lading, which involves the physical movement of the goods; and a letter of credit, which guarantees the credit worthiness of the buyer. We examine each in turn.

The trade draft

The international draft, sometimes called a bill of exchange, is simply a written statement by the exporter ordering the importer to pay a specific amount of money at a specific time. Though the word "order" may seem harsh, it is the customary way of doing business internationally. The draft may be either a *sight* draft or a *time* draft. A sight draft is payable on presentation to the party to whom the draft is addressed. This party is known as the *drawee*. If the drawee, or importer, does not pay the amount specified upon presentation of the draft, he defaults, and redressment is achieved through the letter-of-credit arrangement to be discussed later. A time draft is payable so many days after presentation to the drawee.[5] A 90-day time draft indicates that the draft is payable 90 days after sight. An example of a time draft is shown in Fig. 25-1.

Several features should be noted about the draft. First, it is an unconditional order in writing signed by the drawer, the exporter. It specifies an exact amount of money that the drawee, the importer, must pay. Finally, it specifies an exact interval after sight at which time this amount must be paid. Upon presentation of the time draft to the drawee, it is accepted. The *acceptance* can be by either the drawee or a bank. If the drawee accepts the draft, he acknowledges in writing on the back of the draft his obligation to pay the amount specified 90 days hence. The draft then is known as a trade acceptance. If a bank accepts the draft, it is known as a bankers' acceptance. The bank accepts responsibility for payment and thereby substitutes its credit worthiness for that of the drawee.

---

[5] The draft itself can be either "clean" or "documentary." A clean draft is one to which documents of title are not attached. They are attached to a documentary draft and are delivered to the importer at the time the draft is presented. Clean drafts are usually used for situations in which there is no trade as such and the drawer is simply collecting a bill. Most drafts are documentary.

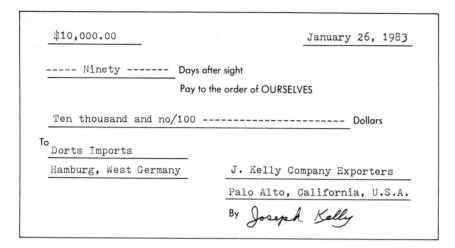

FIGURE 25-1
A trade draft

If the bank is large and well known—and most banks accepting drafts are—the instrument becomes highly marketable upon acceptance. As a result, the drawer, or exporter, does not have to hold the draft until the due date; he can sell it in the market. In fact, an active market exists for bankers' acceptances of well-known banks. A 90-day draft for $10,000 may be accepted by a well-known bank. Say that 90-day interest rates in the bankers' acceptance market are 12 percent. The drawer then could sell the draft to an investor for $9,700, $10,000 − [$10,000 × .12(90/360)]. At the end of 90 days, the investor would present the acceptance to the accepting bank for payment and would receive $10,000. Thus, the existence of a strong secondary market for bankers' acceptances has facilitated international trade by providing liquidity to the exporter.

Bills of lading

A bill of lading is a shipping document used in the transportation of goods from the exporter to the importer. It has several functions. First, it serves as a receipt from the transportation company to the exporter, showing that specified goods have been received. Second, it serves as a contract between the transportation company and the exporter to ship the goods and deliver them to a specific party at a specific point of destination. Finally, the bill of lading can serve as a document of title. It gives the holder title to the goods. The importer cannot take title until he receives the bill of lading from the transportation company or its agent. This bill will not be released until the importer satisfies all the conditions of the draft.[6]

The bill of lading accompanies the draft, and the procedures by which the two are handled are well established. Banks and other institutions able to handle these documents efficiently exist in virtually every country. Moreover, the procedures by which goods are transferred internationally are well grounded in international law. These procedures allow an exporter in one country to sell goods to

---

[6] The bill of lading can be negotiable if specified at the time it is made out. It also can be used as collateral for a loan.

an unknown importer in another and not release possession of the goods until paid if there is a sight draft, or until the obligation is acknowledged, if there is a time draft.

Letters of credit

A commercial letter of credit is issued by a bank on behalf of the importer. In the document, the bank agrees to honor a draft drawn on the importer, provided the bill of lading and other details are in order. In essence, the bank substitutes its credit for that of the importer. Obviously, the local bank will not issue a letter of credit unless it feels the importer is credit worthy and will pay the draft. The letter-of-credit arrangement almost eliminates the exporter's risk in selling goods to an unknown importer in another country. An example of a letter-of-credit form is shown in Fig. 25-2.

Illustration of a confirmed letter. The arrangement is strengthened further if a bank in the exporter's country *confirms* the letter of credit. A New York exporter wishes to ship goods to a Brazilian importer located in Rio de Janeiro. The importer's bank in Rio regards the importer as a sound credit risk and is willing to issue a letter of credit guaranteeing payment for the goods when they are received. Thus, the Rio bank substitutes its credit for that of the importer. The contract is now between the Rio bank and the beneficiary of the letter of credit, the New York exporter. The exporter may wish to work through her bank, because she has little knowledge of the Rio bank. She asks her New York bank to confirm the Rio bank's letter of credit. If the New York bank is satisfied with the credit worthiness of the Rio bank, it will agree to do so. When it does, it obligates itself to honor drafts drawn in keeping with the letter-of-credit arrangement.

Thus, when the exporter ships the goods, she draws a draft in accordance with the terms of the letter-of-credit arrangement. She presents the draft to her New York bank and the bank pays her the amount designated, assuming all conditions of shipment are met. As a result of this arrangement, the exporter has her money with no worries about payment. The New York bank then forwards the draft and other documents to the Rio bank. Upon affirming that the goods have been shipped in a proper manner, the Rio bank honors the draft and pays the New York bank. In turn, it goes to the Brazilian importer and collects from him once the goods have arrived in Rio and are delivered.

Facilitation of trade. From the description, it is easy to see why the letter of credit facilitates international trade. Rather than extending credit directly to an importer, the exporter relies on one or more banks; and their credit worthiness is substituted for that of the importer. The letter itself can be either *irrevocable* or *revocable*, but drafts drawn under an irrevocable letter must be honored by the issuing bank. This obligation can be neither canceled nor modified without the consent of all parties. On the other hand, a revocable letter of credit can be canceled or amended by the issuing bank. A revocable letter specifies an arrangement for payment but is no guarantee that the draft will be paid. Most letters of credit are irrevocable, and the process described above assumes an irrevocable letter.

FIGURE 25-2
Letter-of-credit form

The three documents described—the draft, the bill of lading, and the letter of credit—are required in most international transactions. Established procedures exist for doing business on this basis. Together, they afford the exporter protection in selling goods to unknown importers in other countries. They also give the importer assurance that the goods will be shipped and delivered in a proper manner. The financial manager should be acquainted with the mechanics of these transactions if the firm is engaged in exporting or importing.

The multinational corporation, doing business in two or more countries, has become prominent in recent years. As in domestic operations, its financial manager is concerned with the allocation of capital to investment projects and raising funds. Foreign investments should be judged on the basis of expected returns and risk, the same as a domestic project. Owing to market segmentation, foreign projects sometimes afford risk-reduction properties that are not available in domestic projects.

Expansion abroad is undertaken to go into new markets, acquire less costly production facilities, and secure raw materials. A number of factors make foreign investment different from domestic investment. Taxation is different; risks are present in political conditions and foreign exchange. Forecasting potential political instability and its effect on expected returns is essential at the time an investment is being considered. Foreign exchange risk is the danger that a foreign currency will decline in value relative to the dollar or its convertibility will be restricted. In its currency exposure management, a company can protect itself against exchange risk by balancing foreign monetary assets and liabilities, by use of the forward exchange market, by engaging in a foreign currency swap arrangement, or by adjusting intracompany account arrangements. A good deal of attention was devoted to hedging in the futures market. The interest-rate parity theorem implies a consistent relationship between the forward and spot currency exchange rates and relative differences in nominal interest rates for two countries. Both political and foreign exchange risk must be integrated with business risk in judging the overall risk of a foreign investment.

Raising funds abroad is another major function of the financial manager. Although internal financing—comprised of equity investments and loans from the parent, retained earnings, and depreciation and depletion allowances—is the chief source of funds, external financing is important as well. The major sources of external funds are commercial banks, Eurodollar loans, Eurobonds, and development banks. Financing international trade differs from financing domestic trade in the procedures employed. The differences in procedures are attributable to the lower quality of credit information, poorer communications, slower transportation, and different legal processes in foreign trade. Three principal documents are involved in international trade. The draft is an order by the exporter to the importer to pay a specified amount of money either upon presentation of the draft or a certain number of days after presentation. A bill of lading is a shipping document that can serve as a receipt, as a shipping contract, and as title to the goods involved. A letter of credit is an agreement by a bank to honor a draft drawn on the importer. It greatly reduces the risk to the exporter and may be confirmed by another bank. These three documents greatly facilitate international trade.

QUESTIONS

1. If capital and product markets are perfect, does it make any difference in which country a company invests?

2. Why would a company want to enter a joint venture when it loses partial control over its foreign operations?

3. Explain the function performed by the Eurodollar market.

4. What are the functions of the bill of lading?

5. Many countries require that nationals control more than 50 percent of the voting stock in any venture. Is this wise? Explain.

6. In the early 1970s the Chilean government took over most of the American-owned businesses in Chile. Explain the impact of such action on the short-run and long-run productivity of the assets that were taken over. Project the impact of these actions on future development of the underdeveloped countries.

7. What are monetary assets? Monetary liabilities? With respect to a foreign subsidiary, what if they are mismatched?

8. What is meant by interest-rate parity? Does it work?

9. Identify factors that will prevent the correction of a trade deficit by currency realignment (devaluation or revaluation).

10. In a letter of credit arrangement, who is the borrower? Who is the lender?

11. What is the credit worthiness of a bankers' acceptance? How does it differ from that of the trade draft? What determines the face value of the acceptance?

12. Do income taxes paid by a foreign branch work to the detriment of the U.S. parent company?

PROBLEMS

1. Table 25-1 shows foreign exchange rates. On the basis of this information, compute to the nearest second decimal the number of

   a) British pounds that can be acquired for $100

   b) Dollars that 50 Dutch guilders will buy

   c) Swedish krona that can be acquired for $40

   d) Dollars that 200 Swiss francs can buy

   e) Italian lira that can be acquired for $10 (to the nearest lira.)

   f) Dollars that 1,000 Mexican pesos will buy

2. The U.S. Imports Company purchased 100,000 marks' worth of machines from a firm in Dortmund, West Germany. The value of the dollar in terms of the mark has been decreasing. The firm in Dortmund offers 2/10, net 90 terms. The spot rate for the mark is $0.42, while the 90-day future rate is $0.43.

   a) Compute the dollar cost of paying the account within the 10 days.

   b) Compute the dollar cost of buying a future contract to liquidate the account in 90 days.

   c) The differential between part a and part b is the result of the time value of money (the discount for prepayment) and protection from currency value fluctuation. Determine the magnitude of each of these components.

3. In 1977 the Vermont Maple Industries Company obtained a $100,000 loan in Canadian dollars from the Bank of Quebec to finance an exploratory maple sugar farm in Quebec. At the time of the loan the exchange rate was 1.00 U.S. dollars required to buy one Canadian dollar. Four years later, when the loan was paid, the exchange rate had dropped to .83 U.S. dollars to the Canadian dollar. What gain or loss did the company sustain by virtue of the change in currency value?

4. Financiera de Nuevo León in Mexico offers to pay 12 percent on one-year certificates of deposit. The Mexican government taxes interest income at the source through a with-holding system much like the U.S. system of withholding on personal income. The Mexican tax rate is 21 percent. An American who is in the 40 percent tax bracket in the U.S. invests $50,000 in the Financiera (Savings and Loan).

  a) Determine the taxes paid to the Mexican government.

  b) Determine the taxes paid to the U.S. government on the income from Mexico.

  c) Qualitatively, assess the risks being borne by the American investor.

5. An American manufacturer is going to increase its inventories in Europe financed either by a Eurodollar loan with 18 months maturity at an annual rate of 12 percent payable at maturity or by French francs at an annual rate of 15 percent. If the French francs are chosen, the position will be hedged with an 18-month future contract at $0.16 per franc. The current exchange rate is $0.17 per franc. Choose the better financing alternative.

6. Presently, the dollar is worth 220 Japanese yen in the spot market. The interest rate in Japan on 90-day government securities is 8 percent; it is 12 percent in the United States. If the interest rate parity theorem holds, what is the implied 90-day forward exchange rate in yen per dollar? What would be implied if the U.S. interest rate were 10 percent?

7. Cordova Leather Company of New Mexico is in a 42 percent U.S. tax bracket. It has sales branches in Algeria and in Spain, each of which generate earnings of $200,000 before taxes. If the effective income tax rate is 52 percent in Algeria and 35 percent in Spain, what total U.S. and foreign taxes will Cordova pay on the above earnings?

8. The government of Zwill presently encourages investment in the country. Comstock Inter-national Mining Corporation, a U.S. company, is planning to open a new copper mine in Zwill. The front-end investment is expected to be $25 million, after which cash flows are expected to be more than sufficient to cover further capital needs. Preliminary exploration findings suggest that the project is likely to be very profitable, providing an expected internal rate of return of 34 percent, based on business considerations alone.

   The government of Zwill, like that of many countries, is unstable. The management of Comstock, trying to assess this instability and its consequences, forecasts a 10 percent probability that the government will be overthrown and a new government will expropriate the property, with no compensation. The full $25 million would be lost, and the internal rate of return would be −100 percent. There also is a 15 percent probability that the government will be overthrown but that the new government will make a partial payment for the properties; this would result in an internal rate of return of −40 percent. Finally, there is a 15 percent probability that the present government will stay in power, but that it will change its policy on repatriation of profits. More specifically, it will allow the corporation to repatriate its original investment, $25 million, but all other cash flows generated by the project would have to be reinvested in the host country forever. These probabilities still leave a 60 percent chance that a 34 percent internal rate of return will be achieved.

   Given these political risks, approximate the likely return to Comstock. Should the mining venture be undertaken?

SELECTED REFERENCES

ADLER, MICHAEL, and BERNARD DUMAS, "The Exposure of Long-Term Foreign Currency Bonds," *Journal of Financial and Quantitative Analysis,* 15 (November 1980), 973–94.

AGGARWAL, R., "International Differences in Capital Structure Norms: An Empirical Study of Large European Companies," *Management International Review,* 21, No. 1 (1981), 75–88.

ANDERSON, GERALD L., "International Project Financing," *Financial Executive,* 45 (May 1977), 40–45.

BEAVER, WILLIAM H., and MARK A. WOLFSON, "Foreign Currency Translation and Accounting for Changing Prices in Perfect and Complete Markets," Research Paper, Stanford Business School, 1981.

CALDERON-ROSSELL, JORGE R., "Covering Foreign Exchange Risks of Single Transactions," *Financial Management,* 8 (Autumn 1979), 78–85.

COHN, RICHARD A., and DONALD R. LESSARD, "The Effect of Inflation on Stock Prices: International Evidence," *Journal of Finance,* 36 (May 1981), 277–90.

CORNELL, BRADFORD, "Inflation, Relative Price Changes, and Exchange Risk," *Financial Management,* 9 (Autumn 1980), 30–34.

———, "The Denomination of Foreign Trade Contracts Once Again," *Journal of Financial and Quantitative Analysis,* 15 (November 1980), 933–44.

———, "Spot Rates, Forward Rates and Exchange Market Efficiency," *Journal of Financial Economics,* 5 (August 1977), 55–65.

DAVIS, STEVEN I., "How Risky is International Lending?" *Harvard Business Review,* 55 (January–February 1977), 135–43.

EAKER, MARK R., "Denomination Decision for Multinational Transactions," *Financial Management,* 9 (Autumn 1980), 23–29.

EITEMAN, DAVID K., and ARTHUR I. STONEHILL, *Multinational Business Finance.* 2nd ed. Reading, Mass.: Addison-Wesley, 1979.

ERRUNZA, VIHANG R., and LEMMA W. SENBET, "The Effects of International Operations on the Market Value of the Firm: Theory and Evidence," *Journal of Finance,* 36 (May 1981), 401–18.

FEIGER, GEORGE and BERTRAND JACQUILLAT, "Currency Option Bonds, Puts and Calls on Spot Exchange and the Hedging of Contingent Foreign Earnings," *Journal of Finance,* 34 (December 1979), 1129–39.

———, *International Finance.* Boston: Allyn and Bacon, 1982.

FINNERTY, JOSEPH E., THOMAS SCHNEEWEIS, and SHANTARAM P. HEGDE, "Interest Rates in the Eurobond Market," *Journal of Financial and Quantitative Analysis,* 15 (September 1980), 743–55.

GARMAN, MARK B., and STEVEN W. KOHLHAGEN, "Inflation and Foreign Exchange Rates under Production and Monetary Uncertainty," *Journal of Financial and Quantitative Analysis,* 15 (November 1980), 949–68.

GIDDY, IAN H., "An Integrated Theory of Exchange Rate Equilibrium," *Journal of Financial and Quantitative Analysis,* 11 (December 1976), 883–92.

GITMAN, LAWRENCE J., "A Multinational Firm Investment Model," *Journal of Economics and Business,* 26 (Fall 1973), 41–48.

HAGEMANN, HELMUT, "Anticipate Your Long-Term Foreign Exchange Risks," *Harvard Business Review,* 55 (March–April 1977), 81–88.

HENNING, CHARLES N., WILLIAM PIGOTT, and ROBERT HANEY SCOTT, *International Financial Management,* New York: McGraw-Hill, 1978.

HUGHES, JOHN S., DENNIS E. LOGUE, and JAMES SWEENEY, "Corporate International Diversification and Market Assigned Measures of Risk and Diversification," *Journal of Financial and Quantitative Analysis,* 10 (November 1975), 627–37.

LESSARD, DONALD, "International Portfolio Diversification: A Multivariate Analysis for a Group of Latin American Countries," *Journal of Finance,* 28 (June 1973), 619–34.

———, ed. *International Financial Management, Theory and Application.* New York: Warren, Gorham & Lamont, 1979.

LEVY, HAIM, and MARSHALL SARNAT, "International Diversification of Investment Portfolios," *American Economic Review,* 60 (September 1970), 668–75.

LIETAER, BERNARD A., *Financial Management of Foreign Exchange: An Operational Technique to Reduce Risk.* Cambridge, Mass.: M.I.T. Press, 1971.

LOGUE, DENNIS E., and GEORGE S. OLDFIELD, "Managing Foreign Assets when Foreign Exchange Markets Are Efficient." *Financial Management,* 6 (Summer 1977), 16–22.

OBLAK, DAVID J., and ROY J. HELM, JR., "Survey and Analysis of Capital Budgeting Methods used by Multinationals," *Financial Management,* 9 (Winter 1980), 37–41.

PETTY, J. WILLIAM, II, and ERNEST W. WALKER, "Optimal Transfer Pricing for the Multinational Firm," *Financial Management,* 1 (Winter 1972), 74–87.

RODRIQUEZ, RITA M., "Corporate Exchange Risk Management: Theme and Aberrations," *Journal of Finance,* 36 (May 1981), 427–38.

———, and E. EUGENE CARTER, *International Financial Management,* 2nd ed., Englewood Cliffs, N.J.: Prentice-Hall, 1979.

SHAPIRO, ALAN C., "Exchange Rate Changes, Inflation, and the Valuation of the Multinational Corporation," *Journal of Finance,* 30 (May 1975), 485–502.

———, "Optimal Inventory and Credit-Granting Strategies under Inflation and Devaluation," *Journal of Financial and Quantitative Analysis,* 8 (January 1973), 37–46.

———, and DAVID P. RUTENBERG, "Managing Exchange Risks in a Floating World," *Financial Management,* 5 (Summer 1976), 48–58.

SOLNIK, BRUNO H., *European Capital Markets.* Boston: Lexington Books, 1973.

TECK, ALAN, "Control your Exposure to Foreign Exchange," *Harvard Business Review,* 52 (January-February 1974), 66–75.

VERNON, RAYMOND, et al., *Manager in the International Economy,* 4th ed. Englewood Cliffs, N.J.: Prentice-Hall, 1981.

WELLS, LOUIS T., JR., "The Multinational Business Enterprise: What Kind of International Organization?" *International Organization,* 25 (September 1971), 447–64.

WESTON, J. FRED, *Guide to International Financial Management.* New York: McGraw-Hill, 1977.

The smaller company and financial management

26

The small business, one of the cornerstones of a competitive economy, far outnumbers the large business and often provides more fertile ground for creativity and entrepreneurship. Because new entry into a market is possible, small businesses spring up all the time, keeping the competitive environment lively, a phenomenon that leads to productivity gains and real economic growth. Most of the principles taken up earlier in the book apply to firms of varying size. All companies allocate funds to assets, and they raise funds. The difference is in emphasis. The small firm faces different problems than the large one does, and it has more limited access to financial markets. But it also has connections with certain institutions, such as the Small Business Administration. The focus of this chapter is on the specific aspects that make financial management in the smaller company different from that in the large one.

CHARACTERISTICS OF THE SMALL FIRM

There is no generally accepted definition of what constitutes smallness in a firm. Usually one mentions sales, assets, or number of employees. Frequently, firms with less than $4 million in sales, less than $2 million in assets, and fewer than 200 employees are classified as small. The limits are arbitrary and may be adjusted up or, more likely, down, depending on the situation. Nonetheless, they give the reader some idea of what constitutes smallness.

575

CHAPTER 26
The smaller
company
and financial
management

The growth-oriented smaller firm

A new venture in a growth segment of the economy is a different genre from the more traditional small business that will always remain small. A high technology company may start out small but grow into a larger company, particularly in the electronics, computer, and information systems industries.

For the smaller growth firm, the challenge is to manage growth in an efficient manner. Fast growth brings with it the need to hire large numbers of new employees—often to double the number each year or to even grow more rapidly. With the inevitable turnover of employees, this means an even larger number of new hires who must be assimilated into the organization, and new management must be developed. Frequently, entrepreneurs who start a business are technically oriented and not necessarily good managers of increasing numbers of people. Many a growth firm flounders because its top people, who have been able to do things themselves when the firm was small, cannot manage others.

The growth-oriented smaller business faces a number of strategic decisions in marketing, new products, production, and a host of other areas. Financing is an ever-present problem. For most smaller, growth-oriented, high technology companies, growth in assets outpaces growth in retained earnings. Though these companies typically pay no dividends, the percentage of buildup in receivables, inventories, and fixed assets usually is much greater than the percentage of buildup in retained earnings. Sometimes the problem is alleviated by leasing buildings and equipment and by being labor intensive, instead of capital intensive, in the production process. Even at that, receivables and invenories continue to grow.

Whenever growth in assets outstrips growth in retained earnings, debt increasingly must fill the gap. Debt may take the form of bank loans or increasing reliance on trade payables. Because the firm is small, even though growing, a straight bond issue to the public is out of the question. Consequently, the firm is restricted in its sources of debt funds. With the unbalanced growth mentioned above, debt ratios increase, and these ratios ultimately are questioned by lenders. Eventually it becomes necessary either to raise equity capital or to curtail growth. Equity capital often comes from venture capitalists, a topic considered later in the chapter.

Thus, the small, high technology company faces a number of problems: personnel, marketing, production, and financing. Resolution of the financing problem is instrumental in solving many of the former. Building a company on a proportionally smaller and smaller equity base is precarious. Often the problem is masked by growing profits; but, as long as assets are growing more rapidly, debt ratios deteriorate. The problem often is compounded by using short-term financing—bank loans and payables—to finance long-term funds requirements; that is, permanent buildups in receivables, inventories, and fixed assets. Eventually a day of reckoning must come. It is far better to face the issue of balanced financial growth earlier, rather than later.

The risks of starting and nurturing a growth-oriented, high technology company are many. Usually there is little margin for error. The equity base simply does not provide an adequate cushion. If things go wrong, the smaller company frequently is unable to weather the storm. Although one remedy might be to curtail growth, few entrepreneurs have the temperament to do so. Usually it is forced upon them by outside suppliers of capital, often too late. Thus, there is a higher mortality of small firms than of large ones.

The traditional smaller firm

The traditional smaller company tends to be outside a high technology industry. It may be a retail store, a franchise outlet, a service company, or a small manufacturing company. Even though the company may be quite successful, it probably always will remain small. This forecast does not denigrate the traditional small business, for such firms are essential to the economy. It simply recognizes the fact that high growth is not an appropriate objective. Usually the traditional small firm is heavily dependent upon one or two individuals who own it and are involved in all areas of the enterprise. Indeed, specialization for them is not possible. They are on the firing line all the time, making most of their decisions without elaborate analysis. Their management style is loose and personal; control is informal. They take in stride their day-to-day operations but cannot extricate themselves from these operations for enough time to engage in strategic planning.

Financial management of the small, traditional firm is a good deal different from that of the large firm and even from that of the small, but growth-oriented, high technology firm. For one thing, the small firm cannot sell common stock. All equity capital must come from the owners and from earnings retained in the business. The lack of ability to engage in equity financing seriously limits any expansion plans that management might have. The chief sources of financing are trade payables and bank or finance company loans. Often trade credit serves as a cushion to offset unfavorable cash swings. When the small firm is in a temporary cash bind, it leans on the trade by slowing its payments. If it is desperate, it may use accrual financing as well. It may postpone wages and payments on witholding and income taxes. Of course there frequently are costs to such actions, as discussed in chapter 9. Moreover, such reliance may mask the fact that the funds requirements of the firm are permanent instead of temporary and should be financed by some other means. Bank and finance company loans usually must be secured, usually by receivables and inventories. Often the owners are required to guarantee the loan, to put all their personal wealth at stake and compound their risk.

Any intermediate- or long-term debt also must be secured. Equipment may be purchased on a conditional sales contract or through a secured loan, or it is often leased. If the firm owns its building, it may use a mortgage loan, but the small business usually enters into short-term debt.

Table 26-1 illustrates some financial differences between a small and a large firm. It compares the average balance sheet percentages and financial ratios for two sizes of a machine tool company. These data are compiled by Robert Morris Associates. The smaller firm has a greater need to hold cash than the larger one,

TABLE 26-1 \ **Comparison of balance sheet percentages and financial ratios for small and larger manufacturers of machine tools and metal working equipment**

	Asset size	
	Under $250,000	$10 million to $50 million
Cash	11.6%	4.8%
Receivables	32.3	25.5
Inventories	15.8	37.3
Other current assets	1.8	1.2
Net fixed assets	30.9	24.1
Other noncurrent assets	7.6	7.1
TOTAL ASSETS	100.0	100.0
Notes payable	16.0%	10.4
Accounts payable	16.1	11.5
Accruals	7.0	6.7
Other current liabilities	1.2	3.4
Long-term debt	26.5	15.7
Net worth	33.2	52.3
TOTAL LIABILITIES AND NET WORTH	100.0	100.0
Current ratio	1.8	2.4
Quick ratio	1.3	1.0
Average collection period	53	59
Inventory turnover	6.5	3.0
Debt/Net worth	1.9	0.9
Before-tax profit margin	7.0%	10.6%
Return on assets (before taxes)	16.1%	15.6%

owing to economies of scale in liquidity management. Also, it has far lower inventories, which may be due to differences in the nature of the business. The inventory turnover ratio is more than double that for larger firms, which may support the idea of differences in the nature of the business. With respect to financing, the smaller business uses much more debt and less equity than does the larger business. This relationship may reflect the difficulties of raising equity capital. Also, profitability on sales is less, though the return on assets is about the same, owing to the higher turnover of assets. The other numbers speak for themselves. Thus, the most noticeable differences between the two size categories is the much heavier reliance of the smaller firm on debt financing and the lower level of inventory and higher turnover.

The typical small business is greatly involved, perhaps overly involved, in managing working capital. Because many small businesses are thinly capitalized, management worries a lot about liquidity. Planning cash flows is critical. Receivables must be watched closely, and late payers hounded. In order not to tie up funds unnecessarily, inventories must be managed efficiently. When either receivables or inventories are mismanaged, financial problems typically arise. As mentioned before, current liability management also is important. Many a small business must delay payments to suppliers and sometimes even to employees in order to weather what is hoped to be only a temporary downturn. Some small businesses are franchises, such as fast food outlets and muffler shops, and they usually lease their buildings. Their managements' principle concerns are sales, inventory management, expense control, and planning ahead to pay bills.

In summary, the small business has somewhat different characteristics from those of the large business. Typically, it must rely on internal financing. A great deal of attention should, and indeed must, be paid to working capital management. Continual effort must be devoted simply to remaining solvent. Decision making is concentrated in one or at most only a few individuals. Management is spread thin over all facets of the enterprise, so long-range planning receives little attention. The principles taken up in previous chapters apply to the small business as they do to any business, but the relative emphasis is different.

SPECIAL FINANCING OPPORTUNITIES

We have discussed the differences in financing the small versus the large firm. Previous chapters involving trade and accrual financing, secured short-term lending arrangements, equipment financing, and lease financing (chapters 11, 12, and 20) are particularly germane; however, certain special financing arrangements are applicable to the small business. These include Small Business Administration loans, venture capital, and special Security and Exchange Commission rulings involving small public offerings. The last two are more applicable to the growth-oriented, high technology firm than they are to the more traditional small business. The purpose of this section is to explore these special arrangements.

Small business administration loans

The Small Business Act gives the Small Business Administration, an agency of the federal government, the authority to make loans to small businesses when they are unable to obtain funds elsewhere. The definition of a small business depends upon its sales in relation to those of the industry and upon the number of employees. Any manufacturing firm with less than 250 employees is eligible for an SBA loan. (In some cases, 1,000 employees is the limit.) The SBA seeks to make sound business loans to credit-worthy borrowers, as private lenders do. It thoroughly analyzes every application before it decides whether or not to make a loan. The maximum loan permitted is $350,000.

When possible, the SBA prefers to participate with a private lending institution in extending credit. In fact, it can make direct loans only when borrowing from other sources is not available on reasonable terms. The participation by the SBA may be up to 90 percent of the loan, the balance being provided by the private lender. This participation does not necessarily have to consist of a loan from the SBA. The SBA may, instead, guarantee payment of up to 90 percent of a loan by a private investor. In recent years, participation loans have been stressed and have tended to dominate direct lending.

Venture capital

Venture capital represents funds invested in a new enterprise. Debt funds sometimes are provided; but for the most part, common stock is involved. Almost always this stock is not registered for a period of years. Known as *letter stock*, it cannot be sold until the issue is registered; therefore investors have no liquidity for a period of time. Their hope is that the company will thrive and that after five years or so it will be large and profitable enough to sell its stock in the public market. In turn, venture capitalists hope to sell their stock for many times what they paid for it. This is one scenario. Others, unfortunately, are possible. The risks associated with a new venture are many, and the frequency of failure is significant. With failure, the investor loses everything. The probability distribution of possible returns for most venture capital portfolio investments is highly skewed to the right. That is, there is a significant chance that the investors will lose all their investment, but there also is some probability that their investment will increase in value ten- or even fiftyfold. The overall portfolio return to the venture capitalist is very sensitive to those few investments that do very well, perhaps one or two in ten.[1]

In general, the relative availability of venture capital is closely tied to the tone of the stock market. When the market is buoyant and price/earnings ratios are high, venture capitalists are interested in making investments. The reason is that they can look to a viable and active stock market for ultimate payout. One could argue that it is not the present tone of the market but the expected tone several years hence that is decisive. However, expectations of future market conditions are heavily influenced by present market conditions. On the other hand, when the stock market is in the doldrums, venture capital funds tend to be less available.

Thus the 1960s were characterized by considerable interest in venture capital investments, particularly up to 1968. On average, interest was much lower in the 1970s, when it ebbed and flowed with changes in the stock market. So far in the 1980s, the venture capital market has been robust with considerable competition among venture capitalists to finance the "good idea."

New venture proposals in the high technology area are usually more attractive to venture capitalists than new ventures in a mundane industry. The reason

[1]This phenomenon is confirmed by an excellent survey: Blaine Huntsman and James P. Hoban, Jr., "Investment in New Enterprise; Some Empirical Observations on Risk, Return, and Market Structure," *Financial Management*, 9 (Summer 1980), 44-51. The authors analyzed 110 equity deals put together by three venture capital firms. They found that approximately one in six investments resulted in total failure and many more showed negative or negligible returns. A few investments showed extraordinary returns, the four highest being 318 percent, 160 percent, 110 percent and 109 percent annually. Overall portfolio performance was very sensitive to these "winners." The average portfolio return was nearly 19 percent; but if the best ten investments were eliminated, the overall rate of return on the remaining portfolio was negative.

is simple. In high technology, there is the perceived possibility of substantial growth and ultimate capital gains. Thus there are a number of venture capital firms in the Greater Boston and San Francisco areas, owing to the hotbed of electronic activities in these areas. In addition, there are a number of venture capitalists in New York, Chicago, and Dallas. Perhaps the most prominent venture capitalist in the post-World War II era was Laurence Rockefeller, who was actively involved in a number of young and ultimately successful companies.

The sources of venture capital are several. Wealthy individuals, the traditional source, are still important but no longer dominant. Individuals make venture capital investments directly or indirectly. In a direct investment, the individual or partnership of individuals screens applicants, investigates the investment, and reaches a decision. With an indirect approach, the first step is undertaken by a finder or broker who presents situations and a certain amount of analysis to the investor. Institutional investors such as pension funds, trusts, university endowments, and life insurance companies frequently have venture capital groups or divisions. The intent is to invest a certain portion of the overall portfolio, usually less than 5 percent, in new ventures. Some of these investors have local offices in areas of the country where high technology companies are prevalent. Also, bank holding companies are a source of venture capital. The interest of banks in venture capital increased with the advent of the bank holding company concept, whereby a number of nonbank financial services were placed under the holding company umbrella.

The Small Business Investment Company (SBIC) is another source of venture capital. The Small Business Investment Act of 1958 enabled the Small Business Administration to license SBICs and to provide them with a degree of financing. The SBIC is privately owned and must have at least $150,000 in equity capital. Its investments consist mainly of convertible and debt instruments with warrants attached. In other words, they obtain an indirect equity position in the companies they finance. The SBIC may obtain financing from the Small Business Administration as well as from outside sources. In a number of instances, banks have established SBICs to engage in venture capital investing.

The enterprise seeking financing must convince any of the various sources that sizable returns will offset the substantial risks involved. That may be hard to do, so venture capital is not available to all new companies, but it gives some of them their start.

Public offerings

For the smaller, private company having its first public stock offering, the change in atmosphere is pronounced. Quarterly financial statements are necessary, and information about the company must be released to outsiders on a timely basis. Management's perquisites must be monitored. Whereas the private owner may have felt a company plane was justified, such justification may erode when the firm becomes a public company. Even though the founders may still hold controlling interest in a company, they must consider how their actions affect outside stockholders. When a firm goes public, there is a great concern with quarterly earnings. This preoccupation with short-run profits may be to the detriment of profitability over the longer run. Certain long-term investments and research and development may be curtailed in the pursuit of short-term profits. Another factor is the board of directors. In a public company, it usually includes some outsiders, people not formally affiliated with the company. All of these aspects significantly change the atmosphere as a firm goes from a private company to a public one.

The procedures involved in a public offering of bonds or stock were described in chapter 19; however, the Securities and Exchange Commission (SEC) has special provisions that make it easier for a small company. Under Regulation A, which involves offerings of $1.5 million or less, a company is not required to conform to standard SEC registration procedures. The amount of paper work is much less, and the preliminary circular may be used as a sales tool for the offering. In contrast, the large company must wait for final clearance of the circular by the SEC. For companies with less than $1 million in assets and fewer than 500 stockholders, the S-18 registration form is substantially easier than the standard form. These procedures and more to come are designed to eliminate some of the red tape for the smaller firm making a public security offering.

581
CHAPTER 26
The smaller
company
and financial
management

SUMMARY

A small business may be either a growth-oriented, high technology company or the more traditional small business that will remain small. The key ingredient in the former is rapid growth, and this growth brings with it problems in personnel management, in strategic decision making, and in financial management. A typical problem is that of the assets of the firm growing at a faster rate than retained earnings, which results in debt ratios being stretched. For most of these firms, the risks are high because there is little liquidity to compensate for error. The owner of the traditional smaller firm, involved in all aspects of the enterprise, has little time for forward planning. In most cases, there is no ability to engage in equity financing and little ability to place long-term debt. Financing usually is confined to trade payables, accruals, and short-term secured financing. The balance sheet percentages for the small and for the large firm are not the same, and these differences were illustrated. The typical small business focuses heavily on working-capital management.

Several special financing vehicles are available to the small business. The Small Business Administration makes loans when private lending is not forthcoming, or it will usually participate with a private lender. Venture capital is equity capital invested in a new enterprise. A network of venture capitalists usually invests in high technology companies. In recent years, banks have become an important source of venture capital, often through a Small Business Investment Company (SBIC). Public offerings of securities by small businesses have been made easier by the Securities and Exchange Commission's reducing the registration requirements for smaller offerings.

QUESTIONS

1. How would you define a small business? In terms of sales? Assets? Profits? Employees? Other?

2. What effect do small businesses have on the economy? Are they essential?

3. Identify some of the problems associated with a new enterprise in a high technology, fast growing area.

4. What are some of the repercussions of receivables, inventories, and fixed assets growing at a faster rate than do retained earnings? What are the remedies?

5. Are there dangers to using short-term debt for financing a small but growing company?

6. Identify the characteristics of the traditional smaller business.

7. In the traditional smaller business, with what aspects of finance is management primarily concerned?

8. Under what circumstances might you obtain a Small Business Administration loan if you run a small business and were unsuccessful in obtaining a bank loan?

9. What does a venture capitalist hope to gain from an investment in a new enterprise? How liquid is the investment?

10. Can any small, new business look to venture capital as a source of financing?

11. Why do the Securities and Exchange Commission, the Small Business Administration, as well as other departments of the government try to assist small businesses?

12. If you decide to start a retail store or take on a new franchise, how will you finance it?

SELECTED REFERENCES

BRIGHAM, EUGENE F., and KEITH V. SMITH, "The Cost of Capital to the Small Firm," *Engineering Economist*, 13 (Fall 1967), 1–26.

GILMORE, F.F., "Formulation Strategy in Smaller Companies," *Harvard Business Review*, 49 (May 1971), 71–81.

HUNTSMAN, BLAINE, and JAMES P. HOBAN, Jr., "Investment in New Enterprise: Some Empirical Observations on Risk, Return, and Market Structure," *Financial Management*, 9 (Summer 1980), 44–51.

PLAYFAIR, JOHN L., "New Solutions to the Venture Capital Problem," *CA Magazine*, (September 1976), 26–31.

ROSSITER, BRUCE G., and GENE I. MILLER, "Financing the New Enterprise," in J. FRED WESTON and MAURICE B. GOUDZWAARD, eds., *The Treasurer's Handbook*, Homewood, Ill.: Dow Jones-Irwin, 1976, pp. 861–900.

WALKER, ERNEST W., and WILLIAM J. PETTY II, "Financial Differences between Large and Small Firms," *Financial Management*, 7 (Winter 1978), 61–74.

WHEELRIGHT, STEVEN C., "Strategic Planning in the Small Business," *Business Horizons*, 14 (August 1971), 51–58.

Failure and reorganization

27

Our analysis throughout most of the book has assumed that the firm is a going concern; nevertheless, we must not lose sight of the fact that some firms fail. Internal management must keep this in mind, and so must a creditor who has large amounts due from a company in financial distress. It is a danger that was brought into sharp focus in the 1970s and 1980s with the bankruptcy of large companies such as Penn Central and W. T. Grant and the near collapse of Chrysler Corporation and International Harvester. Previously, bankruptcy was regarded as a phenomenon restricted to small firms, the Depression of the Thirties being the last time major corporations had failed.

The word "failure" is vague, partly because there are varying degrees of failure. A company is regarded as technically insolvent if it is unable to meet its current obligations; however, such insolvency may be only temporary and subject to remedy.[1] Technical insolvency, then, denotes only a lack of liquidity. Insolvency in bankruptcy, on the other hand, means that the liabilities of a company exceed its assets; in other words, the net worth of the company is negative. Financial failure includes the entire range of possibilities between these extremes.

[1]See James E. Walter, "Determination of Technical Insolvency," *Journal of Business,* 30 (January 1957), 30–43.

The remedies for saving a failing company vary in harshness according to the degree of financial difficulty. If the outlook is sufficiently hopeless, liquidation may be the only feasible alternative. With some hope—and luck—many failing firms can be rehabilitated to the gain of creditors, stockholders, and society. Although the major purpose of a liquidation or rehabilitation is to protect creditors, the interests of the owners also are considered. Still, legal procedures favor creditors. Otherwise, they would hesitate to extend credit, and the allocation of funds in the economy would be less than efficient.

Although the causes of financial difficulty are numerous, many failures are attributable either directly or indirectly to management. Very seldom is one bad decision the cause of the difficulty; usually the cause is a series of errors, and the difficulty evolves gradually. Because the signs of potential distress usually are evident prior to actual failure, a creditor may be able to take corrective action before failure occurs. Many companies can be preserved as going concerns and can make an economic contribution to society. Sometimes the rehabilitation is severe, in keeping with the degree of financial difficulty. Nevertheless, these measures may be necessary if the firm is to obtain a new lease on life. In this chapter we take up the full spectrum of remedies available to a firm in financial distress.

VOLUNTARY SETTLEMENTS

Extensions

An extension involves nothing more than creditors' postponing the maturity of their obligations. In cases of temporary insolvency of a basically sound company, creditors may prefer to work the problem out with the company. By not forcing the issue with legal proceedings, creditors avoid considerable legal expense and the possible shrinkage of value in liquidation. Moreover, they maintain their full claim against the company involved; they do not agree to a partial settlement. The ability of creditors to realize the full value of their claims depends, of course, upon the company's improving its operations and its liquidity. In an extension situation, existing creditors often are unwilling to grant further credit on new sales and insist that current purchases be paid for in cash. Obviously, no one creditor is going to extend an obligation unless others do likewise. Consequently, a creditors' committee is usually formed by the major creditors to negotiate with the company and to formulate a plan mutually satisfactory to all concerned.

No creditor is obligated to go along with the plan. If there are dissenting creditors and they have small amounts owing, they may be paid off in order to avoid legal proceedings. The number of dissenters cannot be too large, for the remaining creditors must, in essence, assume their obligations. Obviously, the remaining creditors do not want to be left holding the bag. If an extension is worked out, the creditors can institute controls over the company to assure proper management and to increase the probability of speedy recovery. In addition, they may elect to take security if marketable assets are available. The creditors' ultimate threat is to initiate bankruptcy proceedings against the company and to force it into liquidation. By making an extension, they show an inclination to cooperate with the company.

Composition

A composition involves a pro-rata settlement of creditors' claims in cash or in cash and promissory notes. The creditors must agree to accept a partial settlement in discharge of their entire claim. A debtor may propose a settlement of 60 cents on the dollar. If creditors feel that the settlement is more than they could obtain in liquidation after legal expenses, they will probably accept. Even if it is somewhat less, they may still accept, because no company likes to be responsible for forcing another into bankruptcy. The settlement is a friendly one in the sense that legal proceedings are avoided.

As in an extension, all creditors must agree to the settlement. Dissenting creditors must be paid in full, or they can force the company into bankruptcy. They can be considerable nuisances who may all but preclude a voluntary settlement. Overall, voluntary settlements can be advantageous to creditors as well as to the debtors, for they avoid legal expenses and complications.

Liquidation by voluntary agreement

In certain circumstances, creditors may feel that the company should not be preserved, because further financial deterioration seems inevitable. When liquidation is the only realistic solution, it can be accomplished either through a private settlement or through bankruptcy proceedings. An orderly private liquidation is likely to be more efficient and may result in a significantly higher settlement. Such a voluntary liquidation is known as an *assignment*. A private settlement can also be through a formal assignment of assets to an appointed trustee. The trustee liquidates the assets and distributes the proceeds to creditors on a pro rata basis. Because the voluntary settlement must be agreed to by all creditors, it usually is restricted to companies with a limited number of creditors and outstanding securities that are not publicly held.

SETTLEMENTS INVOLVING LITIGATION

Legal procedures undertaken in connection with a failing company fall under bankruptcy law provided by the Bankruptcy Reform Act of 1978 and the Bankruptcy Act of 1898. The law itself is carried out through bankruptcy courts which exist in every federal judiciary district. Judges of these courts are appointed by the President for a 14-year term, and they hear only bankruptcy cases. Their specialization is an attempt to streamline the bankruptcy process. Bankruptcy law is comprised of many facets, but we are concerned with only two, which pertain to business failure. Chapter 7 of the bankruptcy law deals with liquidation; Chapter 11 deals with the rehabilitation of an enterprise through its reorganization.

In both cases, proceedings begin with the debtor or creditors filing a petition in the bankruptcy court. When the debtor initiates the petition, it is called a voluntary proceeding; whereas if the initiative is taken by creditors, it is said to be involuntary. In voluntary proceedings, merely filing the petition gives the debtor immediate protection from creditors. A stay restrains creditors from collecting their claims or taking actions until the court decides on the merit of the petition. The court can either accept the petition and order relief or dismiss it.

For an involuntary bankruptcy, three or more unsecured creditors with claims totaling $5,000 or more are required. Here the petition must give evidence that the debtor has not paid debts on a timely basis or has assigned possession of most of its property to someone else. The bankruptcy court then must decide whether the involuntary petition has merit. If the decision is negative, the petition is dismissed. Moreover, petitioning creditors sometimes are required to pay the debtor's court costs. (This is designed to protect debtors from nuisance petitions being filed.) If the petition is accepted, the court issues an order of relief pending a more permanent solution. In what follows, we observe the solutions of liquidation and the reorganization of an enterprise.

LIQUIDATION IN BANKRUPTCY

If there is no hope for the successful operation of a company, liquidation is the only feasible alternative. Upon petition of bankruptcy, the debtor obtains temporary relief from creditors until a decision is reached by the bankruptcy court. After issuing the order of relief, the court frequently appoints an interim trustee to take over the operation of the company and to call a meeting of creditors. The interim trustee is a "disinterested" private citizen who is appointed from an approved list and who serves until at least the first meeting of creditors. At the meeting, claims are proven and the creditors then may elect a new trustee to replace the interim trustee. Otherwise the interim trustee serves as the regular trustee, continuing to function in that capacity until the case is completed.

The trustee has responsibility for liquidating the property of the company and distributing liquidating dividends to creditors. Creditors with secured claims are entitled to the value of the property on which they hold a valid lien. Holbrook Leather Company owes Fernandez Machine Company $10,000, and Fernandez has a lien on a machine it previously sold Holbrook. If Holbrook files a Chapter 7 petition, and the machine can be sold for only $6,000, Fernandez's secured claim is $6,000 and its unsecured claim is $4,000. With respect to the latter, Fernandez becomes a general creditor.

In distributing the proceeds of a liquidation to creditors with unsecured claims, the priority of claims must be observed. The order of distribution is as follows:

1. Administrative expenses associated with liquidating the property, including the trustee's fee and attorney fees.

2. Creditor claims that arise in the ordinary course of the debtor's business from the time the case starts to the time a trustee is appointed.

3. Wages of employees earned within 90 days of the bankruptcy petition. These are limited to $2,000 per employee.

4. Claims for contributions to employee benefit plans for services rendered within 120 days of the bankruptcy petition. These claims are limited to $2,000 per employee times the number of employees.

5. Claims of customers who make money deposits for goods or services not provided by the debtor.

6. Income tax claims for three tax years prior to the petition, property taxes for one year prior to the petition, and all taxes withheld from employees' paychecks.

7. Unsecured claims which either filed on time or tardily filed if the creditor did not know of the bankruptcy.

8. Unsecured claims filed late by creditors who had knowledge of the bankruptcy.

9. Fines and punitive damages.

10. Interest that accrued to claims after the date of the petition.

Claims in each of these classes must be paid in full before any payment can be made to claims in the next class. If anything is left over after all of these claims are paid in full, liquidating dividends can then be paid to subordinated debtholders, to preferred stockholders, and finally, to common stockholders. It is unlikely, however, that common stockholders will receive any distribution from a liquidation. Special provision is made in the Bankruptcy Act for damage claims by lessors to the debtor. In general, lessors are limited to the greater of one year of payments or 15 percent of the total remaining payments, but not to exceed three years. (If a company is reorganized, the trustee may assume the lease and is then responsible for future payments on the leased property.)

Upon the payment of all liquidating dividends, the debtor is discharged and relieved of any further claim. The principal objective of bankruptcy proceedings is an orderly liquidation of assets and an equitable, formal distribution to creditors. The disadvantage of these proceedings is that they are slower and usually more expensive than a private liquidation. Some court-appointed officials are inefficient, being more concerned with their remuneration than with the proceeds available to creditors. As a result, a liquidation in bankruptcy may be less efficient than a private liquidation, providing creditors with a lower settlement. When creditors cannot come together in a voluntary manner, however, bankruptcy proceedings are the only recourse.

REORGANIZATION

It may be in the best interests of all concerned to reorganize a company rather than liquidate it. Reorganization is an effort to keep a company alive by changing its capital structure. The rehabilitation involves the reduction of fixed charges by substituting equity and limited-income securities for fixed-income securities.

Procedures

Reorganizations occur under Chapter 11 of the bankruptcy law and are initiated in the same general manner as liquidation in bankruptcy. Either the debtor or creditors file a petition, and the case begins. At this time, the debtor is required to file a list of creditors and the amounts owed. Because creditors are usually numerous in reorganization cases, the bankruptcy court appoints a committee of the seven largest unsecured creditors. This committee acts in behalf of creditors in the administration of the case, and it can request the appointment of a trustee.

The idea in a reorganization is to keep the business going. In most cases, the debtor will continue to run the business, although a trustee can assume operating responsibility of the company. One of the great needs in rehabilitation is interim credit. To provide inducements, Chapter 11 gives post-petition creditors priority over pre-petition creditors. If this inducement is not sufficient, the bankruptcy court is empowered to authorize new creditors to obtain a lien on the debtor's property.

If a trustee is not appointed, the debtor has the sole right to draw up a reorganization plan and to file it within 120 days. Otherwise, the trustee has the responsibility of seeing that a plan is filed. It may be drawn up by the trustee, the debtor, the creditors' committee, or individual creditors, and more than one plan can be filed. All reorganization plans must be submitted to creditors and stockholders for approval. The role of the court is to review the information in the plan, to make sure disclosure is full. If the securities of the debtor are publicly held, the Securities and Exchange Commission (SEC) may want to review the question of disclosure.

In a reorganization, the plan should be *fair, equitable* and *feasible*. This means that all parties must be treated fairly and equitably, and the plan must be workable with respect to the earning power and financial structure of the reorganized company. For example, the reorganized company may not have too great an amount of fixed financial charges relative to its expected earning power. If the future earning power of the company is not estimated fairly or if the fixed financial charges are too great, the reorganized company may have little prospect for success. As a result, the plan would not be considered to be fair, equitable and feasible.

Each class of claimholders must vote on a plan. More than one half in number and two thirds in amount of total claims in each class must vote in favor of the plan if it is to be accepted, *and claimholders may accept more than one plan.*

The next step is for the bankruptcy court to hold a confirmation hearing. If claimholders accept more than one plan, the court must choose the best plan. It may also confirm a plan that has been approved by one class but not by every class of claimholder. In all cases, the reorganization plan must meet certain standards if it is to be confirmed by the court. These standards have to do with its being fair, equitable, and feasible. Upon confirmation of a plan by the bankruptcy court, the debtor then must perform according to the terms of the plan. Moreover, all creditors and stockholders, including dissenters, are bound by the plan.

Reorganization plan

The difficult aspect of a reorganization is the recasting of the company's capital structure to reduce the amount of fixed charges. In formulating a reorganization plan, there are three steps. First, the total valuation of the reorganized company must be determined. This step, perhaps, is the most difficult and the most important. The technique favored by trustees is a capitalization of prospective earnings. If future annual earnings of the reorganized company are expected to be $2 million, and the overall capitalization rate of similar companies averages 10 percent, a total valuation of $20 million would be set for the company. The valuation figure is subject to considerable variation, owing to the difficulty of estimating prospective earnings and determining an appropriate capitalization rate. Thus the valuation figure represents nothing more than a best estimate of potential value. Although the capitalization of prospective earnings is the generally accepted approach of valuing a company in reorganization, the valuation may be adjusted upward if the assets have substantial liquidating value. The common stockholders of the company, of course, would like to see as high a valuation figure as possible. If the valuation figure the trustee proposes is below the liquidating value of the company, common stockholders will argue for liquidation rather than reorganization.

Once a valuation figure has been determined, the next step is to formulate a new capital structure for the company to reduce fixed charges so that there will be an adequate coverage margin. To reduce these charges, the total debt of the firm is scaled down by being partly shifted to income bonds, preferred stock, and common stock. In addition to being scaled down, the terms of the debt may be changed. The maturity of the debt can be extended to reduce the amount of annual sinking-fund obligation. If it appears that the reorganized company will need new financing in the future, the trustee may feel that a more conservative ratio of debt to equity is in order to provide for future financial flexibility.

Once a new capital structure is established, the last step involves the valuation of the old securities and their exchange for new securities. In general, all senior claims on assets must be settled in full before a junior claim can be settled. In the exchange process, bondholders must receive the par value of their bonds in another security before there can be any distribution to preferred stockholders. The total valuation figure arrived at in step one sets an upper limit on the amount of securities that can be issued. The existing capital structure of a company undergoing reorganization may be as follows:

Debentures	$ 9 million
Subordinated debentures	3 million
Preferred stock	6 million
Common-stock equity (at book value)	10 million
	$28 million

If the total valuation of the reorganized company is to be $20 million, the trustee might establish the following capital structure in step two:

Debentures	$ 3 million
Income bonds	6 million
Preferred stock	3 million
Common stock	8 million
	$20 million

Having established the "appropriate" capital structure for the reorganized company, the trustee then must allocate the new securities. In this regard, the trustee may propose that the debenture holders exchange their $9 million in debentures for $3 million in new debentures and $6 million in income bonds; that the subordinated debenture holders exchange their $3 million in securities for preferred stock; and that preferred stockholders exchange their securities for $6 million of common stock in the reorganized company. The common stockholders would then be entitled to $2 million in stock in the reorganized company, or 25 percent of the total common stock of the reorganized company. Before, these stockholders held 100 percent of the stock. It is easy to see why common stockholders would like to see as high a valuation figure as possible. To encourage high valuation, they may attempt to discount the troubles of the company as temporary and argue that the earning potential of the company is favorable.

Thus each claim is settled in full before a junior claim is settled. The example above represents a relatively mild reorganization. In a harsh reorganization, debt instruments may be exchanged entirely for common stock in the reorganized company and the old common stock may be eliminated completely. Had the total valuation figure in the example been $12 million, the trustee might have proposed a new capital structure consisting of $3 million in preferred stock and $9 million in common stock. Only the straight and subordinated debenture holders would receive a settlement in this case. The preferred and the common stockholders of the old company would receive nothing.

These examples show that the common stockholders of a company undergoing reorganization suffer under an absolute priority rule, whereby claims must be settled in the order of their legal priority. From their standpoint, they would much prefer to see claims settled on a *relative priority basis*. Under this rule, new securities are allocated on the basis of the relative market prices of the securities. The common stockholders could never obtain senior securities in a reorganization, but they would be entitled to some common stock if their present stock had value. Because the company is not actually being liquidated, common stockholders argue that a rule of relative priority is really the fairest. The Supreme Court decided otherwise when it upheld the absolute priority rule (*Case v. Los Angeles Lumber Products Company, 1939*).

By and large, the principle of absolute priority is used in reorganization cases, although the Bankruptcy Reform Act of 1978 did provide a degree of flexibility shifting modestly in the direction of relative priority. For example, large creditors may want to allow stockholders to receive some stock in the reorganized company for incentive reasons, even though they are not entitled to it. The court may permit this allocation despite the protest of junior creditors. For the most part, however, the main recourse of stockholders is to question whether a plan is fair and equitable to all securityholders—not whether the absolute priority of claims should be observed. Another example of relative priority occurs when senior claimholders, in order to get junior claimholders to vote for a plan, allow lesser claimholders partial payment, even though their claim is not satisfied in full.

SUMMARY

Business failure, encompassing a wide range of financial difficulty, occurs whenever a company is unable to meet its current obligations. The remedies applied to a failing company vary in severity with the degree of financial difficulty. Voluntary settlements are informal and must be agreed to by all creditors and the company itself. The difficulty with a voluntary settlement is in obtaining agreement of all parties concerned. Voluntary settlements include extensions, compositions, a creditors' committee controlling the operations of the company, and a private liquidation.

Legal settlements are effected under Chapters 7 and 11 of the Bankruptcy Reform Act of 1978. Liquidation of a company occurs under Chapter 7. A trustee has the responsibility of liquidating the property of the debtor in an orderly manner. The proceeds of the liquidation must be made to creditors according to a specified priority of claims. The bankruptcy court oversees the process and makes the final discharge of the debtor.

When a company is rehabilitated through a reorganization, it occurs under Chapter 11. In a reorganization, the capital structure of a company is changed to reduce the total amount of fixed charges. The reorganization plan should be fair, equitable and feasible, as determined by claimholders and the court. In order for a plan to be accepted, it must be approved by one half in number and two thirds in amount of each class of claims. The court must confirm the plan; upon confirmation, it is binding on all creditors and stockholders.

QUESTIONS

1. Contrast a technically insolvent situation with an insolvency-in-bankruptcy situation.

2. Why are taxes and administrative costs involved in the bankruptcy paid prior to any creditor's claim?

3. It is argued that a small number of bankruptcies is a healthy sign of economic development. Explain.

4. As a creditor to a financially troubled concern, would you prefer liquidation or financial reorganization? Why? Would you always prefer liquidation if the market value of the firm was less than the liquidation value?

5. Can you explain why utilities, railroads, and banks are seldom liquidated? Are the risks in these industries less than those in other industrial corporations?

6. Before a firm can be reorganized, a valuation must be placed on it. How should this valuation be arrived at? What conceptual problems would you encounter in the process?

7. Contrast an extension and composition with a reorganization of a firm in distress.

8. When a firm goes through reorganization, what implicit assumption is being made about the profitability of assets? Was this assumption valid in the Penn Central reorganization?

9. Contrast absolute and relative priority bases for settling claims.

10. When liquidation of a company is in litigation, do creditors whose claims originated before the trouble began have priority over recent employees and the federal government's claim for income taxes?

PROBLEMS

1.

Fall Corporation balance sheet

Cash	$ 1,000,000	Note payable	$ 1,000,000
Accounts receivable	2,000,000	Accounts payable	4,000,000
Inventories	5,000,000	Accrued wages	3,000,000
Prepaid expenses	1,000,000	Accrued taxes	1,000,000
Total current assets	$ 9,000,000	Total current liabilities	$ 9,000,000
Fixed assets, net	8,000,000	Long-term debt	12,000,000
Goodwill	5,000,000	Equity	1,000,000
Total assets	$22,000,000		$22,000,000

a) Do you feel that it is likely that the Fall Corporation either is now or will soon be technically insolvent? Why? What steps could management take to correct this situation?

b) Answer part a with respect to the bankruptcy concept of insolvency.

c) Compare and contrast these two concepts of insolvency.

d) Is it possible that attempts to alleviate one form of insolvency could aggravate the other? How?

e) Is the balance sheet the best tool for determining technical or fundamental insolvency? Can you suggest better ones?

2. Merry Land, an amusement park in Atlanta, has experienced increased difficulty in paying its bills. Although the park has been marginally profitable over the years, the current outlook is not encouraging, as profits during the last two years have been negative. The park is located on reasonably valuable real estate and has an overall liquidating value of $5 million. After much discussion with creditors, management has agreed to a voluntary liquidation. A trustee, who is appointed by the various parties to liquidate the properties, will charge $200,000 for his services. The Merry Land Company owes $300,000 in back property taxes. It has a $2 million mortgage on certain amusement park equipment that can be sold for only $1 million. Creditor claims are as follows:

Party	Book value claim
General creditors	$1,750,000
Mortgage bonds	2,000,000
Long-term subordinated debt	1,000,000
Common stock	5,000,000

What amount is each party likely to receive in liquidation?

3. The Vent Corporation has been liquidated under Chapter 7 proceedings. The book and liquidation values are as follows:

	Book	Liquidation
Cash	$ 700,000	$ 700,000
Accounts receivable	2,000,000	1,600,000
Inventory	3,500,000	2,000,000
Office building	5,000,000	3,000,000
Plant	8,000,000	5,000,000
Equipment	7,000,000	3,000,000
Total	$26,200,000	$15,300,000

The liability and equity accounts at the time of liquidation were as follows:

Accounts payable	$ 2,000,000
Accrued federal taxes	500,000
Accrued local taxes	200,000
Notes payable	1,000,000
Accrued wages	500,000
Total current liabilities	$ 4,200,000
Mortgage on office building	$ 3,000,000
First mortgage on plant	3,000,000
Second mortgage on plant	2,000,000
Subordinated debentures	5,000,000
Total long-term debt	$13,000,000
Preferred stock	$ 5,000,000
Common stock	7,000,000
Retained earnings	(3,000,000)
Total	$ 9,000,000
Total	$26,200,000

Expenses of liquidation (lawyers' fees, trustee fees, etc.) came to 20 percent of the proceeds. The debentures are subordinated only to the two first mortgage bonds. All of the accrued wages are less than three months old and less than $2,000 per employee. Determine the appropriate distribution of the proceeds of liquidation.

4. The Greenwood Corporation is in Chapter 11. The trustee has estimated that the company can earn $1.5 million before interest and taxes (50 percent) in the future. In the new capitalization, she feels that debentures should bear a coupon of 10 percent and have coverage of five times, income bonds (12 percent) should have overall coverage of two times, preferred stock (10 percent) should have after-tax coverage of three times, and common stock should be issued on a price-earnings ratio basis of twelve times. Determine the capital structure that conforms to the trustee's criteria.

5. Assume that the Greenwood Corporation (see problem 4) originally had the following capital structure:

	Book value	Market value
Senior debentures	$ 6,000,000	$ 5,500,000
Subordinated debentures	7,500,000	6,000,000
Junior subordinated debentures	2,500,000	1,000,000
Preferred stock (par $100)	2,500,000	500,000
Common stock (1,000,000 shares)	−4,500,000	1,000,000
	$14,000,000	$14,000,000

Determine which of the new securities each class of holders of securities would get under an absolute priority rule.

6. Tara Plantation Company has run into financial difficulty and is facing possible reorganization. It currently has the following capital structure (in thousands):

	Book value
Long-term bonds	$ 40,000
General unsecured debt	30,000
Preferred stock	10,000
Common stock	20,000
	$100,000

Unfortunately, the trustee under Chapter 11 estimates that Tara has a value of only $75 million as a going concern, not the $100 million shown on the books. The trustee has recommended the following capital structure for the reorganized company (in thousands):

Long-term bonds	$10,000
Unsecured debt	20,000
Preferred stock	5,000
Common stock	40,000
	$75,000

If this plan is accepted by the claimholders and confirmed by the bankruptcy court, what will be the distribution of the new securities to the holders of old claims?

7. *Research Project*

Compile data on recent bankruptcy cases involving fairly large companies. Learn as much as you can about "stockholder protective committees"; discover how many of these committees there are for each bankruptcy case you study. Finally, compare the amount of money going for legal fees, court costs, etc., as opposed to the amount the creditors finally receive. Do you begin to feel that there might be "self-interest" as well as "friendly" motives behind the creditors' acceptance of a settlement? Whom do stockholder protective committees really protect? Can you find any parallels between bankruptcy law and probate law?

SELECTED REFERENCES

AHARONY, JOSEPH, CHARLES P. JONES and ITZHAK SWARY, "An Analysis of Risk and Return Characteristics of Corporate Bankruptcy Using Capital Market Data," *Journal of Finance,* 35 (September 1980), 1001–16.

ALTMAN, EDWARD I., *Corporate Bankruptcy in America,* Lexington, Mass.: Heath Lexington Books, 1971.

———, "Financial Ratios, Discriminant Analysis and the Prediction of Corporate Bankruptcy," *Journal of Finance,* 23 (September 1968), 589–609.

———, "Bankruptcy and Reorganization," in Edward I. Altman, ed., *Financial Handbook,* 5th ed. New York: Wiley, 1982.

———, and MENACHEM BRENNER, "Information Effects and Stock Market Response to Signs of Firm Deterioration," *Journal of Financial and Quantitative Analysis,* 16 (March 1981), 35–52.

ALTMAN, EDWARD I., ROBERT G. HALDEMAN, and P. NARAYANAN, "Zeta Analysis: A New Model to Identify Bankruptcy Risk of Corporations," *Journal of Banking and Finance,* 1 (June 1977).

ALTMAN, EDWARD I., and ARNOLD W. SAMENTZ, eds., *Financial Crises.* New York: Wiley, 1977.

BACKER, MORTON, and MARTIN L. GOSMAN, "The Use of Financial Ratios in Credit Downgrade Decisions," *Financial Management,* 9 (Spring 1980), 53–56.

CHEN, KUNG H., and THOMAS A. SHIMERDA, "An Empirical Analysis of Useful Financial Ratios," *Financial Management,* 10 (Spring 1981), 51–60.

COLLINS, ROBERT A., "An Empirical Comparison of Bankruptcy Prediction Models," *Financial Management,* 9 (Summer 1980), 52–57.

Credit Manual of Commercial Laws, 1983. New York: National Association of Credit Management, 1982.

DONALDSON, GORDON, "Strategy for Financial Emergencies," *Harvard Business Review,* 47 (November–December 1969), 67–79.

"The Economics of Bankruptcy Reform," *Law and Contemporary Problems,* School of Law, Duke University, 41 (Autumn 1977).

EPSTEIN, DAVID G., *Debtor-Creditor Law,* 2nd ed. St. Paul, Minn.: West, 1980.

KRUGER, LEWIS, and ARNOLD M. QUITTNER, *Bankruptcy Practice and Procedure Under the New Bankruptcy Act.* New York: Practising Law Institute, 1979.

MOYER, R. CHARLES, "Forecasting Financial Failure: A Re-examination," *Financial Management,* 6 (Spring 1977), 11–17.

VAN HORNE, JAMES C., "Optimal Initiation of Bankruptcy Proceedings by Debt Holders," *Journal of Finance,* 31 (June 1976), 897–910.

WALTER, JAMES E., "Determination of Technical Insolvency," *Journal of Business,* 30 (January 1957), 30–43.

Appendix: present-value tables

TABLE A   Present value of one dollar due at the end of *n* years

N	1%	2%	3%	4%	5%	6%	7%	8%	9%	10%	N
01	0.99010	0.98039	0.97007	0.96154	0.95238	0.94340	0.93458	0.92593	0.91743	0.90909	01
02	.98030	.96117	.94260	.92456	.90703	.89000	.87344	.85734	.84168	.82645	02
03	.97059	.94232	.91514	.88900	.86384	.83962	.81630	.79383	.77218	.75131	03
04	.96098	.92385	.88849	.85480	.82270	.79209	.76290	.73503	.70843	.68301	04
05	.95147	.90573	.86261	.82193	.78353	.74726	.71299	.68058	.64993	.62092	05
06	.94204	.88797	.83748	.79031	.74622	.70496	.66634	.60317	.59627	.56447	06
07	.93272	.87056	.81309	.75992	.71068	.66506	.62275	.58349	.54703	.51316	07
08	.92348	.85349	.78941	.73069	.67684	.62741	.58201	.54027	.50187	.46651	08
09	.91434	.83675	.76642	.70259	.64461	.59190	.54393	.50025	.46043	.42410	09
10	.90529	.82035	.74409	.67556	.61391	.55839	.50835	.46319	.42241	.38554	10
11	.89632	.80426	.72242	.64958	.58468	.52679	.47509	.42888	.38753	.35049	11
12	.88745	.78849	.70138	.62460	.55684	.49697	.44401	.39711	.35553	.31863	12
13	.87866	.77303	.68095	.60057	.53032	.46884	.41496	.36770	.32618	.28966	13
14	.86996	.75787	.66112	.57747	.50507	.44230	.38782	.34046	.29925	.26333	14
15	.86135	.74301	.64186	.55526	.48102	.41726	.36245	.31524	.27454	.23939	15
16	.85282	.72845	.62317	.53391	.45811	.39365	.33873	.29189	.25187	.21763	16
17	.84438	.71416	.60502	.51337	.43630	.37136	.31657	.27027	.23107	.19784	17
18	.83602	.70016	.58739	.49363	.41552	.35034	.29586	.25025	.21199	.17986	18
19	.82774	.68643	.57029	.47464	.39573	.33051	.27651	.23171	.19449	.16351	19
20	.81954	.67297	.55367	.45639	.37689	.31180	.25842	.21455	.17843	.14864	20
21	.81143	.65978	.53755	.43883	.35894	.29415	.24151	.19866	.16370	.13513	21
22	.80340	.64684	.52189	.42195	.34185	.27750	.22571	.18394	.15018	.12285	22
23	.79544	.63416	.50669	.40573	.32557	.26180	.21095	.17031	.13778	.11168	23
24	.78757	.62172	.49193	.39012	.31007	.24698	.19715	.15770	.12640	.10153	24
25	.77977	.60953	.47760	.37512	.29530	.23300	.18425	.14602	.11597	.09230	25

TABLE A \\ Present value of one dollar due at the end of *n* years

N	11%	12%	13%	14%	15%	16%	17%	18%	19%	20%	N
01	0.90090	0.89286	0.88496	0.87719	0.86957	0.86207	0.85470	0.84746	0.84034	0.83333	01
02	.81162	.79719	.78315	.76947	.75614	.74316	.73051	.71818	.70616	.69444	02
03	.73119	.71178	.69305	.67497	.65752	.64066	.62437	.60863	.59342	.57870	03
04	.65873	.63552	.61332	.59208	.57175	.55229	.53365	.51579	.49867	.48225	04
05	.59345	.56743	.54276	.51937	.49718	.47611	.45611	.43711	.41905	.40188	05
06	.53464	.50663	.48032	.45559	.43233	.41044	.38984	.37043	.35214	.33490	06
07	.48166	.45235	.42506	.39964	.37594	.35383	.33320	.31392	.29592	.27908	07
08	.43393	.40388	.37616	.35056	.32690	.30503	.28478	.26604	.24867	.23257	08
09	.39092	.36061	.33288	.30751	.28426	.26295	.24340	.22546	.20897	.19381	09
10	.35218	.32197	.29459	.26974	.24718	.22668	.20804	.19106	.17560	.16151	10
11	.31728	.28748	.26070	.23662	.21494	.19542	.17781	.16192	.14756	.13459	11
12	.28584	.25667	.23071	.20756	.18691	.16846	.15197	.13722	.12400	.11216	12
13	.25751	.22917	.20416	.18207	.16253	.14523	.12989	.11629	.10420	.09346	13
14	.23199	.20462	.18068	.15971	.14133	.12520	.11102	.09855	.08757	.07789	14
15	.20900	.18270	.15989	.14010	.12289	.10793	.09489	.08352	.07359	.06491	15
16	.18829	.16312	.14150	.12289	.10686	.09304	.08110	.07078	.06184	.05409	16
17	.16963	.14564	.12522	.10780	.09293	.08021	.06932	.05998	.05196	.04507	17
18	.15282	.13004	.11081	.09456	.08080	.06914	.05925	.05083	.04367	.03756	18
19	.13768	.11611	.09806	.08295	.07026	.05961	.05064	.04308	.03669	.03130	19
20	.12403	.10367	.08678	.07276	.06110	.05139	.04328	.03651	.03084	.02608	20
21	.11174	.09256	.07680	.06383	.05313	.04430	.03699	.03094	.02591	.02174	21
22	.10067	.08264	.06796	.05599	.04620	.03819	.03162	.02622	.02178	.01811	22
23	.09069	.07379	.06014	.04911	.04017	.03292	.02702	.02222	.01830	.01509	23
24	.08170	.06588	.05322	.04308	.03493	.02838	.02310	.01883	.01538	.01258	24
25	.07361	.05882	.04710	.03779	.03038	.02447	.01974	.01596	.01292	.01048	25

TABLE A \\ Present value of one dollar due at the end of *n* years

N	21%	22%	23%	24%	25%	26%	27%	28%	29%	30%	N
01	0.82645	0.81967	0.81301	0.80645	0.80000	0.79365	0.78740	0.78125	0.77519	0.76923	01
02	.68301	.67186	.66098	.65036	.64000	.62988	.62000	.61035	.60093	.59172	02
03	.56447	.55071	.53738	.52449	.51200	.49991	.48819	.47684	.46583	.45517	03
04	.46651	.45140	.43690	.42297	.40906	.39675	.38440	.37253	.36111	.35013	04
05	.38554	.37000	.35520	.34111	.32768	.31488	.30268	.29104	.27993	.26933	05
06	.31863	.30328	.28878	.27509	.26214	.24991	.23833	.22737	.21700	.20718	06
07	.26333	.24859	.23478	.22184	.20972	.19834	.18766	.17764	.16822	.15937	07
08	.21763	.20376	.19088	.17891	.16777	.15741	.14776	.13878	.13040	.12259	08
09	.17986	.16702	.15519	.14428	.13422	.12493	.11635	.10842	.10109	.09430	09
10	.14864	.13690	.12617	.11635	.10737	.09915	.09161	.08470	.07836	.07254	10
11	.12285	.11221	.10258	.09383	.08590	.07869	.07214	.06617	.06075	.05580	11
12	.10153	.09198	.08339	.07567	.06872	.06245	.05680	.05170	.04709	.04292	12
13	.08391	.07539	.06780	.06103	.05498	.04957	.04472	.04039	.03650	.03302	13
14	.06934	.06180	.05512	.04921	.04398	.03934	.03522	.03155	.02830	.02540	14
15	.05731	.05065	.04481	.03969	.03518	.03122	.02773	.02465	.02194	.01954	15
16	.04736	.04152	.03643	.03201	.02815	.02478	.02183	.01926	.01700	.01503	16
17	.03914	.03403	.02962	.02581	.02252	.01967	.01719	.01505	.01318	.01156	17
18	.03235	.02789	.02408	.02082	.01801	.01561	.01354	.01175	.01022	.00889	18
19	.02673	.02286	.01958	.01679	.01441	.01239	.01066	.00918	.00792	.00684	19
20	.02209	.01874	.01592	.01354	.01153	.00983	.00839	.00717	.00614	.00526	20
21	.01826	.01536	.01294	.01092	.00922	.00780	.00661	.00561	.00476	.00405	21
22	.01509	.01259	.01052	.00880	.00738	.00619	.00520	.00438	.00369	.00311	22
23	.01247	.01032	.00855	.00710	.00590	.00491	.00410	.00342	.00286	.00239	23
24	.01031	.00846	.00695	.00573	.00472	.00390	.00323	.00267	.00222	.00184	24
25	.00852	.00693	.00565	.00462	.00378	.00310	.00254	.00209	.00172	.00142	25

TABLE A — Present value of one dollar due at the end of *n* years

N	31%	32%	33%	34%	35%	36%	37%	38%	39%	40%	N
01	0.76336	0.75758	0.75188	0.74627	0.74074	0.73529	0.72993	0.72464	0.71942	0.71429	01
02	.58272	.57392	.56532	.55692	.54870	.45066	.53279	.52510	.51757	.51020	02
03	.44482	.43479	.42505	.41561	.40644	.39754	.38890	.38051	.37235	.36443	03
04	.33956	.32939	.31959	.31016	.30107	.29231	.28387	.27573	.26788	.26031	04
05	.25920	.24953	.24029	.23146	.22301	.21493	.20720	.19980	.19272	.18593	05
06	.19787	.18904	.18067	.17273	.16520	.15804	.15124	.14479	.13865	.13281	06
07	.15104	.14321	.13584	.12890	.12237	.11621	.11040	.10492	.09975	.09486	07
08	.11530	.10849	.10214	.09620	.09064	.08545	.08058	.07603	.07176	.06776	08
09	.08802	.08219	.07680	.07179	.06714	.06283	.05882	.05509	.05163	.04840	09
10	.06719	.06227	.05774	.05357	.04973	.04620	.04293	.03992	.03714	.03457	10
11	.05129	.04717	.04341	.03998	.03684	.03397	.03134	.02893	.02672	.02469	11
12	.03915	.03574	.03264	.02984	.02729	.02498	.02287	.02096	.01922	.01764	12
13	.02989	.02707	.02454	.02227	.02021	.01837	.01670	.01519	.01383	.01260	13
14	.02281	.02051	.01845	.01662	.01497	.01350	.01219	.01101	.00995	.00900	14
15	.01742	.01554	.01387	.01240	.01109	.00993	.00890	.00798	.00716	.00643	15
16	.01329	.01177	.01043	.00925	.00822	.00730	.00649	.00578	.00515	.00459	16
17	.01015	.00892	.00784	.00691	.00609	.00537	.00474	.00419	.00370	.00328	17
18	.00775	.00676	.00590	.00515	.00451	.00395	.00346	.00304	.00267	.00234	18
19	.00591	.00512	.00443	.00385	.00334	.00290	.00253	.00220	.00192	.00167	19
20	.00451	.00388	.00333	.00287	.00247	.00213	.00184	.00159	.00138	.00120	20
21	.00345	.00294	00251	.00214	.00183	.00157	00135	.00115	.00099	.00085	21
22	.00263	.00223	.00188	.00160	.00136	.00115	.00098	.00084	.00071	00061	22
23	.00201	.00169	.00142	.00119	.00101	.00085	.00072	.00061	.00051	.00044	23
24	.00153	.00128	.00107	.00089	.00074	.00062	.00052	.00044	.00037	.00031	24
25	.00117	.00097	.00080	.00066	.00055	.00046	.00038	.00032	.00027	.00022	25

TABLE B — Present value of one dollar per year, *n* years at *r*%

Year	1%	2%	3%	4%	5%	6%	7%	8%	9%	10%	Year
1	0.9901	0.9804	0.9709	0.9615	0.9524	0.9434	0.9346	0.9259	0.9174	0.9091	1
2	1.9704	1.9416	1.9135	1.8861	1.8594	1.8334	1.8080	1.7833	1.7591	1.7355	2
3	2.9410	2.8839	2.8286	2.7751	2.7232	2.6730	2.6243	2.5771	2.5313	2.4868	3
4	3.9020	3.8077	3.7171	3.6299	3.5459	3.4651	3.3872	3.3121	3.2397	3.1699	4
5	4.8535	4.7134	4.5797	4.4518	4.3295	4.2123	4.1002	3.9927	3.8896	3.7908	5
6	5.7955	5.6014	5.4172	5.2421	5.0757	4.9173	4.7665	4.6229	4.4859	4.3553	6
7	6.7282	6.4720	6.2302	6.0020	5.7863	5.5824	5.3893	5.2064	5.0329	4.8684	7
8	7.6517	7.3254	7.0196	6.7327	6.4632	6.2098	5.9713	5.7466	5.5348	5.3349	8
9	8.5661	8.1622	7.7861	7.4353	7.1078	6.8017	6.5152	6.2469	5.9852	5.7590	9
10	9.4714	8.9825	8.5302	8.1109	7.7217	7.3601	7.0236	6.7101	6.4176	6.1446	10
11	10.3677	9.7868	9.2526	8.7604	8.3064	7.8868	7.4987	7.1389	6.8052	6.4951	11
12	11.2552	10.5753	9.9539	9.3850	8.8632	8.3838	7.9427	7.5361	7.1607	6.8137	12
13	12.1338	11.3483	10.6349	9.9856	9.3935	8.8527	8.3576	7.9038	7.4869	7.1034	13
14	13.0038	12.1062	11.2960	10.5631	9.8986	9.2950	8.7454	8.2442	7.7861	7.3667	14
15	13.8651	12.8492	11.9379	11.1183	10.3796	9.7122	9.1079	8.5595	8.0607	7.6061	15
16	14.7180	13.5777	12.5610	11.6522	10.8377	10.1059	9.4466	8.8514	8.3125	7.8237	16
17	15.5624	14.2918	13.1660	12.1656	11.2740	10.4772	9.7632	9.1216	8.5436	8.0215	17
18	16.3984	14.9920	13.7534	12.6592	11.6895	10.8276	10.0591	9.3719	8.7556	8.2014	18
19	17.2261	15.6784	14.3237	13.1339	12.0853	11.1581	10.3356	9.6036	8.9501	8.3649	19
20	18.0457	16.3514	14.8774	13.5903	12.4622	11.4699	10.5940	9.8181	9.1285	8.5136	20
21	18.8571	17.0111	15.4149	14.0291	12.8211	11.7640	10.8355	10.0168	9.2922	8.6487	21
22	19.6605	17.6580	15.9368	14.4511	13.1630	12.0416	11.0612	10.2007	9.4424	8.7715	22
23	20.4559	18.2921	16.4435	14.8568	13.4885	12.3033	11.2722	10.3710	9.5802	8.8832	23
24	21.2435	18.9139	16.9355	15.2469	13.7986	12.5503	11.4693	10.5287	9.7066	8.9847	24
25	22.0233	19.5234	17.4131	15.6220	14.0939	12.7833	11.6536	10.6748	9.8226	9.0770	25

TABLE B ╲ Present value of one dollar per year, *n* years at *r*%

Year	11%	12%	13%	14%	15%	16%	17%	18%	19%	20%	Year
1	0.9009	0.8929	0.8850	0.8772	0.8696	0.8621	0.8547	0.8475	0.8403	0.8333	1
2	1.7125	1.6901	1.6681	1.6467	1.6257	1.6052	1.5852	1.5656	1.5465	1.5278	2
3	2.4437	2.4018	2.3612	2.3216	2.2832	2.2459	2.2096	2.1743	2.1399	2.1065	3
4	3.1024	3.0373	2.9745	2.9137	2.8550	2.7982	2.7432	2.6901	2.6386	2.5887	4
5	3.6959	3.6048	3.5172	3.4331	3.3522	3.2743	3.1993	3.1272	3.0576	2.9906	5
6	4.2305	4.1114	3.9976	3.8887	3.7845	3.6847	3.5892	3.4976	3.4098	3.3255	6
7	4.7122	4.5638	4.4226	4.2883	4.1604	4.0386	3.9224	3.8115	3.7057	3.6046	7
8	5.1461	4.9676	4.7988	4.6389	4.4873	4.3436	4.2072	4.0776	3.9544	3.8372	8
9	5.5370	5.3282	5.1317	4.9464	4.7716	4.6065	4.4506	4.3030	4.1633	4.0310	9
10	5.8892	5.6502	5.4262	5.2161	5.0188	4.8332	4.6586	4.4941	4.3389	4.1925	10
11	6.2065	5.9377	5.6869	5.4527	5.2337	5.0286	4.8364	4.6560	4.4865	4.3271	11
12	6.4924	6.1944	5.9176	5.6603	5.4206	5.1971	4.9884	4.7932	4.6105	4.4392	12
13	6.7499	6.4235	6.1218	5.8424	5.5831	5.3423	5.1183	4.9095	4.7147	4.5327	13
14	6.9819	6.6282	6.3025	6.0021	5.7245	5.4675	5.2293	5.0081	4.8023	4.6106	14
15	7.1909	6.8109	6.4624	6.1422	5.8474	5.5755	5.3242	5.0916	4.8759	4.6755	15
16	7.3792	6.9740	6.6039	6.2651	5.9542	5.6685	5.4053	5.1624	4.9377	4.7296	16
17	7.5488	7.1196	6.7291	6.3729	6.0472	5.7487	5.4746	5.2223	4.9897	4.7746	17
18	7.7016	7.2497	6.8399	6.4674	6.1280	5.8178	5.5339	5.2732	5.0333	4.8122	18
19	7.8393	7.3658	6.9380	6.5504	6.1982	5.8775	5.5845	5.3162	5.0700	4.8435	19
20	7.9633	7.4694	7.0248	6.6231	6.2593	5.9288	5.6278	5.3527	5.1009	4.8696	20
21	8.0751	7.5620	7.1016	6.6870	6.3125	5.9731	5.6648	5.3837	5.1268	4.8913	21
22	8.1757	7.6446	7.1695	6.7429	6.3587	6.0113	5.6964	5.4099	5.1486	4.9094	22
23	8.2664	7.7184	7.2297	6.7921	6.3988	6.0442	5.7234	5.4321	5.1668	4.9245	23
24	8.3481	7.7843	7.2829	6.8351	6.4338	6.0726	5.7465	5.4509	5.1822	4.9371	24
25	8.4217	7.8431	7.3300	6.8729	6.4641	6.0971	5.7662	5.4669	5.1951	4.9476	25

TABLE B ╲ Present value of one dollar per year, *n* years at *r*%

Year	21%	22%	23%	24%	25%	26%	27%	28%	29%	30%	Year
1	0.8264	0.8197	0.8130	0.8065	0.8000	0.7937	0.7874	0.7813	0.7752	0.7692	1
2	1.5095	1.4915	1.4740	1.4568	1.4400	1.4235	1.4074	1.3916	1.3761	1.3609	2
3	2.0739	2.0422	2.0114	1.9813	1.9520	1.9234	1.8956	1.8684	1.8420	1.8161	3
4	2.5404	2.4936	2.4483	2.4043	2.3616	2.3202	2.2800	2.2410	2.2031	2.1662	4
5	2.9260	2.8636	2.8035	2.7454	2.6893	2.6351	2.5827	2.5320	2.4830	2.4356	5
6	3.2446	3.1669	3.0923	3.0205	2.9514	2.8850	2.8210	2.7594	2.7000	2.6427	6
7	3.5079	3.4155	3.3270	3.2423	3.1611	3.0833	3.0087	2.9370	2.8682	2.8021	7
8	3.7256	3.6193	3.5179	3.4212	3.3289	3.2407	3.1564	3.0758	2.9986	2.9247	8
9	3.9054	3.7863	3.6731	3.5655	3.4631	3.3657	3.2728	3.1842	3.0997	3.0190	9
10	4.0541	3.9232	3.7993	3.6819	3.5705	3.4648	3.3644	3.2689	3.1781	3.0915	10
11	4.1769	4.0354	3.9018	3.7757	3.6564	3.5435	3.4365	3.3351	3.2388	3.1473	11
12	4.2785	4.1274	3.9852	3.8514	3.7251	3.6060	3.4933	3.3868	3.2859	3.1903	12
13	4.3624	4.2028	4.0530	3.9124	3.7801	3.6555	3.5381	3.4272	3.3224	3.2233	13
14	4.4317	4.2646	4.1082	3.9616	3.8241	3.6949	3.5733	3.4587	3.3507	3.2487	14
15	4.4890	4.3152	4.1530	4.0013	3.8593	3.7261	3.6010	3.4834	3.3726	3.2682	15
16	4.5364	4.3567	4.1894	4.0333	3.8874	3.7509	3.6228	3.5026	3.3896	3.2832	16
17	4.5755	4.3908	4.2190	4.0591	3.9099	3.7705	3.6400	3.5177	3.4028	3.2948	17
18	4.6079	4.4187	4.2431	4.0799	3.9279	3.7861	3.6536	3.5294	3.4130	3.3037	18
19	4.6346	4.4415	4.2627	4.0967	3.9424	3.7985	3.6642	3.5386	3.4210	3.3105	19
20	4.6567	4.4603	4.2786	4.1103	3.9539	3.8083	3.6726	3.5458	3.4271	3.3158	20
21	4.6750	4.4756	4.2916	4.1212	3.9631	3.8161	3.6792	3.5514	3.4319	3.3198	21
22	4.6900	4.4882	4.3021	4.1300	3.9705	3.8223	3.6844	3.5558	3.4356	3.3230	22
23	4.7025	4.4985	4.3106	4.1371	3.9764	3.8273	3.6885	3.5592	3.4384	3.3254	23
24	4.7128	4.5070	4.3176	4.1428	3.9811	3.8312	3.6918	3.5619	3.4406	3.3272	24
25	4.7213	4.5139	4.3232	4.1474	3.9849	3.8342	3.6943	3.5640	3.4423	3.3286	25

TABLE B ╲ Present value of one dollar per year, *n* years at *r*%

Year	31%	32%	33%	34%	35%	36%	37%	38%	39%	40%	Year
1	0.7634	0.7576	0.7519	0.7463	0.7407	0.7353	0.7299	0.7246	0.7194	0.7143	1
2	1.3461	1.3315	1.3172	1.3032	1.2894	1.2760	1.2627	1.2497	1.2370	1.2245	2
3	1.7909	1.7663	1.7423	1.7188	1.6959	1.6735	1.6516	1.6302	1.6093	1.5889	3
4	2.1305	2.0957	2.0618	2.0290	1.9969	1.9658	1.9355	1.9060	1.8772	1.8492	4
5	2.3897	2.3452	2.3021	2.2604	2.2200	2.1807	2.1427	2.1058	2.0699	2.0352	5
6	2.5875	2.5342	2.4828	2.4331	2.3852	2.3388	2.2939	2.2506	2.2086	2.1680	6
7	2.7386	2.6775	2.6187	2.5620	2.5075	2.4550	2.4043	2.3555	2.3083	2.2628	7
8	2.8539	2.7860	2.7208	2.6582	2.5982	2.5404	2.4849	2.4315	2.3801	2.3306	8
9	2.9419	2.8681	2.7976	2.7300	2.6653	2.6033	2.5437	2.4866	2.4317	2.3790	9
10	3.0091	2.9304	2.8553	2.7836	2.7150	2.6495	2.5867	2.5265	2.4689	2.4136	10
11	3.0604	2.9776	2.8987	2.8236	2.7519	2.6834	2.6180	2.5555	2.4956	2.4383	11
12	3.0995	3.0133	2.9314	2.8534	2.7792	2.7084	2.6409	2.5764	2.5148	2.4559	12
13	3.1294	3.0404	2.9559	2.8757	2.7994	2.7268	2.6576	2.5916	2.5286	2.4685	13
14	3.1522	3.0609	2.9744	2.8923	2.8144	2.7403	2.6698	2.6026	2.5386	2.4775	14
15	3.1696	3.0764	2.9883	2.9047	2.8255	2.7502	2.6787	2.6106	2.5457	2.4839	15
16	3.1829	3.0882	2.9987	2.9140	2.8337	2.7575	2.6852	2.6164	2.5509	2.4885	16
17	3.1931	3.9071	3.0065	2.9209	2.8398	2.7629	2.6899	2.6206	2.5546	2.4918	17
18	3.2008	3.1039	3.0124	2.9260	2.8443	2.7668	2.6934	2.6236	2.5573	2.4941	18
19	3.2067	3.1090	3.0169	2.9299	2.8476	2.7697	2.6959	2.6258	2.5592	2.4958	19
20	3.2112	3.1129	3.0202	2.9327	2.8501	2.7718	2.6977	2.6274	2.5606	2.4970	20
21	3.2147	3.1158	3.0227	2.9349	2.8519	2.7734	2.6991	2.6285	2.5616	2.4979	21
22	3.2173	3.1180	3.0246	2.9365	2.8533	2.7746	2.7000	2.6294	2.5623	2.4985	22
23	3.2193	3.1197	3.0260	2.9377	2.8543	2.7754	2.7008	2.6300	2.5628	2.4989	23
24	3.2209	3.1210	3.0271	2.9386	2.8550	2.7760	2.7013	2.6304	2.5632	2.4992	24
25	3.2220	3.1220	3.0279	2.9392	2.8556	2.7765	2.7017	2.6307	2.5634	2.4994	25

INDEX

Index

B

C

G

H

I

L

M